MOORFIELDS MANUAL OF
OPHTHALMOLOGY

FOURTH EDITION

MOORFIELDS MANUAL OF OPHTHALMOLOGY

FOURTH EDITION

Timothy L Jackson PhD, FRCOphth
Professor of Retinal Research,
King's College London and
Consultant Ophthalmic Surgeon,
King's College Hospital
London, UK

JP medical publishers

New Delhi • London

Third Edition 2020

Published by JP Medical Ltd,
83 Victoria Street, London,
SW1H 0HW, UK
Tel: +44 (0)20 3170 8910
Email: info@jpmedpub.com
Web: www.jpmedpub.com

EU GPSR Authorised Representative
Logos Europe, 9 rue Nicolas Poussin
17000, La Rochelle, France
Phone: +33 (0) 6 67 93 73 78
E-mail: Contact@logoseurope.eu

ISBN: 978-1-78779-191-6

British Library Cataloguing in Publication Data
A catalogue record for this book is available from the British Library

Library of Congress Cataloging in Publication Data
A catalog record for this book is available from the Library of Congress

Project Manager: Bhavana Sharma
Editorial Assistant: Keshav Kumar Baghel
Cover Design: Seema Dogra

PREFACE

The preface to the last edition of the *Moorfields Manual* considered the impact of online clinical content, and asked if we still need medical textbooks. At that time, the argument in favour of the third edition was that it managed to distil only the most relevant and practical clinical information, whereas the sheer volume of online material detracted from its usefulness.

This time around, another new technology raises existential questions for clinicians who write medical textbooks. It is, of course, artificial intelligence, which has an uncanny ability to distil information into a useable format.

But there remains, I suspect, a role for the *Moorfields Manual*. If you need a reliable recipe for a chocolate brownie, AI is there to help. If you are preparing an intravitreal injection of a potentially toxic drug, there is less room for error. You need sources you can trust.

This book captures the experience and expertise of select clinical experts who know what they are doing, and who I trust to offer good advice. Hopefully, readers will trust them too, to the benefit of those they care for.

Timothy L Jackson

CONTENTS

CHAPTER 3: LACRIMAL

Thomas G Hardy & Geoffrey E Rose

CHAPTER 4: ORBIT

Thomas G Hardy & Geoffrey E Rose

CHAPTER 5: EXTERNAL EYE DISEASE

Guy T Smith & Su-yin Koay

CHAPTER 6: CORNEA

Guy T Smith, Su-yin Koay & Jennifer McMahon

CHAPTER 7: CATARACT SURGERY

Yashin Ramkissoon, Alex Ionides, Carol Cunningham & Alexander Day

CHAPTER 8: GLAUCOMA

David L Lunt, Anthony Khawaja & Peng T Khaw

CHAPTER 11: MEDICAL RETINA

Timothy L Jackson, Catherine Egan, Andrew Webster, Adnan Tufail, Olivia Cundy & Chan Ning Lee

CHAPTER 12: SURGICAL RETINA

Timothy L Jackson & Lyndon da Cruz

CHAPTER 13: PAEDIATRICS

Gillian GW Adams, Lucy Barker & Adam Bates

CHAPTER 14: STRABISMUS

Gillian GW Adams & Naz Raoof

APPENDICES

James E Neffendorf & Timothy L Jackson

CONTRIBUTING AUTHORS

Gillian GW Adams
Chapters 13, 14
Consultant Ophthalmic Surgeon
Moorfields Eye Hospital, London, UK

Adam Bates
Chapter 13
Consultant Ophthalmologist,
Maidstone & Tunbridge Wells NHS
Trust, London, UK

Lucy Barker
Chapter 13
Consultant Ophthalmic Surgeon
Moorfields Eye Hospital
London, UK

Fion Bremner
Chapter 15
Consultant Neuro-Ophthalmologist
National Hospital for Neurology and
Neurosurgery
London, UK

Olivia Cundy
Central Serous Chorioretinopathy
Chapter 11
Clinical Research Fellow
King's College London
London, UK

Emanuel De Carvalho
Chapter 15
Consultant Neuro-Ophthalmologist
Moorfields Eye Hospital
London, UK

Carol Cunningham
Chapter 7
Consultant Ophthalmic Surgeon
Moorfields Eye Hospital, London, UK

Lyndon da Cruz
Chapter 12
Moorfields Eye Hospital and
NIHR BMRC at Moorfields Eye hospital
and the Institute of Ophthalmology
London, UK

Alexander Day
Chapter 7
Consultant Ophthalmic Surgeon
Moorfields Eye Hospital
London, UK

Catherine Egan
Chapter 11
Consultant Ophthalmologist
Moorfields Eye Hospital, London, UK

Avi Gurbaxani
Chapter 9
Consultant Ophthalmic Surgeon
Moorfields Eye Hospital, London, UK

Thomas G Hardy
Chapters 3, 4
Eye Surgery Consultants,
East Melbourne, Australia

Robert Henderson
Hereditary Vitreoretinal Degenerations
Chapter 12
Consultant Ophthalmic Surgeon
Great Ormond Street Hospital for
Children and Moorfields Eye Hospital
London, UK

Alex Ionides
Chapter 7
Consultant Ophthalmic Surgeon
Moorfields Eye Hospital
London, UK

Timothy L Jackson
Chapters 11, 12 and Appendices; Editor
Professor of Retinal Research and
Consultant Ophthalmic Surgeon
King's College London
London, UK

Neringa Jurkute
Chapter 15
Consultant Neuro-Ophthalmologist
National Hospital for Neurology and
Neurosurgery and Moorfields Eye
Hospital, London, UK

Ronald Kam
Chapter 1
Consultant Ophthalmologist
Moorfields Eye Hospital
London, UK

Michelle Khan
Chapter 2
Consultant Ophthalmologist
University of Toronto, Trillium Health
Partners, Toronto, Canada

Peng T Khaw
Chapter 8
Professor of Glaucoma and Ocular
Healing, and Consultant Ophthalmic
Surgeon
NIHR Biomedical Research Centre for
Ophthalmology
Moorfields Eye Hospital and UCL
Institute of Ophthalmology
London, UK

Anthony Khawaja
Chapter 8
Consultant Surgeon
Moorfields Eye Hospital NHS
Foundation Trust, London, UK

Su-yin Koay
Chapters 5, 6
Consultant Ophthalmic Surgeon
Moorfields Eye Hospital, London, UK

Chan Ning Lee
Toxic Retinopathies
Chapter 11
Clinical Research Fellow
King's College London, London, UK

Sue L Lightman
Chapter 9
Professor of Clinical Ophthalmology
and Consultant Opthalmologist
UCL Institute of Ophthalmology &
Moorfields Eye Hospital, London, UK

David L Lunt
Chapter 8
Consultant Ophthalmologist
South Tees Hospitals
Middlesbrough, UK

Samantha Mann
Diabetic Retinopathy and
Maculopathy, Blue Light
Autofluorescence Imaging
Chapter 11
Consultant Ophthalmologist
Southeast London Diabetic Eye
Screening Programme Lead
St Thomas' Hospital
London, UK

Jennifer McMahon
Contact Lenses
Chapter 6
Head of Ophthalmology Services
Great Western Hospital
Swindon, UK

Prithvi Mruthyunjaya
Chapter 10
Ophthalmologist
Byers Eye Institute
Palo Alto, USA

James E Neffendorf
Appendices
Consultant Ophthalmic Surgeon
King's College Hospital
London, UK

Yashin Ramkissoon
Chapter 7
Consultant Ophthalmologist
Sheffield Teaching Hospitals
Sheffield, UK

Naz Raoof
Chapter 14
Consultant Ophthalmic Surgeon
Moorfields Eye Hospital
London, UK

M Ashwin Reddy
Chapter 10
Consultant Ophthalmic Surgeon
Royal London Hospital & Moorfields Eye Hospital
London, UK

Geoffrey E Rose
Chapters 3, 4
Consultant Orbital, Lacrimal and Oculoplastic Surgeon
Moorfields Eye Hospital, London, UK

Mandeep S Sagoo
Chapter 10
Professor of Ophthalmology and Ocular Oncology, UCL Institute of Ophthalmology;
Consultant Ophthalmic Surgeon, Moorfields Eye Hospital & Barts Health NHS Trust, London, UK

Guy T Smith
Chapters 5, 6
Consultant Ophthalmic Surgeon
Great Western Hospital
Swindon, UK

Adnan Tufail
Chapter 11
Consultant Ophthalmologist
Moorfields Eye Hospital
London, UK

David H Verity
Chapter 2
Consultant Surgeon,
Moorfields Eye Hospital
London, UK

Andrew Webster
Chapter 11
Professor of Molecular Ophthalmology, UCL Institute of Ophthalmology & Consultant Ophthalmologist
Moorfields Eye Hospital
London, UK

Sui Chien Wong
Hereditary Vitreoretinal Degenerations
Chapter 12
Consultant Ophthalmic Surgeon
Great Ormond Street Hospital for Children and Moorfields Eye Hospital
London, UK

CONTRIBUTORS TO FIRST, SECOND AND THIRD EDITION

The Editor wishes to thank the contributors listed below who worked on the First, Second and Third Edition of the *Moorfields Manual of Ophthalmology*, alongside the contributing authors listed above.

FIRST EDITION

James F Acheson

GGW Adams

Larry Amure

Richard Andrews

Adam Bates

Keith Barton

Ben Burton

Alan C Bird

Jill Bloom

John Brookes

Helen L Cook

Richard O Collin

Lyndon Da Cruz

Carol Cunningham

Samantha Dandekar

John KG Dart

Catherine Egan

Daniel P Ehrlich

Ahmed N El-Amir

Paul J Foster

Wendy Franks

David Gartry

Ted Garway-Heath

David Goh

Zdenek Gregor

Thomas Hardy

Richard H Hart

Hugo Henderson

Graham E Holder

John L Hungerford

Timothy L Jackson (Editor)

Rajni Jain

Peng T Khaw

Sue Lightman

Natasha Lim

Graham Macalister

Bita Manzouri

Keith Martin

Bernadette McCarry

Patricia McElhatton

Michael Merriman

Michel Michaelides

Moin Mohammed

AT Moore

Prithvi Mruthyunjaya

Ian Murdoch

Anil Nambiar

Winifred Nolan

Narciss Okhravi

Maria Papadopoulos

Carlos E Pavesio

Gordon Plant

Poornima Rai

Madhavan Rajan

Mahesh Ramchandani

Yashin Ramkissoon

Marie Restori

Geoff Roberson

Geoffrey E Rose

Kulwent Sehmi

Dilani Siriwardena

John Sloper

Guy T Smith

Martin Snead

Paul M Sullivan

Chris Timms

Adnan Tufail

Jimmy Uddin

David H Verity

Ananth Viswanathan

SECOND EDITION

James F Acheson

Gillian GW Adams

Richard Andrews

Asaf Bar

Adam Bates

Alan C Bird

Ben JL Burton

J Richard O Collin

Carol Cunningham

Lyndon da Cruz

John KG Dart

Catherine Egan

Paul J Foster

Thomas D Hardy

John L Hungerford

Timothy L Jackson (Editor)

Peng T Khaw

Sue L Lightman

Bita Manzouri

Bernadette McCarry

Prithvi Mruthyunjaya

James E Neffendorf

Gordon T Plant

Yashin Ramkissoon

Geoffrey E Rose

Guy T Smith

Chris Timms

Adnan Tufail

David H Verity

Andrew Webster

THIRD EDITION

James F Acheson
Gillian GW Adams
Adam Bates
Ben Burton
Carol Cunningham
Lyndon da Cruz
John KG Dart
Catherine Egan
Paul J Foster
Gus Gazzard
Thomas G Hardy
Timothy L Jackson (Editor)
Ronald Kam
Peng T Khaw
Anthony Khawaja
Sue L Lightman
David L Lunt
Priscilla Mathewson
Prithvi Mruthyunjaya
James E Neffendorf
Gordon T Plant
Yashin Ramkissoon
Geoffrey E Rose
Mandeep S Sagoo
Guy T Smith
Chris Timms
Adnan Tufail
Oren Tomkins-Netzer
David H Verity
Andrew Webster
Xia Ni Wu

ACKNOWLEDGEMENTS

A big thank to all the authors, and apologies to their nearest and dearest, who will have seen less of them while they gave time to the *Moorfields Manual.* Likewise, many thanks to the staff at Jaypee Brothers Medical Publishers especially Bhavana Sharma.

Timothy L Jackson

DEDICATION

To

- Edward Louis Orpwood Jackson (ELOJ)
- Emily Isabella Orpwood Jackson (EIOJ)
- Miria Diana Jackson (MDJ)
- Lisa Orpwood (LO)
- Purranza 'Archie' Marble Arch (PAMA)

From

- Timothy Llewellyn Jackson (TLJ)

1 TRIAGE

Ronald Kam

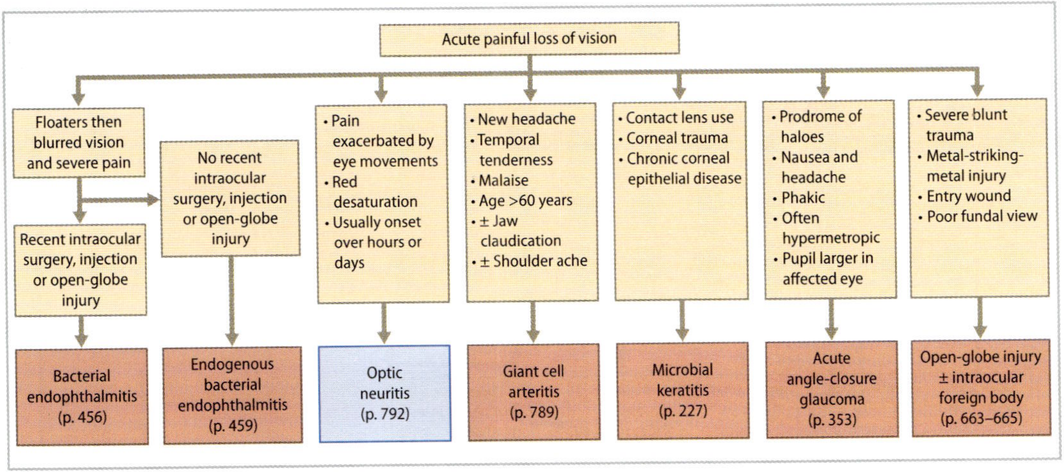

Fig. 1.1: Common causes of painful loss of vision occurring over seconds to hours. Conditions in red boxes require immediate treatment.

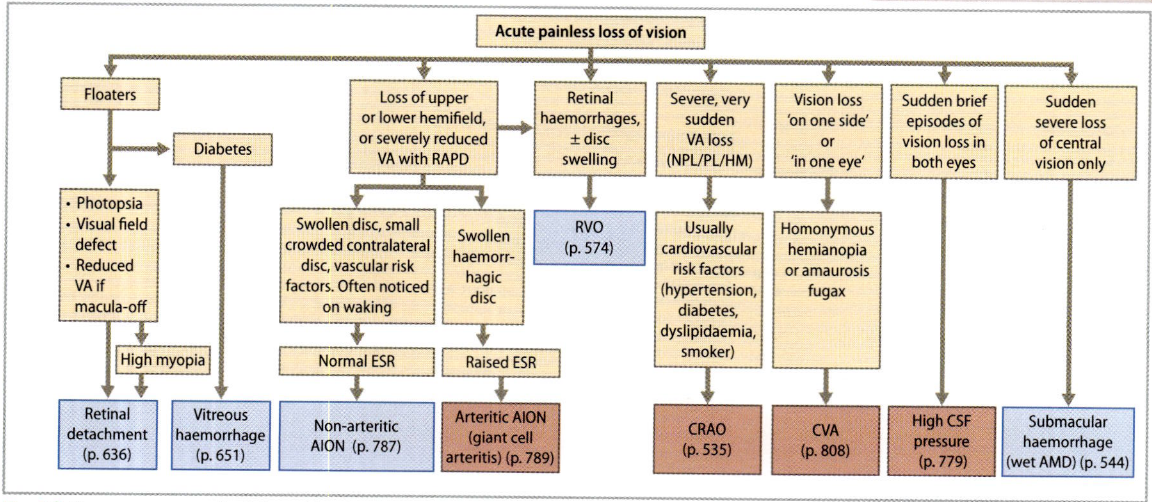

Fig. 1.2: Common causes of painless vision loss occurring over seconds to hours. Conditions in red boxes require immediate treatment.
Abbreviations: AION, anterior ischaemic optic neuropathy; AMD, age-related macular degeneration; CRAO, central retinal artery occlusion; CSF, cerebrospinal fluid; CVA, cerebrovascular accident; ESR, erythrocyte sedimentation rate; HM, hand motions; NPL, no perception of light; PL, perception of light; RVO, retinal vein occlusion; VA, visual acuity

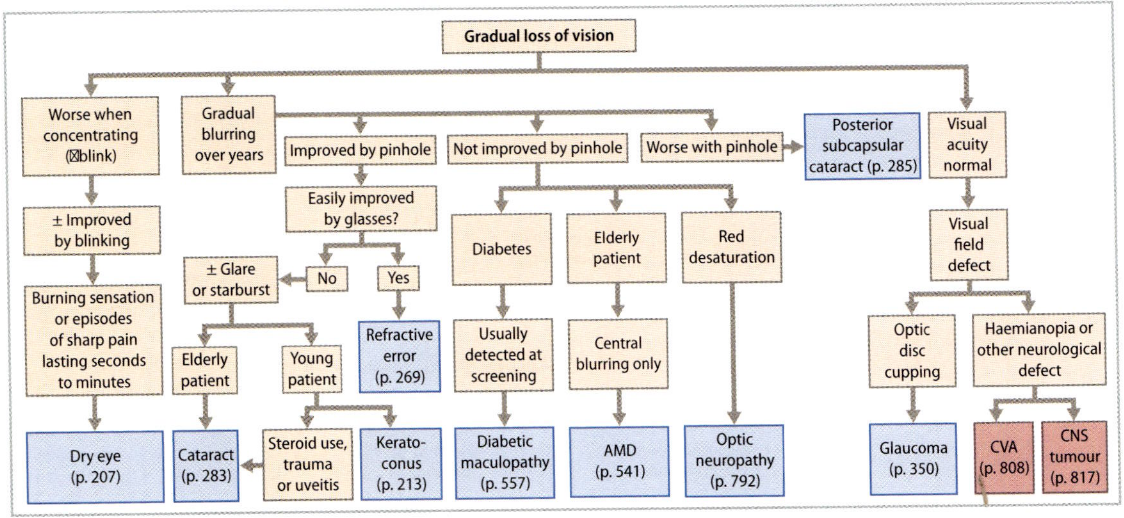

Fig. 1.3: Causes of gradual blurring of vision. Conditions in red boxes require immediate treatment.
Abbreviations: AMD, age-related macular degeneration; CNS, central nervous system; CVA, cerebrovascular accident

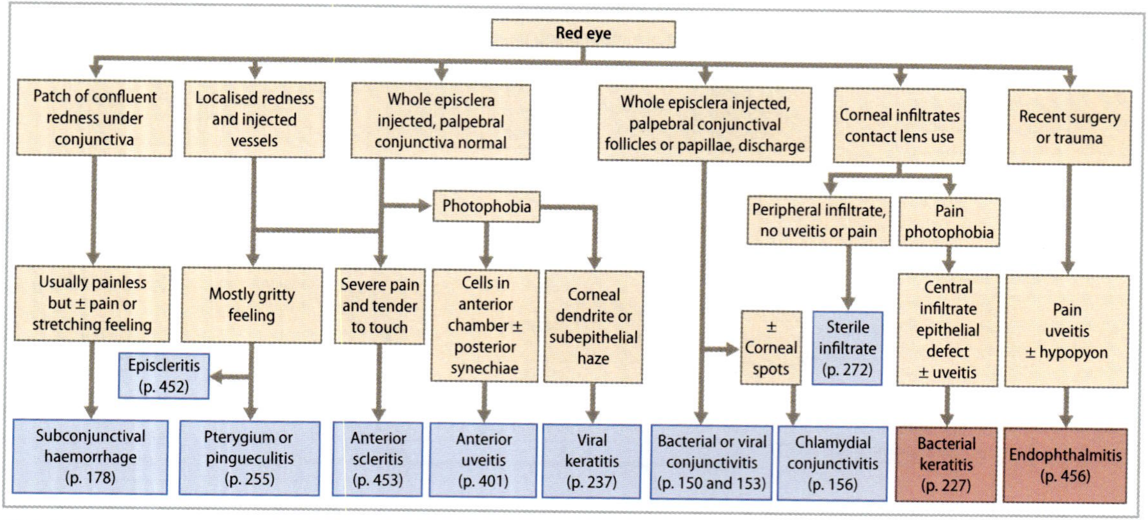

Fig. 1.4: Causes of red eye. Conditions in red boxes require immediate treatment

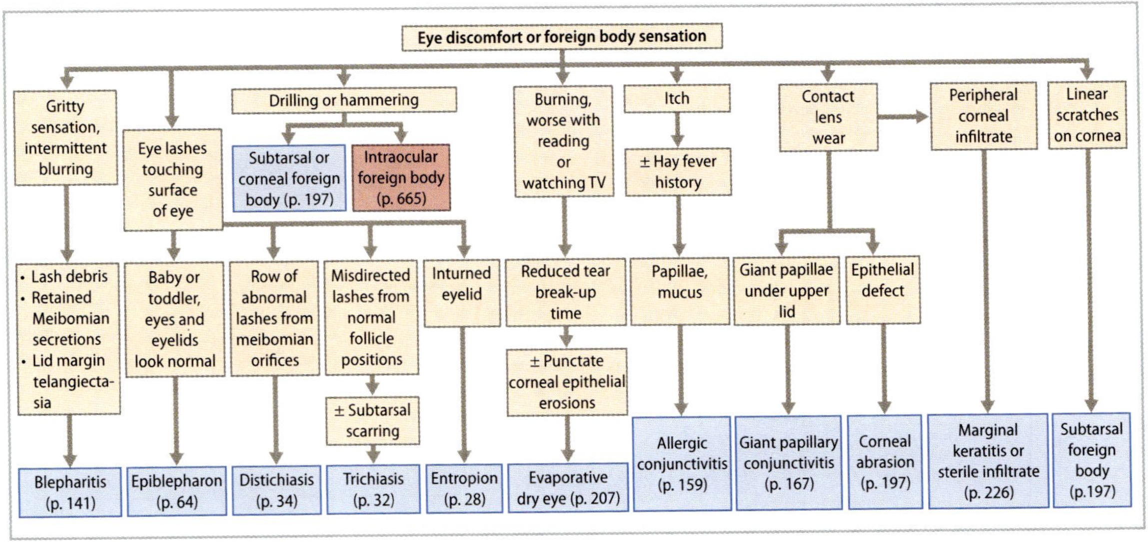

Fig. 1.5: Causes of eye discomfort or foreign body sensation. Intraocular foreign body requires urgent management

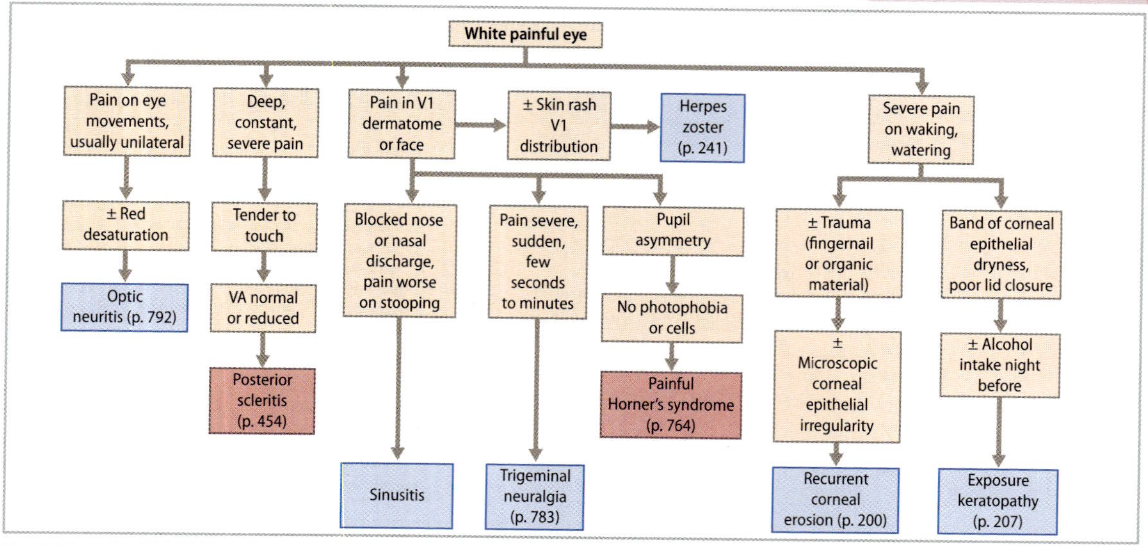

Fig. 1.6: Conditions causing severe or constant eye pain without eye inflammation. Conditions in red boxes require immediate treatment. *Abbreviations:* VA, visual acuity; V1, first division of trigeminal nerve

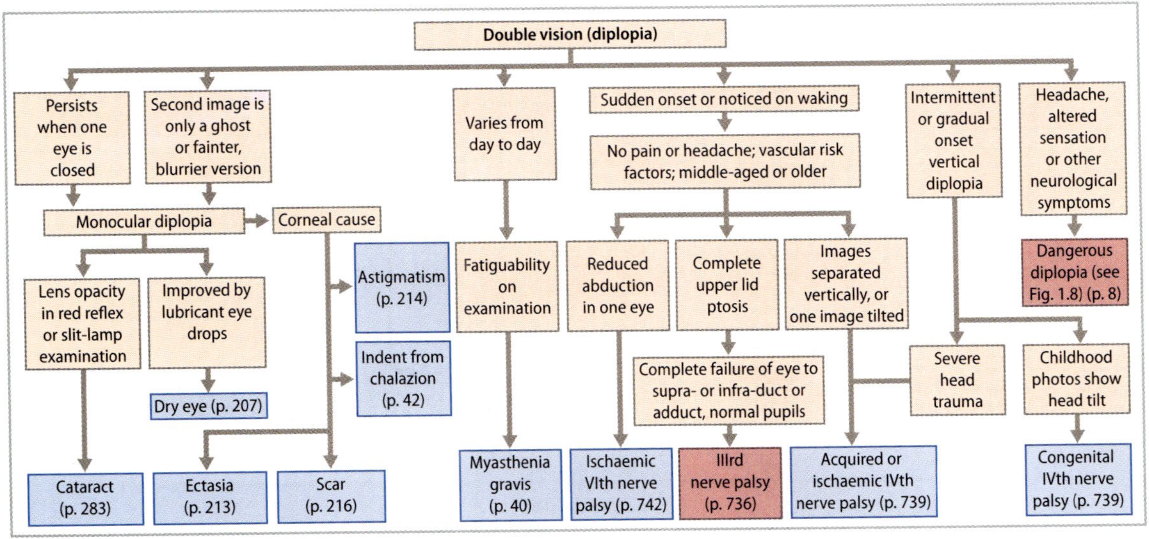

Fig. 1.7: Causes of double vision. Conditions in red boxes require immediate treatment

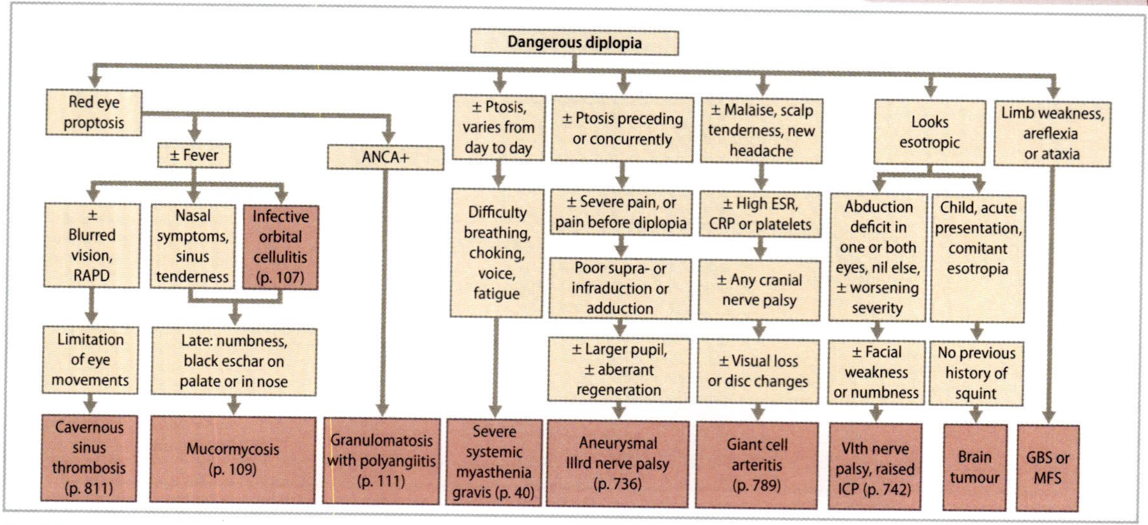

Fig. 1.8: Life-threatening causes of diplopia.

Abbreviations: ANCA, anti-neutrophil cytoplasmic antibody; CRP, C-reactive protein; ESR, erythrocyte sedimentation rate; GBS, Guillain–Barré syndrome; ICP, intracranial pressure; MFS, Miller Fisher syndrome; RAPD, relative afferent pupil defect

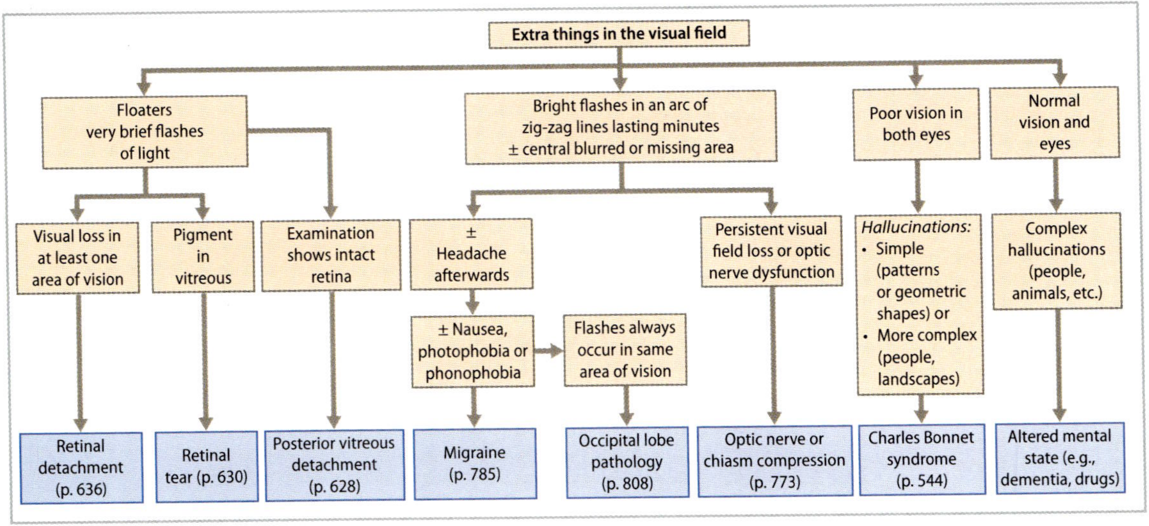

Fig. 1.9: Extra things appearing in the visual field

OCULOPLASTICS

2

David H Verity & Michelle Khan

EYELID ANATOMY REVISION

Surface anatomy

- The upper lid margin lies 1–2 mm below the upper corneal limbus.
- The lower lid margin lies at, or within a few mm of, the level of the inferior corneal limbus.
- The vertical palpebral aperture measures 7–12 mm.
- The upper lid peak lies at, or immediately nasal to, the centre of the pupil.
- The lower lid peak is just lateral to the pupil.
- The adult upper lid crease lies 7–10 mm above the lid margin on downgaze.
- The lateral angle between the two lids is about 1.4 mm (range 2–4 mm) higher than the rounded medial angle, which contains the caruncle lacrimalis, and the plica semilunaris.

Blood supply

- Dual anastomoses of the lateral and medial palpebral arteries in each lid
- Anastomoses with the facial arterial networks
- Posterior conjunctival artery

Lymphatic drainage

- The lateral two-thirds of the lids drain to the superficial parotid nodes.
- The medial lids drain to the submandibular nodes.

Sensory innervation (Fig. 2.1)

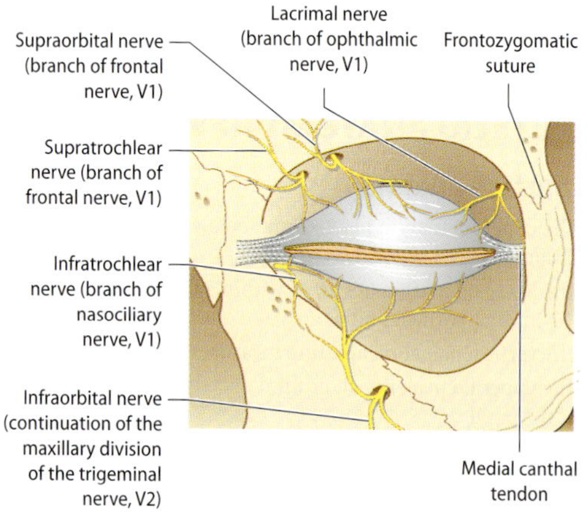

Fig. 2.1: Sensory innervation of the eyelid.

Orbicularis muscle

- The elliptical orbicularis oculi muscle consists of an orbital part which extends onto the cheek and temporal area, a palpebral part which is divided into preseptal, pretarsal and ciliary parts, and a lacrimal part (Duverney or Horner muscle) which arises from the posterior lacrimal crest and extends into the posterior fascia of the lacrimal sac to join the palpebral part.
- Contraction has a purse-string effect, closing the lids and drawing the muscle medially.
- On lid closure, the lacrimal part dilates the lacrimal sac, and with relaxation the sac becomes compressed due to the elasticity of helical fibres within the sac wall (the 'lacrimal pump').
- Innervated by the zygomatic and temporal branches of the facial nerve.

Tarsal plates

- Provide stability and convexity to the lids, and contain meibomian glands and ducts (**Fig. 2.2**).
- Length is 25 mm, thickness is 1 mm, and maximum (central) height is 10 mm (upper tarsus) and is 4 mm (lower tarsus).

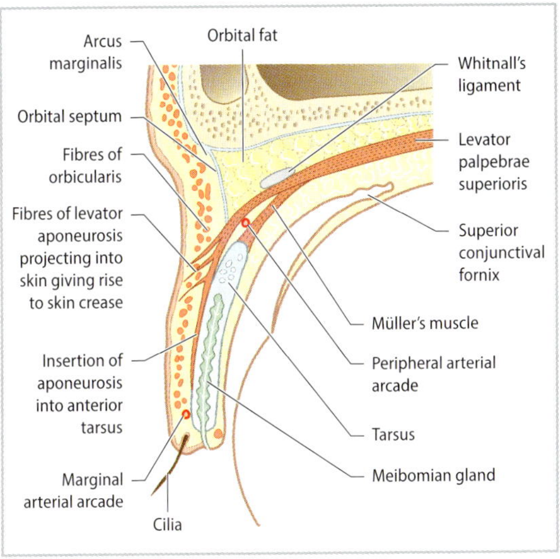

Fig. 2.2: Cross-section through upper eyelid.

Canthal (palpebral) tendons

- Tether the tarsi to the periosteum medially and laterally.
- The anterior limb of the medial canthal tendon inserts anterior to the anterior lacrimal crest, and the posterior limb inserts into the posterior lacrimal crest, the two limbs enveloping the lacrimal sac.
- The lateral canthal tendon attaches the upper and lower tarsal plates to Whitnall's tubercle inside the orbital rim posterior to the septum.

Orbital septum (palpebral fascia)

- Consists of a tough membranous sheet which defines the anterior limit of the orbital soft tissues, and forms a barrier to the spread of infection.
- Fuses with the levator aponeurosis in the upper lid, with the capsulopalpebral fascia in the lower lid, the posterior lacrimal crest medially, and Whitnall's tubercle laterally.
- Prevents anterior herniation of orbital soft tissues; orbital oedema or haemorrhage can therefore lead to an orbital compartment syndrome and optic nerve compression.
- Origin: arcus marginalis at the orbital rim.

Upper lid retractors

- The striated levator palpebrae superioris (LPS) muscle has a common origin with the superior rectus muscle.
- Both are innervated by the superior branch of the oculomotor nerve (CN III). Anteriorly, the LPS becomes the levator aponeurosis, passing anterior to Whitnall's ligament and inserting into the anterior tarsal surface. Medial and lateral horns insert into the periosteum of Whitnall's tubercle laterally, the medial canthal tendon medially, and fibres pass anteriorly through the orbicularis to form the skin crease. Contraction of LPS produces ~12–20 mm of upper lid elevation.
- The sympathetically innervated Müller's muscle arises from the posterior surface of the levator muscle, and inserts into the superior border of the tarsus. Contraction elevates the lid by up to 2 mm.

Whitnall's ligament (superior transverse ligament)

A fascial condensation stretching from the trochlea medially to the lacrimal gland fascia laterally, 10–12 mm above the superior border of the tarsus.

Lower lid retractors

- Arise as the capsulopalpebral head of the inferior rectus, passing forwards as a fascial sheet which envelops the inferior oblique muscle and inserts into the inferior tarsus.
- A sympathetically innervated portion lies posterior to the aponeurosis, arising from the fascial sheath of the inferior rectus muscle and inserting into the inferior tarsus.
- Contraction of the lower lid retractors occurs with down gaze and results in 3–7 mm of lid depression.
- Dehiscence of the retractors contributes to lower lid instability and thus en- and ectropion.

Grey line

- The mucocutaneous junction situated behind the eyelashes.
- Histologically corresponds to the most superficial portion of the orbicularis muscle (the muscle of Riolan).
- A grey line 'split' divides the orbicularis muscle from tarsus, separating the eyelid into anterior and posterior lamellae.

HISTORY

Identify factors which influence disease risk (such as sun exposure, contact lens wear, eczema, and previous surgery) and subsequent management (age, employment and hobbies). Define the duration of symptoms or signs (check old photographs) and any associated ocular symptoms. Preoperatively, ask about antiplatelet and anticoagulant treatment, their indications, and allergies to drugs and plasters. The history and examination is guided by the clinical presentation, which can include the presence of a lesion (**Table 2.1**), abnormal lid position (**Table 2.2**), and lid swelling (**Table 2.3** children and **Table 2.4** adults).

Table 2.1: Lid lesions

Feature	Consider
Discharge	Chalazion, abscess, fistula, canaliculitis and sinus disease
Inflamed cutaneous or subcutaneous lesion	Eczema, discoid lupus erythematosis (DLE), dermatomyositis, sarcoidosis, lymphoma, basal cell carcinoma (BCC) or squamous cell carcinoma (SSC)
Pain, bleeding, change in pigmentation, sensory loss, sun exposure, previous radiotherapy	Malignancy (new or recurrent)
Rapid growth	Keratoacanthoma, SSC, Merkel cell tumour, chalazion, pyogenic granuloma and haemangioma (in young children)
Slow growth	BCC
Postural or diurnal variation in size	Varix or venous-lymphatic anomaly
Previous injury or surgery	Retained foreign body and granuloma

Table 2.2: Abnormal lid height or position

Feature	Consider
Family history	Familial ptosis, myopathy and blepharophimosis
Eyelid movement with jaw action	Marcus Gunn jaw-wink phenomenon
Diurnal variation, diplopia, facial weakness, dysphagia, muscle weakness	Myopathy (e.g. myasthenia gravis)
Thyroid dysfunction, uni- or bilateral proptosis, lid retraction and lateral lid 'flare'	Thyroid eye disease *Note:* Thyroid function tests may be within normal limits
Increased inferior scleral show	Proptosis from thyroid eye disease or orbital mass
Red, uncomfortable eye, contact lens use and topical medication	Ocular surface or conjunctival disease causing ptosis
Lid or facial fasciculations and involuntary lid movement	Blepharospasm and aberrant nerve regeneration (following facial palsy)
'S'-shaped upper eyelid	Lacrimal gland pathology (dacroadenitis, sarcoid involvement, idiopathic orbital inflammation, etc.)
Surgery for acoustic neuroma, or other intracranial disease	Facial nerve paresis or palsy
Diplopia or pupil enlargement	Oculomotor (IIIrd cranial nerve) paresis or palsy
Ptosis in the presence of hypotropia	Pseudoptosis – when the patient fixates with the eye, the lid rises to a normal position
Minimal ptosis and anisocoria, history of head and neck disease, respiratory (apical) disease and thoracic surgery	Horner's syndrome
Sleep apnoea and lid eversion at night	Floppy eyelid syndrome
Involutional facial changes	Involution ectropion and entropion

Table 2.3: Lid swellings – children

Feature	Consider
Localised swelling with minor inflammation	Chalazion
Diffuse swelling with onset within the first 6 months of life, often in upper lid or superonasal quadrant of the orbit	Capillary haemangioma
Very rapidly progressive lid swelling with proptosis, at any age	Rhabdomyosarcoma
Focal swelling overlying orbital rim, frequently overlying frontozygomatic suture, with minimal change over time	Orbital dermoid
Medial canthal swelling with lacrimal symptoms	Congenital dacryocoele
Midline paranasal swelling	Encephalocoele

Table 2.4: Lid swellings – adults

Feature	Consider
Episodic swelling	Blepharochalasis and dacryocystitis (medial canthus)
Swelling beneath the medial canthal tendon (MCT)	Mucocoele of the lacrimal sac
Swelling at the medial canthus extending *above* the MCT	Tumour until proven otherwise (biopsy)
Medial upper eyelid fullness and inflammation	Mucocoele of the anterior ethmoid air cells
Increase in lid swelling with Valsalva manoeuvre	Eyelid or orbital varix
Rubbery consistency, chronic and slow change	Isolated neurofibroma, histiocytic infiltration and low-grade lymphoma
Indurated plaques	Sarcoidosis (±lacrimal gland swelling)
Subcutaneous, with yellow/orange colouration	Xanthogranuloma (histiocytic infiltration)
Lateral upper lid swelling ± 'S'-shaped lid deformity	Lacrimal gland disease – dacryocystitis, pleomorphic adenoma (very slow growth) and malignancy (rapid)

EXAMINATION

Sit directly opposite the patient. Record ocular and eyelid observations with each eye fixating the observer in turn to avoid false measurements. For example, pseudoptosis due to hypotropia can be misdiagnosed as a true ptosis, and apparent lid retraction may be due to contralateral ptosis with consequent increased effort to open the eyes. Note any facial asymmetry and head posture, and record the following:

Margin reflex distance

- Margin reflex distance (MRD) 1: Central corneal light reflex to upper lid margin.
- MRD 2: Central corneal light reflex to lower lid margin.
- MRD gives more information than palpebral aperture (PA, the vertical distance between the upper and lower eyelid margins). For example, the PA in the presence of unilateral lower lid laxity and ptosis can be 'normal'.
- Where the MRD cannot be measured (in young or uncooperative children), the PA often can be.
- If the lid contour is abnormal, record the PA at the medial and lateral limbus, and centrally. The presence of lateral flare is indicative of thyroid eye disease.

Levator function (LF) Typically, 12–18 mm in adults (note, mild forms of previously undetected congenital levator dystrophy may be present in the adult, presenting with ptosis and reduced LF).

- Block compensatory frontalis activity when measuring LF. Hold a ruler vertically before the eye, between thumb and first finger. The second and third fingers rest firmly on the brow to prevent frontalis activity enhancing the recorded LF.
- Measure the maximal vertical excursion of the upper lid margin from downgaze to upgaze. The measurement is repeated for reproducibility.
- Observe the relative lid and globe positions between extreme upgaze and downgaze. Phase lag (delayed lid descent from superior gaze to the horizontal, with a more rapid descent thereafter) *suggests* thyroid eye disease.
- Note the relative lid height in downgaze. With congenital levator dystrophy, and cicatricial changes (previous injury), the lid is higher than the fellow lid, but *lower* in acquired (aponeurotic dehiscence) ptosis.

Upper lid skin crease (SC) height 7–8 mm in men and 9–10 mm in women. Often absent in East Asians, and congenital levator dystrophy, and raised in acquired ptosis. Multiple SCs can exist.

- Marks the fulcrum of activity of the levator palpebrae muscle on the eyelid, and is formed where levator fibres attach to the skin.
- Is measured as the distance between the lid margin and the SC(s) in downgaze.

Upper lid show (ULS) Distance between the lid margin and skin fold (not crease) in primary position. ULS asymmetry can lead to significant aesthetic concerns.

Lagophthalmos Incomplete lid closure. Enquire about nocturnal lagophthalmos, and record (i) completeness of the blink cycle (without instillation of local anaesthesia), (ii) degree of closure with minimal effort, and (iii) with forced closure. Ocular surface symptoms and signs can occur with minimal blink lagophthalmos.

Scleral show (SS) Distance between the lid margins and the superior and inferior corneal limbi, with each eye fixating the target in turn. Inferior SS can be normal, whereas superior SS (at rest) is always abnormal, typically indicating thyroid eye disease.

Hang-up in downgaze Failure of upper lid to descend fully. It can occur with levator dystrophy, previous ptosis surgery, thyroid eye disease and fibrosing orbital disease.

Additional observations

- Colour vision (Ishihara charts – note the number of plates correctly seen, and the speed, being slow or fast) and relative pupil reactions to a bright light in a darkened environment.
- Lash ptosis (drooping of lashes, typically due to slippage of the anterior lamella).
- Laxity (i) of the lid *per se*, (ii) medial and (iii) lateral canthal tendon.
- Lid eversion to examine the conjunctival fornices: conjunctival and forniceal masses are frequently overlooked.
- Cogan's lid twitch in myasthenia gravis (overshoot of upper lid on refixation – after sustained upgaze followed by brief downgaze).
- Jaw movement: Check for abnormal eyelid movement due to medial or lateral pterygoid synkinesis (Marcus Gunn jaw - winking ptosis).
- Synkinetic lid movement with lower facial muscular activity complicating facial palsy.
- Measure the pupil sizes in photopic and scotopic conditions if Horner's syndrome is suspected.

- Document ocular saccades and ductions in all cases. These can be abnormal with central and peripheral lesions affecting the oculomotor nerve, ocular myopathies, Brown's syndrome and aberrant third nerve regeneration.
- Bell's phenomenon (protective elevation of the globe: observe globe movement during attempted forced closure with manual elevation of the upper lid).
- Corneal sensation to light touch with cotton wool. Risk of corneal exposure after ptosis surgery if corneal sensation, Bell's phenomenon, aqueous tear production, or upgaze are impaired.

Record findings as shown in **Figure 2.3**.

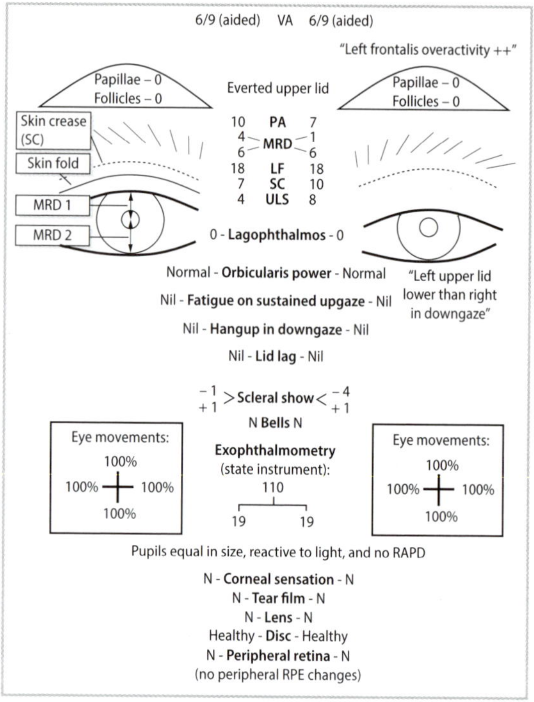

Fig. 2.3: Typical example of notes of a patient with a left aponeurosis disinsertion-type ptosis. *Abbreviations*: LF, levator function; MRD, margin reflex distance; PA, palpebral aperture; ULS, upper lid show; VA, visual acuity

ECTROPION

Background Age-related ectropion is common, but it is important to exclude other causes. Note the degree of laxity (i) of the medial canthal tendon, (ii) of the tarsus (generalised horizontal laxity), and (iii) of the lateral canthal tendon.

Classification

- Age-related: due to collagen laxity.
- Cicatricial: due to skin contracture – may occur with ageing, trauma, previous lower lid surgery, cicatricial diseases such as ichthyosis and eczema, and chronic overflow of tears or topical medication.
- Paralytic: e.g. facial nerve palsy.
- Mechanical: from a lower lid mass such as a meibomian cyst or neoplasia.

Symptoms Epiphora, intermittent red eye, and mucous discharge.

Signs Medial, central or entire lower lid eversion. Other changes reflecting collagen laxity may be present, e.g. dermatochalasis, ptosis, subtle puntal eversion, and punctal stenosis.

History and examination Note any previous lid surgery, trauma, and assess facial nerve power. Look for:
Age-related changes:

- *Horizontal laxity*: lower lid fails to return promptly to the globe surface after distraction.
- *Lateral and medial canthal ligament laxity*: note the degree of punctal displacement with lateral traction, e.g. to the medial limbus, medial pupil, or beyond.
- *Retractor laxity causing tarsal (shelf) ectropion*: the tarsal conjunctiva may be inflamed/thickened from chronic exposure; punctal stenosis is commonly present.
- *Orbicularis muscle weakness*: assess for lagophthalmos, upper lid retraction, Bell's phenomenon, upgaze, and corneal sensation.

Anterior lamella cicatricial changes:

- Ask the patient to open his/her mouth and look up. In the presence of significant cicatricial changes, the lid is distracted from the globe.

Investigations A lower lid mass causing ectropion may require biopsy and, in the case of well-defined masses, intact excision.

Treatment For temporary relief, place a short length of surgical tape horizontally along the lower lid and then up onto the temple region to provide lift and support.

Surgery

- Aims to address horizontal laxity, either with a full-thickness pentagon wedge excision laterally (**Box 2.1**), a lateral tarsal strip (**Box 2.2**) or, for lesser degrees of laxity, lateral canthopexy.
- Medial ectropion with punctual eversion may require a medial (diamond) tarso-conjunctivoplasty. Limited punctoplasty may also be indicated. The 'lazy T' procedure is a medial pentagon excision plus medial tarso-conjunctivoplasty (the configuration of the posterior lamella scar forming a 'T').

Box 2.1: Pentagon wedge excision

1. Consent:

   Benefit: improved lid position.

   Risks: Recurrence of ectropion; over- and undercorrection; scarring; inflammation; infection; suture granuloma (with non-absorbable suture); further surgery. May produce bruising, conjunctival chemosis, and sub-conjunctival haemorrhage.
2. Instil topical anaesthetic into the conjunctival sac.
3. Inject 1–2 mL of 2% lidocaine with 1:200,000 epinephrine through the skin, at either end of the eyelid (30-gauge needle).
4. Use straight scissors to make a full-thickness cut through the eyelid at the junction of the lateral third and medial two-thirds of the eyelid. Overlap the cut edges to decide how much to shorten, and resect this amount, in the form of a pentagon (**Fig. 2.4**).
5. Haemostasis is essential before closing (bipolar cautery).
6. Pass each needle of a double 7/0 Vicryl suture through each 'grey line'. Place the suture on traction with an artery clamp and rest this on the forehead – this aligns the tarsal edges while the tarsal sutures are placed.
7. Align the cut tarsal edges with two 6/0 Vicryl sutures. Take large bites of the tarsus; lay the knots anteriorly. Further deep sutures may be used to close the orbicularis inferior to the tarsus.
8. Now tie the 7/0 Vicryl suture through the grey line, with the knot lying internally. A lash line suture completes correct alignment of the lid edges. If the apposition of the lid margins is imperfect, remove and replace sutures.
9. Close the skin with 3–4 7/0 Vicryl sutures.
10. Apply Oc. chloramphenicol, Vaseline gauze, and an eye pad for 24 hours. The absorbable skin sutures may be left *in situ*, although are frequently removed at first review in 10–14 days.

Box 2.2: Lateral tarsal strip (LTS)

1. Consent: Same risks and benefits as pentagon wedge excision (refer **Box 2.1**).
2. Inject local anaesthetic subcutaneously via a 30-gauge needle to the lateral canthal region, followed by gentle pressure.
3. Perform a lateral canthotomy by making a horizontal cut at the lateral canthus (straight scissors).
4. Ensure haemostasis.
5. Grasp the lateral end of the lower lid (Adson dissecting forceps) and perform cantholysis of the subconjunctival bandlike attachments between the lid and orbital rim (straight sharp scissors).
6. Dissect between orbicularis and the tarsus and divide the two by staying posterior to the grey line (straight scissors). Remove the corresponding mucocutaneous strip of lid margin.
7. Prepare a tarsal strip 3–4 mm wide and ~5 mm long, lower edge parallel to the lid margin. Pare off the conjunctiva on the strip (D15 blade).
8. Perform a lateral (2 mm) upper lid grey line split to enhance subsequent vertical lift (augmented LTS).
9. Attach the LTS to the periosteum using double-ended 5/0 Vicryl. Expose the lateral orbital rim (straight or spring scissors) and spread orbicularis fibres aside (tips of the Moorfields forceps, held in the left hand, straddle the orbital rim and maintain the view of the periosteum).
10. Pass the suture ends through the inner orbital rim periosteum – 2 mm higher than the level of the medial canthus – by rolling the needle from inside the rim anteriorly (**Fig. 2.5A**).
11. Pull both ends through equally, but not completely, to leave a small loop. Place this loop over the LTS. Pass one needle through the end of the LTS laterally, and one medial to the loop, both from the posterior to anterior surfaces of the strip (**Fig. 2.5B**). Tighten the suture to ensure a sufficiently high placement on the orbital rim and reposition if necessary.
12. Place 7/0 Vicryl grey line (buried knot) and lash line sutures (external knot) through the upper and lower lids before tying the strip suture (firm, but do not overtighten – watch the position of the lid on the globe).
13. As the LTS suture ends are pulled upwards, the noose tightens on the strip which is drawn onto the orbital rim, tucked upwards to lie within upper lid grey line split. This provides further vertical support.
14. Close orbicularis and skin with interrupted 7/0 Vicryl sutures.
15. Apply oculentum (Oc.) chloramphenicol, Vaseline gauze, and a firm dressing for 24 hours.
16. Review in 2 weeks for removal of skin sutures; discharge if satisfactory progress.

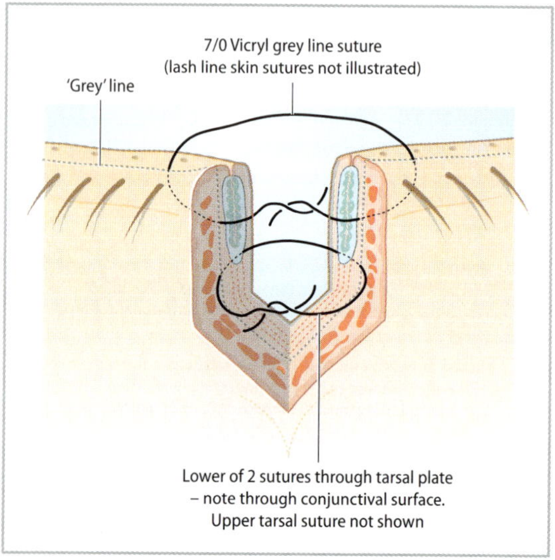

Fig. 2.4: Pentagon wedge excision.

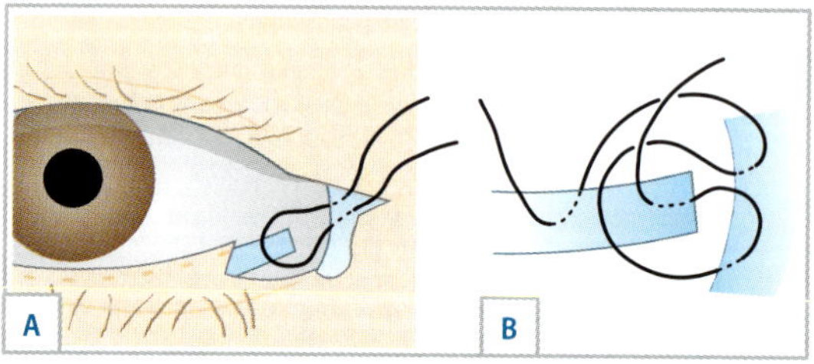

Fig. 2.5: Lateral tarsal strip.

- Marked medial ectropion due to posterior limb canthal tendon laxity will not be addressed by repairing the anterior limb alone. Surgery will entail a medial canthal fixation suture, or medial wedge excision with an anchoring suture between the medial cut end of the tarsus and the periosteum of the posterior lacrimal crest (medial wedge). In paralytic cases, a medial (Lee) canthoplasty helps to raise the lower lid, but where greater support is required, a medial 'pillar' tarsorrhaphy provides significant vertical lift, although reduces the horizontal aperture.

- Tarsal, or 'shelf' ectropion requires lid shortening plus an internal retractor plication, using three 5/0 absorbable synthetic sutures via a conjunctival approach.
- Cicatricial ectropion often resolves with cessation of topical treatment, and a bland moisturising cream to the lower lid. Surgery aims to free all cicatricial bands via a wide subciliary incision, and a full-thickness skin graft, or skin transposition flap into the lower lid.

FLOPPY EYELID SYNDROME

Background Typically presents in middle-aged men with a high body mass index (BMI), and frequently associated with obstructive sleep apnoea. Features include unilateral or bilateral chronic papillary conjunctivitis with mucous production, marked upper lid tissue laxity, and spontaneous tarsal eversion at night. The aetiology is unknown, but repeated lid stretching is thought to alter the quality of the elastic fibres in the tarsus, and lead to collagen accumulation.

Symptoms Irritable red eye with mucous production. Upper lid eversion at night (on the sleeping side).

Signs Ready or spontaneous eversion of the tarsus (**Fig. 2.6**) with rubbery consistency, lash ptosis, papillary conjunctivitis, and superior punctate keratitis.

History and examination Heavy snoring, apnoea and lid eversion at night are common. Horizontal lid laxity is usually marked. Keratitis may be subtle.

Differential diagnosis Allergic conjunctivitis, chlamydial conjunctivitis and age-related lid laxity.

Investigations Refer to a respiratory physician for sleep studies due to the cardiovascular risk of nocturnal hypoxia.

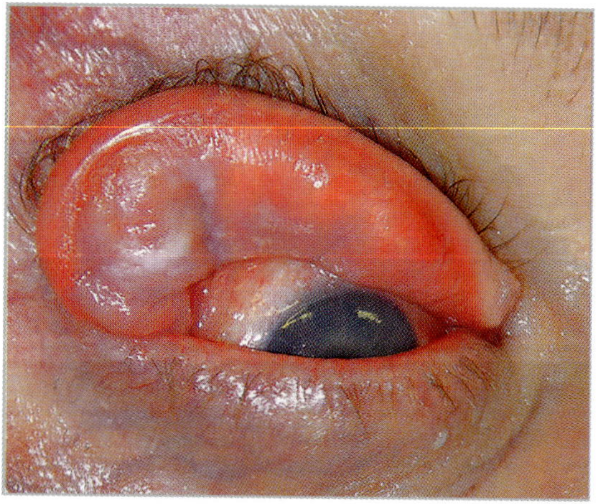

Fig. 2.6: Floppy eyelid syndrome.

Treatment

- *Casualty*: Topical lubricants and mild topical steroid for keratitis.
- *Clinic*: Consider surgical options. Repeated surgery may be necessary.
    1. Anterior lamellar reposition for lash ptosis.
    2. Shortening of the medial and/or lateral upper lid using a lateral tarsal strip (p. 23).
    3. The upper lid can also be shortened by excising a wedge laterally.

Surgical risks include inflammation, infection, scarring, ptosis, reduced lateral visual field (if the horizontal aperture is shortened), and the need for further lid shortening. Patient's expectations are not always met.

LOWER LID ENTROPION

Background Similar aetiology to age-related ectropion (p. 21). Exclude chronic conjunctival disease and cicatricial changes in the posterior lamella. Consider active ocular mucous membrane pemphigoid (OMMP) in elderly patients with a history of ocular surface or oral inflammation; this is often diagnosed late.

Classification

- Congenital (rare).
- Acquired: age-related (common) and cicatricial.

Symptoms Epiphora, mucous discharge and red eye (note, total inversion of the lid margin into the conjunctival fornix may be associated with a white eye and surprisingly few symptoms).

Signs Entropion may be sporadic (on forced closure due to local irritation), or constant. Other features include: subtarsal mucous strands, lash–cornea touch, punctate epithelial keratopathy, conjunctival cicatricial changes, punctal stenosis, skin laxity, and hypertrophic preseptal orbicularis which 'overrides' the pretarsal orbicularis (spastic entropion).

History and examination Ask about previous lid surgery and cicatrising disease, e.g. Stevens–Johnson syndrome, OMMP and allergy to topical medication. Forced lid closure may elicit subtle entropion. Examine for effacement of the plica, an early sign in OMMP. Lower lid entropion may be misdiagnosed as trichiasis, but identification of the meibomian gland orifices always confirms the correct diagnosis and saves the patient from inappropriate electrolysis.

Investigations If OMMP is suspected, perform conjunctival and buccal mucosal biopsies for direct immunofluorescence (DI, place in Michel's transport medium), as well as indirect immunofluorescence (IF) on a blood sample.

Treatment In patients unfit for surgery, or as a temporising measure, consider the following:

- *Transverse lid sutures*: Pass 3–4 double-ended 5/0 absorbable synthetic sutures through the lower lid just beneath the tarsus, bring out through the skin, and tie to create a slight ectropion. Sutures may be left to absorb.
- *Everting sutures*: Pass three double-ended 5/0 absorbable synthetic sutures through the lower fornix and out through the skin 3–4 mm below the lash line (**Fig. 2.7**).

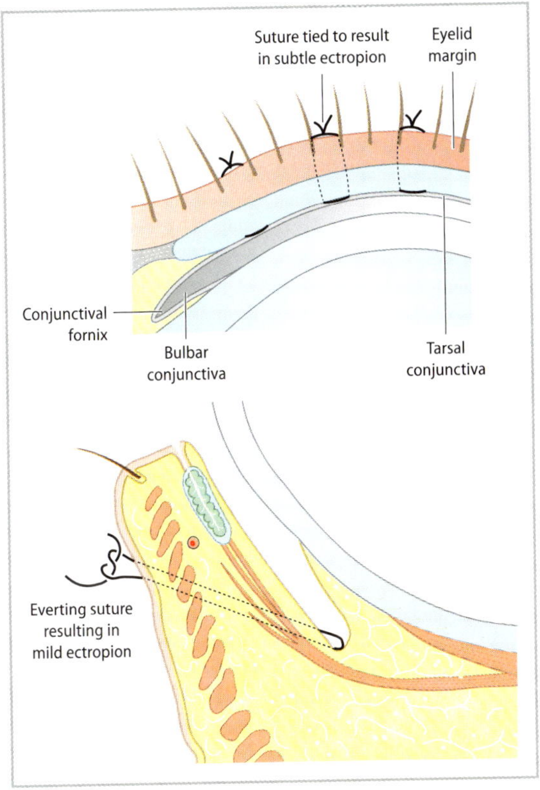

Fig. 2.7: Everting sutures.

- *Botulinum toxin A*: Inject into the preseptal orbicularis (three injections of Dysport 20 units spaced evenly along the lower lid, 1 cm from the margin). May need to be repeated periodically.

Surgery

- Must address horizontal lid laxity (lateral tarsal strip or pentagon wedge excision, pp. 22 and 23) to reduce the risk of recurrence.
- The gold-standard is lid tightening plus Jones procedure, in which, via a subciliary incision, the lower lid retractors are plicated to the anterior lamella using three absorbable sutures, and a horizontal strip of orbicularis is excised. Avoid lower lid

retraction from overtightening. Release or remove the sutures if the lid is inferiorly retracted by the sutures postoperatively.

- Posterior lamella graft (e.g. buccal mucosa) is indicated for cicatricial cases where there is incomplete lid closure with minimal effort. Effective control of conjunctival inflammation should precede surgery in cases of OMMP, with close monitoring for signs of recurrence.

UPPER LID ENTROPION

Background Upper lid entropion is usually due to posterior lamella cicatricial disease, e.g. chronic conjunctivitis, trachoma, ocular mucous membrane pemphigoid (OMMP). In sockets, it can be due to a shortage of lining.

Symptoms Ocular irritation and epiphora.

History and examination Ask about previous injuries, and chronic ocular surface inflammation, e.g. OMMP. Exclude blepharospasm, posterior lamella cicatricial changes, and corneal pannus or epithelial changes.

Differential diagnosis Lash ptosis without true entropion, e.g. floppy eyelid syndrome.

Management For mild cases, anterior lamella reposition may suffice. Make a skin crease incision down to the tarsus, pass three double-armed 5/0 absorbable sutures through the upper tarsus, pass these out through the skin above the lashes, and tie. With all procedures, consider a small recession of the retractors from the anterior tarsal plate, since entropion is associated with lid retraction. Greater eversion is achieved with a grey line split, and, if required, a horizontal wedge excision of the anterior tarsus. Where the tarsus is thin, divide the anterior lamella completely from the posterior lamella and reattach at a higher level (lamellar division). Where there is keratin on the posterior aspect of the tarsus, a terminal tarsal rotation may be required.

TRICHIASIS

Eyelash follicles are in a normal position (unlike distichiasis) but directed towards the globe (**Fig. 2.8**). Causes include chronic lid margin disease (blepharitis) and conjunctival cicatricial diseases, e.g. Stevens–Johnson syndrome and ocular mucous membrane pemphigoid (OMMP). Treat *small* numbers of lashes with electrolysis (**Box 2.3**), **but up to half may re-grow**, and treatment can cause tarsal scarring and further trichiasis. Excision of the anterior lamella bearing the lash follicles (or full-thickness lid excision) is more permanent for localised trichiasis. Manage more extensive areas with cryotherapy (**Box 2.4**), or preferably, complete removal of the anterior lamella if control proves difficult (as in ocular cicatricial pemphigoid). In dark skin, cryotherapy can cause localised skin depigmentation. For small numbers of lashes, direct follicle excision using a feather blade is increasingly the preferred approach, avoiding the complications of electrolysis.

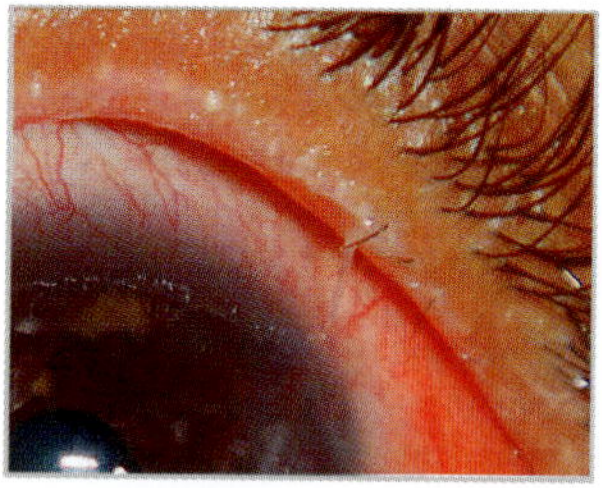

Fig. 2.8: Trichiasis.

Box 2.3: Electrolysis

1. Inject local anaesthesia and use a microscope.
2. Grasp the lid margin with large-toothed forceps, e.g. Adson forceps; direct the electrolysis needle alongside the hair shaft down to the lash follicle. Placing a cut down alongside the shaft with a feather blade can help to deliver electrolysis more directly to the follicle.
3. Deliver the current until gentle blanching occurs. Power and time settings differ between units, e.g. the Ellman Surgitron radiofrequency device uses 'cut/coagulation' setting with power <1 unit.
4. Adequately treated lashes are then easily epilated and the hair bulb visualised.

Box 2.4: Cryotherapy

1. Some units have a thermocouple needle that is inserted into the tissue to check temperature, but this is not essential if the average time it takes to reach –20°C has been assessed on a previous series of patients using the same cryoprobe.
2. Inject local anaesthesia and protect the eye with a plastic lid guard.
3. Use the lid cryoprobe to apply a double-freeze-thaw cycle (to –20°C) with spontaneous thawing between treatments.
4. Prescribe topical antibiotic ointment for 5–7 days.

DISTICHIASIS

Clinical features

In contrast to trichiasis, distichiasis is a congenital disorder in which a separate and more posterior row of metaplastic lashes exists (often growing out of the meibomian gland orifices). The lid margin is in a normal position (**Fig. 2.9**).

Management

- If only a few lashes are affected, evert the eyelid with a meibomian clamp, use a microscope and incise the shaft of the eyelash through a partial-thickness incision of the tarsus to the hair bulb. Electrolyse or excise the follicle bulb under direct view.
- More extensive areas can be treated by splitting the lid at the grey line, freezing the posterior lamella, and reapposing the anterior and posterior lamellae with a running 7/0 absorbable suture. The posterior lamella must be advanced to compensate for the shrinkage after cryotherapy, which could lead to subsequent entropion.

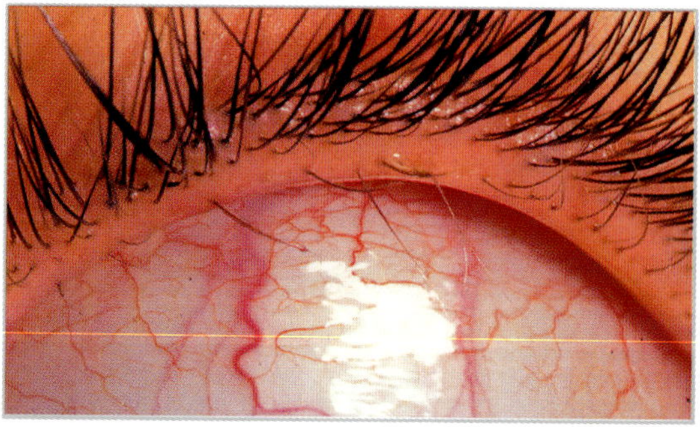

Fig. 2.9: Distichiasis.

FACIAL NERVE PALSY

Background Idiopathic facial nerve palsy (IFNP and 'Bell's palsy') accounts for 75% of cases, but is a diagnosis of exclusion. The facial nerve has five branches: (1) Temporalis, (2) Zygomatic, (3) Buccal, (4) Mandibular, and (5) Cervical (To Zanzibar By Motor Car).

Aetiology

- Idiopathic facial nerve palsy and Bell's palsy:
  - More common in the elderly (>70 years).
  - Spontaneous recovery occurs in >75% of cases, and although may *appear* complete, is often associated with 'functional epiphora' due to residual impaired reinnervation.
  - Exposure keratopathy is unusual in the presence of normal corneal sensation and Bell's response.
- Central or peripheral nervous system lesions.
- Trauma, including iatrogenic causes such as surgery for acoustic neuroma, and facial or parotid surgery.
- Systemic infections and inflammations.
- Herpes zoster oticus (Ramsay–Hunt syndrome) or other middle ear disease – examine the external auditory meatus.
- Mastoiditis
- Parotid tumours
- Previous squamous cell carcinoma (SSC) of the periocular or facial region, with perineural spread along branches of the facial nerve. Also examine the Vth and VIth cranial nerves to exclude disease progression centrally to the brainstem.

Symptoms Related to corneal exposure, failure of the lacrimal pump mechanism causing epiphora, and facial asymmetry.

Signs Include facial weakness (including brow ptosis and droop of the angle of the mouth), upper lid retraction, and lower lid atony (**Fig. 2.10**).

History Ask about prodromal viral illness, earache, previous facial palsy, previous facial skin tumours, middle ear trauma, middle ear disease, headache and dysphonia. Ask about taste sensation and hyperacusis. Risk factors include diabetes, previous IFNP and immunosuppression. Implicated organisms include herpes simplex, herpes zoster, Epstein–Barr virus, cytomegalovirus, adenovirus, rubella, mumps, influenza B and coxsackievirus.

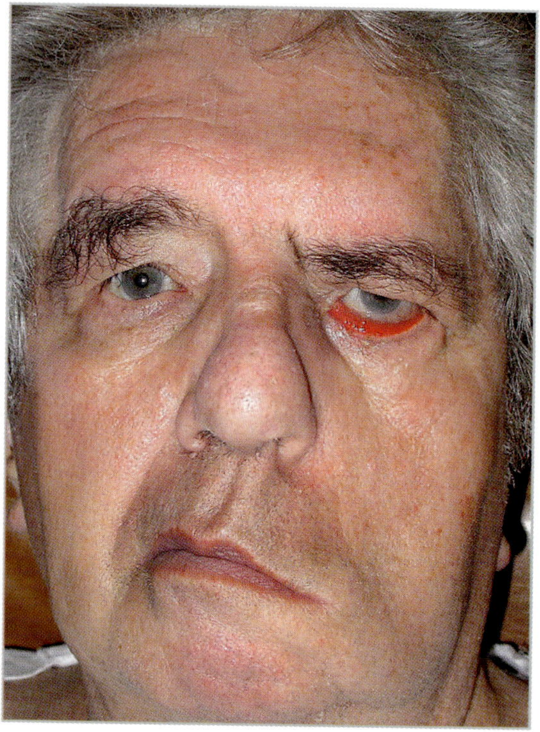

Fig. 2.10: Left facial nerve palsy, with ipsilateral brow and facial droop, including the lateral angle of the mouth, ectropion, and contralateral brow elevation. Ipsilateral lid retraction is present but obscured by brow droop.

Examination Examine for underlying causes (see 'Aetiology' above). Aberrant nerve regeneration syndromes may be missed. Differentiate between lower and upper motor neurone (central) lesions. Central lesions spare the frontalis action due to bilateral innervation. Actively exclude vesicles in the external auditory canal (Ramsay–Hunt syndrome) because of the risk of central nervous system (CNS) complications with immunosuppression which might otherwise be given for IFNP. Test corneal sensation, Bell's phenomenon and upgaze (the corneal prognosis is guarded if these are abnormal). Examine cranial nerves.

Investigations

- Imaging is not immediately indicated for new onset of Bell's palsy in the absence of other neurological or systemic features.
- Consider neuroimaging for patients with concomitant focal neurology or non-resolving facial nerve paresis after 6–8 weeks.

Complications

- Exposure keratopathy and corneal perforation. Contributing factors include upper lid retraction due to unopposed levator activity, lower lid ectropion, lagophthalmos and failure of tear drainage.
- Lower lid atony leading to horizontal laxity and ectropion.
- Aberrant nerve regeneration syndromes including gustatory epiphora in 5%, and facial synkineses, e.g. narrowing of the palpebral aperture with lower facial movement.

Treatment

- *Systemic*: Treat patients older than 16 years of age and presenting within 72 hours of symptom onset with prednisolone 1 mg/kg p.o. or 60 mg p.o. o.d. for 6 days, tailing-off over 10 days. Consider adding antiviral agents (e.g. acyclovir 400 mg five times daily for 7 days or valacyclovir 1,000 mg t.d.s for 7 days) if a viral aetiology is suspected, but only in combination with corticosteroids.
- *Ocular*: Causes other than IFNP frequently require intervention for:
  1. Corneal protection
     a. Topical lubricants, e.g. carbomer gel 1 to 2-hourly, and ointment at night.
     b. Botulinum toxin to the upper lid to induce temporary ptosis (5 iu Botox with a short 27-gauge needle either transconjunctivally at the upper border of the tarsus, or transcutaneously through the skin crease).
     c. Tarsorrhaphy with temporary suture (4/0 Prolene with silicone bolsters), cyanoacrylate glue, or surgery.
     d. A medial (pillar) surgical tarsorrhaphy is preferable to a lateral tarsorrhaphy because it maintains the peripheral visual field.
     e. Lower lid tightening (lateral tarsal strip, which can be 'augmented', i.e. placed higher on the orbital rim to aid tear drainage).
     f. Lower lid elevation with autogenous fascia lata passed through the length of the lid and secured medially to the medial canthal tendon, and laterally to the orbital rim periosteum (via a drill-hole).

   g. A medial (Lee) canthoplasty supports the inner canthus by forming a union between the orbicularis fibres above and below the respective canaliculi. It tends to stretch over time.
   h. For greater support, perform a medial canthal fixation suture, or medial wedge resection (placing an anchoring suture between the cut end of the tarsus and the periosteum of the posterior lacrimal crest).
   i. Upper lid loading with a gold weight or platinum chain (typically for nocturnal lagophthalmos).
   j. Upper lid lowering (Müller's muscle excision for 1–3 mm retraction, or posterior or anterior approach levator recession for larger degrees of retraction).
   k. Sural nerve grafting to improve facial tone.
2. Epiphora
   a. Residual epiphora is managed once ectropion or lid laxity has been addressed.
   b. Gustatory epiphora: botulinum toxin to the lacrimal gland (Dysport 15–20 units transcutaneously, in three divided doses in one clinic visit), or direct surgical denervation of the orbital lobe of the lacrimal gland.
   c. Dacryocystorhinostomy (DCR) to reduce lacrimal outflow resistance.
   d. Glass lacrimal bypass tube if the patient remains symptomatic at least 9 months following DCR.
3. Aberrant regeneration syndromes
   a. These often respond to low-dose botulinum toxin injections.
4. Cosmesis
   a. External or internal brow pexy or lift, or endoscopic brow lift (incision above the hair line)
   b. Lower lid blepharoplasty if there is tissue laxity and oedema.
   c. Angular sling to raise the mouth.
   d. Temporalis muscle transfer to create an encircling sling of fascia, passing laterally to medially in both lids.
   e. Facial reanimation may be achieved by cross-nerve anastomosis, as well as with dynamic muscle and tendon transfer procedures (temporalis tendon transfer, digastric muscle tendon transfer).

Follow-up If there is no recovery of (presumed) Bell's palsy within 6 weeks reconsider the diagnosis: 10% of patients with acute facial nerve palsy have a treatable lesion.

Discharge if all factors contributing to corneal exposure have been addressed and the patient is stable on topical lubricants. This may take months to decades.

PTOSIS

Background Ptosis describes a low position of the upper lid on the globe, and is not a diagnosis. Children with ptosis are at risk of amblyopia if the eyelid covers any part of the pupil, and may require urgent brow suspension. Ptosis may be an indicator of orbital, intracranial or systemic disease.

Aetiology

- *Congenital*: congenital levator dystrophy and congenital Horner's syndrome.
- *Hereditary*: myopathic (myasthenia gravis, ocular myopathy and systemic myopathy)
- *Acquired*: trauma, involutional (aponeurosis dehiscence), oculomotor nerve disease, ocular surface disease or orbital inflammation (e.g. chronic contact lens wear and dacryoadenitis), iatrogenic (lid/orbital surgery), mechanical (upper lid mass), and as part of the post-enucleation socket syndrome.
- *Pseudoptosis*: aberrant facial nerve regeneration, blepharospasm, habit spasm, enophthalmos, hypotropia, hyperglobus, contralateral upper lid retraction or proptosis.

Symptoms Heavy lid, restricted visual field and brow ache (frontalis overaction).

Signs Excess frontalis contraction, raised skin crease, deep upper sulcus, other involutional changes (e.g. dermatochalasis and lower lid ectropion), and abnormal head position. Lid height on downgaze relative to the healthy fellow lid is low in aponeurosis dehiscence and high in congenital (myogenic) ptosis. Congenital cases have a high prevalence of strabismus and refractive errors.

History Ask about: duration; jaw wink; variability; fatigue; diplopia; previous lid surgery; trauma; facial palsy and family history. Elicit risk factors for ptosis (such as contact lens wear and chronic topical steroid use), particularly in young patients.

Examination Full lid examination (p. 18) plus corneal sensation; Bell's phenomenon; orbicularis power; frontalis action; eye movements (risk of postoperative corneal exposure); pupil size/responses; exophthalmometry and peripheral fundal examination. Exclude pseudoptosis (e.g. from hypotropia) by ensuring that lid position is measured with the eye fixating the observer.

Investigation MRI of the sympathetic chain in Horner's syndrome (head, neck and upper thorax). Check antiacetylcholine receptor antibody screen and electromyographic studies in suspected myopathy. In ocular myasthenia gravis, antibodies are absent in ~40% of patients.

Management Children at risk of amblyopia require a frontalis sling procedure within 2–4 weeks. If the upper lid obscures any part of the upper visual field, consider early intervention – a full visual field is required for normal visual development. For mild to moderate ptosis without risk of amblyopia, correction may be delayed until the age of awareness (4–5 years). Otherwise, surgery may reasonably be delayed until early adult years. In adults, bilateral ptosis may cause functional blindness, and warrants early intervention.

Surgical techniques depend on the cause:

- *Congenital ptosis with levator function (LF) ≥5 mm*: Levator muscle advancement on the tarsus (anterior or posterior approach).
- *Congenital levator dystrophy with poor LF (<5 mm)*: Brow suspension with autogenous tissue in children >4 years of age (e.g. autogenous fascia lata), or frontalis muscle suspension. For the younger patient, use synthetic material, e.g. Nylon (Supramid) in children of a few months old, and silicone stenting in children up to 4 years old.
- *Congenital levator dystrophy associated with jaw wink*: Bilateral levator disinsertion and autogenous fascia lata brow suspension. Informed discussion with the parents/carers is essential. Unilateral surgery may cause asymmetry.
- *Involutional ptosis*: Repair/advance the levator aponeurosis onto the tarsus, either via the upper lid skin crease, or via a posterior conjunctival approach, e.g. conjunctivo-Müllerectomy or white-line (posterior aponeurosis) advancement.
- *Myopathy including chronic progressive external ophthalmoplegia and myasthenia gravis*: If LF <8–10 mm (<5 mm in children) consider brow suspension with a non-autogenous material such as silicone, because standard ptosis surgery risks corneal exposure due to orbicularis weakness, reduced Bell's phenomenon and reduced upgaze. Furthermore, a silicone sling can be adjusted. Use local anaesthesia with sedation, with anaesthetic cover. Aim to leave the lid height similar to the preoperative level as frontalis effort will raise the lids above the visual axis. In patients with a third nerve palsy, or where there is a risk of diplopia, silicone is preferred as it can readily be removed or adjusted.

Consent Risk of over or under correction, corneal exposure, lid oedema, infection, asymmetry of skin creases, lid contour and height.

Postoperative care Topical antibiotics q.d.s.; ointment at night, and p.r.n. topical lubricants.

Follow-up One to 3 weeks (sooner if exposure risk), for removal of sutures, then 6–8 weeks. Consider early revision if overcorrected. Manage mild overcorrection with gentle lash traction twice daily. Consider raising the lower lid where there is corneal exposure but minimal clearance of the visual axis by the upper lid (myopathic patients).

CHALAZION

Background Lipogranulomatous inflammatory lid reaction to retained sebaceous secretions (meibomian glands or glands of Zeiss). Histology shows focal or diffuse involvement which may involve the whole lid, and even abscess formation. Associated with lid margin disease (blepharitis), acne rosacea and seborrhoeic dermatitis. Often occurs without significant lid disease.

Differential diagnosis Sebaceous gland carcinoma can masquerade as recurrent chalazion or 'unilateral blepharoconjunctivitis'. Also consider rare Merkel cell tumour (clinically distinct with rapid growth and red appearance). Other periocular infective lesions include acute staphylococcal meibomian gland infection, and infections of a lash follicle and associated gland of Zeiss or Moll. These present as tender swellings which may resolve spontaneously or discharge. Any swelling in the region above the medial canthal ligament suggests neoplasia of the lacrimal sac and requires urgent investigation (CT and biopsy).

History One or more acute or chronic lesions in the eyelid(s). These can resolve spontaneously or become intermittently inflamed.

Examination Focal or diffuse lesion(s) within the lid (**Fig. 2.11**), often with lid margin and tear film changes. Lid eversion may reveal an exophytic inflamed conjunctival granuloma.

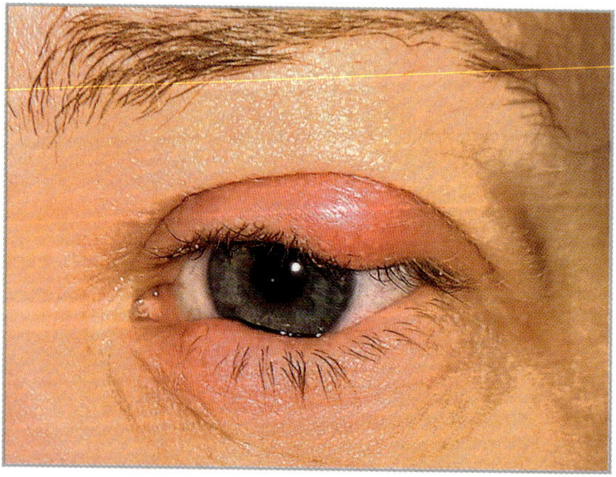

Fig. 2.11: Chalazion.

Medical management

Options include:

- Preventative, and in chronic non-inflamed cases: Twice daily hot compresses to the lids, vertical massage over the Meibomian ducts, and horizontal lid margin hygiene to improve the flow of meibomian gland secretions.
- Various devices are available to deliver heat and compression, of unverified efficacy.
- Oc. chloramphenicol or Oc. fucithalmic b.d.
- Oral doxycycline 100 mg o.d. for 3 months or lymecycline 408 mg o.d. for 8 weeks to treat any associated rosacea, when present.
- Increased omega oils (supplements or fish intake)
- Gutte (G.) azithromycin b.d. for 3 days, repeated the following 3 weeks
- Intralesional 0.1 mL triamcinolone with a 30-gauge needle

Surgical management (incision and curettage)

1. Mark the skin over the lesion with a surgical pen to aid localisation.
2. Instil topical anaesthetic, and inject local subcutaneous anaesthesia (0.5 mL lidocaine 2% with 1:200,000 epinephrine). Use a 30-gauge needle if available and inject slowly to reduce discomfort. Wait for 5 minutes.
3. Position a cyst clamp (open side posteriorly) over the lid and tighten firmly before everting the lid.
4. Make a vertical incision (E11 blade) into the tarsus, no closer than 2 mm to the lid margin.
5. Curette out the granuloma, which may be firm. Larger lesions may require a cruciate incision with excision of tarsus. Clean the granuloma cavity with gauze swaged over the curette end.
6. Send material to histopathology in recurrent or atypical cases.
7. Instil antibiotic ointment and cover the eye with a Vaseline gauze and eye pad for 4–6 hours. Prescribe topical antibiotic q.d.s. for 1 week.

Follow-up Not required for routine cases.

NECROTISING FASCIITIS

Background A destructive microbial infection of the soft tissues which can cause precipitous tissue destruction, septicaemia, disseminated intravascular coagulation (DIC) and death. Causative organisms are classified as type 1 (polymicrobial – anaerobes, gram-negative bacilli and enterococci) and type 2 (group A β-haemolytic *Streptococcus* ± staphylococcal). Early recognition and prompt intervention are critical.

History Risk factors include advancing age, injury (which can be minor, such as an insect bite) and immunosuppression, including diabetes.

Examination Examine for skin discolouration, local sensory loss, frank necrosis and sloughing tissue (**Fig. 2.12**). Check vital signs.

Differential diagnosis Preseptal cellulitis (without progression to orbital cellulitis or necrotising fasciitis), chronic dacryoadenitis (oedema limited to the periorbital region, tenderness in superotemporal quadrant and no skin necrosis), periocular dermatomyositis, and discoid lupus erythematosus.

Investigations Full blood count (FBC), acute-phase inflammatory markers, renal and hepatic profiles.

Management Immediate intravenous (i.v.) benzylpenicillin 2.4 g q.d.s. and i.v. clindamycin 600 mg q.d.s. Debride necrotic tissue down to a healthy (bleeding) bed. Repeat as necessary. Send tissue for culture and sensitivity. Co-manage with intensivist if the patient is unwell. Subsequent reconstructive approaches include 'laissez faire' (granulation), local myocutaneous flaps, and full-thickness grafting.

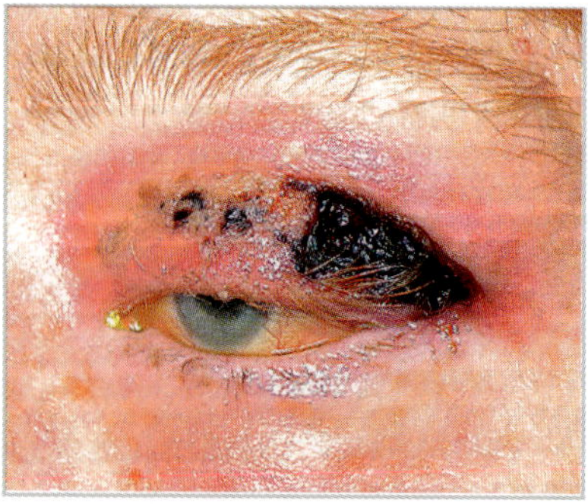

Fig. 2.12: Necrotising fasciitis.

BENIGN LID LESIONS

Epithelial lesions

- *Squamous papilloma*: A sessile or pedunculated lesion of viral origin (**Fig. 2.13**). Manage by shave excision biopsy.
- *Seborrhoeic keratosis (senile verruca)*: Single or multiple plaques or pedunculated lesions occurring in middle-aged to older adults. Perform excision biopsy.
- *Keratoacanthoma*: Solitary, subacute nodule of possible viral origin characterised by a keratin-filled crater, or horn (**Fig. 2.14**). The differential diagnosis includes squamous cell carcinoma (SCC), basal cell carcinoma and seborrheic keratosis. In the absence of spontaneous resolution, perform an excision biopsy which must include deep tissue to exclude SCC.
- *Epidermoid cyst*: Also called sebaceous cyst. Presents as a mobile subcutaneous or dermal mass containing desquamated cells and keratin (**Fig. 2.15**). Manage with complete excision with preservation of overlying skin.

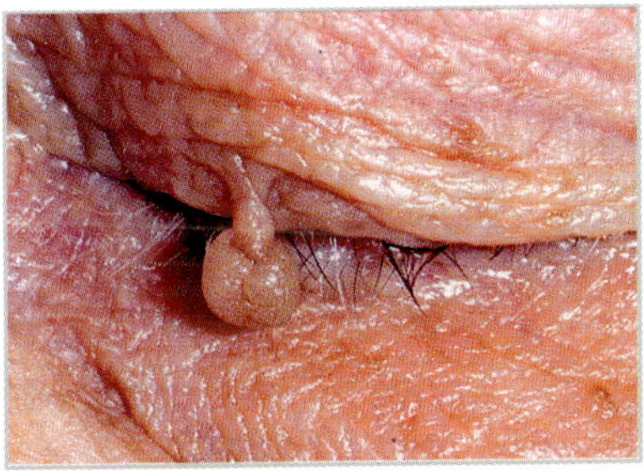

Fig. 2.13: Squamous papilloma.

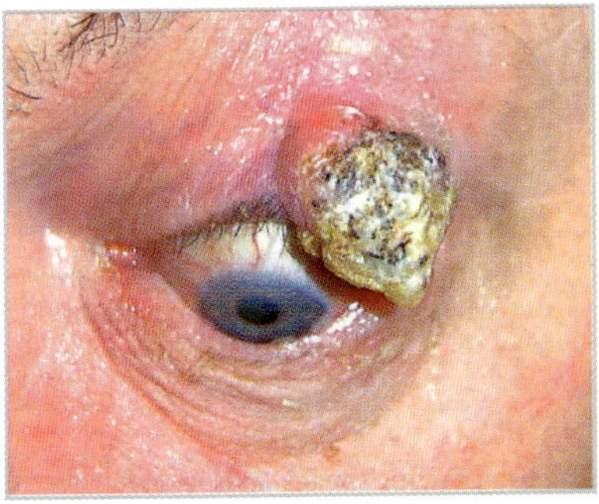

Fig. 2.14: Keratoacanthoma.

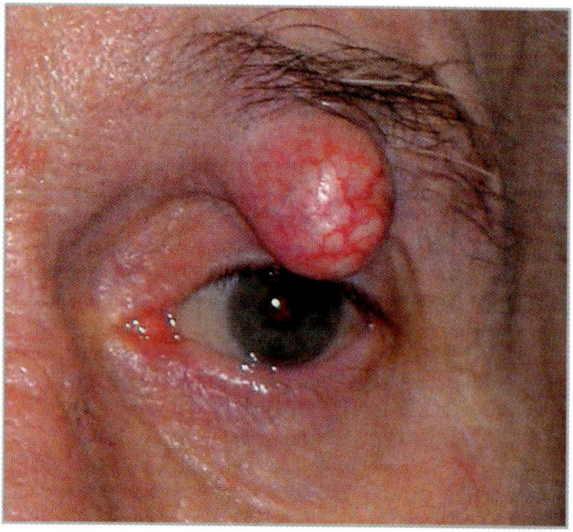

Fig. 2.15: Epidermoid cyst.

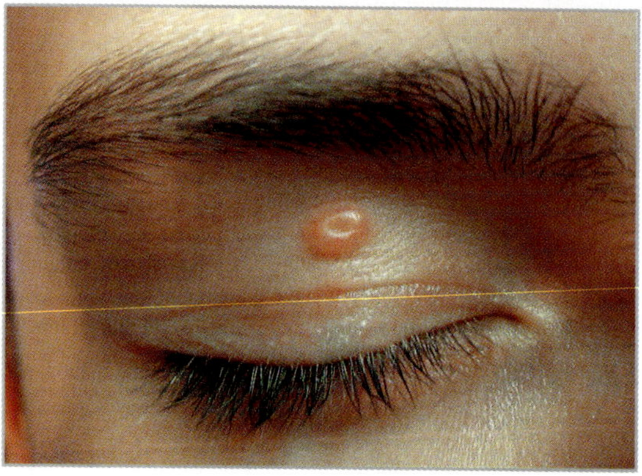

Fig. 2.16: Molluscum contagiosum.

- *Molluscum contagiosum*: Single or multiple periocular lesions which shed poxvirus particles and may present as a chronic follicular conjunctivitis (**Fig. 2.16**). Manage by direct excision.

Adnexal lesions

- Lesions originating from eccrine sweat glands include sudiferous cysts, which may occur as solitary or multiple lesions on the eyelids (**Fig. 2.17**), and syringomata which present as multiple small pale papules on the lower lids. Manage by surgical excision or carbon dioxide laser.

- Lesions of the apocrine glands of Moll include apocrine hidrocystoma which presents as a small fluid-filled cyst on the eyelid margin (**Fig. 2.18**), and cylindroma, a dome-shaped pink nodule. Extensive involvement of the scalp is described as a turban tumour. Excise intact if troublesome.
- Lesions of hair follicles include trichoepithelioma, trichofolliculoma, trichilemmoma and pilomatrixoma. All require excision biopsy.

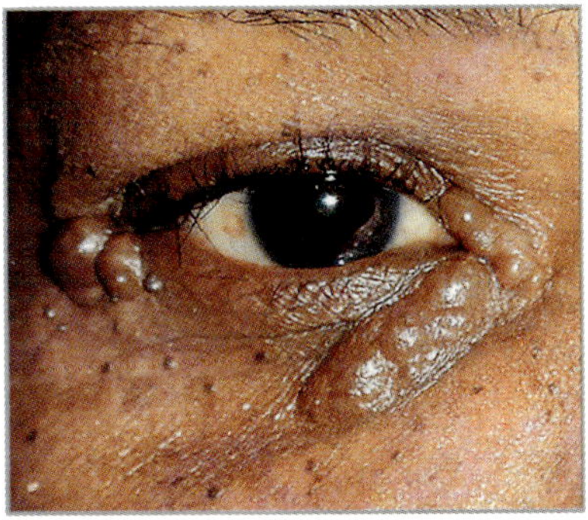

Fig. 2.17: Multiple eccrine (sudiferous) cysts.

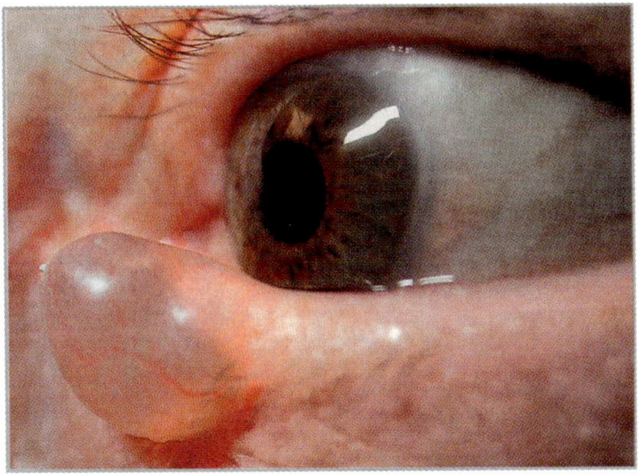

Fig. 2.18: Large cyst of Moll (apocrine hidrocystoma).

Vascular lesions

- *Capillary haemangioma*: Superficial 'strawberry naevi' (**Fig. 2.19**) are the most common, but deeper, orbital lesions can occur (p. 118). An oscillatory decay pattern precedes complete involution within the first decade. Larger lesions may cause astigmatism and mechanical ptosis. Where there is a risk of amblyopia, treatment, typically with topical or systemic β-blockade, is highly effective.
- *Naevus flammeus ('port wine stain')*: This flat red-purple vascular lesion is formed of dilated capillaries, is usually unilateral in distribution, and does not blanch with pressure (unlike a capillary naevus). In addition, it does not involute spontaneously, and is associated with other ocular and leptomeningeal vascular lesions in the Sturge–Weber syndrome (**Fig. 2.20**).
- *Pyogenic granuloma*: Occurs after injury (**Fig. 2.21**), and is neither pyogenic (pus-producing), or granulomatous, but reactive vascular granulation tissue. Histology identifies non-granulomatous inflammatory cells, fibroblasts and blood vessels. Treatment is surgical excision.
- Localised slow flow lesions (varices, **Fig. 2.22**) and high flow lesions (arteriovenous malformations) can occur in the eyelids. Treatment is generally by excision.

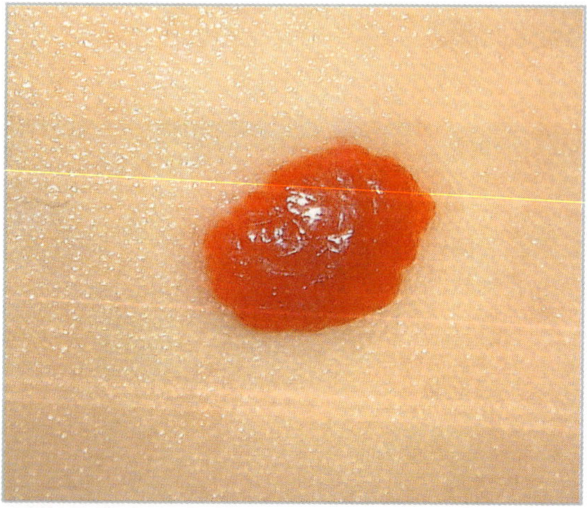

Fig. 2.19: Capillary haemangioma (strawberry naevus).

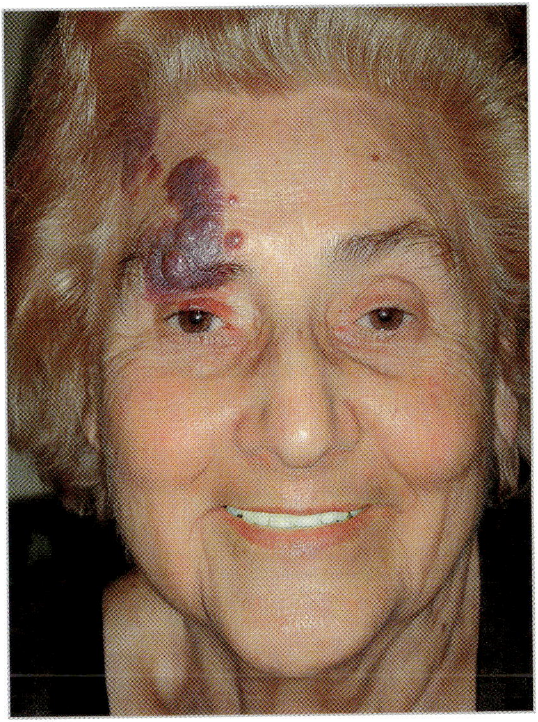

Fig. 2.20: Naevus flammeus associated with Sturge–Weber syndrome.

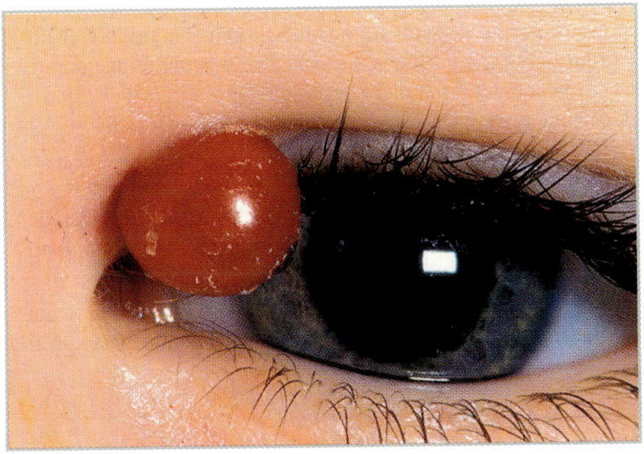

Fig. 2.21: Pyogenic granuloma.

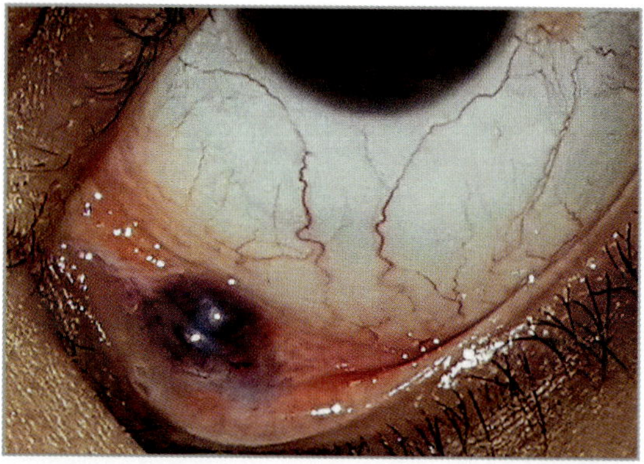

Fig. 2.22: Eyelid varix.

Pigmented lesions

- *Pigmented naevi*: Common lesions that do not require excision in the absence of atypical features such as growth, change in pigmentation, or lash loss (**Fig. 2.23**). Note that basal cell carcinomas may be pigmented, and melanomas may lack pigmentation.
- *Naevus of Ota (oculodermal melanocytosis)*: A small percentage of these can undergo malignant transformation, and can be extensive, involving the eyelid, orbit, maxilla and skull base (see p. 468).

Xanthomatous lesions

- *Xanthelasma*: Presents in the medial eyelids in middle-aged adults **(Fig. 2.24)**, and is associated with hyperlipidaemia in ~50% of cases. Treatment options include surgical excision, carbon dioxide laser, and topical trichloroacetic acid.
- *Juvenile xanthogranuloma*: Presents within the first 2 years of life with raised nodules, typically in the head and neck region, which regress spontaneously within a few years. Associated iris involvement may cause glaucoma, uveitis and spontaneous hyphaema.
- Deeper yellow-orange appearing masses in the lid can be due to orbital xanthogranuloma, and typically require imaging and biopsy.

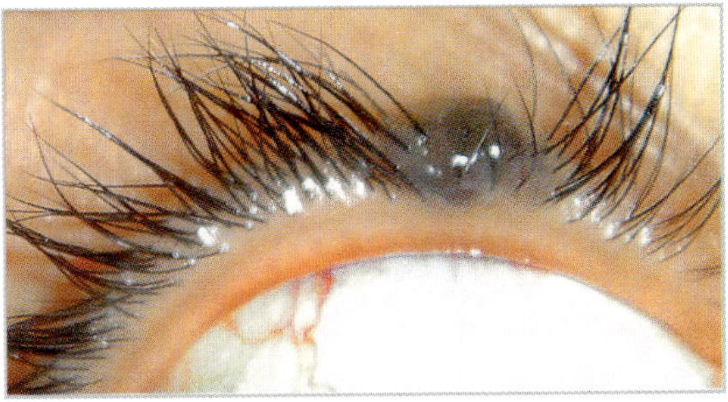

Fig. 2.23: Intradermal naevus with localised lash loss (excision biopsy required).

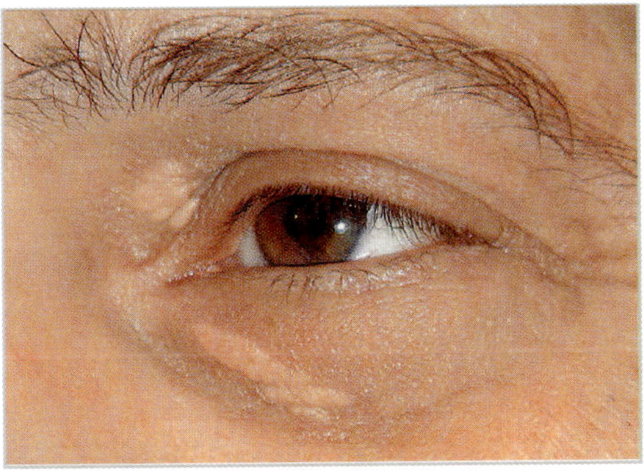

Fig. 2.24: Xanthelasmata.

Neural lesions

Eyelid neurofibroma: can be isolated or associated with neurofibromatosis type I. Lesions occur as a solitary fleshy mass or diffuse lid infiltration with mechanical ptosis (plexiform neuroma) (**Fig. 2.25**). Complete excision is difficult to achieve and recurrence is common.

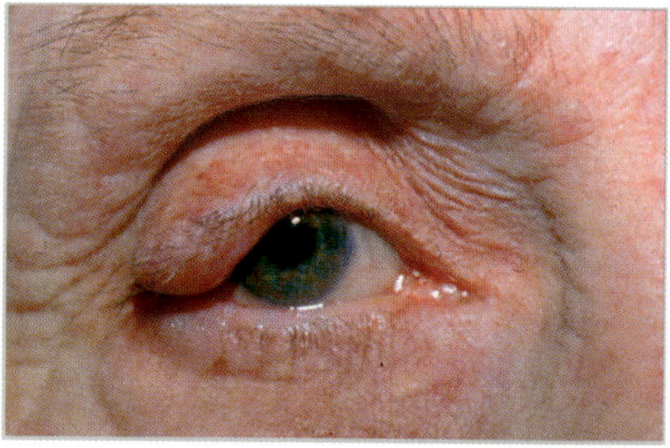

Fig. 2.25: Neurofibroma.

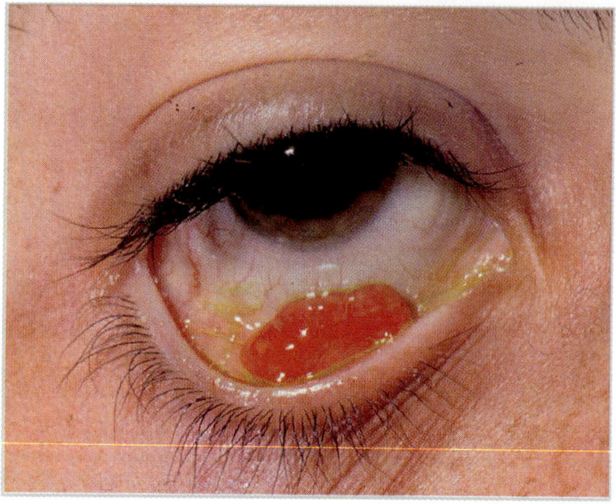

Fig. 2.26: Conjunctival granuloma.

Miscellaneous

- *Exophytic conjunctival granuloma*: A posterior lid lesion associated with chalazia or previous posterior lid surgery **(Fig. 2.26)**. Treat with shave excision biopsy.
- *Cutaneous sarcoid granuloma*: Refer for management of systemic disease. Local lesions are treated with a combination of long- and short-acting intralesional steroid injections (intralesional Depo-Medrone 40 mg/mL, and perilesional dexamethasone 5 mg/mL), repeated empirically.

NEOPLASTIC LID LESIONS

Background There are no pathognomonic features of neoplasia, but a careful history will identify a gradually or rapidly enlarging lid lesion, crusting, bleeding, irritation, red eye, and epiphora, the latter due to mechanical ectropion, corneal irritation, or involvement of the lacrimal drainage system. Biopsy all atypical lid lesions.

Premalignant disease

- *Actinic keratosis*: ~20% of cases progress to squamous cell carcinoma (SCC). Lesions may be widespread and a dermatology opinion is required. Treat by excision or cryotherapy (**Fig. 2.27**).
- *Bowen's disease (intraepithelial neoplasia)*: Cellular atypia is present at the level of the basement membrane, but no deeper. Progresses to SSC in 2–3% of cases; most advocate complete excision unless there is limited tissue, such as around the canaliculi (**Fig. 2.28**). Such cases are managed by debulking and cryotherapy, with full excision in cases of malignant transformation.
- *Lentigo maligna*: Slowly spreading macular lesion, with irregular border. Becomes infiltrative in 33% of cases. Complete excision is preferable, but where this is impractical, monitor the area closely, with excisional biopsy of any enlarging or suspicious areas (**Fig. 2.29**).

Primary eyelid malignant disease

- *Basal cell carcinoma (BCC)*: Accounts for >90% of all neoplastic eyelid lesions, being most prevalent in fair-skinned

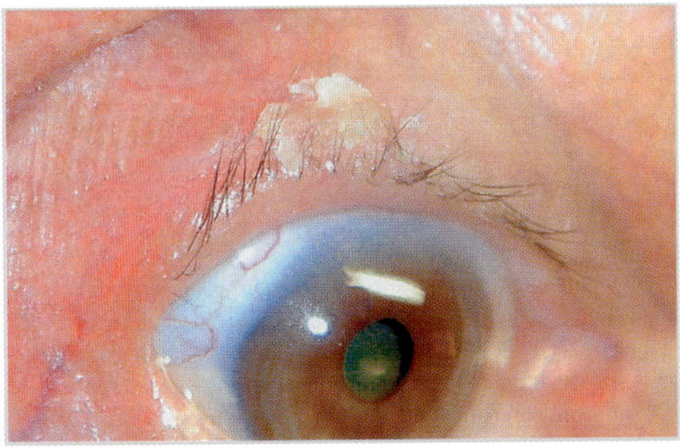

Fig. 2.27: Actinic keratosis.

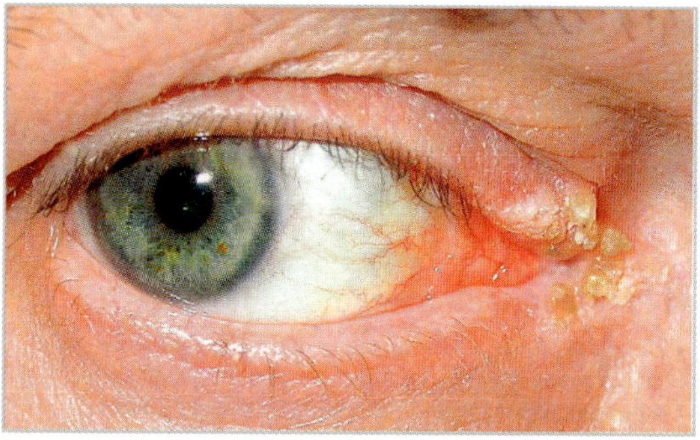

Fig. 2.28: Bowen's disease.

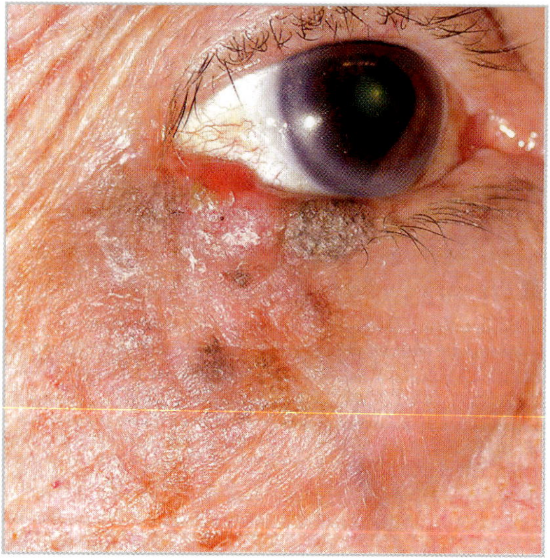

Fig. 2.29: Lentigo maligna with focal infiltrative changes.

individuals. Subtypes are described as nodular, ulcerative, cystic, sclerosing, pigmented or morphoeiform, the latter being the most difficult to manage. Lesions occur most commonly on the lower lid and medial canthus (**Fig. 2.30**), and can be raised (e.g. nodular) or flat (e.g. morphoeiform), and in predisposed individuals multiple BCCs can occur.

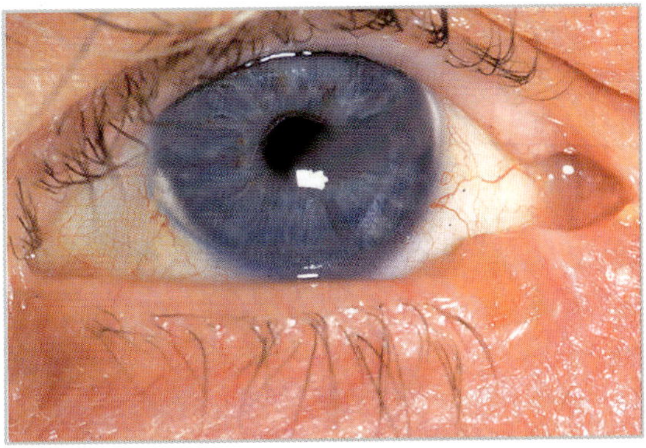

Fig. 2.30: Basal cell carcinoma.

Other features include destruction of the lash follicles, a raised pearly edge with telangiectatic vessels, ulcerated centre, cyst formation and pigmentation.

- Treatment options include surgery (with clear margins, achieved with standard histological sections, or Mohs' surgery), topical imiquimod and oral vismodegib. Exenteration may be required where there is orbital invasion.
- Reconstruction may entail direct closure for small lesions, sliding myocutaneous flaps, and/or full-thickness skin grafting for anterior lamella defects. Small anterior lamella defects can be left to heal by secondary intention, accepting the risk of secondary ectropion. Posterior lamella defects can be reconstructed with local conjunctival advancement, free tarsoconjunctival graft from the upper lid, hard palate graft, and nasal mucosal or labial mucosal grafts. Very small eyelid lesions, and those in elderly, frail patients, may be managed with cryotherapy. Local radiotherapy is not useful; subsequent lesion recurrence may be up to 20% and difficult to control.
- Surgery remains the gold standard, but consider 5% imiquimod cream (a potent inducer of pro-inflammatory mediators) for select patients with nodular BCC. In advanced or syndromic cases, vismodegib, which reduces patched one gene expression (implicated in BCC aetiology), is an alternative.
- *Squamous cell carcinoma*: Represents ~5% of all eyelid malignancies. Lesions occasionally develop from pre-existing areas of actinic keratosis or Bowen's disease. Typically presents as a thickened and erythematous scaly lesion (**Fig. 2.31**), but may also resemble BCC. Surface keratinisation may be marked. SCC is more aggressive than BCC, with

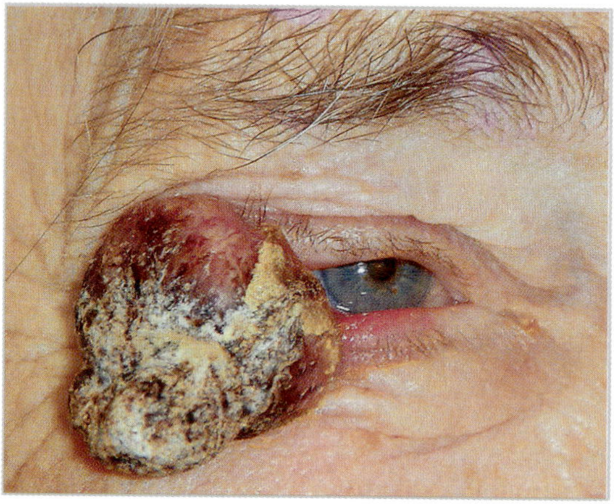

Fig. 2.31: Large squamous cell carcinoma originating from the lateral canthus of the eyelids.

~5% of patients developing local periocular recurrence despite histologically complete excision. Histological misinterpretation of SCC for BCC is not uncommon.

- Excision and reconstruction principles are similar to BCC. SCC has a metastatic potential; mortality is due to local perineural spread to the central nervous system (CNS) (~2%). The alternative to surgical excision includes cryotherapy which is good for small lesions, particularly those close to the lacrimal drainage apparatus. Radiotherapy is effective but is preferably avoided on the upper lid, because of the risk of inducing an irritable eye from keratin production on the tarsal conjunctiva, and for lesions at the medial canthus, which may extend deeply.
- Epidermal growth factor receptor (EGFR) has been implicated in SCC, and anti-EGFR treatment has demonstrated disease control (if not cure) in aggressive forms of periocular SCC, and in frail patients unsuitable for surgery.
- *Sebaceous gland carcinoma*: A rare and aggressive tumour arising from the meibomian glands (**Fig. 2.32**) which carries a high morbidity due to local, haematogenous, and lymphatic spread. A history of chronic, unilateral, atypical or focal 'blepharitis' is suspicious.
- Early diagnosis and complete excision is essential. Head and neck ultrasound, and staging imaging are required due to the aggressive nature of the disease. Perform mapping biopsies

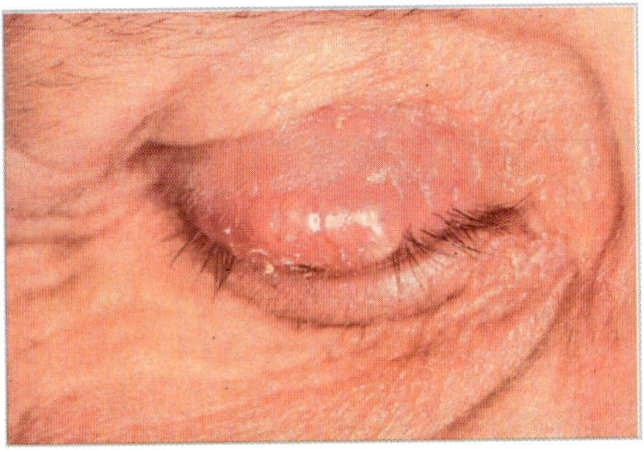

Fig. 2.32: Sebaceous gland carcinoma.

of the superior and inferior tarsal and bulbar conjunctiva to exclude multicentric origin and pagetoid spread.

- Manage localised masses with excision, clear margins, and reconstruction. For diffuse intraepithelial disease, topical mitomycin-C is advocated by some, but many prefer orbital exenteration (where there is diffuse involvement of the lid or conjunctiva) due to the poor prognosis (compared to eyelid BCC and SCC), and inherent uncertainty of the stage of unbiopsied area(s). Include periosteum and lacrimal sac and proximal duct intact with the specimen as pagetoid spread can be extensive. Radiation therapy plays a palliative role. Sentinel lymph node biopsy (SLNB), with clearance if positive, can provide prognostic information but is not proven to influence survival.
- *Melanoma*: <1% of eyelid neoplasms. Lesions are irregularly pigmented (**Fig. 2.33**), but a large minority lack pigmentation. Other features include inflammation and bleeding. Clinical forms include lentigo maligna, superficial spreading, and nodular melanoma. Metastases are common in the latter two forms. The Breslow thickness predicts the average time to metastasis. The cure rate for lesions <0.75 mm thick approaches 100%.
- Excise lesions <1.5 mm thick with wide margins and reconstruct. Lesions >1.5 mm require additional SLNB (see above). Involve nuclear medicine, and head and neck or plastic surgery colleagues. Distant metastasis may occur despite clear histological margins.
- In patients with advanced *BRAF*-gene positive disease, newer anti-monoclonal antibodies (such as the human inhibitory

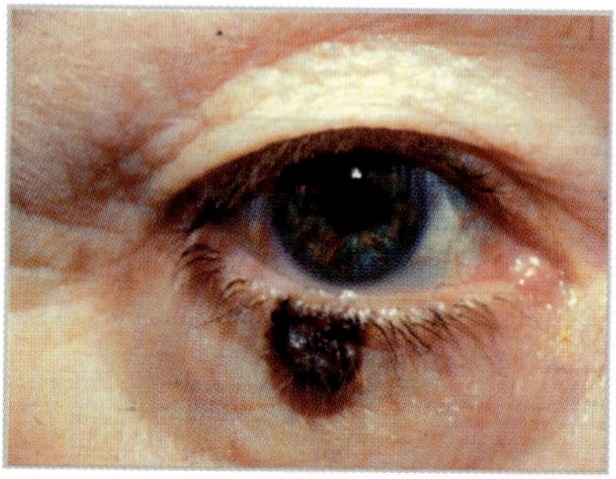

Fig. 2.33: Melanoma.

anti-CTLA-4 antibodies) can delay progression, but carry the risk of severe systemic inflammatory side effects.

- *Merkel cell tumour*: A small-cell undifferentiated/neuroendocrine carcinoma which characteristically presents as a firm, painless nodule with overlying violet skin changes (**Fig. 2.34**). The polyomavirus (MCPyV or Merkel cell polyomavirus) is implicated, and is present in 40–100% of specimens. Growth is rapid, metastases are common, and the prognosis is poor. Early diagnosis and aggressive, histologically guided surgical excisions are important. Adjuvant chemotherapy has not yet been proven to prolong life.

Secondary malignant disease

- *Metastatic disease*: Eyelid involvement is rare. Primary sites include breast and bronchus. Involve physicians.
- *Lymphomatous deposits*: Refer to oncology for systemic investigation and management.
- *Kaposi's sarcoma*: Avascular neoplasm with multicentric cutaneous and extracutaneous involvement which presents as a purplish or red/brown non-pruritic nodule or macule commonly affecting the face, tip of the nose, eyelids or conjunctiva (**Fig. 2.35**). It develops in the presence of Kaposi's sarcoma-associated herpes virus (HHV-8), which is associated with HIV infection and other lymphotrophic disorders. Local control may be achieved with radiation. Management is of the underlying immune deficiency.

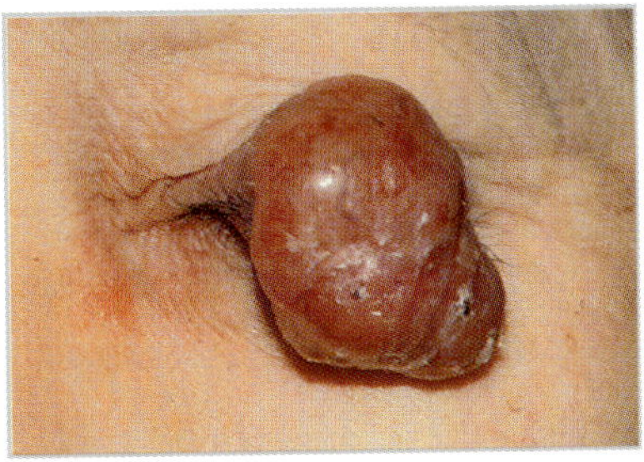

Fig. 2.34: Large Merkel cell tumour.

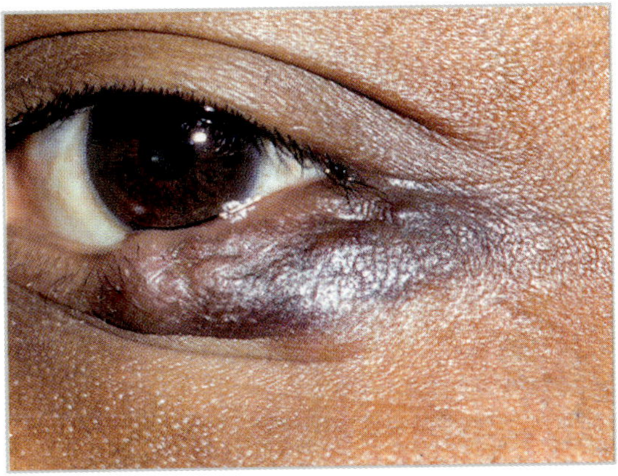

Fig. 2.35: Kaposi's sarcoma.

FACIAL DYSTONIAS

Clinical features The facial dystonias include benign essential blepharospasm (a focal dystonia characterised by repeated involuntary contractures of the orbicularis oculi, procerus and corrugator muscles), Meige syndrome (blepharospasm + midface musculature spasm) and hemifacial spasm. Increasingly frequent blinking and periocular spasms may lead to social embarrassment, anxiety, depression, and functional blindness.

Examination Draw the position and degree of spasm or fasciculation. Perform a full ocular and cranial nerve examination (including corneal sensation). Note any lid margin disease or tear film abnormalities. Evert the lids.

Investigations Refer patients with hemifacial spasm, recent or rapid onset blepharospasm, or blepharospasm with other neurological features (e.g. reduced corneal sensation) to a neurologist for assessment and neuroimaging. Those with longstanding, stable symptoms and without other neurological signs do not require investigation.

Management Minimise the sensory stimulus for blepharospasm. Treat any ocular surface disease, including meibomian gland dysfunction (p. 143), and dry eye (with frequent lubricants, p. 207). Consider uveitis and glaucoma as precipitating causes. Consider FL-41 tinted lenses and PressOp pressure device attached to the glasses to apply pressure to the temples (sensory trick).

Chemodenervation with botulinum toxin type A (BoNTA) improves symptoms in the majority of patients. An empirical approach is required to identify the optimum dose: repeat treatment may be needed to control symptoms. Inform patients about support groups, e.g. The Dystonia Society, and provide an information leaflet if available.

Botulinum toxin injections All volumes and dosages given below are for Dysport and are not applicable to other BoNTA formulations, e.g. Botox and Xeomin. It is essential to review the manufacturer's advice for each agent. Xeomin has the highest neurotoxin activity per unit.

Complications: Ptosis, diplopia, entropion, ectropion, exposure keratitis, and allergy.

Contraindications: Known hypersensitivity, history of myopathy, bleeding disorders, and pregnancy/lactation.

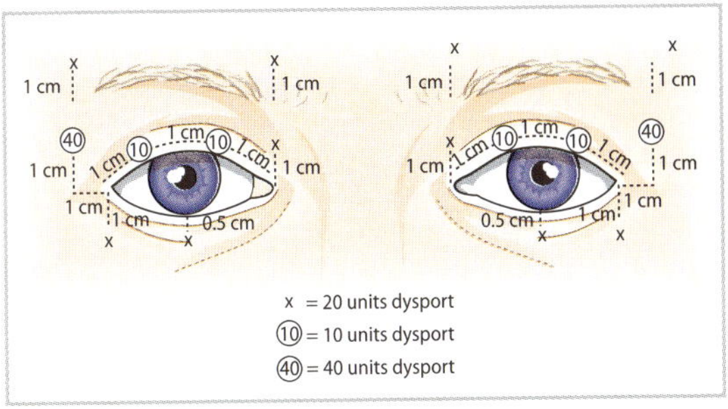

Fig. 2.36: Botulinum toxin injections for blepharospasm and hemifacial spasm.

Week 1 (first clinic visit):

1. *Blepharospasm and hemifacial spasm*:
   - Give Dysport in six locations around the eye, each location receiving 20 units (**Fig. 2.36**) with the exception of the lateral upper lid, where 40 units are given.
   - For patients with evidence of pretarsal spasm give 10 units of Dysport in two locations on the upper lid (topical anaesthetic cream may be required).
2. *Aberrant facial nerve regeneration and myokymia*: reduce initial doses.

Week 4:

1. *Spasm controlled*: review in 3 months. If further botulinum toxin is indicated, the dose is the sum of the previous two injections.
2. *Spasm not controlled*: further injection(s) to muscles that remain in spasm. Review 1 week later (week 5).

Continue this cycle until either the spasm is controlled or the side effects of treatment become intolerable.

Surgery

- Consider surgery for patients with an inadequate response to conservative measures and BoNTA.
- Protractor myectomy (via a blepharoplasty incision) may be effective in some cases, although injections may still be required.
- Frontalis suspension may be considered in cases of apraxia of eyelid opening, ± removal of pretarsal orbicularis, or for pre-tarsal apraxia (inability to open the eyelids due to spasms of the pre-tarsal orbicularis).
- Consider deep brain stimulation of the internal globus pallidus for very severe cases.

Further management options

- *Induced ptosis as side effect of controlling pretarsal spasm*: trial of ptosis props; if tolerated, consider brow suspension with supramid or (reversible) silicone stents.
- Pharmacological augmentation of chemodenervation, e.g. trihexyphenidyl, a cholinergic receptor antagonist (caution in those with urinary retention, dementia and narrow angles) can be useful in refractory cases or for spastic Bell's phenomenon (eyeball rolls under upper eyelid despite adequate control of spasm).

CONGENITAL EYELID DISEASE

Blepharophimosis-ptosis-epicanthus inversus syndrome

Clinical features An autosomal dominant disorder with a global prevalence of ~1 in 50,000, caused by mutations in the single-exon gene forkhead box L2 (*FOXL2*). In type I BPES, complex eyelid malformations occur with premature ovarian failure. Type II only has lid defects. Ocular features include variable degrees of ptosis with poor levator function, epicanthus inversus, blepharophimosis (narrowing of the horizontal palpebral aperture), telecanthus (canthal displacement due to soft-tissue anomaly), hypertelorism (canthal displacement due to a wide nasal bridge), and lower lid ectropion. Other associated features include hypoplasia of the tarsal plate, prominent vertical brow hair, flat brow, and female infertility.

Management Urgent brow suspension where there is a risk of amblyopia. Elective surgery may be deferred until the age of 3–4 years, when nasal bridge growth begins, the tissues are larger, and the epicanthic folds reduce in size. Correct mild epicanthic folds with a Y–V plasty over the medial canthal tendon (MCT). A Z-plasty alone over the epicanthic fold(s) is indicated where there is no telecanthus. Correct telecanthus by resecting the middle portion of the MCT and suturing the ends together. A transnasal wire, which draws the MCTs towards the midline, may be indicated in hypertelorism, and in severe cases of telecanthus, where medial canthal bone requires removal in addition to medial canthal soft tissue. Ptosis surgery is carried out after the medial canthoplasty, and usually requires brow suspension with autogenous fascia lata. A full-thickness skin graft to the upper and lower lids may also be required.

Genetic counselling BPES is usually autosomal dominant, but *de novo* mutations may account for >50% of cases. Consider prenatal testing for at-risk pregnancies, if the family mutation is known. Involve a senior clinician or refer to a geneticist.

Eyelid coloboma

Clinical features May be idiopathic, or associated with developmental first arch or clefting syndromes. Upper lid colobomas are more common, representing a spectrum from a small localised absence of the tarsus and associated lashes, to complete absence of the upper lid with corneal exposure (**Fig. 2.37**). Ocular and systemic associations include forniceal conjunctival choristomas, bands and foreshortening,

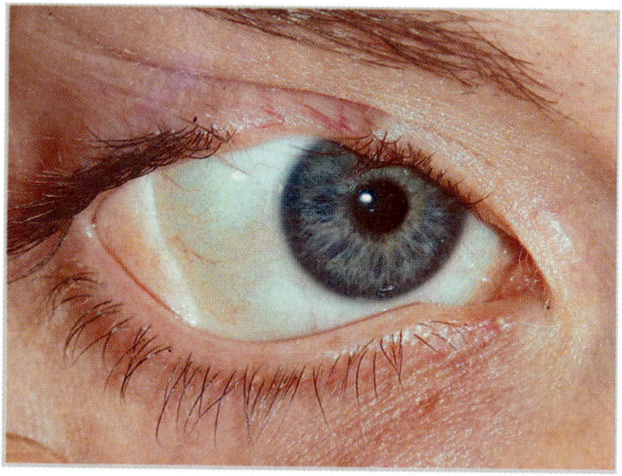

Fig. 2.37: Upper eyelid coloboma – note associated ocular dermolipoma.

anophthalmos, cryptophthalmos, limbal dermoids and Goldenhar's syndrome. Lower lid colobomata may be associated with lower facial clefting syndromes.

Management Complete ocular, orthoptic, and systemic evaluation are required. Corneal exposure is treated aggressively, and is an indication for urgent upper lid surgery. Small- to medium-size defects (<50% of lid width) may be repaired by pentagon wedge excision of the anomalous tissue with direct closure, with or without lateral cantholysis. Larger defects require staged surgery with a lower to upper lid switch flap and subsequent division of the flap. A forced duction test is performed, conjunctival traction bands are excised, and forniceal foreshortening is managed with buccal mucous membrane graft(s). Monitor for amblyopia.

Distichiasis

See page 34.

Epiblepharon

Clinical features An excess fold of skin and muscle in the lower lid, typically with vertically orientated eyelashes irrespective of the amount of skin redundancy, and without true entropion (**Fig. 2.38**). In severe cases, lash–globe contact may occur.

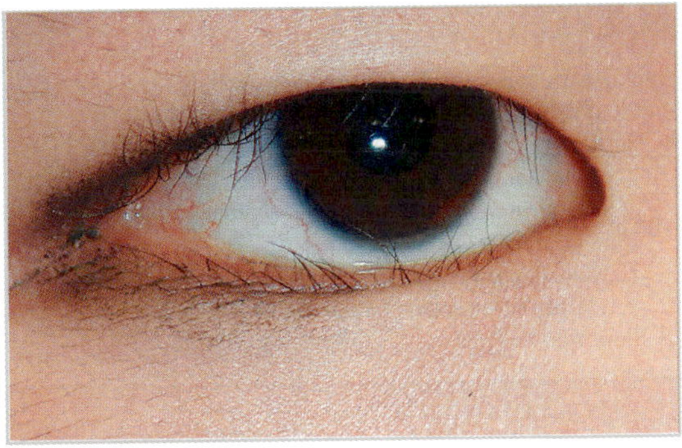

Fig. 2.38: Epiblepharon showing skin and muscle fold in the lower eyelid, with vertical orientation of the eyelashes.

Management The majority of cases resolve spontaneously. Where there is no entropion, excise a strip of skin and muscle (Hotz procedure). Add everting sutures if there is entropion, but keep them deep to avoid an unwanted skin crease.

EYELID TRAUMA

Background Broad groups of eyelid injury are recognised, but any combination may occur:

- Lacerating trauma:

  Uncomplicated:
  ± lid margin laceration, ± lacrimal gland prolapse.
  Complicated by injury to: levator complex, orbital septum, lacrimal apparatus, globe, orbit, sinuses and cranium.
  ± retained lid or orbital foreign body.
- Blunt trauma (contusion and avulsion of lid).
- Chemical injury (alkalis tends to be the most severe, but acids can be equally destructive).

History A carefully documented history, with imaging, is medicolegally critical. Note the following:

- The time and nature of an alleged assault or foreign body (FB), as well as the distance and trajectory.
- The FB material and structure, and whether all parts have been recovered.
- Other ocular symptoms.
- ENT symptoms including epistaxis and cerebrospinal fluid (CSF) rhinorrhoea.

Examination

- Record VA.
- Accurately document and photograph the extent of the injury. Note any involvement of the lid margin(s), lacrimal drainage apparatus, or posterior lamella.
- Exclude anterior segment, (p. 267), posterior segment (p. 661) and orbital injury (p. 127). *Always* consider a possible intracranial injury with sharp upper lid injuries.

Investigations Imaging is chiefly to exclude bony injury, retained FB, gas and pus. A plain skull X-ray has limited value. Dedicated orbital (not head) CT scan is preferable, with fine cuts and coronal reformats. Examine the soft-tissue windows for FBs, and bone windows for fractures.

General principles of repair

- Cranial, systemic and ocular injuries take priority over eyelid repair.
- Extensive lid, globe, orbital, and even intracranial injury may occur through a small eyelid laceration. Such lacerations often appear small or healed, concealing severe underlying injuries.

- Corneal protection remains paramount when considering reconstruction.
- In canalicular injuries, repair all involved canaliculi. Intubate with a monocanalicular stent(s) for 2–3 weeks (see below).
- Involve a paediatrician if children are injured. Consider non-accidental injury (p. 698). Children with traumatic ptosis are at risk of developing amblyopia and may require urgent brow suspension.
- Provide tetanus toxoid coverage.
- Animal bites to the face can safely be closed primarily. Cover with oral antibiosis, e.g. co-amoxiclav 375 mg t.d.s. p.o.
- Repair under general anaesthesia unless there is limited injury to the lid alone.
- Thoroughly clean all dirty wounds.
- Do not discard tissue unless necrotic or infected.
- Primary repair aims to approximate tissue planes – posterior lamella, tarsus and skin. Undertake complex procedures (e.g. skin grafting) secondarily.
- Avoid vertical shortening as tissue contracture leads to ectropion.
- In most situations use a standard 2–1–1 knot: draw the suture in opposite directions with each throw and tie knots anteriorly to avoid corneal abrasion.
- Use deep 5/0 absorbable sutures (e.g. Vicryl) to draw planes together and anchor tissues. Skin sutures should not bear tension.
- *Skin*: Use continuous 7/0 absorbable or 6/0 Nylon sutures, or 6/0 absorbable interrupted.
- *Tarsus*: Use 6/0 absorbable sutures × 2–3.
- *Grey line and lash line*: Use buried 7/0 absorbable suture.
- Skin sutures can be left to absorb, or can be removed after 7–10 days.
- Avoid silk sutures as these can cause inflammation.

Specific injuries

- *Lid margin*: Repair using the same principles as a pentagon wedge excision (p. 22).
- *Levator palpebrae complex*: Thoroughly clean the wound and approximate corresponding tissue as accurately as possible. Do not extend the wound to identify further structures because spontaneous resolution of the ptosis may occur up to 6 months post-injury, and the ptosis may be partly due to a neuropraxia.
- *Medial canthal tendon*: Even in cases of avulsion, a residual stump of deep canthal tendon can be grasped with toothed (e.g. Adson) forceps, and approximated to the medial cut end

of the tarsus using a 5/0 suture (absorbable or nonabsorbable) on a complex-curve, fish-hook or half-circle needle.

- *Canaliculus*: Always repair the upper and inferior canaliculi, preferably under general anaesthesia. Identification of the cut proximal end of the canaliculus within the wound is aided by application of 10% epinephrine on a cotton bud (transected end appears as a pale 'ring'), or by syringing through the fellow canaliculus with fluorescein or air. Insert the heel of a monocanalicular silicone stent into the punctal ampulla flush with the punctum. The stent itself requires no suturing and can be removed at 2–3 weeks. However, a stent will not prevent annular tissue contracture, and epiphora can still occur despite a patent lumen postoperatively. This technique avoids the use of the pigtail probe which risks injury of the healthy canaliculus. Alternatively, if sufficient distal canaliculus is present, this can be opened along its posterior surface and marsupialised into the conjunctival sac with an 8/0 absorbable suture. Where both canaliculi are injured, repair by an experienced surgeon is indicated. A silicone rod may be used and tied in the nose. If subsequent dacryocystorhinostomy with retrotubes fails, a Lester Jones tube may be indicated.

OPTOMETRY AND GENERAL PRACTICE GUIDELINES

Refer children with any eyelid abnormality early to detect and manage amblyopia. Adult eyelid malpositions such as ptosis and ectropion can be managed routinely unless there is ocular surface irritation, either from a stagnant tear film or aberrant lashes. Manage entropion with greater urgency due to the risk of corneal abrasion. Where there is lid laxity, a length of half-inch micropore tape applied along the lower lid and brought up onto the temple will tighten the lid and provide a temporary correction.

The majority of cases of facial palsy are idiopathic (Bell's palsy) and will not require tarsorrhaphy, but refer urgently to determine other risk factors for corneal exposure (e.g. reduced corneal sensation or Bell's phenomenon). Similarly, urgently deal with corneal exposure from any cause of lid malposition (e.g. entropion). Look for staining with 2% fluorescein dye in the exposed corneal areas. Refer suspected tumours urgently.

Give stat i.v. antibiotic (e.g. co-amoxyclav) to any patient with presumed eyelid infection with breakdown or frank necrosis of the overlying skin and refer immediately. Necrotising fasciitis is rare but has a high mortality.

Injuries to the eyelids require urgent attention, in particular upper eyelid trauma where there may be a risk of corneal exposure, and a risk of undetected globe, orbital, or even intracranial injury. The risk of corneal exposure is higher where there is eyelid margin injury. Refer patients with canalicular trauma urgently, as successful anatomical union is more difficult after 24–36 hours.

The following guidelines for hospital referral urgency are not prescriptive, as clinical situations vary.

Immediate

- Periorbital infection with suspected skin necrosis (necrotising fasciitis) p. 44

Same day

- Eyelid lacerations p. 66
- Canalicular laceration p. 68
- Acute adult ptosis associated with motility disorder and non-reactive pupil indicating a IIIrd nerve palsy (refer to neurosurgeon or neurologist) p. 736

Urgent (within 2 weeks)

- Suspected eyelid neoplasia, and atypical or recurrent eyelid lesions p. 53
- Entropion with corneal epitheliopathy, evidence of lash–cornea touch, or corneal scarring p. 28
- Ectropion or upper lid retraction with evidence of corneal exposure p. 21
- Bell's palsy p. 35
- Trichiasis with corneal fluorescein staining p. 32
- Keratoacanthoma p. 45

Soon (within 1 month)

- Paediatric ptosis p. 39
- Molluscum contagiosum p. 46
- Pyogenic granuloma p. 48
- Recent onset or unilateral facial dystonia (muscle spasm) p. 60
- Trichiasis without corneal fluorescein staining p. 32

Routine

- Adult ptosis p. 39
- Eyelid malposition without corneal exposure or irritation p. 21, 28
- Floppy eyelid syndrome p. 26
- Chalazion p. 42
- Squamous papilloma p. 45
- Actinic keratosis p. 53
- Epidermoid cyst p. 45
- Cyst of Moll p. 47
- Eyelid naevus p. 50
- Xanthelasma (check for dyslipidaemia) p. 50
- Longstanding bilateral facial dystonia (muscle spasm) p. 60

LACRIMAL

3

Thomas G Hardy & Geoffrey E Rose

THE WATERY EYE

Anatomy and physiology The tear film provides corneal lubrication, nourishment and protection, has anti-infective properties, aids removal of bacteria, cells and debris, and optimises the optical interface between air and cornea. It is triphasic, comprising a mucous layer (from goblet cells), aqueous layer (basal production from the accessory glands of Krause and Wolfring; reflex production from the main lacrimal glands), and lipid layer (meibomian glands).

Symptomatic watering results from reduced tear removal (normally by evaporation and drainage) and/or overproduction. Obstructive epiphora refers to reduced tear drainage. Tear distribution is also important, as is eyelid movement (lacrimal pump) and position. Patient tolerance of watering varies widely.

The lacrimal drainage system comprises three compartments:

1. Tear lake
2. Lacrimal sac
3. Nasal cavity

Relatively high-resistance conduits connect these compartments; the canaliculi (connecting compartments 1 and 2), and nasolacrimal duct (NLD, connecting compartments 2 and 3) **(Fig. 3.1)**:

- *Canalicular obstruction produces 'flow' symptoms*: 'Eyes well up with water', blur on downgaze, e.g. reading. 'Volume' symptoms are minimal or absent.
- *Nasolacrimal duct obstruction (NLDO) produces 'volume' symptoms* due to backwash from the lacrimal sac, e.g. recurrent conjunctivitis; morning stickiness; mucous debris in the tear film; dacryocystitis; lacrimal sac mucocoele or abscess. If tears cannot reflux from the sac via the canaliculi or valve of Rosenmüller, then the sac may become distended, painful and/or infected.

History Assess severity – symptoms indoors are more significant than those outdoors in cold, windy weather; frequency of dabbing with tissues; ± Munk score (0 = no watering; 1 = occasional watering with dabbing less than twice daily; 2 = dabbing 2–4 times daily; 3 = 5–10 times daily; 4 = >10 times daily or constant). Ask about onset, time relationships,

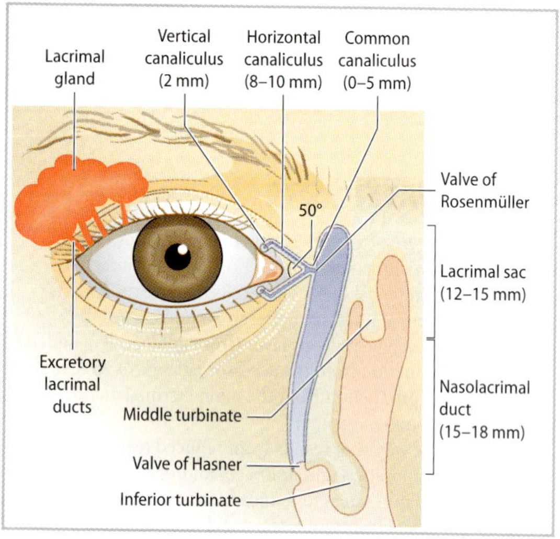

Fig. 3.1: Lacrimal drainage anatomy. The angle between the horizontal and common canaliculi in the axial plane is ~135°. Therefore, one must pull the lid laterally when probing the common canaliculus (during intubation, e.g. at dacryocystorhinostomy) to straighten out this angle and avoid a 'false passage' from canalicular perforation.

duration, and site of tear spillover. Medial spillage suggests impaired drainage; lateral spillage may relate to lower lid laxity, or upper lid dermatochalasis contacting the tear film with chronic skin wetting by capillary action. Reflex watering from tear-film deficiency is often worse in dry, warm or evaporative environments, bright light, or when blinking is reduced, e.g. concentrating on reading, computer use, and Parkinson's disease. Simultaneous rhinorrhoea suggests overproduction. Bloody tears suggest a sac tumour (rare), canaliculitis, or trauma to the canaliculi/sac (including iatrogenic injury and factitious disorder). Ask about surface irritation or itch (atopy), a history of facial/nasal trauma, and previous sinonasal or lacrimal surgery. 'Crocodile tears' are associated with facial palsy and involve neurogenic reflex watering, often sudden, from the thought of food, eating, or chewing. Lacrimal sac swelling may be secondary to a dacryocoele (a congenital cyst), mucocoele (see below), pyocoele, dacryocystitis or acute tear retention (both painful), tumour (usually painless ± bloody tears), or occasionally air (± pain).

Examination Examine for causes of overproduction or impaired drainage.

- *Overproduction*: Look for–
  1. Lid or lash malposition – trichiasis, distichiasis, entropion, exposure keratopathy due to ectropion or lagophthalmos.
  2. Lid margin disease.
  3. Tear film deficiency – perform Schirmer's test (p. 209) and tear film break-up time (p. 209).
  4. Corneal foreign body/erosions or subtarsal foreign body.
  5. Conjunctivitis – look for allergic papillae, follicles.
  6. Corneal disease, especially superficial punctate keratopathy from tear film anomalies or exposure keratopathy, and early dendritic keratitis.
  7. Uveitis and scleritis.
- *Impaired drainage*: Look for–
  1. Eyelid laxity or malposition of the lower lid or punctum, particularly ectropion.
  2. Punctal or canalicular stenosis, cicatrising conjunctival disease (e.g. pemphigoid and lichen planus), eye drops (e.g. glaucoma therapy), systemic chemotherapy (especially 5-FU and docetaxel), and trauma (including iatrogenic, e.g. lid tumour resection).
  3. Canaliculitis.
  4. Fistula – congenital or acquired (following dacryocystitis) – and accessory (duplicated) punctum/canaliculus.
  5. Lacrimal pump failure – especially facial palsy, scarring (trauma and surgery).
  6. Lacrimal sac mucocoele – this is a chronic collection of mucopurulent material due to low grade colonisation/infection of stagnant tears. Pressing on the sac causes reflux of mucus or pus (**Fig. 3.2**).
  7. Lacrimal sac mass – consider tumour or tense mucocoele. In general, a mass below medial canthal tendon (MCT) originates from the sac; lesions above the MCT may indicate non-sac origin (e.g. encephalocele) or lacrimal sac tumour.
  8. Dacryocystitis – active or resolved.
  9. Nasal obstruction, e.g. mass, inflammation and scarring. Perform nasal endoscopy if suspect obstruction/stenosis distal to lacrimal sac.
  10. Altered facial/lid relationship – including proptosis/prominent eyes, lower lid retraction and hypoplastic midface.
  11. Prior surgery or trauma – look for scars.

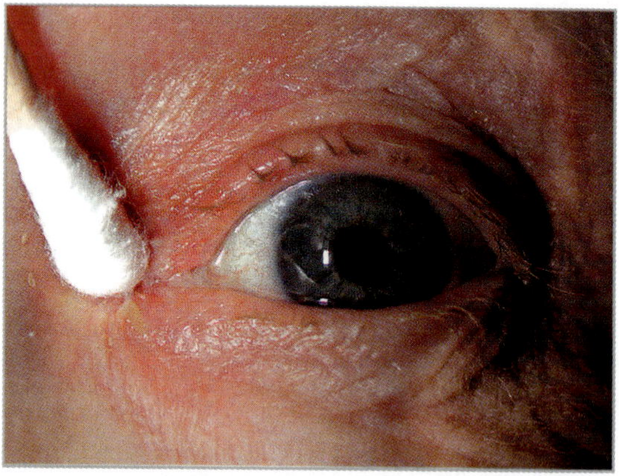

Fig. 3.2: Mucocoele with mucous reflux.

Clinical tests

- *Fluorescein disappearance test (FDT)*: Instil a tiny drop of fluorescein 2% in both eyes at the start of history taking. After ~5 minutes, look at tear film height ± asymmetry. High + diluted = overproduction; high + undiluted = impaired drainage.
- *Syringing*: Perform diagnostic lacrimal syringing in all patients with epiphora (including ectropion), except those with acute dacryocystitis in whom the procedure is usually painful. Consider patient's comfort and use a reclining chair with head support. Be very gentle to avoid canalicular trauma. Instil topical anaesthetic. If necessary, dilate the punctum, but avoid tearing the fibrous annulus and avoid sharp dilators. Keep the lower lid under firm lateral tension to eliminate the angle between the horizontal and common canaliculus to avoid canalicular perforation (false passage). Gently inject saline using a 2.5 mL syringe with a lacrimal cannula, inserted no more than ~5 mm into the horizontal canaliculus. It is seldom necessary to check for a 'hard' or 'soft stop' by pushing the cannula up against the medial sac wall, which is often uncomfortable. Lower canalicular reflux suggests obstruction proximal to the common canaliculus. Upper canalicular reflux with fluorescein or mucus reflux suggests a mucocoele due to NLDO. Early reflux via the upper canaliculus without fluorescein suggests common canalicular obstruction. Syringe the upper canaliculus if the lower punctum is occluded. The site of canalicular obstruction may be measured (hold cannula

with forceps at punctum and withdraw cannula; measure forceps-cannula tip distance).

- *Jones I dye test*: Assesses physiological drainage. Instil fluorescein 2% and then insert a cotton bud under the inferior turbinate – if there is dye on the cotton bud, the test is positive. Nasal endoscopic visualisation is more accurate. A negative result indicates non-patency, partial patency, or functional NLDO. The test is most useful following dacryocystorhinostomy (DCR) with nasal endoscopy or cotton bud placement at the surgical ostium; otherwise, it is less reliable.
- *Jones II assisted dye test (non-physiological)*: As per Jones I, but after syringing. Not needed if Jones I is positive.

Investigations

- *Dacryocystogram (DCG)*: Indications include non-compressible lacrimal sac mass, failed DCR or trauma without mucocoele (surgery for post-traumatic or recurrent mucocoele is relatively straightforward in experienced hands, so DCG is not needed), suspected functional NLDO (shows narrow NLD ± dilated sac, with delayed clearance from sac on late erect films), and bloody epiphora (mass/filling defect). Assess for anatomy, filling defects, NLD calibre and delayed lacrimal drainage system emptying on late erect films.
- *CT-DCG (bone ± soft-tissue window CT facial bones performed immediately after DCG)*: Indications include sinonasal disease, lacrimal tumours (widened NLD canal, soft-tissue mass and bony destruction), and in some cases following trauma, especially if metallic implants are suspected.
- *Dacryoscintigraphy*: Semi-functional test; may distinguish between delayed drainage between compartments 1 and 2 ('pre-sac delay' or lacrimal pump failure), and 2 and 3 ('post-sac delay', NLD stenosis or obstruction).

Management (Fig. 3.3)

- *Overproduction*: Treat the underlying cause, e.g. lid hygiene, lash removal, topical lubricant, steroid, or antibiotic.
- *Impaired drainage*:
  - Lid malposition: Surgical correction.
  - Punctal stenosis: Punctoplasty **(Box 3.1)**.
  - *Canalicular stenosis*:
    - *Proximal*: DCR + retrograde canaliculostomy (canaliculi are intubated from within the opened lacrimal sac and a 'cut-down' performed lateral to the site of obstruction).
    - *Distal*: canaliculo-dacryocystorhinostomy (C-DCR; canaliculi are joined to the sac flaps after excision or

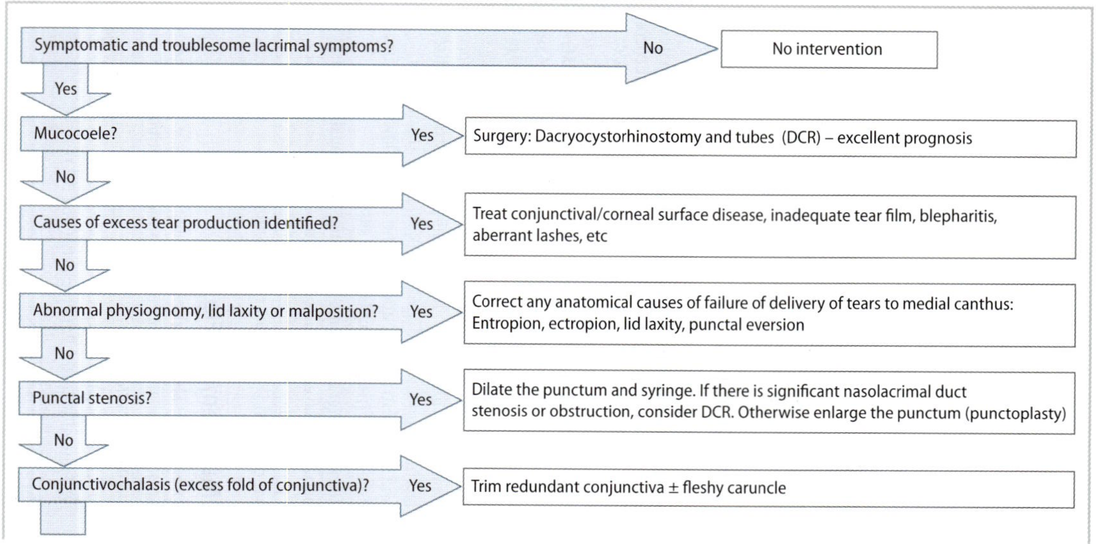
Symptomatic and troublesome lacrimal symptoms?
No
No intervention
Yes
Mucocoele?
Yes
Surgery: Dacryocystorhinostomy and tubes (DCR) – excellent prognosis
No
Causes of excess tear production identified?
Yes
Treat conjunctival/corneal surface disease, inadequate tear film, blepharitis, aberrant lashes, etc
No
Abnormal physiognomy, lid laxity or malposition?
Yes
Correct any anatomical causes of failure of delivery of tears to medial canthus: Entropion, ectropion, lid laxity, punctal eversion
No
Punctal stenosis?
Yes
Dilate the punctum and syringe. If there is significant nasolacrimal duct stenosis or obstruction, consider DCR. Otherwise enlarge the punctum (punctoplasty)
No
Conjunctivochalasis (excess fold of conjunctiva)?
Yes
Trim redundant conjunctiva ± fleshy caruncle

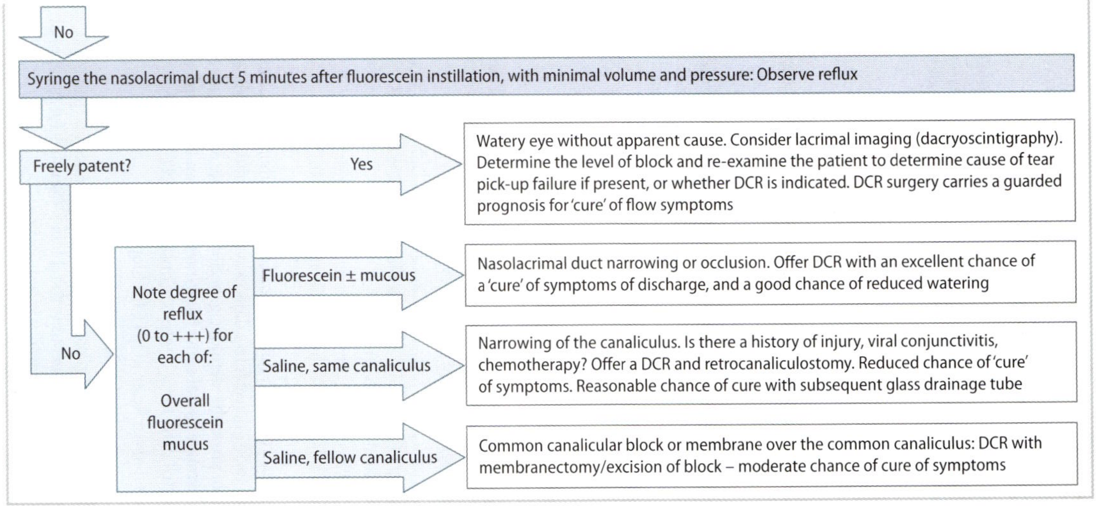

Fig. 3.3: Management of epiphora in adults.

Box 3.1: Punctoplasty ('3-snip' or posterior ampullectomy)

1. Instil topical anaesthetic.
2. Dilate lower punctum with a punctum dilator, e.g. Nettleship.
3. Make two parallel cuts (medial and lateral) in the posterior wall of the vertical canaliculus (ampulla) and join at the bottom with fine, straight scissors (e.g. Vannas).
4. Gently cauterise conjunctiva at wound edges.
5. Prescribe G. chloramphenicol q.d.s. and mild topical steroid q.d.s. for 2 weeks.
6. Review in 2–3 weeks.

trephination of intervening scar tissue, or the scar is excised from within the sac until the probes are seen (stents passed directly into the sac) ± lacrimal canalicular bypass, e.g. Lester Jones tube (LJT).

- *Canaliculitis*: see page 86.
- *Acute dacryocystitis (lacrimal sac abscess)*: see page 87.
- *Mucocoele or functional NLDO*: DCR (see below).
- *Lacrimal sac tumour (biopsy sac)*: If discovered intraoperatively perform incisional (±frozen section) biopsy, abandon DCR and plan later definitive excision of lacrimal drainage system (e.g. dacryocystectomy).
- *Lacrimal pump failure (atonic canaliculi)*: Difficult to treat. Tighten/shorten lid ± punctoplasty ± DCR ± lacrimal canalicular bypass (e.g. LJT).
- *Nasal congestion*: Prescribe a nasal decongestant, e.g. xylometazoline hydrochloride nasal spray 0.1%, one spray per nostril, 2–3 times daily for up to 7 days. Beware interactions with monoamine oxidase inhibitors, etc. Restrict use to 5–7 consecutive days to avoid rebound rhinorrhoea. Also, prescribe steroid, e.g. beclomethasone dipropionate (Beconase) nasal spray 50 µg/metered spray, two sprays per nostril daily for 2–3 weeks. Consider an ENT opinion.
- *Nasal mass*: Refer to ENT for biopsy.
- *Congenital NLDO*: See page 84.
- *Botox to lacrimal gland*: 5-10 U, transconjunctival (palpebral lobe) or transcutaneous (orbital lobe). Consider for functional obstruction or if surgery inappropriate.

DACRYOCYSTORHINOSTOMY

Background Aims to create a mucosal-lined anastomosis between the lacrimal sac and nose using an external (open) or endoscopic approach. An external approach is absolutely indicated if sac tumour is suspected [if confirmed, biopsy the sac but do not complete dacryocystorhinostomy (DCR)], and for proximal canalicular disease. For external and endonasal techniques see **Boxes 3.2 and 3.3**.

Box 3.2: External dacryocystorhinostomy

1. Select general anaesthetic (GA) or local anaesthetic (LA) with sedation (bupivacaine 0.5% with 1:200,000 epinephrine on side of nose, medial peribulbar, infraorbital nerve block, plus cocaine 5% 3 mL intranasal packing around middle turbinate; avoid cocaine in children).
2. Haemostasis under GA is assisted by head-up position, BP control, intranasal 0.1% epinephrine moistened cotton buds or cocaine 5% nasal pack. Consider tranexamic acid 1g i.v.
3. Consider prophylactic antibiotics in cases of dacryocystitis.
4. Make a straight incision 1 cm anterior to the medial canthus, ~1.5 cm long, raise skin flap and expose the medial canthal tendon (MCT) using blunt dissection (Rollet's rougine).
5. Dissect MCT and periosteum from anterior lacrimal crest, release sac, especially superiorly, and mobilise laterally.
6. Start rhinostomy by opening suture between nasal and lacrimal bones with Traquair periosteal elevator. Use bone punch, e.g. Kerrison's rongeurs, to extend as far superiorly and anteriorly as possible, inferiorly (level with inferior orbital rim) and posteriorly (to just behind the posterior lacrimal crest). Rhinostomy should measure about 2–3 cm in diameter **(Fig. 3.4)**. Protect nasal mucosa from inadvertent perforation.
7. Perform anterior ethmoidectomy (with, e.g. curved haemostat) as required to allow posterior nasal mucosal flap to mobilise laterally.
8. Fully open sac from fundus to duct and fashion sac and nasal mucosal flaps, using all available rhinostomy space. Incise nasal mucosa >3 mm anterior to root of middle turbinate – the anterior nasal mucosal flap should be larger than posterior **(Fig. 3.5)**. Suture flaps with 6/0 Vicryl. 'Suspend' anterior flaps to overlying orbicularis.
9. Consider O'Donoghue tubing or similar stent if canalicular obstruction. Tie tubing in the nose and place a marker stitch, e.g. 5/0 silk, to aid later stent removal.
10. Carefully close skin with 6/0 non-absorbable suture. Keep closure flat and avoid 'bow-stringing'.

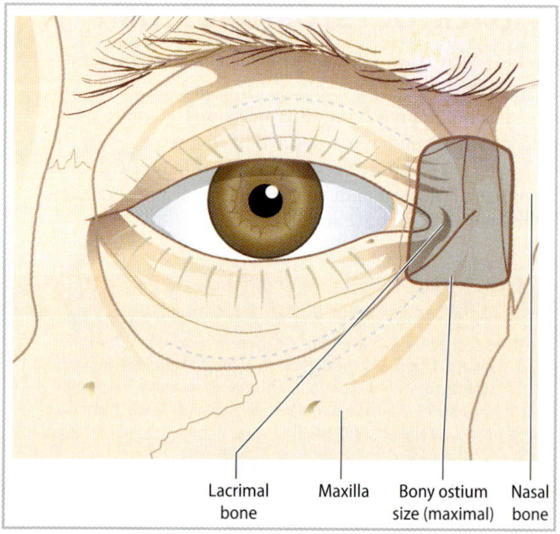

Fig. 3.4: Dacryocystorhinostomy: rhinostomy.

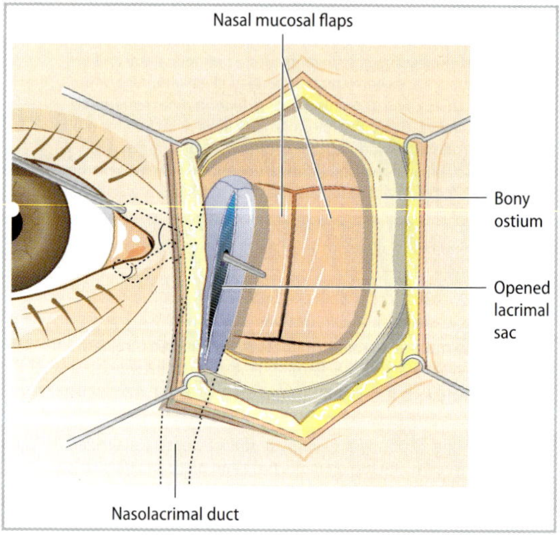

Fig. 3.5: Dacryocystorhinostomy: mucosal flaps.

Box 3.3: Endonasal dacryocystorhinostomy

1. Steps 1–3 as for external DCR, but endonasal anaesthesia and haemostasis require additional local infiltration of the lateral nasal wall under direct vision, and placement of cocaine-soaked neurosurgical patties at the operative site.
2. Perform septoplasty as required for access.
3. Using a crescent blade or similar, place a vertical incision along the maxillary line, with posteriorly-directed horizontal relieving incisions at the upper (just above middle turbinate origin) and lower (middle of middle turbinate) ends of this primary incision. Use a periosteal elevator (e.g. suction Freer) to raise the flap posteriorly and reflect medially over the turbinate.
4. Identify the very thin lacrimal bone and pass an anteriorly – directed angled 3 mm rongeur to engage and remove the frontal process of the maxilla. Repeat to remove the majority of the process, revealing the lacrimal sac and upper nasolacrimal duct.
5. Remove bone alongside the upper part of the lacrimal sac with a guarded high-speed diamond burr (avoiding perforation of the skull base).
6. Remove any lacrimal bone or ethmoid encroaching medially to the lacrimal sac. Consider opening the agger nasi air cell.
7. Vertically open the lacrimal sac (angled keratome or crescent blade) after passage of a suitable lacrimal probe, with the flaps relieved at their upper and lower ends to encourage them to lay flat on the lateral nasal wall. Inspect the sac for stones or masses (biopsy if in doubt) and common canalicular opening.
8. When the sac is opened widely, consider silicone stent and secure within the nose, e.g. ligature clip.
9. Trim nasal mucosal flap leaving mucosa to cover any areas of raw bone, particularly at the maxillary frontal process. Place a dissolving intranasal dressing to keep the flaps widely open.

Consent

- *Benefit*: External DCR success rate is similar to powered mechanical endoscopic DCR (85–95%); endoscopic laser DCR has lower success rates (~60%). Success with primary surgery varies with definition of success (anatomic vs. symptomatic), symptoms (near 100% cure from mucocoele stickiness with correctly performed DCR), and underlying disease (mucocoele > functional nasolacrimal duct obstruction (NLDO) ~70% > canalicular block ~30–50%).
- *Risk*: Visible scar (1–2% at 1 year); significant post-operative epistaxis (2–3%, occasionally requiring nasal packing,

admission and monitoring for hypovolaemia), sinusitis (~1%), infection (~1%); CSF leak (exceedingly rare).

Post-operative care No hot drinks for 12 hours; no nose blowing for 5–7 days. Prescribe a steroid-antibiotic combination eye drop q.d.s. 2 weeks, then b.d. 2 weeks, and nasal saline ± steroid spray (e.g. mometasone furoate one puff daily) for 1 month.

Follow-up Remove sutures at 7 days and stent at 4 weeks, unless canaliculo-dacryocystorhinostomy (2–3 months) or retrograde canaliculostomy (2–3 weeks).

LESTER JONES' CANALICULAR BYPASS TUBE

Provides a permanent fistula connecting the conjunctival sac to the nose. Requires prior or simultaneous dacryocystorhinostomy (DCR) and carunculectomy. Use a 'bull-horn' dilator or specific Lester Jones' tube (LJT) insertion set followed by passage of the LJT down the dilated tract; place the LJT just behind the medial canthus, angled about 30° inferiorly **(Fig. 3.6)**. Avoid abutting the nasal septum. Secure LJT with silk suture and bolster over medial lower lid in primary placement. Avoid nose blowing for 1 week postoperatively (risk of tube coming out), and review at 6 weeks. Advise the patient to place finger over the tube if sneezing or blowing nose, and perform daily 'sniff' test to confirm patency (inhale through nose with ipsilateral nostril blocked; sniffing water into nose may aid cleaning). Attend within 1–2 days if tube dislodges, when replacement without LA/GA is sometimes successful. Review annually for internal cleaning and saline irrigation.

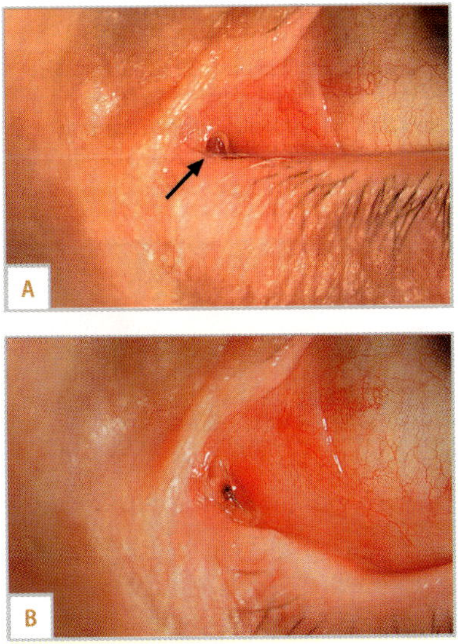

Fig. 3.6: Lester Jones tube (arrow). (A) Tip of well-positioned Jones tube just visible above medial lower eyelid; (B) Tube seen more easily on eversion of lower lid.

CONGENITAL NASOLACRIMAL DUCT OBSTRUCTION

Background The lacrimal system usually canalises by 7 months of fetal life. In the first year postpartum, 96% of cases of nasolacrimal duct obstruction resolve; a further 60% resolve in the second year with some slow resolution thereafter.

Examination Perform the fluorescein disappearance test (p. 74). Check for an expressible mucocoele and dacryocoele (a tense, bluish sac swelling usually in the first month of life). Look for 'accessory' fistulae (duplicated punctum-canaliculus), typically in the medial lower lid (skin or lid margin); these may drain fluorescein **(Fig. 3.7)**.

Differential diagnosis

- *Watery eye*: Atopy, punctal ageneis or incomplete canalisation (rare), conjunctivitis and blepharitis.
- *Lacrimal sac mass*: Dermoid; tumour, e.g. haemangioma, rhabdomyosarcoma; meningo-encephalocoele.

Management Explain the natural history. Massage the sac six times daily by firm pressure on the medial upper lid, behind the anterior lacrimal crest; demonstrate to parents. Use topical antibiotics for episodes of conjunctivitis. Defer probing until 12 months, unless dacryo(cysto)coele, acute/recurrent dacryocystitis and/or abscess occur, but only probe after the acute episode resolves **(Box 3.4)**.

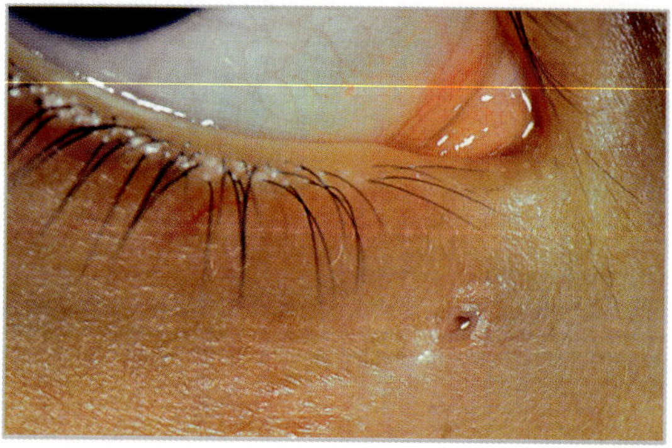

Fig. 3.7: Typical location for congenital lacrimal fistula, joining the common canaliculus by passing below the anterior limb of the medial canthal tendon.

Box 3.4: Syringe and probe (probing)

1. Explain the procedure:

   Benefit: Complete symptom resolution rates (approximate): >90% if done at the age of 1 year, 90% at 2 years, 80% at 3 years, 70% at 4 years and 40% at 5 years.

   Risk: False passage, bleeding, failure and bronchospasm.

2. Examine (under GA) lids, conjunctiva and puncta. Look for fistulae and expressible mucocoele. Perform nasal endoscopy.
3. Perform dacryocystogram (DCG) if redo, to clarify anatomy.
4. Inject saline and fluorescein mixture using a lacrimal cannula. Feel for resistance. If not able to easily introduce cannula, dilate puncta gently. Place a fine suction catheter or endoscope up nose to look for fluorescein.
5. Consider probing even if patent to syringing, e.g. if significant symptoms or prior failed probing. Try to start with a '0' Bowman for lower punctum, '00' for upper. Try to avoid smaller probes or sizes larger than '1'.
6. Insert probe vertically (2 mm) then horizontally with lid on lateral traction. Feel for 'hard stop' as probe contacts medial sac wall against nasal bones. Otherwise, compressed tissue results in a 'soft stop'.
7. Direct probe vertically down into the nasolacrimal duct (NLD), angled slightly posteriorly and medially. Feel for a 'pop' as the probe perforates the membrane of a non-patent NLD. Feel for tight 'gritty' sensation (stenosed bony canal). Inability to pass probe may indicate absent NLD; look for 'buried probe' (anomalous submucosal NLD).
8. Check probe is below inferior turbinate – feel using large probe along floor of nose or look with an endoscope.
9. Repeat syringing. This also assists sac washout.
10. Prescribe a steroid-antibiotic combination drop t.d.s. and continue effective lacrimal sac massage for 1 week.

Follow-up Review as required if first probing, or 6–8 weeks if a redo. Consider balloon dacryoplasty and/or intubation (silicone stent) if multiple endoscopically monitored probings fail.

CANALICULITIS

Background Canaliculi become grossly dilated with intraluminal deposits of granules caused by low-grade infection, classically *Actinomyces*, but also fungi.

Symptoms Chronic discharge with lids stuck together especially in mornings. Epiphora is often mild but worse in mornings.

Signs Swollen inflamed lid medial to prominent 'pouting' punctum **(Fig. 3.8)**. Features may be subtle.

Management Usually responds to canaliculotomy – dilate and open 5 mm of horizontal canaliculus. Use a pair of cotton buds (rolled medial to lateral) to compress the canaliculus and express deposits; consider small curette to remove granules. Consider microbiology and prescribe G. chloramphenicol q.d.s. for 10 days.

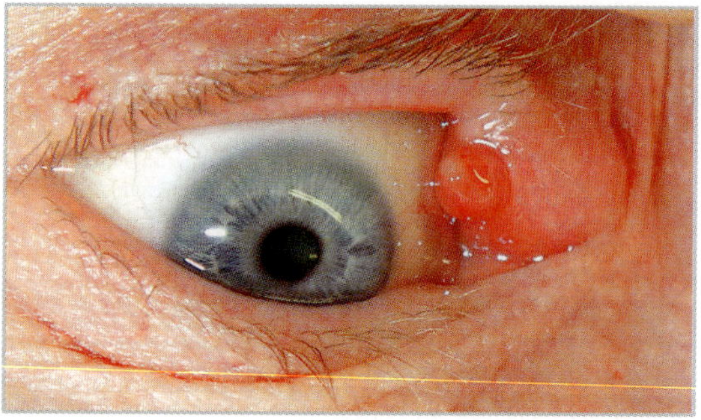

Fig. 3.8: Canaliculitis (*Actinomyces*) with punctal granuloma and stringy discharge from dilated upper canaliculus (Courtesy D Verity).

ACUTE DACRYOCYSTITIS/ LACRIMAL SAC ABSCESS

Background A purulent lacrimal sac infection/abscess with surrounding cellulitis, often associated with nasolacrimal duct obstruction. Caused by superinfection of a mucocoele. May form a discharging cutaneous fistula below the medial canthal tendon (MCT).

Clinical features Tense, painful erythematous swelling below the MCT, often with a history of stickiness and epiphora **(Fig. 3.9)**.

Management Hot compresses 4–6 times daily, G. chloramphenicol q.d.s until resolved, and oral cefalexin 250–500 mg q.d.s. 1–2 weeks or until cellulitis resolves. If febrile or acutely unwell treat as preseptal cellulitis (p. 107). Incise and drain if fails to respond after 5–7 days, or if worsens. Apply topical skin anaesthetic e.g. eutectic mixture of local anaesthetics (EMLA), for 30 minutes, then inject LA slowly around the abscess and then into the abscess cavity; this may be very painful if not performed slowly. Incise with a blade, drain, and send pus to microbiology; packing with ribbon gauze is rarely required except for very large abscesses. Arrange definitive treatment with dacryocystorhinostomy (DCR) when cellulitis is resolved (or occasionally, in acute setting).

Children with non-resolving acute dacryocystitis or infected dacryocoele require systemic antibiotics, examination under anaesthesia, and drainage via the nasal cavity (probing or endoscopic DCR).

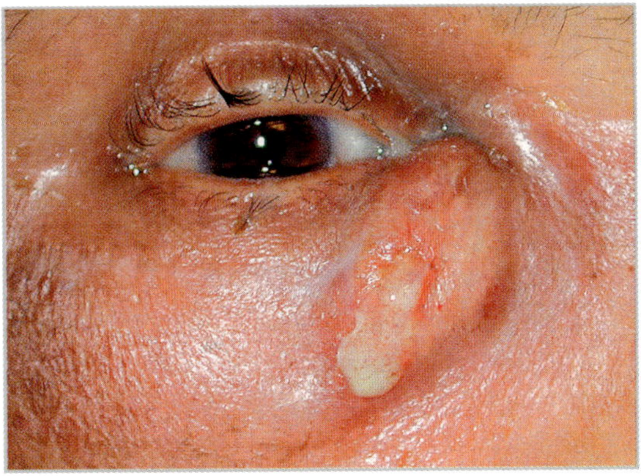

Fig. 3.9: Acute dacryocystitis with purulent discharge from acquired lacrimal sac fistula.

LACRIMAL DRAINAGE SYSTEM TUMOURS

Background and clinical features Inflammatory (e.g. granuloma and lymphoid hyperplasia) and neoplastic (transitional cell carcinoma, papilloma, squamous cell carcinoma, lymphoma and melanoma) lesions of the lacrimal sac/duct are rare, but must be considered in cases of lacrimal sac mass, non-compressible mucocoele, bloody tears and/or mass or filling defect on dacryocystogram (DCG)/CT-DCG.

Management Biopsy via external approach. Further treatment depends on underlying disease and may involve radical *en bloc* excision of the entire lacrimal drainage system ± radiotherapy ± chemotherapy.

OPTOMETRY AND GENERAL PRACTICE GUIDELINES

Most lacrimal problems are non-urgent. Reassure patients who have very mild watering, e.g. only outdoors in cold, windy weather. In those with troublesome epiphora, treat or refer any sinonasal disease to an ENT surgeon (e.g. rhinitis, polyps and mass) before referral to an ophthalmologist, the latter preferably one experienced in lacrimal disorders. Also consider epiphora secondary to eye disease and ask if the eye becomes red and painful or if vision is blurred. Treat or refer any readily identifiable ocular surface problem (e.g. tear film deficiency, blepharitis, allergic conjunctivitis and trichiasis). Look specifically for eyelid/lash malpositions, e.g. lower lid ectropion/entropion.

A firm and non-reducible mass in the lacrimal sac fossa or blood-stained tears suggest a lacrimal sac neoplasm, so refer urgently; sac mucocoeles are generally compressible. Any swelling presenting in the region above the medial canthal tendon is neoplasia until proven otherwise.

Instruct parents of children with congenital nasolacrimal duct obstruction to massage firmly over the nasolacrimal sac (not just on the side of the nose) six times daily. Refer if symptoms fail to resolve after a year, or sooner if frequent conjunctivitis or dacryocystitis occurs.

The following guide to referral urgency is not prescriptive, as clinical situations vary.

Same day

- Canalicular injuries p. 68
- Acute dacryocystitis/lacrimal sac abscess (commence G. chloramphenicol q.d.s. and systemic antibiotics, e.g. cefalexin 250–500 mg p.o. q.d.s.) p. 87

Urgent (within 1 week)

- Epiphora with blood-stained tears p. 72, 88
- Non-compressible lacrimal sac mass p. 88

Routine (non-urgent)

- Isolated epiphora p. 71
- Epiphora with recurrent conjunctivitis (treat episodes with G. chloramphenicol q.d.s. 1 week) p. 71
- A child with epiphora since birth unless suspected dacryocoele, recurrent problematic conjunctivitis, or any dacryocystitis p. 84
- Suspected canaliculitis (prescribe G. chloramphenicol q.d.s. 2 weeks) p. 86
- Lacrimal sac mucocoele p. 73

ORBIT

4

Thomas G Hardy & Geoffrey E Rose

ANATOMY

Bones of the orbit

Frontal, zygoma, maxilla (thin), sphenoid (greater and lesser wings), ethmoid (thin), lacrimal (thin) and palatine (**Fig. 4.1**).

Anatomic relations of the bony orbit

- *Roof:* Anterior cranial fossa and frontal sinus.
- *Medial:* Ethmoid air cells and sphenoid sinus.
- *Floor:* Maxillary antrum.
- *Lateral:* Temporalis fossa and middle cranial fossa.

Orbital septum

Separates the lids from the orbit and acts as barrier to the spread of infection; arises from orbital rim, and encloses the lacrimal sac which straddles the pre- and post-septal spaces.

Surgical spaces

Pre- and post-septal, subperiosteal (potential space), extraconal, intraconal and sub-Tenon's (**Fig. 4.2**).

Lacrimal gland

The larger orbital lobe is separated from the palpebral lobe by the lateral horn of the levator aponeurosis; ductules pass through the palpebral lobe to the superolateral fornix.

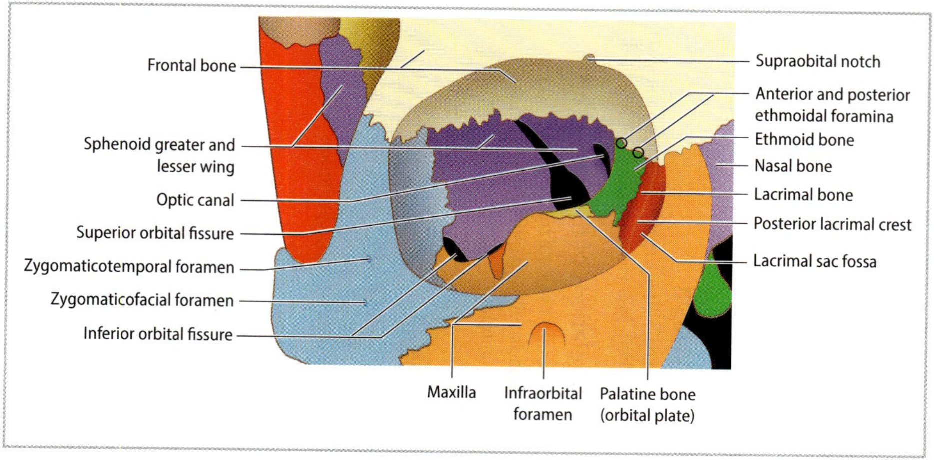

Fig. 4.1: Anatomical structures of orbit.

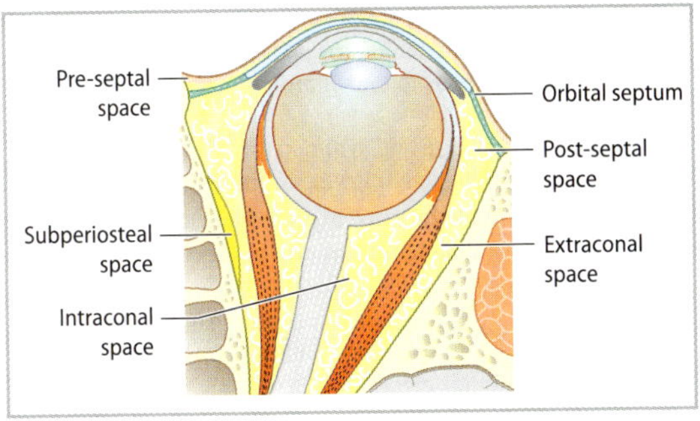

Fig. 4.2: Surgical spaces of the orbit (axial view).

HISTORY AND EXAMINATION

History

Ask about the following:

1. *Proptosis:* 'bulging' and 'prominent' eye.
2. *Pain:* causes include inflammation, infection, acute pressure changes (e.g. haemorrhage) and bony/neural invasion.
3. *Progression:* symptoms may occur over minutes (e.g. haemorrhage); hours–days (e.g. inflammation); weeks–months (e.g. malignancy); months–years (e.g. benign tumour and cyst).
4. *Past medical history:* in particular, thyroid disease, malignancy, trauma and sinusitis.
5. *(Perceptual) visual problems:* diplopia, blurring, altered colour perception and refractive change.
6. *Palpable* or *visible* mass.
7. *Periorbital abnormalities:* including sensory change (paraesthesia and numbness), facial weakness, redness, swelling, tenderness, watering and lid anomalies.

Examination

Note the following:

1. *General inspection* ('Panoramic'): note facial scars, asymmetry, swellings/masses, and goitre or thyroidectomy scar. Old photos (e.g. driver's licence) may clarify disease onset.
2. *Visual function* ('Perception'): VA, colour vision (Ishihara), red desaturation, reduced brightness perception and confrontation testing/formal perimetry, if relevant.
3. *Pupils*: test for a relative afferent pupillary defect (RAPD, p. 747).

4. *Exophthalmometry* (***Proptosis***): for a rough estimate look from above and behind the patient, but perform exophthalmometry as follows if proptosis or enophthalmos is suspected:
   - Check the location and symmetry of the lateral orbital rims (often recessed following orbito-facial fracture).
   - Rest an exophthalmometer gently against each lateral orbital rim and note the distance between the callipers (base distance) from the rule.
   - Ensure the eye being tested is fixating on the examiner's opposite eye and record the anterior corneal position, avoiding parallax error.
   - Record the instrument make and base distance for subsequent readings.

   Average upper limit of normal:
   a. *Caucasian:* 21 mm (equator in front of the lateral orbital rim, e.g. on axial CT scan).
   b. *African-Caribbean:* 22–23 mm.
   c. *Southeast Asian:* 19 mm.

   Asymmetry ≥2 mm is generally abnormal. Beware of pseudoproptosis from high myopia/contralateral microphthalmos, or gross orbito-facial asymmetry. Axial proptosis suggests thyroid eye disease or an intraconal mass. Enophthalmos suggests an expanded orbital volume (e.g. blowout fracture) or contracted orbital contents (e.g. scirrhous metastatic breast carcinoma). A change with Valsalva manoeuvre or head-down posture suggests a distensible low-flow (venous) malformation.
5. *Non-axial globe displacement*: using a horizontal clear plastic ruler, measure from the midline to the corneal reflex of the fixating eye on both sides to look for a difference. Compare the vertical positions of each fixating eye against a horizontal axial plane. Distinguish the following:
   - *Telecanthus:* increased distance from the midline to the medial canthus (normal is 15–19 mm).
   - *Hypertelorbitism (hypertelorism):* increased separation of otherwise normally-sized orbits.
   - *Pseudohypertelorbitism:* lateral displacement of the medial walls with normally-located lateral walls (narrow orbits).

   Causes of non-axial displacement include:
   - *Inferior displacement:* lacrimal gland mass, frontal sinus mucocoele or tumour, encephalocoele, sphenoid meningioma, orbital roof fracture (typically displaced inferiorly) and nerve sheath tumour.

- *Superior:* maxillary sinus tumour and orbital cyst/tumour.
- *Lateral:* ethmoid sinus mucocoele or tumour and subperiosteal collection.
- *Medial:* lacrimal gland enlargement and sphenoid meningioma.

6. ***Palpation***: examine orbital rim, soft tissues, and feel for masses (note location, shape and size). Gently palpate all quadrants using little finger (eyes closed for upper orbit).
7. ***Pulsation***: check for globe pulsation, thrill, or bruit using the bell of the stethoscope over a closed eye.
8. *Full ocular examination*: check conjunctival fornices. Intraocular pressure (IOP) may be elevated by lesions compressing globe (e.g. tight inferior rectus in thyroid eye disease). Note choroidal folds (from retrobulbar mass including extraocular muscle enlargement), disc swelling, disc pallor or collateral vessels (e.g. optic nerve sheath meningioma).
9. *Ocular motility*: distinguish neuropathic, myopathic and mechanical (restrictive) dysmotility. Consider formal documentation (e.g. Hess chart), especially in thyroid eye disease and orbital fractures, and forced duction testing. Painful eye movement suggests inflammation.
10. *Periorbital examination*: skin (erythema, oedema and induration); lid position (e.g. retraction and/or lateral eyelid flare in thyroid eye disease); regional lymph nodes; and cranial nerves V and VII. Note fullness of the periorbital regions (e.g. temporalis fossa in sphenoid meningioma), nose abnormalities, or facial asymmetry.

INVESTIGATIONS

Imaging

Patients with proptosis require imaging, with a few exceptions such as mild thyroid eye disease. Examine all aspects of imaging including extraorbital regions, prior to reading report. When viewing an orbital mass consider the following:

1. *Physical characteristics:* size, shape (round suggests benign) and internal structure (e.g. fluid level).
2. *Location:* likely tissue of origin and surgical space; relationship to normal structures.
3. *Biologic behaviour:* longstanding benign masses may induce bone remodelling or 'scalloping', whereas malignant lesions often destroy tissue, producing irregular bony erosion. Causes of calcification include phleboliths in chronic venous malformation, dystrophic calcium in lacrimal gland carcinoma, ossifying (complex) choristoma and teratoma. Contrast enhancement reflects vascularity.

Plain X-ray Redundant when CT is available. Blowout fracture is a clinical diagnosis and easily missed on plain X-ray.

Computed tomography (CT) Except in children, the first-line imaging modality for orbital disease as very fast acquisition avoids movement artefact. Indications include proptosis, orbital masses, bony lesions, trauma and hyperacute haemorrhage. CT is relatively cheap, readily available, and good for showing bone detail and metal foreign bodies. Main disadvantages are radiation exposure and contrast reactions. Radiation dosage can be halved by using solely non-contrast scans for structural studies (e.g. fractures, pre-decompression planning), and solely a 'with-contrast' run for suspected inflammatory and neoplastic disease. Contrast is often helpful, especially with tumours, but is contraindicated in patients with iodine allergy, dehydration, cardiac failure, hyperthyroidism, or renal impairment. Diabetics have a ~9% risk of contrast-induced renal failure. Request fine axial cuts and reformatted coronal ± sagittal sections. View bone using bone 'windows', looking for hyper- and hypo-ostotic lesions, bony erosion, or fractures. Use soft-tissue 'windows' to systematically examine extraocular muscles, optic nerve, lacrimal gland, fat, vessels, extraorbital structures (brain, sinuses and nose), any mass lesions, or vascular changes. Three-dimensional reconstructions are useful in trauma and craniofacial disorders. CT angiography is mainly useful for neuro-ophthalmic problems. CT-venography may show dural venous sinus thrombosis (intracranial hypertension); consider dynamic vascular studies for venous malformations.

Magnetic resonance imaging (MRI) Mainly indicated for disease at the orbito-cranial junction, e.g. optic nerve sheath tumours, and for detailed examination of soft-tissue lesions and inflammatory processes. Orbital MRI requires fat-suppression to delineate soft-tissue structures. Cortical bone has a very low signal intensity and appears black. Cancellous bone has a moderate signal intensity. Key sequences include T1- and T2-weighted imaging with and without fat suppression, diffusion-weighted studies (diffusion restriction indicates highly cellular tissue, e.g. abscess, and very cellular tumours, e.g. lymphoma), and contrast (typically Gadolinium) enhanced studies. Dynamic contrast-enhanced studies detail vascularity. Beware of common MRI artefacts (e.g. failure of fat suppression) and liaise with an experienced head and neck/orbital radiologist as required. MRI is contraindicated if metal foreign bodies are suspected. Select MRI for children, except for trauma and orbital cellulitis/suspected sinus disease (CT is first line). See also page 759.

Ultrasound Internal tumour reflectivity may aid diagnosis and discriminate cystic versus solid lesions. Doppler flow studies may help to diagnose and monitor vascular lesions such as infantile haemangioma and arteriovenous malformation (AVM).

Angiography Usually reserved for arteriovenous fistulae/ malformations.

Other tests

Blood tests As appropriate, e.g. thyroid function tests, inflammatory markers and autoantibodies.

Perimetry Useful for assessing optic nerve function and change over time.

Optical coherence tomography (OCT) (especially retinal nerve fibre layer and ganglion cell layer) Useful to assess optic nerve structure and change over time.

Biopsy In general, it is preferable to obtain tissue by open biopsy (incisional or excisional), rather than CT-guided or ultrasound-guided fine-needle aspiration cytology, as histology gives better structural representation than cytology, and multiple stains are available.

CONGENITAL DISORDERS

Dermoid and epidermoid cysts

Background A choristoma (normal tissue in abnormal location) arising from surface ectoderm trapped at sites of embryologic folding. Cysts are classified by their contents and lining:

- *Epidermoid:* squamous epithelial lining only, with associated keratin.
- *Dermoid:* lined by squamous epithelium and dermis. Hairs, sebaceous glands/oil and keratin may be present.
- *Conjunctival:* conjunctival lining with mucous contents.

Epidermoid and dermoid cysts may have intra- and extra-orbital components (temporalis fossa, central nervous system, and nose) with an interconnecting 'stalk' traversing bone, a so-called 'dumb-bell' configuration.

Clinical features Typically, a firm, mobile and non-tender lump is noted soon after birth in the superotemporal quadrant (STQ) (**Fig. 4.3**) or less commonly, superonasal quadrant (SNQ), sometimes attaching to the zygomatico-frontal or fronto-nasal suture. Patients may have episodes of inflammation following trauma, or skin discharge with very superficial, ruptured or incompletely excised lesions. Deep orbital lesions can present in adolescence or adulthood with proptosis and recurrent orbital inflammation.

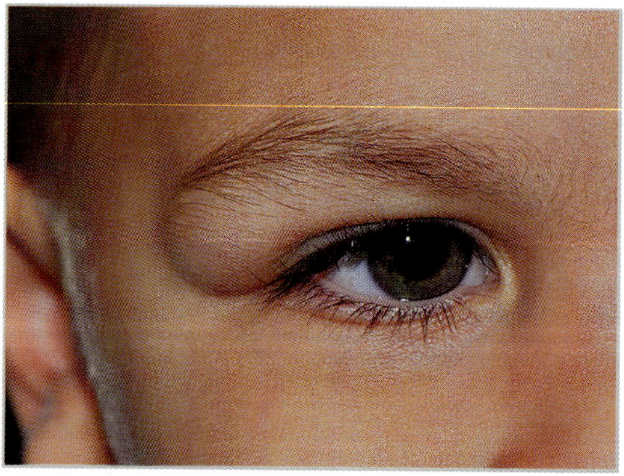

Fig. 4.3: Superotemporal quadrant dermoid with temporal fossa extension.

Investigations Imaging is generally only indicated for superolateral lesions when it is not possible to palpate behind the equator of the cyst or there are signs of orbital or extra-orbital involvement. Imaging of superomedial lesions (preferably MRI) rules out encephalocoele and other differentials. MRI is preferred; CT may be indicated for lesions extending beyond the orbit, especially if intracranial.

Management Arrange non-urgent complete excision before school age, when the risk of trauma increases. Removal may require periosteal dissection ± bone removal (e.g. 'dumb-bell' cyst). The preferred approach for superior lesions is via the upper lid skin crease. If deep extension is found unexpectedly and the surgeon is not familiar with removal of complex lesions, leave the cyst intact, close the incision, and refer to an experienced orbital surgeon: do not remove lesions incompletely. If accidental rupture occurs, perform a thorough washout of the surgical field to remove the pro-inflammatory cyst contents.

Dermolipoma

Background A choristoma of dermal elements (ectopic skin, subcutaneous fat; occasionally 'complex' containing other tissues, e.g. bone) occurring on the ocular surface, typically the STQ.

Clinical features Discharge and irritation from abnormal conjunctival wetting and surface hairs, and poor cosmesis. Look for a firm, immobile, pale-yellowish mass closely applied to the globe (**Fig. 4.4**). Occasionally associated with craniofacial

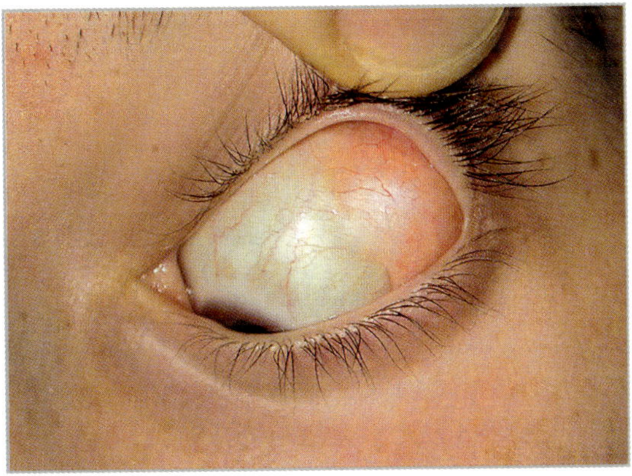

Fig. 4.4: Dermolipoma.

microsomia (e.g. Goldenhar's syndrome, below) and Duane's retraction syndrome.

Differential diagnosis Orbital fat prolapse, subconjunctival lipoma (mobile under the conjunctiva) and lacrimal gland prolapse.

Management Conservative microsurgical excision by an experienced surgeon, avoiding damage to the lacrimal gland ductules and lateral rectus. Careful conjunctival closure without tension, ± flap or graft, helps to prevent ocular motility restriction.

Corneolimbal (epibulbar) dermoid

A choristoma of conjunctival origin, often protruding over the cornea (**Fig. 4.5**). It may produce discomfort, exposure, or astigmatism. It can be associated with craniofacial microsomia or Goldenhar's syndrome, that may also feature eyelid colobomas, accessory auricular appendages, poor hearing, facial weakness and vertebral abnormalities. Manage symptomatic corneolimbal dermoids with topical lubricants/steroids or excision (superficial sclerokeratectomy/lamellar keratoplasty). Asymptomatic conjunctival lesions tend to be stable and excision is rarely required.

Microphthalmos and anophthalmos

Background Rare, often sporadic, uni- or bilateral idiopathic disorder of multifactorial aetiology. It may be associated with:

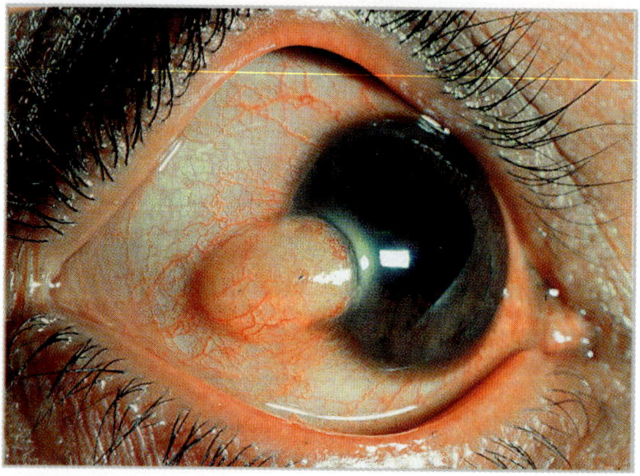

Fig. 4.5: Limbal dermoid.

chromosomal anomalies (e.g. trisomy 13 and 18); genetic mutations (e.g. *PAX6* and *SOX2*); craniofacial microsomia (see previous section); renal, cardiac and cerebral abnormalities; CHARGE and other rare congenital syndromes; cleft palate; and polydactyly. Other rare developmental ocular/orbital anomalies include cryptophthalmos (failure of lid-fold development with congenital 'symblepharon') and congenital cystic eye.

Clinical features An absent or small eye is noted soon after birth or on antenatal ultrasound. Microphthalmos may be associated with a variably-sized cyst arising from the eye or its vestigial remnant; reduced lid and orbit growth ('micro-orbitism'); microcornea; colobomata; cataract; glaucoma and aniridia.

Management Refer for genetics, audiology, and general paediatrics review (renal ultrasound and intrauterine infection screening) and arrange MRI brain and orbit. Examine parents and fellow eye for anomalies (e.g. coloboma). Leave cysts intact to stimulate orbital and lid growth, unless excessively large. In the absence of a cyst, insert progressive orbital and socket expanders, either as serial solid shapes or expanding (e.g. hydrophilic) implants. Once final orbital and lid growth is achieved, further expansion of the orbit (orbital implants and bony grafts), fornices (mucous membrane grafts), and lids is often required.

THYROID EYE DISEASE

Background Thyroid eye disease (TED) is an idiopathic autoimmune disorder resulting in an 'active' orbital inflammatory phase (months–years) and subsequent 'inactive' fibrotic phase, largely involving extraocular muscles and orbital fat/connective tissues. There is a female preponderance, with peak incidence at age 30–50 years. Severe cases are more common in older patients, males and smokers. Usually associated with Graves' hyperthyroidism, but patients may be hypo- or euthyroid. Unilateral or asymmetric in ~15%. A minority of cases (≤5%) develop sight-threatening optic neuropathy or exposure keratopathy. For strabismus issues see page 735.

Classification Determine activity (inflammation) and severity.

Activity Clinical Activity Score (CAS): scores 1 for each of 10 features:

- *Pain:* (i) retrobulbar and (ii) on eye movement.
- *Redness:* (iii) lid and (iv) conjunctiva.
- *Swelling:* (v) lids, (vi) conjunctiva, (vii) plica/caruncle and (viii) ≥2 mm increase in proptosis over 1–3 months.
- *Loss of function:* (ix) >8° decrease in eye movement over 1–3 months and (x) loss of ≥1 Snellen line over 1–3 months.

VISA grade (also measures severity):

- *Vision (optic nerve function):* document acuity, colour vision, RAPD, disc pallor/oedema (no numeric score).
- *Inflammation/congestion:* VISA inflammatory score is the numeric sum of: orbital pain (none = 0, at rest = 1, and with gaze = 2), chemosis (0–2), eyelid oedema (0–2), conjunctival injection (0–1), eyelid injection (redness) (0–1), giving a total out of 8.
- *Strabismus/motility:* grade diplopia as none (0), with gaze (1), intermittent (2), or constant (3) (Gorman score)
- *Appearance/exposure:* grade lid retraction, proptosis, tearing, foreign body sensation, exposure keratopathy (and other signs) as none (0), mild (1), moderate (2) or severe (3).

Severity Use the NOSPECS classification, VISA disease grade, or the European Group on Graves' Orbitopathy (EUGOGO).

NOSPECS: used less often but considers:

- No symptoms or sign.
- Only lid retraction ± lid lag.
- Soft-tissue involvement (lid and conjunctival inflammation).
- Proptosis.
- Extraocular muscle involvement ± diplopia.

- Corneal disease.
- Sight-threatening optic neuropathy.

EUGOGO: Has the advantage of incorporating quality of life (QoL).

- *Mild:* one or more of the following – minor impact on QoL, nil/transient diplopia, <2 mm lid retraction, <3 mm proptosis (for race and gender), minor soft-tissue involvement, or minor corneal exposure.
- *Moderate to severe:* Two or more of the following – impact on QoL justifies medical or surgical intervention, ≥2 mm lid retraction, ≥3 mm proptosis, moderate or severe soft tissue involvement, and significant (constant or inconstant) diplopia.
- *Sight-threatening:* Urgent treatment required for sight-threatening optic neuropathy or corneal exposure.

Symptoms Include change in appearance ('bulging', 'staring' and lid swelling), redness, foreign body sensation, watering, photophobia, ache, visual loss (colour, VA and fields), globe subluxation and diplopia. Ask about QoL, thyroid autoimmunity, smoking, family history of thyroid autoimmunity or TED or other autoimmune disorder.

Signs Look for proptosis (usually axial); optic neuropathy (reduced VA; colour vision; RAPD; field loss); exposure keratopathy; upper lid retraction (**Fig. 4.6**); lid 'lag' on downgaze (descent of upper lid less than that of the globe); lagophthalmos; increased IOP typically on upgaze, but also primary position; conjunctival inflammation and chemosis; caruncle oedema; superior limbic keratoconjunctivitis; lid inflammation; orbital fat and lacrimal gland prolapse; ocular dysmotility (restrictive). The most commonly affected muscle is the inferior rectus, followed by medial, superior, then lateral rectus. Elderly patients may present with relatively inactive orbitopathy and progressive, typically vertical, strabismus ('cold TED').

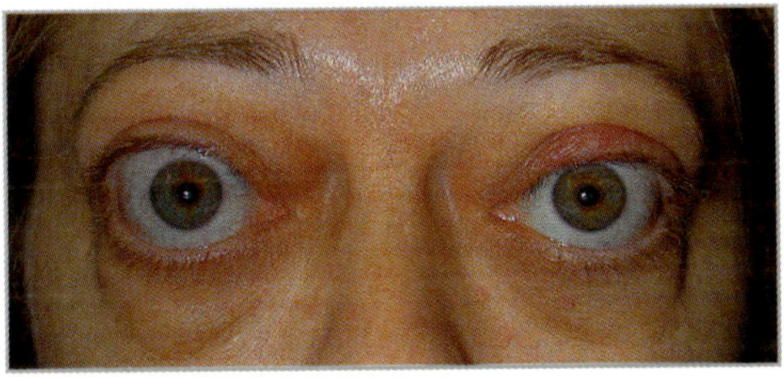

Fig. 4.6: Moderately severe and inactive thyroid eye disease (left upper lid erythema secondary to chalazion).

Differential diagnosis Consider idiopathic orbital inflammatory disease and other orbital inflammatory disorders; lymphoproliferative disorders, and carotico-cavernous fistula (enlarged arterialised superior ophthalmic vein on imaging). Consider myasthenia gravis (may coexist) in elderly males with inactive TED.

Investigations Request thyroid function tests and thyrotropin receptor antibodies (TRAb), especially thyroid stimulating immunoglobulin (TSI) which is better correlated with presence, activity and severity of TED than other TRAb. Anti-thyroid peroxidase, anti-thyroglobulin and thyroid microsomal antibodies have poor sensitivity and specificity and are not helpful in Graves' disease, but may have a role in hypothyroid or euthyroid orbitopathy. CT (**Fig. 4.7**) is indicated if orbital decompression is planned, for uncertain diagnosis, or asymmetry >2 mm on

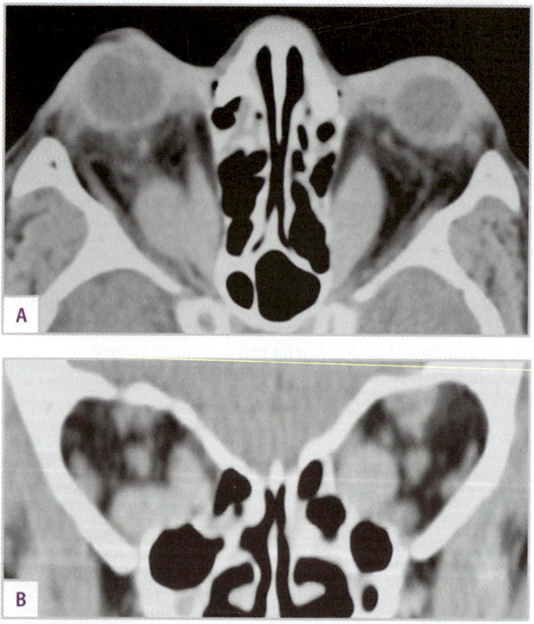

Fig. 4.7: Thyroid eye disease – axial (A) and coronal (B) CT scans showing marked right inferior rectus and left medial rectus enlargement, together with moderate right medial rectus enlargement and bilateral congestion of orbital fat.

exophthalmometry. MRI (STIR sequence and T2) can assess the degree of muscle oedema during the inflammatory phase.

Management

- Grade activity and severity.
- *Casualty*: Refer as follows.
  - *Sight-threatening:* Same-day orbital opinion.
  - *Active*: Orbital clinic within 1–2 weeks.
  - *Inactive*: Routine referral (preferably to a specialist orbital clinic).
- *Clinic*: Urge smokers to stop. Achieve and maintain euthyroidism and avoid sudden fluctuations in thyroid hormone levels. Consider endocrinology referral.
  - *Conservative:* Ocular lubricants, elevation of head at night, and sunglasses. Consider selenium (selenite, 100 μg b.d. for 6 months) if active, mild (per EUGOGO) TED. Consider vitamin D supplementation (500-1,000 units D3 daily) and treat hyperlipidaemia.
  - *Immunosuppression*: Consider i.v. methylprednisolone (IVMP) if active inflammation coexists with moderate or severe (EUGOGO) TED. Intravenous steroids have greater efficacy (74% vs. 51%) and fewer side effects (56% vs. 81%) than oral steroids. For moderately severe TED, consider weekly infusions of IVMP 500 mg, repeated for 6 weeks, then reassess response and, if needed, repeat at 250 mg weekly for another 6 weeks. Consider adding mycophenolate sodium with IVMP as first line, or if there is a poor response after 3 weekly doses. Note baseline tests, side effects, and monitoring required for patients on systemic steroids (p. 413). For sight-threatening disease consider IVMP 1 g daily (or alternate days) for three doses and review at 1 week – if responding, consider repeat IVMP – if no response, arrange for urgent orbital decompression. Avoid a total IVMP dose >8 g, since this is associated with increased hepatotoxicity and mortality. For oral steroids, start with enteric-coated prednisolone 1 mg/kg/day but reduce if less severe or comorbidity. Taper steroids gradually (1–3 months) depending on clinical response and comorbidities. Consider gastric ulcer prophylaxis with proton-pump inhibitor or H2 antagonist, pneumocystis pneumonia prophylaxis and bisphosphonates. Consider steroid-sparing agents (e.g. mycophenolate, azathioprine and ciclosporin) if steroid-intolerant or contraindications, and co-manage with physicians. Biologic agents, e.g. rituximab (anti-CD20), tocilizumab (anti-interleukin-6) have shown promise in certain studies but their roles in mainstream management are not yet clear. Teprotumumab

(anti-insulin-like growth factor-1 receptor) has shown great promise for both active and inactive TED with significant improvement in proptosis, ocular motility and inflammation; however, it is costly and has limited availability outside the US.

- *Radiotherapy (RT)*: The evidence-base is uncertain, but consider low dose (e.g. 20 Gy in 10 fractions) lens-sparing orbital irradiation with corticosteroids (i.v. or oral, e.g. 20 mg prednisolone daily) for sight-threatening disease or significant soft-tissue inflammation, including ocular dysmotility. Proptosis and lid retraction are typically not responsive to orbital radiation.
- *Surgery*:
  - Orbital decompression should precede any planned strabismus surgery, which should precede lid surgery.
  - *Orbital decompression (bone ± fat)*: Consider when TED is inactive and stable, unless sight is threatened. The main indication is facially disfiguring, non-sight-threatening proptosis. Bony decompression for >28 mm proptosis involves three walls (medial and lateral walls and floor); for 24–28 mm consider two or two-and-a-half walls (lateral and medial, ± medial floor), and consider only lateral wall decompression if <24 mm.
    - *Benefit:* Between 3 and 15 mm of globe retroplacement (dependent on extent of decompression).
    - *Risks:* Visual loss (<1:3,000); new diplopia ('nil' for lateral wall decompression; 10–15% for floor decompression); other risks are low (permanent infraorbital nerve numbness, haemorrhage, infection, late overcorrection or maxillary atelectasis, troublesome scar, redo surgery, temporalis atrophy, persistent masticatory oscillopsia and CSF leak).
  - *Strabismus surgery:* Generally involves recessions, once orthoptically stable for ≥6 months (p. 735). Consider early surgery where a gross deviation requires maximal surgery.
  - *Lid surgery:*
    - *Upper lid retraction:* Retractor recessions (Müller's muscle ± levator) are often required and very rarely a spacer (e.g. hard palate mucosa or xenograft) may be used. Consider tarsorrhaphy, although aesthetic results are limited.
    - *True lower lid retraction (as opposed to displacement from proptosis):* Retractor release with placement of spacer material.

CELLULITIS

Background Preseptal and orbital cellulitis constitutes a medical emergency, requiring immediate administration of high-dose, broad-spectrum systemic antibiotics before imaging or referral to an orbital specialist. Orbital cellulitis may be life-threatening if it spreads to the intracranial space. Possible sources of infection include paranasal sinuses (most common), oropharynx (including teeth), skin, foreign bodies, trauma (including iatrogenic), and haematogenous spread. Bacteria are the most common cause, especially streptococci and staphylococci. *Haemophilus influenzae* is much rarer since routine immunisations. Anaerobes and other gram-negative organisms are less common. In certain areas, community-acquired methicillin-resistant *Staphylococcus aureus* (MRSA) is becoming a common cause of sinusitis, dacryoadenitis (with abscess), and orbital cellulitis. Consider rarer organisms in immunocompromised patients or those from endemic areas (mucormycosis, aspergillosis, tuberculosis and viruses, e.g. Herpes zoster).

Clinical features Preseptal cellulitis produces fever and periocular pain, swelling, ptosis, tenderness and redness (± chemosis) (**Fig. 4.8**). Orbital cellulitis is similar but with greater chemosis and conjunctival injection, reduced eye movements ± diplopia, vision loss, RAPD and proptosis.

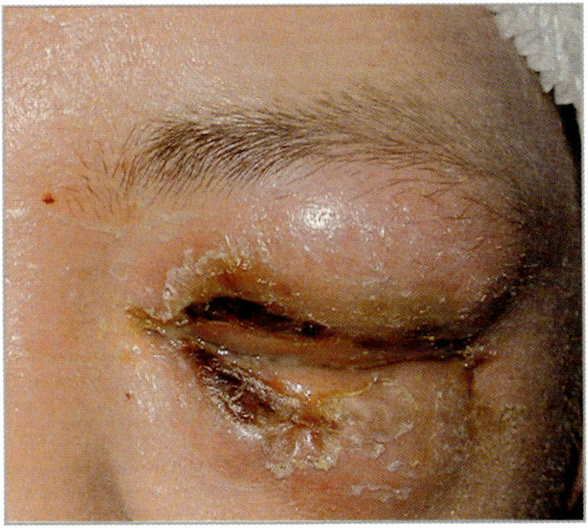

Fig. 4.8: Preseptal cellulitis.

History and examination Ask about sinus disease, trauma, surgery, skin infection, dental infection, immunocompromise and diabetes. Check temperature, general status (hydration, etc.), visual function (VA, colour vision, confrontation fields and RAPD), eye movements, globe displacement (axial and non-axial) and full ocular examination noting optic disc appearance. Mark the extent of skin inflammation to determine if it is subsequently improving or worsening.

Investigations Investigate all cases except mild preseptal cellulitis responding to treatment. Request CT orbits and facial bones (sinus disease, orbital or intracranial abscess), MRI if suspected non-metallic foreign body, FBC (neutrophilia), blood culture if systemically septic, and blood glucose. Swab any sources of pus for microbiology. Include brain imaging (MRI preferred) if any suspicion of neurological impairment.

Management Start treatment immediately. Doses given are for adults, but consult with local infectious disease physicians as guidelines, organisms and susceptibilities vary across time and region:

- *Preseptal cellulitis:*

  Mild: Amoxicillin/clavulanate 500/125 mg p.o. t.d.s. or flucloxacillin 500 mg p.o. q.d.s., both for 10 days. Review daily until there is a definite improvement, then every 2–7 days until complete resolution. Treat as severe (see below) if the patient fails to respond, or is ≤5 years old, septic, or potentially noncompliant.

  Severe: Admit for ceftriaxone 1–2 g i.v. daily in divided doses until responding (1–2 days), then treat as for mild disease.

- *Orbital cellulitis:*

  Admit. Monitor orbital and visual functions 2–3 times daily. Give ceftriaxone 1–2 g i.v. daily plus flucloxacillin 1–2 g i.v. q.d.s. (beware of cholestatic jaundice). Consider vancomycin, clindamycin, linezolid, teicoplanin or other appropriate antibiotics for MRSA. In patients >10 years old or those with chronic sinonasal disease, add metronidazole 500 mg i.v. t.d.s. Continue i.v. treatment for 3–5 days, provided condition improves. Request CT, blood glucose, FBC, ± blood culture (if septic). Refer any sinus disease to ENT. Repeat CT to exclude abscess if any deterioration occurs. Arrange urgent neurosurgical referral if there is neurologic deterioration or intracranial abscess. Change to oral antibiotic (see preseptal cellulitis above) when there is definite improvement. Review every 2–5 days after discharge until complete resolution. Consult again with infectious disease physicians if there is a poor response to initial therapy.

- *Subperiosteal orbital abscess:*
  Subperiosteal abscess ('empyema') is far more common than true intraorbital abscess. Drain if superior or large medial location, >10 years old, clinical/visual deterioration, or failed medical therapy. Consider surgical decompression if the orbit is very tense or not responding to antibiotics. Consider systemic steroids especially if visual loss occurs despite the above measures.

Invasive fungal orbital infection A potentially vision and life-threatening subset of orbital cellulitis. Suspect in patients with poorly controlled diabetes, who are poorly responsive to standard antimicrobial therapy, immunocompromised, debilitated, or with iron overload or haematologic disease. The most common organisms are *Rhizopus* species (in the Mucorales order, hence called mucormycosis), and aspergillosis. *Mucormycosis* most commonly spreads from the sinuses in immunocompromised hosts (rhino-orbital-cerebral mucormycosis). It may present with typical orbital cellulitis, minimal external inflammation (e.g. painful orbital apex syndrome), sinonasal inflammation, ulceration and crusting or necrosis. Mucormycosis in the context of coronavirus disease 2019 (COVID-19) is particularly high-risk for life and vision. Arrange urgent multiple biopsies, and CT and MRI looking for sinus disease, bony destruction, T2 low signal and/or poor mucosal contrast enhancement (**Fig. 4.9**). Manage with ENT, infectious disease physicians ± neurosurgery. Surgery involves debridement and biopsy of the sinuses ± orbital apex. Commence empiric antifungals (e.g. i.v. ± intraorbital amphotericin B and oral voriconazole) and address any immune compromise or metabolic disturbance. Prognosis is often poor, especially with intracranial infection.

Necrotising fasciitis This is a severe, rare, rapidly progressive infection of deep subcutaneous tissues associated with high morbidity (14% blindness) and mortality (up to 10%), and may follow trivial trauma. Periorbital infections generally have better outcomes than other sites. There may be no identifiable immune compromise. Common organisms include group A beta-haemolytic Streptococci, and Staphylococci including MRSA. Necrotic skin/subcutaneous tissue ± subcutaneous emphysema are highly suggestive. Management includes general acute medical care, high dose i.v. antibiotics, and usually aggressive debridement of necrotic tissue.

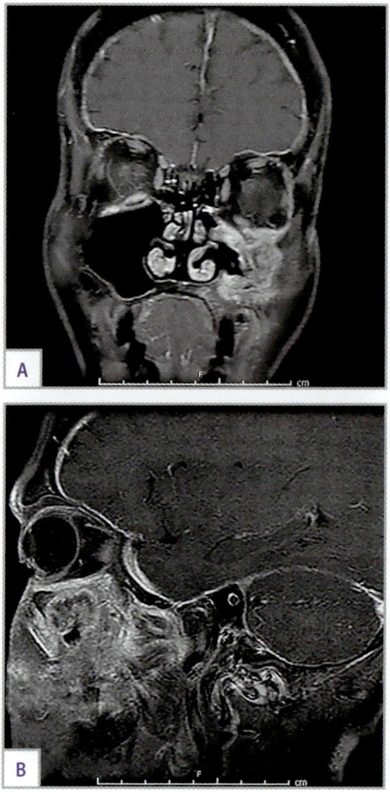

Fig. 4.9: Left invasive fungal (*Aspergillus*) maxillary sinusitis with inferior orbital invasion. (A) Coronal and (B) Sagittal MRI T_1-weighted fat suppression with contrast.

IDIOPATHIC ORBITAL INFLAMMATORY DISEASE

Background Inflammation is not a diagnosis, but a tissue response to trauma, infection, tumour necrosis, ischaemia, toxins, allergy, etc. Idiopathic orbital inflammatory disease (IOID) is, by definition, a diagnosis of exclusion and most cases require a biopsy. Avoid the term 'pseudotumour' which implies an established diagnosis. Any orbital tissue can be involved and presentation varies from acute to chronic. Corticosteroids alter both the clinical course and histopathologic findings in a number of inflammatory processes, including IOID, lymphoma, and metastatic carcinoma. Use steroids only after a tissue diagnosis is established, with the following exceptions:

- Inflammatory superior orbital fissure (Tolosa-Hunt) or orbital apex syndrome (beware of invasive fungal disease).
- Classic orbital myositis.
- Classic thyroid eye disease.
- Sight-threatening orbital inflammatory disease awaiting urgent biopsy.

Clinical features Inflammation produces the following cardinal features:

- '*Rubor*': redness of lids, conjunctiva and extraocular muscle insertions.
- '*Dolor*': pain on eye movement ± tenderness.
- '*Calor*': warmth.
- '*Tumor*': lid swelling, mass or enlarged lacrimal gland.
- *Loss of function:* ptosis, restricted eye movements and diplopia, visual loss and sensory loss (less commonly).

Take a careful general medical history for underlying systemic (especially inflammatory and autoimmune) diseases and arrange full medical examination as required.

Differential diagnosis Infective cellulitis; haematologic or lymphoproliferative disorders (leukaemia and lymphoma); sinus disease; autoimmune disease, including thyroid eye disease, sarcoidosis and granulomatosis with polyangiitis (GPA); carotico-cavernous fistula; primary or secondary orbital malignancy.

Investigations Arrange orbital CT or MRI. Consider the following tests: FBC; erythrocyte sedimentation rate (ESR); C-reactive protein (CRP); urea and electrolytes (U&E); liver function test (LFT); autoantibodies; immunoglobulin (Ig)G4; antineutrophil cytoplasmic antibody (ANCA); angiotensin-converting enzyme (ACE); calcium; chest X-ray (CXR) and CT chest.

Management Attempt to determine the underlying aetiology. See the following pages for management of more common orbital inflammatory conditions: dacryoadenitis (p. 113); orbital myositis (p. 115), superior orbital fissure syndrome (p. 117). Consider referral to a physician, rheumatologist or oncologist. In the absence of a classic presentation of orbital myositis or superior orbital fissure syndrome, consider nonsteroidal anti-inflammatory drugs (NSAIDs), e.g. flurbiprofen 100 mg p.o. t.d.s. for 2 weeks, then 50 mg t.d.s. for 1–2 months; warn of side effects including exacerbation of asthma, gastrointestinal (GI) upset and bleeding, and consider prophylaxis with omeprazole 20 mg p.o. daily, or ranitidine 150 mg p.o. b.d. If no response to NSAIDs, arrange orbitotomy ('opening of the septum') and biopsy for histopathology ± microbiology. Systemic steroids (typically prednisolone up to 1 mg/kg/day) may be commenced after biopsy. Taper over 1–3 months, monitoring for response. Be aware of steroid side effects and required monitoring (p. 413). If inflammation recurs, repeat the biopsy before increasing prednisolone. Consider low-dose, lens-sparing orbital radiotherapy (20 Gy per orbit) in refractory cases after a biopsy and other investigations have excluded other diseases. Steroid-sparing agents (e.g. mycophenolate and methotrexate) may be required for chronic disease – co-manage with a rheumatologist/immunologist.

DACRYOADENITIS

Background Lacrimal gland inflammation is most commonly idiopathic, but may be associated with infection (mostly viral, e.g. mumps, Epstein–Barr virus, cytomegalovirus and varicella-zoster), sarcoidosis, IgG4-related-disease, Sjögren's syndrome, granulomatosis with polyangiitis (GPA), lymphoproliferation and occasionally bacterial, e.g. community-acquired MRSA. Persistent lacrimal gland inflammation raises the suspicion of carcinoma.

Clinical features Typically, pain, erythema, swelling ± ptosis of lateral upper lid, and disturbed tear production (**Fig. 4.10**). Numbness or paraesthesia are rare and suggest carcinoma.

Differential diagnosis Consider lacrimal gland carcinoma (sensory disturbance, bony destruction on CT) (p. 124). Consider sarcoidosis if – bilateral; respiratory disturbance; rash; hilar lymphadenopathy on CXR; raised serum calcium and ACE. GPA typically features destructive sinonasal ± pulmonary disease ('limited' form) or renal ('systemic' form) involvement and may be associated with orbital involvement elsewhere, keratitis and scleritis. IgG4-related disease may cause typically bilateral dacryoadenitis, orbital nerve (especially infraorbital) enlargement, extraocular muscle enlargement, sinus disease, lymphadenopathy and other systemic disease.

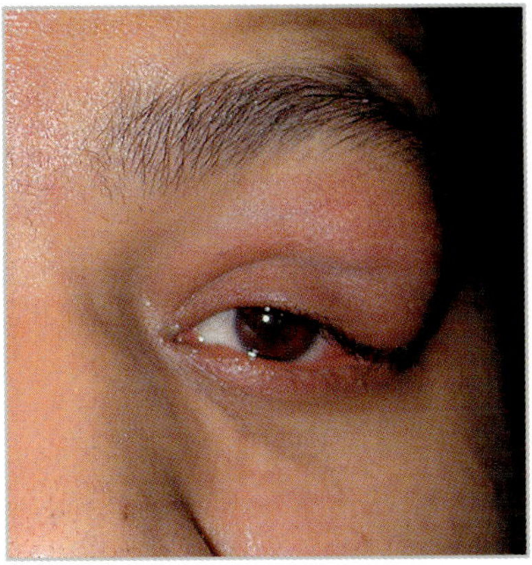

Fig. 4.10: Dacryoadenitis.

Investigations CT or MRI for increasing symptoms >2–3 weeks. Biopsy if there is a poor response after several weeks' treatment, >3–4 weeks of pain, suspicion of malignancy or serious systemic inflammatory disease (e.g. GPA), or a persistent lacrimal fossa mass at 3–4 months.

Management Treat as idiopathic orbital inflammatory disease (p. 111). Disease-specific management as required. Follow-up for 6 months then discharge if there is complete resolution and no suspicious features (persistent pain or mass; sensory disturbance).

ORBITAL MYOSITIS

Background Idiopathic inflammation of the extraocular muscles. It may be associated with systemic inflammatory disease (e.g. Graves' disease, IgG4-related disease or inflammatory bowel disease).

Clinical features Prodrome of periorbital ache exacerbated by eye movement, followed 12–24 hours later by diplopia. More common in young adults and females; usually single muscle and unilateral. Symptoms are worst looking away from the field of action of the affected extraocular muscle (EOM); typically with a paretic motility pattern. Patients may have proptosis, redness over EOM insertions, upper or lower lid retraction, or ptosis. Repeated attacks may cause muscle fibrosis and a permanent restrictive squint.

Investigations CT or MRI shows (typically single) EOM enlargement, classically (but not reliably) involving the insertion (thyroid eye disease classically spares the EOM insertion), high T2 signal, and typically homogeneous contrast enhancement (**Fig. 4.11**).

Differential diagnosis Includes metastasis, vascular malformation, and lymphoproliferative disease. Multiple EOM involvement suggests other disease, e.g. thyroid eye disease (p. 102), inflammatory bowel disease (may be granulomatous myositis) or IgG4-related disease.

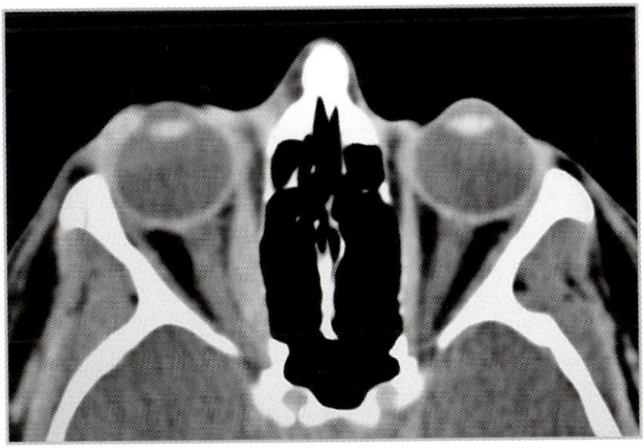

Fig. 4.11: CT of right medial rectus myositis.

Management For classic presentation, prednisolone up to 1 mg/kg/day usually produces a response within 24 hours. Taper to 10 mg over 10–14 days, and then much more slowly over 1–2 months. Biopsy if there is a poor response to treatment, or recurrence. Radiotherapy is helpful if cases are recurrent, chronic, or for failed medical treatment with non-specific inflammation on biopsy.

SUPERIOR ORBITAL FISSURE SYNDROME (TOLOSA-HUNT SYNDROME)

Background Idiopathic inflammation involving the superior orbital fissure (SOF) region. May also involve the cavernous sinus.

Clinical features May include retrobulbar ache, ophthalmoplegia, and periorbital sensory loss/disturbance (V1 and V2). Inclusion of visual loss is sometimes referred to as 'orbital apex syndrome'.

Investigations CT/MRI shows an infiltrative mass at the orbital apex and loss of the normal fat pad at the SOF (applies to any infiltration at the SOF). Look for features of infiltrative/destructive sinus disease on imaging (e.g. granulomatosis with polyangiitis) or loss of mucosal enhancement on MRI (e.g. angioinvasive fungal disease).

Differential diagnosis Exclude intracranial spread of lymphoma. Trauma may produce similar signs (see p. 127), as may tumours and granulomas at the orbital apex.

Management Treat with high-dose prednisolone 1 mg/kg/day if tolerated, tapering according to response. Expect a rapid and good response; significant pain and/or poor response raises suspicion of invasive fungal disease or tumour. Biopsy recurrent or suspicious cases, however, biopsy carries a relatively high risk of visual loss, permanent ophthalmoplegia, or sensory loss. Radiotherapy may be appropriate.

ORBITAL VASCULAR LESIONS

Classification

The International Society for the Study of Vascular Anomalies (ISSVA) classifies vascular anomalies as follows:

- *Tumours:* Usually absent at birth, and result from endothelial proliferation followed sometimes by involution. They are well circumscribed, may cause mass effect, and connect to otherwise normal vascular channels.
- *Malformations:* Typically present at birth but may be subclinical. Further classified by their vessel(s) of origin and/or haemodynamics: fast or high-flow (arterial/arteriovenous), slow or low-flow (venous) and 'no-flow' (lymphatic or capillary). Classically grow commensurately with the patient.
- *Shunts:* Abnormal communications between arterial and venous circulations. May be congenital (including malformations) or acquired (e.g. traumatic).

Tumours

Haemangioma Infantile haemangiomas (**Fig. 4.12**) present in the early weeks and months of life with rapid growth over weeks to months, and gradual involution, typically resolving before age of 10 years, often with a fibro-fatty residuum. Superficial, dermal, 'strawberry naevi' account for around 90% (p. 48); 10% are deeper. Mass effects include ptosis, astigmatism, globe displacement and ocular dysmotility. Extensive lesions may cause Kasabach–Merritt syndrome (red blood cell or platelet sequestration) and circulatory stress. Lesions may pulsate (unusual), or slightly enlarge with Valsalva manoeuvre (e.g. crying). Large segmental lesions, especially facial, raise the possibility of PHACES syndrome (Posterior fossa anomalies; Haemangioma; Arterial

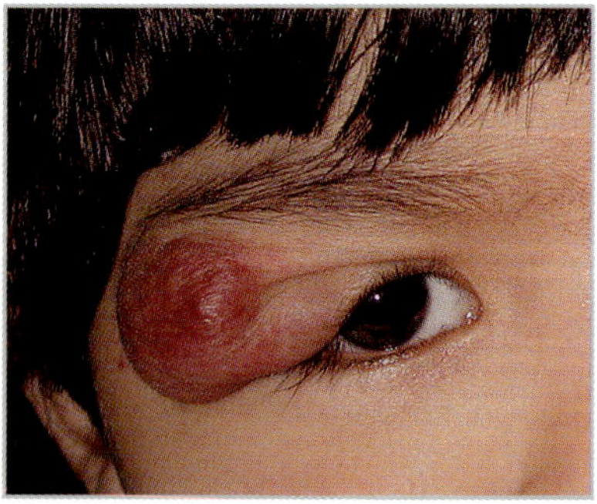

Fig. 4.12: Haemangioma.

anomalies especially cerebral stenoses; Cardiac anomalies especially coarctation; Eye anomalies, e.g. cataract, coloboma, morning glory disc; and Sternal clefting or Supraumbilical raphe). MRI may be required to determine the depth and usually shows well-defined, enhancing lesions with arterial flow voids. It is possible to monitor size and internal flow rates with serial Doppler ultrasound. For periocular lesions carefully monitor VA to identify and treat any amblyopia. Explain the natural history. First-line therapy is oral propranolol under the care of paediatricians; most effective when treated in first year of life (98% response rate). Consider laser (especially pulsed dye) and topical timolol for superficial lesions. Intralesional corticosteroids are now rarely required, e.g. dexamethasone 4 mg in 1 mL to periphery of lesion + Depo-Medrone 40 mg in 1 mL to centre of the lesion. Surgical excision/debulking may help. Systemic steroids and chemotherapeutic agents are rarely required.

Other tumours Include 'pyogenic granuloma' (lobular capillary haemangioma), and other rare lesions, e.g. angiosarcoma and Kaposi's sarcoma.

■ Malformations

Fast-flow or arteriovenous malformations Comprises arterial feeding vessels, an arterialised vascular network with no capillary bed ('nidus'), and dilated venous drainage. May produce pulsatile mass or proptosis, bruit, conjunctival arterialisation, chemosis, lid swelling, pain from thrombosis or haemorrhage, impaired vision, and dysmotility. CT or MRI shows an irregular, rapidly enhancing mass, flow voids, with high-flow on Doppler ultrasound. Angiography provides precise anatomic delineation. Treated by surgery or interventional radiology (e.g. intravascular coils or glue) followed by excision. Recurrences are common.

Slow-flow vascular malformations *Orbital cavernous venous malformation* (a.k.a. '*cavernous haemangioma*'). Formed by small arterial feeders with thin-walled vessels and venous drainage, most common in middle-aged females. It may also present as an incidental finding on imaging, or with slowly progressive axial proptosis ± globe indentation, producing hypermetropia and choroidal folds. Apical lesions may cause retrobulbar ache, visual loss (including gaze-evoked amaurosis) and ocular dysmotility. Imaging shows a well-defined, round, irregularly and/or heterogeneously 'patchy' progressively enhancing mass. May be soft and compressible on ultrasound. Traditionally, non-apical lesions not affecting vision are observed; however, excision of small lesions has low morbidity and confirms the diagnosis.

Excision may be warranted for lesions with significant mass effect and vision loss, especially if progressive. Radiotherapy may shrink these lesions.

Venous malformation: These irregular venous dilatations may enlarge with dependent posture or Valsalva manoeuvre ('distensible'). May cause ache, pain and proptosis if they bleed or undergo thrombosis. Superficial lesions have visibly dilated veins (**Fig. 4.13**). Repeated haemorrhages, inflammation and scarring may cause enophthalmos due to fat atrophy. There may be involvement of contiguous structures (central nervous system, face, sinuses, and temporalis fossa). Static CT or MRI shows multiple irregular masses, often along the course of a vein ± signs of prior bleeding. There may be a thin hyperdense rim or calcification ('phleboliths') on CT. Angiography is rarely required and frequently only shows a venous 'blush'. Dynamic CT, MRI, or ultrasound may show filling with Valsalva manoeuvre. Ultrasound shows cystic spaces. Management may involve amblyopia therapy or surgical excision for unremitting pain, severe cosmetic disfigurement, or massive expansion. Surgical risks are significant and include blindness, loss of motility, ptosis, haemorrhage and recurrence. Drainage of acute haemorrhage ('chocolate cysts') is possible. Interventional radiologic injection of a sclerosant, such as bleomycin, may reduce the lesion size but is less efficacious than for lymphatic malformations; injection of glue plus excision may be considered.

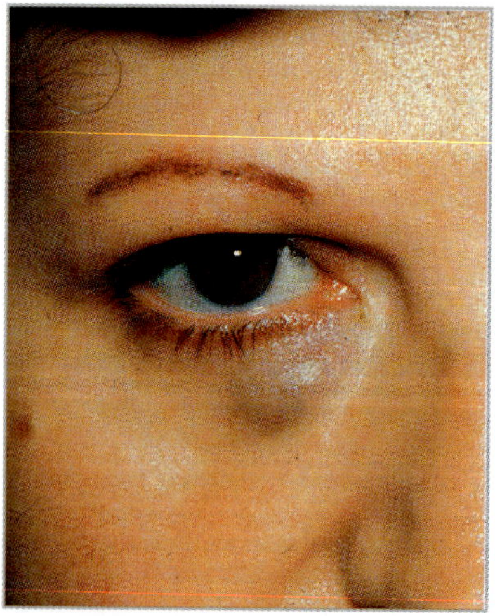

Fig. 4.13: Orbital venous malformation.

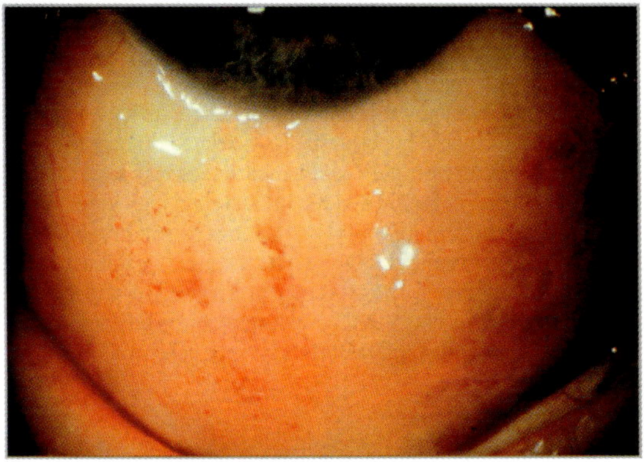

Fig. 4.14: Orbital lymphatic malformation.

'No-flow' vascular malformations

Lymphatic malformations Superficial lesions (**Fig. 4.14**) produce intermittent swelling, ecchymoses, and disfigurement of the lids and conjunctiva; deeper lesions produce intermittent haemorrhage, with episodic swelling, visual disturbance, or dysmotility. Acute inflammatory exacerbations can occur with viral infections. These may have mixed venous/lymphatic elements, or extraorbital involvement, e.g. face and oropharynx. Imaging may show large fluid-filled space ('macrocysts') and/or an infiltrative 'microcystic' pattern. Management includes observation, sclerotherapy (e.g. bleomycin and doxycycline), often best for macrocystic lesions, whereas microcystic lesions generally require debulking surgery. Sirolimus may be effective for microcystic lesions.

Capillary malformations Seen in in Sturge–Weber syndrome ('port wine stain'; associated ocular and central nervous system anomalies) and hereditary haemorrhagic telangiectasia (HHT). Treatment includes LASER and surgery.

Arterio-venous shunts (carotico-cavernous fistula)

See page 811.

Other vascular lesions

Aneurysm (rare); orbital venous thrombosis (post-inflammatory and idiopathic); spontaneous orbital haemorrhage (subperiosteal or related to extraocular muscles; occurring in elderly, haemorrhagic diathesis, anticoagulation and malignancy).

ORBITAL LYMPHOPROLIFERATIVE DISORDERS

Background Orbital lymphoproliferations are divided into reactive lymphoid hyperplasia, IgG4-related disease and lymphoma. Primary orbital T-cell lymphoma is very rare. B-cell lymphoma is histologically divided into low and high grade, the former being much more common; the most common orbital B-cell lymphoma is marginal zone type, followed by follicular and diffuse large B cell. The orbit may be involved secondarily from adjacent or distant B-cell lymphoma. Conversely, orbital lymphoma may spread to extraorbital sites, e.g. central nervous system.

Clinical features Typically, gradual onset of a painless infiltrative mass in the sixth and seventh decade, often with non-axial proptosis (**Fig. 4.15**). Disturbed ocular motility may occur, but neurovascular or visual compromise is uncommon. Lacrimal gland involvement is common. Conjunctival involvement is classically a 'salmon patch' in colour and texture. High-grade tumours have a more rapid, progressive course.

Investigation Exclude non-neoplastic or idiopathic inflammatory disorders (p. 111). CT or MRI typically shows a well-defined, enhancing, infiltrating or 'moulding', extraconal, homogeneous and soft-tissue mass with restricted diffusion (less restriction in non-neoplastic infiltrates). Calcification is very rare. Biopsy, sometimes repeated, is mandatory, and immunohistochemistry ± gene rearrangement studies [Ig heavy chain polymerase chain reaction (PCR)] are usually required. A fresh specimen may be required for flow cytometry.

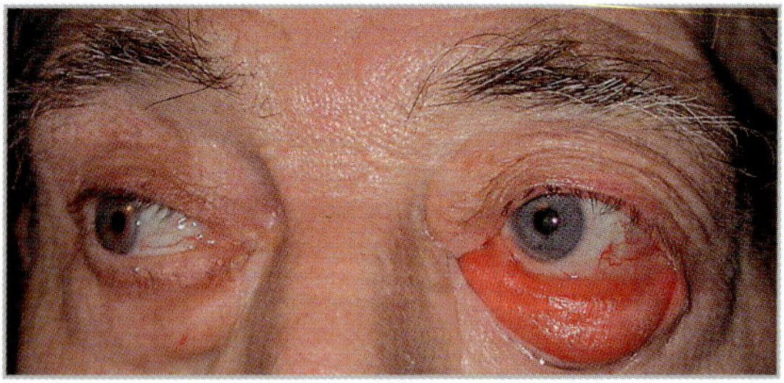

Fig. 4.15: Orbital lymphoma with restricted adduction of the left eye.

Management

- *Reactive lymphoid hyperplasia (RLH)*: Extraorbital, especially lymph node, involvement is not uncommon. Progression to lymphoma occurs rarely. The response to systemic prednisolone is generally excellent; low-dose radiotherapy may be required for functional disturbance. Debulking or decompressive surgery may be required for a gross mass effect or proptosis.
- *Immunoglobulin-G4-related orbital disease*: Similar to RLH, but associated with fibro-inflammatory masses in the orbit and systemically (sclerosing sialadenitis, pancreatitis, cholangitis and thyroiditis; retroperitoneal and pulmonary fibrosis). Raised titres of serum IgG4 may be seen. May predispose to subsequent lymphoma. Biopsy and treat as for RLH; consider rituximab. Repeat biopsies, if there is a poor response to treatment or later relapse.
- *B-cell lymphoma*: Refer all patients to a haematologist/oncologist for systemic investigation. The risk of systemic disease varies with site (eyelid > orbit > conjunctiva) and is higher with bilateral disease. About 25% have prior or concurrent systemic disease, and 50% subsequently. Low-grade lymphoma is usually treated with radiotherapy (~24 Gy; occasionally very low dose 2 × 2 Gy) often with a good response. Higher-grade, systemic disease generally requires chemotherapy (e.g. cyclophosphamide, doxorubicin, vincristine and prednisolone, often with rituximab: 'R-CHOP') and radiotherapy (30–35 Gy). As the prognosis is generally good, consider the risk versus benefit of treatment. Monitor clinically and radiologically.

LACRIMAL GLAND TUMOURS

Pleomorphic adenoma

Background The most common benign lacrimal gland tumour. It may involve the orbital (majority) or palpebral lobe.

Clinical features Classically presents in the second to fifth decades as very slowly progressive proptosis, inferomedial globe displacement, and superotemporal quadrant mass. Ocular indentation may cause blurred vision and/or choroidal folds; impaired motility is rare. Pain, sensory disturbance, and inflammation are very rare and suggest malignancy.

Investigations CT typically reveals a round or bosselated, well-circumscribed, enhancing mass indenting the globe and lacrimal fossa (bone remodelling). MRI shows heterogeneous intermediate signal intensity on T1 and T2 with heterogenous contrast enhancement. Calcification occurs in 3%.

Differential diagnosis (of superotemporal quadrant mass) Other benign lacrimal gland tumours (rare), malignant lacrimal gland tumours, lymphoproliferation, neural tumours (e.g. neurofibroma), chronic dacryoadenitis (idiopathic orbital inflammatory disease, Sjögren's syndrome, Ig-G4-related disease, sarcoidosis and granulomatosis with polyangiitis, dermoid or lacrimal cysts and extrinsic tumours.

Management Refer routinely to an experienced orbital surgeon. Clinico-radiologic features should suggest the diagnosis. Incisional biopsy is contraindicated as it increases the risk of recurrence and malignant transformation. Complete excision with an intact pseudocapsule is required, sometimes via a lateral orbitotomy. Keratoconjunctivitis sicca may occur postoperatively, even with preservation of the palpebral lobe.

Follow-up None required with intact excision, but at least 15 years if there is disruption of the tumour during surgery. If histological foci of malignant change are found, consider postoperative radiotherapy as for lacrimal gland carcinoma and extend follow-up to 20 years.

Lacrimal gland carcinoma

Background Primary lacrimal gland malignancies have a high mortality. The most common is adenoid cystic carcinoma; *de novo* adenocarcinoma, squamous cell carcinoma (SCC), mucoepidermoid carcinomas and carcinoma ex-pleomorphic adenoma ('malignant mixed tumour') are less frequent.

Differential diagnosis Similar to pleomorphic adenoma (see previous section), which must itself be excluded clinico-radiologically. Consider carcinoma in cases of non-resolving dacryoadenitis.

Clinical features Typically, a brief (<1 year) history of a superotemporal quadrant mass with pain, sensory loss, and paraesthesia. Inflammation may occur. Invasion of orbital structures, e.g. levator and extraocular muscles may occur.

Investigations CT often shows an infiltrative tumour moulding to the globe, extending back towards the superior orbital fissure (SOF), with finely irregular bony erosion, and calcification in ~33%.

Management Refer to an experienced orbital surgeon for urgent diagnostic incisional biopsy. Treatment involves complete local macroscopic excision and high-dose radiotherapy to the orbit, SOF and anterior cavernous sinus. Intra-arterial neo-adjuvant chemotherapy (cisplatin or 5-fluorouracil) promotes tumour shrinkage. Exenteration or radical craniofacial resection does not reduce local recurrence or increase survival, but postoperative chemotherapy may delay disease recurrence.

Follow-up Review lifelong to treat the inevitable dry eye, radiation-induced cataract, and monitor for local or systemic recurrence, particularly pulmonary.

RHABDOMYOSARCOMA

Background The most common primary malignant mesenchymal tumour of childhood. May be spontaneous (majority) or familial.

Clinical features Orbital involvement typically presents in the first decade with rapid proptosis (weeks), non-axial globe displacement, erythematous lid swelling, and ptosis. Pain, visual loss and watering are uncommon. Occasionally, it arises from extraorbital sites with secondary orbital spread. It may, very rarely, present in the elderly.

Differential diagnosis Consider inflammatory disorders (e.g. orbital cellulitis), haemangioma, venolymphatic malformation, aggressive neurofibroma, and other malignant tumours (e.g. haematological, neuroblastoma, Ewing's and other sarcomas).

Investigations CT/MRI usually shows a homogeneous, well-defined, enhancing, soft-tissue mass with restricted diffusion and usually without bony destruction – typically not centred on the muscles. Arrange incisional or excisional biopsy for histologic typing and testing for *FOXO1* fusion with *PAX3* or *PAX7* which, if positive, herald a worse prognosis. Embryonal type is more common and better prognosis than alveolar and other types.

Management Although controversial, treat with excisional biopsy if possible. Refer to a paediatric oncologist for staging and multi-agent chemotherapy, which generally has a good prognosis unless alveolar variant. Radiotherapy is often required. Follow-up long term.

SOLITARY FIBROUS TUMOUR

The most common adult mesenchymal orbital tumour with various histopathologic morphologies (e.g. the most cellular form: haemangiopericytoma); *NAB2-STAT6* gene fusion is a sensitive and specific marker. Usually presents in middle age with a slow-growing, firm, superonasal mass, proptosis, and visual loss. Dysmotility, pain, lid swelling, and ptosis are less common. Local recurrence is typical with incomplete excision; malignant change and metastases are rare. Treatment involves complete (preferably intact) local resection, and occasionally radical excision or exenteration if the lesion is infiltrative or diffusely recurrent. Radiotherapy may be considered for incompletely excised or recurrent lesions, or those with malignant features. Chemotherapy may be required for advanced or metastatic disease; the role of biologic and antiangiogenic agents is unclear.

ORBITAL TRAUMA

Background The most common orbital injury is a 'blowout' fracture, typically involving the floor and/or medial wall. If the injury results from an alleged assault or workplace injury, make detailed notes documenting the timing and circumstances of the injury, and measure or preferably photograph all injuries. For traumatic optic neuropathy, see page 796.

History Ask about the nature of the injury (typically blunt trauma, e.g. fist), any visual symptoms including diplopia, blurred vision or field loss, and periorbital sensory loss. Dental malocclusion and trismus (inability to open the mouth) suggest extraorbital involvement of the maxilla/zygoma. High velocity and/or penetrating injury significantly increase the risk of neurological and craniofacial injuries.

Examination Check VA, RAPD, colour vision, infraorbital sensation, ocular motility, exophthalmometry, non-axial globe dystopia, and bony orbital rims. Perform a careful head, ocular, and general assessment to exclude other injuries.

Management Consider the following diagnoses:

- *Orbital floor fracture*: Features include – periorbital ecchymoses; subconjunctival haemorrhage (SCH); enophthalmos; limited eye movement, especially upgaze (from inferior rectus entrapment, bruising, oedema or neuropraxia); infraorbital nerve hypoaesthesia/numbness/pain; subcutaneous emphysema. Children may have a 'greenstick' fracture with significant fascia or muscle entrapment but minimal bruising ('white eye blowout') and nausea and vomiting, especially on upgaze. Request non-contrast CT (same or next day) (**Fig. 4.16**) with fine cuts of orbits and face (axial, coronal ± sagittal). Consider skull and cervical CT as indicated. Ban nose-blowing for 10 days.
  - *Surgery is required for:*
    - Children – a 'white eye blowout' requires surgery within 24–48 hours.
    - Enophthalmos >2 mm and symptomatic: may present weeks after injury.
    - Consider repair if >50% of the floor is involved, as there is a higher risk of late enophthalmos.
    - Consider repair if diplopia fails to resolve after 4–6 weeks and duction test shows restricted movement.

  Monitor diplopia carefully; consider serial Hess charts. Some diplopia on extreme up- or downgaze may persist,

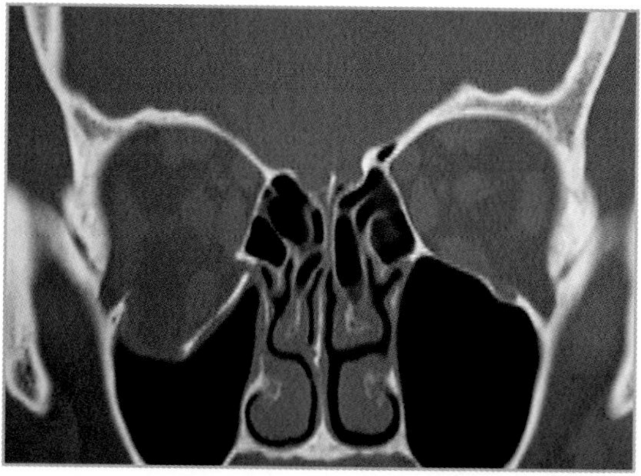

Fig. 4.16: CT of a right orbital floor blowout fracture.

but if restriction affects the primary position or the field of binocular vision at 4–6 weeks then consider orbital exploration and fracture repair.
Persistent diplopia may require inferior rectus recessions, and/or Faden procedures of the superior rectus and contralateral inferior rectus. Consider ipsilateral inverse Knapp procedure if improvement ceases after 6 months, but results are often disappointing. Consider decompressing the infraorbital canal if there is significant persistent neuralgic pain in the infraorbital nerve territory. Options for repair include alloplastic material (e.g. titanium mesh and porous polyethylene) or autogenous material (e.g. cranial bone).

- *Medial orbital wall fracture*: Often has subcutaneous emphysema, variable ecchymosis, medial rectus (MR) dysfunction, enophthalmos, or proptosis. Repair if there is significant MR entrapment causing pain or diplopia, or for enophthalmos >2 mm. Otherwise observe. Ban nose-blowing for 10 days.
- *Lateral orbital wall and roof fracture*: Isolated lateral wall fractures are rare and are usually associated with zygomatico-maxillary complex fractures. Small and undisplaced roof fractures may be monitored for neurologic and ophthalmic complications with broad-spectrum antibiotic cover (e.g. co-amoxiclav); large roof fractures may require neurosurgical repair.
- *Orbital haematoma*: May occur after surgery, blunt trauma, bleeding diatheses, spontaneously, or with underlying vascular

anomalies. Features include: severe orbital or ocular pain; proptosis; ptosis; restricted eye movements, periorbital oedema; progressive visual loss and optic neuropathy; marked subconjunctival haemorrhage; IOP. Most cases are mild and observable. If there is moderate to severe visual loss and/or optic neuropathy, admit and consider urgent lateral cantholysis, orbitotomy, and evacuation of the haematoma. Formal bony orbital decompression may very rarely be required. Consider the following, after consultation with an orbital surgeon, if there is no response to surgical decompression: mannitol (0.5–2 g/kg i.v. over 30–60 minutes), acetazolamide (500 mg i.v.), and high-dose corticosteroids (e.g. methylprednisolone i.v. 0.5–1 g daily; unproven benefit, beware of use in neurotrauma). Consider prophylactic antibiotics in cases associated with sinus fracture. Monitor visual and orbital function regularly (up to 2–3 times a day), depending on response to treatment.

- *Superior orbital fissure syndrome*: Severe impact to the lateral wall may produce oedema, haemorrhage, or bony compression of adjacent soft tissues with subsequent ophthalmoplegia (cranial nerves III, IV, and VI), ptosis (III), mydriasis, efferent pupillary defect (III), loss of accommodation (III), and V1 sensory loss (including cornea). Management is generally supportive, but may include high-dose corticosteroids, e.g. i.v. methylprednisolone for 48 hours (up to 1 g, then prednisolone 1 mg/kg/day rapidly reducing), but beware of use in neurotrauma, steroid side effects and contraindications (p. 413). Consider delayed reduction of significantly displaced fractures. It may also occur with orbital apex tumours, granulomas and idiopathic orbital inflammation (p. 111).
- *Orbital apex syndrome*: Consists of superior orbital fissure syndrome with optic neuropathy. Management is similar to superior orbital fissure syndrome.
- *Traumatic optic neuropathy*: The optic nerve may be damaged by direct (e.g. penetrating) trauma or more commonly by indirect mechanisms (e.g. diffuse craniomaxillofacial trauma). Management is controversial and uncertain. High-dose steroids (i.v.) carry risk of increased mortality if there is coexisting neurotrauma, and may worsen the visual outcome. Surgical decompression of the optic canal may be performed via a transcranial or transnasal endoscopic approach, but is also controversial and unproven. See also page 796.
- *Orbital foreign bodies*: Occur in up to 3% of orbital trauma. A clear history of penetrating trauma may not be forthcoming, especially in children. Look for small entry wounds. Request CT (also excludes metallic objects prior

to MRI), or MRI if organic matter is suspected. Beware of intracranial and intraocular penetration. Remove if organic (e.g. wood), copper-containing (copper and brass), infective (e.g. associated with an abscess, discharging sinus), or for a functional deficit (e.g. optic neuropathy and ocular motility disturbance).

EYE SOCKET DISORDERS

Post-enucleation socket syndrome (PESS) Caused by an absent or small orbital implant following eye removal; attempted correction with a large and heavy prosthesis may result in poor prosthetic retention, rotation, and instability. Clinical features form the mnemonic, PESS: Ptosis, Enophthalmos, deep upper lid Sulcus, and lower lid Sag (retraction, laxity and/or ectropion) (**Fig. 4.17**). Upper lid entropion or retraction and lagophthalmos may also occur.

Consider a larger artificial eye, but this may worsen lower lid sag, retention, and stability. If no implant is palpable, augment volume with a secondary ball implant. If an implant is present, exchange for larger ball implant, or add orbital floor implant (e.g. porous polythene), or autogenous material to the socket and/or postseptal upper lid sulcus fillers (e.g. hyaluronic acid, dermis-fat graft or micro-fat graft). A shortage of socket lining (conjunctiva) may lead to poor prosthesis retention; treat with mucosal grafting, generally after correcting volume deficiency.

Discharge is a common and often minor problem, relating mainly to the presence of the prosthesis (a foreign body). Regular prosthetic care, including cleaning with contact lens solutions and polishing, helps to reduce protein surface biofilm. Evert the lid to exclude giant papillary conjunctivitis and if present treat with topical steroids, e.g. G. dexamethasone 0.1% q.d.s. for 1 month. Exclude exposed sutures or implants – these generally require removal of exposed material (± simultaneous or later reinsertion of implant or dermis-fat graft). True socket infection is rare and relates to bacterial contamination at the time of implant insertion, implant exposure, and host factors, e.g. prior radiotherapy, diabetes or immunosuppression.

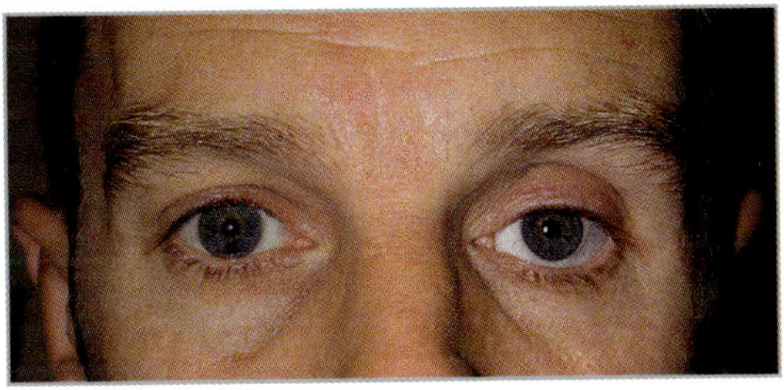

Fig. 4.17: Left post-enucleation socket syndrome.

Implant exposure generally relates to inadequate surgical implantation. Failure to widely open the posterior intraconal space and dragging of anterior tissues leads to insufficiently posterior placement. Restitution of dragged tissues further shallows the implant ('cactus syndrome'). Other factors include poor host conditions (e.g. prior radiotherapy), insufficient socket lining (limiting closure over implant), abnormally small bony socket (e.g. prior radiotherapy and microphthalmos/anophthalmos), and possibly use of non-absorbable sutures.

Poor prosthetic motility is common after eye removal ± orbital implantation, especially in horizontal gaze (shorter fornices); it is less common after evisceration than enucleation. Distinguish motility of the socket (often poor after trauma, multiple surgeries) from that of the prosthesis. Optimise prosthetic fitting and volume augmentation. The use of pegged implants may slightly improve prosthetic motility but has a very high long-term complication rate (~80–90%), e.g. granuloma, exposure, infection, peg extrusion, 'clicking' noise, and poor prosthesis retention.

PROCEDURES (ENUCLEATION AND EVISCERATION)

Box 4.1: Enucleation

1. Obtain fully informed consent and agreement from two consultant ophthalmologists. Mark the side.
2. Surgery is usually performed under general anaesthesia (GA), but retrobulbar local anaesthesia (LA) with sedation is possible. Give i.v. antibiotic prophylaxis on induction (e.g. cefazolin 2 g).
3. Confirm the side by examining the eyes, notes, and consent form.
4. Perform 360° peritomy using spring scissors and blunt dissect Tenon's capsule from the globe. Conjunctival traction sutures are advisable.
5. Preplace 5/0 Vicryl in the recti near their insertion, then disinsert. Disinsert obliques (may reattach the inferior oblique).
6. Divide the optic nerve using enucleation scissors or snare. Gently handle the eyes with ocular tumours to minimise the risk of seeding; examine the eye carefully. Send the eye for histopathology.
7. Obtain central retinal artery haemostasis using bipolar cautery and pressure.
8. Select an implant, typically 22 mm size. Acrylic is much cheaper than other choices. For implants other than porous polyethylene (Medpor), a wrap (e.g. Vicryl mesh) is required for muscle attachment. Donor sclera is generally avoided if there is a risk of prion disease transmission.
9. Insert the implant behind posterior Tenon's capsule using a 'no-touch' technique, e.g. insert through the thumb from a polythene surgical glove and 'glide' the implant into place through a hole cut in the end of the thumb.
10. Suture the extraocular muscles to the implant/wrap using the preplaced sutures.
11. Close Tenon's capsule (interrupted 5/0 Vicryl) and conjunctiva (continuous 7/0 Vicryl).
12. Insert the largest possible conformer into the fornices, leaving 2–3 mm lagophthalmos. Place a temporary suture tarsorrhaphy. Apply antibiotic ointment.
13. Apply a pressure dressing for 5–7 days.
14. Review in 5–7 days. Early complications include conjunctival prolapse, dislodged conformer, orbital haemorrhage, oedema and infection. Late complications include post-enucleation socket syndrome, implant extrusion, exposure or malposition, and lining deficiency.
15. Refer for an ocular prosthesis in 4–6 weeks.

Box 4.2: Evisceration

1. Consent, precautions, anaesthesia and peritomy are similar to enucleation (Steps 1–4 above).
2. Perform a 360° limbal keratectomy (blade then spring scissors).
3. Remove the intraocular contents using a metal scoop.
4. Carefully debride all uveal tissue with a cotton bud. Avoid alcohol as this may cause scleral necrosis. Cauterise the vortex veins and any bleeding vessels.
5. Split sclera diagonally across the macula into two halves (each with two recti attached).
6. 'Islandise' the optic nerve with a small scleral rim. This prevents neuroma.
7. Insert an unwrapped implant into the posterior orbit via a 'glide'. As per enucleation, avoid the implant contacting the surgeon or lids. Unlike enucleation, an implant wrap is not required.
8. Close the sclera (5/0 Vicryl) with a 4–5 mm overlap, avoiding closure under tension over the implant.
9. See 'Enucleation', points 12–16.

OPTOMETRY AND GENERAL PRACTICE GUIDELINES

Infection of the skin and the eye is not uncommon, but it is important to distinguish minor soft-tissue infection from pre-septal cellulitis, and especially orbital cellulitis. Reduced visual acuity, restricted eye movements, diplopia, and proptosis suggest orbital cellulitis.

Orbital cellulitis requires immediate referral to a specialist to exclude life- or vision-threatening complications. Commence broad-spectrum i.v. antibiotic therapy (cefuroxime, and in patients over 10 years old, metronidazole) immediately, before investigation or referral. This measure may be sight and life-saving.

Orbital trauma also requires urgent assessment; small penetrating entry points may be hard to detect. Exclude and stabilise other injuries to head, neck, and spine before arranging ophthalmic review.

The following guide to referral urgency is not prescriptive, as clinical situations vary.

Immediate

- Pre- or post-septal orbital cellulitis p. 107
- Necrotising fasciitis suggested by violaceous skin discoloration or frank necrosis p. 44
- Significant trauma p. 127

Urgent (within 1 week)

- Proptosis with visual dysfunction p. 94
- Proptosis with corneal exposure (commence G. hypromellose 0.3% 2-hourly) p. 94
- Orbital inflammation (exclude cellulitis) p. 111
- Structural and congenital lesions where there is suspicion of globe displacement, reduced vision, or incipient amblyopia, e.g. orbital haemangioma in an infant p. 98-101; 118

Routine

- Chronic proptosis (months to years) without visual dysfunction p. 94
- Structural and congenital lesions with documented normal acuity p. 98-101; 118

EXTERNAL EYE DISEASE

Guy T Smith & Su-yin Koay

5

CONJUNCTIVAL ANATOMY

- The bulbar conjunctival epithelium includes goblet cells that produce the mucous layer of the tear film.
- The conjunctival stroma comprises a superficial adenoid layer and a deep fibrous layer. The former contains lymphoid tissue that results in follicle formation with appropriate stimuli (it is undeveloped in infants who cannot develop a follicular response). The conjunctiva is firmly anchored to the tarsus and limbus, resulting in tarsal papillae or limbal papillae when there is conjunctival inflammation/infiltration with inflammatory cells, whereas the bulbar conjunctiva is only loosely attached to the globe so that papillae do not develop when there is inflammation/infiltration.
- Lymphatics drain to the submandibular and preauricular lymph nodes.
- The accessory lacrimal glands of Wolfring and Krause are located in the conjunctival stroma at the superior margin of the upper tarsus and the superior fornix, respectively.
- The meibomian glands are located in the tarsal plates of the eyelids and share some characteristics of hair follicles but without a hair shaft; if diseased (e.g. chronic blepharitis), they can develop a hair (distichiasis).
- The conjunctiva has comparatively few pain fibres from the trigeminal nerve (ophthalmic division), so pain is poorly localised.

HISTORY AND EXAMINATION

History Key symptoms include redness, surface irritation, itching, discharge, watering, conjunctival swelling, and mildly blurred vision if the tear film is disturbed. More severe vision loss may indicate corneal or other disease.

Examination Systematically examine the lid position and margin, lashes, meibomian gland orifices, puncta, fornices, tarsal plates, tear film, limbus, cornea, and conjunctiva. Record the following:

- *Conjunctival hyperaemia*: may be diffuse or localised.

- *Subconjunctival haemorrhage*: May be fine punctate haemorrhages, larger blotches or a solid sheet.
- *Discharge*: Note if serous or watery (viral and toxic aetiology), mucopurulent (bacterial/viral conjunctivitis), or stringy (allergic).
- *Chemosis*: Oedematous conjunctiva appears milky and may swell beyond the lid margins.
- *Follicles*: Focal lymphoid hyperplasia in the tarsal conjunctiva produces rounded, avascular elevations that emerge from deep in the adenoid layer, often surrounded by more superficial papillae, with whitish-grey centres surrounded by small vessels (**Fig. 5.1**). Fluorescein pools around the elevations making them easier to see.
- *Papillae:* Elevated accumulations of inflammatory cells in the superficial tarsal conjunctiva with a central vascular tuft (**Fig. 5.1**). Small papillae produce a velvety appearance but may fuse to form elevated compound 'giant' papillae, sometimes with apical scars and a cobblestone appearance (**Fig. 5.2** and see **Fig. 5.13**, p. 162). At the limbus, giant papillae appear as gelatinous mounds, usually in the palpebral aperture.
- *Pigment*: Assess the extent and whether this is associated with increased conjunctival thickness, as in neoplasia.
- *Coagulated inflammatory exudate*: Adherent to the tarsal or forniceal conjunctiva. May bleed when peeled off (**Fig. 5.3**).

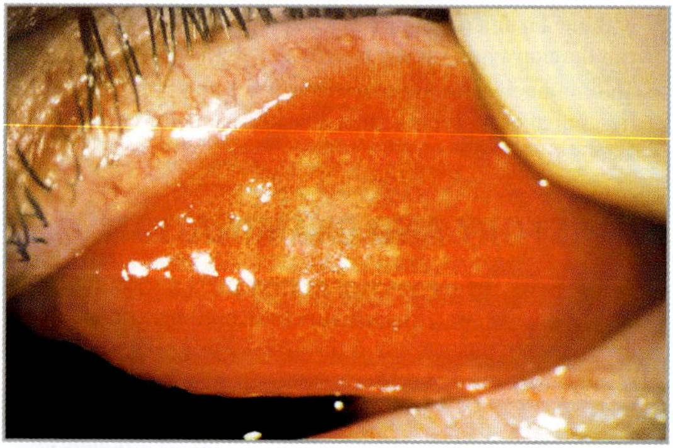

Fig. 5.1: Follicles (large pale elevations) surrounded by micropapillae (smaller superficial vascularised elevations).

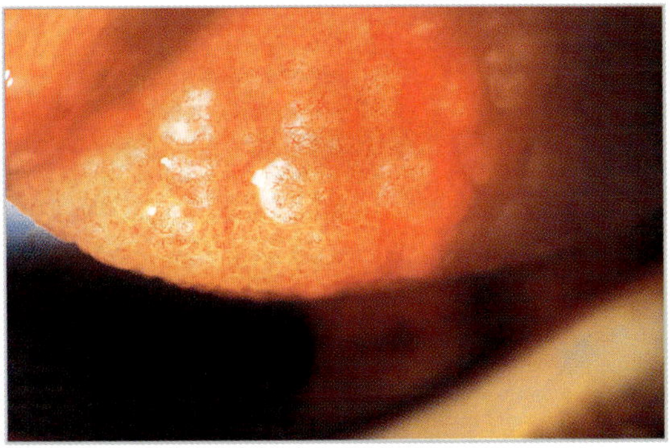

Fig. 5.2: Compound 'giant' papillae with scarred apices surrounded by micropapillae.

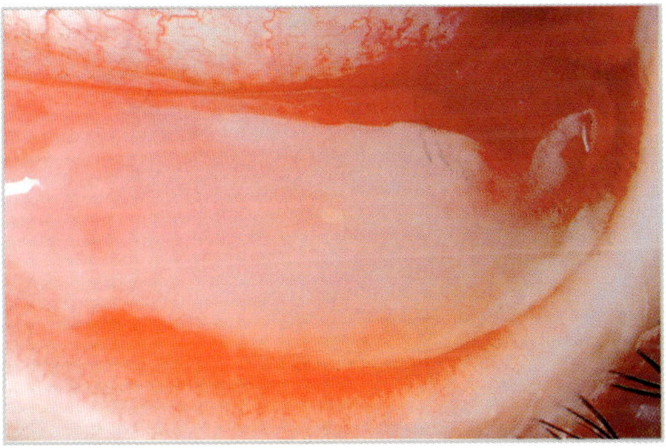

Fig. 5.3: Pseudomembrane (Courtesy DH Verity).

- *Symblepharon*: identify the position (medial, lateral, or superior fornices) and extent (**Fig. 5.4**).
- *Punctal orifice*: may be normal, occluded, absent, stenosed, or with a plug *in situ*.
- *Meibography*: images the meibomian gland silhouette to assess atrophy/drop out. It is not clear if dropout indicates glandular tissue loss, or reduced visibility from glands that assume the characteristics of surrounding tarsal tissue, and how this relates to gland function.

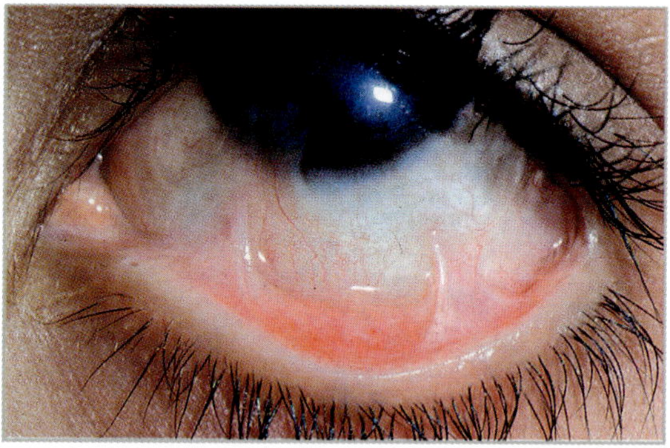

Fig. 5.4: Symblephara (Courtesy DH Verity).

ANTERIOR BLEPHARITIS

Background Blepharitis describes inflammation of the whole lid. Classification is difficult due to heterogeneous presentation and the complex and incompletely understood pathogenesis and natural history. *Marginal blepharitis*: Lid margin inflammation that includes both anterior and posterior blepharitis. *Anterior blepharitis*: Lid margin inflammation anterior to the grey line (p. 14), centred around the lashes. Anterior blepharitis may be accompanied by squamous debris, collarettes or cylinders (**Fig. 5.6,** p. 145) around the lash base and vascular changes of the lid skin. Historically, anterior blepharitis was believed to have a primarily bacterial origin. *Demodex folliculorum/ brevis* overgrowth in the lash follicles may contribute to anterior blepharitis. As *Demodex* mites consume epithelial cells at the hair follicle they cause microabrasions that induce epithelial hyperplasia. Their presence is strongly associated with hair follicle duct dilatation, hyperkeratinisation, perifollicular non-granulomatous inflammation and a type 1 allergic response. Cylindrical dandruff is pathognomonic of *Demodex* overgrowth.

History Ask about lid margin erythema, ocular irritation and burning sensation. *Demodex*-related itching may be worse at night or early morning following mite activity. Risk factors for *Demodex* overgrowth include rosacea, diabetes, increasing age, local or systemic immunosuppression, stress, alcohol, sun exposure and smoking.

Examination

- *Skin*: Seborrhoea of the scalp, brows, and ears.
- *Lids*: Collarettes (waxy, cylindrical debris at the base of the lashes, formed as bacterial debris clinging to the shaft of the lash as it grows). *Demodex* damage to the hair follicle causes lash loss and misdirection. Seborrhoeic greasy lash debris and lid margin erythema with focal lid margin ulceration may occur (**Fig. 5.5**).
- *Conjunctiva*: Reactive conjunctivitis and keratitis occur with higher numbers of lash follicle mites.

Anterior blepharitis is commonly associated with posterior blepharitis (p. 143) and ocular rosacea (p. 148).

Treatment

- Advise lid hygiene to remove debris and the biofilm that harbours bacteria. Use a cotton-tipped bud dipped in boiled or sterile water, contact lens solution or dilute bicarbonate of soda (one teaspoon in one cup of cooled boiled water). Avoid surfactants, e.g. baby shampoo. Aim to create an environment

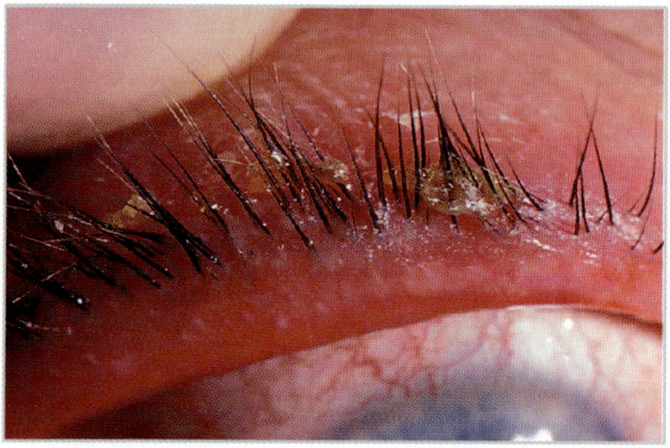

Fig. 5.5: Anterior blepharitis showing collarettes and lid margin erythema.

that favours the normal commensal bacteria rather than sterilising the lid margin. Avoid corneal trauma.

- Treat >10 basal collarettes as *Demodex* overgrowth. The mite's life cycle (larva-nymph-adult) is ~14–23 days, necessitating prolonged eyelid treatment, e.g. commercially available tea tree oil preparations or wipes (e.g. Optase) b.d. for at least 6 weeks; or off-label ivermectin 1% cream nocte for 3 months. Lotilaner 0.25% eye drops can be used b.d. for 28 days but are not yet available in the UK.
- For staphylococcal disease (diagnosed with culture from conjunctival swabs), prescribe Oc. chloramphenicol or Oc. ciprofloxacin b.d. to the lid margins for 3 weeks.

Follow-up 1 month if there is corneal involvement; otherwise, not routinely required.

POSTERIOR BLEPHARITIS

Background Posterior blepharitis is inflammation of the posterior lid margin. It can be caused by meibomian gland dysfunction (MGD), conjunctivitis (p. 150), allergic conjunctivitis (p. 159) and systemic conditions such as acne rosacea (p. 148), see **Flowchart 5.1**.

Obstructive MGD describes meibum accumulation within the gland's ductal system. Contributors include increasing age, hormonal disturbances (e.g. during menopause), environmental factors (e.g. dust), meibomian gland breakdown products, changed meibum composition with increased melting point, chemicals (e.g. makeup) and medication toxicity. Initially, MGD may show few signs other than reduced tear film stability, but continued meibum production widens the ducts and then the secretory acini. Resultant acinar atrophy causes posterior lid margin notching.

Stasis induces overgrowth of *Demodex* mites and commensal bacteria (e.g. coagulase-negative staphylococci, *Staphylococcal aureus*, and *Propionibacterium acnes*) that release irritative free fatty acids (FFAs) that destabilise the tear film. Bacterial enzymes and FFAs promote inflammation. Conjunctival irritation stimulates keratinisation.

History Chronic and non-specific symptoms include crusting of lashes (80%), ocular redness (80%), foreign body sensation (65%), chalazia (60%), blurred vision (45%), tearing (40%) and a burning sensation (40%). The symptoms of meibomian seborrhoea are worse than the signs. Ask about isotretinoin exposure.

Examination Similar to dry eye disease (p. 207). Symptoms may not correlate well with signs.

- *Skin:* look for seborrhoeic dermatitis and acne rosacea.
- *Lids:* meibomian seborrhoea has excessive fluid meibomian secretions with little inflammation initially. With MGD there are dilated, prominent meibomian gland orifices (100%), meibomian gland plugs (100%), pouting meibomian gland orifices (35%) (**Fig. 5.6**) and papillary hypertrophy (100%). Chalazia may be present. Express the meibomian glands to grade the ease of expression and appearance: clear, cloudy, cloudy with debris (granular) and thick like toothpaste. With time lash loss (madarosis) (60%), lid notching (45%), lid margin telangiectasia, posterior migration and loss of definition of the mucocutaneous junction, and whitening of the lashes (poliosis) may occur (**Figs. 5.7 and 5.8**).

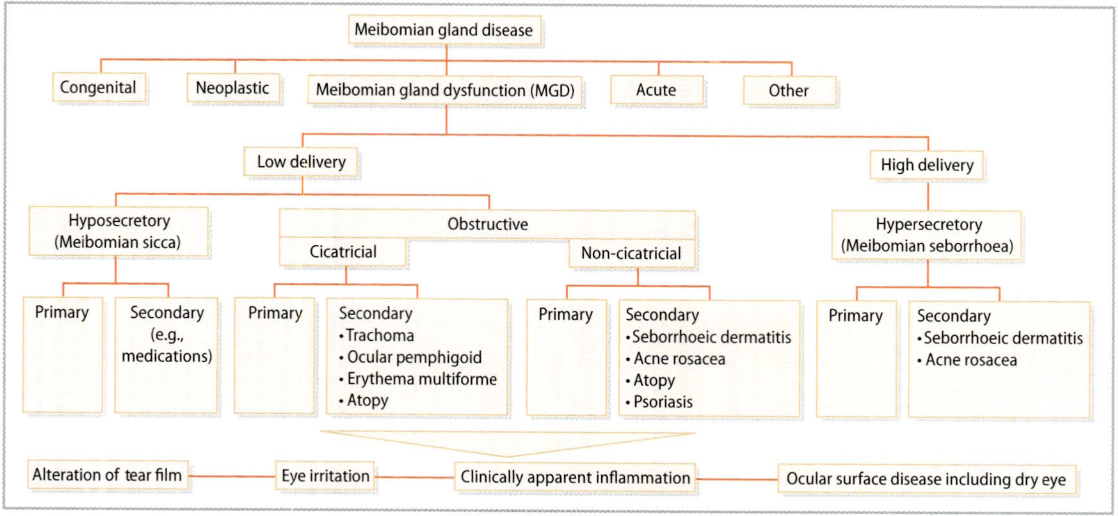

Flowchart 5.1: Classification from the International Workshop on Meibomian Gland Dysfunction: Report of the Definition and Classification Subcommittee. (Nelson JD et al. Invest Ophthalmol Vis Sci. 2011;52:1930-7.)

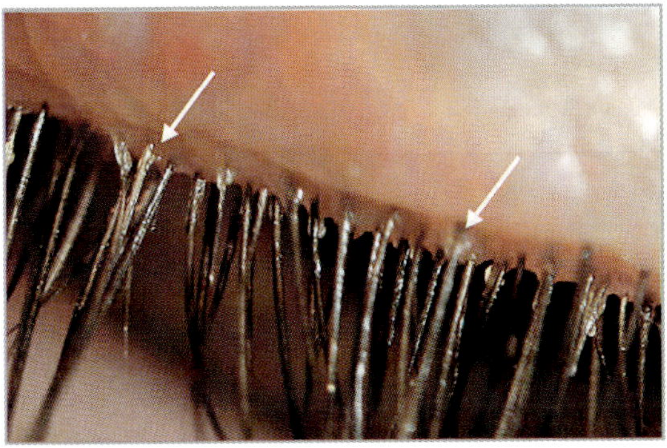

Fig. 5.6: Demodex with cylindrical dandruff on lashes.

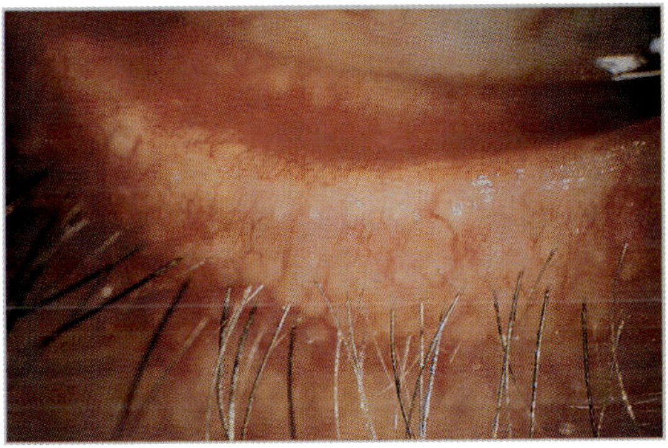

Fig. 5.7: Posterior blepharitis.

- *Conjunctiva*: diffuse hyperaemia (100%).
- *Cornea and tear film*: reduced tear break up time (100%), tear film debris (55%), and foamy tear film (60%). In meibomian keratoconjunctivitis, there is superficial punctate keratopathy (SPK) adjacent to the lower lid margin (100%). Corneal vascularisation, marginal ulceration and corneal perforation can occur.

Treatment Emphasise that this is a chronic condition needing prolonged treatment. There is a large overlap with dry eye treatment (p. 210). Treat any associated *Demodex* species (p. 142).

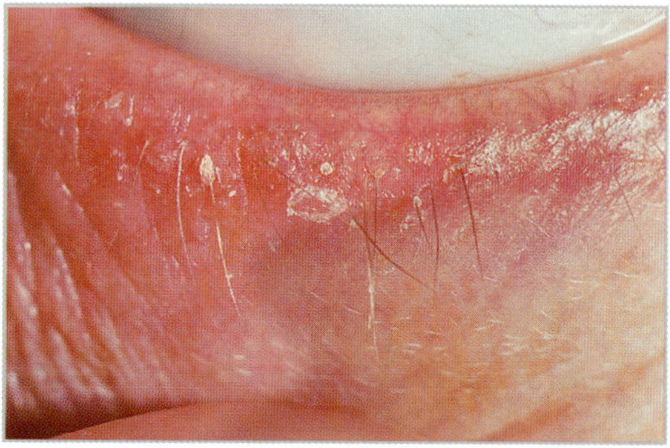

Fig. 5.8: Poliosis (white lashes), madarosis (lost lashes) and collarettes.

Normalise lipid consistency:

- Apply warm compresses for 7–10 minutes using a microwavable, or USB heating pad. Ensure good contact between the pad and the eyelid. Time the treatment.

Release meibomian gland obstruction:

- After warm compresses express stagnant meibomian gland secretions by massaging from top to bottom along the length of the upper lid (massage up in the lower eyelid) or advise to carry out two tight blinks/squeezes of the eyelids. If symptoms persist, consider:
  - A single thermal pulsation session, e.g. Lipiflow
  - Three to four treatments with intense pulsed light (IPL) therapy
  - Intraductal probing with a thin wire, to enable meibum expulsion

Reduce inflammation:

- Topical lubricants rinse and dilute debris, toxins, cytokines and other proinflammatory molecules in the tears, e.g. sodium hyaluronate 0.03% q.d.s.
- Lid hygiene (p. 141) removes lid margin debris and biofilm to restore usual commensal flora and control *Demodex* overgrowth.
- Consider short-term topical corticosteroids, e.g. G. prednisolone 0.5% b.d. for 2 weeks in severe inflammation, or steroid ointment (e.g. hydrocortisone, betamethasone

and dexamethasone) for very inflamed lid margins. Avoid long-term topical steroids as not proven and may encourage *Demodex* overgrowth.

- For chronic steroid-dependent cases, add topical ciclosporin b.d. as a 3-month trial, using whichever formulation is available or tolerated. Advise patients that its effect takes 3 months to build.
- Avoid topical NSAIDs, as longer-term dosing can cause corneal epitheliopathy.

If necessary, consider macrolide antibiotics. These work by reducing inflammation and biofilms; any bacteriocidal effects are likely incidental, as MGD is not thought to be caused primarily by bacterial infection. For corneal involvement prescribe G. azithromycin 1.5% b.d. for 3 days then once at night for 1 month, repeated as needed.

The production of toxic enzymes by lid commensals such as *Staphylococcus epidermidis* and *P. acnes* is highly responsive to low dose of tetracyclines. To a lesser extent, this applies to both sensitive and resistant strains of *S. aureus*. The doses of doxycycline used are not microbiocidal, e.g. doxycycline 100 mg o.d. p.o. for 8 weeks (some clinicians use 50 mg o.d. for 1 week then 50 mg b.d for 7 weeks to increase tolerance to doxycycline). Enhancing gut biome (e.g. consuming kefir) may improve tolerance. Warn about the risk of sunburn and changes to international normalised ratio (INR) when on tetracyclines. Contraindications include age of <8 years and pregnancy. Alternatively, use azithromycin 500 mg b.d. oral for 1 day then 250 mg oral daily for 4 days.

Treat frankly infected lids, e.g. Oc. chloramphenicol or Oc. ciprofloxacin b.d. to the lid margins for 3 weeks.

Follow-up For moderate-to-severe disease, review routinely in clinic. Expect improvement in 2–3 months, then reduce lid hygiene to the minimum required to prevent symptoms. Continue warm compresses.

OCULAR ROSACEA

Background A chronic inflammatory facial dermatosis characterised by exacerbations and remissions. There are multiple pathogenic pathways, but mast cell upregulation is central. More common with light skin, but may be missed with darker skin tones. Ocular involvement is common and can occur without cutaneous features. Prevalence of 0.4–1% of adult population, onset any age after 30 years. Children may be affected. Associated with dyslipidaemia, hypertension and gastrointestinal disorders. See also anterior and posterior blepharitis (pp. 141 and 143).

History Similar to posterior blepharitis (p. 143). Symptoms may be triggered ultraviolet (UV) exposure, heat, strenuous exercise, alcohol or spicy food.

Examination Look for a fixed (non-moving) centrofacial erythema in a characteristic pattern that may periodically intensify (**Fig. 5.9**). This can also affect other locations, e.g. neck, chest, scalp, ears and back. Major cutaneous signs include papules, pustules, flushing and telangiectasia. Periodic exacerbation and remission of burning and stinging are characteristic. Ocular changes occur in ~25% of cases, and are the primary feature in up to 20%. The severity of ocular disease

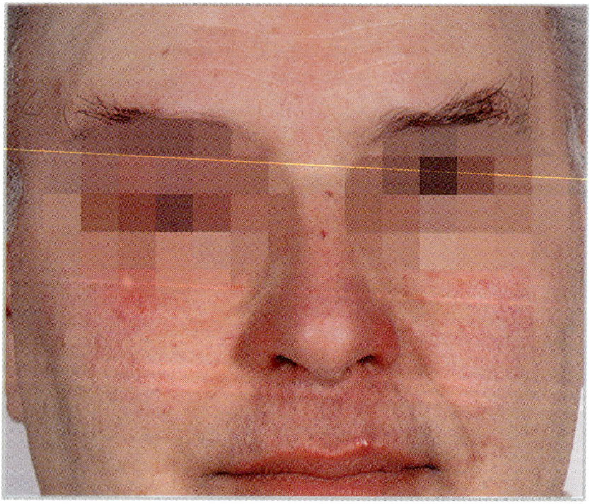

Fig. 5.9: Cutaneous rosacea showing telangiectasia, erythema, papules and one pustule.

may not correlate with cutaneous disease. Ocular symptoms and signs are non-specific and usually, but not always, bilateral:

- *Lids*: Posterior blepharitis and chalazia.
- *Conjunctiva*: Variable diffuse injection ± small grey nodules on the bulbar conjunctiva near the limbus (phlyctens). These may ulcerate. Inferior cicatrisation may occur in chronic disease.
- *Cornea*: Involved in 5–30%. Inferior superficial neovascularisation may progress, ± deep neovascularisation, ± lipid keratopathy. Ranges from superficial punctate keratitis to marginal keratitis, scarring and peripheral ulceration that may progress to perforation.
- May develop episcleritis or scleritis requiring treatment.

ROSacea COnsensus expert panel (ROSCO) grading of ocular rosacea:

- *Mild*: blepharitis
- *Mild to moderate*: blepharitis and conjunctival injection
- *Moderate to severe*: corneal involvement with punctate keratitis, infiltrates and vascularisation
- *Severe:* sclerokeratitis, with or without anterior uveitis

Investigations Clinical diagnosis.

Treatment Identify and avoid environmental and lifestyle triggers to minimise flushing and irritation. Treat as for severe meibomian keratoconjunctivitis (p. 145), although high frequency or potent topical steroids may prove necessary. G. cyclosporine 0.1% up to q.d.s. daily, as for vernal keratoconjunctivitis, may help, as may doxycycline 100 mg o.d. Prolonged treatment may be required, but increases the incidence of adverse effects, e.g. photosensitivity and gastrointestinal disturbance. Avoid doxycycline in children, pregnant or lactating women. Consider co-management with a dermatologist.

Follow-up Depends upon the severity and response to treatment. May need frequent review when very symptomatic, to prevent progressive corneal disease.

BACTERIAL CONJUNCTIVITIS

Background Adult bacterial conjunctivitis is most often caused by staphylococcal species, followed by *Haemophilus influenzae* and *Streptococcus pneumoniae* and a smaller, but increasing, incidence of *Neisseria gonorrhoeae*. In children, *H. influenzae* is the most common, followed by *S. pneumoniae* and *Moraxella catarrhalis*. Contact lens wearers are more susceptible to gram-negative infections. *Pseudomonas aeruginosa* is more likely in the critically ill. Neonates can be affected by the vertical, oculogenital transmission of *N. gonorrhoeae* and *Chlamydia trachomatis*. For conjunctivitis of the newborn see page 689. Infection can spread via hand-to-eye, fomites, e.g. door handle, and respiratory droplets.

Symptoms Presentations vary, but features suggesting bacterial infection are gluey or sticky eyelids in the morning, absence of burning sensation and lack of watery discharge. Usually it starts in one eye, then spreads to the other. Presentation may suggest the causative organism:

- Hyperacute (<12 hours): *N. gonorrhoeae, Neisseria meningitidis* and *S. pneumoniae*.
- Acute (<3–4 weeks): *Haemophilus aegyptius, Streptococcus* and *Pseudomonas* spp.
- Subacute: *H. influenzae* (thin watery discharge), *Escherichia coli* and *Proteus* spp.
- *Chronic (>4 weeks)*: *Chlamydia*.

Ask about contact with conjunctivitis, trauma, prior episodes, treatment, contact lens use, immune status, sexual history, and ear symptoms in children.

Signs Record VA. Mucoid or purulent discharge suggest bacterial infection (**Fig. 5.10**), often with eyelash crusting or gluing. The lids may be variably oedematous. There is diffuse conjunctival injection ± papillae, with membranes in severe diseases. Exclude uveitis, epithelial defects, ulceration and keratitis (**Fig. 5.11**, p. 154). Unlike viral conjunctivitis, lymphadenopathy is usually absent except with *Chlamydia* or gonococcus. Gonococcus can produce a secondary iritis and keratitis.

Differential diagnosis Consider viral keratoconjunctivitis (systemic viral features such as sore through, cough, fever; less discharge; follicles and punctate corneal infiltrates or erosions), allergic conjunctivitis (atopy; itch; papillae and stringy discharge), blocked nasolacrimal duct (usually unilateral; look for reflux with pressure on a mucocoele), blepharitis, and acute mucous membrane pemphigoid.

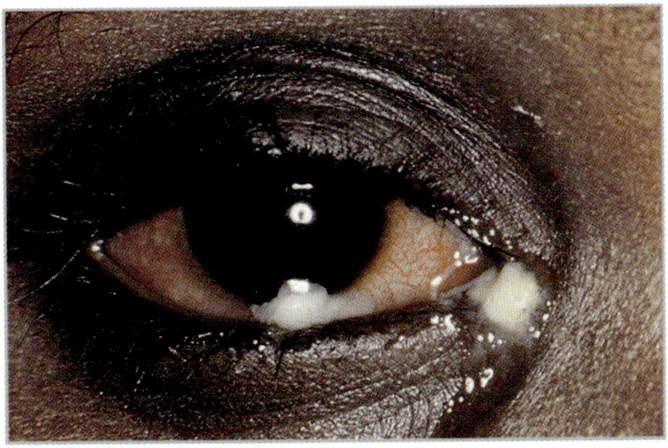

Fig. 5.10: Bacterial conjunctivitis.

Investigations Send conjunctival cultures for ophthalmia neonatorum, suspected gonococcal or chlamydial infection, recurrence and failed therapy. Hyperacute cases require blood and chocolate agar cultures and smears.

Treatment Untreated, bacterial conjunctivitis usually resolves within a week, but topical antibiotics speed resolution. Hence the decision to start antibiotics must balance patient's clinical particulars and needs, with antibiotic stewardship. Treat if there is immunocompromise, contact lens use, and suspected gonococcal or chlamydial infections. Advise how to avoid transmission: clean away discharge; wash hands; and avoid direct contact or sharing towels. If straightforward, consider G. chloramphenicol 4–6 times daily for 5 days. Use a quinolone (e.g. G. levofloxacin or G. ofloxacin 4–6 times daily for 5 days) for contact lens users who may be infected by *Pseudomonas*. Instruct contact lens wearers to avoid lenses until completion of the treatment course and resolution of symptoms. Discard or carefully sterilise potentially infected lenses and cases. If there is no response, reconsider the diagnosis; prolonged or repeated treatment is contraindicated. Topical steroids may reduce the scarring often seen following membranous conjunctivitis, but obtain specialist advice. If microscopy shows gram-negative intracellular diplococci treat for *Neisseria* with hourly G. cefuroxime 5% and a single dose of 1 g intramuscular (i.m.) ceftriaxone. Bacterial conjunctivitis secondary to gonococcal or chlamydial infections requires systemic treatment (check the latest treatment protocols for treatment with a sexually transmitted infection service). Regularly irrigate the fornices with saline and refer to a sexual health clinic for contact tracing. Delay may lead to perforated cornea, endophthalmitis, septicaemia, or meningitis. Prescribe oral antibiotics for bacterial conjunctivitis with concurrent acute otitis media, e.g. Augmentin 625 mg t.d.s. for 1 week.

Follow-up Most cases are seen once and discharged, but advise patients to return if there is no improvement after 2 days of antibiotics. For hyperacute and membranous conjunctivitis, examine daily until improving, then every 2–3 days until resolved.

ADENOVIRAL KERATOCONJUNCTIVITIS

Background The most common acute viral infection of the external eye is caused by many different serotypes. Virus may spread systemically and shed via tears, resulting in secondary ocular infection. External spread may occur by aerosol or direct contact, e.g. hands and clinical instruments. The virus can remain infectious on porous surfaces for 10 days and non-porous surfaces for over 1 month. In immuno-compromised patients undergoing haematopoietic stem cell or solid organ transplantation, disseminated infections can be life-threatening, particularly in the paediatric population.

History Incubation period is ~8 days with three typical presentations, which may overlap:

- *Acute non-specific follicular conjunctivitis*: Produces a red eye initially with mild irritation and tearing, but little photophobia. Lid swelling occurs after 48 hours. Usually bilateral, separated by 1–3 days. Usually resolves rapidly. Patients may have an upper respiratory tract infection (URTI).
- *Pharyngoconjunctival fever (PCF)*: The most common presentation which often occurs in children. Features follicular conjunctivitis with punctate keratopathy and rarely late subepithelial infiltrates associated with regional lymphoid hyperplasia and systemic viral features (fever, pharyngitis, rhinitis, sometimes vomiting and diarrhoea).
- *Epidemic keratoconjunctivitis (EKC)*: Can be epidemic or sporadic, and is the most severe type. Patients may have an URTI, gastrointestinal symptoms, urethritis or cervicitis. Occurs most commonly in winter and autumn, with acute onset of largely unilateral conjunctivitis ± haemorrhages, and variable preauricular and submandibular lymphadenopathy. Punctate keratopathy and focal keratitis appear early and rarely with later corneal scarring. Membranous conjunctivitis occurs on day 7 (may scar) and subepithelial infiltrates (SEIs) on day 14 (may persist for months or years).

Examination

- Tender preauricular lymphadenopathy.
- *Lids*: mild-to-moderate swelling.
- *Conjunctiva*: diffuse injection ± haemorrhages, chemosis, serous or mucopurulent discharge, tarsal conjunctival follicles and papillae (**Fig. 5.1**, p. 238).
- *Cornea*: variable involvement (30% in PCF, ~80% in EKC). At the outset, there may be fine pin-point epithelial infiltrates/erosions which persist for 1–2 weeks. Pseudodendrites,

corneal erosions and filamentary keratitis occur rarely. At ~14 days coarse SEIs may develop (**Fig. 5.11**) causing photophobia, a gritty sensation and, when in the central cornea, affect vision.

- *Anterior chamber*: may have a mild cellular reaction in the second week.

Wash hands and clean the slit lamp after use. Use a disposable tonometer head if it is necessary to check the IOP. Minimise patient's time in the hospital to reduce the risk of transmission to others.

Differential diagnosis Bacterial conjunctivitis (more purulent discharge, rarely follicles, no keratopathy, and no systemic viral features), acute haemorrhagic conjunctivitis caused by enterovirus 70, coxsackievirus A24, or *S. pneumoniae* (usually resolves within 2–4 days), and allergic conjunctivitis (more likely to have itch, atopy, papillae and stringy discharge).

Investigations Not routinely required, but perform if the diagnosis is uncertain, or needed to support advice about quarantine. PCR is the gold standard (sensitivity 95% and specificity 100%). Immunochromatography (with the RPS AdenoPlus) is an in-clinic diagnostic kit with a high specificity (90–98%) but lower sensitivity of (85–90%).Virus is rarely detectable after 7–10 days from the onset. RPS AdenoPlus detects the presence of viral particles, the results may correlate with disease infectivity and, thus, allow patients a speedier return to school and work when the virus is no longer detectable.

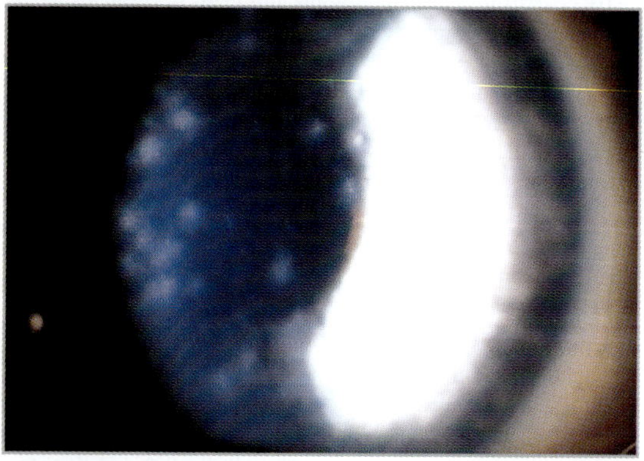

Fig. 5.11: Adenoviral keratoconjunctivitis with subepithelial infiltrates.

Treatment

- *Patient advice*: Explain that the disease is highly contagious for 7–14 days, so avoid work and contact with family members (separate towels and face cloths), wash hands, and keep hands out of eyes.
- *Antivirals*: There is no effective licensed antiviral. Oc. ganciclovir 0.15% has shown marginal benefit; use five times daily for severe cases.
- *Antibiotics*: Use G. chloramphenicol q.d.s. if there is bacterial superinfection and Oc. chloramphenicol q.d.s. for pseudomembranes.
- *Topical lubricants*: Single dose lubricants may help to relieve irritation.
- *Topical steroids*: Intensive potent topical steroids are effective in membranous conjunctivitis and may reduce conjunctival scar formation when combined with conjunctival treatment to break down early synechiae formation. Symptomatic corneal SEIs are treated on their merits for relief of symptoms and vision improvement and may prevent scarring in severe early disease. Persistent SEIs rarely, if ever, scar and can be treated with lubrication or low potency topical steroids (e.g. fluorometholone 1–4 times daily as required until symptoms controlled). SEIs may reappear when steroids are tapered off. Corticosteroids may increase the viral load if given in the first week when there is active viral replication. After a week, steroids probably do not alter the basic pathogenesis, but merely suppress inflammation.
- *Topical NSAIDs*: Not useful for adenoviral keratoconjunctivitis.
- *Topical disinfectant/steroid combination*: G. povidone iodine 1.0% q.d.s. + G. dexamethasone 0.1% q.d.s. for 7 days increases recovery but also reduces the risk of development of SEIs more effectively than steroids alone.
- *Topical ciclosporin*: Can be effective for managing recurrence of persistent SEIs after initial reduction with steroids.
- *Transepithelial excimer laser + 0.02% mitomycin C*: For patients with chronic adenoviral corneal opacification following resolution of acute infection. Improvements in photophobia, VA and contrast sensitivity, and decrease in coma, secondary astigmatism, and total higher-order aberrations reported.

Follow-up Most cases spontaneously resolve within 8–10 weeks, often sooner. Review those with keratitis in clinic and assess for steroid-induced ocular hypertension. Viral persistence and reactivation may occur. Permanent visual loss is very rare, but corneal subepithelial infiltrates may recur for several years.

CHLAMYDIAL CONJUNCTIVITIS

There are three species of chlamydiae: *C. trachomatis*, *C. psittaci* and *C. pneumoniae*. Almost all ocular diseases are caused by *C. trachomatis* with three distinct ocular syndromes: adult inclusion conjunctivitis (AIC), neonatal inclusion conjunctivitis (p. 689) and trachoma.

Adult inclusion conjunctivitis

Background AIC is a sexually transmitted infection (STI) caused by serotypes D–K. This can manifest as cervicitis and pelvic inflammatory disease in women, and epididymitis and prostatitis in men. Both sexes may experience urethritis, proctitis, pharyngitis, perihepatitis, reactive arthritis, lymphogranuloma venereum, and conjunctivitis. More frequently, patients remain asymptomatic reservoirs of *Chlamydia*. Chlamydial infection in women, especially if untreated, increases the risk of infertility and ectopic pregnancy. Spread is usually through direct contact with infected genital secretions, but rarely also by direct eye-to-eye contact or by poorly chlorinated swimming pools.

Symptoms Acute, or more usually subacute, onset of conjunctival redness, irritation and mucopurulent discharge occurring within 2–19 days from inoculation. Partial ptosis is common. May be unilateral or bilateral.

History Sexual transmission is almost invariably the cause and should be assumed in PCR-positive cases.

Examination

- Check for preauricular lymphadenopathy.
- *Conjunctiva*: Inflammation worse in the inferior tarsus and fornix than superiorly, with well-developed follicles. Bulbar conjunctival follicles can occur in adults. Significant conjunctival scarring is rare.
- *Cornea*: About 2 weeks after the onset, fine or coarse superficial punctate keratitis, subepithelial infiltrates, and small perilimbal infiltrates may develop, with a microvascular pannus.

Investigation PCR has largely replaced culture and smears, with comparable sensitivity (88%) and specificity (100%) to tissue culture. In acute cases, also perform bacterial cultures, and *Herpes simplex* and adenoviral PCR to exclude other causes.

Treatment ~50% of AIC has concurrent *C. trachomatis* genital tract infection, whether symptomatic or not, so refer to a sexual health clinic for contact tracing, investigation and treatment of the genital reservoir. After all ocular and genital swabs are taken, treat AIC with either G. azithromycin b.d. for 3 days or G. fluoroquinolone (e.g. moxifloxacin or levofloxacin) six times daily for 5 days. Aminoglycosides are ineffective. Symptoms improve over 2–4 weeks, but conjunctival follicles may last months and corneal infiltrates months to years. Untreated disease may become chronic.

Trachoma

Background Caused by immunotypes A–C. Rare in the developed world but endemic to North Africa, the Middle East, India and Southeast Asia. Usually self-limiting, but repeated infection leads to conjunctival cicatrisation and corneal scarring. Acute infection begins 5 days after inoculation.

Examination

- ± tender preauricular lymphadenopathy.
- *Conjunctiva*: Bilateral hyperaemia, infiltrate, watery or purulent discharge and a mixed follicular and papillary response: follicles become more prominent as the disease progresses to involve the fornix and palpebral conjunctiva. Diagnosis requires at least two of the following:
  - ≥5 follicles on the superior tarsal conjunctiva
  - Limbal follicles or their sequelae (Herbert's pits, **Fig. 5.12**)
  - Tarsal conjunctival scarring
  - Vascular pannus

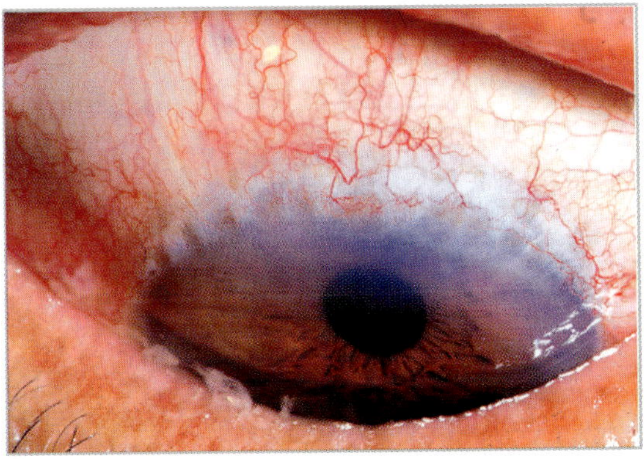

Fig. 5.12: Herbert's pits (Courtesy DH Verity).

Treatment Infection provides no immunity, so endemic areas require control with community health education and mass treatment with oral antibiotics such as azithromycin or doxycycline. Surgery may be required for lid deformities such as entropion and aberrant lashes, or severe corneal opacity.

ACUTE, SEASONAL AND PERENNIAL ALLERGIC CONJUNCTIVITIS

Background Common with increasing prevalence. Largely benign but can impair patients' quality of life. An IgE-mediated hypersensitivity reaction (Type I) triggered by direct contact between an allergen and the ocular surface, leading to mast cell degranulation and release of inflammatory modulators, e.g. histamine. Allergic (or atopic) conjunctivitis is an umbrella term that can more accurately be labelled as acute allergic conjunctivitis, seasonal allergic conjunctivitis (SAC) or perennial allergic conjunctivitis (PAC). Often (70%) associated with atopy or a family history of atopy. For vernal keratoconjunctivitis (see p. 161), atopic keratoconjunctivitis (p. 165), giant papillary conjunctivitis (p. 167), including contact lens-associated papillary conjunctivitis (p. 167) and contact hypersensitivity (p. 169).

History Transient acute or subacute episodes of ocular itch (the hallmark symptom), tearing/clear watery discharge. SAC is the most common in spring/summer, PAC throughout the year but generally worse in autumn due to exposure to house dust mites, animal dander, and fungal spores. Ask about past occurrences. Acute reactions, often unilateral, may occur with marked conjunctival swelling as well as systemic reactions. These episodes are commonly associated with sneezing, nasal congestion, and other symptoms of allergic rhinitis. Note major (hay fever, asthma, atopic dermatitis and eczema) and minor (idiopathic urticaria, non-hereditary angioedema and food allergies) atopies.

Examination In SAC, ocular inflammation varies from mild to severe lid swelling, diffuse bulbar and tarsal conjunctival injection without papillae, and conjunctival oedema, whereas in the most chronic PAC papillary conjunctivitis is typical.

Differential diagnosis Viral conjunctivitis, bacterial conjunctivitis, molluscum contagiosum, giant fornix syndrome, chlamydial conjunctivitis, non-allergic eosinophilic conjunctivitis, contact allergic blepharoconjunctivitis, mucous membrane pemphigoid, Stevens–Johnson syndrome/toxic epidermal necrolysis (Lyell's syndrome), superior limbic keratoconjunctivitis, ligneous conjunctivitis, Parinaud's oculoglandular syndrome and factitious conjunctivitis.

Treatment Follows a step ladder approach based on symptom severity:

- For mild symptoms, preservative free (PF) 'thin' lubricating eye drops dilute antigens, e.g. hyaluronic acid 0.03% over spring/summer for acute and seasonal cases, and long-term for perennial cases.
- If possible, identify and avoid the allergic trigger. Consider skin prick or serum allergy testing.
- Discourage eye rubbing, which causes mast cell degranulation and potentially keratoconus.
- Contact lenses may not be tolerated.
- Explain the sometimes relapsing remitting clinical course and importance of sustained eye drop compliance.
- Cool compresses reduce acute allergic conjunctival swelling. Consider also antihistamines, e.g. G. azelastine 0.05%.
- For long-term management, consider topical mast cell stabilisers, e.g. G. ketotifen 0.25% PF b.d. or G. olopatadine 0.1% b.d., for a few weeks. Explain that they may take time to work.
- Topical NSAIDs can improve comfort by blocking non-histamine mediators, e.g. G. diclofenac 0.1% PF t.d.s. for 2 weeks.
- For severe acute exacerbations and severe unresponsive cases with corneal involvement, use topical steroids at high frequency then rapidly tailed off on a weekly basis, e.g. G. hydrocortisone 0.335% PF, G. fluorometholone 0.1%, or loteprednol etabonate 0.5% 1–6 times daily. Measure baseline IOP and repeat measurements if treating for >1 month.
- Consider oral antihistamines for systemic symptoms, e.g. loratadine (Clarityn) 10 mg daily over spring/summer for acute and seasonal cases, and long-term for perennial cases.

Follow-up Only for severe and recurrent disease requiring topical steroids.

VERNAL KERATOCONJUNCTIVITIS

Background A rare but serious form of chronic allergic conjunctivitis, mediated by Type I and IV hypersensitivity reactions. Male preponderance (2–3:1), with onset age 5–15 years, especially in Middle-Eastern and Afro-Caribbean patients. Management can be challenging.

History There is often a family or personal history of atopy. Symptoms typically occur in spring or summer, but may persist throughout the year. Itch is the main symptom, but a copious sticky mucous discharge, photophobia, lacrimation, blurred vision and pain/foreign body sensation occur during exacerbations.

Examination There are two phenotypes—palpebral and limbal vernal keratoconjunctivitis—a few cases have both; palpebral disease is the most severe and difficult to manage.

Palpebral vernal keratoconjunctivitis:

- *Lids*: A mild mechanical ptosis may be present. Evert the upper lids to look for macropapillae (smaller than 1 mm in size, flat-topped lesions with a polygonal appearance); may be focal or diffuse in distribution. In more severe cases, whitish inflammatory infiltrates occur. Giant papillae/ cobblestone, which are >1 mm (**Fig. 5.13**), arise from small lesions that amalgamate when the dividing septa rupture. Mucous deposits seen between giant papillae indicates active disease. Cobblestone papillae are absent in the inferior tarsal conjunctiva. Tarsal conjunctival scarring indicates chronicity.
- Acute exacerbations produce copious and stringy mucous discharge.
- *Conjunctiva*: Mild conjunctival injection and reduced mucous production are characteristics of decreased disease activity.
- *Cornea*: Superficial punctate keratitis indicates active disease. There may be epithelial macroerosions (vernal ulcer), followed by mucus, calcium and phosphate deposition, as well as delayed-healing vernal shield ulcers (also called 'vernal plaques'), usually in the superior cornea, but centrally if severe (**Fig. 5.14**). Surgically removed or resolved shield ulcers leave greyish ring-shaped scars.

Limbal vernal keratoconjunctivitis:

- *Lids*: Micropapillae of the tarsal conjunctiva.
- *Conjunctiva*: Gelatinous conjunctival papillae, typically observed at the limbal region with Horner-Trantas' dots

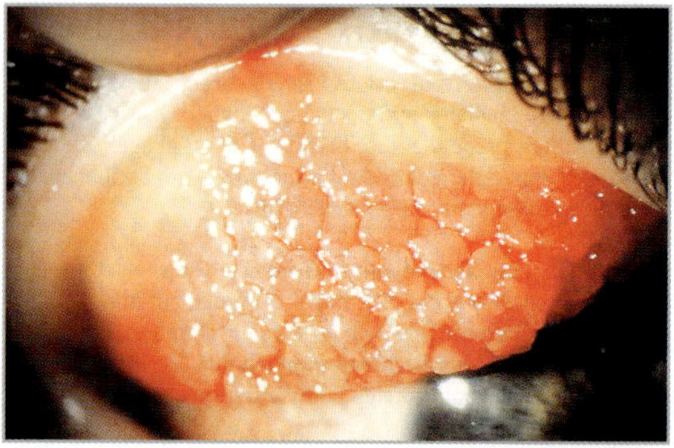

Fig. 5.13: Cobblestone papillae in severe vernal keratoconjunctivitis.

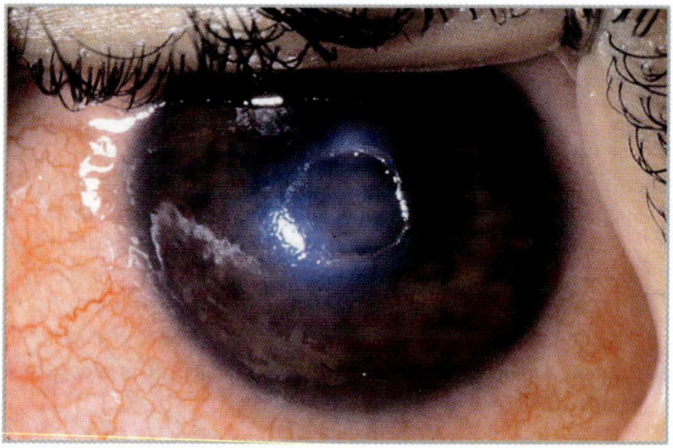

Fig. 5.14: Vernal shield ulcer (Courtesy DH Verity).

(chalk-white, raised accumulations of inflammatory cells and necrotic debris), most commonly at the apices of limbal papillae (**Fig. 5.15**).

- *Cornea*: Pseudogerontoxon (paralimbal band of superficial lipid that resembles arcus senilis) occurs close to the inflamed segment of the limbus. Limbal vascularisation is generally less prominent, although some superficial vessel ingrowth can occur, especially superiorly.

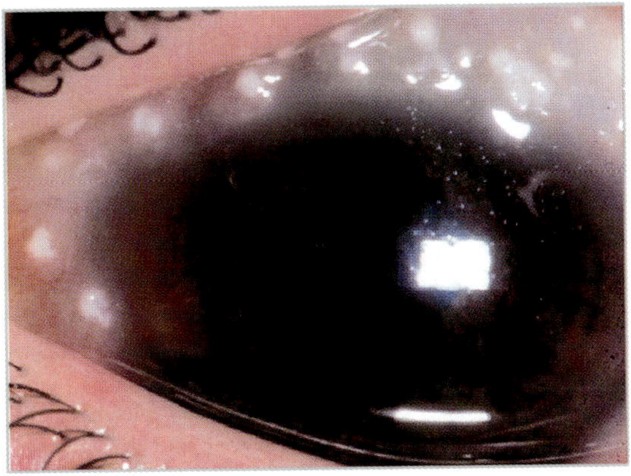

Fig. 5.15: Trantas' dots on the apices of limbal papillae (Courtesy DH Verity).

Treatment The same for both types, but limbal vernal keratoconjunctivitis (VKC) responds better to topical therapy. Use a therapeutic stepladder, from simple to complex, as needed:

- For patient's advice about allergen avoidance, allergy testing, lubricants to dilute allergens, avoiding eye rubbing, contact lens intolerance and the importance of drop compliance, see the allergic conjunctivitis section (p. 160).
- Topical ciclosporin and mast cell stabilisers (as above) are poorly tolerated during exacerbations, so ideally start these before anticipated seasonal exacerbations.
- Topical mast cell stabilisers, e.g. G. ketotifen 0.25% preservative free b.d. or G. olopatadine 0.1% b.d. can be used long term.
- If unresponsive to combined mast cell stabilisers and antihistamine, and for flare-ups, add topical steroid for the minimum period necessary, escalating from 'safe steroids' (e.g. G. hydrocortisone 0.335%) to more potent steroids (e.g. G. dexamethasone 0.1%), with frequency or concentration titrated against disease activity. Regularly check IOP.
- G. ciclosporin 0.1% (Ikervis—adults and Verkazia—children) is effective, with less frequent requirement for topical steroid rescue therapy when used q.d.s. compared to b.d. in severe VKC, after partial control with topical steroids
- Consider Oc. tacrolimus 0.1% (Protopic) skin ointment for those who cannot tolerate, or are only partially responsive to, topical ciclosporin.

- If unresponsive to intensive topical steroids use either 1 mL subconjunctival triamcinolone acetonide 40 mg/mL via a fornix injection and/or oral prednisolone at 0.5 mg/kg for 2 weeks.
- For very severe disease consider oral ciclosporin, oral montelukast or subcutaneous omalizumab or dupilumab. Use may be limited by side effect profile, so co-manage with an allergy specialist. For those over 16 years, consider a trial of oral aspirin 900 mg b.d.
- Vernal plaques (shield ulcers) may heal spontaneously once the conjunctival disease is controlled. If an epithelial defect persists despite disease control, then peel off the vernal plaque with a crescent blade to help to prevent recurrence.
- Consider a bandage contact lens for persistent epithelial defects.
- G. acetylcysteine 5% (Ilube) 1–4 times daily is useful in VKC and atopic keratoconjunctivitis for dissolving mucous filaments, deposits and early plaque development.

Follow-up Review every 1–2 weeks until inflammation is controlled, then every 2–3 months for those on long-term topical steroids. Corneal scars (from plaques and secondary infections), steroid-induced glaucoma and cataracts are the principal causes of visual loss in VKC, which resolves after puberty in 90–95% of cases. The remaining individuals may develop atopic keratoconjunctivitis.

ATOPIC KERATOCONJUNCTIVITIS

Background An uncommon severe form of atopic conjunctivitis associated with keratitis. It coexists with atopic dermatitis in >90% of cases. Caused by Type I and IV hypersensitivity to ocular allergens exposure, with a male preponderance (2–3:1). Can occur before adolescence, but peak prevalence is between 30 and 50 years.

History Chronic itching, burning, foreign body sensation, photophobia, tearing and mucoid discharge. Some cases occur following vernal keratoconjunctivitis (VKC). Symptoms are perennial, often worse in winter.

Examination

- *Skin*: Patients usually have widespread eczema, although this may be restricted to the periorbital skin. It ranges from mild eczema to lichenification. Eczema, erythema, dryness and scaly skin are often associated with thickening. Epidermal integrity is disrupted, leading to fissures/cracks and scratches from intense itching (excoriation).
- *Lids*: Chronic staphylococcal blepharitis, keratinisation of the lid margins, ectropion and mild ptosis.
- *Conjunctiva*: Inferior palpebral conjunctival involvement is more common than the superior involvement seen in VKC. Papillary conjunctivitis ± cobblestone papillae and excessive mucous can occur. Chronic inflammation commonly causes tarsal conjunctival scarring (cicatrising conjunctivitis). The discharge is usually watery compared to the stringy discharge typically seen in VKC.
- *Cornea*: Punctate epithelial erosions are commonly observed, particularly in the inferior cornea. Persistent epithelial defects can occur, leading to corneal thinning, descemetocoele formation and perforation. Stromal scarring and peripheral vascularisation are common. Bacterial or *Herpes simplex* virus (HSV) keratitis are common in severe diseases and can damage vision. Keratoconus can occur due to chronic ocular rubbing.

Subcutaneous dupilumab is sometimes used to treat atopic dermatitis, but side effects can include eye pruritus, blepharitis, dry eye, conjunctivitis, and rarely ulcerative keratitis.

Treatment As for VKC (p. 161), but also treat acute HSV (p. 237) as required and consider chronic, prophylactic, oral acyclovir 400 mg b.d. or valaciclovir 500 mg o.d. for susceptible patients. Prolonged treatment is often required. A poor response to topical therapy may require oral ciclosporin and/or either azathioprine or mycophenolate. Systemic treatment may control eczema but cause exacerbations when withdrawn; so, liaise with a dermatologist who can also help to control periocular eczema. Consider periocular E45 cream as required, steroids, e.g. 1% hydrocortisone skin ointment o.d. or b.d. (with care, due to the risks of systemic absorption, depigmentation and superinfection), and tacrolimus 0.1% (Protopic) applied up to the lid margin for eyelid eczema (conjunctival spillover may help to control eye disease).

Follow-up As for VKC.

GIANT PAPILLARY CONJUNCTIVITIS (INCLUDING CONTACT LENS-ASSOCIATED PAPILLARY CONJUNCTIVITIS)

Background Most commonly seen with contact lenses, ocular prostheses and occasionally protruding sutures. Occurs secondary to direct mechanical irritation, leading to Type I and IV hypersensitivity reactions. Shares the conjunctival features of atopic keratoconjunctivitis and vernal keratoconjunctivitis (pp. 161 and 165), but without corneal involvement.

History Typically develops 1–2 years after initiating soft contact lens use, but other ocular foreign bodies have more variable onset. Ask about decreased contact lens tolerance, contact lens cleaning and maintenance practices, infrequent lens replacement, mucous discharge and ocular itch. The symptoms usually worsen after contact lens removal.

Mucous fishing syndrome describes a chronic papillary reaction due to repeated mucus removal by the patient (the mucus originating from various anterior segment disorders).

Examination

- *Lids*: Evert the eyelid and look for hyperaemia, infiltrate and a papillary response (best seen using fluorescein). Papillae are often small, but giant papillae (>1 mm) occur and may have epithelial erosions and scarring of the apices. Giant papillae occur rarely since the widespread introduction of disposable and frequently replaced contact lenses (**Fig. 5.16**). Ptosis can occur due to tissue laxity, irritation, and tissue spasm from chronic inflammation.
- *Conjunctiva*: Look for protruding sutures or exposed scleral buckles.

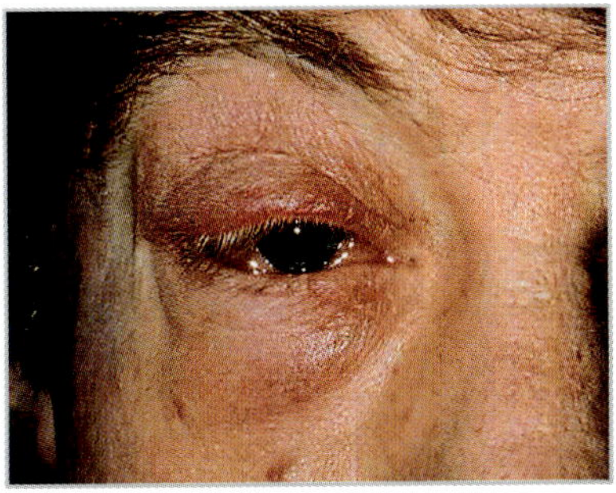

Fig. 5.16: Giant papillary conjunctivitis. (Courtesy DH Verity).

- *Contact lens*: Look for the excessively mobile contact lenses, with scratches and gross deposits.
- *Prosthesis*: Examine for scratches and gross deposits.

Treatment Start by removing the mechanical irritant. For contact lens wearers, a switch to daily disposable soft lenses is usually effective. If these are not available (e.g. high toric prescriptions) increase the frequency of lens replacement to whatever is practicable, with once or twice weekly protein removal and rigorous lens cleaning. Replace damaged rigid gas permeable lenses, remove broken sutures and repolish ocular prostheses. For ocular prostheses, washing and cleaning with detergent and a protective coating are essential to maintain hygiene and comfort. General allergic eye care should be practiced, such as avoiding eye rubbing, using artificial tears and cool compresses, and allergen avoidance, especially for patients with keratoconus. Cessation of lens wear is rarely necessary.

Follow-up Review contact lens wearers only if symptoms persist. Advise regular contact lens practitioner's review if not under medical review. Arrange regular assessment, maintenance and fitting of prostheses.

DROP TOXICITY/OCULAR SURFACE MEDICAMENTOSA (CONTACT HYPERSENSITIVITY AND TOXIC CONJUNCTIVITIS)

Background A relatively common condition, particularly with certain eye drops including neomycin and atropine; however, prolonged use of any preserved drop (especially those containing benzalkonium chloride-BAK) may cause either a Type IV contact hypersensitivity or toxic response. The corneal and conjunctival epithelial cells absorb and retain preservatives for days after a single application. Contact lens solutions and eye lid cosmetics are also implicated.

History Ask about itch and lid swelling. Toxic conjunctivitis may take days to years to develop, but most typically occurs after ~3 months' exposure, most often with glaucoma medications. There appears to be a dose-response, reflecting the number of drops and their preservative concentration. List all topical medications and note their preservatives/excipients.

Examination

- *Lids*: Look for erythematous, dry, scaly dermatitis, particularly in the lower lid but often extending to the cheek (**Fig. 5.17**), and follicles (pilocarpine, apraclonidine, brimonidine and atropine), especially in the lower fornix. A mild-to-severe papillary reaction may evolve over time.
- *Conjunctiva*: There is diffuse conjunctival injection, often worse inferiorly. Bulbar follicles are uncommon but, when present, are highly suggestive of a toxic aetiology. Punctate

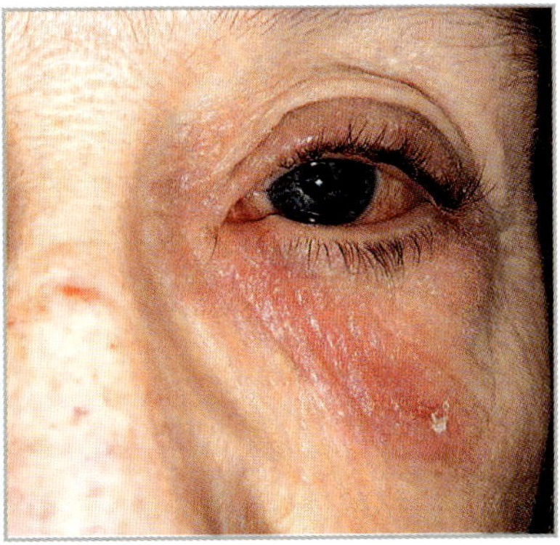

Fig. 5.17: Contact hypersensitivity secondary to eyedrops.

staining of the conjunctival epithelium may be seen. Asymptomatic subconjunctival fibrosis can occur with long-term eye drop use. In a small minority, a more severe, progressive subconjunctival scarring develops, which can lead to fornix contraction, symblepharon, punctal stenosis, and corneal pannus (drug-induced cicatricial pemphigoid).

- *Cornea*: The cornea is rarely involved. Punctate staining of the corneal epithelium (occasionally in a whorl pattern), erosive changes, and greyish subepithelial corneal infiltrates with a clear zone between the lesions and the limbus is typically associated with aminoglycoside antibiotics, antiviral agents, or medications preserved with BAK and all indicate direct toxicity. The most severe cases may present with an inferior or central corneal epithelial defect, stromal opacification, and neovascularisation, and may be associated with extensive limbal stem cell damage.

Investigation If the cause is not obvious, patch testing via dermatology may occasionally identify a cause.

Treatment Usually resolves quickly on stopping medications, but significant toxic reactions may take 2–12 weeks to settle. Topical skin steroids may help, e.g. hydrocortisone 0.5% skin ointment b.d. 5 days. Restrict eye drops to p.r.n. G. saline 0.9% preservative and excipient free until resolved, then cautiously reintroduce necessary medication one at a time.

Follow-up Review any changes in long-term ocular medications as required.

STEVENS–JOHNSON SYNDROME – TOXIC EPIDERMAL NECROLYSIS SPECTRUM

Background Immune reactions within a disease spectrum that is divided into erythema multiforme (EM) (minor and major) and Stevens–Johnson's syndrome (SJS) – toxic epidermal necrolysis (TEN; previously called Lyell's syndrome).

Erythema multiforme minor is milder, often triggered by viral illness (typically *Herpes simplex* virus), and is less often drug related (~10%). Has symmetrically distributed, typical target lesions (papules with central pallor/erythematous surround or central erythema/pale surround; **Fig. 5.18**) that spread proximally along the limbs, and bullae on the back of hands, palms, forearms, feet and soles, or dependent parts in prostrate patients. There is minimal mucosal involvement.

Erythema multiforme major: Typical target lesions or raised, oedematous papules with similar distribution to EM minor; epidermal detachment (but <10% of body surface area) and involvement of one or more mucous membranes without long-term sequelae.

Stevens–Johnson's syndrome and toxic epidermal necrolysis spectrum: SJS and TEN are severe cutaneous adverse reactions mostly caused by medications. The two conditions are considered as the same disease with different spectrums of severity. Dermal detachment is <10% for SJS and >30% in TEN. Overlapping SJS–TEN is defined as 10–30% skin detachment.

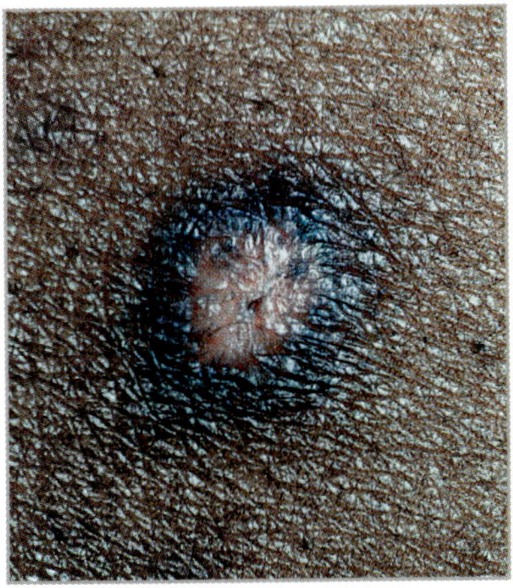

Fig. 5.18: Target lesion in Stevens–Johnson's syndrome (Courtesy DH Verity).

History Rarely, the initial presentation is with conjunctivitis, but usually the systemic diagnosis is already established. The skin rash is often preceded by malaise, fever, and upper respiratory tract (flu-like) symptoms. Drugs are associated with 85% of cases: most commonly sulfas, NSAIDs and anticonvulsants, e.g. carbamazepine. Lesions typically begin to appear 4–28 days after the trigger. Other causes include mycoplasma infection and idiopathic.

Examination SJS/TEN is characterised by painful blisters, purpuric macules, and atypical target lesions predominantly on the face and trunk. Nasal and oral mucosae are commonly affected, with ruptured bullae and haemorrhagic crusting (**Fig. 5.19**). The vagina and anus may be affected. Acute ocular involvement in SJS/TEN usually occurs concurrently with skin disease, but may develop before or after. Ocular manifestations are the same for SJS and TEN: bilateral conjunctivitis ± bullae. There may be superficial punctate keratopathy and mild anterior uveitis. Cardiovascular, pulmonary, gastrointestinal, urinary tract and other body systems may be affected.

Treatment Due to the high morbidity and mortality of SJS (~5%) and TEN (~15%), care is usually provided in a specialised burns unit. Key is withdrawal of the offending drug and multi-disciplinary supportive care by dermatologists, intensive care doctors, skin care nurses and ophthalmologists.

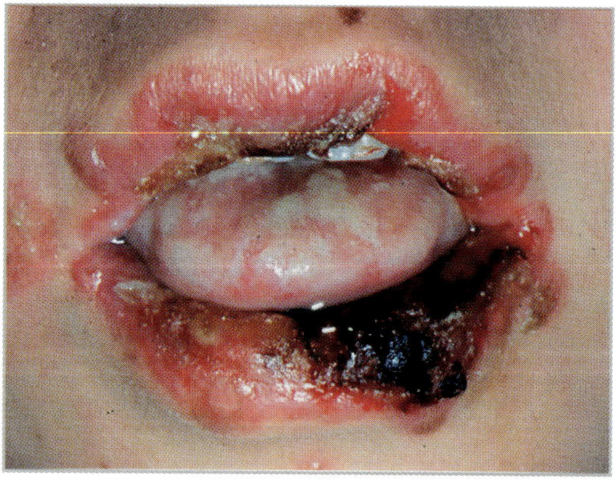

Fig. 5.19: Stevens–Johnson's syndrome (Courtesy DH Verity).

- Apply non-preserved ocular lubricants 2-hourly (day and night), e.g. sodium hyaluronate or hypromellose.
- An ophthalmologist or eye nurse should remove inflammatory debris and break down conjunctival adhesions daily, using topical anaesthetic, saline irrigation, and a squint hook with forceps. Scissors may be needed for well-developed adhesions that cannot be broken down with forceps alone. Avoid blind sweeping of the fornices with a cotton bud or glass rod.
- For any unconscious patient, prevention of corneal exposure is mandatory. Use a polyethylene film to create a moist chamber over the eye. Secure to skin; if the skin is damaged, first apply ointment to damaged/ulcerated lid skin.
- Use a broad spectrum preferably preservative-free topical antibiotic (e.g. G. levofloxacin q.d.s.) as prophylaxis even in the absence of epithelial loss, but alter the antibiotic based on microbial sensitivities and local bacterial resistance.
- Topical steroids (e.g. G. dexamethasone 0.1% preservative free b.d.), supervised by an ophthalmologist, may reduce ocular surface damage in the acute phase of SJS/TEN, but can mask corneal infection so use with caution in the presence of a corneal epithelial defect. Monitor IOP if on steroids.
- In the presence of corneal fluorescein staining or frank ulceration, apply amniotic membrane (vacuum-dried Omnigen or fresh) with a scleral conformer or a 18-mm hydrogel contact lens. Protect the entire ocular surface including the cornea, tarsal conjunctiva and lid margins with amnion. Consider also allogeneic serum eye drops q.d.s. for supportive therapy.
- The use of systemic steroids, i.v. immunoglobulin (IVIG) or immunomodulatory therapy depends on the extraocular manifestations of SJS/TEN: there is no good evidence that they benefit ocular disease.

Follow-up Provide daily ophthalmology review of all inpatients. Taper any topical steroids and antibiotics after eye lesions have stabilised, then review weekly for 1 month, for at least 12 months, and then as required. Use the Cicatrising Conjunctivitis Assessment Tool (p. 174). The disease may fully resolve, but possible sequelae include dry eyes, eyelid deformities, conjunctival and corneal scarring. Lid margin keratinisation suggests a poor prognosis. Late recurrences are probably infrequent but include recurrent conjunctival inflammation, late cicatrising conjunctivitis, and late sclerokeratitis, all of which can exacerbate ocular surface failure and require specialist management.

MUCOUS MEMBRANE PEMPHIGOID

Background Mucous membrane pemphigoid (MMP) is a heterogeneous group of chronic, autoimmune, subepithelial blistering diseases predominantly affecting the mucous membranes. It may occur as MMP with ocular involvement or at a single-site, including ocular MMP (OcMMP, previously termed 'ocular cicatricial pemphigoid'). OcMMP is a rare type II hypersensitivity disease with antibodies to basement membrane and subsequent conjunctival scarring, with Caucasian predominance and typical onset age of 60–70 years (range 30–90). It is the most common cause of cicatrising conjunctivitis. Younger patients may present with more severe ocular and systemic disease and, despite immunosuppression, deteriorate faster. Limbal involvement suggests a more severe phenotype.

History Chronic or intermittent redness, tearing, burning and foreign body sensation often misdiagnosed as infectious conjunctivitis. May have decreased vision, or sometimes minimal symptoms. Ask specifically about mucosal lesions of the mouth (85%), nasopharynx (35%), uro- and anogenital region (35%), skin (20%), larynx (12%), and trachea and oesophagus (5%). Involve skin and oral medicine specialists as required, and ENT for those with dysphagia and dyspnoea. Ask about topical glaucoma medications.

Examination About 10% of patients present with a fulminating conjunctivitis, accompanied by rapid scarring, leading to a dry eye and surface failure within months, but most have more slowly progressive disease.

- *Lids*: Entropion, trichiasis, scarring of meibomian glands.
- *Conjunctiva*: Hyperaemia of bulbar and tarsal conjunctiva, loss of plica semilunaris, subepithelial fibrosis, conjunctival keratinisation, occlusion of lacrimal ductules, fornix shortening, symblepharon and ankyloblepharon.
- *Cornea*: Inflammation, limbitis (12–28%), corneal neovascularisation, keratinisation, stem-cell failure, erosion, ulceration, perforation, scarring and secondary infection.
- *Eye movement*: May be restricted.

Grade using the *Cicatrising Conjunctivitis Assessment Tool* to aid diagnosis and quantify disease progression and treatment response. Some components are recorded but do not contribute to the overall composite disease severity score as they showed inadequate levels of agreement in validation testing. Scores from 0 (best) to 34 (worst):

- *Inflammation (disease activity)*: Bulbar conjunctival hyperaemia (scored 0–4) in all quadrants, maximum score 16/eye; limbitis (record as 0–4 quadrants affected).
- *Scarring (disease progression)*: Subconjunctival fibrosis (present/absent); upper and lower fornix symblephara (score 0 if absent, score 1 if <½ horizontal involvement, score 2 if >½ horizontal involvement); upper and lower fornix depth measure (mm), compare to normal values to assess foreshortening, not scored.
- *Ocular morbidity (sight-threatening effects of disease)*: Sequelae of inflammation and scarring—distichiasis (present/absent), conjunctival keratinisation of bulbar conjunctiva, lid margin/tarsal conjunctiva and cornea (present/not present), corneal vascularisation in central 4 mm (score 0 if absent or 1 if present); quadrants of corneal neovascularisation (score 0–4 for quadrants involved); central corneal opacity (score 0 if absent, score 5 if present); peripheral corneal opacity (score 0–4 for quadrants involved).

Differential diagnosis Other causes of conjunctival cicatrisation include surface neoplasia, rosacea, topical medication toxicity, and other autoimmune conditions, e.g. IgA and graft-versus-host disease, sarcoidosis, and Stevens–Johnson's syndrome–toxic epidermal necrolysis.

Investigations Delayed diagnosis is common with moderate to severe conjunctival inflammation and advanced cicatrising disease often seen at presentation. Alongside signs consistent with OcMMP, a positive direct immunofluorescence (anti-BP180) biopsy at a non-ocular site establishes the diagnosis. For patients without extraocular MMP, biopsy the conjunctival (anti-integrin β4) and buccal mucosa for direct immunofluorescence and take blood for indirect immunofluorescence. Arrange dermatology, oral medicine and ENT consultations as required. Use specialist histology services for immunofluorescence studies (e.g. St John's Dermatology Unit, St Thomas' Hospital, London). False negatives are common in ocular disease (only 60–80% are positive) although not in buccal or skin disease. A positive biopsy or indirect immunofluorescence is not mandatory to treat typical ocular disease, if other causes of conjunctival cicatrisation are excluded.

Treatment Untreated, ocular involvement in MMP eventually destroys the lacrimal gland ductules and meibomian gland orifices, impairing both the aqueous and the lipid constituents of the tear film, resulting in secondary dry eye. Eyelid malposition, symblepharon and trichiasis combine with dry eye, chronic limbitis and subsequent limbal stem-cell failure, to cause keratopathy. The latter ultimately results in reduced vision due to corneal epithelial defects, neovascularisation or even corneal perforation and eye loss. Treatment requires specialised knowledge. For mild-to-moderate disease, use dapsone starting at 25 mg p.o. b.d., increasing up to 150 mg/day as required. Contraindications include sulpha allergy and glucose-6-phosphate dehydrogenase deficiency (screen for G6PD deficiency before starting dapsone); anaemia is common. Sulfasalazine, an alternative to sulfonamide, may be better tolerated at 1–2 g orally daily. If the response is incomplete consider adding azathioprine 2–3 mg/kg p.o. o.d., or mycophenolate 1 g p.o. b.d. If there is no response to a sulfonamide, then discontinue this and use azathioprine or mycophenolate alone. For severe or moderate but unresponsive disease, use oral cyclophosphamide 1–2 mg/kg/day (or as monthly 500 mg infusions) ± oral prednisolone 1 mg/kg/day and taper off steroids once the inflammation is controlled, usually over 3 months. As an alternative to cyclophosphamide, consider anti-CD20 antibody infusions (e.g. rituximab or truxima), usually 3-monthly, but it is unlcear if this is superior to cyclophosphamide or *vice versa*. Each can be used as second line for severe disease if the other has been used first. All these drugs require mandatory screening for side effects (pp. 413–415). Screen for tuberculosis (TB) prior to steroid therapy (p. 413). Topical and subconjunctival steroids can relieve symptoms but are ineffective for treatment of the underlying disease and may cause secondary glaucoma. There is limited information about the value of methotrexate. Ciclosporin is probably not effective. Intravenous immunoglobulin is reserved for treatment failures with cyclophosphamide and anti-CD20 treatments.

Local treatment is important. Epilate lashes abrading the cornea. Seemingly trivial surgical intervention and conjunctival trauma can lead to serious exacerbation of disease, so ensure effective immunosuppression beforehand. Entropion, which is the cause of most trichiasis, usually responds to a grey line split and anterior lamellar reposition, ideally once the inflammation is controlled, but tends to recur. Electrolysis and cryotherapy are rarely helpful, except for treating small numbers of recurrent localised lashes, and cause increased lid scarring. Treat tear film deficiencies with punctal occlusion and preservative-free tear substitutes. Optimise meibomian gland function with warm compresses and lid massage. Use bandage contact lenses with caution. Oculoplastic surgery may be needed to reconstruct the fornices as part of entropion correction, or to treat lagophthalmos. Transcorneal cataract surgery does not require added immunosuppressive therapy, providing the disease is controlled at the time, but access and surgery may be difficult because of both conjunctival and corneal scarring. Postoperative epithelial defects may be difficult to heal. Osteo-odonto-keratoprosthesis can benefit patients with corneal blindness in controlled disease.

Follow-up About 20% of patients have mild disease and can be reviewed annually to assess progression, or more frequently if ongoing local therapy is required. Progressive conjunctival fibrosis can occur despite clinical quiescence. Patients on systemic drugs require blood and sometimes urine tests to screen for toxicity according to specific protocols (see p. 413 and Table 9.2, p. 415). These can often be undertaken via the general practitioner (GP), with 2–3 monthly ophthalmology review of treatment effect.

SUBCONJUNCTIVAL HAEMORRHAGE

History Most cases are idiopathic but ask about hypertension, Valsalva (coughing/constipation/heavy lifting), bleeding diathesis, anticoagulant and antiplatelet drugs, and trauma.

Examination Fresh haemorrhage appears bright red, often over a large area (**Fig. 5.20**). Haemorrhage without a posterior margin may be associated with an intracranial bleed.

Investigations Check blood pressure (BP), but arrange a coagulation screen and FBC only if recurrent.

Treatment None required. Reassure patients that the haemorrhage will fade over 2–3 weeks.

Follow-up Discharge with referral to a haematologist if a bleeding diathesis is detected, or GP if hypertensive. Otherwise, no follow-up is required.

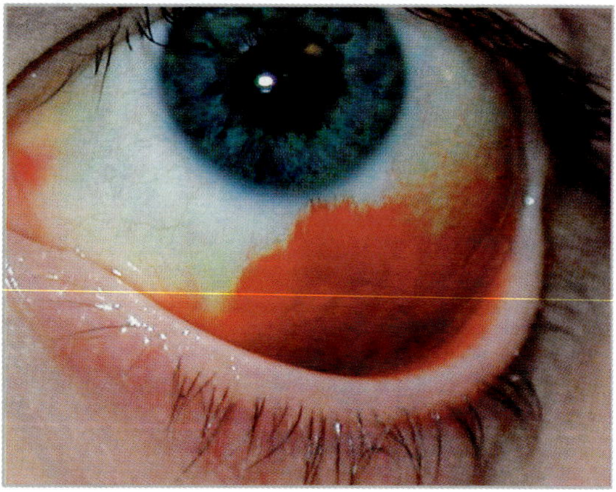

Fig. 5.20: Subconjunctival haemorrhage (Courtesy Y Ramkissoon, K Mireskandari).

SUPERIOR LIMBIC KERATOCONJUNCTIVITIS

Background A rare inflammatory conjunctivitis, of unknown aetiology, also affecting the superior third of the cornea and limbus.

History Patients typically describe remissions and exacerbations of foreign body sensation, burning, pruritus, mild photophobia, mucoid discharge, and tearing. Ask about contact lens wear, ocular surgery, and symptoms of thyroid dysfunction.

Examination Signs are usually bilateral but asymmetrical, and less severe than symptoms:

- *Lids*: Superior tarsal papillae (20%).
- *Conjunctiva*: Conjunctival hyperaemia and thickening most intense at the superior limbus (100%) (**Fig. 5.21**), and fading towards the fornix, ± conjunctival keratinisation, and redundancy and laxity of the upper bulbar conjunctiva. Conjunctiva stains with lissamine green.
- *Cornea*: Superior, superficial punctate keratitis (75%) and micropannus, with filamentary keratopathy in 33% of cases. Tear deficiency may be present.

Investigations Thyroid function tests (30% have thyroid dysfunction).

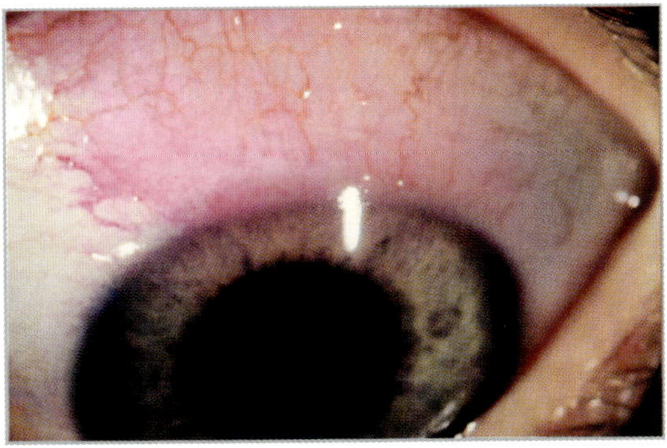

Fig. 5.21: Superior limbic keratoconjunctivitis with Rose Bengal staining of conjunctiva and limbus. Lissamine Green produces similar staining.

Treatment Treat any thyroid dysfunction. G. acetylcysteine 5% q.d.s. reduces filaments. Offer preservative free tear substitutes as required. Advise paraffin eye ointment with retinol palmitate, e.g. Oc. HyloNight nocte. Consider topical steroids for severe diseases, e.g. G. fluorometholone (FML) 0.1% q.d.s for 2 weeks. Bandage contact lenses may help. In severe cases, consider surgical resection of the superior limbal conjunctiva, thermal cauterisation, ± amniotic membrane implantation; but there are variable results. The disease often remits after 2–4 years.

MISCELLANEOUS CONDITIONS OF THE CONJUNCTIVA

Graft-versus-host disease (GVHD) Ocular complications occur in 60–90% of patients in both acute and chronic GVHD. The acute stage features conjunctival hyperaemia, which may progress to a pseudomembranous conjunctivitis with corneal epithelial desquamation. In the chronic form, there is secondary inflammation resulting in lacrimal and meibomian glandular fibrosis and dry eye symptoms (70–75%) (p. 207). This can be compounded by ocular toxicity from chemotherapy, meibomian gland destruction from total body irradiation, and immunosuppression. Intraocular involvement may lead to visual impairment. Signs of cicatricial conjunctival changes with consequent lid scarring and lid malposition (entropion and ectropion) develop.

Pingueculum A yellowish raised area of bulbar conjunctiva in the palpebral aperture along the horizontal meridian (**Fig. 5.22**). May gradually thicken or become inflamed, but often asymptomatic, and only noticed when the background conjunctiva becomes red, e.g. conjunctivitis. No treatment is usually required, but if the area becomes inflamed consider topical lubricants or weak topical steroid, e.g. G. FML t.d.s. reducing over 3 weeks. Excision biopsy is occasionally needed for symptomatic relief, combined with a conjunctival autograft to reduce postoperative scarring.

Kawasaki disease A rare condition occurring most commonly in girls aged 2 months to 9 years, with 1–2% mortality. Produces

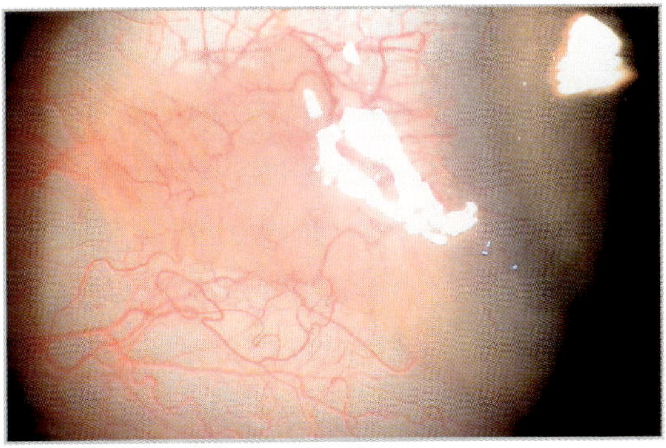

Fig. 5.22: Pingueculum.

conjunctivitis that does not require treatment, but which may be the presenting feature and hence requires urgent paediatric referral for management of extraocular features. These include cervical lymphadenopathy, dry lips, 'strawberry' tongue, arthralgia, arthritis, palmar erythema, and desquamation of fingertips.

Oculoglandular syndrome Also called cat-scratch fever and Parinaud's conjunctivitis. Caused by *Bartonella* spp. or a more rarely pathogens such as *M. tuberculosis*, *T. pallidum*, and *C. trachomatis*. Produces grossly visible preauricular lymphadenopathy, low-grade fever, and unilateral conjunctival granulomata with focal necrosis ± ulceration. Resolves spontaneously over 2–3 months. Excision of solitary granulomata may be curative. A course of oral tetracyclines speeds resolution.

CHEMICAL INJURY

Background Compounds include alkalis, acids, solvents, and detergents. Alkalis penetrate ocular tissue and are the most harmful, e.g. ammonia, lye in drain cleaner, caustic potash, $Mg(OH)_2$ from 'sparklers', and lime in wet plaster, cement and mortar. Acids usually produce more superficial damage, but concentrated acids may produce effects that are indistinguishable from alkalis, as can hydrofluoric acid. Treat as an emergency, even before vision testing.

Immediate treatment Measure the pH of both eyes (normal: 7.3–7.6). Instil topical anaesthetic and eyelid speculum and irrigate the eye(s) copiously with saline or Ringer's lactate solution delivered via i.v. tubing, for at least 30 minutes. Avoid acidic solutions to neutralise alkalis or *vice versa*. Pull down the lower lid and double-evert the upper lid to irrigate the fornices and remove any particulate matter. This may rarely require a general anaesthetic. Five minutes after ceasing irrigation, retest the pH. Continue irrigating until neutral. Persistently abnormal pH suggests retained material.

History Document the chemical, time, nature of exposure, and any first aid measures. If available, examine the chemical container labels and test its pH. Contact a poison centre for more information if required, e.g. UK National Poisons Information Service.

Examination Record VA and facial injuries. Apply fluorescein and systematically note:

- *Lids*: May be burned or oedematous.
- *Conjunctiva*: Extent of epithelial loss, chemosis, and haemorrhage. Grade any limbal ischaemia to determine prognosis:
  - I = little or none: good
  - II = <1/3: Good (**Fig. 5.23**)
  - III = 1/3 to 1/2: Guarded
  - IV = >1/2: Poor
  - VI = total: Poor. Severe ischaemia may produce a deceptively white eye.
- *Cornea*: clarity (ranges from epithelial damage to corneal haze but iris details visible, total epithelial loss with iris details obscured, cornea opaque with iris and pupil detail obscured); note the size and depth of any defects. Total epithelial defects may be easy to miss: Bowman's layer takes up fluorescein slower than basement membrane and stroma.

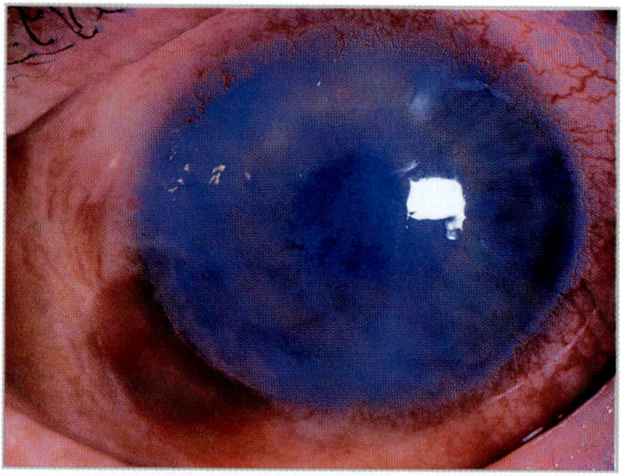

Fig. 5.23: Grade II limbal ischaemia with associated corneal damage (Courtesy DH Verity).

- *Anterior chamber*: depth and activity.
- *Lens*: clarity.
- *Intraocular pressure*
- *Retina*: retinopathy may result from penetration of alkali through the sclera. Do not use phenylephrine for dilation as it causes vasoconstriction, reducing blood flow to damaged tissues and potentially worsening the injury.

Subsequent treatment Aim to close the epithelium, control inflammation, promote repair/prevent ulceration and avoid long-term sequelae. The majority of injuries are mild (I); if there is no limbal ischaemia or epithelial defect, no treatment is required. For cases with epithelial defects (moderate to severe) give a broad-spectrum topical antibiotic q.d.s. (e.g. G. chloramphenicol 0.5%), unpreserved if available, and review in 1–2 days as ischaemia may not be apparent immediately. If there is limbal ischaemia treat as follows:

1. *Acute phase (day 0–7)*: Debride clearly necrotic corneal and conjunctival epithelium which may stimulate inflammation and contain residual chemicals. Use preservative-free eye drops if available. Prevent corneal melting with G. sodium ascorbate 10% 2-hourly and vitamin C 1 g p.o. daily. For grade II–IV injuries add G. sodium citrate 10% 1-hourly. Control anterior uveitis with topical steroid, e.g. dexamethasone 0.1% 4–6 times daily and taper as soon as this is controlled;

otherwise, avoid steroids in the acute phase. Prescribe G. chloramphenicol q.d.s., cycloplegia, and analgesics. If IOP is raised add acetazolamide 250 mg q.d.s. p.o., and topical medication if further IOP reduction is required. Lyse conjunctival adhesions. Review grade II–IV burns weekly.

2. *Early repair phase (day 7–21)*: Monitor re-epithelialisation. Epithelial defects should be closed in grade I and healing in grade II. Grades III and IV epithelial defects persist. The degree of ischaemia may initially be under or overestimated, so reassess. Continue ascorbate and citrate drops until the epithelium has healed. Taper off corticosteroids to promote repair. Once the epithelium has closed, topical corticosteroid may be restarted if necessary.
3. *Late repair phase (from day 21)*: Grade II corneal injuries may heal with conjunctival epithelium in the ischaemic sector. Grade III injuries may also re-epithelialise from the conjunctiva with associated superficial and deep stromal vascularisation, persistence of goblet cells in the epithelium, and poor epithelial basement membrane adhesion. Grade IV injuries usually re-epithelialise over months with conjunctival derived tissue. In more severe chemical injuries, corneal inflammation, collagen synthesis, and collagenase activity peak at this time. Continue treatment to minimise corneal melting and add oral doxycycline 100 mg o.d. Avoid NSAIDs if there are epithelial defects, as they can delay healing and promote corneal melting.

Surgery For severe disease (no epithelialisation ± corneal melting unresponsive to 10–14 days of conservative measures), use an amniotic membrane retained with a conformer. This probably has better outcomes than sutured membranes (sutured over the entire ocular surface and secured to the lid skin and fornices) providing the conformer extends into the fornices. Use tissue glue to seal impending or small (<1 mm) perforations (p. 203). Tectonic keratoplasty may be required for larger perforations. Stem cell transplants usually fail until the ocular surface has stabilised and inflammation subsided. Use a conjunctival flap or, when there is inadequate conjunctiva, a buccal mucosal transplantation for unresponsive corneal melts. The success of surgical rehabilitation, e.g. penetrating keratoplasty, is dependent upon an adequate tear film and the population of limbal stem cells. These may be harvested from the contralateral eye in uniocular injuries, or as an allograft. Keratoprosthesis may be required for severe bilateral chemical injuries.

OPTOMETRY AND GENERAL PRACTICE GUIDELINES

Conjunctivitis is one of the most common eye diseases, and although there are numerous causes, most community cases are allergic, viral or bacterial. Without specialist examination or equipment, it can be difficult for GPs to exclude other causes of red eye and the history is critical. Optometrists have slit lamps to look for cellular infiltrate, papillae, follicles, membranes and cicatrisation.

Refer perilimbal redness, intraocular pain, photophobia, or vision loss, which are more typical of uveitis or corneal disease. Other important causes of a red eye include angle-closure glaucoma, episcleritis and scleritis. Microbial keratitis results in a white corneal spot, which often stains with fluorescein, with adjacent conjunctival hyperaemia. Vision loss is minimal in acute conjunctivitis but may occur with diseases that also involve the cornea, including viral keratoconjunctivitis and blepharokeratoconjunctivitis, both of which are common in primary care. A baseline visual acuity can help to detect subsequent decline.

- Never diagnose bacterial conjunctivitis in the absence of purulent discharge. Topical antibiotics reduce disease duration from 10 to 3–4 days, e.g. G. chloramphenicol q.d.s. for 1 week.
- If bacterial conjunctivitis is possible but uncertain, prescribe 5 days of G. chloramphenicol q.d.s. then stop all treatment except preservative-free topical lubricants (e.g. G. hypromellose p.r.n.) for symptomatic relief. For contact lenses wearer, prescribe a fluoroquinolone (e.g. moxifloxacin, levofloxacin or ofloxacin 4–6 times daily for 5 days) due to the risk of resistance or *Pseudomonas*.
- Viral conjunctivitis often occurs following contact with family or friends with conjunctivitis and has a watery or purulent discharge. It is commonly caused by adenovirus and many, but not all, cases have systemic symptoms (upper respiratory tract infection, sore throat, diarrhoea and malaise). There is no proven treatment, but most cases resolve in 2–3 weeks; lubricants may improve comfort. Advise about infection control: wash hands, avoid sharing towels, TV remotes, computer keyboards and sex.
- Most cases of infectious conjunctivitis can be treated in primary care. Swabs are not necessary for typical cases but send viral, bacterial, and chlamydial swabs if there is no improvement in 5–10 days. Refer if there is no improvement in 2 weeks or if the vision deteriorates.
- A personal or family history of atopy and ocular itching are typical of allergic conjunctivitis. Use a combined mast cell

stabiliser and antihistamine (e.g. G. olopatadine b.d.) as first-line treatment and continue for as long as needed. If recurrent, advise antigen avoidance (house pets, pollen, hypoallergenic bedroom and domestic environment) as for asthma protocols.

- Do not prescribe steroid eyedrops in primary care because they can potentiate infection and elevate intraocular pressure. Subconjunctival haemorrhages do not require investigation or referral unless recurrent, but ask about bleeding diatheses and exclude hypertension.
- The following guide to referral urgency is not prescriptive, as clinical situations vary.

Immediate

- Chemical injury: instil anaesthetic eyedrops (if available) then rinse immediately with clean neutral liquid, e.g. sterile saline. Following copious irrigation transfer all serious injuries to an eye unit by an ambulance. p. 183
- Suspected gonococcal conjunctivitis p. 689

Same day

- Suspected chlamydial conjunctivitis p. 156
- Stevens–Johnson's syndrome (systemic features may require more urgent referral to physicians.) p. 171

Urgent (within 1 week)

- Non-resolving conjunctivitis p. 150
- Viral conjunctivitis with corneal involvement (keratoconjunctivitis) p. 154
- Vernal keratoconjunctivitis, atopic keratoconjunctivitis p. 161
- Drop toxicity p. 169

Soon (within 1 month)

- Inflamed pingueculum p. 181
- Cicatrising conjunctivitis including ocular mucous membrane pemphigoid (unless severely inflamed) p. 174

Routine

- Blepharitis and rosacea p. 141–149
- Giant papillary conjunctivitis p. 167
- Uninflamed pingueculum causing ocular discomfort p. 181
- Superior limbic keratoconjunctivitis p. 179
- Recurrent subconjunctival haemorrhage p. 178

CORNEA

6

Guy T Smith, Su-yin Koay & Jennifer McMahon

ANATOMY

The normal cornea

- The air–tear interface is the most powerful refracting interface of the eye.
- The cornea is aspheric, with the central cornea steeper than the periphery, i.e. prolate.
- The refractive power of the optical zone (central 4 mm) is ~43D.
- The average adult transverse corneal diameter is 11–12 mm and 9–11 mm vertically.
- Corneal clarity depends upon an ordered lamellar collagen structure and relative dehydration, requiring a minimum endothelial cell density of ~1,000 cells/mm^2. The mean endothelial cell density falls by ~0.6% per year.
- The central corneal thickness remains constant between the second and sixth decades but varies with measurement technique, time of day (thickest in the morning) and race: Afro-Caribbeans and Chinese ~530 ± 30 μm; Caucasians ~550 ± 30 μm.
- Normal corneal innervation is essential for the maintenance of an intact epithelial surface.
- Stem cells that generate the epithelium are located at the junction between the cornea and sclera, probably in the palisades of Vogt.
- The normal cornea is avascular.

HISTORY AND EXAMINATION

History

Ask about the presenting symptoms, past ocular and medical history, medications, allergies, family and social history. Document the presence or absence of the following key symptoms and determine their severity, nature, duration, and any relieving or exacerbating factors:

- *Reduced vision*
- *Abnormal sensation*: Direct stimulation of the corneal nerves usually gives rise to severe and sharp pain. Inflammation produces a duller and aching pain. Photophobia is a spasmodic pain on exposure to light caused by ciliary spasm. Irritation or grittiness is a symptom of epithelial disturbance. Itch usually indicates allergy. A diseased anaesthetic cornea may be asymptomatic.
- *Tearing*: Multiple causes including corneal epithelial breakdown and stromal inflammation (see also p. 71).
- *Conjunctival injection*: Ask if friends or family are affected, suggesting infection.
- *Discharge*: Ask if this is purulent, mucoid, or ropey/stringy. Ask if friends and family are affected. Discharge is most often secondary to ocular surface infection (purulent) or allergy (ropey/stringy).
- *Contact lens*: Ask about contact lens wear including the type, cleaning routine, pattern of wear (daily or overnight), duration of use and contact with water (see also p. 269).

Examination

Corneal structure and function are dependent upon the lids, tears, conjunctiva, and sclera. Examine as follows, documenting relevant positive and negative findings.

- *General habitus, hands and face*: For example, rheumatoid hand changes may help to diagnose the cause of peripheral corneal thinning.
- *Vision*: Record uncorrected visual acuity (UCVA), best-corrected visual acuity (BCVA), and pinhole visual acuity. High-contrast Snellen VA may be maintained despite reduced contrast sensitivity from corneal opacity or astigmatism.
- *Eyelids*: Note inflammation, abnormal contour, incomplete closure, misdirected lashes, and lid margin disease (blepharitis).
- *Tears*: Note the quality (discharge and debris) and quantity (meniscus height). If the tears appear abnormal, measure tear

break-up time (p. 193), and tear volume with Schirmer I test (p. 209).

- *Bulbar conjunctiva*: Note scarring (location and extent) and subconjunctival haemorrhage. If inflamed, note depth (conjunctival, episcleral and scleral) and location (perilimbal, sectoral, diffuse and localised).
- *Tarsal conjunctiva*: Evert the upper and lower lids to look for keratinisation, scarring, foreign bodies (FBs), and the presence of membranes, papillae and follicles.
- *Corneal epithelium*: Note any defects (size, location and pattern, e.g. superficial punctate keratitis, dendritic and geographic), FBs, infiltrates (pattern, size, location and depth), oedema (extent and severity, e.g. bullae), deposits (location, pattern and material, e.g. iron, calcium and filaments).
- *Corneal stroma*: Record the size, location, depth and pattern of opacities. Infiltrates have fuzzy margins, whereas scars have well-defined edges and often corneal thinning. Areas of oedema have soft, diffuse edges on retroillumination and increased corneal thickness. Note the depth, number of clock hours and distance of corneal new vessels from the limbus. Ghost vessels carry no blood and appear grey. Inactive vessels may have blood flowing through them but appear to have sharp edges on retroillumination. Active vessels have a cuff of oedema producing a less-defined edge.
- *Corneal endothelium and Descemet's membrane*: Note thickening, guttata, folds or breaks in Descemet's membrane, and the extent and distribution of deposits [keratic precipitates (KPs), pigment and blood].
- *Drawings*: Draw any corneal abnormalities using a frontal and slit view. Baseline photographs and anterior segment optical coherence tomography (OCT) scans may help to quantify changes seen at subsequent examinations.

Further clinical tests (see next page) may be indicated based on the history and examination.

INVESTIGATIONS

Consider the following tests and investigations, as indicated by the history and examination.

Corneal sensation Corneal anaesthesia may be due to corneal disease or predispose to it. Warn the patient, and then lightly touch the peripheral cornea with a cotton-tipped bud. Compare sides. Be aware that testing can affect vital staining and spread infection between eyes. If the results are uncertain use a Cochet and Bonnet aesthesiometer which is more sensitive, and quantitative.

Vital dyes

1. *Undiluted 2% fluorescein*, viewed with a cobalt blue light, has multiple uses:
   - *Tear drainage*: Jones tests and fluorescein disappearance test, see page 74.
   - *Aqueous leakage (Seidel's test)*: Apply 2% fluorescein to areas of suspected leakage. The usually dark-orange 2% fluorescein is diluted by leaking aqueous, turning bright green under a blue light (**Fig. 6.1**).
2. *Dilute fluorescein* viewed with cobalt blue light. Fluorescein 2% does not fluoresce well (quench) leading to misleading

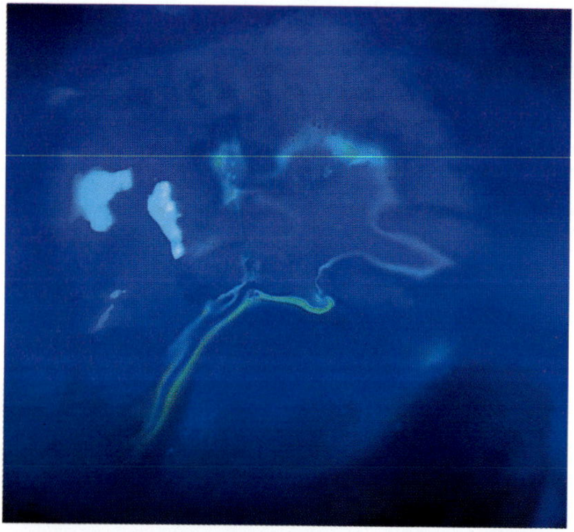

Fig. 6.1: Positive Seidel's test in corneal perforation.

results for both tear film and corneal fluorescein staining assessment, and qualitative assessment of tear film meniscus height. Prepare dilute fluorescein from 2% fluorescein by wetting a fluorescein impregnated strip with one drop of non-preserved saline, shaking off the excess, and touching the strip onto the lower tarsal conjunctiva. Alternatively, pipette 2 μL of 2% fluorescein into the lower fornix. Use to assess:

- *Fluorescein break-up time (FBUT)*: Time between a complete blink and the appearance of a corneal tear film defect (dark blue spot). Also called tear break-up time (TBUT). Used for dry eye diagnosis (p. 207). Measure a minute after adding dilute fluorescein. Fluorescein reduces tear film stability so normal (>8 seconds) is less than without dye (>10 seconds).
- *Ocular surface staining*: Fluorescein stains corneal cells with compromised integrity. Look for staining shortly after instillation, before the dye disappears or becomes diffusely absorbed, masking focal abnormality. The ocular staining score is 0 for 0–9 dots, 1 for 10–32 dots, 2 for 33–100 dots, and 3 for ≥100 dots. Give a score for the cornea and both the temporal and nasal conjunctiva. For filaments, staining in the pupillary area and confluent patches of corneal staining add 1 for each (maximum score = 12). See also Dry Eye page 207.
- *Corneal thinning and ulceration*: Raised areas have a thinner overlying layer of fluorescein and appear bluer. Thinned cornea with an intact epithelium 'pools' fluorescein, appearing green. To distinguish pooling from staining/ulceration flush with saline, wait for 10 minutes and re-examine—pooled fluorescein will have dispersed and areas of damaged epithelium/stroma remain green, e.g. corneal abrasion.

3. *Lissamine green* stain indicates degenerate cells, dead cells and mucus. To achieve the 1% required for effective staining, cut the ends off 4 Lissamine strips with sterile scissors, into a sterile tonometer well. Add four drops from a saline Minim. After 1 minute, draw up the lissamine green and deposit the full drop into the lower fornix. Ocular staining score is 0 for 0–9 dots, 1 for 0–32 dots, 2 for 33–100 dots, 3 for ≥100 dots for the cornea, temporal and nasal conjunctiva separately (maximum score = 9).

Matrix metalloproteinase-9 test InflammaDry® assays tear matrix metalloproteinase-9 (MMP-9) levels in 10 minutes. The test is positive (abnormal) if ≥40 ng/mL, indicating non-specific ocular surface inflammation. MMPs tend to increase with age.

Pachymetry Measuring the central corneal thickness (CCT) is useful for monitoring corneal grafts, prior to refractive surgery, and for normalising IOP measurements. For normal CCT values, see page 189. There are several devices that measure CCT.

- *Scanning slit system* (Orbscan) and rotating *Scheimpflug camera systems* (Galilei, Pentacam and Sirius) have the advantages of being noncontact and producing a thickness map. It may not be possible to capture data with some corneal curvatures and the posterior corneal surface must be visible (standard deviation, SD ~10 μm).
- *Ultrasound* requires topical anaesthesia. Any area of the cornea can be measured (record which). Touch the probe gently onto the cornea, perpendicular to the surface, to avoid overestimating corneal thickness (SD ~3 μm).
- *Optical low coherence reflectometry* (Lenstar LS900 and Aladdin HW3.0) provides fast non-contact CCT measurement along the line of sight. It can be acquired with a contact lens *in situ* (SD ~3 μm with low interobserver variability).
- *Swept source OCT* (Argos, IOLMaster 700, Casia, Anterion and MS-39) provides fast non-contact CCT measurement along the line of sight. Can be acquired with a contact lens *in situ* (SD ~3 μm with low interobserver variability).

Keratometry Dedicated instruments for measuring central corneal curvature, such as the Javel–Schiotz and Bausch & Lomb keratometers, express the corneal curvature as a radius of curvature or in dioptric power, based on the Placido image from the tear film. Automated devices such as the Lenstar, IOLMaster, rotating Scheimpflug camera systems and videokeratoscopes also provide measures of corneal curvature; all require a good tear film for accurate measurements.

Corneal topography Measures the corneal shape or curvature.

- *Placido-based videokeratoscopy* measures the corneal reflection of circles of light (mires) of known radius. Tear film abnormalities degrade the image. It does not measure beyond the surface and therefore the corneal power is derived mathematically. The reconstruction algorithms vary. Peripheral measurements are less accurate because the relationship between the corneal curvature and the refractive power varies, and fewer points are analysed.
- *Scanning slit-beam system*: Computerised corneal mapping devices that use a calibrated video and slit-beam system, e.g. Orbscan. A mathematical representation of the true topographic anterior and posterior corneal surfaces is formed, from which the surface curvature is calculated. The image must be captured in 30 msec to prevent degradation from eye movement.

- *Rotating Scheimpflug camera systems* use slit illumination to give an optical section, i.e. photographed inside view by a Scheimpflug camera. The camera is oriented according to the Scheimpflug principle to create a sharp image from the anterior corneal surface to the posterior crystalline lens surface. The system swivels around the eye generating a series of radially oriented images that are reconstructed with the Placido derived surface image to derive the anterior and posterior corneal surfaces, iris and crystalline lens.
- *Optical coherence tomography*: Spectral-domain systems designed for anterior segment imaging use a longer 1,310 nm wavelength to better image the angle structures. A-scan rates from 20 kHz to 400 kHz allow three-dimensional imaging of the anterior segment with axial resolution < 10 µm and a transverse resolution of 30 µm. Various line arrangements can be chosen. It produces typical topography maps, but also angle metrics. Some devices combine Placido disc topography with OCT, (e.g. MS-39), but some are entirely OCT-derived (e.g. Casia and Anterion).

All methods produce similar results in the visually important, central 3 mm of the cornea. Data points taken along meridians from centre to periphery are converted into colour-coded contour maps. Typically, yellows and greens represent normal corneal powers; cool colours represent lower power, and warm colours, higher power. Scales are not standardised and need to be selected carefully for meaningful interpretation. Topography of fellow eyes usually produces mirror images (enantiomorphs). Videokeratography of regular astigmatism results in a bow-tie pattern (**Fig. 6.2**).

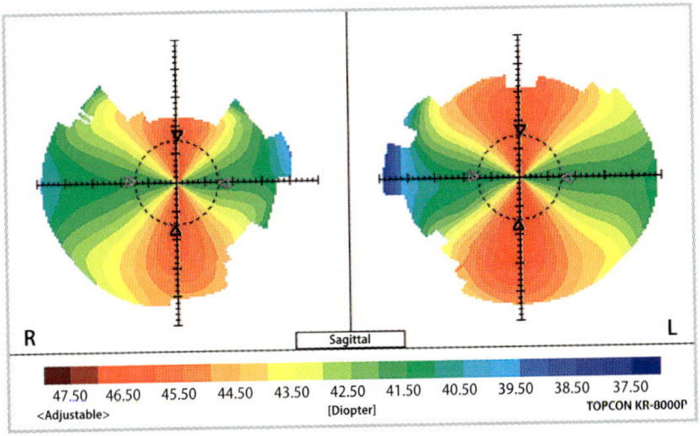

Fig. 6.2: Corneal topography showing with-the-rule astigmatism (Topcon videokeratoscope). Compare with Figure 6.11.

Wavefront scanning technology Can be used to measure the total ocular aberrations. Data acquisition and manipulation vary between manufacturers. Maps show the difference between the ideal planar wavefront and the wavefront distorted by the eye's aberrations, including lower-order aberrations (prism, sphere and cylinder), higher-order aberrations (all the rest), and point spread function (light scatter).

Specular microscopy Permits visualisation and photography of the endothelium. Computer analysis produces quantitative and qualitative indices that can be used to monitor cell loss from contact lens wear, intraocular surgery or corneal dystrophies.

***In vivo* confocal microscopy** Can help diagnose fungal and *Acanthamoeba* keratitis, and rare conditions like epithelial ingrowth and irido-corneal-endothelial syndrome.

CORNEAL ABRASIONS AND FOREIGN BODIES

Background A shearing force or foreign body breaches the corneal epithelium to expose the subepithelial nerve plexus.

Symptoms Pain, photophobia, foreign body (FB) sensation, and tearing.

History Ask about the material (organic, metallic, or other) and mechanism of injury. Could a high-velocity FB have entered the eye from metal striking metal? Were safety glasses worn?

Examination Instil proxymetacaine 0.5%. Evert both lids to exclude subtarsal FBs (**Fig. 6.3**). Use 2% fluorescein to show conjunctival defects. If these coexist with subconjunctival haemorrhage that obscures the sclera, dilate the pupil to exclude an intraocular FB. Subconjunctival pigment may indicate uveal prolapse from scleral perforation. Note the pattern of corneal fluorescein staining such as a geographic abrasion, superficial punctate keratitis or linear scratches. Draw the abrasion location, size (in millimetres), and depth (percentage of corneal thickness). Iron FBs may be surrounded by a rust ring or sterile infiltrate, especially if present >24 hours (**Fig. 6.4**). The base of uninfected abrasions should be clear. Mild anterior uveitis may be present but iris or lens defects suggest an intraocular FB.

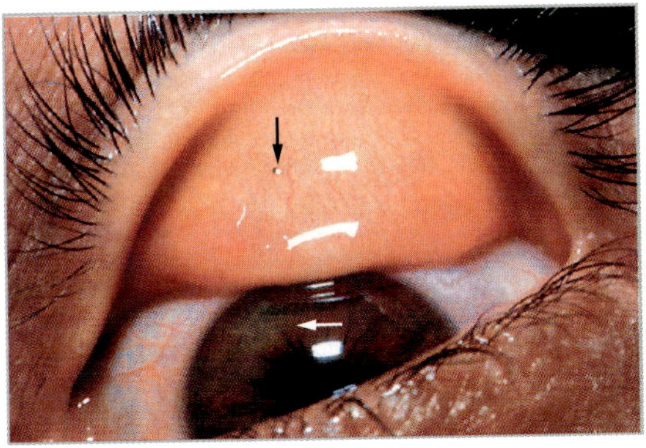

Fig. 6.3: Subtarsal foreign body (vertical black arrow) with associated corneal fluorescein uptake (horizontal white arrow).

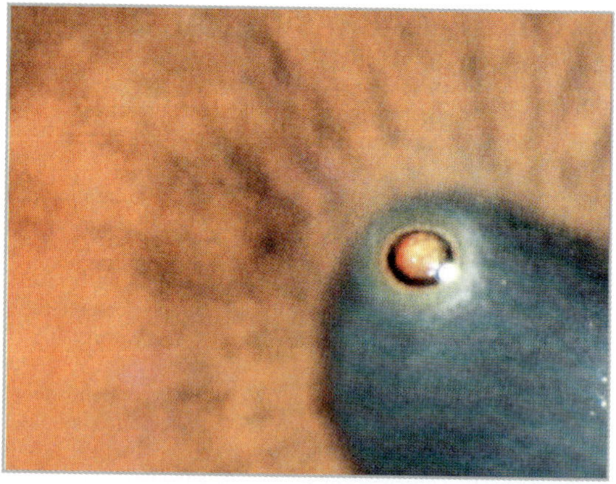

Fig. 6.4: Corneal foreign body with rust ring.

Differential diagnosis Treat expanding or new infiltrates associated with purulent discharge, severe redness, or pain as bacterial keratitis (p. 227). For apparently spontaneous epithelial defects consider corneal dystrophy (p. 245) and recurrent erosion syndrome (p. 200). Exclude chemical and penetrating injury.

Investigations Obtain an X-ray to exclude an intraocular metallic FB if high-speed fragments may have hit the eye.

Management Remove FBs (**Box 6.1**). Stat G. atropine 1% or cyclopentolate 1% relieve pain from ciliary spasm. Offer oral analgesics as required. Without a clear history of injury an 'abrasion' in contact lens wearers is often the first sign of bacterial keratitis. If in doubt, treat as bacterial keratitis (p. 227).

Follow-up

1. Contact lens wearers.
   - Prescribe a quinolone antibiotic (e.g. levofloxacin 0.5% or moxifloxacin 0.5%) q.d.s. until the eye is comfortable, indicating epithelialisation. Ask the patient to return immediately if symptoms deteriorate, suggesting infection.
   - Re-start contact lens wear 1 week after the epithelium has healed.
2. Non contact lens wearers.
   - Small abrasion at low risk of infection: Remove any pad after 24 hours. Use Oc. chloramphenicol q.d.s. for 5 days then stop. Review only if symptoms persist.

Box 6.1: Removal of superficial corneal foreign body

1. Explain the procedure and warn that discomfort may increase when the anaesthetic wears off.
2. Instil topical anaesthesia, e.g. three drops of proxymetacaine 0.5%.
3. Multiple superficial FBs are sometimes more easily removed by irrigation.
4. Remove embedded FBs at the slit lamp using a 20-gauge needle with a bent tip. Remove any rust ring with a needle or dental burr. Deep rust rings in the visual axis that cannot easily be removed should be left to resolve spontaneously. Mild iron-staining is not visually significant.
5. Document the epithelial defect size (post-removal).
6. Apply Oc. chloramphenicol and paraffin embedded mesh, e.g. Jelonet, and pressure pad unless there is a risk of infection, e.g. organic matter, fingernail scratch, or contact lens wearer.

- *Larger abrasions or high risk of infection:* Use Oc. chloramphenicol q.d.s. and review at 24 hours. If the abrasion is healing well and the patient is comfortable, continue ointment for 5 days then stop. If not, instil G. atropine 1%, continue Oc. chloramphenicol q.d.s. and review again in 24 hours.

RECURRENT CORNEAL EROSION

Background Traumatic, dystrophic, or degenerative damage interferes with corneal epithelium–basement membrane adhesion, resulting in recurrent epithelial breakdown (recurrent erosion syndrome). Determine the cause, because this determines the treatment. See also persistent corneal epithelial defects (p. 202).

Symptoms Recurrent attacks of pain, tearing, and redness, typically during sleep or upon wakening.

History Ask about prior corneal abrasions, especially those from organic material such as a tree branch or fingernail. Ask if there is a family history of recurrent erosions or corneal disease.

Examination Epithelial defects vary from focal superficial punctate keratopathy (SPK) or immature epithelium (**Fig. 6.5**), to full-thickness defects. The anterior chamber (AC) may have scanty cells. Examine the other eye with fluorescein and retroillumination for signs of a corneal dystrophy.

Differential diagnosis Epithelial basement membrane dystrophy (also known as Cogan's, or map-dot-fingerprint dystrophy, p. 245) is the most common cause and often presents with recurrent erosion. Also frequent in Thiel-Behnke (p. 247), Reis–Bücklers (p. 247), Lattice (p. 247), Granular type I and II (p. 249), and Meesman's (p. 249) dystrophies.

Fig. 6.5: Recurrent corneal erosion with subsequent subepithelial cysts in the affected area in a patient with epithelial basement membrane dystrophy.

Management Most cases respond to conservative management with stat G. atropine 1%, Oc. chloramphenicol and pressure pad, with review in 24 hours if not settled. Repeat if the epithelium has not healed. If not healed in 3 days, insert a bandage contact lens (BCL), ideally a silicone hydrogel plano lens, to relieve discomfort and promote healing. Inflamed eyes may better tolerate a BCL if treated with topical NSAID (G. preservative free diclofenac 0.1% b.d.) and cycloplegic (G. preservative free atropine 1% b.d.) for 2 days. Use the BCL for 2–3 months. Cases not responding to padding and BCL may benefit from focal debridement of loose epithelium using a cellulose sponge under topical anaesthesia. Remove any residual strands with plain forceps. Avoid sharp instruments. Recalcitrant cases may respond to oral doxycycline 100 mg daily, ± a weak topical steroid b.d., for 4–6 weeks. Focal abnormalities occurring outside the optical zone may respond to anterior stromal puncture using the needle on an insulin syringe (bend the tip at 90° to the shaft with tying forceps, leaving a point shorter than the corneal thickness to avoid a corneal perforation)—make multiple fine punctures through Bowman layer in the affected area. Use surgical superficial keratectomy or phototherapeutic keratectomy (PTK) for recalcitrant cases, particularly if there is excessive aberrant epithelial basement membrane and subepithelial collagenous pannus (the most common in epithelial basement membrane dystrophy). Once healed, prescribe a lubricant ointment at night until asymptomatic for at least 3 months.

Follow-up Review daily until the epithelial defect closes (see comments above). Those with ocular surface disease, BCLs or on topical steroids are at increased risk of microbial superinfection and require close follow-up.

PERSISTENT EPITHELIAL DEFECT

Background Persistent corneal epithelial defects (PCEDs) occur in association with a large and heterogeneous group of ocular and systemic diseases. Detection and treatment of any underlying autoimmune diseases may promote corneal healing and avoid potentially lethal vasculitis.

History and examination Look for abnormal eyelid closure and tear film. Test corneal sensation (ideally with a Cochet–Bonnet aesthesiometer). Note the location and size of epithelial defects (usually oval with slightly heaped edges, in the palpebral aperture), the percentage of stromal thinning, and presence of any infiltrate. Exclude the following potential causes:

- *Local*: Eyelid or eyelid margin disease; neurotrophic keratitis; neuroparalytic keratitis (e.g. Bell's palsy); following corneal infections, burns, and surgery (including keratorefractive procedures); atopic or vernal keratoconjunctivitis; Mooren's ulcer; staphylococcal marginal ulcer; herpetic keratitis and allograft rejection.
- *Systemic*: Nutritional disorders (e.g. keratomalacia); diabetes; skin disease (e.g. acne rosacea and psoriasis); leukaemia; Sjögren's disease; graft-versus-host disease; collagen vascular disorders (rheumatoid arthritis, ocular mucous membrane pemphigoid, Stevens–Johnson syndrome/toxic epidermal necrolysis, relapsing polychondritis, systemic lupus erythematosus, polyarteritis nodosa and granulomatosis with polyangiitis).

Treatment Aim to control any known underlying disease. Move up the following ladder of interventions, until responsive:

- Discontinue unnecessary topical medications and use ointment to reduce eyelid shearing forces on the corneal epithelium.
- A low-toxicity unpreserved antibiotic drop or ointment such as chloramphenicol or quinolone is usually used as prophylaxis against bacterial infection.
- Use preservative-free drops if possible, especially if the patient requires more than four drops daily.
- Manage infiltrates as microbial keratitis (p. 227). Patients on topical steroids may have infection without an infiltrate.
- Treat dry eye with tear substitutes, serum tears, or punctal occlusion. Avoid continuous use of hydrogel bandage contact lenses if there is aqueous tear deficiency; the risk of microbial keratitis is high.
- Lid closure with Botox injection (p. 37) or a temporary central tarsorrhaphy with a 4/0 mattress suture and bolster.

- For recalcitrant cases consider human amniotic membrane patch or graft. This can be performed in theatre (glued and/or sutured), or in clinic (OmniLenz or Prokera).
- Consider topical human autologous or allogenous 20% serum, finger-prick autologous blood, or nerve growth factor (Oxervate), all six times daily.
- Consider G. insulin (e.g. 1 unit of Humulin S in 1 mL of ocular lubricant) q.d.s for cases refractory to medical treatment.
- Treat small perforations (<1 mm) with tissue glue (**Box 6.2**), a contact lens and prophylactic topical antibiotics. For larger perforations use a therapeutic lamellar or penetrating keratoplasty.
- If all these treatments fail, a conjunctival flap will sacrifice vision but reduces discomfort and ocular inflammation and promotes healing. If no conjunctiva is available due to scarring, a free buccal mucous membrane graft will usually result in a stable epithelium.

Follow-up Weekly until stable or healed.

Box 6.2: Applying corneal glue

1. Apply topical anaesthetic, e.g. proxymetacaine 0.5%.
2. Trephine a circular patch of clear plastic from a sterile drape using a 4-mm skin punch. To one side apply a drop of KY jelly or carbomer gel. This allows the patch to be picked up using an applicator, such as a cotton-tipped stick.
3. Lift the patch and turn it over. To the other side apply a small drop of cyanoacrylate (e.g. Histoacryl) tissue glue (**Fig. 6.6**).
4. Dry the corneal defect with a cellulose (e.g. Weccel) sponge. Remove epithelium at the edge of the perforation as glue does not stick well to epithelial cells.
5. Place the patch over the defect, glue-side down (**Fig. 6.7**). Leave the polythene patch in place.
6. Use a cellulose sponge to confirm that the defect is sealed.
7. For small punched-out corneal lesions, too small to patch, apply glue directly to the cornea (**Fig. 6.8**).
8. Apply a bandage contact lens both for comfort and to stabilise the glue.
9. Loose glue has a high risk of infection; remove with a needle and re-glue if necessary. It is not possible to assess whether healing has occurred without removing the glue, unless it has displaced spontaneously.

Complications include early loss of glue, neovascularisation, and infection. Advise patients not to rub the eye and use preservative-free drops while the contact lens remains *in situ*. Review within 24 hours. Consider tectonic corneal grafting if the leak continues.

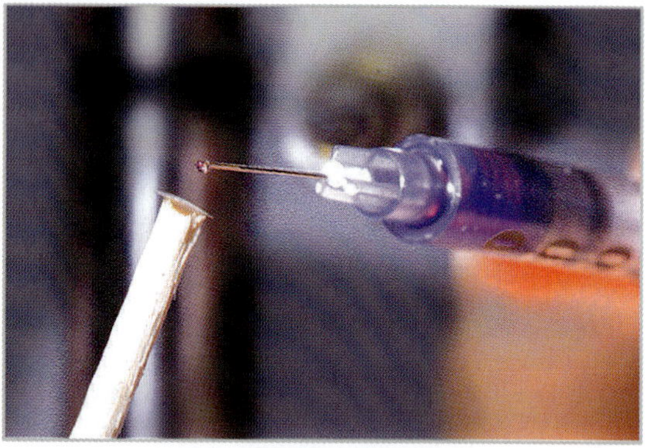

Fig. 6.6: Application of glue to a polythene patch.

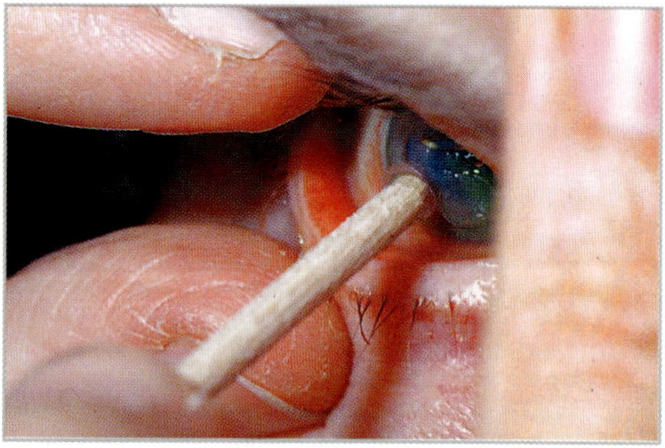

Fig. 6.7: Application of a polythene patch to a corneal ulcer.

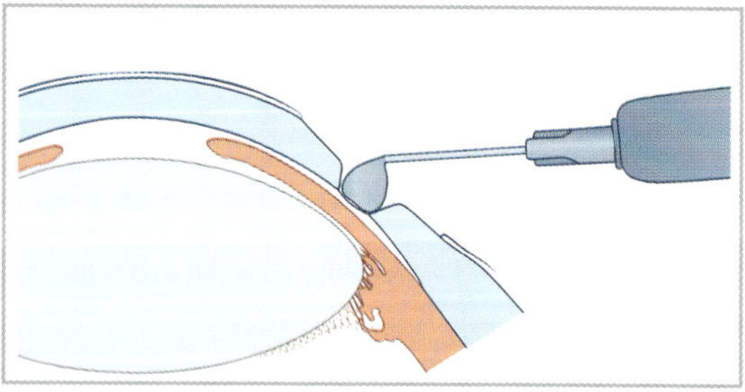

Fig. 6.8: Direct application of glue to a small punched-out corneal ulcer.

NEUROTROPHIC KERATITIS

Background Caused by damage to the trigeminal nerve, with partial or complete loss of corneal innervation and sensation. It can occur as a result of congenital abnormalities, ocular disease (most commonly herpetic infections), neurological conditions or surgery, and systemic conditions such as diabetes mellitus (**Table 6.1**).

Examination Assess corneal sensation with a cotton-tipped bud, or a Cochet and Bonnet aesthesiometer.

Signs The Mackie classification details three stages. Stage 1 features epithelial changes, including hyperplasia and irregularity, punctate keratopathy, dellen, decreased tear break-up times, stromal scarring and superficial vascularisation. In Stage 2, persistent epithelial defects occur. These are usually oval in shape with a characteristic rolled and smooth edge. Stromal oedema, Descemet's membrane folds or AC inflammatory cells may also be seen. In Stage 3, a corneal ulcer with stromal involvement is present. This may progress to corneal melting and subsequent perforation.

Table 6.1: Causes of neurotrophic keratitis

Inherited and congenital • Familial dysautonomia (Riley–Day syndrome) • Familial corneal anaesthesia • Hereditary and sensory autonomic neuropathy types IV and V • Mobius' syndrome • Goldenhar's syndrome	**Ocular** • Herpes simplex keratitis (p. 237) • Herpes zoster keratitis (p. 241) • Corneal surgery (keratoplasty and refractive surgery) • Contact lens wear • Chemical or physical burns (p. 183) • Chronic ocular surface inflammation • Corneal dystrophies (granular and lattice) (p. 247) • Drug toxicity (timolol and diclofenac) • Orbital neoplasia
Neurological • Traumatic/surgical resection of trigeminal nerve • Surgical ablation for trigeminal neuralgia • Compressive/infiltrative lesion, e.g. acoustic neuroma, aneurysm • Stroke	**Systemic** • Diabetes mellitus • Leprosy • Vitamin A deficiency

Treatment Ocular lubricants are used in all stages of neurotrophic keratitis. If an epithelial defect is present, use prophylactic topical antibiotics such as G. chloramphenicol 0.5% q.d.s. Matrix metalloproteinases inhibitors such as oral doxycycline and oral erythromycin can reduce the risk of corneal melt in Stage 3 disease, e.g. doxycycline 100 mg o.d. for 6 weeks. Treat severe cases with autologous or allogenic serum eye drops, or insulin eye drops (e.g. 1 unit of Humulin S in 1 mL of ocular lubricant) q.d.s. until the epithelial defect heals. Consider cenegermin 0.002% (Oxervate) for refractory cases (not available in the United Kingdom). Surgical treatment may be necessary, including amniotic membrane grafting, tarsorrhaphy, and corneal neurotisation.

Follow-up See Stage 1 every 3–4 weeks; see Stage 2/3 weekly until stable or healed.

DRY EYE DISEASE

Background Dry eye disease (DED) is a multifactorial condition characterised by a loss of tear film homeostasis accompanied by ocular symptoms. Tear film instability and hyperosmolarity, ocular surface inflammation and damage, and neurosensory abnormalities play aetiological roles. Divided into aqueous deficient and evaporative (the most common), but they often overlap. Tear dysfunction affects 5–30% of the population, with a female preponderance, increasing with age.

History

- *Symptoms:* May include surface discomfort, photophobia, redness, itch, watering, eyelid fatigue, pressure, and transient blurring especially for tasks requiring sustained visual attention such as reading, driving at night, watching television and working on a computer. Delineate symptom duration, laterality and any relieving and exacerbating factors, including the effect of blinking and artificial tears. Symptoms may correlate poorly with signs.
- *Contact lens (CL) wear:* Consider CL-induced dry eye (CLIDE) and CL-associated dry eye (CLADE).
- *Previous lid and ocular surgery:* Ask about LASIK, surgical manipulation of the conjunctiva, exposure to anti-fibrotic adjuncts and exposure to topical drugs toxic to the ocular surface, e.g. anaesthetics, NSAIDs, glaucoma medications and povidone-iodine.
- *Full drug history:* Topical medications can cause DED due to their allergic, toxic and immuno-inflammatory effects. Preservatives, e.g. benzalkonium chloride (BAK), may aggravate DED. Multiple systemic drugs can induce DED secondary to decreased tear production, altered nerve input and reflex secretion, inflammatory effects on secretory glands, or direct irritation effects through secretion into the tears (amiodarone, aspirin, bisphosphonates, isotretinoin, ibuprofen and clofazimine). Ask about adrenergic agents [β-blockers (odds ratio, OR 1.98), and α-agonists), anti-cholinergics (antidepressants/antipsychotics, OR 2.54), neuroleptics, anti-Parkinson's disease drugs, H_1-antihistamines, decongestants, antispasmodics, benzodiazepines (OR 2.25), and HRT especially oestrogen use alone (OR 1.69). Complex interactions with multiple drugs may amplify effects.
- *Full medical history*: Ask about dry mouth, lymphadenopathy, continuous positive airway pressure (CPAP) use, Parkinson's disease, radiation exposure and anterior pituitary disease (hormones influence the ocular surface and adnexa directly, or via steroids, thyroxine or insulin). Insulin resistance and DED

are associated with polycystic ovary syndrome, pregnancy, anti-androgen therapy and complete androgen insensitivity syndrome. In types I and II diabetes, hormonal and metabolic dysregulations cause lacrimal gland dysfunction, plus type I diabetes has cross-reactive autoimmune components. Sex hormones modulate growth hormone, insulin-like growth factor and insulin. Many androgen effects on the lacrimal gland depend on an intact hypothalamic-pituitary axis. Androgen deficiency is linked to corneal and conjunctival epitheliopathies but not aqueous tear deficiency (in the absence of autoimmune disease). Patients with DED have an increased prevalence of sleep and mood disorders, anxiety and depression.

- *Ocular surface disability index (OSDI):* Measures the frequency of symptoms, environmental triggers and vision-related quality of life. It is useful for managing patients with more severe dry eye, e.g. Sjögren's disease. Ranges from normal (0–12 points), to mild (13–22), moderate (23–32), and severe (33–100) disease. Useful for monitoring the progression of DED and response to treatment, although it is mainly used as a research tool.

Examination Findings are heterogenous and often vary over time. Examine in the following order:

- *Non-invasive tear break-up time (NITBUT):* Measures tear film stability without fluorescein. Ask the patient to blink naturally three times and then to keep their eye open until asked to blink again. Close the other eye to prevent it driving the blink response. Record the time until dry spots appear (ideally the median of three measurements per eye). If either eye is <10 sec, diagnose DED. NITBUT can be objectively measured by some machines, e.g. MS-39 and CA-800.
- *Lid contour and blinking:* The normal spontaneous blink rate is 10–15/min, higher in women than men. Blinking clears debris, provides mechanical protection, and spreads meibomian gland lipids from the lower lid to the superior ocular surface. The percentage of incomplete blinks correlates with DED symptoms. Note any proptosis.
- *Tear film quantity:*
  1. Meniscometry measures the inferior tear strip meniscus height against the slit-lamp beam height. Record in the centre of the lower eyelid without lid manipulation, shortly after a blink. Normal is 0.5–1.0 mm, but influenced by the time after a blink, position along the lid, time of day, temperature, humidity, air speed, and illumination. Digital and OCT readings are more repeatable and objective.
  2. The Schirmer test without anaesthetic can confirm severe aqueous deficiency (e.g. Sjögren's disease), but its variability

and uncomfortableness preclude routine use. Bend a Schirmer strip by 90° at the preformed notch and place into the conjunctival sac at the junction of the middle and temporal thirds of the lower lid, without touching the strip with your fingers. Conduct the test in ambient lighting, with patient's eyes closed. Record how far down the paper fluid moves by capillary action over 5 mins: ≤9 mm indicates severe dry eye; ≤22 mm mild to moderate dry eye. However, due to wide confidence intervals, values from 8 to 25 mm are inconclusive.

- *Fluorescein break-up time (FBUT):* See page 192.
- *Ocular surface damage:*
  1. *Corneal punctate keratopathy:* >5 corneal spots following instillation of dilute fluorescein indicates keratopathy, but not necessarily DED. See page 192 for techniques. Corneal and conjunctival staining correlate with disease severity in severe DED, but not with mild-to-moderate DED. A positive stain is not required to diagnose DED.
  2. Look for corneal focal abnormal wetting with pterygium, thinning (dellen), infection, keratinisation, scarring, and filaments (strands of mucous anchored to corneal epithelium).
  3. Assess bulbar and tarsal conjunctiva (evert lid) for conjunctival injection, scarring, keratinisation and symblephara. The most common clinical sign suggestive of ocular surface inflammation is conjunctival redness, but it can exist despite a white eye. The conjunctiva may redden quickly during examination. Staining of the marginal tarsal conjunctiva (lid wiper epitheliopathy) indicates epithelial disruption and damage to this area.
- *Meibomian glands (see also p. 71):*
  1. *Position:* The openings should be just anterior to the mucocutaneous junction. Posterior gland migration is abnormal.
  2. *Appearance:* Pouting, plugging, absence and notching are abnormal.
  3. *Secretions:* Cloudy, granular, or "toothpaste" are abnormal. Should be clear.
  4. *Expressibility:* Normally, 25–65% are non-expressible (non-secretory) with nasal gland function > central > temporal. Hence, the presence of non-expressible glands in the central lid does not necessarily mean there is meibomian gland dysfunction.
- Exclude the following conditions which can be confused or associated with dry eye:
  1. Allergic conjunctivitis (p. 159).
  2. Conjunctivochalasis (excess conjunctival folds). Discomfort made worse by blinking.

3. Superior limbic keratoconjunctivitis (p. 179).
4. Corneal epithelial basement membrane dystrophy (p. 245)
5. Toxicity from glaucoma eye drops, preservatives, ethylenediaminetetraacetic acid (EDTA) and cosmetics.
6. Lagophthalmos (p. 19).
7. Cicatrising conjunctivitis (Stevens–Johnson syndrome—toxic epidermal necrolysis p. 171; ocular mucous membrane pemphigoid p. 174).

Investigations

Osmolarity: Can be assessed with the TearLab/Trukera device. Normal is 302 mOsm/L, with an inter-eye difference of 7 mOsm/L. DED produces elevated, unstable and asymmetric readings. Use the highest value of the two eyes. Readings >308 mOsm/L indicate loss of homeostasis, while an inter-eye difference of >8 mOsm/L indicates tear film instability. Osmolarity generally increases with disease severity, readings > 308 mOsm/L indicate mild-to-moderate DED while values > 316 mOsm/L indicate more severe DED. Record the test time and when eye any drops were last instilled. As FBUT alters the tear film, it should follow osmolarity measurement.

Interferometry (e.g. LipiView) is a noninvasive method for quantifying the lipid layer at the surface of the tear film, and can be used to assess tear film stability. It also evaluates blink rate and can perform dynamic meibomian gland imaging.

Corneal *in vivo* confocal microscopy often shows an abnormal neural network in patients with neuropathic corneal pain (see below).

Management

Determine the symptoms and cause(s) of DED before crafting a treatment plan. As needed, address: meibomian gland abnormalities and orifice patency; tear osmolarity production, stability, loss and runoff; lipid quality/quantity; and inflammation. Where possible, distinguish aqueous deficiency from evaporative aetiologies.

First-line

- Educate about the condition, its management and prognosis. Explain there is no panacea.
- Modify local environment, e.g. humidify the room; turn off the air conditioner; do not overheat living space; and reduce airflow over ocular surface.
- Advise diet rich in omega-3, e.g. fish (salmon, mackerel and sardines); and reduce the omega 6:3 ratio. Consider supplements of maqui berry (Maquibright 60 mg od po), and omega 3 ± omega 7 (dry omega).

- Reduce, modify or eliminate causative systemic and topical medications.
- Use preservative free ocular lubricants, e.g. Celluvisc (the many available products have similar efficacy). These can help to reduce osmolarity by disrupting the hyperosmolar environment and breaking the cycle of inflammation, and lubricate any lid-wiper epitheliopathy. For punctate staining treat early, before chronic pain emerges, and use hyaluronic acid for its wound healing properties, e.g. HyloTear. Hydroxypropyl guar (HP-guar)-based products increase mucous layer thickness and reduce inflammation, e.g. Systane. Trehalose has very high water-retention capabilities, and offers bio- and osmoprotection; some drops have an antinociceptive action if instilled cold, e.g. Thealoz Duo.
- For meibomian gland dysfunction, consider lipid-containing lubricants, e.g. Optive Plus, VisuEvo, Evotears, Thea Lipid, HyloDual Intense, plus lid hygiene and warm eyelid compresses (p. 145).

Second-line

- Check compliance with first-line treatment.
- Increase the frequency of preservative free ocular lubricants.
- Add overnight ointment, e.g. Xailin Night.
- Add perfluorohexyloctane, e.g. Miebo or Evotears q.d.s.
- Tear conservation:
  - Spectacles and moisture-chamber goggles
  - Punctal plugs for aqueous dry eye (use in evaporative disease is controversial), but control inflammation first. Complications include canalicular migration of the plug, pyogenic granuloma, punctal enlargement, tumors (rare) and infections (keratitis, conjunctivitis, canaliculitis and dacryocystitis). Silicone plugs have the advantage of being visible.
- Drug therapy:
  - Pretreat with topical steroid for 1 week before starting ciclosporin 1 mg/mL nocte. Then taper the steroid by one drop per week. Advise patient that it may take 3 months to work.
  - Oral pilocarpine, starting at 5 mg b.d.
- Treat posterior blepharitis (p. 145).

Third-line

- Autologous/allogeneic serum eye drops, e.g. 20% solution six times daily.

- Longer duration steroids, e.g. prednisolone 0.5% or hydrocortisone 0.335% 1–3 times daily, until symptoms improve (up to 4–6 months, some may require long-term use).
- Consider a therapeutic contact lens, balancing risks and benefits for each case:
  - *Soft-bandage lenses:* Best for filaments with some residual tear production.
  - *Scleral lenses:* Create a precorneal reservoir of fluid. Can be worn overnight for nocturnal lagophthalmos.
- *Surgical punctal occlusion:* Consider if removeable plugs not tolerated or retained (60%). Epiphora can be a potential problem if both the upper and lower puncta are totally and permanently closed.

Fourth-line

- Lifitegrast 5%, e.g. Xiidra; a lymphocyte function-associated antigen-1 (LFA-1) antagonist, b.d., for 3 months
- Amniotic membrane graft
- Lateral tarsorrhaphy
- Salivary gland transplantation

For patients with chronic symptoms but limited signs, that are refractory to treatment, consider neuropathic pain ('pain without stain'; keratoneuralgia; neuropathic pain syndrome; corneal neuralgia and corneal dysaesthesia) rather than DED. Occurs due to overt damage within the somatosensory nervous system or local tissue damage, e.g. laser refractive surgery. Corneal nociceptors, that transmit somatosensory 'pain' information to the central nervous system, have the potential to be 'wound up' by repeated physiological stimulation or by noxious stimuli, e.g. hyperosmolarity or inflammation.

Management may not be required if there only signs, but no symptoms of DED. Corneal nerve damage secondary to longstanding DED can reduce corneal sensitivity and mask discomfort, as may other diseases associated with reduced corneal sensation (post herpetic, diabetes, Riley-Day syndrome); manage each as appropriate.

Follow-up Severe disease often requires long-term follow-up, but otherwise discharge once stable.

KERATOCONUS

Background The most common primary corneal ectasia, characterised by noninflammatory, central corneal thinning, typically presenting in the second and third decades.

History Ask about blurred vision, rapidly changing spectacle prescription, eye rubbing and contact lens (CL) wear. Review past refractions if available. Family history exists in ~8%. Conditions associated with keratoconus (KC) include atopic dermatitis, vernal keratoconjunctivitis, Down's syndrome, Ehlers–Danlos syndrome, Laurence-Moon-Bardet-Biedl syndrome, and others.

Examination Irregular astigmatism can reduce spectacle VA. Corneal changes are nearly always bilateral, but may be asymmetrical. The cornea has a variably shaped cone (**Fig. 6.9A**), that is thinned at the apex. This produces a focal lid convexity in downgaze (Munson's sign, **Fig. 6.9B**). The corneal substrate may appear normal but several signs may be present including: a rust-coloured Fleischer ring at the base of the cone (best seen using oblique cobalt blue illumination); Vogt's striae (deep stromal vertical stress lines); fine subepithelial scarring at the cone apex; a scissor reflex on retinoscopy; an oil drop red reflex; and prominent corneal nerves.

Investigations Corneal topography is the most sensitive investigation and may show KC before symptoms or signs emerge. An initial *forme fruste*, with inferior protrusion of the posterior cornea and epithelial thinning over the cone apex, may mask classic KC (anterior KC), which features steepening and thinning of the inferior cornea (**Figs. 6.10** and **6.11**).

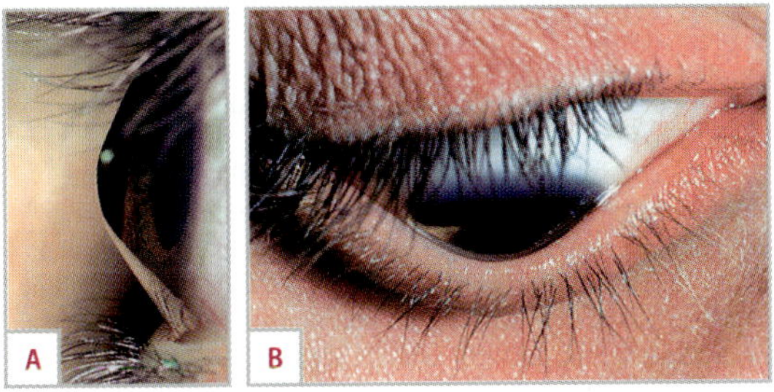

Fig. 6.9: (A) Keratoconus. (B) Munson's sign (Courtesy DH Verity).

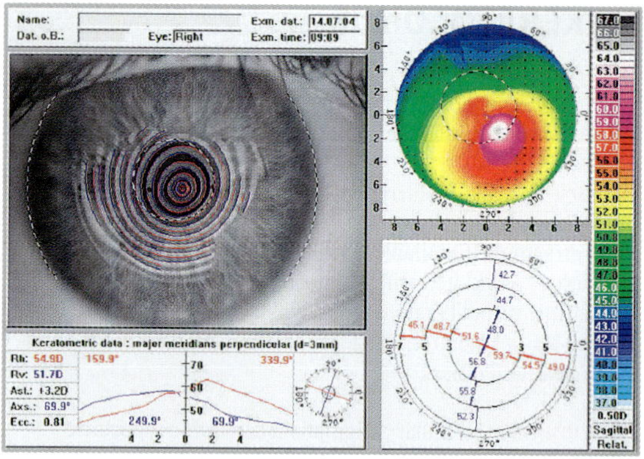

Fig. 6.10: Corneal topography showing keratoconus. Normal astigmatism is shown in Figure 6.2 (p. 195).

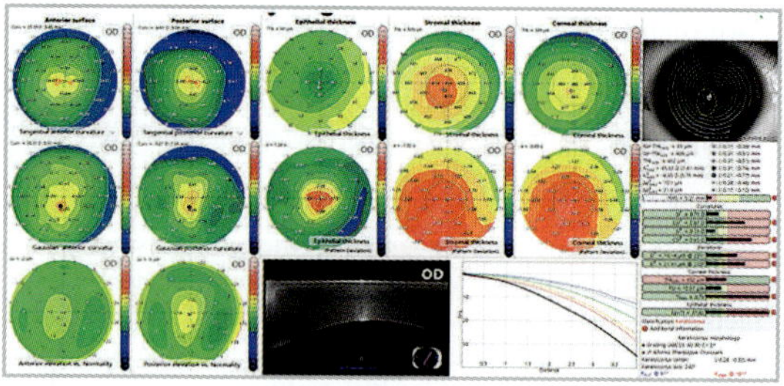

Fig. 6.11: Keratoconus summary report on the MS-39 device, showing anterior surface versus posterior surface elevation, epithelial thickness, corneal thickness, a Placido disc image and indices.

Management Treat allergic eye disease to discourage eye rubbing.

- *Collagen cross-linking (CXL):* Aims to stabilise the corneal shape in progressive KC (**Box 6.3**). Avoid with thin corneas (<375 µm including epithelium) due to a risk of endothelial damage and decompensation. Beware of epithelial thickening over areas of stromal collapse, producing falsely thick corneal measurements; perform anterior segment OCT if unsure. Under current protocols (subject to change) offer CXL for early KC (steepest K reading, Kmax, ≤55D) if there is topographic evidence of progressive ectasia, namely one or more of: ≥1.0D increase in Kmax; ≥1.0D increase in K2 or K1 front; ≥0.5D

Box 6.3: Corneal cross-linking (Dresden protocol)

1. Consent: 81–100% have stabilised or improved corneal curvature. Complication rate is ~3% including corneal infiltrates, bacterial keratitis, stromal scarring, endothelial cell loss and occasional corneal decompensation. All cases have transient stromal haze that usually resolves by 2 weeks, but may persist up to a year. Corneal sensation is typically reduced for 12 months. Retreatment rates are low (~2.5% per year).
2. Under topical anaesthesia, delineate the central 9.0 mm of corneal epithelium with a corneal marker and remove with a hockey knife or epilasik blade.
3. Apply riboflavin for 30 minutes from a syringe and cannula (confirm absorption of green solution at the slit lamp). For corneas < 400 µm use isotonic or hypotonic solution (rather than the standard hypertonic riboflavin) and recheck pachymetry after 30 minutes. If the pachymetry is <400 µm then apply two drops every 10 seconds for 90 seconds or until the corneal thickness is at least 400 µm before starting treatment.
4. Irradiate the cornea with 365 nm UVA at 3 mW/cm^2 for 30 minutes, applying riboflavin every 2–5 minutes. There are also accelerated CXL protocols. The shorter duration treatments may be easier for the patient but may not produce such consistent results.
5. Fit a bandage contact lens for 1 week.
6. Prescribe topical steroids (unpreserved dexamethasone 0.1% q.d.s.), antibiotics (unpreserved chloramphenicol 0.5% q.d.s.) and lubricants (unpreserved hyaluronate drops) with oral pain relief (e.g. codeine and paracetamol).
7. Expect epithelial healing at first review at 1 week. Follow-up until healed, then 6-monthly for a year, then annually.

increase in K2 back; or ≥16 µm decrease in the minimum thickness. For moderate/advanced keratoconus (Kmax > 55D) consider if there is one or more of: ≥2.5D increase in Kmax; ≥2.5D increase in K2 or K1 front; ≥22 µm decrease in the minimum thickness. Also consider if refraction shows ≥1.0D increase in astigmatism with good VA.

- *Correct irregular astigmatism:* If VA is reduced, use spectacles, toric soft, or rigid gas permeable contact lenses (RGP CLs). If RGP CLs are poorly tolerated, try a piggy-back system (soft silicone hydrogel CL under the RGP lens) or a hybrid rigid gas permeable/soft lens. Treat any external eye disease, especially allergic conjunctivitis, to improve contact lens tolerance. For advanced KC with unstable corneal CLs, fit scleral CLs (often better tolerated).
- *Intracorneal ring segments (ICRS):* Reduce the sphere, cylinder and spherical equivalent in KC, and may permit continued spectacle wear, and improve CL tolerance and fitting, but

do not stop cone progression. Consider for the few patients with inadequate spectacle vision who do not tolerate CLs. The cornea should be at least 400 µm thick at the ICRS insertion site. Postoperative segment extrusion, corneal neovascularisation, segment migration, infectious keratitis, channel deposits, corneal haze, corneal melting, persistent incisional gaping, chronic pain, and focal oedema may occur, but serious problems are rare as ICRS implantation is reversible, no corneal tissue is removed, and the central optical zone is not invaded.

- *Intraocular lens:* Consider phakic intraocular lens (IOL) or clear lens extraction and toric lens implantation for the few patients who have stable KC and almost regular astigmatism. If astigmatism is irregular enough to require CLs a toric IOL will exacerbate CL vision problems and require spectacle overcorrection.
- *Corneal transplant surgery:* Consider if CL lens fitting is no longer possible, not tolerated, or most commonly when the CL vision is inadequate. Deep anterior lamellar keratoplasty (DALK) is safer than penetrating keratoplasty (PK), with equivalent outcomes. Epikeratophakia (onlay lamellar keratoplasty) is only occasionally used as the resulting VA is relatively poor, typically in high-risk cases, e.g. Down's syndrome. Corneal allogenic intrastromal ring segments (CAIRS) involve intrastromal transplantation of donor cornea stromal segments, similar to ICRS, but may have less risk of extrusion.
- *Scarring:* PK is usually required if scarring limits the corrected VA. DALK is technically more difficult with deep anterior scarring or previous hydrops, often resulting in a posterior lamellar split. DALK avoids the risk of endothelial rejection, but residual scar tissue degrades the postoperative VA.
- *Hydrops:* Acute rips in Descemet's membrane occur in ~5% (higher in Down's syndrome or allergic eye disease), resulting in a sudden onset of profound stromal hydration with pain, redness, photophobia and loss of vision (**Fig. 6.12**). Usually resolves in 8–10 weeks but may take 6 months. About 15% of patients regain good vision with CL wear. Offer G. hypertonic sodium chloride 5% q.d.s. and G. atropine 1% or G. cyclopentolate 1% b.d. Examine every 2–4 weeks until resolved, or more frequently when peripheral and inflamed as vascularisation may occur. Consider G. dexamethasone 0.1% for vascularisation, but not all respond. A large diameter DALK or PK may be required if there are no signs of improvement at 3 months, or earlier if there is vascularisation.

Follow-up Every 6 months for 2 years then annually. If progressing, consider CXL.

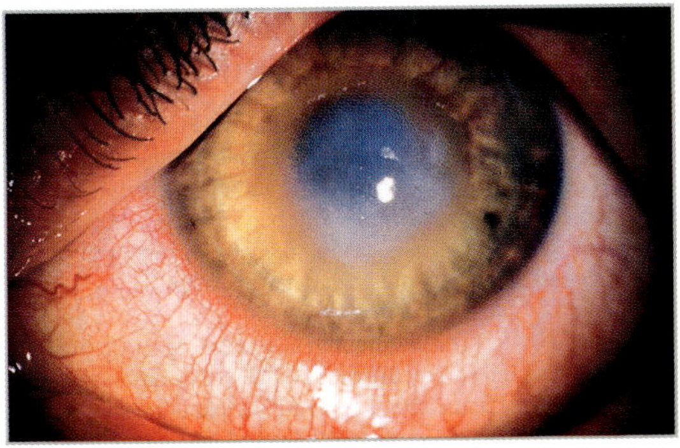

Fig. 6.12: Acute hydrops.

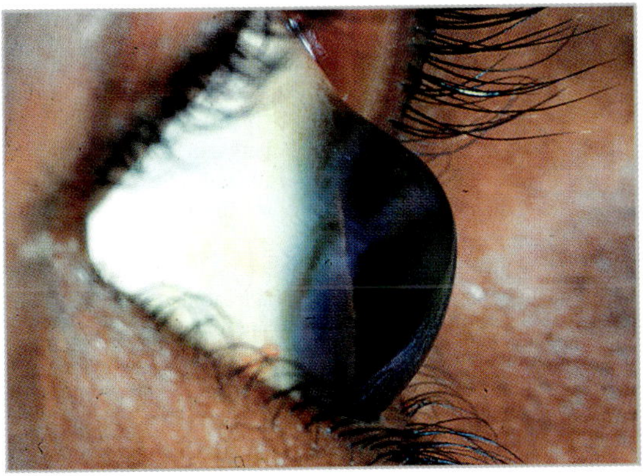

Fig. 6.13: Keratoglobus (Courtesy DH Verity).

Other corneal ectasias

Pellucid marginal degeneration Onset from age 20–40 years. A characteristic arcuate band of thinning 1–2 mm wide is seen from 4 to 8 o'clock, located 1–2 mm central to the limbus.

There may be marked central corneal flattening along the vertical meridian before inferior thinning is detectible.

Keratoglobus Stromal thinning extends to the peripheral cornea resulting in a globular corneal profile (**Fig. 6.13**).

PERIPHERAL CORNEAL ULCERATION AND THINNING

Background Peripheral ulcerative keratitis (PUK) is often idiopathic (Mooren's ulcer). It may also be associated with rheumatoid arthritis (RA) and type III autoimmune diseases, most commonly granulomatosis with polyangiitis (GPA, previously known as Wegener's granulomatosis), and rarely relapsing polychondritis and polyarteritis nodosa.

Examination Scleritis is absent in Mooren's ulcer, variably present in RA, and severe, usually necrotising, in autoimmune diseases. PUK is destructive, beginning peripherally and progressing centrally, circumferentially, and posteriorly, leaving thinned neovascularised cornea.

Differential diagnosis See **Table 6.2**.

Investigations PUK may be the presenting feature of potentially fatal systemic, vasculitic disease. Check cytoplasmic antineutrophil cytoplasmic antibodies (cANCA), perinuclear antineutrophil cytoplasmic antibodies (pANCA), rheumatoid factor (RhF), antinuclear autoantibodies (ANA), extractable nuclear antigen (ENA), ESR, CRP, serum angiotensin converting enzyme (sACE), CXR, and urine for protein and casts.

Treatment Involve experienced clinicians. Unilateral Mooren's ulcer may resolve with topical treatment (steroids, acetylcysteine, antibiotic and ciclosporin), bandage contact lenses and minor surgery (conjunctival resection/tissue glue), with oral doxycycline. However, many cases (typically severe or bilateral Mooren's ulcer and PUK associated with type III autoimmune disease) progress rapidly and require complex, urgent management, including systemic immunosuppression, to avoid irreversible damage.

Follow-up Aim for 1 year of remission (and ANCA normalisation in GPA) then taper immunosuppressants. Monitor for side effects of systemic treatment (p. 413). 'Burnt-out' Mooren's ulcers may reactivate with cataract or corneal graft surgery, so consider the risks versus benefits of prophylactic immunosuppression.

Table 6.2: Differential diagnosis of peripheral corneal thinning

Condition	Sex	Pain	Epithelium intact?	Age	Most common site	Laterality	Progression	Perforation	Comments
Terrien's marginal degeneration (**Fig. 6.14**)	M = F	No	Yes	3–4th decade	Superior or superonasal, but may extend around the entire corneal periphery	Bilateral	Yes, slowly	No, unless trauma	Variable and intermittent limbal inflammation, AC uninflamed. Lipid in vascularised, superficial cornea. Topical steroids control inflammation. For details (see p. 259)
Herpes zoster ophthalmicus (HZO) and herpes simplex virus (HSV)	M = F	No	No	Usually adults	Any quadrant	Unilateral	Yes	Yes	Reduced corneal sensation, mild uveitis. For treatment see page 241 (HZO) or page 237 (HSV)
Peripheral ulcerative keratitis associated with systemic vasculitis	M = F	Yes	No	Usually middle-aged or older	Any	Unilateral or bilateral	Usually rapid	Yes	Typically with rheumatoid arthritis, granulomatosis with polyangiitis (may be the presenting sign), polychondritis, or polyarteritis nodosa

Table 6.2: Differential diagnosis of peripheral corneal thinning—*Contd...*

Condition	Sex	Pain	Epithelium intact?	Age	Most common site	Laterality	Progression	Perforation	Comments
Mooren's ulcer	M = F	Yes	No	Any age	Any	Typically, bilateral in young Afro-Caribbeans, and unilateral in Caucasians	Rapid	Yes	May progress more slowly in elderly unilateral cases, some of which can be managed topically. Can be rapid in some cases, often bilateral, requiring systemic immunosuppressive therapy in Afro-Caribbeans
Pellucid margin degeneration	M = F	No	Yes	2–3rd decade	Inferior	Bilateral	Yes, slowly	No unless trauma	Conjunctiva and AC uninflamed. No lipid deposition. Abnormal topography. No treatment
Marginal keratitis and ocular rosacea	M = F	No	Yes	Any	Multifocal	Uni- or bilateral	Yes, with recurrent episodes	No	For treatment see page 226 (marginal keratitis) and page 148 (ocular rosacea)

Table 6.2: Differential diagnosis of peripheral corneal thinning —*Contd...*

Condition	Sex	Pain	Epithelium intact?	Age	Most common site	Laterality	Progression	Perforation	Comments
Furrow degeneration	M = F	No	Yes	Elderly	Peripheral to arcus senilis	Bilateral	Very slowly	No	Conjunctiva and AC uninflamed. Associated with rheumatoid arthritis or idiopathic in the elderly. Treatment rarely needed
Dellen (**Fig. 6.15**)	M = F	No	Yes	Any	Adjacent to limbal or corneal elevation	Unilateral	Very slowly	No	Conjunctiva and AC uninflamed. Eliminate elevation if possible. Topical lubricants

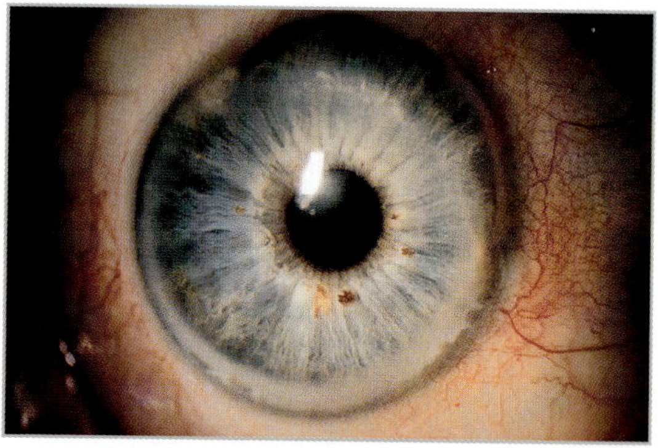

Fig. 6.14: Terrien's marginal degeneration.

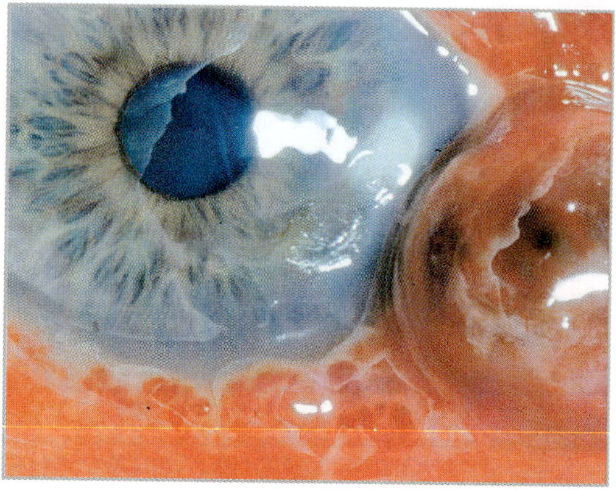

Fig. 6.15: Dellen from an adjacent, elevated subconjunctival haemorrhage (Courtesy DH Verity).

INTERSTITIAL KERATITIS

Background Interstitial keratitis (IK) is a sign, not a diagnosis. It describes corneal stromal inflammation, without epithelial involvement, with or without stromal vascularisation. IK is caused by direct invasion of microorganisms, or by an immune response thought to be due to foreign antigen, or altered corneal antigen, associated with the underlying condition. It may be necrotising or non-necrotising. The most common causes are listed in **Table 6.3**.

Symptoms Red eye, irritation, tearing, photophobia, and reduced VA (if the optical zone is involved). May be asymptomatic prior to visual symptoms.

History Ask about previous eye or systemic disease; especially herpetic eye disease, sarcoidosis, maternal syphilis (congenital syphilis may present age 5–20 years), previous sexually transmitted infection (syphilis and chlamydia), reduced hearing (syphilis and Cogan's syndrome), rashes (measles, mumps and syphilis), and contact lens wear.

Table 6.3: Causes of interstitial keratitis (those in *italics* are due to actively replicating organisms requiring specific antimicrobial therapy)

Bacterial • Syphilis • Lyme • Lyme disease • Infectious crystalline keratopathy	**Fungal** • *Microsporidia*
Mycobacterial • *Atypical mycobacteria*	**Parasitic** • *Acanthamoeba* • *Onchocerciasis*
Viral • Herpes simplex • Herpes zoster • Epstein–Barr • Adenovirus	**Non-infectious systemic** • Cogan's syndrome • Reactive arthritis
Phlyctenular keratitis • Fascicular keratitis (linear inflammation, vascularisation and scarring often crossing the optical zone)	**Nummular opacities** • Sarcoid • Herpes simplex virus • Herpes zoster ophthalmicus • Cogan's syndrome • Lyme disease • *Acanthamoeba* (late)

Examination

- *Face:* Look for features of congenital syphilis (saddle nose; frontal bossing; Hutchinson's triad of IK, notched upper central incisors and sensorineural deafness). Herpes zoster ophthalmicus (HZO) may leave scars in the Vth nerve distribution, but may occur without a rash.
- *Conjunctiva:* Exclude follicles due to sarcoid.
- *Cornea:* May show bilateral or unilateral involvement: infectious causes and herpes simplex virus (HSV) are usually unilateral, HZO almost always unilateral. Early syphilis may initially be unilateral. Focal lesions are due to phlyctenular keratitis (see next section) and nummular causes (see **Table 6.3**). There may be active vessels or ghost vessels from previous disease.
- *Uveitis:* May coexist.
- *Pupil/iris:* Nodules (sarcoidosis) and miosis (syphilis, secondary to uveitis).
- *Fundus:* Salt and pepper chorioretinopathy of syphilis. Optic atrophy.

Investigations Based on the likely causes (**Table 6.3**).

Treatment First exclude infectious causes and treat. Then control inflammation with topical steroids with or without infection prophylaxis. For active corneal vascularisation unresponsive to control of inflammation use anti-vascular endothelial growth factor (VEGF) therapy, e.g. bevacizumab 2.5 mg in 0.1 mL subconjunctival injection given adjacent to the area of most active corneal new vessels. Give at weeks 0, 4 and 8 ± 1 week. Inactive corneal vessels, identified using ICG angiography, can be treated with fine-needle cautery to feeder arteries.

Follow-up Depends upon underlying cause. HZO may progress without symptoms until the vision is affected, particularly after withdrawal of topical steroids, so review for a year. HZO and HSV may relapse after years, so advise patients to promptly seek specialist care if symptomatic.

PHLYCTENULOSIS

A fleshy swelling of the interpalpebral conjunctiva that can expand to involve the cornea (**Fig. 6.16**). Thought to be a type IV hypersensitivity reaction. Corneal phlyctens occasionally occur without a significant lid or conjunctival component. May intermittently become inflamed. Associated with blepharokeratoconjunctivitis in children, adult ocular rosacea, areas where pulmonary TB is endemic, *Staphylococcus*, *Candida*, herpes simplex virus (HSV), varicella zoster virus and intestinal worms. Topical steroids resolve inflammation in 2–4 days. Treat any staphylococcal lid disease with lid hygiene, topical antibiotic, or tetracycline as appropriate (p. 145). Use oral aciclovir prophylaxis for suspected HSV. Severe cases may perforate.

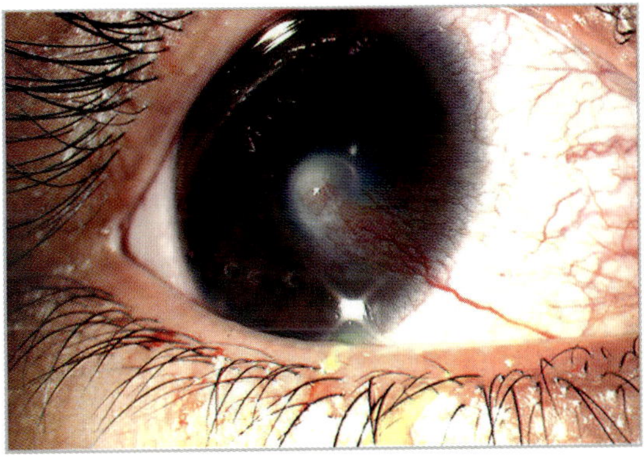

Fig. 6.16: Phlycten.

MARGINAL KERATITIS

Peripheral corneal infiltrates may develop without any clear precipitating factors, especially in patients with blepharitis (**Fig. 6.17**). Thought to be an immunological response to lid organisms or their toxins. An initially intact epithelium may later break down. No culture is required. The infiltrates resolve with topical steroids (e.g. G. prednisolone 0.5% q.d.s.). Treat any lid margin disease (lid hygiene and topical antibiotics for any acute lid disease, pp. 141 and 145) and ocular rosacea (p. 148).

Peripheral infiltrates can occur secondary to contact lens surface antigens (corneal infiltrative events or CIE). CIE is often asymptomatic. Symptomatic cases differ from bacterial keratitis in having an infiltrate, ± an overlying epithelial defect, that is outside the central 4 mm, without uveitis or pain.

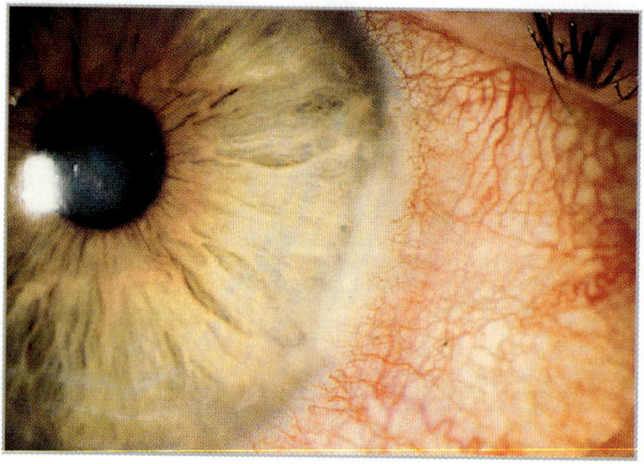

Fig. 6.17: Marginal keratitis.

BACTERIAL KERATITIS

Symptoms Unilateral red eye, pain, discharge, tearing and blurred vision.

History Ask about onset, risk factors (trauma, contact lens wear, and ocular surface or systemic disease), rate of progression, previous treatment and level of discomfort.

Examination Examine eyelids, conjunctiva, and cornea of both eyes for predisposing factors, e.g. dry eyes. Test corneal sensation. Draw the size, location, depth, shape and colour of the corneal infiltrate (**Figs. 6.18A and B**). Obtain anterior segment OCT and/or photographs to document baseline and change. Perform Seidel's test (p. 192) if perforation is suspected. Document AC cellular activity, including the height of any hypopyon. Bacterial keratitis does not cause endophthalmitis unless Descemet's membrane is breached, or has been previously (by trauma or surgery).

Differential diagnosis Bacterial keratitis has a sudden onset, rapid progression and a usually well-defined infiltrate with ulceration, typically in contact lens users and after trauma.

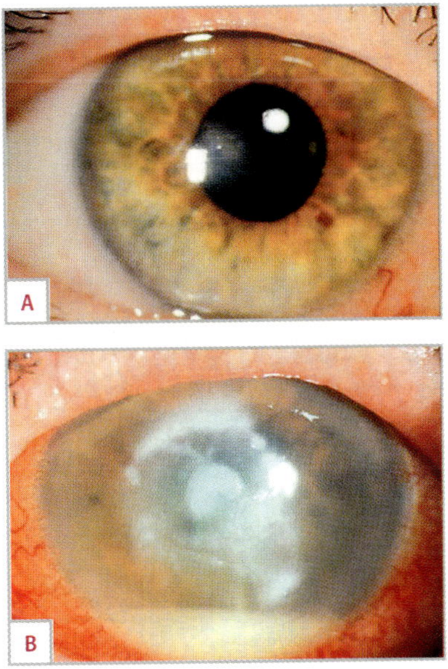

Fig. 6.18: Bacterial keratitis. (A) Small pneumococcal infiltrate. (B) Severe pseudomonal keratitis with hypopyon.

In the UK, ~98% of keratitis cases are bacterial, including 90% of culture-positive cases. Fungal and amoebic keratitis comprise ~2% of all and 10% of culture-positive cases, so exclude both if there is a less acute onset, more diffuse disease, raised infiltrates, or ocular surface disease. An initial bacterial co-infection occurs in 10% of *Acanthamoeba* cases. Rare causes of progressive keratitis include: polymicrobial infection with two or more of bacteria, fungus and *Acanthamoeba*; anaerobic bacteria (*Propionibacterium* and *Capnocytophaga*); *Nocardia*; *Mycobacterium*; and *Microsporidia*. Non-infectious causes include corneal infiltrative events (p. 271) in contact lens users (40% of contact lens keratitis), marginal keratitis (p. 226) and phlyctenular keratitis (p. 225).

Investigations Large, rapidly progressive and severely symptomatic cases require a corneal scrape (**Box 6.4**) to guide

Box 6.4: Taking a corneal scrape

1. Liaise with microbiology staff. Request an urgent Gram stain for severe disease.
2. Warm refrigerated media to room temperature.
3. Explain the procedure.
4. Instil G. proxymetacaine 0.5%.
5. At the slit lamp, use a 20-gauge needle to remove superficial debris from the ulcer, and then scrape the edges and base using a fresh needle for each inoculation (if using a blade instead, flame and allow to cool for 20 seconds between scrapes).
6. Streak material onto two glass slides for Gram and Giemsa staining (or other preferred stain). Air dry and label with pencil.
7. Take additional scrapes, one for each culture medium. Streak material onto agar plates without breaking the surface.
8. Plate onto blood agar, chocolate agar, and Sabouraud's agar.
9. If acanthamoeba is suspected, streak onto the centre of a non-nutrient agar plate. Use a Lowenstein–Jensen slope for suspected mycobacterial keratitis.
10. Tape the covers onto the plates to prevent evaporation.
11. Inoculate brain–heart infusion and cooked meat broth by agitating the needle in the media, or rub a sterile cotton swab onto the needle and then use the media container lid to break the tip of the swab into the media.
12. Culture contact lenses, cases, and solutions. Document that the patient understands these will be destroyed in the process.
13. Label all material, and transport immediately to the laboratory.
14. Cultures may be positive in 24 hours, but can take up to 2 weeks for fungi, acanthamoeba, or anaerobes.

therapy; if this cannot be done refer urgently to a centre that can, before starting therapy.

If available, corneal impression membranes (CIM) are a safer and easier alternative (**Fig. 6.19**), with similar culture positive rates for bacteria. Performed without a slit lamp. Instil G. proxymetacaine then place the membrane on the corneal surface for 3 seconds, avoiding the lid margins and lashes. Place the membrane into brain-heart infusion broth and send to microbiology.

Management In the UK, quinolone resistance is uncommon so start empiric therapy with a third or fourth generation quinolone, e.g. levofloxacin 0.5% or moxifloxacin 0.5%. For severe keratitis, use hourly overnight for two nights (omit overnight treatment for mild disease), then hourly by day for 3 days, then q.d.s. until the epithelial defect heals. Alternatively, use dual therapy with preservative free fortified aminoglycoside, e.g. G. gentamicin 1.5% and cephalosporin, e.g. G. cefuroxime 5% following a similar regimen. Admit if unable to comply with therapy. For more severe ulcers, prescribe G. cyclopentolate 1% b.d. If the cornea is thinned, apply a Cartella shield, without padding, and consider starting doxycycline 100 mg o.d. p.o for 6 weeks, or until re-epithelialised.

Review the patient with microbiology results after 2 days; change therapy only if microbiology results indicate resistance. Gram-negative keratitis may transiently deteriorate after the start of subsequently effective therapy, but with reduced pain. Review again in a corneal clinic 1–5 days after starting treatment, and if improving reduce antibiotics to q.d.s. and consider adding

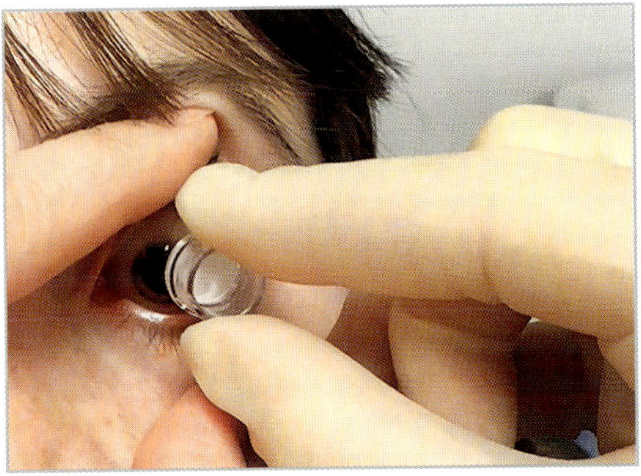

Fig. 6.19: Corneal impression membrane (CIM) sampling.

G. prednisolone 0.5% q.d.s. to reduce inflammation and speed healing. A large Indian RCT found that earlier introduction of topical steroids (within 3 days of onset) improves outcomes for severe bacterial keratitis other than *Nocardia*, but avoid in UK as fungal and *Acanthamoeba* keratitis is relatively common in contact lens users. Address any precipitating factor.

If not responding at day 5, ensure compliance, then refer to a subspecialist to exclude rare causes and resistant organisms with: confocal microscopy; specimens for identification of microbial DNA by PCR; re-culturing (± discontinuing therapy for 48 hours beforehand); and altering antibiotics based on antimicrobial sensitivities.

Corneal cross-linking is under investigation as a treatment for early bacterial keratitis and early fungal keratitis. Avoid for *Acanthamoeba*, fungal and deep-seated keratitis.

FUNGAL KERATITIS

History Ask about risk factors: contact lens wear, ocular surface disease, trauma or systemic disease. *Candida* keratitis occurs typically in patients with ocular surface disease. Contact lens wear is associated with *Fusarium* spp. and ocular trauma with both this and other filamentous fungi, most commonly *Aspergillus* and *Paecilomyces* spp., although many other species may cause keratitis.

Symptoms Unilateral red eye, tearing and blurred vision. Pain and photophobia are initially mild, but become severe relative to the clinical signs.

Signs The corneal surface typically appears grey with an elevated, rough texture often having a serrated edge (**Fig. 6.20**). Fibrin is less prevalent than with bacterial keratitis. Rarely, *Fusarium* spp. may be very rapidly progressive and indistinguishable from bacterial keratitis. *Candida* produces a small ulcer with expanding infiltrate, sometimes in a collar-stud configuration, often in patients using steroids for ocular surface disease. There may be an endothelial plaque under fungal lesions (easily visualised on OCT). Suppurative keratitis, fibrinoid uveitis, hypopyon, and elevated IOP may occur, particularly if advanced.

Differential diagnosis Herpes simplex virus, *Acanthamoeba*, and atypical bacterial keratitis, e.g. *Nocardia*, *Mycobacterium* and *Propionibacterium* spp.

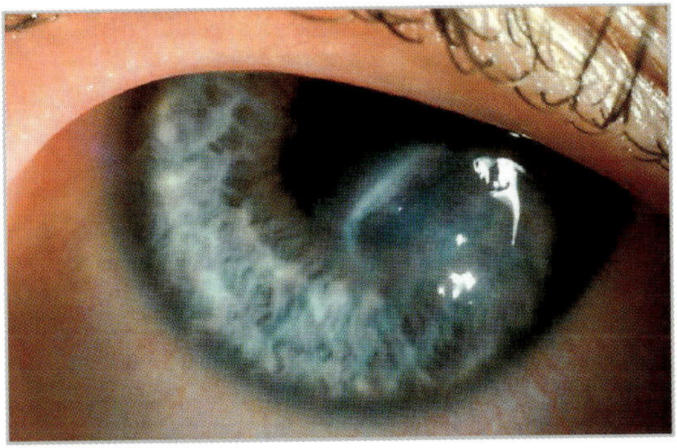

Fig. 6.20: Fungal keratitis (*Aspergillus fumigatus*) (Courtesy SJ Tuft).

Investigations Take a corneal scrape for smear and culture (**Box 6.4,** p. 228). The smear often makes the diagnosis. Liaise with microbiology. If the diagnosis is uncertain, obtain *in vivo* confocal microscopy and PCR; if not available and not responding, consider referral. PCR is commercially available, e.g. www.micropathology.com. If culture negative after 7 days, in unresponsive cases, perform a partial-thickness corneal biopsy. This must be large (3 mm) and deep enough to include the affected areas or alternatively mid-lamellar. Send half to microbiology, half in formalin to histology.

Treatment

- Stop topical steroids immediately.
- Start with G. natamycin 5% hourly day and night for 1–2 days, then hourly day only. Reduce dosing as signs improve. Switch to amphotericin 0.15% (same dosing) if *Candida* is isolated.
- If after 5–7 days the clinical signs are deteriorating add G. chlorhexidine 0.2% one drop half hourly for the first 3 hours, then 1-hourly for 2 days, 2-hourly for 5 days, and 3-hourly for 2 weeks.
- If any of natamycin, chlorhexidine or amphotericin is ineffective or unavailable, use G. voriconazole 1%.
- Use cycloplegics for pain relief and if there is significant uveitis.
- Use oral therapy for deep or peripheral fungal keratitis, e.g. voriconazole at the recommended doses for systemic disease (check liver and renal function at baseline and then weekly). Continue until clear signs of improvement, toxicity or intolerance.
- If there is suspected extension into the AC or sclera, consider anterior segment OCT or ultrasound to delineate tissue involvement and refer to a senior subspecialist.
- Recurrence is common, so continue treatment for 4–8 weeks after the ulcer and inflammation resolve.
- For culture-proven isolates, liaise with a microbiologist or infectious disease consultant.
- For severe keratitis (peripheral and deep corneal involvement), add oral fluconazole at the recommended doses for systemic therapy.
- If there is no response to above measures after 2–3 weeks, arrange therapeutic penetrating keratoplasty.
- Patients improving slowly may benefit from an intrastromal injection of voriconazole 50 μg in 0.1 mL, repeated at 1–2 weekly intervals as required.

Follow-up Initially 1–2 times weekly until there are signs of improvement or deterioration halts. This may take days or weeks. Fungal keratitis may be very difficult to manage and loss of vision, enucleation or evisceration are relatively common outcomes.

ACANTHAMOEBA KERATITIS

Background 85% of cases wear contact lenses, but trauma is also important. Protozoa may be isolated from contact lenses, water (fresh, salt, tap, swimming pools and hot tubs), dust, soil, or sewage.

History Ask about contact lens schedule (daily disposable or reusable), cleaning regimen, disinfection solution if used, swimming and showering in lenses, and the use of tap water to clean lenses or lens case. Initially, pain and photophobia exceed the clinical signs.

Examination Signs are usually unilateral and highly variable. The cornea may show superficial punctate keratitis, reduced sensation, and dendritiform lesions. Perineural infiltrates may be peripheral or central, and transient. Stromal infiltrates are initially minimal, patchy and widespread. Focal lesions are uncommon. Paracentral infiltrates may coalesce to form characteristic ring infiltrates (**Fig. 6.21**), but rarely in the the first month. Other features include disciform oedema, scleritis and mild uveitis. Hypopyon suggests bacterial superinfection.

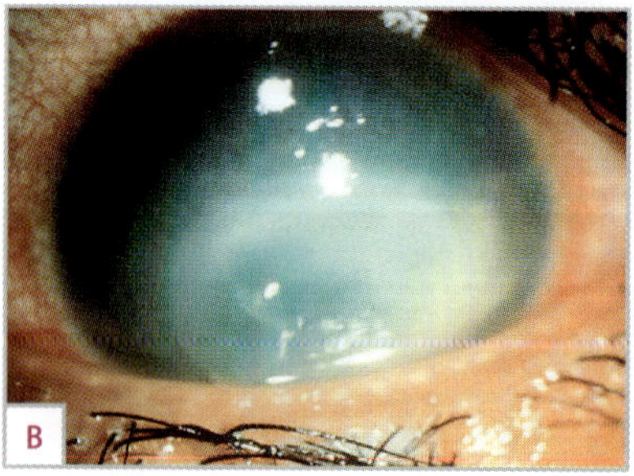

Fig. 6.21: *Acanthamoeba* keratitis. (A) Perineural infiltrates. (B) Ring infiltrate.

Differential diagnosis Can appear very similar to herpes simplex keratitis. Do not diagnose Herpes simplex keratitis in a contact lens wearer until *Acanthamoeba* is excluded. Also consider fungal or bacterial keratitis, e.g. *Nocardia*.

Investigations Arrange confocal microscopy before a corneal scrape (p. 228) to include PCR. Culture contact lenses, cases, and solutions. Explain that these will be destroyed in the process. A corneal trephine biopsy may be necessary if culture-negative cases progress.

Treatment *Acanthamoeba* cysts are highly resistant and *in vitro* susceptibility correlates poorly with *in vivo* activity.

- Discontinue topical steroids.
- *First line:* Use biguanides disinfectants, G. PHMB 0.02% or G. chlorhexidine 0.02%, hourly initially. As signs resolve, reduce to q.d.s.
- *Second line:* Add either G. propamidine 0.1% or G. hexamidine 0.1% hourly. Both are relatively epitheliotoxic.
- For resistant disease or exacerbations thought due to replicating *Acanthamoeba*, consider G. chlorhexidine 0.2% and G. PHMB 0.06% or 0.08%.
- Topical voriconazole 1% and oral voriconazole (at recommended doses for systemic disease with recommended hepatotoxicity testing) may also have a role in resistant disease.
- Superinfection, most commonly bacterial, is common both at onset and subsequently. Treat as necessary (p. 227).
- The use of topical steroids to control inflammation is controversial. Consider only if there is unacceptable pain (usually due to scleritis unresponsive to oral NSAIDs) or deteriorating corneal inflammation, and delay for at least 2 weeks after starting effective anti-amoebic therapy. Use the minimum potency and frequency needed to achieve the effect.
- For analgesia, start with oral NSAIDs, e.g. flurbiprofen 50–100 mg t.d.s. p.o, as inflammation drives the pain. If these and paracetamol are ineffective then add co-codamol or codeine phosphate. For painful scleritis unresponsive to NSAIDs and intensive topical steroids, oral prednisolone (1 mg/kg) with a steroid-sparing drug, e.g. ciclosporin and/or mycophenolate can be eye saving. The disease takes too long to control to safely use oral prednisolone as single therapy.
- Cure rates are ~85% at 12 months for medical treatment.

- The largest series of therapeutic keratoplasties reported poor outcomes so reserve for those with controlled scleritis, after 8–10 months of biguanide therapy, or for corneal perforation.

Follow-up 1–4 weekly until signs of resolution occur, then monthly as treatment is tapered off.

HERPES SIMPLEX KERATITIS

Background Herpes simplex virus keratitis (HSVK) may occur as a primary infection (first eye manifestation) in adults and children, but the first manifestation of HSVK is more commonly due to reactivation of latent viral infection arising from symptomatic or asymptomatic orofacial infection.

History Ask about potential triggers for recurrence such as UV light, trauma, cold, menstruation, psychological stress, systemic illness and immunosuppression. Ask about previous labial, genital, or ocular HSV.

Examination Test corneal sensation: hypoaesthesia occurs early. Examine the eye fully, as multiple sites may be involved.

- Primary HSVK may manifest as punctate keratitis, dendritic ulcers, corneal stromal keratitis (more common in children) and disciform keratitis, sometimes with lid and conjunctival signs.
- Recurrent HSVK:
  1. *Epithelial HSV:* Blotchy, stellate, or a filamentary keratitis usually progresses in 1–2 days to a classic dendritic pattern (branching lesions with feathery edges, and bulbs at the end) that stain with fluorescein (**Fig. 6.22**). There may be slightly larger underlying subepithelial ghost infiltrates. With prolonged infection or steroid use, a geographic or amoeboid ulcer may occur. There may be a mild AC cellular reaction.

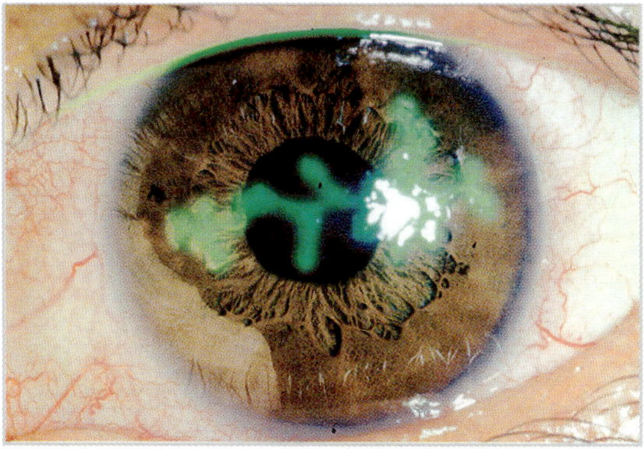

Fig. 6.22: Dendritic corneal ulcer (Courtesy DH Verity).

2. *Stromal HSV:* Three main patterns of disease exist:
   a. *Disciform ± endotheliitis:* A circular area of oedema with minimal infiltrate or vascularisation (except in recurrent disease) (**Fig. 6.23**). Fluorescein staining shows an intact epithelium, pushed forward by the underlying oedema. Oedema also produces folds in Descemet's membrane. Granulomatous keratic precipitates (KPs) occur under the disciform or elsewhere. There may be AC cells and the IOP is often raised.
   b. *Necrotising interstitial keratitis:* Typically shows intact epithelium, greyish-white stromal patches, corneal thinning and neovascularisation.
   c. *Necrotising interstitial keratitis with ulceration:* Beware of rapid corneal melting. A hypopyon may occur with stromal necrosis or secondary to bacterial superinfection.

Differential diagnosis

- *Epithelial disease:* Varicella-zoster keratitis, recurrent corneal erosion, healing abrasion, contact lens pseudodendrites and *Acanthamoeba* keratitis.
- *Stromal disease:* Other causes of interstitial keratitis (**Table 6.3, p. 223**), *Acanthamoeba* and bacterial keratitis. Do not diagnose HSVK in UK contact lens users without first considering *Acanthamoeba*.

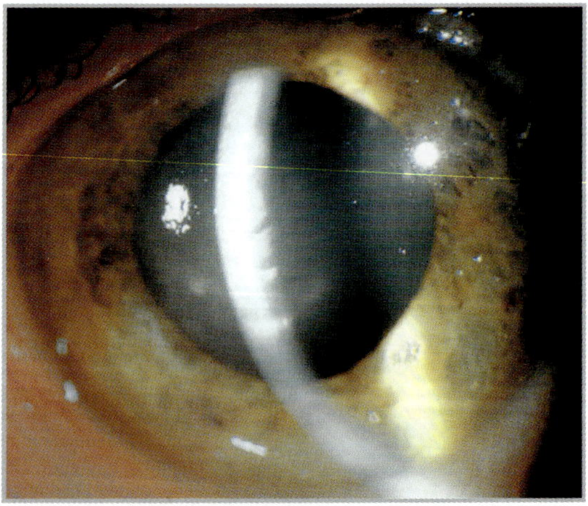

Fig. 6.23: Disciform lesion.

Investigations Viral cultures are not routinely available. Request PCR in all cases with epithelial involvement – HSV DNA is detectable in 30–80% if taken within 2–3 days and prior to antiviral therapy, however, false positives can occur. Epithelial PCR is not helpful for stromal keratitis but is positive in 50% of stromal biopsies. Request serology for stromal disease without a history of labial HSV, when the diagnosis is uncertain: IgG is usually positive after primary infection in the immunocompetent; IgM is high in primary infection and then falls. About 10% of the population converts per decade, e.g. 50% positive in 50-year-old people; negative serology excludes HSV but positive IgG serology does not confirm the diagnosis.

Treatment

- *Epithelial HSV:*
  1. Debride loose epithelium using topical anaesthetic and a cotton wool swab. Instil G. cyclopentolate 1%, Oc. chloramphenicol and pad overnight. Avoid if there is stromal involvement.
  2. Oc. ganciclovir 0.15% five times daily for 14 days, or at least 7–10 days after healing. Treatment may initially aggravate subepithelial ghosting. This usually fades within a year and does not require steroid therapy.
  3. Treat mild uveitis with G. cyclopentolate 1% b.d.
  4. While ulceration persists use G. chloramphenicol q.d.s. as prophylaxis against bacterial superinfection.
  5. Do not use topical steroids.
- *Stromal HSV:*
  1. Treat with G. prednisolone 1% q.d.s. or G. dexamethasone 0.1% q.d.s. depending on severity. Steroid treatment increases the viral load so combine with topical ganciclovir.
  2. Oc. ganciclovir 0.15% gel five times daily for 14 days with aciclovir 400 mg 5/day p.o. for 7 days then b.d. until resolution.
  3. G. chloramphenicol q.d.s. if there is an epithelial defect.
  4. Systemic steroids are not indicated.
  5. If epithelial healing has not occurred within 3 weeks, this may be toxic or neurotrophic requiring a change of preserved topical steroids to unpreserved. Failure to improve may also be due to a resistant strain (see below).
  6. Infection may be prolonged and damaging in immunocompromised patients.
  7. Threatened or actual corneal perforation requires glue or tectonic keratoplasty. Penetrating keratoplasty has a high risk of HSV recurrence and rejection, so defer until the eye is uninflamed and steroid free.

- *Endotheliitis (disciform keratitis):*
  1. This may result in endothelial cell loss and corneal decompensation. Treat promptly as described for stromal keratitis in 1 and 2 above.

For recurrent corneal epithelial or stromal disease use prophylactic aciclovir 400 mg b.d. p.o. for 1–2 years (reduces recurrences by 50%).

Aciclovir resistance occurs in ~5% of cases, indicated by epithelial disease taking >3 weeks to heal or >2 recurrences of stromal disease despite antiviral prophylaxis. Reference laboratories can perform a plaque resistance assay using viral culture, or PCR for thymidine kinase gene mutations. Treat resistant disease with combined ganciclovir gel 5–6 times daily, G. trifluorothymidine 6–9 times daily, oral aciclovir 800 mg five times daily, and, for stromal and endothelial disease only, add topical steroids as required.

HERPES ZOSTER OPHTHALMICUS (OPHTHALMIC SHINGLES)

Background Years to decades after primary varicella infection (chickenpox), latent virus in the trigeminal ganglion may reactivate. This produces eye disease and frontal/eyelid/nasal rash (ophthalmic division, V1).

Symptoms Headache, fever, malaise, chills and neuralgia. Ask about precipitating factors such as physical trauma, surgery, immunosuppression and systemic illness.

Signs Multiple sites may be involved:

- *Skin/lids:* Crops of clear vesicles on inflamed hyperaesthetic skin with V1 distribution, typically occurring 2 days after neuralgia. Vesicular fluid becomes turbid and remains contagious until scabbed (**Fig. 6.24**). Occasionally dermatitis does not develop.
- *Conjunctiva:* A follicular or papillary conjunctivitis is extremely common.
- *Episclera/sclera:* Focal inflammation.
- *Cornea:* Keratitis develops in ~65% of patients, often with a marked decrease in corneal sensation and a varied appearance. Fine or coarse punctate epithelial keratitis occurs. 'Dendrites' differ from those of herpes simplex virus (HSV, p. 227) in that they are fine, greyish, non-ulcerated, elevated, linear lesions that appear painted on (**Fig. 6.25**). They stain poorly with fluorescein and lack terminal bulbs. Gentle debridement does not produce a fluorescein-staining ulcer, unlike HSV. Coarse, nummular, anterior stromal infiltrates may occur subsequent to epithelial disease. Neurotrophic

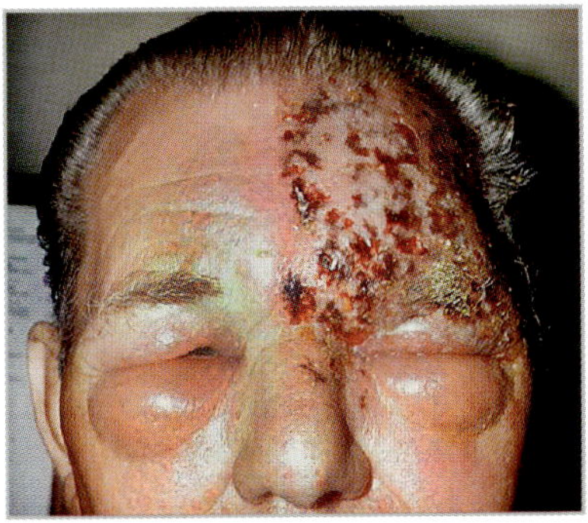

Fig. 6.24: Herpes zoster ophthalmicus (HZO).

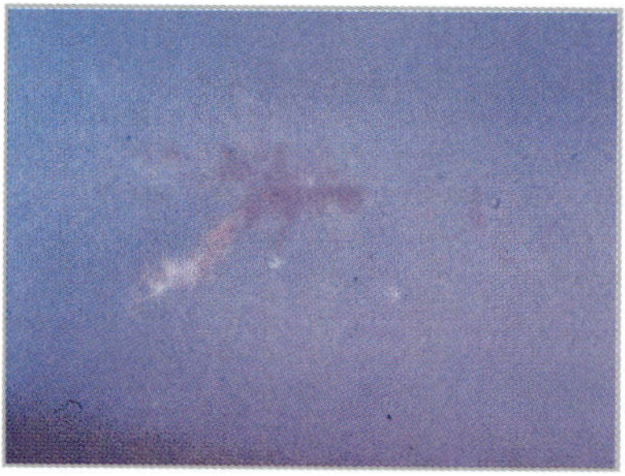

Fig. 6.25: Microdendrites.

keratitis occurs in ~50%. Disciform, necrotic, interstitial or peripheral ulcerative keratitis, or sclerokeratitis, may occur.

- *Anterior chamber:* 40% have cells and flare.
- *Intraocular pressure:* May be low, normal, or elevated. Marked elevation occurs in 10% (33% if keratouveitis).
- *Fundus:* Optic neuritis, central retinal vein occlusion, central retinal artery occlusion, necrotising retinitis (acute retinal necrosis), thrombophlebitis, localised arteritis ± exudates may occur.
- *Cranial nerves:* Palsies are not uncommon.

Investigations Herpes zoster ophthalmicus (HZO) is a clinical diagnosis, but virus may be cultured from vesicles for 3–5 days. Take a careful history to exclude immunocompromise and investigate if suspected.

Acute treatment

- Aciclovir 800 mg five times daily p.o. for 7–10 days or famciclovir 500 mg t.d.s. p.o. for 7 days, ideally starting within 72 hours of onset.
- Use skin toilet with or without topical disinfectants to prevent bacterial superinfection.
- For epithelial defects prescribe Oc. chloramphenicol 1% q.d.s for 7 days, or until epithelium heals.
- Use Oc. ganciclovir 0.15% five times daily for 2 weeks if there are pseudodendrites.
- For iritis or moderate to severe disciform disease with intact epithelium, use topical steroids commensurate with the severity.
- For unstable tear film or exposure keratitis, add tear substitutes, e.g. preservative free hyaluronic acid 0.2% 2-hourly.

- Offer appropriate analgesia and cycloplegia as required.
- For neurotrophic ulcers, consider botulinum toxin protective ptosis or central tarsorrhaphy.

The use of systemic steroids, bandage contact lenses, tissue glue, tarsorrhaphy, and corneal grafts all require senior input, as do immunocompromised patients.

Treatment and follow-up of chronic disease Corneal anaesthesia recovers fully in 60% in 2–3 months, but 25% develop permanent anaesthesia and neurotrophic keratitis. Disciform immune keratitis responds slowly and may require long-term, low-dose topical steroids to prevent recurrence. Skin lesions may take weeks to heal, and leave scars. Exacerbations of chronic disease may be associated with live virus in the cornea, so treat with a week of aciclovir 800 mg five times daily (along with the measures described above).

Post-herpetic neuralgia (neuralgia persisting for >1 month after the skin heals) may be severe. Topical capsaicin cream 0.075% to affected skin takes 2–3 weeks for onset of action. Use 3–4 times daily for 2–6 weeks, then as required once effect achieved. Continue for several months in older patients; 75% respond. Amitriptyline may help (initially 25–50 mg p.o. nocte, increasing in 25 mg increments every 3–4 days until taking 75–100 mg). If the pain is uncontrolled with these treatments refer to a pain clinic.

THYGESON'S KERATITIS

Background An uncommon superficial punctate keratitis of unknown aetiology.

Symptoms Intermittent episodes of irritation/foreign body sensation/pain ~50%, photophobia ~50%, blurred vision ~50%, redness ~15%, and tearing ~15%. May rarely be asymptomatic.

Signs VA is only mildly affected (6/9 or better in ~80%), and rarely worse than 6/18. Usually bilateral, but may be very asymmetrical. The cornea has discrete, elevated, whitish, crumb-like epithelial opacities that stain with fluorescein. Subepithelial ghosts may be present. Opacities are mainly in the pupillary area (**Fig. 6.26**).

Differential diagnosis Viral keratoconjunctivitis, granular dystrophy, and superficial punctate keratopathy.

Treatment G. FML 0.1% q.d.s. If unresponsive, try G. dexamethasone 0.1% q.d.s. Bandage contact lenses give symptomatic relief as an alternative to steroids.

Follow-up Review at 1 week; if settling, taper steroids slowly. Control of symptoms may require long-term treatment, used as necessary. The clinical course is characterised by exacerbations and remissions with a good visual prognosis (corneal scarring and vascularisation do not occur). Monitor for complications of long-term steroid use.

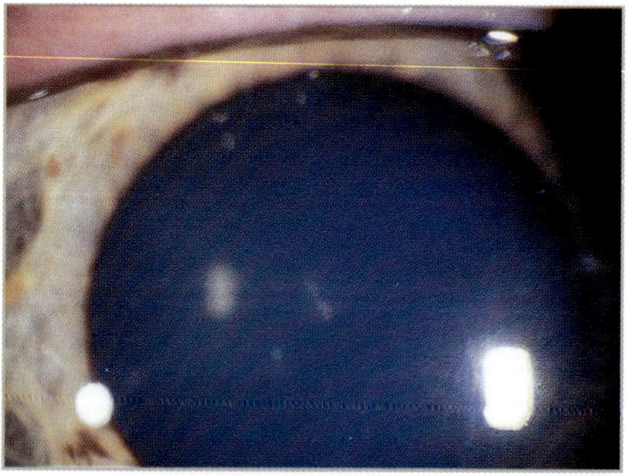

Fig. 6.26: Thygeson's keratitis (Courtesy SJ Tuft).

CORNEAL DYSTROPHIES

In the absence of genetic tests, most corneal dystrophies are diagnosed clinically. Opaque corneal deposits, epithelial and stromal oedema secondary to endothelial dysfunction, and stromal scarring from repeat epithelial erosions and chronic stromal oedema may all reduce vision. Management aims to improve visual function and relieve discomfort from epithelial damage.

Many corneal dystrophies have Mendelian inheritance, so draw a family tree (p. 493) and if possible, examine near relatives.

Epithelial and subepithelial corneal dystrophies

- *Epithelial basement membrane dystrophy* (EBMD) (map-dot-fingerprint dystrophy and Cogan's dystrophy): Common; no gene identified. Abnormal attachment between the epithelium and Bowman's layer causes recurrent erosions and persistent epithelial defects. These result in subepithelial 'maps' (geographic opacities), 'dots' (intraepithelial microcysts) and 'fingerprints' (subepithelial ridges) (**Fig. 6.27**). Any condition with repeated epithelial breakdown may produce a similar clinical picture, e.g. chronic epithelial oedema.

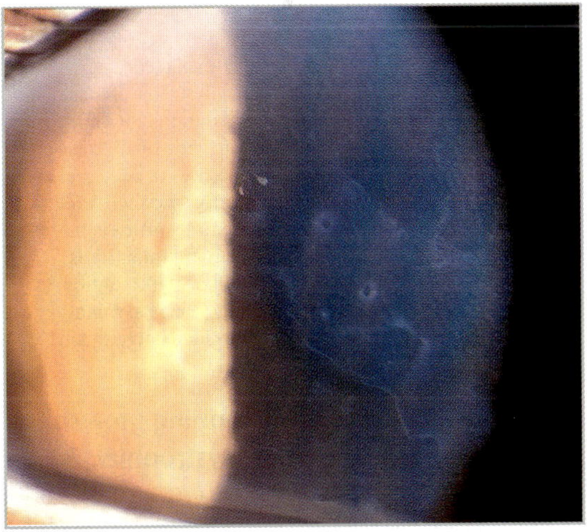

Fig. 6.27: Epithelial basement membrane dystrophy (Courtesy SJ Tuft)

Symptoms are usually nocturnal or on waking, varying from mild-to-severe depending on the erosion size. Minor trauma can trigger major epithelial breakdown. Symptom severity may not parallel slit-lamp findings. Fluorescein may show localised epithelial irregularity and epithelial defects. High-magnification examination of the other eye against the red reflex of a dilated pupil may uncover subtle abnormalities when the affected eye is too uncomfortable to examine in detail. No need to treat if asymptomatic. Otherwise, start with the least invasive treatment: preservative free lubricant drops, gels, or hyperosmotic agents during the day and/or ointments at bedtime. Escalate to bandage contact lenses to stabilise the epithelium, for 6–12 weeks. Consider oral tetracyclines, e.g. doxycycline 100 mg p.o. daily for 2 months, combined with low potency topical steroids, e.g. G. FML for 4–6 weeks, for recalcitrant erosions. Superficial keratectomy to remove devitalised epithelium, subepithelial pannus or deposits can improve epithelial–stromal adhesion and reduce irregular astigmatism. For persistent erosions outside the visual axis use anterior stromal micropuncture. For severe erosions in the visual axis mechanically debride loose epithelium (with a 21-gauge needle, corneal spatula or D15 blade) ± diamond burr-assisted polishing. Excimer laser phototherapeutic keratectomy (PTK), to create a focal 5–10 μm ablation just into Bowman's layer, is useful if irregular astigmatism involves the visual axis or if there is underlying anterior corneal haze/scarring. Mitomycin C can reduce postoperative scarring/haze from deeper stromal ablations.

- *Meesmann's dystrophy* (Meesman's epithelial corneal dystrophy, juvenile familial epithelial dystrophy, Stocker–Holt dystrophy): Rare and autosomal dominant (AD). Presents in the first few months of life with small, clear or grey-white, bubble-like epithelial opacities in both eyes (**Fig. 6.28**). Bowman's layer is unaffected and there are no associated systemic disorders. The central cornea is more affected than the periphery. Initially asymptomatic, as it slowly progresses symptoms of mild ocular irritation, photophobia, and blurred vision may occur. Basement membrane thickening may cause irregular astigmatism. Treat epithelial erosions as per EBMD.

Epithelial-stromal transforming growth factor β-induced corneal dystrophies

The transforming growth factor β-induced (TGFBI) dystrophies have overlapping clinical features that may cause diagnostic confusion. Histology and genotyping are required to confirm the diagnosis.

Fig. 6.28: Meesmann's dystrophy (Courtesy SJ Tuft).

- *Thiel–Behnke corneal dystrophy (TBCD)* (curly fibre corneal dystrophy, corneal dystrophy of Bowman's layer type II, honeycomb-shaped corneal dystrophy and Waardenburg–Jonkers' dystrophy): AD inheritance. Painful corneal erosions start during childhood. Subepithelial corneal opacities with honeycomb pattern are seen centrally with a clear zone at the corneoscleral junction. Recurrent erosions result in subepithelial scarring, irregular astigmatism, and reduced VA by the second decade. Erosions reduce with time. Manage erosions as per EBMD. Consider superficial keratectomy or PTK for visually significant opacities.
- *Reis–Bücklers' corneal dystrophy* (corneal dystrophy of Bowman's layer type I, geographic corneal dystrophy, atypical granular corneal dystrophy, granular corneal dystrophy type 3, anterior limiting membrane dystrophy, type 1): AD inheritance. Painful recurrent corneal erosions can occur throughout life, from early childhood. They may occur before corneal opacities. Confluent irregular and coarse geographic-like opacities with varying densities develop at the level of the Bowman's layer and the superficial stroma, initially central and discrete, then extending to the limbus and deeper stroma. Often confused with TBCD, but shows more irregular diffuse opacities with clear interruptions, whereas TBCD exhibits multiple flecks with reticular formation especially in the corneal centre. Manage erosions as per EBMD, and visually significant opacities per TBCD.
- *Lattice corneal dystrophies (LCDs):*
  a. Classic LCD (LCD I, Biber–Haab–Dimmer): AD inheritance of TGFBI R124C mutation. Presents with

central, superficial, fleck-like opacities, usually by the age of 10 years. In retroillumination, scanty isolated, subtle, and peripheral lattice lines are seen in the deeper layers. Thin-branching refractile lines and/or subepithelial, whitish, ovoid dots start centrally and more superficially, then spread centrifugally and deeper, sparing the far peripheral stroma (**Fig. 6.29**). Often asymmetric. Descemet's membrane and the endothelium are uninvolved. Corneal sensation is diminished. Diffuse, subepithelial, ground-glass haze of the central and paracentral cornea develops concurrently with the central and paracentral lattice lines and subsequently progresses. Recurrent epithelial erosions are common by the age of 10 years; manage as per EBMD. Visual impairment occurs by the fourth decade due to progression of diffuse central haze and may necessitate surgery. Deep anterior lamellar keratoplasty (DALK) is advantageous in sparing the unaffected corneal endothelium and although recurrence occurs, it may occur later (~3 years) than with PTK, superficial keratectomy and penetrating keratoplasty (PK).

b. Lattice corneal dystrophy variants (LCD type III, IIIA, I/IIIA, IV, atypical LCD, deep LCD and polymorphic corneal amyloidosis): Caused by >80 TGFBI mutations. AD inheritance. The phenotype may differ between eyes, and those sharing the same gene defect. Ocular discomfort ranges from severe discomfort in those with anterior geographic amyloid deposition to minimal or no pain in those with deep deposits. Treat erosions as per EBMD. Visual impairment also varies.

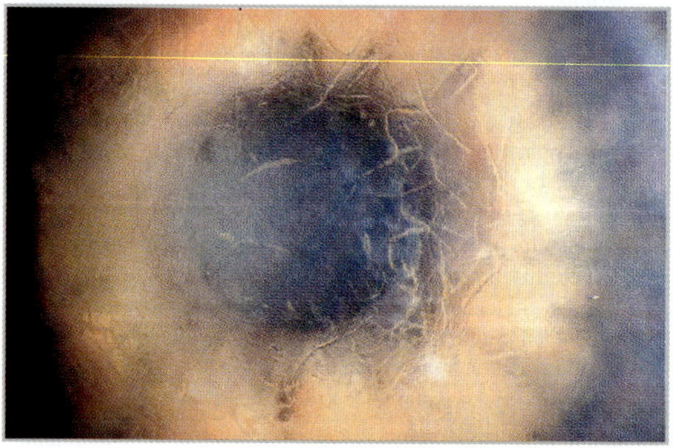

Fig. 6.29: Classic lattice corneal dystrophy-1 (LCD1)

- *Familial amyloid polyneuropathy type IV* (Finnish or Meretoja type; Meretoja syndrome): AD inheritance of gelosin mutation. More severe disease in homozygous patients. Not a corneal dystrophy, but a systemic disease with corneal findings similar to LCD. Reduced or absent corneal sensation may result in neurotrophic keratopathy, with epithelial erosions and persistent epithelial defects. Surface healing issues may occur after surgery. The corneal abnormalities are accompanied by a progressive bilateral neuropathy involving the cranial and peripheral nerves, dysarthria, and a dry and lax itchy skin with amyloid deposits in the arteries and sclera. Look for characteristic mask-like expression with protruding lips, pendulous ears and blepharochalasis.
- *Granular corneal dystrophy (GCD):*
  a. GCD type I (classic granular dystrophy, Groenouw type I dystrophy): AD inheritance of R555W mutation. Small white sharply demarcated spots that resemble breadcrumbs or snowflakes become apparent in the central cornea beneath Bowman's layer by the age of 10 years (**Fig. 6.30**). VA gradually decreases and painful recurrent erosion syndrome (RES) is common (~60%). The peripheral 2–3 mm remains clear, as does tissue between the opacities. Manage RES as per EBMD (p. 245); manage deep stromal opacities as per LCD (p. 247). Patterns of recurrence after surgery are highly variable, with recurrence appearing as early as 1 year after surgery.
  b. GCD type II (GCD with amyloid, Avellino dystrophy, combined lattice-granular dystrophy): AD inheritance of

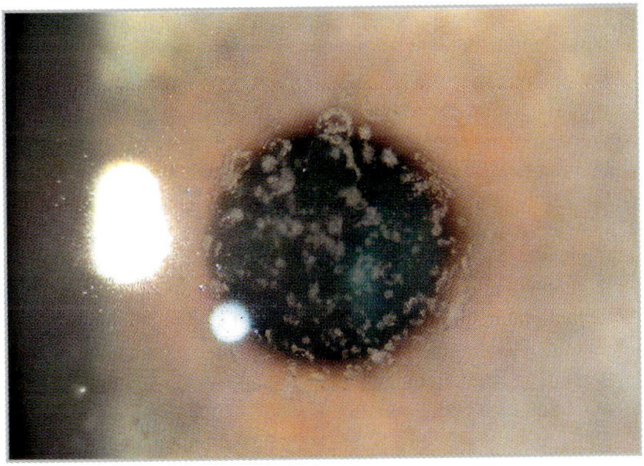

Fig. 6.30: Granular Corneal Dystrophy (type I) (GCD I).

R124H mutation. Mostly diagnosed during adolescence or early adulthood, but homozygous patients may be diagnosed as early as 18 months, heterozygous patients as early as 8 years. Phenotypic expressivity varies considerably; in heterozygotes initial signs are tiny, subtle, superficial, whitish stromal dots which typically develop small spokes or thorns. Heterozygous mutations produce fewer stromal opacities than GCD1. Homozygous patients demonstrate numerous small dots in the superficial cornea that by adulthood progress to deeper, larger, very dense, irregularly shaped opacities. Later, all eyes show superficial whitish discoid or ring-shaped patches with a moth-eaten appearance. Most patients also develop translucent spiky anterior to midstromal deposits. Patients may also have entirely translucent, short, dash-like linear or dot-like deposits in the posterior stroma. The lines or dashes are thicker and whiter, less commonly cross each other, and may have attached bulbs or spikes compared to the thinner lines of classic LCD, which are more refractile and characteristically intersect. Vision decreases slowly as the central cornea becomes more affected. Versus GCD1, there are fewer erosive episodes (~15%), less corneal opacification, and hence better vision. Corneal injury accelerates opacification, so excimer and femtosecond laser treatments are strongly contraindicated. Manage erosions as per EBMD (p. 245). PK may be required.

Stromal corneal dystrophies

- *Central crystalline dystrophy (SCD)* (Schnyder's crystalline corneal dystrophy, Schnyder's crystalline dystrophy sine crystals, hereditary crystalline stromal dystrophy of Schnyder, crystalline stromal dystrophy, and central stromal crystalline corneal dystrophy): AD inheritance. May present in childhood, but diagnosis is usually made by the second or third decade. Initially, a yellow/white central ring of needle-shaped, polychromatic crystals occurs in Bowman's layer, later arcus lipoides then midperipheral panstromal haze eventually cause the entire cornea to appear hazy. Corneal sensation decreases with age. Diagnosis may be delayed in patients who have the acrystalline form of the disease (~50%). The epithelium, Descemet's membrane, and endothelium are normal. VA decreases and complaints of glare increase with age. Although scotopic vision may be remarkably good, most patients >50 years of age have severely reduced photopic vision. Usually stabilises after childhood, but gradual corneal opacification may reduce VA to the point that corneal grafting is required. Infrequently recurs in the graft. Both affected and unaffected members of the pedigrees may have hyperlipoproteinemia (type IIa, III, or IV), xanthelasma and genu valgum.

- *Macular corneal dystrophy* (Groenouw type II dystrophy and Fehr speckled dystrophy): Three immunotypes (I, IA, and II) appear similar clinically. Initially, central, superficial, irregular whitish fleck-like opacities (macules) develop, that later involve the limbus (unlike GCD) and the deep stroma down to Descemet's membrane. Simultaneously, a slowly progressive diffuse haze involves the entire stroma. Larger central macules appear in the superficial stroma, with smaller and more discrete peripheral opacities in the deep stroma. The cornea is thin with reduced sensitivity. The epithelium remains smooth; recurrent erosions rarely occur. As the disorder progresses, Descemet's membrane becomes greyer and develops guttate excrescences, although frank endothelial decompensation only rarely occurs. Severe visual impairment occurs between age of 10 and 30 years requiring DALK. Clinically significant recurrence in the graft is rare.

Endothelial corneal dystrophies

- *Congenital hereditary endothelial dystrophy (CHED)* (Maumenee's corneal dystrophy): AR inheritance. Congenitally decreased corneal endothelial cell density (~10% of age-matched controls) gives rise to bilateral, often asymmetric corneal clouding that varies from milky ground-glass opacification to mild haze (**Fig. 6.31**), occasionally with focal

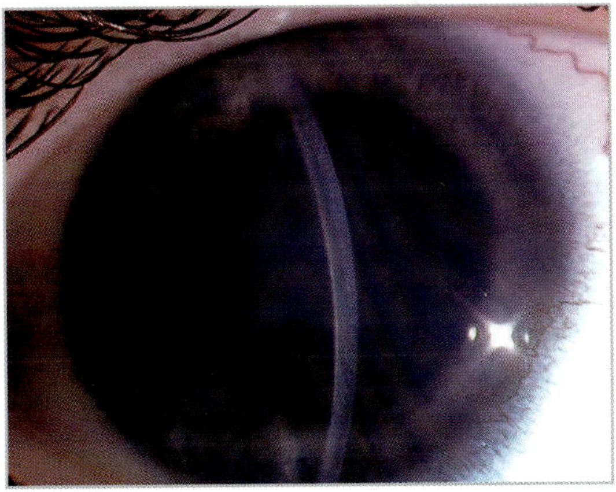

Fig. 6.31: Congenital hereditary endothelial dystrophy (CHED) (Courtesy SJ Tuft).

grey spots. Severe stromal thickening (about half normal) can occur but with minimal epithelial microbullae and minimal to no tearing or photophobia. Often accompanied by nystagmus. Check IOP. Harboyan's syndrome is characterised by CHED and progressive, postlingual sensorineural hearing loss.

- *Posterior polymorphous corneal dystrophy (PPCD)* (Schlichting dystrophy): AD inheritance. Three different gene mutations give rise to three subtypes: PPCD-1, 3 and 4. PPCD does not typically cause congenital corneal clouding. Often asymmetric and sometimes uniocular. Opacities of Descemet's membrane and the endothelium, best seen with retroillumination, have a wide variety of morphologic features: geographic grey opacities; vesicular lesions (typical for PPCD3), either single or grouped, often surrounded by grey circular opacity; parallel grey-white endothelial bands with white "flaky" material along the edges that may extend across the entire cornea (railroad tracks) often unilateral; occasionally, diffuse opacification of Descemet membrane and multiple larger vesicular endothelial opacities (**Fig. 6.32**). Endothelial changes are often unchanged over years. Possible slow progression of polymorphic vesicles and thickening of Descemet's membrane over years and decades is often asymptomatic, but occasionally causes endothelial decompensation. Visual impairment and pain may develop

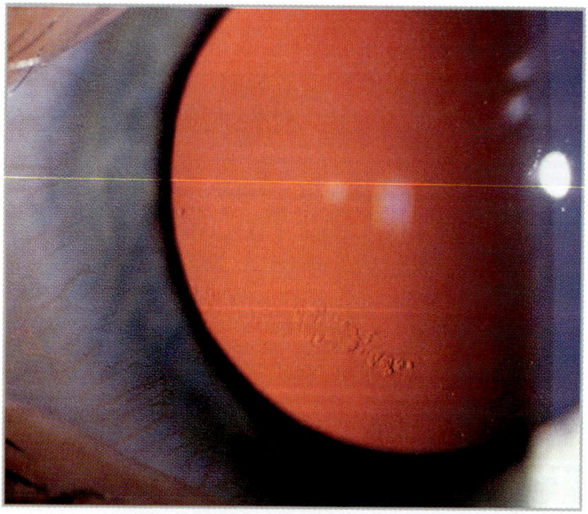

Fig. 6.32: Posterior polymorphous corneal dystrophy (PPCD) (Courtesy SJ Tuft).

secondary to corneal oedema, necessitating endothelial keratoplasty in 20–25% of cases. Both keratoconic and non-keratoconic corneal steepening are reported, with PPCD-3 usually demonstrating corneal curvatures > 48.0 diopters in both eyes. Peripheral iridocorneal adhesions occur in ~25% of cases and IOP in ~15–35%.

- *Fuchs' endothelial dystrophy (FECD)* (late hereditary endothelial dystrophy): Although AD, the genetics are complex and heterogeneous, demonstrating variable expressivity and incomplete penetrance. Usually presents in the fifth to sixth decade, sometimes earlier, with irritation or blurred vision, often worse on waking. Females predominate, 3:1. Corneal guttae start centrally and spread peripherally (Stage 1). Nonpigmented guttata may also occur with degenerative corneal disease, trauma, or inflammation. Nonprogressive guttata in the peripheral cornea of young patients (Hassall–Henle bodies) may have an AD inheritance and are of no clinical significance. The corneal endothelium may have a beaten metal-like appearance with or without pigment dusting. Descemet's membrane is irregularly thickened. Pachymetry shows corneal thickening. Specular microscopy shows increasing polymegathism and polymorphism. There is a strong correlation between central corneal thickness and endothelial cell count. It can advance to endothelial decompensation and stromal oedema (Stage 2), which may progress to involve the epithelium, causing intraepithelial and interepithelial oedema (epithelial bullae) and bullous keratopathy (Stage 3) (**Fig. 6.33**). Treatment includes

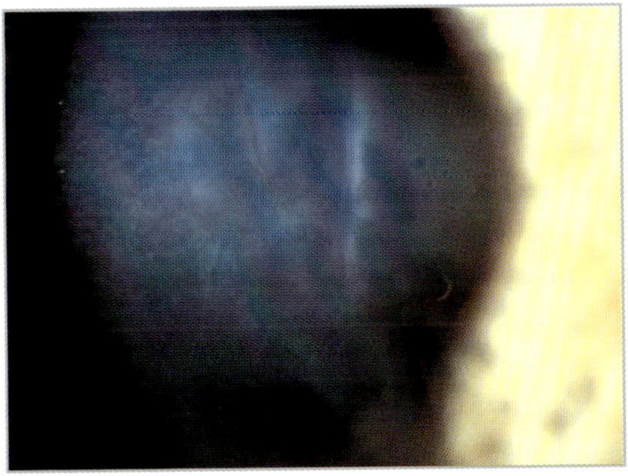

Fig. 6.33: Fuchs' endothelial corneal dystrophy (FECD) (Courtesy SJ Tuft).

G. hypertonic sodium chloride 5% q.d.s. to dehydrate the epithelium. Bandage contact lenses may relieve discomfort but use with caution, due to the high risk of microbial keratitis. Treat ruptured bullae as RES (p. 200). Intraocular surgery may accelerate disease progression, so take precautions (p. 320). May require posterior lamellar keratoplasty, e.g. Descemet's stripping endothelial keratoplasty (DSEK) or Descemet's membrane endothelial keratoplasty (DMEK), before subepithelial fibrosis, stromal scarring, and peripheral superficial or deep vascularisation from chronic oedema occur (Stage 4). Consider Descemet's stripping only (DSO) surgery if confined to the central cornea. Topical Rho kinase inhibitors (ripasudil and netarsudil) used q.d.s. can facilitate endothelial cell migration following DSO, and hasten recovery of post-operative corneal oedema.

For SCD, LCDs and GCD1 exclude paraproteinemic keratopathy (PPK) associated with monoclonal gammopathy of undetermined significance (MGUS), smouldering plasma cell myeloma and Waldenström macroglobulinaemia. Suspect PPK, if there is late and possibly unilateral corneal disease without a family history; test serum protein immunoelectrophoresis to exclude monoclonal gammopathy.

PTERYGIUM

Background Conjunctival growth into the cornea, typically in young to middle-aged patients, with a male preponderance. There may be history of exposure to high UV levels, wind, and low humidity, e.g. outdoor work in hot dry climates.

Signs A fleshy triangular growth encroaches a variable distance onto the cornea, with the base arising from the conjunctiva (**Fig. 6.34**). The lesion is usually on the horizontal meridian, particularly the nasal side, and may be inflamed. There may be subepithelial scarring or iron deposition at the apex (Stocker's line), and dellen with elevated pterygia. Measure the distance onto the cornea.

Differential diagnosis

- *Goldenhar's syndrome (oculoauriculovertebral dysplasia):* See page 100.
- *Inflammatory pannus:* Usually less bulky, often not on the horizontal meridian, and often associated with ocular rosacea and underlying corneal thinning.
- *Ocular surface squamous neoplasia (OSSN):* Dysplastic epithelium arising from the limbus which may coexist with pterygium. Previously termed corneal intraepithelial neoplasia (CIN).

Treatment Sunglasses to reduce sunlight ultraviolet A and B exposure. Treat ocular irritation with tear substitutes. If

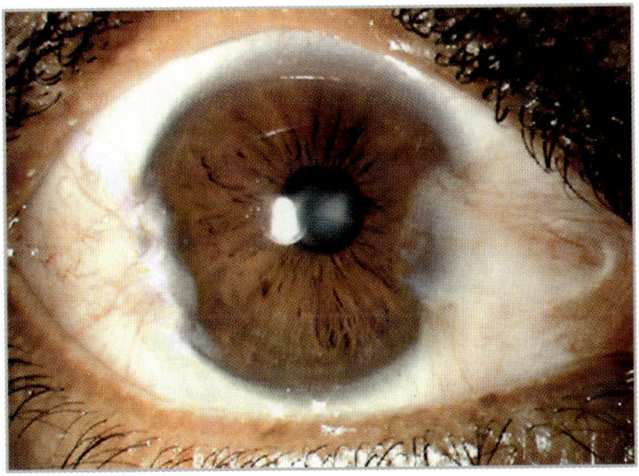

Fig. 6.34: Pterygium.

inflamed, try G. FML 0.1% q.d.s. for 1 month. Excise, or avulse, with conjunctival autografting, if symptoms are uncontrolled by conservative therapy or if there is encroachment into the visual axis. Send specimens for histology.

Follow-up If asymptomatic, review as necessary. If on topical steroids, check IOP in 4–6 weeks. Taper by one drop per fortnight when inflammation settles, then see as required.

BAND KERATOPATHY

Background Calcium deposits in the basement membrane, Bowman's layer, and anterior corneal stroma. A sign, not a diagnosis, of uncertain pathogenesis. Possibly related to exposure/evaporation, tear pH, and tear composition. Often idiopathic, but also associated with a range of ocular diseases—chronic low-grade uveitis (10–50% of juvenile chronic arthritis); corneal dystrophies (posterior polymorphous and congenital hereditary endothelial dystrophy); phthisis; silicone oil keratopathy; prolonged glaucoma; longstanding corneal oedema; metabolic abnormalities including hypercalcaemia and hyperphosphataemia. May be inherited (juvenile and mature type).

History and examination Take a full ocular and systemic history and examine for underlying causes. The amorphous pale grey deposits are seen peripherally in the anterior cornea, mainly in the palpebral aperture (**Fig. 6.35**). With time, the central cornea becomes affected. There is a transparent limbal zone.

Investigations Consider serum calcium and phosphate, if there is no obvious ocular cause.

Treatment
- Manage the underlying condition.
- *Mild irritation*: topical lubricants.

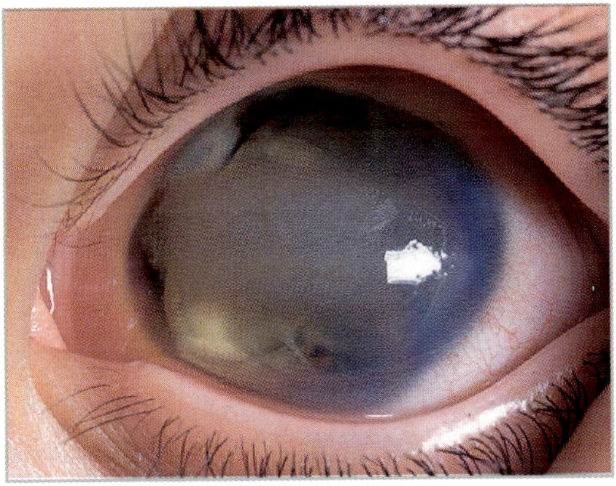

Fig. 6.35: Band keratopathy in an eye with buphthalmos (Courtesy DH Verity).

- *Moderate irritation:* bandage contact lens and preservative-free topical lubricants.
- *Severe irritation and reduced VA:* superficial keratectomy ± EDTA chelation, or excimer phototherapeutic keratectomy (PTK).

Follow-up Review 3–12 months, depending on the symptoms and underlying cause.

CORNEAL DEGENERATIONS AND DEPOSITS

Distinguish corneal degeneration from corneal dystrophies (p. 245). Corneal degenerations are structural abnormalities secondary to factors such as trauma, infection, increasing age, and others. Corneal dystrophies arise from an inherited or *de novo* genetic defect.

Climatic droplet keratopathy (Spheroid degeneration of the cornea, Labrador keratopathy, Bietti's keratopathy and pearl diver keratopathy) **(Fig. 6.36)**. Occurs mainly in men who work outdoors due to UV light exposure. Early on, fine subepithelial yellow droplets form superficially in the peripheral cornea. Later, droplets become central with subsequent corneal clouding and reduced vision. Excimer phototherapeutic keratectomy (PTK) may be necessary.

Terrien's marginal degeneration An uncommon bilateral peripheral corneal thinning disorder, without systemic associations, in men and women of all ages but often presenting in their 30s and 40s. Progression is variable but usually slow. Causes progressive peripheral corneal thinning usually starting in the superior or superonasal quadrant and progressing both centrally and peripherally, resulting in 360° involvement in advanced cases. White deposits occur relatively early at the

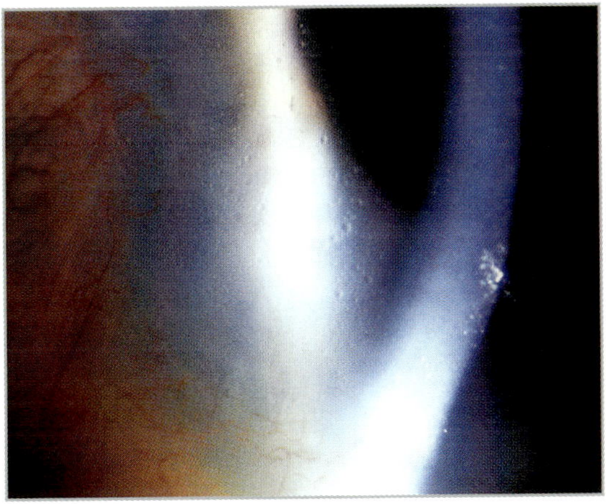

Fig. 6.36: Climatic droplet keratopathy (Courtesy SJ Tuft).

leading edge (**Fig. 6.14**, p. 222). Presents with both reduced vision due to progressive corneal astigmatism, and episodes of recurrent discomfort associated with limbal/anterior bulbar inflammation and photophobia. Inflammatory cells may be present in the ulcer and on confocal microscopy. The differential diagnosis (**Table 6.2**, p. 219) includes pellucid marginal degeneration, Mooren's ulcer and peripheral ulcerative keratitis (PUK). Carefully exclude the systemic associations of PUK (p. 218). Treat with spectacles, rigid gas permeable contact lenses when astigmatism becomes high or irregular, and scleral contact lenses when corneal lenses fail. Spontaneous corneal rupture is uncommon and keratoplasty is usually reserved for the few cases whose visual requirements cannot be met by conservative measures.

Band keratopathy See page 257.

Lipid keratopathy Extracellular lipid deposition from corneal vessels (**Fig. 6.37**). It may be idiopathic ± vessels, or associated with previous keratitis or disordered lipid metabolism (e.g. Fish-eye syndrome). If previous keratitis, treat any active inflammation to avoid further corneal neovascularisation.

Salzmann's nodular degeneration Degeneration of the superficial cornea involving the epithelium, Bowman's layer, and stroma, preceded by chronic ocular surface inflammation

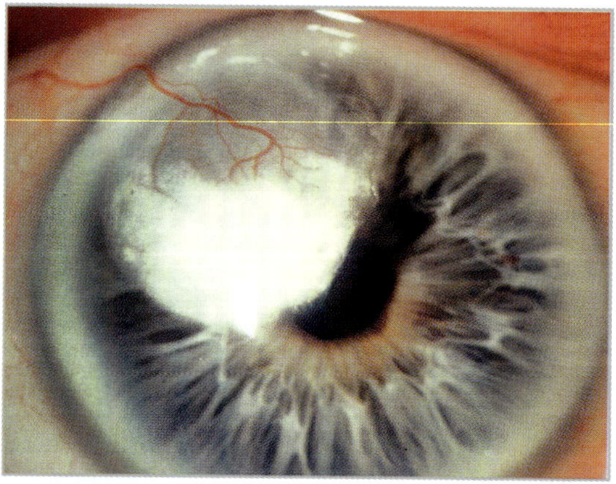

Fig. 6.37: Lipid keratopathy from herpes keratitis (Courtesy SJ Tuft).

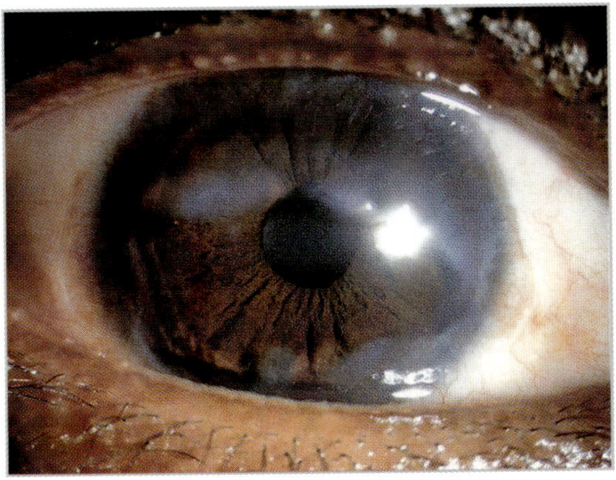

Fig. 6.38: Salzmann's nodular degeneration (Courtesy SJ Tuft).

accompanying any chronic ocular surface disease. May cause red eyes, irritation, and blurred vision. Bluish-white nodules of amyloid result in irregular astigmatism (**Fig. 6.38**). Treat the underlying cause. Consider superficial keratectomy ± PTK. The nodules may recur after surgical removal. A lamellar graft is rarely required.

Peripheral hypertrophic subepithelial corneal degeneration Has a similar appearance to Salzmann's nodular degeneration, but with a peripheral circumferential distribution, and is not associated with ocular surface disease. It usually occurs in white Caucasian females. The adjacent corneal limbus may have vessels and sometimes a pseudopterygium. A superficial keratectomy may be required for comfort, or to improve vision when the lesions encroach on the pupillary zone. The clinical course is relatively benign.

Corneal degenerations and deposits not requiring treatment

Arcus senilis (corneal annulus and anterior embryotoxon). Extremely common, bilateral, benign and peripheral corneal degeneration. Appears as a hazy grey ring ~2 mm in diameter with a lucent zone between it and the limbus (**Fig. 6.39**). Caused by lipid droplets in all layers of the cornea, especially the anterior and deep stroma. Check lipids in those under the age of 50 years.

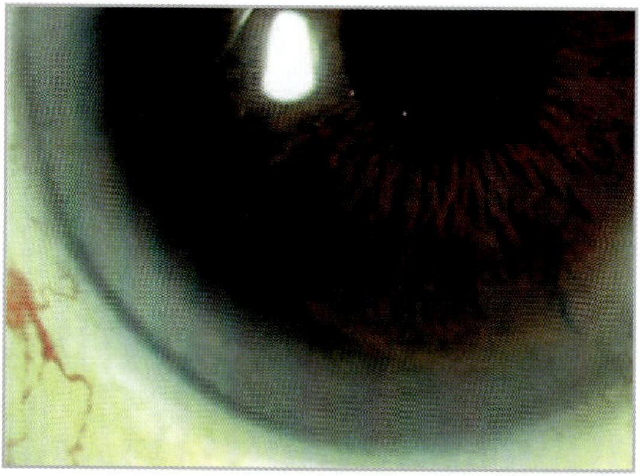

Fig. 6.39: Arcus senilis.

Kayser–Fleischer ring Copper deposition immediately superficial to Descemet's membrane, 1–3 mm inside the limbus—usually only visible with gonioscopy. Variable colour: brown, ruby red, bright green, blue, or yellow. Associated with hepatolenticular degeneration (Wilson's disease) and chronic hepatobiliary disease. Disappears with penicillamine treatment used to treat the systemic disease.

Fleischer ring Accumulation of ferritin within and between basal epithelial cells at the base of a keratoconus cone.

Vortex keratopathy (vortex corneal dystrophy, corneal verticillata of Fleischer, hurricane keratopathy and striate melanokeratosis): Pigmented whorl-shaped lines in the epithelium (**Fig. 6.40**). Associated with chloroquine, indomethacin, amiodarone, phenothiazine (e.g. chlorpromazine), and tamoxifen use, and clofazimine toxicity. Seen in Fabry's disease (X-linked recessive) and asymptomatic female carriers, so examine family members if there is no drug cause.

Hudson–Stähli line Horizontal iron deposition line at the junction of the lower and middle thirds of the cornea corresponding to the line of lid closure. Normal in the elderly.

Ferry's line Iron deposition line adjacent to limbal filtering blebs.

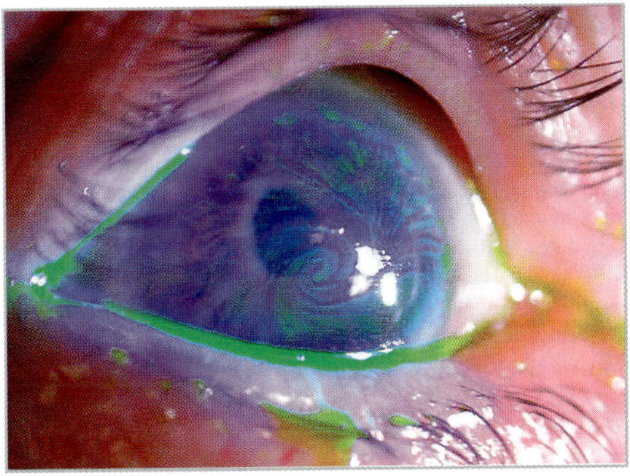

Fig. 6.40: Vortex keratopathy.

Stocker's line Iron line at the apex of a pterygium.

Phototherapeutic keratectomy An iron deposition line may occur at the perimeter of treatment.

Haemosiderin Golden-brown stromal deposits can follow a large hyphaema with prolonged raised IOP. Tends to resolve with time.

Corneal farinata Small grey punctate opacities seen pre-Descemet's membrane in the elderly. Does not affect VA. May be associated with ichthyosis and keratoconus. Sometimes larger, more polymorphous types of comma, circular and dot-like opacities are seen.

Mosaic (crocodile) shagreen Grey-white polygonal opacities, separated by clear spaces, in anterior or posterior corneal layers. Usually bilateral and most prominent centrally. Rarely, it reduces VA. Usually occurs in the elderly, but one juvenile autosomal dominant form is described.

Limbal girdle of Vogt Involves the interpalpebral and superficial stroma. Type I has no clear zone at the limbus with chalky-white deposits due to actinic damage. Type II has a clear zone at the limbus with lucent areas in superficial opacity. May be indistinguishable from early band keratopathy.

CORNEAL GRAFT REJECTION

Background Immunologically mediated graft rejection may occur at any time, but most often within 2 years of penetrating keratoplasty (PK). It may affect any part of the graft. A "classic" allograft rejection has acute inflammation with anterior bulbar hyperaemia, fresh keratitic precipitates, ± uveitis. However, the only sign may be reduced VA with increased corneal thickness, best detected using baseline then routine, regular pachymetry or anterior segment OCT. Treat stromal and endothelial rejection as an emergency. While "classic" rejection can occur after Descemet's membrane endothelial keratoplasty (DMEK) and Descemet's stripping endothelial keratoplasty (DSEK), more often the only findings are VA loss and increased corneal thickness reversible with prompt intensive topical steroids. Rejection rates for PK and DSEK are both ~20% within 5 years versus 1–2% for DMEK at 2 years, possibly because less stroma is transplanted.

Epithelial rejection A slightly raised linear opacity, confined to the epithelium, starts peripherally and migrates centrally over several days (**Fig. 6.41**). Mild perilimbal injection may be present, but there are usually few symptoms. Complete by 3 weeks after grafting. No change in treatment or review schedule is required, as it seldom leads to endothelial rejection.

Subepithelial rejection May occur up to 1 year following PK. Small, round, and subepithelial infiltrates in Bowman's layer are confined to the graft (Krachmer spots). There may be mild irritation, perilimbal injection, photophobia, keratic precipitates

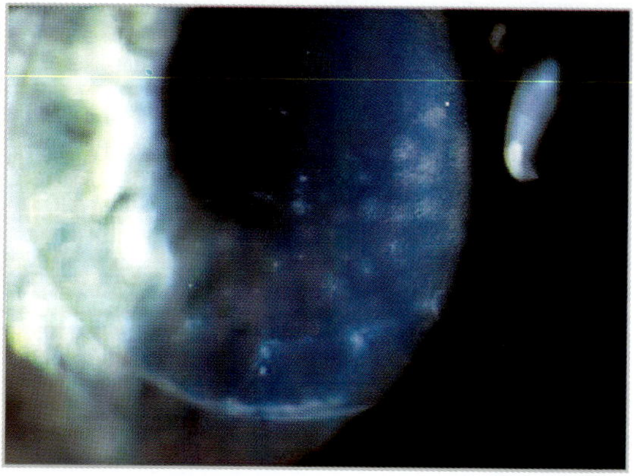

Fig. 6.41: Epithelial graft rejection.

(KPs), flare and AC cells. Only infrequently progresses to endothelial rejection, but treat with topical steroids to speed resolution of the infiltrates, e.g. G. prednisolone 0.5% q.d.s., until inflammation is resolved, then taper gradually.

Stromal rejection Only 1–2% of rejections. Rapidly spreading, dense, even infiltrate affecting all stromal layers, but confined to the graft. Vascularisation occurs late. Treat as per endothelial rejection. It usually fully resolves.

Endothelial rejection Carries potential for irreversible damage to the endothelium and subsequent corneal decompensation (**Fig. 6.42**). Two patterns occur:

i. *Focally progressive (25–45% of rejections):* Begins at the graft host junction. Cytotoxic lymphocytes from marginal vessels then form an advancing demarcation line (Khodadoust line) with clear cornea centrally and stromal oedema behind it. KPs, cells and flare are present. The differential diagnosis includes diffuse rejection, suture abscess, and epithelial ingrowth (usually occurs later and without uveitis or stromal swelling behind the line).
ii. *Diffuse (25–45% of rejections):* Tends to occur later than focally progressive cases. Variable severity. Cytotoxic lymphocytes from the uvea result in AC cells and flare. KPs are confined to the graft endothelium. The graft may be oedematous or remain clear if there is only mild rejection. DSEK and DMEK transplant rejection may be asymptomatic,

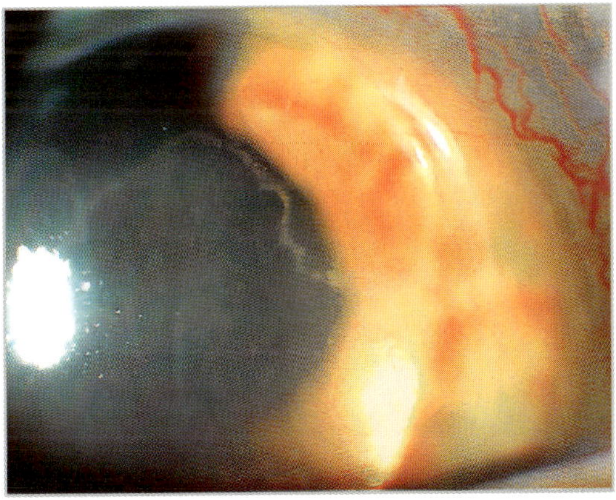

Fig. 6.42: Endothelial corneal graft rejection.

often precipitated by stopping topical steroids. The differential diagnosis includes anterior uveitis (KPs not confined to graft, more AC cells), and herpes simplex keratitis (raised IOP, no new KPs, AC quiet). Treat as follows:

1. Admit if compliance with treatment is uncertain.
2. Intensive topical steroids (e.g. G. prednisolone 1% hourly day and night for a day, then 0600 to 2400 hours, with Oc. Betnesol 0.1% nocte).
3. Cycloplegia (e.g. G. atropine 1% o.d.).
4. Systemic steroids if not responding within 24–48 hours, or for recurrent episode (e.g. prednisolone 40–80 mg o.d. p.o. with omeprazole 20 mg o.d. p.o.).
5. Control IOP if raised (e.g. acetazolamide SR 250 mg b.d. p.o.).
6. Review every 3–7 days until there are signs of improvement, then taper steroids.

ANTERIOR SEGMENT TRAUMA

Common traumatic ocular injuries described elsewhere include corneal abrasion (p. 197), angle recession (p. 367), retinal commotio, tears and ruptured globe (pp. 661–665), and optic neuropathy (p. 796). If an injury results from an alleged assault or workplace injury, carefully document the timing and circumstances of the injury and measure or preferably photograph all wounds. Consider tetanus prophylaxis and examine both eyes.

Conjunctival laceration

Look for a laceration with rolled or retracted edges and foreign bodies (FBs). Prolapsed Tenon's capsule appears white and oedematous. Brown pigment suggests a scleral laceration and prolapse of uveal tissue. Be aware of the potential for involvement of the extraocular muscles or of a scleral perforation obscured by subconjunctival haemorrhage. Remove FBs and prolapsed Tenon's capsule. Small, clean conjunctival lacerations require no suturing. Prescribe Oc. chloramphenicol q.d.s. 1 week. Larger (>15 mm) more complex lacerations may require suturing with interrupted 8/0 Vicryl. Avoid suturing the plica or caruncle. Be careful to appose the conjunctiva rather than Tenon's capsule. If sutured, review at 1 week.

Corneal laceration

History Pain, red eye, foreign body sensation, watering, and reduced vision.

Examination If the globe is ruptured, pressure on the globe may risk further ocular injury, so avoid tonometry, gonioscopy, and indented fundoscopy. Note the site, location, extent, and depth of the corneal wound. Seidel testing (p. 192) may be negative with full-thickness shelving wounds that self-seal. Note the AC depth, cellular activity, and any hyphaema. Look for pupil irregularity or iris prolapse through the wound. Traumatic mydriasis is common. Test for a RAPD due to traumatic optic neuropathy or retinal detachment. The IOP may be low, normal, or elevated. Dilate and examine the posterior pole and periphery.

Management

- *Partial-thickness:* Use topical anaesthetic, e.g. G. proxymetacaine 0.5%, and remove any debris. Only suture gaping wounds, in theatre, with 10/0 Nylon.
- *Full-thickness:* Apply a protective shield and prescribe antiemetic if required. Treat clean, self-sealing, full-thickness lacerations with prophylactic moxifloxacin 400 mg daily p.o.

(co-amoxiclav t.d.s. for children) and G. chloramphenicol 0.5% q.d.s. Treat minimally leaking lacerations with a bandage contact lens and G. unpreserved chloramphenicol 0.5% q.d.s. Leaking full-thickness lacerations with AC shallowing requires debridement and suturing (10/0 Nylon) in theatre. Admit, nil by mouth, except for prophylactic oral antibiotics. For more extensive damage, treat as a ruptured globe (p. 663).

Follow-up Review daily until the epithelium heals. Stop topical and oral antibiotics at 1 week if healed. Explain the symptoms of retinal detachment, endophthalmitis, and sympathetic ophthalmia, with advice to attend promptly if these develop.

CONTACT LENSES

Background In the UK, the fitting and review of contact lenses for most refractive error is carried out by community optometrists; while hospital optometrists undertake the fitting and monitoring of contact lenses for mostly complex indications such as:

- *Complex refractive error:* High myopia (>15D); high hypermetropia (>10D); aphakia; significant anisometropia; aniseikonia; irregular astigmatism secondary to corneal irregularity due to keratoconus; other corneal ectasias; corneal graft; infective events; trauma; and refractive surgery.
- *Therapeutic relief:* Commonly known as 'bandage lenses', soft or rigid lenses may be used for: pain relief; mechanical protection of the ocular surface; maintaining corneal hydration; or to tamponade leaking wounds. Examples include: recurrent erosion syndrome; bullous keratopathy; keratinised lids; misdirected eyelashes and corneal exposure.
- *Cosmetic improvement with or without therapeutic effect:* To provide an iris effect in aniridia or iris coloboma, to improve the appearance of scars, to improve the lid position in ptosis, or to enable refractive correction where spectacles cannot be worn due to facial deformity.
- *Occlusion:* To reduce vision partially or completely in the management of intractable diplopia, or to reduce light in cone dystrophies or ocular albinism.

The modulus of contact lenses measures their stiffness, influencing how rigid or flexible they are. High modulus lenses are easier to handle but may be less comfortable, while low modulus lenses are softer and more comfortable but can be more challenging to insert and remove.

History Ask about:

1. *Lens type:*
    - *Material:* Rigid gas permeable (also referred to as hard, GP or RGP), soft (hydrogel or silicone hydrogel) or hybrid (RGP centre with soft skirt).
    - *Size:* Most standard soft and hybrid lens diameters are 13.8 to 14.5 mm. RGP lenses may be described as corneal (≤ corneal diameter), limbal (the lens bears on the peripheral cornea), or scleral (the lens bears solely on the sclera and usually vaults the limbus and cornea).
    - *Frequency of replacement:* Soft lenses are usually either daily disposable, frequent replacement (weekly, 2-weekly, monthly or 3-monthly) or continuous wear (also known as extended or overnight wear with maximum recommended period of 6 nights). Most rigid lenses have a lifespan ≥ 12 months.

- *Refractive correction type:* Distance vision, monovision (typically one eye for distance, one for near), extended depth of focus (EDOF) and multifocal.

2. *Pattern of wear:* Average wearing time per day (in hours), number of days per week, any overnight wear and if so the number of nights, maximum wearing time per day, and last time contact lens worn before consultation.
3. *Cleaning regimen:* All-in-one solutions (AIO) are now almost universally dispensed for soft-lens users. The contact lens should be removed from the eye with clean, dry hands, rubbed in the palm of the hand with the AIO solution, rinsed with the AIO and stored/disinfected in the AIO overnight. Storage cases should be rinsed daily with the AIO, wiped out with a tissue and left open to air dry plus scrubbed with a brush and boiled weekly, and replaced monthly. Daily lens cleaners are still available for soft lens users struggling with lens surface deposits, but are not widely used outside hospital contact lens departments. Two-step solutions (daily cleaner and disinfecting/conditioning solution) are still in widespread use for rigid lenses, although multipurpose solutions are also available. Hydrogen peroxide solutions are available for use with both soft and rigid materials, and are useful if preserved solutions cause allergy and for persistent deposits. Protein deposits can be removed with enzyme tablets, usually once weekly.
4. *Hygiene:* Advise to wash and dry hands before handling contact lenses. Avoid lens contact with water due to the risk of *Acanthamoeba* keratitis (do not wash face, shower or swim in contact lenses). Do not wear contact lenses during sleep unless prescribed for this purpose.
5. *Use of topical medications:* Unless instructed otherwise by the prescriber, advise patients to remove contact lenses before instilling any topical ocular medication, and keep out for at least 15 minutes after. Soft lenses absorb water-soluble compounds, and accumulated preservatives can cause ocular surface toxicity, lens clouding, and increased drug bioavailability.
6. *Any adverse symptoms* (**Table 6.4**).

Examination Note the presence of scratches, defects, deposits on the lens, and the wettability of the surface. Remove the lens and examine the eye for the common contact lens-related problems shown in **Table 6.4**.

Investigations Arrange refraction and corneal topography to validate unexplained reduced vision, unexpected refractive change or suspected corneal structural changes.

Table 6.4: Summary of contact lens related problems, symptoms, signs, aetiology and treatment

Complication	Aetiology	Symptoms	Primary clinical features	Other signs	Treatment
Microbial keratitis	Bacterial infection with common pathogens including *Pseudomonas aeruginosa and Staphylococcus.* Associated with microtrauma, tear stagnation, poor hygiene, reusable lenses and overnight wear	Acute onset and rapidly worsening pain, redness, watering, photophobia, reduced vision	Central epithelial defect (ulcer) with underlying stromal infiltrate and oedema	Conjunctival hyperaemia, AC activity, lid oedema	See page 227
Acanthamoeba keratitis	Infection with *Acanthamoeba*. Associated with contamination by non-sterile water, poor hygiene, overnight wear	Pain far in excess of clinical signs. Slow onset over days	Irregular epithelium, possible dendritic keratopathy and patchy stromal infiltrates	Later signs: keratoneuritis (inflammation of corneal nerves), limbitis	See page 234
Fungal keratitis	Infection with pathogens such as *Fusarium* (the most common), *Aspergillus* and *Candida*	Slow onset over days	Dense, grey-white, raised stromal infiltrate with some ulceration and serrated margins	Minimal uveitis	See page 231

Table 6.4: Summary of contact lens related problems, symptoms, signs, aetiology and treatment—*Contd...*

Complication	Aetiology	Symptoms	Primary clinical features	Other signs	Treatment
Contact lens associated infiltrative events (CIEs)	Inflammatory response to bacterial toxins on the lens or lid margin	Mild watering, redness, irritation but no pain	Small, peripheral subepithelial infiltrate(s) ± overlying epithelial defect	Localised conjunctival hyperaemia	Discontinue lens wear until resolved. Monitor closely for the first 24-48 hours. Treat as microbial keratitis if any doubt. Review lens hygiene, modality, and treat lid margin disease before recommencing wear
Corneal abrasion	Mechanical trauma during contact lens application or removal or trapped foreign bodies	Sudden onset of pain and watering	Linear or sharply circumscribed epithelial break without infiltrate	Localised conjunctival or limbal hyperaemia	See page 197

Table 6.4: Summary of contact lens related problems, symptoms, signs, aetiology and treatment—*Contd...*

Complication	Aetiology	Symptoms	Primary clinical features	Other signs	Treatment
3 and 9 o'clock staining	Associated with poor tear movement, poor blink or over rigid contact lens edge	Often asymptomatic, variable discomfort during wear	Punctate epithelial stain at temporal and nasal peripheral cornea in rigid corneal lens wear	Interpalpebral conjunctival hyperaemia. Later stages show dellen and vascularised scarring	Refit with soft lens, larger diameter rigid lens or modify rigid lens edge profile
Inferior closure stain (inferior arcuate 'SMILE' stain)	Incomplete blink, dehydration of soft contact lens	Inferior redness and discomfort in soft lens wear	Punctate stain in inferior third of cornea	Inferior limbal/conjunctival hyperaemia	Blink hygiene, refit to lower water content or silicone hydrogel soft lenses
Superior epithelial arcuate lesion (SEAL)	Mechanical pressure from tight-fitting contact lens	Irritation and photophobia	Full-thickness linear epithelial lesion in the peripheral superior cornea	Superior limbal/conjunctival hyperaemia	Discontinue wear until healed, refit to lower modulus lens material

Table 6.4: Summary of contact lens related problems, symptoms, signs, aetiology and treatment—*Contd...*

Complication	Aetiology	Symptoms	Primary clinical features	Other signs	Treatment
Solution-induced corneal staining (SICS)	Toxicity and/or hypersensitivity response to compounds adsorbed onto or into the contact lens	Stinging on insertion of contact lens, dryness, redness at the end of wearing time, itching and mucous discharge	Diffuse or midperipheral annular corneal punctate staining	Low-grade inflammation, diffuse conjunctival hyperaemia	Change to daily disposable lens, or use non-PHMB-based or preservative free care solutions
Dimple veil	Static air bubbles under rigid corneal contact lens	Possible blurred vision	Fluorescein pooling in localised epithelial depressions	None	Refit rigid corneal lens to improve alignment or change lens type
Hypoxia	Metabolic stress resulting from limited oxygen transmission to the cornea in contact lens wear, due to contact lens material or ineffective tear pump	None or mild irritation, blurred vision in some cases	Epithelial microcysts, oedema and vacuoles; superficial or deep vascularisation; stromal striae or folds; endothelial polymegathism and pleomorphism	Circumlimbal flush, diffuse, punctate or coalesced fluorescein staining	Stop wear until settled then review contact lens material, contact lens fit and wearing schedule

Table 6.4: Summary of contact lens related problems, symptoms, signs, aetiology and treatment—*Contd...*

Complication	Aetiology	Symptoms	Primary clinical features	Other signs	Treatment
Contact lens-associated papillary conjunctivitis (CLAPC)	Inflammatory response, either mechanical from contact lens fit/design, or hypersensitivity to deposits on contact lens surface	Itching, irritation, increasing mucous discharge, smearing of vision in contact lenses	Mild to 'giant' papillae and associated diffuse hyperaemia of upper tarsal conjunctiva ± mucus	Mild superficial punctate keratopathy	Remove current contact lens, review lens hygiene, frequency of replacement, material and fit
Lid wiper epitheliopathy (LWE)	Mechanical friction due to poor lubrication between lid margin and anterior contact lens surface	Discomfort	Linear lissamine green/ fluorescein staining of marginal conjunctiva	None	Review contact lens material, modality and improve lubrication
Corneal warpage	Mechanical or hypoxic effect of rigid or high modulus lenses	Good vision in contact lens and poor vision with spectacles	Irregular corneal topographical changes	Variable refractive endpoint and visual symptoms	Refit with high-oxygen transmission lenses. Topography usually normalises unless this is the first sign of keratoconus

Therapeutic (bandage) contact lens fitting Aim to fit a lens that is stable on the cornea, produces minimal ocular surface disruption, and is comfortable. Most therapeutic soft lenses are silicone hydrogel with a choice of back optic zone radius (BOZR, typically 8.40–8.60 mm) and overall diameter (typically 13.50–14.20 mm) in plano or low minus powers. Choose a larger overall diameter lens for a less regular cornea to improve stability. The lens should be well-centred on the cornea, move freely on intentional displacement using the lower lid, but not >0.5 mm on blink. Allow the lens to settle for 20 minutes then recheck the fit to exclude tight lens syndrome (lens tightens after insertion). If the lens is too static, replace with a flatter (larger) BOZR lens and/or a smaller diameter.

LASER REFRACTIVE SURGERY

Background Excimer laser refractive surgery procedures are commonly used to correct myopia, hypermetropia and astigmatism. In the UK, this is predominantly undertaken in the private sector, but treatment can influence the management of conditions seen in the National Health Service, e.g. cataract and glaucoma. Some postoperative complications may present acutely to emergency departments, e.g. dislocated laser-assisted *in situ* keratomileusis (LASIK) flaps or deep lamellar keratitis. A basic understanding is therefore worthwhile.

Basic principles Excimer (excited dimer) laser photoablation can remove corneal tissue with submicron accuracy, without thermal build up or adjacent tissue damage. Myopia can be corrected by removing tissue from the central cornea, resulting in central flattening and reduced refractive power. In hyperopia, tissue is removed from the peripheral cornea resulting in steepening of the central cornea and increased refractive power.

Femtosecond lasers emit light pulses of short duration (10^{-15} seconds) at 1,053 nm wavelength that causes photodisruption of the tissue with minimum collateral damage. This enables bladeless incisions to be performed within the tissue at various patterns and depth with high precision, safety and repeatability. Femtosecond laser can be used for many anterior refractive procedures; LASIK flap creation, keratorefractive lenticule extraction (KLEx), corneal graft surgery, astigmatic keratectomy, and channel cutting for insertion of intracorneal ring segments.

Contraindications Relative ocular contraindications include severe dry eyes, severe atopy, keratoconus, previous herpetic keratitis, neurotrophic corneas and nystagmus. Relative systemic contraindications include collagen vascular diseases, pregnancy, hormone replacement therapy, and immunocompromise, e.g. HIV infection.

Surgical techniques There are four main refractive procedures (**Table 6.5**)—photorefractive keratectomy (PRK), LASIK, laser subepithelial keratomileusis (LASEK) and KLEx. All use topical anaesthesia.

- Photorefractive keratectomy

  Involves removal of the corneal epithelium followed by photoablation of Bowman's layer and the anterior stroma.

Trans-PRK is a modification of PRK where the epithelial cells are removed by the excimer laser, prior to reshaping of the stromal bed. After treatment, a bandage of contact lens is inserted. Mild-to-severe foreign body sensation is normal for 3–4 days

Table 6.5: Efficacy and safety of excimer laser refractive procedures

Parameters	PRK	LASEK	LASIK	KLEx
Ablation	Surface	Surface	Intrastromal	Intrastromal
Refractive predictability (±1D)	91%	98%	98%	98%
Refractive stability	1–3 months	3–4 weeks	2–3 weeks	1 week
Visual recovery	3–7 days	3–7 days	24 hours	24 hours
Postoperative pain	Moderate, 24–48 hours	Mild, 24–48 hours	Very mild, 12 hours	Very mild, 12 hours
Postoperative topical steroids	3 weeks to 3 months	3 weeks to 3 months	1–2 weeks	1 week to 3 months
Significant intraoperative complications	Rare	Rare	Flap-related problems (0.3%)	Rare
Postoperative complications	Corneal haze (1–2%)	Corneal haze	Flap and interface problems (4%), infectious keratitis (1:7,500), epithelial ingrowth (<1%), diffuse lamellar keratitis (<1%), dry eyes, keratectasia	Trace corneal haze (4–19%), interface inflammation (0.3–1.6%), keratitis (0.3%)
Recovery from dry eyes	4 weeks to 6 months	4 weeks to 6 months	Up to 12 months	Up to 6 months

(KLEx, keratorefractive lenticule extraction; LASEK, laser subepithelial keratomileusis; LASIK, laser-assisted *in situ* keratomileusis; PRK, photorefractive keratectomy) postoperatively, until the corneal surface has re- epithelialised. PRK is safe and effective for correcting low myopia. The use of PRK was limited by the corneal wound healing response, causing corneal haze, with subsequent reduced contrast sensitivity and VA, and unpredictable refractive regression. More recently, intraoperative topical mitomycin has been used to limit the wound healing response.

- *Laser-assisted* in situ *keratomileusis:* A hinged flap is cut in the anterior stroma with a femtosecond laser or mechanical microkeratome. The flap is usually 110–180 μm thick and 8–9 mm in diameter. The hinge may be superior or nasal. The flap is lifted and the excimer laser treatment applied to the exposed stromal bed. The flap is then repositioned. Visual recovery is rapid and stable. There is minimal damage to the epithelium, so postoperative foreign body sensation is mild and short-lived. Haze is only seen at the periphery of the flap where Bowman's layer has been cut. However, the procedure is technically more challenging with the risk of intraoperative and postoperative flap-related complications and ectasia if a residual stromal bed of >250 μm has not been left, or the patient had *forme fruste* keratoconus preoperatively.
- *Laser subepithelial keratomileusis:* A modification of PRK that preserves the epithelial sheet. The epithelium is peeled back with a modified mechanical keratome (Epi-LASIK) or manually after application of 20% ethanol (LASEK). The excimer laser treatment is applied to the stromal bed. The epithelium is then repositioned and a bandage lens applied to protect the epithelium while it heals. The retention of the epithelium is said to reduce postoperative pain and speed visual recovery. Intraoperative application of mitomycin C limits postoperative haze.
- *Keratorefractive lenticule extraction:* A femtosecond-only procedure that removes stromal tissue (the lenticule) without a flap. Multiple commercial options exist: small-incision lenticule extraction (SMILE), corneal lenticule extraction for advanced refractive correction (CLEAR), smooth incision lenticule keratomileusis (SILK), and small incision–guided human-cornea treatment (SmartSight). The femtosecond laser creates the posterior surface, vertical sides and anterior surface of the lenticule, and a small tunnel for extraction of the lenticule. The cap thickness (above the lenticule) is typically 100–120 μm. The lenticule thickness depends on the refractive error. KLEx shows excellent efficacy, safety, predictability, and avoids flap-related complications. There is reduced damage to Bowman's layer with better biomechanical integrity and corneal stability. The basal nerve plexus is minimally disrupted, reducing dry eye and patient discomfort.

Outcomes

- Results obtained with different lasers and microkeratomes are not directly comparable.
- Excimer laser refractive procedures are safe and effective for the correction of mild-to-moderate myopia. The predictability decreases in myopia > 8D, hypermetropia > 4D, astigmatism > 3D, and therapeutic treatments, e.g. correction of post-penetrating keratoplasty astigmatism.
- Complications occur in ~5%, but ≤1% are sight-threatening. Complications include: scarring; flap trauma and button holes; epithelial ingrowth; flap folds; keratectasia; inflammation (diffuse lamellar keratitis); microbial keratitis; dry eye; retinal detachment; decentred optical zone; and irregular astigmatism.
- Dislocated or wrinkled flaps of short duration can be floated back into position in the operating theatre or sutured. Amputation of the flap may be necessary.
- Following LASIK, the interface between the flap and stroma may become inflamed (deep lamellar keratitis, DLK). DLK may occur in the immediate postoperative period, or later in response to epithelial abrasion or superficial infection. Treat the triggering event with frequent topical steroids, unless contraindicated, e.g. G. prednisolone 1% six times daily. As the inflammation settles, taper off steroids. The differential diagnosis includes interface infection (below).
- Interface infection is rare and often caused by low virulence organisms, e.g. *Mycobacteria*. Emergency treatment is required. It is usually necessary to lift the flap to obtain material for culture and sensitivity testing (p. 228). Apply frequent and fortified broad spectrum topical antibiotics. Amikacin is particularly useful for its activity against low virulence organisms, e.g. *Nocardia* and *Mycobacteria*. Flap amputation may be necessary.
- Epithelial ingrowth is unusual unless the flap has been button-holed or lifted for retreatment.
- Treatment dry eye for at least 6–8 months following LASIK, and any retreatment.
- Most keratometers and topography systems assume that the cornea has a spherical profile with a constant relationship between the anterior and posterior corneal surfaces. Following excimer refractive surgery these assumptions no longer hold true. As a consequence, conventional biometry is inaccurate. Following treatment for myopia biometry tends to underestimate IOL power required, resulting in postoperative hypermetropia. Following refractive surgery, advanced biometric calculations are required (pp. 287 and 290).

OPTOMETRY AND GENERAL PRACTICE GUIDELINES

General comments

The most urgent corneal referral is microbial keratitis. Compared to conjunctivitis, there is less likely to be a history of contact with eye infection or systemic viral features such as a sore throat, and more likely to be history of contact lens wear or pre-existing corneal disease, with pain and reduced vision. Look for a white corneal infiltrate and focal fluorescein staining. Corneal scrapes taken prior to antibiotic therapy have a higher yield, so if microbial keratitis is suspected refer urgently without starting treatment. Conjunctival swabs have a low yield in corneal infection. Advise contact lens wearers to bring their lenses, solutions, and cases for testing.

Immediately refer patients with corneal grafts if they notice blurred vision, inflammation, or pain. The risk of graft rejection is life-long, and may occur decades after successful corneal transplant surgery.

General practice

Use magnification to visualise small corneal abnormalities such as foreign bodies, ulcers, and abrasions. The ophthalmoscope with a plus lens dialled up to focus on the cornea, or an auroscope with the earpiece removed, both give a magnified view of the cornea; much can be seen with the naked eye and a good light. Fluorescein is extremely helpful in this setting—one drop of proxymetacaine in both eyes may also make the examination easier. Many corneal conditions such as herpes simplex keratitis, Thygeson's keratitis, and recurrent erosion syndrome run a relapsing and remitting course, with recurrence even while the patient is being treated. It is preferable to refer back urgently rather than to alter medication. The use of steroid eye drops should be supervised by an ophthalmologist.

Optometrists

Patients with corneal diseases and poor spectacle-corrected acuity may have irregular astigmatism improved by fitting a rigid contact lens; this is typical of early keratoconus. Tear film abnormalities may cause visual changes when the patient concentrates and the blink rate reduces, such as when driving or reading. Tear substitutes such as hyaluronic acid are available over the counter, but treat any accompanying blepharitis.

Corneal infiltrates associated with contact lenses (corneal infiltrative events or CIE) and marginal keratitis need to be differentiated from bacterial keratitis (pp. 226 and 227). If in doubt, refer urgently to rule out bacterial keratitis.

Immediate

- Penetrating corneal trauma p. 267
- Bacterial keratitis p. 227

Same day

- Herpes simplex keratitis p. 237
- Herpes (varicella-) zoster keratitis p. 241
- Corneal graft rejection p. 264

Urgent (within 1 week)

- Severe dry eyes with rheumatoid arthritis p. 207

Routine

- Suspected corneal dystrophy p. 245
- Keratoconus p. 213
- Dry eyes p. 207
- Corneal degenerations p. 259

CATARACT SURGERY

7

Yashin Ramkissoon, Alex Ionides,
Carol Cunningham & Alexander Day

Background Cataract is the leading cause of treatable blindness globally, primarily affecting older adults. About 30% of people over 65 years of age and 70% of those over 85 years old develop visually significant (<6/12) cataract. Although age is the main risk factor, the process is multifactorial. Surgery is the only effective treatment. Phacoemulsification with intraocular lens (IOL) implantation allows rapid visual rehabilitation with generally low complication rates. For infantile cataract, see page 674.

Indications for cataract surgery

Reduced visual function: If the patient is coping visually and the cataract causes minimal symptoms of glare or difficulty with small print, consider if surgery is needed, especially for low myopes who can read well at a comfortable distance, and emmetropes with good unaided distance vision. For uniocular surgery consider if postoperative anisometropia might necessitate clear lens or early cataract surgery in the fellow eye.

Limited fundal view: Consider cataract surgery if lens opacity prevents adequate posterior segment assessment. Symptoms may help to determine if macular disease or cataract explain vision loss. If reading is the major symptom, then this suggests macular disease predominates, while glare and blurred vision may implicate cataract.

Lens-induced disease: Including phacolysis, phacoanaphylaxis, phacomorphic secondary angle-closure or primary angle-closure glaucoma.

To improve stereopsis and reduce anisometropia: Consider second eye cataract surgery for symptomatic anisometropia (up to 2 dioptres is usually tolerated).

Refractive lens extraction (RLE) for spectacle independence: This involves clear lens extraction with multifocal IOL implantation, or sometimes monovision IOLs (one focussed for distance, one for near). Carefully discuss the risks and benefits. Hyperopes benefit most, as RLE gives good unaided distance vision and reduced reliance on reading glasses. Emmetropes gains less, as they already have good distance vision. Myopes are special cases, as they lose their ability to read up close without glasses.

History

- *Symptoms*: Ask about the duration and character of any visual loss (reduced VA, contrast sensitivity, or glare), and the impact on daily activities. Validated symptom questionnaires may help to determine the need for surgery. Ensure symptoms are sufficient to warrant surgery and set realistic expectations for improvement if cataracts are mild.
- *Past ocular history*: Spectacle or contact lens use, amblyopia, strabismus, previous anisometropia, glaucoma, surgery including refractive procedures such as LASIK, trauma, uveitis or scleritis, and blepharospasm. In patients with a pre-existing squint, it is generally better to operate on the fixing eye first, to avoid fixation switch and possible diplopia.
- *Past medical and surgical history*: Especially deafness, confusion, neck disease, orthopnoea, difficulty lying flat, and seizures.
- *Drug history*: Especially tamsulosin, risperidone and paliperidone (all associated with intraoperative floppy iris syndrome), anticoagulants and allergies to iodine or antibiotics (some surgeons avoid cephalosporins in those with a severe penicillin allergy).
- *Social history*: Identify pre- and postoperative social support and any occupation or hobbies with specific visual requirements.

Examination

- *Corrected VA*: Measure near and distance, and pinhole VA which may predict postoperative vision better than corrected VA. Contrast sensitivity and glare disability are useful if symptoms are disproportionate to the VA loss, or the degree of cataract.
- *Binocular balance*: Cover test and ocular motility, when indicated.
- *Lids and adnexae*: Blepharitis, ectropion, entropion, orbital, or lacrimal disease may need treatment prior to cataract surgery.
- *RAPD*: Check before dilating pupils.
- *Slit-lamp examination*: Assess the anterior segment including ocular surface disease, corneal clarity, guttatae, AC depth, pupil size, evidence of previous intraocular inflammation or trauma, pseudoexfoliation, IOP, and gonioscopy if angle disease is suspected.

- *Cataract*: Note the type (nuclear, cortical, posterior subcapsular, and mixed) and grade (1+ to 5+) of cataract. Cortical cataracts are characterised by spokes, water clefts and vacuoles due to osmotic imbalances in lens epithelial cells. Nuclear cataracts result from accumulation of protein aggregates in the central lens, becoming progressively harder and more brunescent with time. Posterior subcapsular cataracts occur at the posterior pole immediately beneath the lens capsule and may be associated with diabetes, steroid use and ocular inflammation.
- *Fundoscopy*: Note posterior vitreous detachment (reduced risk of postoperative retinal detachment) or vitreous pigment cells, and exclude optic nerve or macula disease, retinopathy and peripheral retinal breaks or degenerations (especially in high myopes. Exclude posterior polar cataracts (a type of congenital cataract), due to their high risk of posterior capsule rupture.

Investigations

- *Blood pressure*: Control preoperatively – there is an increased risk of suprachoroidal haemorrhage with systolic BP ≥ 180 mmHg or a diastolic > 100 mmHg.
- *BM*: Diabetics have an increased risk of postoperative cystoid macular oedema (CMO), so consider adding NSAID eye drops (p. 566) to postoperative steroids. Consider also for other macular diseases, as these can also increase the risk of CMO.
- *Other blood tests and ECG*: Only if clinically indicated – routine testing does not reduce morbidity and mortality. If taking warfarin, ensure the INR is in the therapeutic range (discontinuing warfarin increases the risk of stroke 1:100). Warfarin is now increasingly rare as newer anticoagulants prevail. Patients take their anticoagulants for life-threatening reasons, so do not stop these for cataract surgery.
- *Optical coherence tomography*: Before and after cataract surgery.
- *Special investigations*: As indicated, including B-scan ultrasound to exclude retinal detachment or mass lesion if there is no fundal view; corneal topography (particularly if high or irregular astigmatism or history of corneal laser refractive surgery); specular microscopy and pachymetry to assess endothelial compromise.

Consent

- *Benefits*: These may include—
  1. Improved quality of vision; ~95% of patients without ocular co-pathology achieve a BCVA of 6/12 or better.

2. Improved fundal view to monitor or treat posterior segment disease.
3. Reduced spectacle dependence.
4. Improved control of primary angle-closure or primary angle-closure glaucoma (EAGLE study).

- *Risks*: Complications are infrequent and most can be treated. The overall risk of blindness is <1 in 1,000, with an estimated 1 in 10,000 chance of losing the eye as a result of surgery. There is almost no risk to the fellow eye. Potentially sight-threatening complications include: infectious endophthalmitis (<0.1%), retinal detachment (<1%), suprachoroidal haemorrhage (0.03%), cystoid macular oedema (1–2%), and corneal decompensation (<0.3%). Other specific complications include: ecchymosis (common), ptosis, posterior capsule (PC) rupture and/or vitreous loss (<1%), dropped nuclear fragments (<0.2%), postoperative IOP rise (common), subluxation of IOL implant, iris prolapse/wound leak, uveitis, spectacle correction for best vision, drop allergy, diplopia, further surgery, and posterior capsule opacification (PCO). There may be a guarded prognosis if there is coexisting ocular disease. Patients with a longstanding unilateral cataract and a divergent eye are at risk of intractable postoperative diplopia.
- *Also discuss*:
  1. The diagnosis and natural history of cataract.
  2. Alternative non-surgical options such as spectacles.
  3. The patient's preferred refractive target and the risk of refractive surprise (greater if there is a history of previous corneal refractive surgery). Discuss standard monofocal, increased range of focus and multifocal IOLs, and monovision.
  4. The surgical procedure, what to expect, and postoperative care.
  5. Same day bilateral cataract surgery or delayed sequential approach.
  6. *Anaesthetic options*: Topical, LA (with or without sedation) or GA.
  7. *Admission*: Day case (inpatient care rarely required).
  8. Provide written information and time to consider the options.

Preoperative assessment

Evaluate not just the eye but also the general health of the patient, including BP, patient's ability to lie flat and still during surgery, and anaesthetic issues. It is not usually necessary to stop antiplatelet or anticoagulant medications.

BIOMETRY

Selecting the correct IOL power for the desired refractive outcome relies on careful biometry. Measure the corneal curvature, axial length (AL), focimetry (or refraction) and, if keratometry is impossible, corneal topography.

Keratometry (K) Central corneal curvature is measured by automated keratometry with paired readings taken in two orthogonal meridia. Take the average of three pairs of readings including axes. Corneal power in dioptres (D) = 337.5/ keratometry in mm (where 337.5 is the hypothetical refractive index of the cornea).

All contact lenses can alter the corneal contour and adversely affect the biometry measurements, particularly rigid contact lenses. Tightly fitting contact lenses can induce a reversible corneal flattening which can cause a postoperative gradual myopic shift. Leave out soft contact lenses for a week and rigid lenses for a month before biometry.

For previous refractive surgery perform corneal topography to confirm whether the patient had myopic or hyperopic LASIK/ PRK, as this affects the biometry formula selection (see below). If in doubt, long AL and flatter corneal power indices suggest myopic laser treatment, whereas shorter AL and steeper corneal indices suggest hyperopic treatment. Warn those with previous refractive surgery of the greater risk of refractive surprise; for radial keratotomy, consider a low myopic outcome anticipating a future hyperopic shift.

Axial length of the eye Usually measured using either optical interferometry (e.g. IOLMaster, Carl Zeiss) or A-Mode ultrasound.

- *Optical interferometry*: Noncontact and measures AL to the retinal pigment epithelium (rather than the vitreoretinal interface as in ultrasound). A trace with a signal-to-noise ratio (SNR) of ≥2.0 is acceptable; however, the higher the SNR, the more accurate the reading. AL readings are typically 0.1 mm longer with the IOLMaster compared to A-scan. Take care in selecting the correct lens-constant (optimised for either ultrasound or optical biometry) when performing IOL calculations. For emmetropia, choose an IOL power targeting plano to –0.3D. Improved refractive targeting can be achieved by optimising IOL constants for optical biometry. The IOLMaster has a built- in keratometer, facilities to measure preoperative 'anterior chamber depth' (ACD, the distance from the anterior corneal vertex to the anterior lens along the visual axis), horizontal white-to-white (HWTW) measurement, optional settings, e.g. 'pseudophakia' (PMMA, silicone, and acrylic) or 'silicone oil filled vitreous', and software to calculate IOL implant powers using a selection of formulae.

- *A-mode ultrasound*: Essential if cataract is dense or other ocular opacity prevents optical measurement of AL, but more user-dependent. Immersion A-scan methods offer a reduced chance of foreshortening eye by indentation (small potential error of 0.1 mm) but a much greater chance of misaligning the probe with respect to visual axis, which can lead to very large errors (~mms). A small and high-frequency (typically 10 MHz) transducer is placed on the anaesthetised cornea (usually supported in spring-loaded assembly such as a tonometer holder).

  Between pulses, echoes are received from the ocular tissues and plotted as spikes on a display (**Fig. 7.1**). The height of the spike indicates the amplitude of the echo and the position along the X-axis indicates time delay (converted to distance using assumed velocities in ocular tissue). A major source of error is poor alignment of the ultrasound probe; ensure central fixation with a perpendicular incidence (indicated by strongest echo with steepest rise time from baseline). The AL of silicone oil filled eyes = anterior cornea to posterior lens, plus the measured vitreal length × 0.64, as the measured length of the vitreous must be scaled to allow for the reduced velocity of sound in oil.
- *B-Mode ultrasound*: Invaluable in babies, poorly cooperative patients, and to exclude staphyloma. Provides a cross-sectional image of the eye (**Fig. 7.2**) and orbit through a closed eyelid (with a good system the anterior cornea and foveal pit can be imaged). Assumes a single velocity in ocular tissues, but adjust

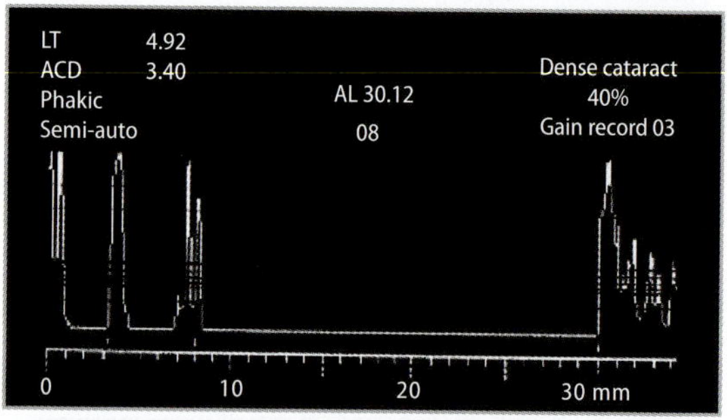

Fig. 7.1: A-scan: axial length (AL) 30.12 mm; anterior chamber depth (ACD) 3.40 mm; lens thickness (LT) 4.92 mm: cursors at base of trace mark (from left to right) the anterior lens interface, posterior lens interface and vitreo-retinal interface.

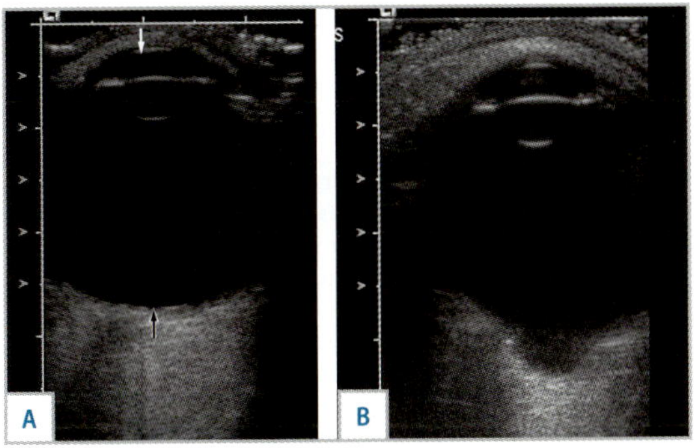

Fig. 7.2: Transverse (horizontal) central B-scan sections. (A) Average length eye, cornea (white arrow) and foveal pit (black arrow). (B) Highly myopic eye with gross posterior pole staphyloma.

for silicone oil-filled eyes as above. Requires a skilled operator for accurate AL measurement; take care not to indent the globe as the probe is hand-held and considerably heavier than the A-scan probe.

Focimetry or refraction Assess spherical and astigmatic error in each eye to ensure they are consistent with other biometry data. Review pre-cataract refraction if available. Aim to minimise anisometropia to 2 D or less, unless monovision is desired (e.g. dominant eye focussed for distance; non-dominant for near). However, if the patient is adapted to longstanding anisometropia, correcting this can cause problems with image size disparity and diplopia.

Corneal topography Use keratometry rather than topography for IOL calculation. Topography can quantify significant keratometric astigmatism and exclude irregular astigmatism or keratoconus prior to surgery, and help to plan for incision placement, limbal relaxing incisions, or toric IOL use.

Intraocular lens power calculation formulae Select the Barrett Universal II formula, but if there is prior refractive laser or surgery select a specialised formula (see below). An online IOL calculator is available, at iolcalculator.escrs.org. Formulae such as Hoffer Q, SRK-T are now obsolete.

An interocular difference in AL of >0.3 mm or K >1 D should be checked with multiple readings and ideally with the patient's refractive history or focimetry of old spectacles (before cataract development, as nuclear sclerosis often induces myopic shift). If the axial lengths differ by >0.6 mm between fellow eyes and the history or focimetry are not consistent, use A-scan to cross-check the readings obtained by optical interferometry, e.g. IOLMaster.

Specialised formulae: Select the Barrett True K formula (available on the IOLMaster700) following laser refractive surgery or radial keratometry, after establishing if it was myopic or hyperopic laser treatment. The Haigis-L formula is also widely used after refractive laser for myopia or hyperopia, and uses AL, Ks and ACD. Many other formulae are available for use after myopic or hyperopic laser refractive treatment or radial keratotomy, which importantly include posterior corneal curvature measurements. Consider using one of several IOL calculators to compute an average recommended IOL power, such as iolcalc.ascrs.org

Unexpected postoperative refractive outcome In the event of a confirmed refractive surprise:

- Re-check IOL choice, lens constant used, formula used, and target refraction. Ensure that a positive or negative powered lens was accurately chosen.
- Repeat biometry to exclude a biometry error and perform corneal topography. Measure distance from the anterior cornea to the anterior surface of the IOL with either A- or B-scan (be careful not to measure to the posterior implant surface): too shallow or too deep will lead to myopic or hyperopic surprises, respectively (usually due to excess anterior or posterior vaulting of the implant, often due to crimping of haptics).
- In cases of myopic surprise, also consider retained viscoelastic behind the implant – a distended bag may be visible on examination or with B-scan.
- Beware manufacturing/pack errors with mislabelled implant power (implant thickness can be measured *in situ* on B-scan and compared to a correctly labelled implant of the same model).
- Discuss treatment options with the patient.
- If the refractive outcome is tolerated, leave the IOL *in situ* and/or offer spectacle or contact lens correction.
- If not tolerated and no obvious biometry error, consider: IOL exchange, piggyback IOL or corneal refractive surgery.
- If the refractive outcome is not tolerated and if there is obvious biometry error, offer IOL exchange based on refraction or corneal refractive surgery. If the fellow eye has cataract, consider equalising refraction with second eye surgery or electing for anisometropic monovision.

MANAGEMENT OF ASTIGMATISM

Background Visually significant keratometric astigmatism of ≥1.0 D is present in ~42% of eyes undergoing cataract surgery. Cylindrical targeting using incision placement, limbal relaxing incision (LRI), opposite clear corneal incision (OCCI), toric IOL or a combination of techniques can reduce or eliminate pre-existing corneal astigmatism and improve unaided distance vision (**Fig. 7.3**).

Incision placement Placing clear corneal incisions (CCI) on the steep meridian causes wound-induced flattening sufficient to control 0.75–1.50 D with wound sizes of 2.8–3.4 mm, but is less effective with wounds of 1.5–2.4 mm. Temporal CCIs are almost (0.25 D) astigmatically neutral if ≤3.4 mm and are recommended if there is negligible corneal astigmatism. Superior CCIs induce up to 1.50 D flattening. It is not always possible to operate on the steep meridian (e.g. if superonasal in the right eye or inferotemporal in the left eye), unless left-handed or ambidextrous. OCCIs treat up to 1.5 D of corneal astigmatism: operate on the steep axis and place another corneal incision opposite the main wound to increase corneal flattening.

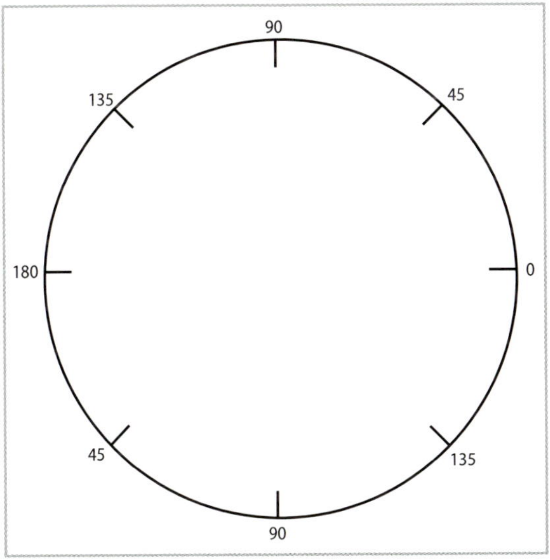

Fig. 7.3: Corneal axis marking convention for surgical toric markers (it is the same for right and left eyes).

Limbal relaxing incisions (LRI) Safe and viable means to correct up to 3.00 D of corneal astigmatism, especially if toric IOLs are contraindicated or unavailable (**Box 7.1**). Paired arcuate limbal incisions centred on the steep meridian flatten the central cornea, and are usually combined with a neutral temporal CCI. Measure the axis and amount of corneal astigmatism by keratometry or topography. Identify requisite LRI length (degrees of arc) from preferred nomogram, e.g. modified Gills or Nichamin (**Table 7.1A and B**). Variability of refractive correction is a significant drawback and is surgeon dependent. Regression is another important factor. Complications include: wrong axis, perforation (rare), infection, misalignment, under/over correction, induced irregular astigmatism, decreased corneal sensation, and weakened globe.

Toric intraocular lenses Toric IOLs incorporate a cylindrical correction on a spherical optic for correction of pre-existing regular keratometric astigmatism. Consider for astigmatism ≥1 D, when an LRI is inadequate or less predictable, or in young patients (beware a *forme fruste* of keratoconus). Successful outcome relies on careful lens power calculation and selection, minimising surgically induced astigmatism, meticulous cortical clean-up/capsule polish, and precise alignment of IOL cylindrical correction axis with the steep corneal meridian. Make corneal reference marks preoperatively as described below for LRIs or consider intraoperative digital alignment. Significant IOL

Box 7.1: Limbal relaxing incision

1. Mark the limbus at the 90° position preoperatively, with the patient sitting upright at the slit lamp (avoids alignment error from cyclotorsion when supine or after orbital block). Perform LRI at the start of surgery when the eye is firm and there is less risk of 'dragging' the corneal epithelium (if a large LRI is required at the site of the main wound, extend the LRI at the end of surgery).
2. Align a degree gauge (e.g. Mendez ring) on the cornea using the limbal reference marks (**Fig. 7.4**). Locate and mark the steep meridian. Confirm with intraoperative keratoscopy (reflected mires appear closer on the steep axis).
3. Define the required arc length centred on the steep meridian using either ink marks or a fixation ring with increment markers (e.g. Fine–Thornton–Nichamin ring).
4. Use a guarded diamond knife-style blade set at a depth of 600 μm according to nomogram. Make accurate incisions at the most peripheral clear cornea (irrespective of vessels), keep the blade perpendicular and pull towards you. Wait 4–6 weeks for stable refraction.

Table 7.1A: Nichamin nomogram for clear corneal phaco surgery (minimal or 'against-the-rule' astigmatism)

Astigmatic status = 'spherical': (+0.75 × 90; +0.50 × 180)
Astigmatic status = 'against-the-rule': (steep axis 0–30°/150–180°):
Intraoperative keratoscopy determines exact incision location
Incision design = 'Neutral' temporal clear corneal (3.5 mm or less, single plane, just anterior to vascular arcade) along with the following peripheral arcuate incisions

Preoperative cylinder	30–40 y.o.	41–50 y.o.	51–60 y.o.	61–70 y.o.	71–80 y.o.	81–90 y.o.	>90 y.o.
+0.75 → +1.25 *Paired limbal arcs on steep axis	55°	50°	45°	40°	35°	35° Nasal limbal arc only on steep axis	
+1.50 → +2.00 *Paired limbal arcs on steep axis	70°	65°	60°	55°	45°	40°	35°
+2.25 → +2.75 *Paired limbal arcs on steep axis	90°	80°	70°	60°	50°	45°	40°
+3.00 → +3.75 *Paired limbal arcs on steep axis	90° reduce o.z. to 8 mm	90° reduce o.z. to 9 mm	85°	70°	60°	50°	45°
			Degrees of arc to be incised				

* The temporal incision is made by first creating a two-plane, grooved phaco incision (600 μm depth), which is then extended to the appropriate arc length at the conclusion of surgery. o.z., optic zone; y.o., years old.

Table 7.1B: Nichamin nomogram for clear corneal phaco surgery ('with-the-rule' astigmatism)

Astigmatic status = 'with-the-rule': (steep axis 45–145°)
Intraoperative keratoscopy determines exact incision location
Incision design = 'Neutral' temporal clear corneal (3.5 mm or less, single plane, just anterior to vascular arcade) along with the following peripheral arcuate incisions

Preoperative cylinder	30–40 y.o.	41–50 y.o.	51–60 y.o.	61–70 y.o.	71–80 y.o.	81–90 y.o.	>90 y.o.
+1.00 → +1.50 Paired limbal arcs on steep axis	50°	45°	40°	35°	30°		
+1.75 → +2.25 Paired limbal arcs on steep axis	60°	55°	50°	45°	40°	35°	30°
+2.50 → +3.00 Paired limbal arcs on steep axis	70°	65°	60°	55°	50°	45°	40°
+3.25 → +3.75 Paired limbal arcs on steep axis	80°	75°	70°	65°	60°	55°	45°
	Degrees of arc to be incised						

Source: Reproduced with kind permission from Louis D. 'Skip' Nichamin, M.D., Laurel Eye Clinic, Brookville, PA, USA.

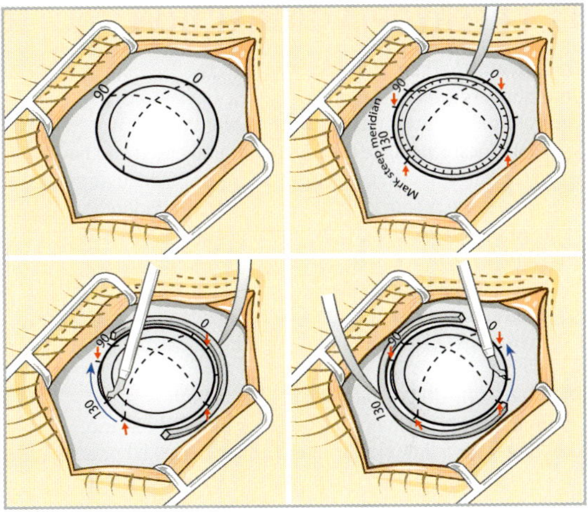

Fig. 7.4: Limbal relaxing incision.

rotation/axis shift can occur after implantation in up to 10% of eyes, reducing astigmatism correction (two-thirds of effect is lost with a 20° deviation) and requiring repositioning within 2 weeks. Insert the lens into viscoelastic filled capsular bag, leaving it just counterclockwise to the intended axis, before removing all viscoelastic then make final clockwise adjustment of the IOL to the desired axis. Residual postoperative astigmatism is pseudophakic and cannot be corrected with a rigid contact lens (only with spectacles or soft-toric contact lens). Measuring the posterior corneal curvature may improve biometry precision for toric IOLs.

Occasionally, corneal laser refractive surgery is required to correct residual postoperative astigmatism.

PRESBYOPIA CORRECTION

Background There is debate over IOL classification, but common terms include monofocal, toric (astigmatism correcting), simultaneous vision and accommodating.

Monofocal lenses are the most commonly used and have a single point of focus, typically set for clear unaided distance vision (see also monovision below). The terms 'monofocal plus', 'enhanced monofocal' and 'premium monofocal' describe minor adjustments to the surface asphericity to improve unaided intermediate distance vision.

Simultaneous vision IOLs are often divided into extended depth of focus (EDOF) and multifocal intraocular lens (MFIOL).

Monovision Utilises monofocal IOLs in both eyes. The dominant eye is normally corrected for unaided distance vision and the fellow eye for intermediate (−1.00 D) or near vision (−1.50 D to −2.50 D). In carefully selected patients, this technique can be highly effective with a high degree of patient satisfaction. Patients must be counselled on the loss of stereoacuity and depth perception, and potential anisometropic symptoms. Patients must be well-motivated and ideally have a preoperative trial with contact lenses to ascertain if they can tolerate anisometropia.

Extended depth of focus EDOF lenses IOLs have a single elongated point of focus that can provide clear unaided distance and intermediate vision. They can be defined as providing a monocular depth of focus at least 0.5 D wider than a monofocal control at 0.2 logMAR (6/9.5 Snellen equivalent).

Multifocal intraocular lenses Multifocal IOLs incorporate multiple focussing elements in a single fixed lens, aiming to provide clear unaided distance, intermediate and near vision. They are classified as:

- Diffractive, whereby incoming light is diffracted by an interference grid producing separate focal points simultaneously. Includes some EDOF IOLs and trifocal IOLs that offer improved intermediate and near vision.
- Refractive, use different zones on the lens surface to focus light at different distances
- Combined refractive and diffractive.

In select, motivated patients MFIOLs can produce a high level of success. The main problem of dysphotopsia (glare, haloes, or dazzle, particularly at night) has been reduced with newer IOL designs and symptoms often dissipate over 6 months or more due to neuroadaptation. Many patients may require spectacles for reading small print or reading in dim light and some may require spectacles for driving. Patient selection and counselling are paramount. Motivated patients who understand the limitations of MFIOLs and have realistic expectations, particularly hyperopes with little or no astigmatism, are ideal candidates. Contraindications may include myopes who have previously enjoyed excellent uncorrected near vision, highly demanding patients, and ocular comorbidity such as macular degeneration, diabetic retinopathy, corneal scarring, or uveitis. Correct corneal astigmatism >0.75 D with a combined toric multifocal IOL.

Accommodating intraocular lenses These aim to mimic physiological accommodation and avoid the optical side effects of MFIOLs. For example, the Lumina (Akkolens) has sulcus placement and aims to exploit residual ciliary muscle contraction and relaxation, but currently there is no optimal design and further research is needed to overcome issues such as capsular fibrosis.

LOCAL ANAESTHESIA

Background Most cataract surgery is performed under local anaesthesia (LA), with the advantage of reduced morbidity and mortality, reduced hospital stays, and increased patient satisfaction compared to general anaesthesia (GA). Anaesthesia can be achieved by topical ± intracameral anaesthetic, but akinesia (paralysis of ocular movements) requires regional orbital block (sub-Tenon's, peribulbar, or retrobulbar). The choice of LA technique must be tailored to surgery, the patient's expectations, and the comfort of both patient and surgeon.

- *Patient selection*: Good communication before and during surgery reduces anxiety and improves cooperation. The patient should be able to lie still and relatively flat for the duration of surgery.
- *Monitoring*: All patients must be monitored (usually only pulse oximetry required) by suitably trained personnel.
- *Sedation*: Useful in certain patients, e.g. anxious or claustrophobic, may improve mild head tremor, but not for pain relief. Risks include inducing confusion, restlessness, falling asleep then waking with a jolt, and airway compromise. Requires postoperative monitoring and appropriate escort/ transport arrangements.
- *General anesthesia*: Preferred if the patient is unable to comply with instructions (e.g. confusion and learning difficulties), very severe claustrophobia, history of panic attacks, significant psychiatric disease, marked resting head tremor, young patient, previous adverse reaction, allergy or complication associated with LA, or if the patient declines LA.

Topical anaesthesia For many surgeons, this has become the standard choice. Select well-motivated patients, routine cases, and an experienced surgeon. Caution if there is a language barrier, significant hearing impairment, 'lid squeezers', extreme anxiety, dementia/confusion, nystagmus, seizure history, and combined or long surgical procedures. Warn the patient of pressure sensation and preservation of vision during surgery. Avoid unnecessarily bright illumination.

- *Advantages*: Non-invasive and quick, rapid visual recovery, avoids complications of orbital blocks/GA, inexpensive, and useful if anticoagulated or long axial length.
- *Disadvantages*: Not suitable for all, limited to short procedures, drops can cause superficial punctate keratitis, epithelial haze/ impaired view, and without akinesia surgery may be challenging if the patient is uncooperative or if complications arise.
- *Technique*: Apply G. proxymetacaine 0.5% (or G. benoxinate 0.4%) initially (less stinging than tetracaine) then 2–3 drops G. tetracaine 1% (better anaesthesia during surgery than

proxymetacaine or benoxinate) 5 minutes preoperatively. Ensure application to the cornea, bulbar conjunctiva, inferior and superior fornices (to reduce speculum discomfort). Also instill G. proxymetacaine 0.5% once to the fellow eye. Instill a further two drops during surgery: before the first corneal incision and before IOL insertion. Give additional drops at any stage as required, remembering that tetracaine can cause epithelial haze.

- Adjunctive intracameral anaesthesia is often used and eliminates the pressure sensation/pain sometimes experienced under topical alone: irrigate the AC with 0.5 mL preservative-free 1% lidocaine without epinephrine in balanced salt solution (BSS) after the first incision or use for hydrodissection.

Sub-Tenon's block

- *Technique*: See **Box 7.2** and **Figure 7.5**. There are also techniques with no dissection, using a small nick in conjunctiva/sub-Tenon's tissue with Westcott scissors, then the LA cannula is advanced without dissecting a pocket.
- *Agents*: Use shorter-acting lidocaine 1% or 2% (without epinephrine), or longer-acting bupivacaine 0.5%, or a mixture of both, with or without hyaluronidase diluted to 15 i.u./mL (Hyalase may prevent loculation of fluid behind the globe, reducing the risk of increased posterior pressure and its complications). The maximum safe dose of lidocaine without epinephrine is 3 mg/kg and bupivacaine 2 mg/kg (0.5% = 5 mg/mL, 1% = 10 mg/mL, 2% = 20 mg/mL), e.g. maximum safe dose of 2% lidocaine for a 70 kg patient is (3 × 70)/20 = 10.5 mL.

Box 7.2: Sub-Tenon's block

1. Position the patient supine, apply G. benoxinate 0.4% then 5% povidone iodine, and insert the lid speculum. Button-hole the conjunctiva and Tenon's capsule 4 mm from the limbus in the inferonasal quadrant using spring scissors and forceps. Apply conjunctival cautery if required **(Fig. 7.5A)**.
2. Blunt dissect to open sub-Tenon's space **(Fig. 7.5B)** then insert a curved blunt sub-Tenon's cannula between Tenon's and sclera. Gentle hydrodissection assists passage **(Fig. 7.5C)**.
3. Keep the tip adjacent to the globe and pass posteriorly; there is usually some resistance at the equator **(Fig. 7.5D)**.
4. Push beyond equator and inject 3–5 mL of LA to spread around globe and into the intraconal space. This often causes proptosis. If there is resistance to injection, reflux, or subconjunctival swelling, reposition the cannula or dissect more posteriorly before re-injecting.

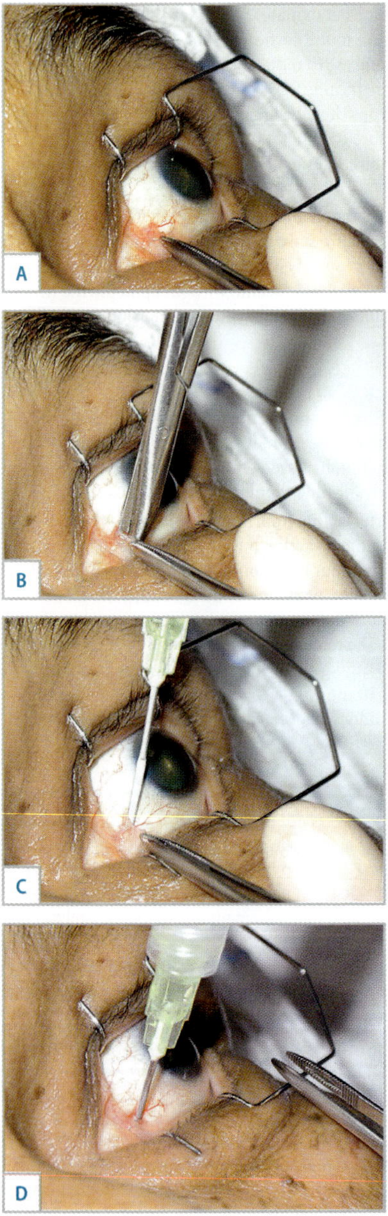

Fig. 7.5: How to perform a sub-Tenon's block. See **Box 7.2**.

- *Advantages*: Safest orbital block (avoids sharp needle), relatively rapid action.
- *Disadvantages*: Less effective akinesia if poorly administered, subconjunctival chemosis or haemorrhage, and may be difficult to perform if previous buckle/conjunctival surgery.

Peribulbar block and retrobulbar block These sharp needle techniques are rarely used due to their higher risk of complications (**Fig. 7.6**).

Complications of sharp needle blocks Retrobulbar haemorrhage (check central retinal artery perfusion on fundoscopy and if compromised consider immediate lateral canthotomy; can also occur with sub-Tenon's LA), globe penetration/perforation (<0.1%, longer eyes at increased risk), optic nerve sheath haemorrhage, extraocular muscle trauma/ toxicity causing diplopia, ptosis, rarely subarachnoid injection with brainstem anaesthesia (confusion, seizures, paralysis, respiratory arrest, and circulatory collapse), intravascular injection of LA (seizures and resistant ventricular fibrillation).

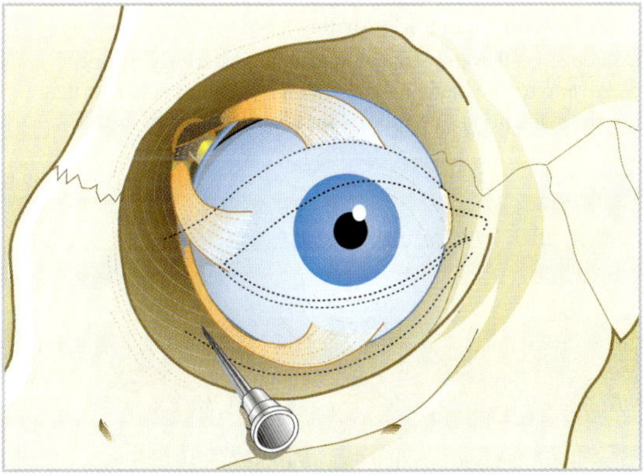

Fig. 7.6: Peribulbar block.

BASIC SURGICAL TECHNIQUES

A 'standard' method of phacosurgery is described, recognising that surgeons will evolve their own techniques.

Preparation and draping

Antiseptic preparation of the surgical field (ocular surface, lids, lashes, cheek, and forehead) for at least 2 minutes with aqueous povidone-iodine 5–10% (or aqueous chlorhexidine) and draping of the eyelashes reduces the risk of postoperative endophthalmitis.

Main incision

Construct a small self-sealing clear (or near-clear) corneal incision as either a single plane stab or two- or three-step incisions (three-step is more secure). Stabilise the globe using a Thornton-Fine 'C-ring' or micro-grooved forceps **(Fig. 7.7)**:

- *Step 1*: Groove the cornea anterior to the limbus using a diamond or steel keratome (avoid incising the conjunctiva to prevent chemosis during phaco).
- *Step 2*: Create a stromal tunnel about 1 mm long using a 2.2–2.4-mm keratome (a longer tunnel is less likely to leak and essential if the AC is shallow).
- *Step 3*: Deliberately tilt the keratome posteriorly before advancing the blade to enter the AC (note expected corneal striae on entry). A temporal incision is preferred as it is

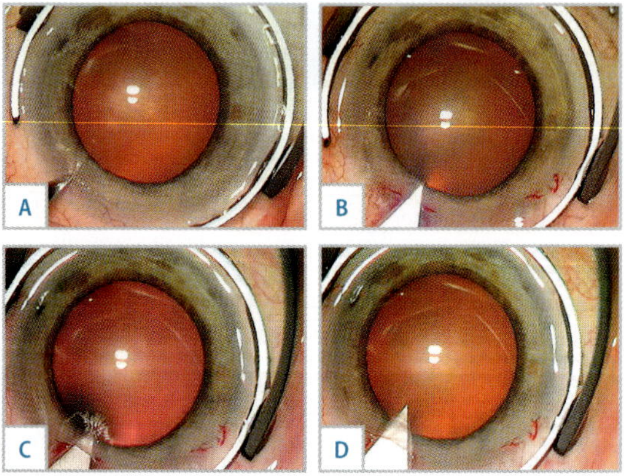

Fig. 7.7: Three-step corneal incision. (A) Groove. (B) Stromal tunnel. (C) Tilt keratome posteriorly. (D) Enter AC.

astigmatically neutral (if <3.2 mm) and allows better access. The site of incision may be tailored to reduce pre-existing corneal astigmatism (p. 291).

Side port incision

Inject viscoelastic to stabilise the AC. Create a second, limbal side-port incision (paracentesis) 45–90° from the main wound using a keratome or 15° blade; do not make this too wide to avoid leaking or iris prolapse. If utilising bi-manual irrigation and aspiration of cortex use a 20-G microvitreoretinal (MVR) blade and make an additional side port ~180° apart.

Continuous circular capsulorrhexis

Use a cystotome (preformed or bent insulin syringe needle) and/or rhexis forceps **(Figs. 7.8 and 7.9)**. Puncture the capsule at the centre and extend radially, ending with a 'J'-turn to create a curvilinear fold in the favoured direction (clockwise or anticlockwise). Grasp the capsular flap just in front of the tearing point, then pull circumferentially to create a continuous circular capsulorrhexis (CCC) of 5–6 mm diameter. To reduce the risk of

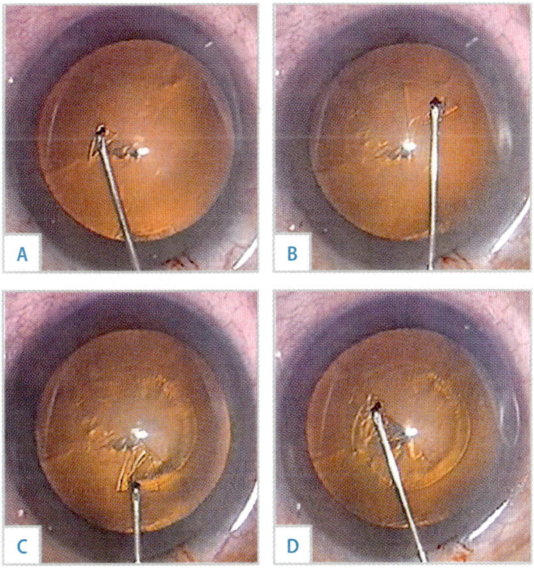

Fig. 7.8: Needle capsulorrhexis. Clockwise capsulorrhexis with a bent insulin syringe needle.

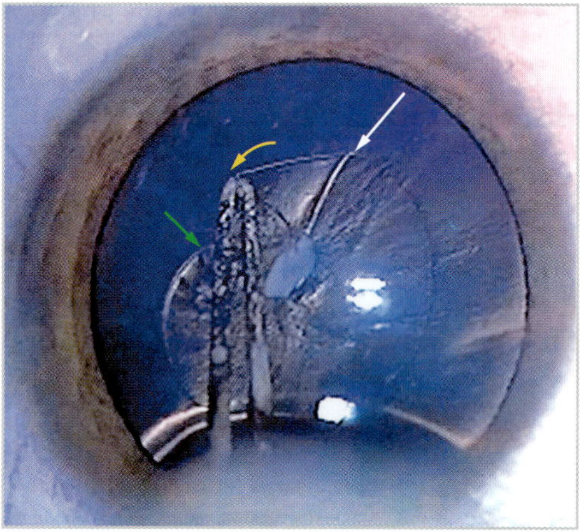

Fig. 7.9: Forceps capsulorrhexis. Start point (green arrow), tearing point (white arrow) and direction of pull (yellow curved arrow) are shown. Note anterior polar lens opacity adherent to anterior capsule.

losing control, re-grip the outer flap edge near the tearing point, ensure the AC depth is maintained with viscoelastic, and avoid pressure on the posterior lip of the wound. If the capsulorrhexis needs enlarging or if an irregular edge must be stabilised, cut the rhexis margin tangentially with Ong scissors to create a new flap to grip and extend with forceps (safest after IOL insertion). If the red reflex is poor/absent, stain the anterior capsule with trypan blue 0.06% (e.g. VisionBlue™). Wash out after 30 seconds. In young patients, beware anterior insertion of the zonular fibres (identifiable by staining with trypan blue) and the more elastic capsule as both increase the risk of the capsulorrhexis tearing out. For management of anterior capsule tears see page 327.

Hydrodissection

Separates the cortex from the capsule to mobilise the lens in the bag. Use a Rycroft or 27-gauge hydrodissection cannula (Pierce or J-cannula) on a syringe of BSS. Place the tip of the cannula under the rhexis margin, immediately adjacent to the capsule, advance slightly, then gently inject BSS. A 'fluid wave' behind the lens confirms the correct cleavage plane **(Fig. 7.10)**. Gently depress the nucleus to help move fluid around the lens. A single injection is usually sufficient, but repeat the hydrodissection

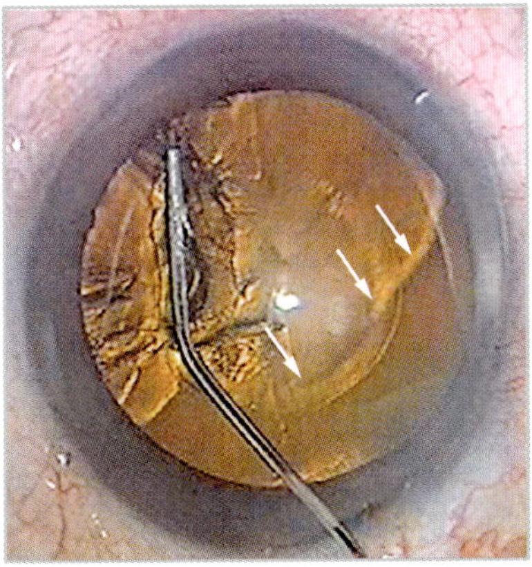

Fig. 7.10: Hydrodissection. Wavefront of fluid between lens and posterior capsule is shown by arrows.

if necessary, at a different site, until the lens is freely mobile. Hydrodelineation cleaves the adult nucleus from the epinucleus: inject BSS into the lens matter and watch for the 'golden ring' sign – the epinuclear shell may not be easy to remove later but provides useful protection to the posterior capsule (PC) for phaco-chop techniques.

Phacoemulsification

A piezoelectric crystal in the hand-piece oscillates the titanium phaco needle at 35–45 kHz, generating ultrasonic energy in front of the tip. Emulsified lens matter is removed via a central aspiration port. The AC is maintained by fluid entering via the irrigation sleeve, also serving to cool the phaco needle (ensure the holes of the sleeve are positioned horizontally so flow is not impeded and is directed away from the corneal endothelium). Most phaco machines are either flow-based (usually a peristaltic pump) or vacuum-based (usually Venturi). Standard linear foot pedal control positions are:

- *Position 1*: off.
- *Position 2*: irrigation on (set by the infusion bottle height) with aspiration (set by flow rate and vacuum) increasing with pedal depression.
- *Position 3*: phacoemulsification increasing to the set maximum energy.

Phaco techniques A variety of methods are possible according to the type of cataract and surgical skill. Aim to develop an adaptable technique, minimise phaco energy and fluid flow, and maintain a stable AC. AC stability is determined by irrigation (height of infusion bottle), vacuum setting, fluidic technology of the machine and integrity (construction and instrument positioning).

- *Divide and conquer*:
  1. Aims to split the nucleus into quadrants for emulsification. The easiest technique to master. Set 20–60% phaco power and 30–50 mmHg vacuum for the first stage. Make a central groove 1.5 times the width of phaco tip **(Fig. 7.11)**, sculpting deeper centrally than peripherally; beware of the rhexis margin. Advance the tip at the same speed as emulsification (increase power as required) to avoid pushing the lens. Rotate the nucleus 180° to complete a long groove before sculpting a second long groove at right angles to the first. Alternatively, rotate the nucleus 90° at a time, dividing into quadrants with four short grooves. Bimanual rotation minimises zonular stress; if there is resistance to rotation consider repeating the hydrodissection. The depth of the groove for successful cracking varies with nucleus density; when the red reflex becomes apparent through the base of the groove, the depth is usually sufficient **(Fig. 7.12)**.
  2. To crack the nucleus **(Fig. 7.13)** make certain the second instrument and phaco tip are at the base of the groove. Separate the instruments using an upward pivoting motion (rather than pure lateral movement); this is mechanically more efficient and reduces zonular stress. Ensure the crack extends along the full length. If unsuccessful, the groove is usually not deep enough in the centre. For quadrant removal, use 40–60% phaco power but increase the vacuum

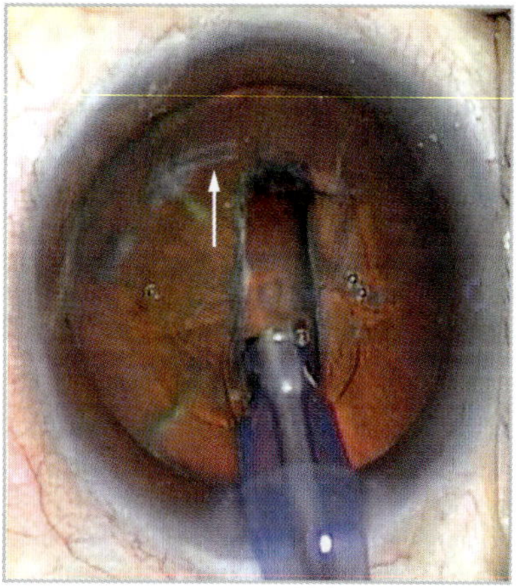

Fig. 7.11: Sculpting.

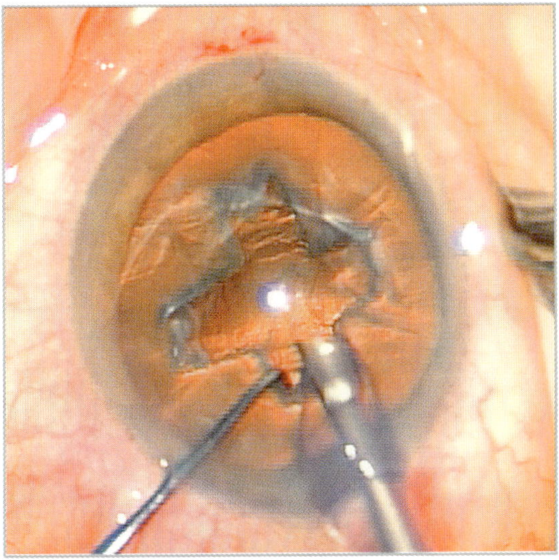

Fig. 7.12: Divide and conquer.

to 250–350 mmHg (flow rate 25–35 mL/min). Position the quadrant to be removed opposite the phaco tip. Use vacuum and phaco to impale the centre of the fragment (tilting the apex of the quadrant anteriorly aids this manoeuvre). Maintain occlusion without phaco energy (foot position 2) and pull the quadrant to the centre of the bag for emulsification. Power modulations (micropulse or burst modes) reduce the total phaco energy required, especially in harder cataracts. Other advances to minimise ultrasound energy but maintain efficiency of nucleus removal include torsional (Ozil, Alcon) and transversal (WhiteStar signature handpiece, AMO) excursions of the phaco tip. Protect the posterior capsule during quadrant removal by keeping the second instrument below the phaco tip at all times.

- *Stop and chop*: Stop and chop shortens phaco time, is useful for hard nuclei, and may reduce stress on the capsule when the zonules are weak or the rhexis incomplete. Sculpt a single long groove, crack the nucleus into two halves, then 'stop' and 'chop' each heminucleus. Rotate the nucleus so that the groove is at 30° to the phaco needle, then align the bevel of the tip parallel to the heminucleus to optimise tip occlusion. Increase vacuum (250–380 mmHg) to embed the phaco tip into the heminucleus aided by a short pulse of

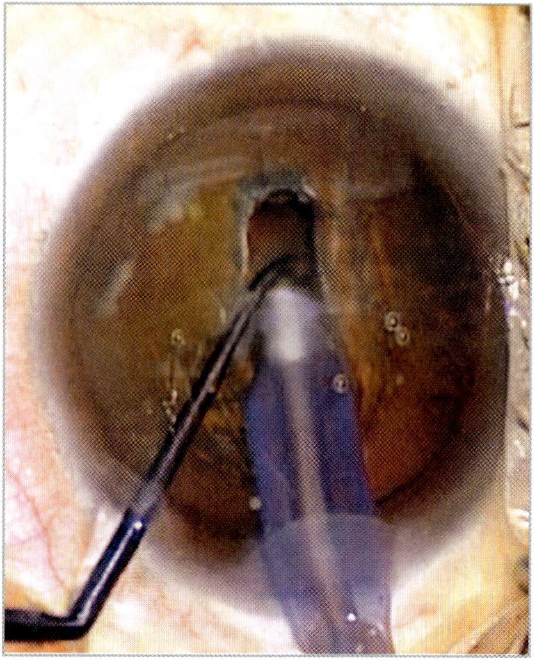

Fig. 7.13: Cracking the nucleus.

phaco. To perform a horizontal chop, pass the chopper flat under the capsulorrhexis edge, engage opposite the equator of the nucleus, then pull the chopper towards the phaco tip to split the nucleus (**Fig. 7.14**). Just before the instruments meet, move the chopper at right angles to release the wedge of nucleus for emulsification. For a vertical chop technique, use sharp-tipped chopper to vertically incise the heminucleus (within the capsulorrhexis) towards the embedded phaco tip. Lift the engaged nucleus slightly to facilitate cleavage before lateral separation of the chopper and phaco tip to complete fracture. Rotate the nucleus clockwise and repeat the chopping action until the nucleus is completely removed.

- *'Primary chop'*: No sculpting is required for this technique. Impale the nucleus with the phaco tip just proximal to the centre and immobilise with high vacuum (phaco power 40–60% on burst and vacuum 320–380 mmHg). Follow with either horizontal or vertical chop (as above).

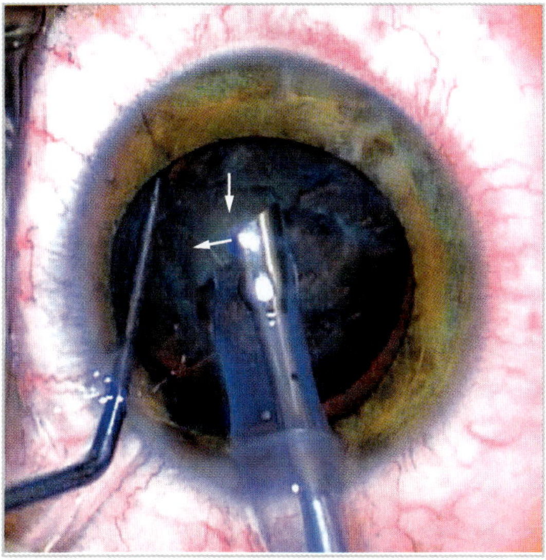

Fig. 7.14: Horizontal chop. Arrows indicate the direction of pull of the chopper.

- *'Taco' technique*: Useful for soft nuclei that are too soft to crack after sculpting a central groove. Fold the nucleus into the groove using aspiration and second instrument manipulation to 'tyre iron' the heminucleus into the phaco tip (minimal or no phaco energy is required).

Cortical clean up

Residual cortical or soft lens matter (SLM) is removed using manual (Simcoe), automated irrigation and aspiration (I&A) systems **(Fig. 7.15)** or bimanual I&A **(Fig. 7.16)**. Engage SLM beneath the anterior capsule with the tip of the cannula and use aspiration to strip from the periphery to the centre. Excessive pulling (versus aspiration) risks PC rupture if the capsule is inadvertently engaged (indicated by star-shaped capsular striae). If the capsule is engaged, keep the instrument still and reflux immediately (if using automated I&A check the correct pedal action beforehand). Proceed circumferentially until all SLM is cleared. Difficult-to-remove sub-incisional SLM can be tackled via the second instrument port or a second-side port placed opposite the main incision. Ninety-degree angled tips for the automated I&A are also available. Alternatively, remove the

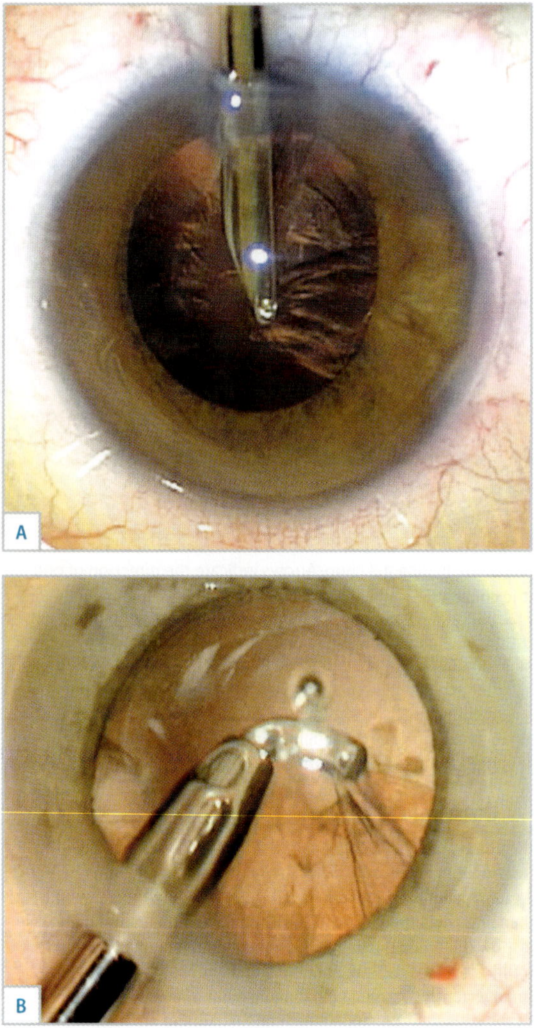

Fig. 7.15: Cortical clean up. (A) Simcoe aspiration of SLM. (B) Automated I&A using 90° tip.

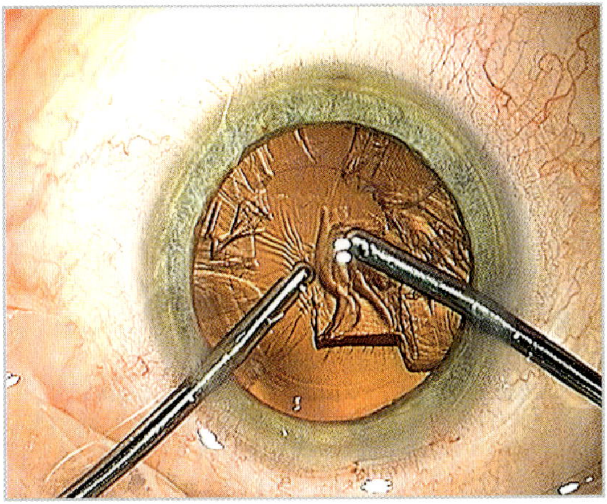

Fig. 7.16: Bimanual irrigation and aspiration (Courtesy P Sullivan).

remaining SLM after IOL insertion – dialling the IOL in the bag can loosen material with the optic protecting the PC. Residual SLM may prolong postoperative inflammation and cause early posterior capsular opacification (PCO), but better to leave small amounts than risk a PC tear.

Capsule polishing

The PC can be polished with automated I&A or a dedicated polisher with a roughened surface under viscoelastic. Manual focal irrigation after filling the bag with viscoelastic is also effective at stripping residual cortex/plaque ('jet-wash' technique) which can reduce the incidence of PC fibrosis by 50%. If there is a resistant plaque, try viscodissection to raise the edge then peel with rhexis forceps (very risky). Routine removal of residual lens epithelium from the equator (and anterior capsule) may reduce the risk of capsular fibrosis/PCO.

Insertion of posterior chamber intraocular lens

Fill the capsular bag with viscoelastic and deepen the AC to protect the endothelium. Enlarge the section if required for manual implantation or injection of the IOL. For manual insertion, fold the optic in half on the long axis of the haptics. Insert the leading haptic (haptic and curve always pointing to the left) beneath the rhexis margin into the capsular bag. As the folded optic passes through the incision, keep pressed against the posterior lip of the wound to avoid Descemet's membrane tears. Once the leading haptic and part of optic are in the bag, rotate forceps 90° clockwise before slowly releasing to allow unfolding. Remove forceps then dial the trailing haptic into the bag with minimal manipulation, or place with McPherson forceps. Injector systems have the advantage of avoiding contact between the IOL and ocular surface, and permit smaller incisions (**Fig. 7.17**).

Final steps

Remove all viscoelastic from the AC and behind the IOL to minimise postoperative IOP rise or capsular distension syndrome. Tilt the optic gently with the cannula (rock and roll) to dislodge viscoelastic from behind the IOL or place the tip behind the optic. Finally, deepen the AC with BSS via a side port and check wound integrity. A well-constructed incision is self-sealing and stromal hydration is unnecessary. If the wound leaks, suture with 10/0 Nylon or 10/0 Vicryl. Inject intracameral cefuroxime 1.0 mg in 0.1 mL (if there is a history of severe penicillin allergy consider intracameral moxifloxacin or intracameral vancomycin). Most surgeons place a clear shield to protect the eye, or use a pad and shield if the blink reflex is absent following an orbital block.

Postoperative care

A typical postoperative eye drop regimen includes G. dexamethasone 0.1% q.d.s. 4 weeks, and G. levofloxacin 0.5% q.d.s. 1 week. In Asian, Afro-Caribbean, or diabetic patients, who are prone to more vigorous or prolonged postoperative inflammation, use 2-hourly steroid for the first 1-2 weeks then taper to q.d.s. for 2 weeks then b.d. for 2 weeks before discontinuing. NSAIDs, such as nepafenac 0.1% or ketorolac 0.5% three times daily for 4–6 weeks postoperatively may reduce risk of macular oedema in diabetic patients (see page 566).

Patient advice

Advise patients to return immediately if they experience visual loss, pain, or increasing redness. Wear the shield at night for 1 week. Avoid splashing or rinsing water in the eye for 1 week; avoid swimming until off steroid eye drops. Avoid heavy lifting and prolonged bending for 1 week.

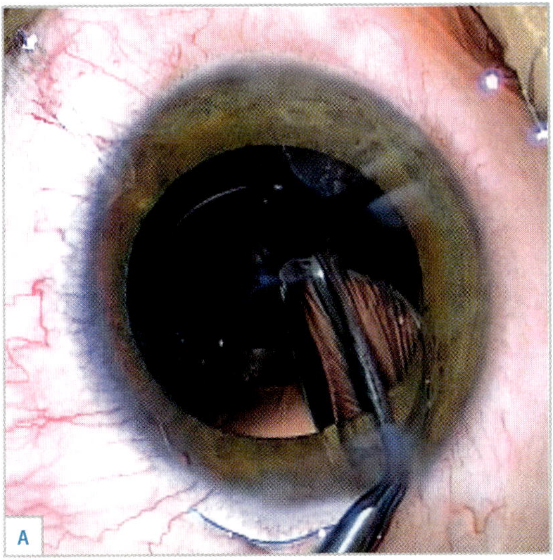

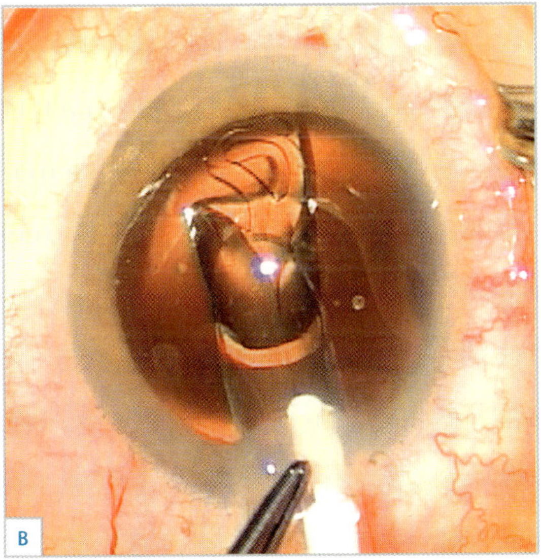

Fig. 7.17: Intraocular lens insertion. (A) Manual insertion of an Acrysof MA60 IOL. (B) Injection of Akreos Adapt aspheric optic (note the leading haptic orientation curving to left being introduced beneath anterior capsule rim).

Follow-up

See at postoperative day 21–28 to assess visual outcome and inflammation, with dilated retinal examination for all cases. If satisfactory then discharge or list for second eye surgery. If surgery was complicated, there is a history of glaucoma, or any other concerns then examine on the day of surgery, or day after, with further review according to progress. Recommend refraction 4–6 weeks postoperatively in routine cases.

DIFFICULT CASES

Small pupil Anticipate in diabetes, pseudoexfoliation (PXF) syndrome, chronic miotic use, α-1 adrenergic blocker use, advanced age, and posterior synechiae. Consider the following:

- *Optimise mydriasis*: Stop miotics in advance, dilate with cyclopentolate 1%, phenylephrine 2.5% (or 10% but beware BP elevation) plus NSAID (e.g. G. flurbiprofen 0.03%), all three times preoperatively. If the pupil is still light-responsive, give more drops. Consider a Mydriasert pellet (containing 0.28 mg tropicamide and 5.4 mg phenylephrine), placed in the inferior conjunctival sac 1–2 hours preoperatively. Consider intracameral phenylephrine (undiluted preservative free 2.5% phenylephrine) or commercially available intracameral mydriatics, e.g. Mydrane, particularly for patients taking α-1 adrenergic blockers such as tamsulosin, risperidone or paliperidone.
- *Highly cohesive viscoelastic*: E.g. Healon GV or 5 helps to splint the pupil open.
- *Posterior synechiolysis*: Inject viscoelastic under the pupil margin and sweep the iris free with a cannula or iris repositor. Consider pupil stretch. Remove any pupillary membrane with forceps.
- *Iris hooks*: Make limbal stab incisions parallel to the iris (or angled slightly posteriorly) with a 25-gauge orange needle or the tip of an MVR blade; avoid the main wound or side ports. Ensure the proximal two hooks are close to the main incision to avoid 'tenting' and consequent iris trauma by the phaco tip. Insert the hooks into the AC, engage the pupil margin and retract (**Fig. 7.18**). Only adjust to final tension after all hooks are *in situ* – do not overstretch. If placing hooks is difficult due to a deep AC, indent the globe at the limbus for easier iris capture. To remove hooks, simply disengage the iris and pull.
- *Pupil expander rings*: Such as the Malyugin ring can provide good pupil expansion with minimal iris sphincter trauma (**Fig. 7.18**). Insert through the main corneal incision into the AC. Gently advance the plunger to deploy the ring, allowing the scrolls to engage the pupillary margin. Use a manipulator through a side port to help engage all four iris points if needed. For removal, disengage the scrolls using micro-instruments, then grasp the distal scroll and guide the ring into the injector cartridge while slowly retracting it with the plunger. Carefully withdraw the injector, ensuring the ring is fully loaded and the iris is free.

Zonular weakness/dehiscence Beware in PXF, advanced age, previous trauma or surgery, vitrectomised eyes, high

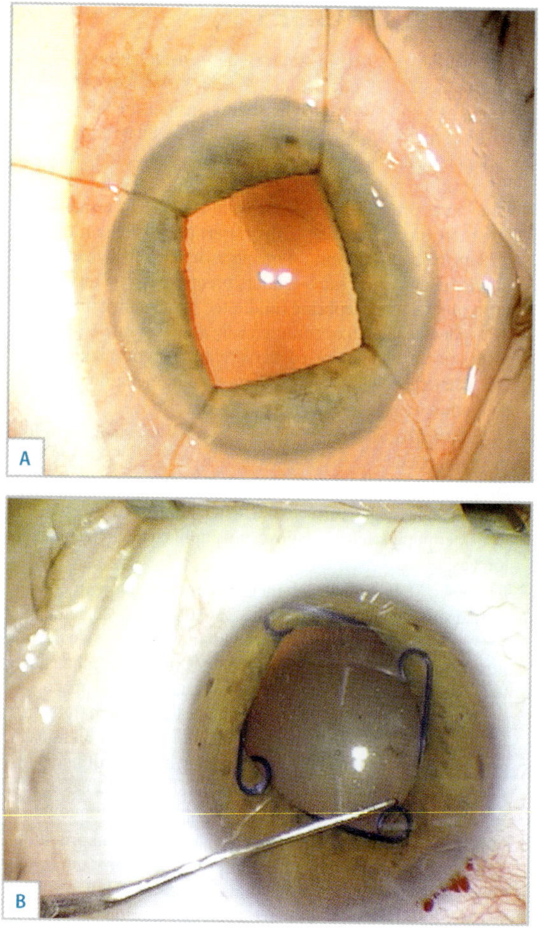

Fig. 7.18: (A) Iris hooks (Courtesy N Islam). (B) Malyugin ring (Courtesy B Little).

myopia, Marfan's syndrome, homocystinuria, Weill–Marchesani syndrome, and sulfite-oxidase deficiency. Look for phaco- or iridodonesis and identify the location of zonular deficiency preoperatively. Aim to minimise zonular stress. Use viscoelastic generously to tamponade areas of zonular dehiscence. Consider each surgical step in turn:

- *Main incision*: Place opposite the zonular weakness if possible.

- *Capsulorrhexis*: Initiate the capsulorrhexis towards the weak zonules using the intact zonules for countertraction. Iris hooks or a second instrument at the capsulorrhexis margin can provide extra stability. Ensure an intact capsulorrhexis is large enough for easy removal of nuclear fragments.
- *Hydrodissection*: Ensure good cortical cleavage and hydrodelineation, but inject extremely gently.
- *Phaco*: Use sufficient phaco power to avoid 'pushing' the nucleus during sculpting and rotate carefully. Horizontal phaco-chop technique produces less zonular stress (p. 307). Beware of a floppy posterior capsule (PC) when removing the last fragments; lower the vacuum and flow rate and consider pulse mode. For 90–180° of zonular dehiscence consider inserting a capsular tension ring (CTR, see below) before phacoemulsification.
- *Cortical removal*: Strip the soft lens matter (SLM) tangentially (c.f. radial) to spread forces. Consider using viscoelastic to keep the capsular bag open or stabilise by preplacing an IOL or CTR.
- *Intraocular lens implantation*: Insert the leading haptic into the bag towards the area of zonular weakness and gently direct the trailing haptic into the bag with McPherson forceps (avoid aggressive dialling). Alternatively, inject the IOL so both haptics unfold directly in the bag. Position the IOL with haptics on the axis of zonular weakness to achieve the best centration. If the IOL is significantly decentred, consider a CTR or place in the sulcus. Avoid silicone plate haptic IOLs as they are more likely to decentre.
- *Capsular tension ring*: Stretches and stabilises the capsular bag by redistributing forces from weak to intact zonules (**Fig. 7.19**). Also reduces capsular phimosis, IOL decentration, and possibly PCO. The open ring is made of PMMA, available in a range of sizes denoted by the diameter of the open ring/compressed ring in millimetres, e.g. 12/10. Insert as large a ring as possible, especially in high myopes. Overlapping of the ends of the CTR is acceptable. Contraindications include incomplete capsulorrhexis or anterior capsule tear, posterior capsule tear if not concentric, and >180° zonular dialysis. Insert into the bag at any point after capsulorrhexis using forceps or injector, but aspiration of SLM trapped under the CTR may be difficult, so delay until after cortical clearance if possible. If zonular loss is marked consider a sutured CTR with one or two eyelets positioned anterior to the capsule for scleral fixation (e.g. Cionni ring) or use sutured capsular tension segments to stabilise capsular bag, alternatively if the capsule cannot be salvaged then consider a secondary scleral fixated PC-IOL, AC-IOL or iris fixated IOL.

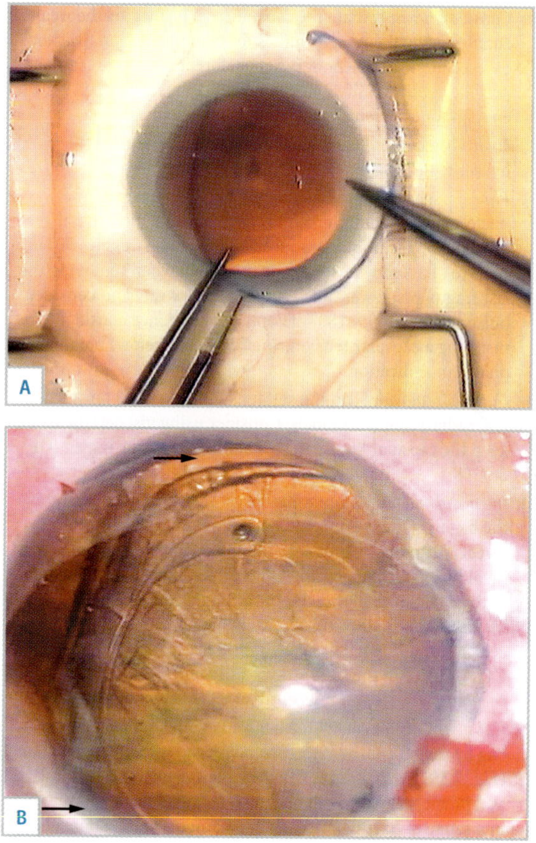

Fig. 7.19: Inserting capsular tension rings (CTR). (A) CTR (Ophtec) being introduced into the capsular bag via a temporal corneal section. (B) CTR (Morcher) insertion before nucleus removal in a patient with aniridia and 160° zonular dialysis.

Brunescent lens Dense and large nuclei are at high risk of PC tear, zonular dehiscence, corneal endothelial damage, and phaco wound burns. Use a 'soft shell' viscoelastic technique (see below). Ensure a large capsulorrhexis for safer phaco and manipulation. Keep the bottle height low to reduce irrigation volume if surgery is prolonged. Chop techniques reduce phaco time and zonular stress; horizontal chop can be effective in cleaving hard nuclei.

Move the phaco tip slowly when sculpting; avoid pushing the lens and use sufficient power to emulsify. Beware of grooving too deep as the epinucleus is thin or absent. Reduce the total phaco time using burst mode or pulse mode (also reduces 'chatter' during fragment removal, i.e. fragments being pushed away from the tip). Alternatively, transversal or torsional modalities, with the appropriate tip, can be more efficient. Dense adhesions in the epinuclear layer at the base of the groove may preclude adequate cracking/chopping and a residual plate may require separate phaco removal.

White cataracts Absent red reflex, release of 'lens milk', and risk of peripheral capsular tears makes capsulorrhexis difficult. Use trypan blue 0.06% (e.g. VisionBlue) to improve capsule visualisation **(Fig. 7.20)**. Increased pressure from the intumescent lens may cause the capsulorrhexis to tear peripherally ("Argentinian flag"), so aim to make a slightly smaller capsulorrhexis and enlarge. Consider using a highly cohesive viscoelastic, e.g. Healon GV. See also brunescent lens above.

High myopia Exclude peripheral retinal breaks pre- and postoperatively. Discuss refractive targeting and the increased risk of retinal detachment and refractive surprise. If the patient wants unaided reading vision, aim for –1.50 D to –2.50 D; for emmetropia aim for –0.50 D. Beware of posterior staphyloma so consider a B-scan cross-check to confirm the axial length (p. 288). Avoid sharp needle LA techniques. The AC is deep, so make a short tunnel incision to avoid distorting the cornea. Capsulorrhexis is more difficult with a deep AC but keep fully formed with viscoelastic to avoid a peripheral tear, observe for anteriorly-placed zonule insertions which may make the rhexis

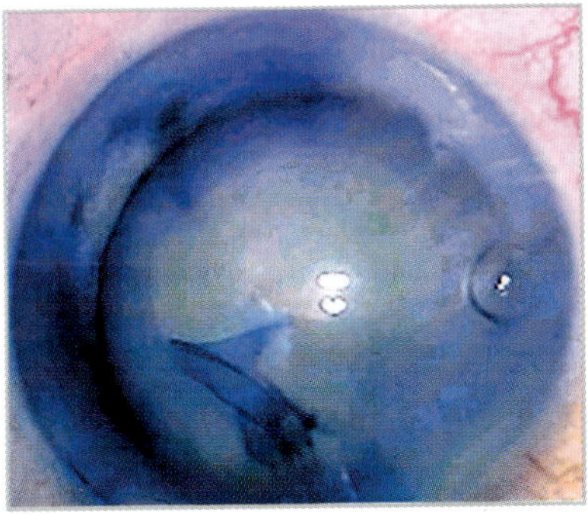

Fig. 7.20: Trypan blue use in white cataract surgery.

run out, and ensure the capsulorrhexis is not too large as the position of the dilated pupil margin in highly myopic eye may mislead sizing. A steep approach with phaco makes sculpting and vertical chopping more difficult – a horizontal chop is easier. The depth of the AC can be decreased by permitting some leakage through a side port with the second instrument. Use hydrophilic or hydrophobic acrylic IOLs with square-edged design to reduce posterior capsular opacification (optic diameter ≥ 6 mm). Avoid silicone IOLs and consider a CTR. Review the postoperative refractive outcome to check biometry accuracy, then quickly perform second eye surgery to minimise the duration of anisometropia/aniseikonia.

Posterior polar cataract This may conceal a defect in the PC. Perform gentle hydrodissection, if any. Most perform hydrodelineation alone with viscodissection of cortex after nucleus removal. Ensure a stable AC with low vacuum and bottle height. Avoid divide and conquer; use phaco-chop or bowl technique instead (the nucleus is usually soft).

Shallow AC/hypermetropia Make a watertight, long tunnel with three-step incision and small side ports to prevent leaks. Maximise the AC depth and stability with highly cohesive viscoelastic (Healon 5 or GV). Consider debulking the lens by phacoemulsification before hydrodissection. Avoid endothelial trauma; use a 'soft-shell' viscoelastic method (see below). Reduce the total phaco power using chop technique and pulse/burst/ozil/cool phaco mode. In extremely shallow ACs, a single port pars plana anterior vitrectomy can create enough working space to perform surgery.

Fuchs' endothelial dystrophy/guttatae Minimising endothelial cell loss is paramount. Use a 'soft-shell' technique: inject dispersive viscoelastic (e.g. Viscoat) adjacent to the endothelium then expand the AC below using cohesive viscoelastic, thus spreading the dispersive agent against the endothelium. Phaco as far from the endothelium as safely possible and reduce total energy with phaco-chop and torsional, or IOP-maintaining phacoemulsification programmes with lower energy output. Avoid applying phaco power within dispersive viscoelastics as they may coagulate, block aspiration, and cause a phaco burn. Consider G. sodium chloride 5% q.d.s. and Oc. sodium chloride 5% nocte to prevent postoperative corneal oedema.

Uveitis Explain the increased risks of surgery (relapse of uveitis/cystoid macular oedema, CMO) and the need for careful follow-up. Ideally, uveitis should be controlled for 3 months preoperatively and treatment stable. Prescribe G. dexamethasone 0.1% b.d.–q.d.s. and G. ketorolac 0.5% b.d.–q.d.s 1 week preoperatively. For extensive posterior synechiae likely to need significant iris manipulation, or those with prior posterior uveitis, especially if associated with CMO, use oral prednisolone EC 40 mg o.d. from 3 days to 2 weeks preoperatively and tapered by 5 mg/week postoperatively to the preoperative dose; if contraindicated, consider intravitreal triamcinolone 4 mg (e.g. Triesence or Trivaris which are licensed for intravitreal use) at the time of surgery (if not a steroid responder). Use a clear corneal incision, foldable acrylic IOL, intensive postoperative topical steroids (initially G. dexamethasone 0.1% 1–2-hourly), and tropicamide 1% b.d. until review at 1 week.

Glaucoma Be aware that nuclear sclerosis may give the false impression of preserved neuroretinal tissue at the optic disc. Patients with a past history of primary angle-closure glaucoma are likely to have a shallow AC and may get postoperative corneal decompensation. Those with advanced glaucoma may lose VA if postoperative IOP elevation 'snuffs out' the small remaining island of vision (although this is very rare). Avoid oral acetazolamide in those with functioning trabeculectomies as reduced aqueous flow may promote fistula closure. Small pupils are common in those on miotics; where possible discontinue 2 weeks preoperatively. Temporal clear corneal incisions help to avoid conjunctival manipulation at the site of existing or future trabeculectomy blebs. Those with functioning trabeculectomy blebs require longer and more intensive postoperative steroids, e.g. dexamethasone 0.1%, 2-hourly for the first week then q.d.s., tapering off over 3 months. Some clinicians advocate subconjunctival 5-FU at the time of surgery.

Diabetes See page 566.

Intraoperative floppy iris syndrome (IFIS) Characterised by iris billowing, pupillary constriction and iris prolapse during intraocular surgery. IFIS is associated with the use of α-1 adrenergic antagonist use (even after a single dose) such as tamsulosin, doxazosin, and risperidone. There is no advantage to stopping medication preoperatively. IFIS potentially increases the risk of iris trauma, posterior capsular tears and vitreous loss, therefore consider intracameral phenylephrine (undiluted preservative free 2.5% phenylephrine) or commercially available intracameral mydriatics (e.g. Mydrane), iris hooks or Malyugin ring.

INTRAOPERATIVE COMPLICATIONS

When surgical complications occur: Stop, take a deep breath, and plan carefully what to do next.

Posterior capsule tears Posterior capsule tears (PCT) during phacoemulsification occur at <1% amongst experienced surgeons, but the rate is higher for trainees due to a steep learning curve. Identification of predisposing factors, timely recognition, and appropriate management significantly minimises the associated morbidity. Signs of PCT include sudden deepening of the AC and momentary pupil dilatation, direct visualisation of the capsule defect or vitreous prolapse, sudden shallowing of the AC during hydrodissection, unstable or immobile lens, and occlusion of the phaco handpiece by vitreous.

Figure 7.21 outlines the management of PCT. If suspected, do not immediately remove instruments from eye; instead, inject viscoelastic first and assess:

- Extent of the PCT and vitreous loss into the AC.
- Amount of residual lens matter – if the nucleus is remaining, the priority is to safely prevent dropped fragments.
- Remaining capsular support – is there sufficient capsule present to secure a posterior chamber IOL, either in the bag or sulcus?

The key principles are to stabilise the AC, preventing extension of the PCT/further vitreous prolapse, and to perform as few manoeuvres as possible to achieve the desired repositioning of the vitreous. If no vitreous prolapses from a small PCT with intact anterior hyaloid face, it may sometimes be possible to convert it to a primary posterior capsulorrhexis after visco-tamponade, then remove residual nucleus by careful phaco (low vacuum/flow rate), thus avoiding anterior vitrectomy entirely. If there is vitreous loss into the AC, perform anterior vitrectomy **(Box 7.3)** before attempting to remove any lens material trapped by vitreous. Scissor/swab vitrectomy may be used if the prolapse is minimal **(Fig. 7.22)**, but is generally not advised because of uncontrolled vitreous traction. A hydrophobic IOL with Prolene haptics (3-piece IOL) can be safely positioned in the sulcus, with optic capture behind the anterior capsule to insure IOL stability and prevent further vitreous prolapse into the AC, intra- or postoperatively.

Posterior dislocation of nucleus or nuclear fragments into the vitreous (dropped nucleus) Resist the temptation to retrieve dropped lens material as there is a high risk that vitreous traction will cause retinal breaks. Refer to a retinal surgeon for vitrectomy, after clearing the AC vitreous and as much SLM as possible. Lens insertion is decided according to

Posterior capsular tear (PCT):
Keep instruments in eye, lower bottle height to minimum and assess.
Stabilise AC with viscoelastic via side port before removing phako probe

↓

Vitreous loss → No → Convert PCT to 1° posterior capsulorrhexis if possible or tamponade with viscoelastic prior to gentle SLM removal

Yes ↓

Anterior vitrectomy:
Remove any free lens fragments manually before performing anterior vitrectomy to clear AC and release trapped nuclear material **(Box 7.3 and Fig. 7.22)**

↓

Nucleus remaining in bag? → No or dropped nucleus → Proceed to SLM clear up

Yes ↓

Extract nucleus:
Float nuclear fragments into AC and express out of wound, aspirate or phaco (use low bottle height, vacuum and aspiration)

↓

SLM clear up:
Further anterior vitrectomy until AC clear

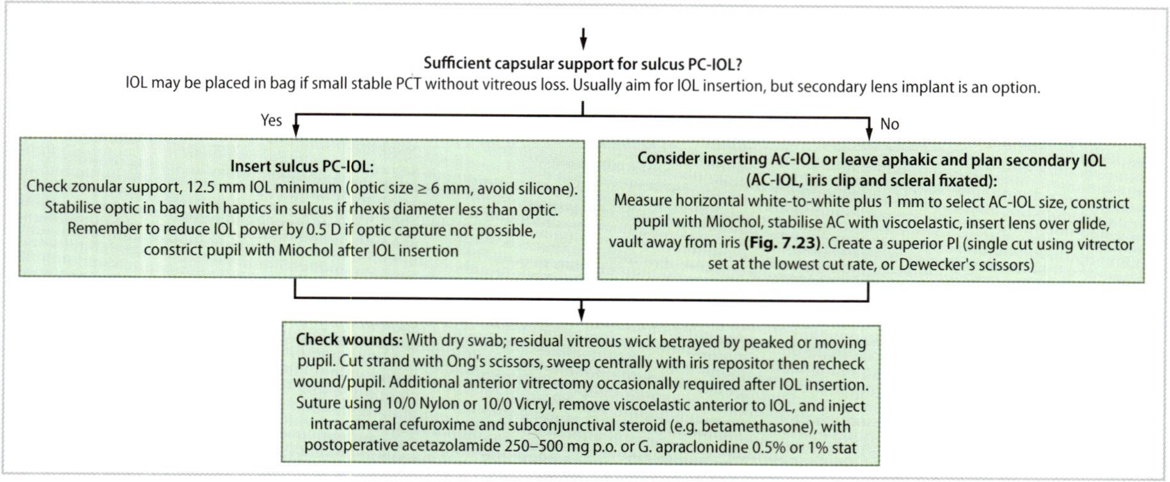

Fig. 7.21: Algorithm for management of posterior capsule rupture.

(AC, anterior chamber; PC-IOL, posterior capsule-intraocular lens; PI, peripheral iridotomy; SLM, soft lens matter)

Box 7.3: Anterior vitrectomy (Fig. 7.21)

1. Be familiar with the anterior vitrector before it is required; know how to set up the machine.
2. A bimanual method is preferred to limit hydration and further vitreous prolapse. Separate the 20-gauge cutter from the infusion. If there is minimal vitreous prolapse, perform a 'dry' vitrectomy (no infusion), maintaining the AC with viscoelastic. Otherwise, insert the infusion cannula via a side port.
3. Check the vitrector is cutting and aspirating in BSS before using in the eye; if the vitrector blows bubbles, the tubes are incorrectly connected.
4. Insert the vitrector via a side port or corneal section. A pars plana approach 3.5 mm behind limbus is an alternative for experienced surgeons, who are also then able to examine the peripheral retina to exclude iatrogenic retinal breaks. Set at low vacuum but use the maximum cut rate.
5. Place the cutter tip through the PCT and hold steady just behind the capsule, with the cutting port facing anteriorly and visible at all times.
6. Vitreous is difficult to see; visualise using use pupil asymmetry, iris movement and intracameral triamcinolone.
7. To minimise vitreous loss avoid shallowing the AC, tamponade with viscoelastic each time before resuming anterior vitrectomy, and lower the bottle height to reduce vitreous hydration. Limit the vitrectomy to the least required to clear the AC to the plane of the PCT and minimise capsular loss.
8. Considering suturing the wounds with 10/0 Nylon or 10/0 Vicryl to ensure positive AC pressure and to decrease the potential for vitreous migration to the wounds.

(AC, anterior chamber; BSS, balanced salt solution; PCT, posterior capsule tears)

local preference but if safe to do so, place an IOL so that pars plana vitrectomy and fragmatome lens removal can be completed without re-entering the anterior segment. Suture the main wound to ensure AC stability during subsequent vitrectomy surgery.

Postoperatively prescribe G. dexamethasone 0.1% preservative free (PF) 1–2 hourly for 1 week then taper slowly over 8 weeks minimum; G. chloramphenicol 0.5% PF q.d.s. 2 weeks; acetazolamide SR 250 mg b.d. p.o. if the IOP is raised or significant viscoelastic is retained. Consider G. ketorolac 0.5% q.d.s. 1 month as prophylaxis against CMO. Review at day 1 for raised IOP, lens and pupil position, wound integrity, and dilated retinal examination. Thereafter, review at day 7, 30, 60 or more

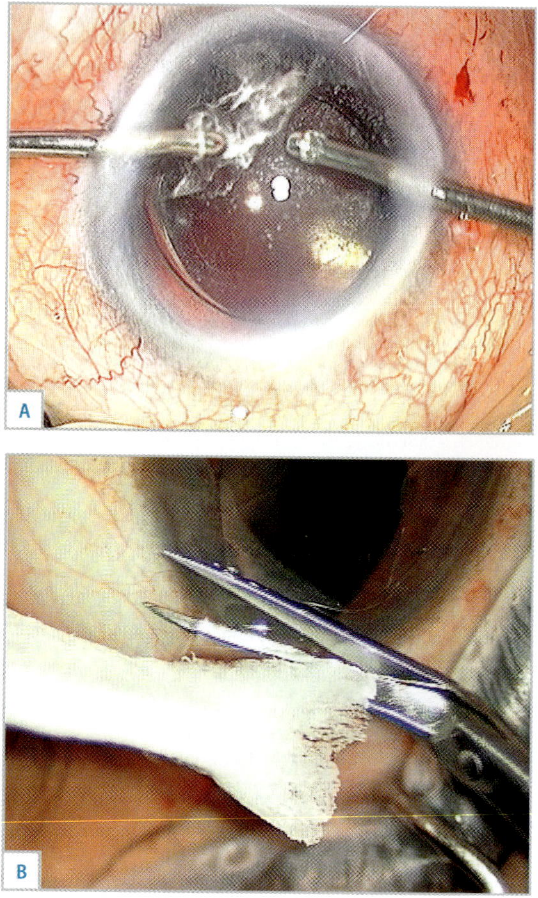

Fig. 7.22: (A) Anterior vitrectomy using bimanual technique with separate cutter and infusion. Intracameral triamcinolone stains prolapsed vitreous white (Courtesy B Little). (B) Scissor swab vitrectomy at wound (rarely needed if there is adequate anterior vitrectomy).

frequently as required. Visual rehabilitation is often delayed, but optimal management can minimise the higher risk of CMO, chronic anterior uveitis, IOL decentration, secondary glaucoma, endophthalmitis, and retinal detachment.

Suprachoroidal haemorrhage A rare (<0.1%) but devastating complication, due to rupture of bridging vessels crossing the suprachoroidal space. Risk factors may include age >65 years, atherosclerosis, anticoagulation (warfarin, rivaroxaban, apixaban), anti-platelet drugs (aspirin, clopidogrel), tachycardia, hypertension, Valsalva manoeuvre, myopia, unstable AC, glaucoma, uveitis, and previous ocular surgery. Early recognition is critical. Look for a sudden shallowing of the AC with positive posterior pressure and iris prolapse. Self-sealing wounds of small-incision surgery usually limit the bleed, but early recognition is critical in minimising the extent – never convert to extracapsular cataract extraction (ECCE) as there is a high risk of expulsion of the intraocular contents. Deepen the AC if possible and close the eye immediately. Examine the fundus on the table for dark choroidal elevation. Consider i.v. 20% mannitol (1 mg/kg over 30 minutes) on the table. If the bleed is limited, surgery may be completed after waiting at least 30 minutes for the blood to clot. Immediate drainage via a sclerostomy is controversial and should not be attempted. Seek the opinion of a retinal surgeon to exclude retinal detachment and consider drainage of large or macular involving suprachoroidal haemorrhage when the clot liquefies. While small haemorrhages may do well, large bleeds usually do badly.

Anterior capsule tears/discontinuous capsulorrhexis

Radial capsulorrhexis tears risk extending to the equator and the posterior capsule. To prevent losing a peripherally tearing capsulorrhexis, ensure the AC is fully formed with a highly cohesive viscoelastic (e.g. Healon GV) and attempt to redirect the tearing forces towards the centre by gripping the capsule as close to the tearing point as possible. If the capsulorrhexis is lost under the iris, try to visualise the endpoint by retracting the iris with the second instrument or an iris hook. Rescue may be possible using 'Little's manoeuvre', whereby the advancing capsulorrhexis flap is unfolded, grasped with forceps near the tearing point and pulled backwards which redirects the tear centrally, before refolding the flap forward and continuing the tear. Alternatively, start a new tear in the opposite direction to include the deviation. If rescue is not feasible, an experienced surgeon may proceed with 'gentle' phaco in the presence of a single tear: use gentle and minimal hydrodissection; avoid overinflation (or collapse) of the AC; use slow bimanual rotation of the nucleus; employ chop techniques and careful cortical aspiration. If the IOL is placed in the bag, position the haptics perpendicular to the tear, or else insert in the sulcus. If it is not possible to secure a sulcus lens consider an AC IOL (**Fig. 7.23**), or alternatively scleral fixated lenses (e.g. Carlevale lens) are used increasingly, often via a vitreoretinal referral.

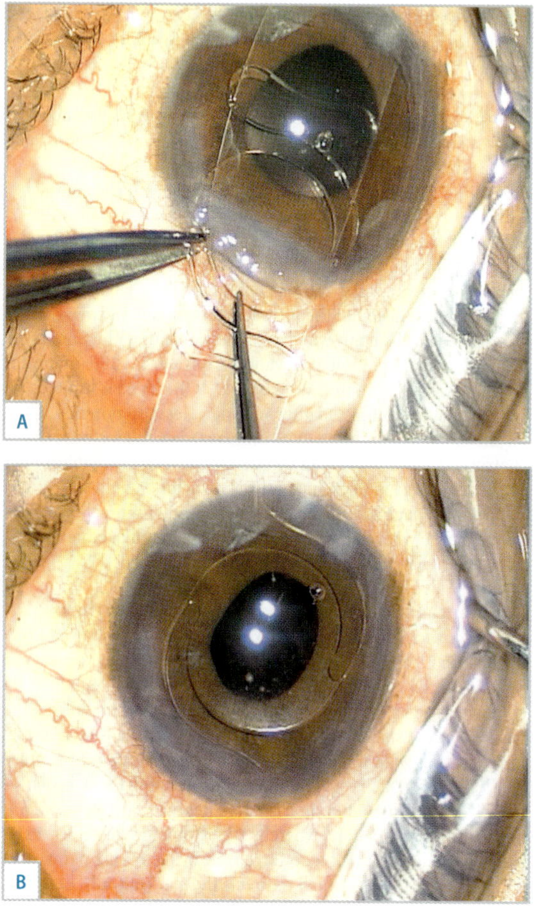

Fig. 7.23: Anterior chamber intraocular lens (AC-IOL): (A) AC-IOL is inserted over a Sheet's glide. (B) AC-IOL in situ with haptics in the angle; peripheral iridotomy yet to be performed.

Intraoperative iris prolapse This is often due to a short corneal tunnel opening into the AC too posteriorly. Prolapse is also more likely if the AC is shallow or if the iris is 'floppy' – beware of patients taking tamsulosin, risperidone or paliperidone. If so, ensure good wound construction, create a long tunnel, and consider hydrodissection via a paracentesis rather than the main wound. If prolapse occurs tamponade the iris away from the wound with viscoelastic and use an iris repositor via a side port to gently sweep it back into the AC. If minor prolapse/iris trauma recurs consider proceeding with surgery. Otherwise, consider iris hooks either side of the wound and subincisionally to secure the iris, suturing the wound and making a new incision with a longer tunnel, or creating a peripheral iridectomy in the prolapsing iris (beware of the risk of postoperative glare from temporal iridectomies). Securely suture the corneal wound at the end of surgery. As iris prolapse is associated with an increased risk of cystoid macular oedema (CMO), so add a NSAID agent (e.g. ketorolac 0.5% three times daily for 4 weeks) to the postoperative regimen.

Corneal phaco burn The phaco tip heats significantly when emulsification continues without flow of irrigation fluid, resulting in a thermal corneal burn at the main incision, compromising wound integrity and causing significant astigmatism (**Fig. 7.24**). Wounds frequently require multiple sutures to remain watertight. Phaco burns are much less likely using burst mode, ozil or hyper-pulse (cool phaco). Causes include:

- *Obstruction to flow by viscoelastic*: This results in 'smoke' (emulsified viscoelastic) appearing at the phaco tip. Ensure adequate aspiration of viscoelastic before starting phaco.
- Wound too tight, constricting the infusion sleeve. Enlarge the wound appropriately.
- Hyphaema increases heat build-up at the phaco probe.

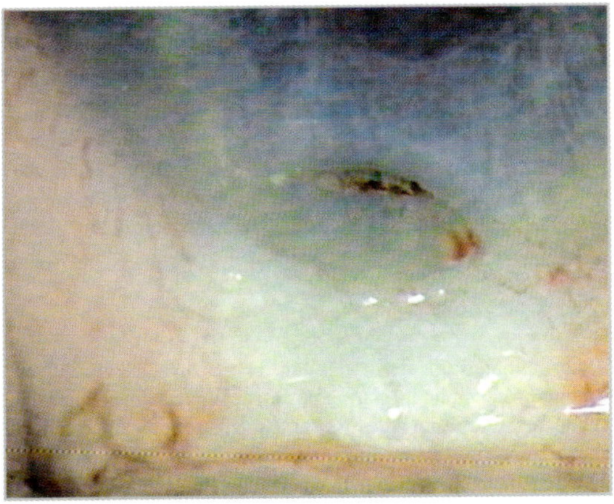

Fig. 7.24: Phaco burn (Courtesy GS Bhermi).

POSTOPERATIVE COMPLICATIONS

Although highly successful, modern phaco surgery is not without complications. See page 298 for anaesthetic complications and page 322 for intraoperative complications.

Elevated intraocular pressure Postoperative IOP elevation is common and usually self-limiting. Causes of raised IOP include retained viscoelastic, over-pressurised AC on completion of surgery, inflammation, pre-existing glaucoma, posterior capsule rupture, vitreous loss, and less commonly pupil block (p. 350) and aqueous misdirection (p. 371). Exclude chronic inflammation and retained lens matter. Short-term topical IOP-lowering agents and/or systemic acetazolamide are usually successful in treating elevated IOP. Late (>2 weeks, typically 4–6 weeks) postoperative IOP rise after uncomplicated surgery is usually secondary to steroid response (p. 364) – stop steroid and use a topical NSAID, or if steroid is still required to control inflammation consider G. loteprednol 0.5%, which induces less steroid response.

Wound leak Prevention is better than cure! Causes include poor wound construction, phaco burn, inadequate suture closure, and postoperative trauma. If the AC remains deep, observe or insert a bandage contact lens. If there is persistent or brisk leak, iris prolapse, flat AC or excess against-the-wound astigmatism, return to theatre to re-suture the wound.

Postoperative iris prolapse This may be avoided with well-constructed, self-sealing wounds or adequate suture closure in those at risk (shallow AC; 'floppy iris' in those on tamsulosin, paliperidone or risperidone; intraoperative prolapse; risk of rubbing eye postoperatively). G. pilocarpine 2% in the early postoperative period may reduce minor incarceration but surgery is usually required if the iris is prolapsed through the wound. Reposition viable iris if not epithelialised (<48 hours), excise any non-viable tissue, and suture the wound. Following repositioning, prescribe intensive topical steroids (G. prednisolone 1% 2-hourly) and topical antibiotic (G. levofloxacin q.d.s.) to reduce the risk of severe inflammation or infection.

Decentred, subluxed, or unstable intraocular lens May be asymptomatic, or result in reduced best-corrected vision, dysphotopsia, diplopia, glare, or uveitis-glaucoma-hyphaema syndrome. Causes include loss of capsular support (anterior rhexis tear, posterior capsule tear, zonular dehiscence), asymmetric haptic placement, and pupil capture (if rhexis larger than optic or sulcus posterior chamber-IOL). According to symptoms and signs, manage by early or late IOL repositioning, lens exchange with posterior chamber scleral fixated (e.g.

haptic fixated or Carlevale lens), iris claw, or AC IOL. Minimise intervention if the endothelial count is low and beware of the eccentric pupil (c.f. IOL subluxation). An IOL dislocated into the vitreous does not necessarily require retrieval, but may be removed via a vitrectomy if the mobile lens gives troublesome symptoms. Refer routinely for vitreoretinal review.

Corneal decompensation Risk factors include pre-existing endothelial compromise (symptomatic diurnal variation in vision, guttatae, pachymetry >630 μm) and intraoperative endothelial trauma. Exclude postoperative IOP rise. To minimise endothelial cell loss, use highly dispersive viscoelastic protection (Viscoat), reduce phaco energy with pulse, burst, ozil or cool phaco mode, and use chop techniques. Allow at least 3 months for oedema to resolve and assess vision and pachymetry before considering corneal graft surgery. Consider interim treatment with topical hypertonic saline (G. sodium chloride 5% q.d.s. or Oc. sodium chloride 5% nocte). If intraoperative endothelial trauma causes a tear or flap, consider a total AC air bubble tamponade.

Rhegmatogenous retinal detachment The reported incidence after uncomplicated phaco-surgery ranges from 0.2% to 3.6% (average 0.7%). The excess risk in the first 10 years is five-fold, with most occurring in the first year. The risk increases with posterior capsule rupture or vitreous loss (4–13-fold), high myopia (10-fold), peripheral lattice degeneration, ocular trauma, or previous retinal detachment. Some studies show increased risk in myopic males compared to females.

Refractive surprise See page 290.

Cystoid macular oedema See page 593.

Endophthalmitis See page 456.

Posterior capsular opacification (PCO) The most common complication (<10% at 2 years) occurring months to years after cataract surgery due to proliferation and migration of residual lens epithelial cells across the posterior capsule. Symptoms include gradual blurring, glare, or reduced contrast sensitivity. May be asymptomatic. Exclude coexisting disease accounting for visual loss. Patient-, surgical-, and IOL-related factors influence the risk of developing PCO:

- *Patient factors*: Young age (~100% occurrence in children) and uveitis.
- *Surgical factors*: In the bag IOL fixation and 360° overlap of the capsulorrhexis margin onto the anterior optic surface provide biomechanical barriers to posterior lens epithelial cell migration. Good cortical clean-up reduces the risk.

Irrigation of the posterior capsule with balanced salt solution after cortical removal to 'jet- blast' off any residual cellular remnants reduces PCO.

- *Intraocular lens factors*: Barriers to cell migration include square-edged optic and contact between the optic and posterior capsule (facilitated by angled haptics); large optic diameter; convex posterior optic surface; IOL material, e.g. hydrophobic acrylic versus hydrophilic.

Treatment involves neodymium-doped yttrium aluminum garnet (YAG) laser posterior capsulotomy **(Box 7.4 and Fig. 7.25)** or rarely surgical capsulotomy.

Box 7.4: YAG posterior capsulotomy

1. Consent:
    - *Benefit*: Improve VA and contrast sensitivity, reduce glare and improve fundal view to manage posterior segment disease.
    - *Risk*: IOP rise, inflammation, IOL pitting (not usually visually significant unless in the visual axis), and subluxation or posterior dislocation of the IOL (especially silicone plate haptic IOLs). Very rarely bleeding, iris damage, endophthalmitis (release of loculated bacteria), corneal decompensation, macular oedema (less likely if capsulotomy is delayed ≥3 months postoperatively), and retinal detachment (0.5–1% or greater if axial length >24 mm).
2. Check the pupil position and visual axis on the slit lamp before dilating the pupil to confirm PCO is present and significant.
3. Instill topical anaesthetic before applying a capsulotomy contact lens (e.g. Abraham lens).
4. Set the laser to a single pulse. Defocus by +1.50 D. Minimise laser energy: start with 0.7 mJ, then increase the power until sufficient to open the capsule (rarely need >1.5 mJ). Focus the aiming beam on or just behind capsule.
5. Start peripherally to avoid pitting the IOL in the visual axis. Aim to clear the visual axis to the largest physiological mydriatic pupil size or more if a clear peripheral fundal view is important, e.g. diabetic retinopathy. An inverted-'U' (horseshoe) opening avoids the potential of pitting in the visual axis (unlike a cruciate capsulotomy) and minimises 'floaters' (unlike full-'circular' capsulotomy). Treating areas under tension allows the capsule to spring apart, minimising the number of shots (and total energy) required. Usually requires 30–40 shots.
6. For prophylaxis against post-YAG IOP spike, instill 1 drop of G. apraclonidine 1% before and after treatment. Alternatively, give a single dose of oral acetazolamide SR 250 mg. Some check IOP 1-hour post-laser.
7. To minimise inflammation, prescribe a short course of topical steroid, e.g. G. dexamethasone 0.1% q.d.s. 5–7 days.

Box 7.4: *Continued*

8. Warn about new floaters and distinguish from retinal detachment symptoms.
9. Follow-up is not routinely required, but patients with raised IOP at 1 hour despite prophylactic treatment should be monitored for glaucoma.

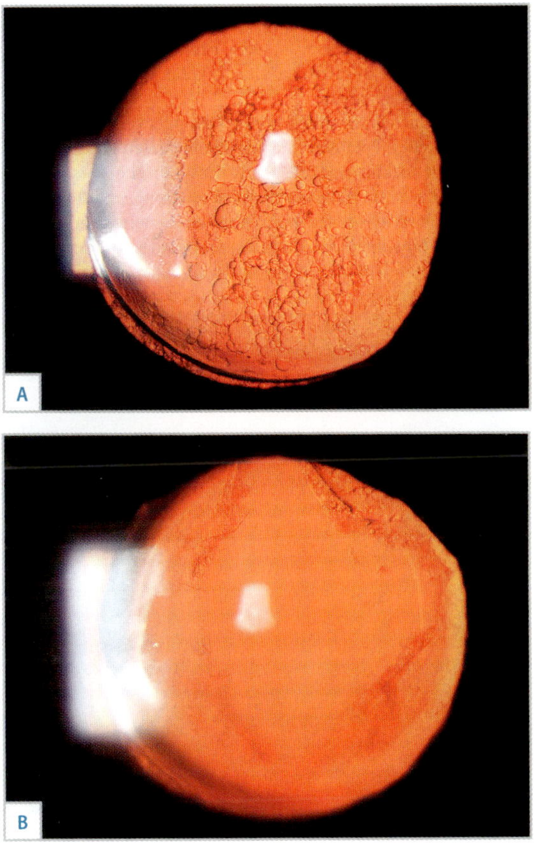

Fig. 7.25: Cruciate YAG laser posterior capsulotomy before (A) and after (B) treatment. Note the capsule retracts in each quadrant to create a quadrilateral opening.

FEMTOSECOND LASER-ASSISTED PHACOEMULSIFICATION SURGERY

The femtosecond laser, first used for corneal refractive surgery, delivers ultra-short pulses producing photodisruption via microcavitation bubbles which are much smaller than conventional lasers, therefore allowing greater precision with less collateral tissue damage. It has been used in cataract surgery to create corneal incisions, lens capsulotomy and fragmentation **(Fig. 7.26)**. Lens fragmentation **(Fig. 7.27)** may reduce phacoemulsification time by 84–96%. Femtosecond laser can also quickly create intrastromal arcuate keratotomies to reduce keratometric astigmatism.

Femto-phaco is not suited to eyes with poor dilation or corneal opacities. Potential risks include increased IOP during laser/patient docking and capsular block syndrome, possibly due to increased nuclear volume after laser 'softening', and sealing of the capsulorrhexis to the lens. There is a learning curve, particularly for surgeons without laser refractive experience.

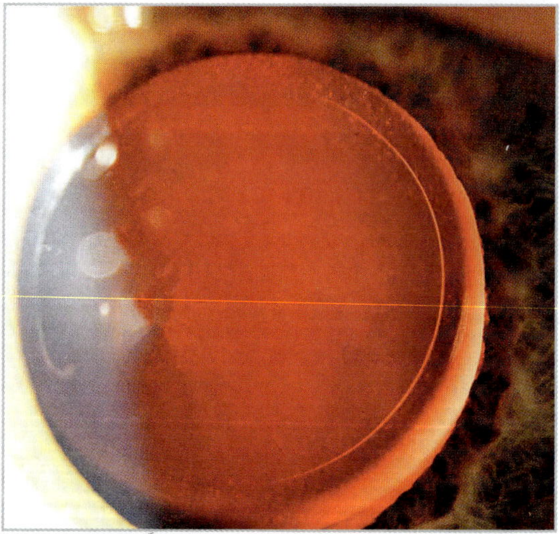

Fig. 7.26: Femtosecond laser capsulorrhexis (Courtesy JD Stevens).

Fig. 7.27: Femtosecond nucleus fragmentation – cube pattern (Courtesy JD Stevens).

Multiple studies in a public health care setting report that the visual outcomes and complication rates are similar to those in manual phacoemulsification, with no cost benefit.

OPTOMETRY AND GENERAL PRACTICE GUIDELINES

General comments

Age-related cataracts produce a gradual reduction in visual acuity (VA). The diagnosis is seldom difficult using slit-lamp examination. The red reflex is often altered when viewed with a direct ophthalmoscope, although nuclear sclerotic cataracts may be less evident than cortical lens opacities or posterior subcapsular cataracts. If the vision deteriorates below the patient's requirements and they would like to discuss surgery, then arrange routine referral.

Optometrists

- If symptoms are disproportionate to VA, ask about quality of vision in different lighting conditions or glare from car headlights at night or in bright sunlight. If possible, measure contrast sensitivity, which may give a better indication of 'real world' visual function.
- Where possible, include the following when referring:
  1. Visual symptoms attributable to cataract, including the effect on the patient's desired lifestyle, occupation, and driving.
  2. Any known ocular comorbidity.
  3. Up-to-date spectacle refraction and best-corrected VA in each eye.
  4. Desired refractive target if known.
  5. Any relevant medical or social history and any special circumstances.

General practitioners

- Remember the cataractogenic effect of long-term corticosteroids (including eye drops, face cream, oral or inhaled steroids).
- Consider reduced VA as a cause of falls in the elderly. Gradually progressing cataracts may mean patients are unaware of very poor VA.
- Exclude diabetes mellitus, especially in younger patients with cataract.
- Measure VA if possible. Consider referral to an optometrist to confirm the diagnosis of cataract, and to check the best-corrected VA with updated refraction before referral for surgery.
- Identify systemic disease which may compromise surgery or anaesthetic, e.g. orthopnoea, respiratory or cardiovascular disease.

- Provide a list of current medications. Tamsulosin and other α-blockers (e.g. risperidone, paliperidone), anticoagulants and antiplatelet drugs are particularly relevant.
- Poorly controlled hypertension or diabetes increases the risk of complications and may result in cancellation of surgery. Initiate measures to improve control prior to referral and monitor in the run-up to surgery.
- Explain that smoking increases the risk of cataract. Stopping may slow progression.

GLAUCOMA

8

David L Lunt, Anthony Khawaja & Peng T Khaw

BACKGROUND

Glaucoma describes a group of disorders with characteristic structural optic neuropathy (disc cupping) and associated visual field loss. Intraocular pressure (IOP) is the major modifiable risk factor. Recognised types of glaucoma include:

- Primary open-angle glaucoma
- Angle-closure glaucoma
- Secondary glaucoma (due to uveitis, trauma, etc.)
- Congenital glaucoma

Reducing IOP is the only proven means of preserving the visual field, although it is not effective in every case.

HISTORY

Ask about:

- Active problems, mode of presentation, and the patient's worries.
- Presenting and highest IOPs, if recorded at source of referral.
- Past ophthalmic history (e.g. uveitis and trauma).
- Surgery and complications, especially glaucoma, cataract, retinal procedures, and refractive surgery (alters corneal thickness and IOP measurements) as these can alter future management.
- Refractive error.
- Contact lens usage (may be affected by surgery and influence the choice of medication and surgical technique).
- Medical history for conditions linked with glaucoma (hypotensive crises, migraine and Raynaud's phenomenon) and those affecting the choice of medication, e.g. bradyarrhythmias, angina, asthma, renal stones and sickle cell disease.
- Medication used previously and currently, especially: systemic beta (β)-blockers; other antihypertensive medication; systemic, inhaled, or topical steroids; and bronchodilators. Any side effects from ocular medications including preservatives.
- Ethnic/racial group and preferred language
- Family history of glaucoma or blindness
- Occupation
    - *Driving status*: Heavy goods, or own vehicle? Has the patient informed the driving authorities that they have glaucoma?
- Social support and care arrangements

INTRAOCULAR PRESSURE

Background IOP is the cardinal modifiable risk factor for glaucoma. The prevalence of glaucoma rises with IOP, but 30–50% of cases have normal IOP. Mean IOP rises with age in Caucasians and tends to be the highest in the morning. Glaucoma is associated with greater IOP fluctuations. IOP is measured by flattening or indenting the cornea, hence corneal abnormalities (scars and extremes of thickness) may significantly influence results and lead to inappropriate treatment. Inaccuracies of ±6 mmHg may occur at the extremes of corneal thickness. The use of correction tables and formulae to adjust for the effect of corneal thickness is not recommended, as the relationship is more complex and not linear. Some modern non-contact tonometers measure and account for corneal hysteresis/rigidity to some degree.

Equipment Commonly used tonometers include the Goldmann (slit-lamp mounted), iCare (rebound tonometer, especially helpful for children), Ocular Response Analyser (non-contact air puff tonometer that additionally measures corneal biomechanical properties and derives a corneal-compensated IOP that is less influenced by corneal artefact), Corvis (uses high-speed video to measure corneal response to an air puff and derive IOP readings less influenced by corneal artefact), Tonopen (may offer advantages in scarred/abnormal corneas), Perkins (Portable Goldmann principle useful for examination under anaesthesia and home visits) or iCare Home (a rebound tonometer for self-testing at home).

Goldmann tonometer Ensure adequate corneal anaesthesia and that the prism is clean and free from contaminants. Avoid excess fluorescein. If corneal astigmatism is >3.0 D, rotate the prism so the minus cylinder axis on the prism graduation corresponds to the red mark on the prism holder. If necessary, hold the lids against the orbital rim but avoid pressure on the globe. Be aware, breath-holding increases IOP. If the mires pulsate, measure at the mid-pulse amplitude. Record the time of measurement.

Confirming calibration: Mount the tonometer on the slit lamp with the prism inserted. Fit the calibration bar into the socket on the side of the tonometer. Graduations on the bar correspond to different IOPs: Centre or with calibration bar absent (0 = 0 mmHg), second (2 = 20 mmHg) and third (6 = 60 mmHg). The longer part

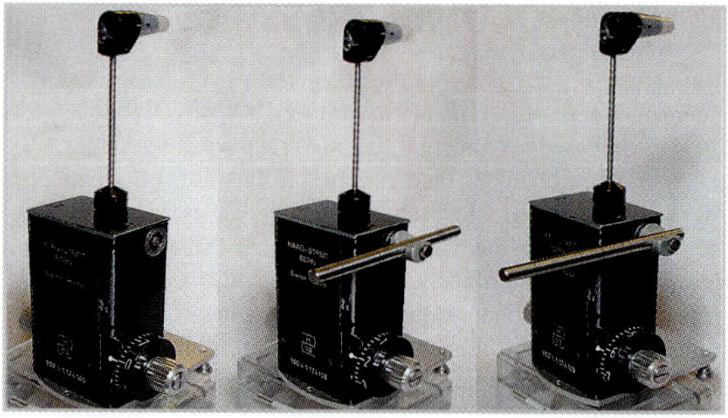

Fig. 8.1: Goldmann tonometer with calibration bar attached, showing calibration to 0, 20 and 60 mmHg (left to right).

of the calibration bar is on the side opposite the prism **(Fig. 8.1)**. Dialing the appropriate reading should cause the bar to pivot with adjustments ±2 mmHg either side of the correct reading.

GONIOSCOPY

Background Examine the drainage angle of all patients with suspected glaucoma or ocular hypertension, both at diagnosis and periodically thereafter.

Equipment Goldmann one- or two-mirror lenses are steeper than corneal curvature (K) and require a coupling medium. Four-mirror lenses (Zeiss, Posner and Sussman) are flatter than K. Steeper-than-K lenses provide a stable, clear view and are easier to use. They can be used to perform dynamic (compression) examination. Four-mirror lenses are superior for difficult dynamic examinations.

Examination Dim ambient illumination and ensure adequate topical anaesthesia. Apply a low-viscosity coupling fluid (e.g. carbomer 0.2% or hypromellose 0.5%) to the Goldmann lens. Use a narrow-slit beam, 1 mm long, to avoid pupil constriction and widening of the angle. Identify Schwalbe's line at the apex of the corneal wedge reflex **(Fig. 8.2)**. The trabecular meshwork lies immediately posterior to this. Estimate the geometric width of the angle (in degrees) between the surface of the trabecular meshwork and a line tangential to the peripheral one-third of the iris. Note the profile of the iris (plateau, concave, regular and steep), its first point of contact with corneoscleral coat and its point of true insertion (modified Spaeth classification). The angle width is often recorded as 1 = 10° and 2 = 20°. Care is necessary with shorthand notation, as this may lead to confusion with some grading systems, e.g. the Shaffer system ranges from 0 to IV, with IV a wide open angle, whereas the Scheie system ranges from 0 to IV, but IV denotes a closed angle. It may be more helpful to document the number of degrees that the iris contacts the trabecular meshwork, and if >180° then the angle is occludable. The angle structures visible are heavily influenced by the orientation of the eye and gonioscope. It is important to grade the angle with the eye in primary position and the gonioscope not tilted, so as to not inadvertently open a closed angle.

After assessing the angle width, widen the beam and examine the four quadrants again for the presence of pigment (intratrabecular, diffuse or geographic and blotchy deposits on trabecular surface), Sampaolesi's line (granular pigment on Schwalbe's line), and abnormalities such as neovascularisation, membranes, angle recession or iridodialysis. Peripheral anterior synechiae are identified with a Goldmann lens; ask the patient to look towards the mirror and gently indent the cornea with the edge of the lens. If the angle does not open, perform indentation gonioscopy with a four-mirror lens to differentiate between appositional and synechial angle-closure. A normal angle is shown in **Figures 8.2A and 8.3.**

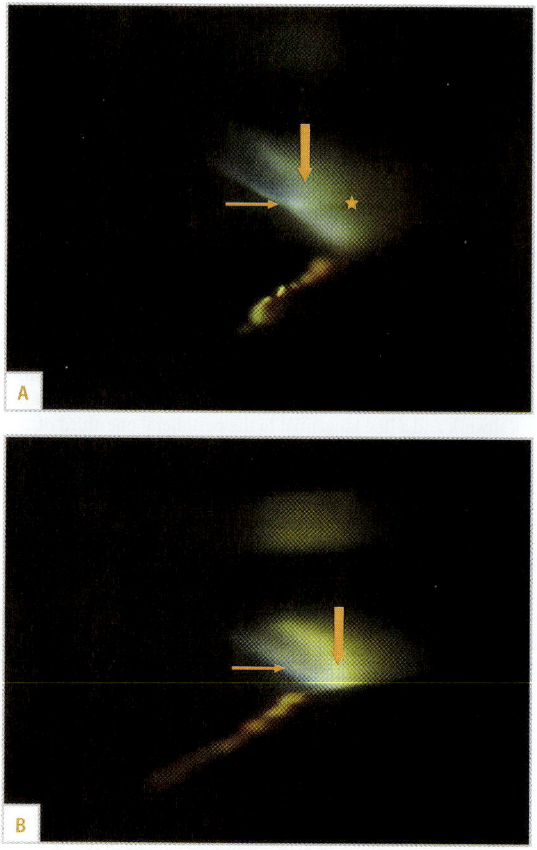

Fig. 8.2: Gonioscopy showing a wide-open angle (A) and a closed angle (B). The corneal wedge is formed by the junction of the reflex from the corneoscleral junction (broad arrow) and the corneal endothelium (thin arrow). The apex of the wedge indicates the location of Schwalbe's line. The star in image A represents the horizontal extension of Schwalbe's line. The posterior meshwork is visible posterior to this. See also Figure 8.3.

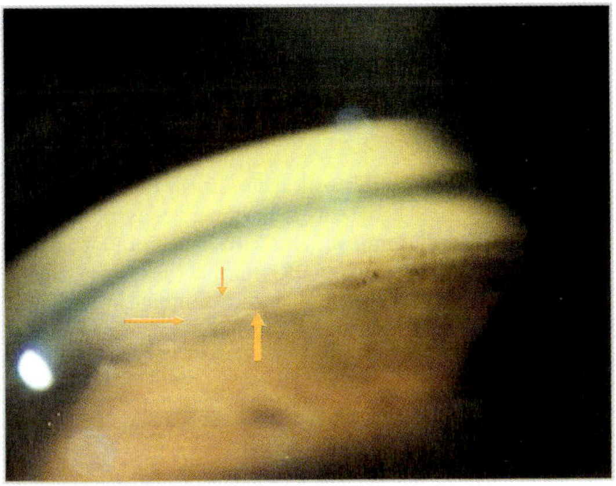

Fig. 8.3: Gonioscopy showing ciliary body band (upward arrow), scleral spur (horizontal arrow), junction of pigmented and non-pigmented trabecular meshwork (downward arrow).

OPTIC DISC EXAMINATION

Background Identification of characteristic optic disc changes facilitates the diagnosis of glaucoma, and the detection of disease progression.

Examination Measure the vertical disc size by reducing the height of the focussed light beam to the same size as the disc. Note the beam height (mm) and lens used (magnification factor). Measure the cup-to-disc ratio (CDR). Normal CDR varies with disc size **(Fig. 8.4)**. Assess the rim for focal thinning or notches. Check the 'ISNT rule': normal rim thickness is inferior > superior > nasal > temporal.

Other features: Look for tilting, peripapillary atrophy, disc haemorrhages, and 'bayoneting' (double angulation) or 'baring' (exposing) of blood vessels. Nerve fibre layer defects are best seen using either white light or red-free light, carefully focussed, particularly in superotemporal or inferotemporal nerve fibre bundles. Record all observations. An asymmetric CDR is suspicious of glaucoma if the discs are the same size.

Imaging A baseline record of disc appearance (photograph or OCT image) aids detection of change.

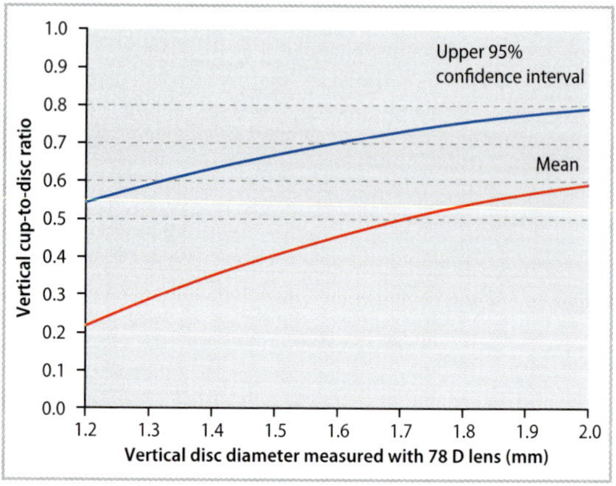

Fig. 8.4: Normal cup-to-disc ratio relative to disc size (Courtesy DF Garway-Heath).

OPTIC DISC OPTICAL COHERENCE TOMOGRAPHY

The circumpapillary retinal nerve fibre layer (RNFL) analysis is a useful adjunct to clinical examination, and helps to monitor trends over time.

A traffic light colour-coded computer analysis system is incorporated into scanning machines to depict the statistical divisions of normative data, but first confirm the accuracy of the scan. It is important to note there is only a finite number of scans within the normative database for age, against which all scans are compared. For small, large or tilted discs, the database is much smaller, and ring measurement placement is variable, so that the computer algorithms often interpret these discs as abnormal. For non-glaucomatous disc abnormalities (such as disc pit or optic disc drusen), the analysis can be similarly abnormal and therefore unsuitable for offering additional information with regard to glaucoma progression. A system for reporting RNFL images is presented below:

1. Complete a full clinical examination, with visual field, before interpreting the OCT. Confirm patient's name, date of birth, date of OCT, diagnosis, and any historical scans.
2. View the fundus images, and the size and alignment of the scanning circle (if misaligned or a different size scanning circle is used, you cannot compare with previous scans).
3. Confirm the disc-fovea line is similar in previous scans. Adjust manually, if incorrect.
4. Image quality: Note if image quality is poor and consider why, e.g. cataract.
5. Review the TSNIT (temporal, superior, nasal, inferior and temporal) graph. Check for the 'double hump' seen in a normal scan, and smooth scanning lines showing good segmentation.
6. Review the pie graphs of quadrants of RNFL. Red is abnormally thin, yellow is borderline, and green is normal thickness when compared against age-matched normals.
7. Do not simply interpret red scans as abnormal and green scans as normal.

OCT assessment of macula inner retinal thickness is also helpful for diagnosing and monitoring glaucoma, and may detect early change. Relevant macular parameters include the ganglion cell layer (GCL) alone or together with the inner plexiform layer (GCIPL), RNFL, or the ganglion cell complex (RNFL + GCIPL). See also pages 752 to 756 for more detail.

Anterior segment OCT (AS-OCT) can assess angle width and the risk of occlusion, but unlike gonioscopy does not show the trabecular meshwork, pigment and new vessels.

HUMPHREY VISUAL FIELD TESTS

Background Static, white-on-white and semi-automated perimetry is the standard method for identifying and assessing progression of functional visual loss from glaucoma. Monocular fields determine management. Binocular field determines quality of life and function, e.g. ability to drive.

Single field test Ask is the field: 1. Reliable and 2. Glaucomatous?

- The best measure of reliability given by the machine is the false-positive level: high levels of fixation losses and false negatives may not indicate unreliability.
- Causes of artefact include inattention (producing a 'clover-leaf' field), small pupil size, uncorrected refractive error, lens rim, lid/brow, media opacities, and macular disease.
- Characteristic sites of early glaucomatous damage are paracentral, nasal, and arcuate.
- 'Raw' thresholds give the height of the 'hill of vision' (in dB of attenuation: high dB values mean a dim stimulus was seen) at test locations.
- Total deviation compares the patient's 'hill of vision' to age-matched normals.
- Pattern deviation highlights focal rather than diffuse loss (total deviation shows both).
- Global indices attempt to summarise plots in a single number: Mean deviation (MD) for total deviation, pattern standard deviation (PSD) for the pattern of deviation.
- The Glaucoma Hemifield Test compares corresponding clusters in superior and inferior hemifields. Repeatable abnormality suggests glaucoma.
- Always evaluate fields in light of other clinical findings, including the the optic disc appearance, ability to do field test, and media opacities. If in doubt, repeat.

Field series Ask if a field defect is: 1. Progressing and 2. If so, how fast?

- Ideally, all fields in the series should be same type, e.g. all standard full threshold (FT) or all Swedish interactive thresholding algorithm (SITA). If the series is mixed FT/SITA use pattern deviation for progression. SITA-FAST and SITA-FASTER algorithms offer shorter test times.
- Software (e.g. FORUM Glaucoma Module for the Humphrey perimeter) can help to detect pointwise or global progression.
- Sources of error include fluctuation (short- and long-term), learning effects, inappropriate change criteria, inappropriate frequency of testing, artefact (see Single field test, above), poor

reliability (see Single field test, above), and field loss beyond the dynamic range of the perimeter.

- Central (10-2) field testing is useful to monitor advanced peripheral loss extending within 10° and to detect early glaucoma that has predominantly affected the macula (e.g. the macular vulnerability zone is a central area that is particularly susceptible to glaucomatous damage and often affected in early glaucoma).
- Newer combined algorithms such as the 24-C programme include standard peripheral and more central field points.

PRIMARY OPEN-ANGLE GLAUCOMA

Background A progressive optic neuropathy associated with distinctive, excavated disc appearance and a pattern of visual field loss localising damage to the optic nerve head. Usually bilateral, but often asymmetric. Affects 2% of people over 40 years of age. Risk factors include Black African or Caribbean origin, positive family history (stronger risk factor if >1 first-degree relative), myopia, and increasing age. Elevated IOP is the most important modifiable risk factor for the development of primary open-angle glaucoma (POAG). Like most biological risk factors (e.g. BP and stroke), there is no one IOP threshold that defines POAG and segregates risk, and the usual upper limit of normal (21 mmHg) is simply the population average plus 2 standard deviations. However, POAG with IOP consistently ≤21 mmHg is defined separately as normal tension glaucoma (NTG; also known as normal pressure glaucoma). IOP-independent mechanisms may contribute more to NTG than the most common high-tension POAG, but this is controversial, and IOP remains the only proven modifiable risk factor for NTG.

Symptoms Typically asymptomatic until advanced visual field loss occurs. Occasionally, early disease presents with non-specific visual symptoms due to paracentral field loss.

History Ask for a family history of glaucoma and glaucoma blindness. Exclude causes of secondary glaucoma (history of trauma, uveitis, or steroid usage). Ask about migraine and peripheral vasospasm, e.g. Raynaud's phenomenon.

Examination

- *Slit lamp*: The anterior segment is normal in POAG. Exclude signs of secondary glaucoma, e.g. pigment dispersion, pseudoexfoliation, neovascularisation, anterior segment dysgenesis, angle-closure and aphakia. Measure IOP; the risk of POAG increases with IOP.
- *Gonioscopy*: By definition the angle must be open, not occludable, and with no peripheral anterior synechiae. Gonioscopy is essential to differentiate POAG from other forms of glaucoma.
- *Optic disc*: Shows progressive, pathological loss of neuroretinal rim and associated nerve fibre layer defects, manifesting as enlargement of the cup-to-disc ratio.

Investigations

- *Visual field*: Look for progressive field loss anatomically consistent with the area of neuroretinal rim loss. Monitor with regular automated perimetry every 3–4 months if progression is suspected.
- *Optic disc imaging*: A baseline photograph and/or OCT image is very useful for future comparison and detection of change.
- *Central corneal thickness*: Affects measured IOP, with thick corneas registering artefactually higher IOP readings on average (thin corneas vice versa). Population average thickness is ~550 μm (standard deviation, 30–35 μm), but varies by race (p. 189).
- *Rarely*: Consider 24-hour ambulatory BP and sleep apnoea monitoring to look for nocturnal BP dips/sleep apnoea.

Diagnosis Moderate/advanced POAG is easily diagnosed with typical disc and field change. Early glaucoma is more difficult and may need monitoring for months or years before progression confirms the diagnosis.

Differential diagnosis

- *Ocular hypertension*: IOP > 21 mmHg but no glaucomatous optic neuropathy.
- Previous elevated IOP causing stable, non-progressive signs of optic neuropathy.
- Non-glaucomatous optic neuropathy
- Other lesions of the visual pathway

Treatment All current treatments principally aim to lower IOP and reduce or eliminate glaucomatous progression. Options are medical, laser, or surgery. Very elderly patients with slow disease progression may have a low risk of significant visual function loss in their remaining lifetime, so consider observation of their disease trajectory before commencing treatment.

- *Casualty*: Only start treatment if the diagnosis is certain and IOP > 28 mmHg, or if there is advanced disc damage. Start with single therapy regardless of IOP, using topical prostaglandin analogues as first-line. Arrange routine clinic referral.
- *Clinic*: Tailor treatment to the patient's circumstances (consider age, stage of glaucoma, etc.). Aim initially for a 30% IOP reduction medically or with selective laser trabeculoplasty (SLT). Stop ineffective treatments and use alternatives. Avoid polypharmacy. Monitor regularly for disc and field progression. If IOP reduction is inadequate to stop progression

on maximal medical therapy (2–3 drops) consider SLT if this has not already happened (p. 377) or trabeculectomy surgery (p. 385). The 'target pressure' for an individual patient is the estimated IOP needed to prevent progression: it may be different in each eye and may vary with time and changing circumstances **(Fig. 8.5)**. The target may be below 10 mmHg in patients with vulnerable optic nerves whose disease is progressing despite IOP at the lower end of the normal range.

- *Optic nerve head blood flow*: Although not directly measurable *in vivo*, vasospasm or fluctuation in systemic BP may have an affect on optic nerve head perfusion. This may be a separate factor contributing to disease progression.
- *Neuroprotection*: Currently, no definitive proof but undergoing clinical trials.

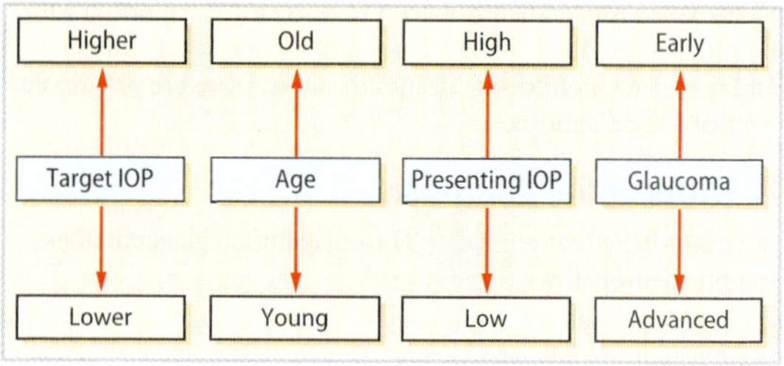

Fig. 8.5: Factors influencing the target intraocular pressure.

PRIMARY ANGLE-CLOSURE

Background Angle-closure is contact between the iris and trabecular meshwork (iridotrabecular contact, or ITC) accompanied by a significant impairment of aqueous outflow. It may be primary or secondary, with 75% of primary cases due to pupil block. Frequently associated with glaucomatous optic neuropathy. The symptomatic form ('acute' angle-closure) is a common ophthalmic emergency.

Classification The traditional classification of acute, intermittent, chronic, and latent phases fails to identify the disease stage and mechanism of closure. Classify as follows:

- *Stage*:
  1. Occludable angles, defined as >180° ITC measured with gonioscopy in the primary gaze (primary angle-closure suspect, PACS). Perform dynamic (also termed indentation) gonioscopy to open an angle that is closed in static gonioscopy in primary position, and to identify peripheral anterior synechiae (PAS). Dynamic gonioscopy is carried out by indenting the cornea using either direct pressure with a 4-mirror lens that has a smaller area of contact with the central cornea, or by using a gonioscopy lens that has a larger flanged area of contact and asking the patient to look in the direction of the mirror and tilting the lens to use the edge of the lens to indent the central cornea.
  2. *Primary angle-closure (PAC)*: >180° ITC with either high IOP or PAS.
  3. Primary angle-closure with glaucomatous optic neuropathy (PACG).
- *Mechanism of angle-closure*:
  1. Pupil block
  2. Anterior and non-pupil block (includes plateau iris)
  3. Lens induced
  4. Causes behind the lens, e.g. aqueous misdirection (p. 371).

Nuclear sclerosis is almost invariably present. This is part of the primary disease and distinct from phacolytic/phacomorphic glaucoma (p. 365).

Symptoms Blurring of vision sometimes accompanied by haloes around lights, redness and periocular or hemicranial pain. There may be nausea and vomiting. However, angle-closure is often asymptomatic, especially in Asian people.

Signs Signs mirror symptoms in acute disease; VA is reduced, there is circum-limbal injection with corneal oedema, raised IOP, and an immobile pupil. Refraction is often (but not always) hypermetropic.

History and examination A positive family history is common. Dynamic gonioscopy is essential to make the diagnosis. Record the estimated geometric angle width, angle structures visible, iris profile (steep, regular, or plateau), iris pigment on the trabecular meshwork, and extent of PAS. Asymmetry between the two eyes suggests a secondary cause.

Differential diagnosis Consider primary open-angle glaucoma; phacolytic and phacomorphic glaucoma; irido-ciliary cysts; retinopathy of prematurity; uveitis; nanophthalmos; Weill–Marchesani syndrome; Marfan's syndrome; persistent hyperplastic primary vitreous and lens subluxation; posterior segment pathology and iatrogenic causes (including vitreoretinal surgery). PAC is extremely uncommon below the age of 30 years. In older people, rule out neovascularisation and hypertensive uveitides. Numerous drugs can precipitate angle-closure (topical mydriatics; anticholinergic agents including bronchodilators; antispasmodics; antidepressants; proprietary cold and flu medication and anticonvulsants).

Investigations Anterior segment OCT is a useful adjunct to clinical examination. B-mode ultrasound is invaluable in identifying posterior segment disease (e.g. ciliary effusions) when the fundal view is inadequate.

Management This ranges from community observation to emergency outpatient (and occasionally inpatient) management.

- *Primary angle-closure suspect*: Manage asymptomatic patients with occludable angles in the community, after informing them of the symptoms to look out for. Consider laser iridotomy if any 'PLUS' features apply:
  1. Patients with only one functioning eye
  2. Family history of significant angle-closure disease
  3. Conditions requiring regular pupil dilatation, e.g. diabetic retinopathy
  4. Vulnerable adults who may not report symptoms
  5. Using medications with anticholinergic action (includes several used for depression, hay fever, bladder dysfunction, heart conditions and pain)
  6. People living or working remotely, with poor access to emergency care
- *Primary angle-closure/PACG*: Offer peripheral iridotomy. If <30 mmHg and early disease consider IOP-lowering eye drops at first-line treatment, with ongoing observation of disease trajectory and changes to angle morphology with repeated gonioscopy. For eyes with PAC and IOP >30 mmHg, or with PACG, the EAGLE trial found that lens extraction

(even in the absence of significant cataract) was more effective than laser iridotomy.

Emergency management of symptomatic acute PAC

Immediately initiate medical and/or laser treatment to control IOP. Consider admitting patients with IOP > 40 mmHg in an eye with useful vision.

- *Stat*: G. dorzolamide 2%/timolol 0.5% combination, G. apraclonidine 0.5%, G. prednisolone 1%, G. pilocarpine 2%, and i.v. acetazolamide 250–500 mg (dose depending on body weight and renal function). Lie the patient supine. Provide analgesics/antiemetics as required.
- Check IOP at 30–60 minutes.
  1. If responding, unless there is a clear reason not to, perform Yttrium Aluminum Garnet (YAG) laser iridotomy in both eyes as soon as corneal clarity allows **(Box 8.1)**.
  2. If partially responding, add further doses of acetazolamide 250 mg q.d.s. p.o., G. prednisolone 1% 1–2-hourly, and G. pilocarpine 2% q.d.s.
  3. If no response within 2 hours, consider laser iridoplasty **(Box 8.2)** or diode laser cycloablation. In units with adequate medical support, consider glycerol 50% 1 g/kg bodyweight p.o., or i.v. mannitol 20% 1 g/kg. A controlled AC paracentesis can rapidly end a non-responsive angle closure attack (use a 29.5-gauge insulin syringe with the plunger removed, inserted parallel to limbus and iris to avoid lens contact).

Box 8.1: YAG laser iridotomy

This is the cornerstone of management.

1. Premedicate with G. apraclonidine 0.5% and pilocarpine 2% (4% for dark brown irises) 30 minutes and 5 minutes before.
2. Always use a lens (Wise or Abraham's). Try to treat in the base of an iris crypt **(Fig. 8.6)**
3. Create an iridotomy that will be covered by the upper lid (usually 11–1 o'clock), or that is clear from the tear meniscus (i.e. 3 or 9 o'clock). Try to avoid treating in an area under the marginal tear strip; this may cause glare/linear dysphotopsia.
4. If bleeding occurs, a little pressure with the contact lens helps to stop this.
5. Argon pretreatment is useful in patients with thick brown irises: 10–40 shots, 0.05–0.1 seconds, 50 μm, 200–1,000 mW power. Avoid charring.
6. Iridotomies should be ~200 μm in diameter.
7. Check IOP 1 hour post laser. Prescribe G. prednisolone 1% hourly for 24 hours, then q.d.s. 7 days.

Box 8.2: Laser peripheral iridoplasty

Applying large, slow-contraction burns to peripheral iris is useful in both symptomatic and asymptomatic cases. Premedication and lenses are as for iridotomy **(Box 8.1)**.

- Using an argon laser, select a 500 µm spot size, 0.5 seconds for all iris colours. Power: 100 mW increasing as required.
- End-point: Brisk contraction of the stroma without charring or a pop.
- Target the peripheral iris, but ensure there is a gap between the endothelium and iris. This may mean starting in the mid-peripheral iris and spiralling out to the far periphery as a gap opens with treatment.
- Apply five evenly spaced shots per quadrant.

If used for medically unresponsive cases of acute angle-closure, a peripheral iridotomy must be completed at the earliest opportunity within hours of pressure normalisation. Monitor pressure and give topical steroids as for iridotomy.

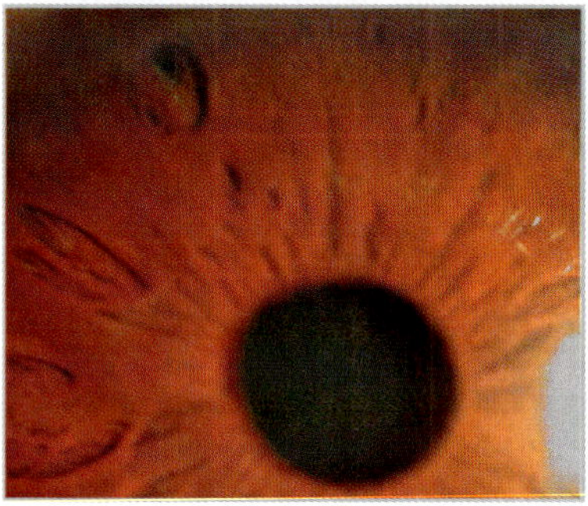

Fig. 8.6: Laser iridotomy in the 11 o'clock position.

Subsequent management targets the specific mechanism of closure. If the mechanism is at or anterior to the lens, lens extraction will open the angle.

The presence of >6 clock hours of PAS extending across the trabecular meshwork and glaucomatous optic neuropathy both suggest that laser and medical treatment are unlikely to control IOP satisfactorily. A trabeculectomy may be needed. Because of the poor success rate and increased complications, avoid trabeculectomy soon after an acute attack, unless absolutely necessary.

Follow-up Once IOP is controlled, continue medication until next review of patient at 1 week, 1 month, then annually.

PSEUDOEXFOLIATION SYNDROME

Background Pseudoexfoliation syndrome (PXS) is characterised by the deposition of grey flecks of amyloid-like fibrillar material on the lens capsule and many extraocular tissues. It is more common with increasing age, with geographical and racial clustering. Associated trabecular dysfunction may cause elevated IOP and pseudoexfolative glaucoma (PXG). Associated with polymorphisms in the *LOXL-1* gene.

Symptoms May be an incidental finding or present late with glaucomatous field loss. Two-thirds are unilateral on presentation.

Signs Radial lens–iris contact may rub off pseudoexfoliation (PXF) material from the lens, leaving a 'bull's-eye' pattern (a clear intermediate zone). Central iris transillumination occurs due to abrasion of iris pigment epithelium, and PXF material may be seen on the iris and pupil margin **(Fig. 8.7)**. Gonioscopy shows 'salt and pepper' pigmentation on the trabecular meshwork and pigment deposition anterior to Schwalbe's line (Sampaolesi's line). Often the pupil dilates poorly.

History and examination Record family history, VA, IOP, iris transillumination, gonioscopy, RAPD, and disc examination (with pupils dilated). Note cataract density and post-dilation pupil size. Look for phacodonesis – lens subluxation may occur due to weak zonules.

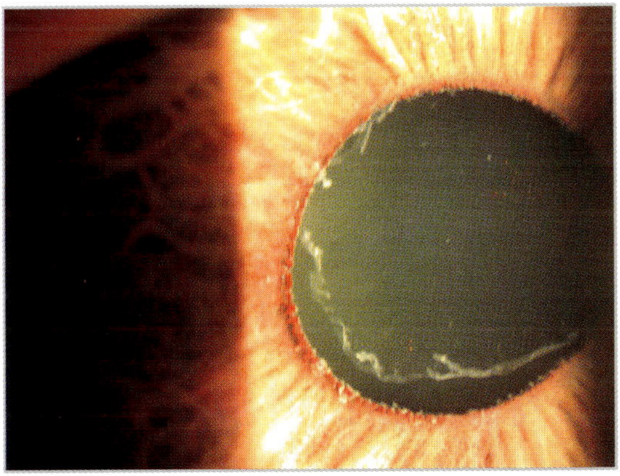

Fig. 8.7: Pseudoexfoliation.

Investigations Arrange baseline disc imaging and visual fields. Further investigations are not routinely required.

Treatment Manage ocular hypertension and glaucomatous optic neuropathy as for primary open-angle glaucoma (p. 350). Laser trabeculoplasty may be effective but may also fail abruptly. High IOP spikes may lead to rapid progression of disc damage. Trabeculectomy is usually effective. Cataract surgery may be complicated (~five-fold increase in vitrectomy rate) due to weak zonules and small pupils, so manage accordingly (p. 315). Postoperative capsule phimosis may be significant.

Follow-up With PXF only (no glaucomatous optic neuropathy or ocular hypertension), review 12 monthly. For PXG, review 3–12 monthly as indicated by the stability of IOP, disc and field.

PIGMENT DISPERSION SYNDROME

Background Pigment dispersion syndrome (PDS) is characterised by pigment shedding from iris pigment epithelium and deposition on other intraocular structures. It is more common in Caucasians, myopes, and the 35–50 years of age group, and can occur with an autosomal dominant inheritance pattern with variable penetrance. Posterior bowing of the mid-peripheral iris results in abrasion of the iris by lens zonules. Pigment deposits in the trabecular meshwork are associated with raised IOP and glaucoma.

Symptoms Transient visual blurring or haloes, with IOP spikes, often following physical exertion. May present late with glaucomatous field loss.

Signs Pigment loss results in iris transillumination, typically seen as radial spokes in the mid-periphery **(Fig. 8.8)**. Pigment deposition on the corneal endothelium is usually concentrated

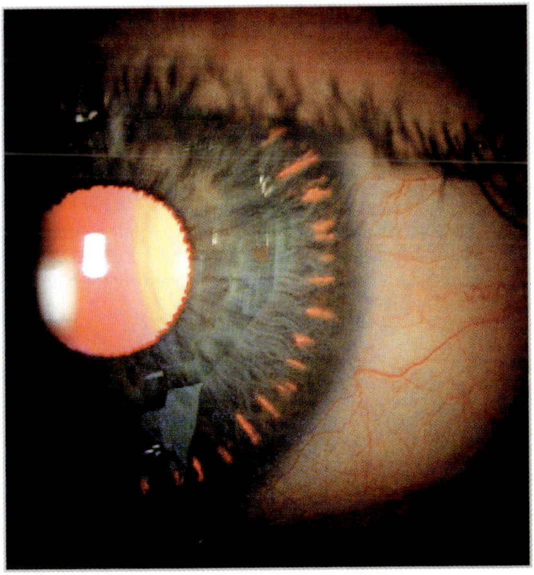

Fig. 8.8: Pigment dispersion syndrome with peripheral iris transillumination (Courtesy K Barton).

in the vertical midline by aqueous convection (Krukenberg's spindle). The AC is deep. Gonioscopy shows diffuse pigment deposition around 360° of the trabecular meshwork. The angle is open and the peripheral iris may be appreciably bowed posteriorly. Pigment granules may be seen on the iris surface and among zonular insertions at the lens equator (Scheie stripe).

Differential diagnosis Angle pigmentation can occur in angle-closure, pseudoexfoliation, and following trauma and iritis. Iritis may cause iris transillumination.

History and examination Ask about visual disturbance, particularly following exercise. Record family history, VA, IOP, corneal pigment deposits, AC depth and cellular activity, iris transillumination, gonioscopy, RAPD, and disc examination (with pupils dilated). Exclude peripheral retinal holes, especially if prescribing pilocarpine.

Investigations Request a baseline disc image and visual field.

Treatment Consider IOP measurement following exercise. Pigment dispersion may 'burn out' prior to causing elevated IOP. Iris–zonule contact may be reduced by low-dose pilocarpine, but this is often not tolerated. Treatment with laser peripheral iridotomy to reduce 'reverse pupil block', which may cause backward bowing of the iris, is controversial. Manage pigmentary glaucoma as for primary open-angle glaucoma (p. 350). Laser trabeculoplasty may be effective but has a high failure rate; use low-power settings. Trabeculectomy is often effective.

Follow-up With PDS only (no glaucomatous optic neuropathy or ocular hypertension), review 6–12 monthly; for pigmentary glaucoma, 3–12 monthly as indicated by stability of the IOP, disc and fields.

NEOVASCULAR GLAUCOMA

Background A secondary glaucoma with an open angle, but angle-closure mechanisms result from iris neovascularisation.

Symptoms Redness, pain, photophobia and blurred vision.

Signs Poor VA, high IOP, conjunctival congestion, corneal oedema, iris new vessels (NVI or rubeosis iridis, **Fig. 11.22**, p. 528), ectropion uveae, vessels crossing the trabecular meshwork on gonioscopy, and peripheral anterior synechiae (PAS).

Differential diagnosis: For the causes of rubeosis iridis, see page 528.

Investigations Carotid Doppler imaging if relevant.

Treatment

- *Control IOP*: As shown in **Figure 8.9**. Arrange physician review as required.
- *Urgent panretinal photocoagulation (PRP)*: Use slit lamp, indirect, or endolaser. For technique see page 523. Consider cryotherapy or trans-scleral diode laser retinal ablation if an inadequate fundal view prevents laser treatment under direct vision.
- *Medical treatment*: Topical glaucoma medication is required in eyes with navigational vision or better. If the eye is painful with no useful navigational vision, manage with G. dexamethasone 0.1% q.d.s. and G. atropine 1% b.d.
- *Surgical treatment*: For eyes with good potential visual function, consider glaucoma drainage devices, or mitomycin C (MMC) augmented trabeculectomy; consider using an anti-VEGF agent with surgery.
- *Intravitreal anti-VEGF drugs*: E.g. ranibizumab or bevacizumab, but a Cochrane review was inconclusive.
- *Ciliary ablation by diode laser*: See page 396.
- *Retrobulbar alcohol or enucleation*: Reserved for painful blind eyes not controlled medically or with cyclodestruction.

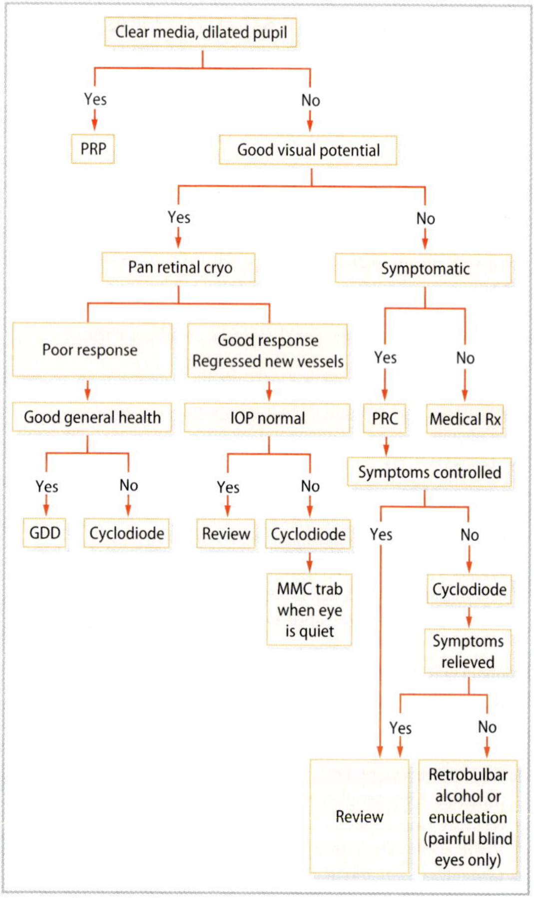

Fig. 8.9: Neovascular glaucoma treatment algorithm. Abbreviations: GDD, glaucoma drainage device; PRC, pan retinal cryotherapy; PRP, panretinal photocoagulation

UVEITIC GLAUCOMA

Background 10% of uveitic eyes develop secondary glaucoma.

Signs Look for keratic precipitates, flare, iris atrophy/nodules, and posterior synechiae. Gonioscopy may show peripheral anterior synechiae, pigment, or debris in the angle.

Management Problems include frequent recurrence, variable IOP, pupillary membranes and secondary cataracts precluding disc assessment and reliable field testing, and the need for long-term steroid treatment. Collaborate with uveitis specialists and physicians, especially for immunosuppression. Treatment depends on the mechanism(s):

- *Secondary open-angle glaucoma*: Treat medically and control the uveitis.
- *Closed-angle glaucoma with pupil block*: Examine the other eye to rule out primary angle-closure. Treat as acute angle-closure but without miotics. Surgical iridectomy is preferable to laser.
- *Steroid pressure response*: See next page.
- *Closed-angle without pupil block*: Medical management of IOP.
- *All mechanisms*: If medical therapy fails, consider mitomycin C-augmented trabeculectomy or a glaucoma drainage device. Do not combine cataract and filtering surgery. Use postoperative steroids and 5-fluorouracil (5-FU) judiciously after trabeculectomy, using the minimum steroid potency and dosage needed to adequately control inflammation to avoid cataract formation in phakic eyes.

STEROID PRESSURE RESPONSE AND ASSOCIATED GLAUCOMA

Background Usually caused by topical steroids, especially prednisolone and dexamethasone, but may be caused by intraocular, periocular, inhaled, intranasal, or systemic steroids. G. dexamethasone 0.1% q.d.s. for 6 weeks is associated with an IOP rise of >6 mmHg in 35% of normal adults, versus 95% of patients with primary open-angle glaucoma (POAG). Higher IOP rises occur in POAG patients and their first-degree relatives. Most often seen following cataract surgery, but can with other eye operations including otherwise successful glaucoma filtration surgery.

Classification Low response (<6 mmHg IOP rise); intermediate response (6–15 mmHg); and high response (>15 mmHg). Diagnosis is confirmed by IOP fall on steroid reduction.

Symptoms Often asymptomatic unless there is advanced field loss or very high IOP.

Signs Raised IOP, usually after 4–6 weeks of steroids (rarely before 2 weeks, except in children). Optic disc cupping with visual field loss may suggest steroid-induced glaucoma.

History and examination Record the steroids used, their concentration, frequency and duration, IOP, and optic disc assessment. Perform gonioscopy. Exclude posterior subcapsular cataract.

Differential diagnosis Undiagnosed or co-existing ocular hypertension/POAG.

Investigations Disc imaging and visual field assessment.

Treatment
- Reduce the potency and frequency of steroid treatment.
- Consider FML, rimexolone, or loteprednol (less steroid response in adults).
- Treatment as for POAG if IOP remains above target (p. 350).
- Consider topical NSAIDs for the management of inflammation.

Follow-up The rate of IOP fall is variable (days to months). Occasionally, IOP rise is permanent.

PHACOLYTIC AND PHACOMORPHIC GLAUCOMA

Background Disease of the lens may cause raised IOP. Identifying the underlying mechanism is important before deciding on the appropriate therapeutic options.

Classification

- *Phacolytic*: Leakage of protein from mature or hypermature cataract through an intact capsule obstructing trabecular meshwork.
- *Phacomorphic*: Secondary angle-closure from lens intumescence. Increases relative pupil block.

Symptoms: Unilateral pain, reduced VA, lacrimation, and photophobia.

Signs: Intumescent mature or hypermature (Morgagnian) cataract, conjunctival hyperaemia, corneal oedema, and IOP > 21 mmHg.

History: Record duration and severity of symptoms, previous history of cataracts, ocular surgery or uveitis.

Examination

- *Phacolytic*: Angles open on gonioscopy, intense AC flare with small white particles of lens matter.
- *Phacomorphic*: Closed angles on gonioscopy, shallow AC, typically with contralateral eye showing deeper AC and open angles.

Differential diagnosis

- *Symptomatic primary angle-closure*: Characteristically has symmetrically narrow angles. A mature/hypermature cataract is not present.
- *Inflammatory/uveitic glaucoma*: Exclude other uveitides by thorough examination.
- *Phacoanaphylactic glaucoma*: Granulomatous uveitis with keratic precipitates and hypopyon is usual, with a history of cataract surgery.

Investigations B-scan ultrasonography [±ultrasound biomicroscopy (UBM)] helps to define the anatomical relationships and exclude retrolental disease. Record axial length, AC depth, lens thickness, or posterior capsule configuration in both eyes.

Treatment The immediate aim is to control IOP and inflammation. The definitive treatment is cataract extraction as soon as IOP and inflammation are controlled:

- Topical β-blockers (e.g. timolol 0.25% b.d.), and/or topical α-agonist (e.g. apraclonidine 0.5% t.d.s.)
- Oral carbonic anhydrase inhibitors (e.g. acetazolamide 500 mg stat dose, then 250 mg q.d.s.)
- Topical steroid (e.g. prednisolone 1% 2-hourly)
- Cycloplegics (e.g. cyclopentolate 1% t.d.s.)
- Hyperosmotic agents (e.g. oral glycerol 50% up to 1 mL/kg) may be necessary.
- Avoid miotics, since they may shift the iris–lens diaphragm forward, exacerbating angle-closure, and possibly increase inflammation.

TRAUMATIC GLAUCOMA

Background Trauma may lead to early or late IOP elevation, progressing to glaucomatous optic neuropathy. Hyphaemas may cause very high IOP. The trabecular meshwork may be directly damaged (alkalis, siderosis and angle-recession) but this may not reduce outflow for many years. Angle-recession results in glaucoma in 5% (10% of those with 360° recession). Traumatic cataract, significant iris injury, and lens subluxation/dislocation are also important risk factors for glaucoma.

Symptoms Acutely – pain, reduced vision, or haloes. May present late with glaucomatous field loss.

Signs Iris sphincter ruptures, deep AC, AC cells (hyphaema and ghost cells), flare, or phacodonesis. Gonioscopy may show peripheral anterior synechiae, angle recession **(Fig. 8.10)**, cyclodialysis clefts, or blood. Look for 360° angle recession by comparing both eyes. Exclude vitreous haemorrhage and posterior segment sequelae of trauma.

Differential diagnosis Primary open-angle glaucoma.

History and examination Record the details of the injury and subsequent treatment; VA; IOP; iris defects; AC depth and cellular activity; pupil size; gonioscopy; RAPD; and dilated disc examination. If the injury resulted from a workplace accident or alleged assault, make careful and complete notes. Carefully examine the orbit, anterior segment, posterior segment and peripheral retina for other injury.

Fig. 8.10: Angle recession. A normal angle is shown in Figure 8.3 (p. 345).

Investigations Baseline visual field and optic disc photography/imaging.

Treatment

- *Casualty*: If the IOP is elevated, commence medical treatment. Request early clinic review.
- *Clinic*: AC washout (hyphaema), vitrectomy (ghost cells), or cataract extraction (lens trauma) may be necessary if the IOP is not responsive. Treatment is determined by the likely mechanism of pressure rise. Laser trabeculoplasty is unlikely to be effective. Non-augmented trabeculectomy has a high failure rate due to prior inflammation and conjunctival scarring. Mitomycin C trabeculectomy or a glaucoma drainage device (e.g. Baerveldt tube) is often considered as a primary procedure.

Follow-up As indicated by IOP, disc and field. Annual IOP measurement is required for eyes with angle recession. Always check IOP when reviewed, even years later. The presence of recession may have medicolegal implications.

GLAUCOMA FOLLOWING VITREORETINAL SURGERY

Background Temporarily raised IOP after vitreoretinal surgery is common. Progression to glaucoma occurs in <5% of cases. Risk factors include pre-existing glaucoma, trauma, angle recession, steroid response, high myopia, pigment dispersion syndrome, chronic inflammatory disease, proliferative retinopathies, use of silicone oil (remains a risk even if removed), and vitreous haemorrhage.

Mechanism

- *Scleral buckling procedures*: Ciliary body rotation with angle-closure; anteriorly placed buckle causing angle-closure; high buckle with vortex vein compression; shed photoreceptor outer segments occluding outflow (Schwartz–Matsuo syndrome; not peculiar to buckle cases and often presents prior to surgery).
- *Vitrectomy*: Ghost cell glaucoma; retained lens material; pigment dispersion after cryotherapy; chronic inflammation and neovascular glaucoma.
- *Vitrectomy with intravitreal tamponade*: Pupil block with overfill of tamponade and direct angle-closure or intratrabecular obstruction and damage from emulsified silicone oil.

Signs Look for raised IOP, corneal oedema, cells or emulsified silicone oil in the AC, absence of an inferior gas/fluid interface from vitreous gas overfill, and iris bombé. Gonioscopy may show an open or closed-angle, peripheral anterior synechiae, silicone oil, or new vessels. Check the patency of any inferior iridectomy in aphakic silicone-filled eyes. Large silicone oil bubbles in the AC are easily seen, but a 100% AC oil fill is easily missed, and often lacks corneal oedema despite sometimes very high IOP.

Natural history IOP often settles when postoperative inflammation resolves. Steroid response within 2 weeks of surgery is unlikely. Removal of emulsified silicone oil does not affect IOP.

Medical management

- *Open-angle*: First-line treatment is topical β-blocker and α-adrenergic agonists b.d. Consider prostaglandin agonists o.d. if postoperative inflammation is not severe. Oral acetazolamide may be required.

- *Closed-angle*: Difficult to control medically. Aqueous suppressants are first-line, such as oral acetazolamide 250 mg q.d.s. orally, topical β-blocker b.d. and an α-adrenergic agonist.
- *Pupil block*: Mydriatics, e.g. atropine 1% b.d.

Surgical management: Overfill of tamponade with pupil block requires partial removal of gas or silicone. Glaucoma surgery is often needed in eyes with closed angles and aphakic eyes. Trans-scleral diode laser ciliary ablation is used in most cases, but more than one treatment is often needed. If oil is *in situ*, reduce the power. Consider drainage tube implants if there is potential for good navigational vision (VA >6/60 and/or visual field >10°).

Prognosis No perception of light in 50% of eyes with IOPs persistently >30 mmHg or hypotony after treatment. Optic disc cupping may progress despite IOP control. Cases with closed angles have the poorest prognosis.

AQUEOUS MISDIRECTION (MALIGNANT GLAUCOMA)

Background Characterised by axial shallowing of the AC and raised IOP. Occurs in 2% of patients undergoing trabeculectomy for angle-closure. May occur after any type of intraocular surgery. Crowding of the ciliolenticular space (possibly from anterior rotation of the ciliary body) is believed to block aqueous flow. Posterior aqueous diversion into the vitreous increases retrolenticular pressure and shallowing of the AC. Risks are high in nanophthalmic and small and short eyes.

Symptoms Blurred vision and altered refractive error. Unilateral pain, lacrimation, and photophobia if IOP is elevated.

Signs Shallow or flat AC, with or without elevated IOP. Choroidal detachment, haemorrhage, or signs of pupil block are absent.

History Ask about the duration/severity of symptoms, previous history of angle-closure, and recent ocular surgery.

Examination Record VA and IOP. Shallowing of the AC is axial, unlike iris bombé in pupil block. Consider and exclude hypotony/overdrainage or choroidal effusions. Confirm patency of any iridotomy.

Differential diagnosis

- Symptomatic angle-closure
- *Choroidal detachment*: IOP is typically low with choroidal elevation visible on fundoscopy.
- *Choroidal/vitreous haemorrhage*: Sudden onset of elevated IOP associated with severe pain. Blood may be visible.

Investigations Arrange preoperative biometry ± ultrasound to identify nanophthalmic/small and short eyes prior to glaucoma surgery (axial length < 21 mm, posterior scleral thickness ≥ 2 mm). B-mode ultrasound is useful in excluding choroidal detachment or haemorrhage.

Treatment Identify high-risk eyes preoperatively – suture the scleral flap watertight using releasable sutures, and give postoperative cycloplegia.

Established cases:

- *Cycloplegia:* G. atropine 1% t.d.s. and phenylephrine 10% b.d.
- *Reduction of aqueous production (if IOP is elevated):*
  1. Topical β-blockers (e.g. timolol 0.25% b.d.) and topical α-agonist (e.g. apraclonidine 0.5% t.d.s.).
  2. Oral carbonic anhydrase inhibitors (e.g. acetazolamide 250 mg q.d.s.).
- *Reduction of vitreous volume:* If raised IOP is unresponsive consider hyperosmotic agents (e.g. oral glycerol 50% up to 1 mL/kg, or intravenous mannitol up to 2 g/kg).

In 50% of cases, IOP is lowered and the AC deepens with atropine and ocular hypotensive drugs. If unsuccessful, or when lens–cornea touch is present, laser and/or surgical intervention is required.

Laser/surgical management Perform YAG laser disruption of the posterior capsule/anterior hyaloid in pseudophakic eyes. It is important to extend the capsulotomy to the periphery. If this fails, pars plana vitrectomy is effective in two-thirds of cases. In phakic eyes, direct argon laser through an existing peripheral iridectomy to shrink the ciliary processes: trans-scleral diode can also be used. Vitrectomy alone has a poor success rate. Combined cataract extraction with primary posterior capsulotomy and anterior vitrectomy (with rupture of the anterior hyaloid face, not achieved with core vitrectomy) is recommended in any patient with even mild lens opacity. With no opacity, clear lens extraction is an option. The treatment algorithm in **Figure 8.11** outlines the management of malignant glaucoma.

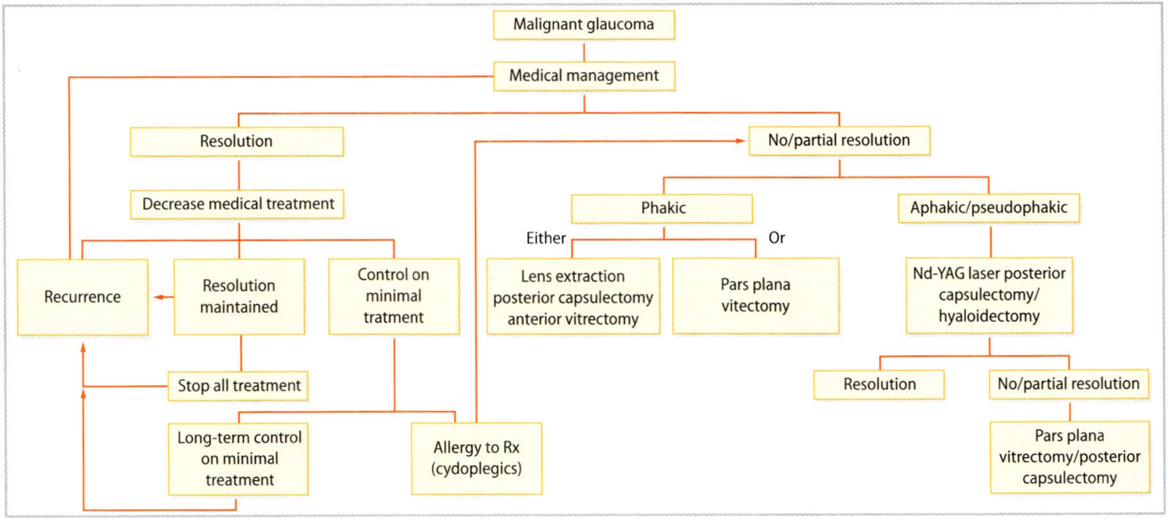

Fig. 8.11: Management of aqueous misdirection.

Source: Adapted with permission from Rubin, Tsai, and Hitchings (Br J Ophthalmol 1997).

CONGENITAL GLAUCOMA

Background Congenital glaucoma is rare, with an incidence of 1:20,000 Caucasians. Cases are usually sporadic, but can be autosomal recessive.

Classification

- *Primary congenital glaucoma (isolated trabeculodysgenesis)*: The most common form of neonatal glaucoma.
- *Secondary to ocular disease*: Anterior segment dysgenesis (Axenfeld–Rieger's syndrome and Peters' anomaly), aniridia, aphakic glaucoma and uveitic glaucoma.
- *Secondary to systemic disease*: Metabolic, chromosomal, and connective tissue disorders.

Clinical features Classic triad of epiphora, photophobia, and blepharospasm. May also present with enlarged cornea (buphthalmos, **Fig. 6.35**, p. 257), corneal clouding, or after screening in families with early-onset glaucoma. Late presentation may lead to reduced vision and nystagmus, strabismus and rapidly progressing myopia.

History and examination Record any complications during pregnancy and labour, age at onset of symptoms (earlier onset indicates a worse prognosis), developmental milestones, family history, and consanguinity. Full examination usually requires anaesthesia.

Differential diagnosis

- *Enlarged cornea*: Axial myopia, megalocornea, and connective tissue disorders.
- *Haab's striae*: Birth trauma and posterior polymorphous dystrophy.
- *Corneal oedema/opacity*: Congenital hereditary endothelial dystrophy, sclerocornea, infections, metabolic, e.g. mucopolysaccharidoses.
- *Watering/red eye*: Conjunctivitis, nasolacrimal obstruction and ocular inflammation. All have normal IOP and an absence of disc cupping.

Examination under anaesthesia (EUA) EUA is performed using ketamine anaesthesia. The gold standard for IOP measurement is Perkins' tonometry (without fluorescein, in case goniotomy required). Important findings include:

- *Cornea*: Note oedema/opacity, posterior embryotoxon, and horizontal corneal diameter (>11 mm in newborn or >12 mm in children under 1-year is suspicious of glaucoma; >13 mm is abnormal at any age, as is disc asymmetry). Haab's striae **(Fig. 8.12)** are linear ruptures in Descemet's membrane that are a characteristic of raised IOP in children, usually occurring in the first 18 months of life.

- *Iris and gonioscopy:* Look for any secondary causes and anterior segment dysgenesis, e.g. thin and hypoplastic irides with corectopia (off centre pupils) or polycoria (multiple pupils).
- *Cup-to-disc ratio (CDR):* >0.3 in a newborn or >0.5 at any age is suspicious, as is asymmetry (use small pupil indirect if available). Do not dilate pupils if goniotomy is required.
- *Refraction* (progressive myopia) and *B-scan* are essential to assess axial length and coexistent disease.
- Systemic evaluation and blood can be taken for genetic studies if indicated during EUA.

Treatment Surgery is the mainstay of treatment although initially IOP can be controlled medically. β-blockers or pilocarpine are usually first-line; avoid brimonidine in young children due to apnoea and CNS effects. Goniotomy or trabeculotomy (*ab interno* or *ab externo*, including 360° using iTrack) are commonly performed operations in primary congenital glaucoma. Goniotomy may require corneal epithelial debridement with alcohol. The success rate is up to 90%, although surgery may need repeating. Trabeculectomy with antiscarring therapy can also be performed, sometimes

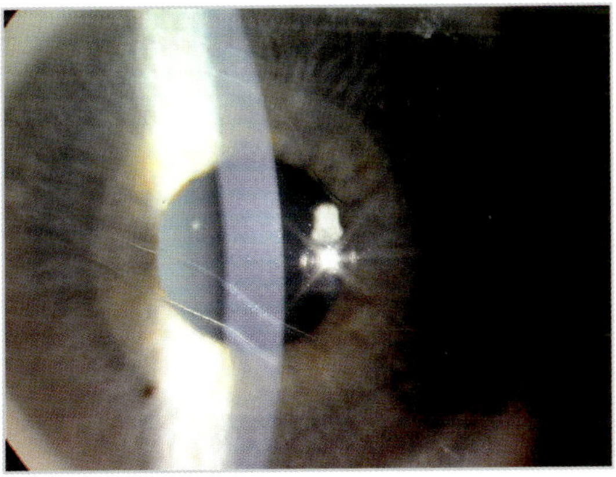

Fig. 8.12: Haab's striae.

combined with trabeculotomy, particularly in the Middle East and Asia. All patients require anti-scarring agents due to a high rate of failure in children. Broad iridectomy is useful if there is central opacity. Tube drainage devices are used if trabeculectomy fails or as a primary therapy in poorer prognosis cases including aphakia and uveitic glaucoma. Cyclodestruction is used if surgery fails, if there is poor visual prognosis, or penetrative surgery is not technically possible. There is a significant risk of intraocular inflammation and phthisis, particularly if used on multiple occasions. Occlusion therapy and correction of refractive error are essential.

Follow-up Intensive surveillance is required, particularly postoperatively. This is usually carried out in specialists units. Education, social support and counselling are important in managing the family as a whole.

SELECTIVE LASER TRABECULOPLASTY

Indications Consider using as the first-line treatment for ocular hypertension and primary-open angle glaucoma, and also for inadequate IOP control despite medications. Can decrease dependency on topical medication which is relevant for those with poor compliance, adverse effects, and pregnancy. Can be effective in normal tension glaucoma but may be less effective due to lower target IOPs.

Contraindications Poor angle visualisation; patient unable to sit at laser or maintain a steady gaze. Caution in eyes with pseudoexfoliation, pigment dispersion or uveitis.

Consent

- *Benefit*: 360° laser is equivalent to prostaglandin monotherapy. Reports to suggest 65–90% get a 7–10 mmHg drop, with 10% attrition/year; 78.2% eye drop free at 3 years and 69.8% at 6 years. Can be repeated at any time point as long as they have some initial benefit.
- *Risk*: Ineffective, elevated IOP, transient blurring of vision, pain, vasovagal attacks, iritis and haemorrhage.

Technique See **Box 8.3**.

Box 8.3: Selective laser trabeculoplasty (SLT)

- Continue all glaucoma medications before and after treatment.
- Instill G. proxymetacaine 0.5%, and G. apraclonidine 0.5% or 1%.
- Select a Goldmann or SLT-specific gonioscope.
- Target the circular aiming beam at the pigmented meshwork (see **Fig. 8.3**, p. 345).
- Apply 100 non-overlapping shots across 360°. Increase power from 0.3 mJ upwards (to a maximum of 1.4 mJ), until small 'champagne' bubbles seen occasionally. Pigmented meshwork requires less energy.
- Prescribe G. ketorolac 0.5%, for pain/discomfort, on a p.r.n. basis t.d.s. 1 week. There is conflicting evidence about post procedure steroid use.
- Check IOP at 1-hour; treat acute pressure spikes.
- Review at 1 and 4–6 weeks.

PHARMACOLOGY OF INTRAOCULAR PRESSURE-LOWERING DRUGS

Prostaglandin analogues have superseded β-blockers as the first-choice therapy due to greater efficacy at lowering IOP and fewer side effects, but in primary open-angle disease selective laser trabeculoplasty should also be considered first-line. If the first-choice of monotherapy alone is not effective or not tolerated, switch to another monotherapy, such as a β-blocker. Consider preservative-free formulations in pre-existing ocular surface disease.

If monotherapy is well-tolerated but insufficient to reach the target IOP, consider adding a second drug or using a combined drug preparation. Commonly prescribed combination drugs are:

- Timolol and carbonic anhydrase inhibitor (e.g. Cosopt, Azarga and generics) – this has additive effect with pilocarpine.
- Timolol and prostaglandins analogues (e.g. Xalacom and Ganfort).

Pilocarpine is less commonly prescribed because of the ocular side effects and the frequent daily dosage, but is still useful in primary angle-closure with plateau iris configuration, in acute angle-closure with pupillary block mechanism, and in aphakic glaucoma.

Side effects and precautions Occlusion of the nasolacrimal duct by placing a finger over the caruncle or closing the eye may help to reduce the incidence of the side effects shown in **Table 8.1**. For drug use in pregnancy, see page 840. SLT may also be a useful adjunct in pregnancy.

Table 8.1: Common side effects

Category	Generics	Main mechanism of action	Most common or severe side effects	Contraindications (CI), precautions (P), and theoretical risks (T)
Prostaglandin F2α analogues	Latanoprost Travoprost Bimatoprost (also available in some countries as a sustained release pellet injected into the AC) Tafluprost	Increased uveoscleral outflow (IUSO)	Increased skin and iris pigmentation, excessive lash growth, aphakic cystoid macular oedema, orbital fat loss. Rarely, reactivate herpes keratitis and uveitis. Latanoprost less likely to cause red eye than bimatoprost or travoprost	T: risk of abortion
Non-selective β antagonists	Timolol Levobunolol Carteolol Metipranolol	Reduced aqueous production (RAP)	Bradycardia, arrhythmia, heart failure, bronchospasm, syncope, nocturnal hypotension, headache and depression. Mild corneal hypoaesthesia with prolonged use	CI: asthma, chronic obstructive airways disease (COAD), bradycardia, heart block and heart failure. Avoid in normal pressure glaucoma. T: Patients on oral hypotensives
Selective β1 antagonist	Betaxolol	RAP	Similar to other β-antagonists but theoretically fewer respiratory side effects	P: Asthma, COAD, bradycardia, heart block and heart failure
α2 agonists	Brimonidine Apraclonidine	RAP and IUSO	Allergy and red eye, taste disturbance. Respiratory failure and fatigue in children. Fatigue may also occur in adults.	CI: Oral monoamine oxidase inhibitor users and children

Table 8.1: Common side effects—*Contd...*

Parasympatho-mimetics	Pilocarpine	Increased aqueous outflow	Miosis, pseudomyopia, brow ache and ciliary spasm. Rarely pupil block. Theoretical increased risk of retinal detachment	P: Urinary outflow obstruction and asthma. T: Parkinsonism and peptic ulcers
Carbonic anhydrase inhibitors (CAI)	Brinzolamide Dorzolamide	RAP	Blurred vision, aesthenia, paraesthesia and induced myopia	CI: Sulphonamide allergy and severe renal impairment. P: Corneal endothelial dysfunction
Rho-kinase inhibitors	Netarsudil (in Europe, only available as a combination drop with latanoprost)	Increased aqueous outflow	Conjunctival hyperaemia, small subconjunctival haemorrhages and corneal verticillata	
Oral CAI	Acetazolamide	RAP	Paraesthesia, nausea, vomiting, diarrhoea, depression and electrolyte imbalance. Rarely, blood dyscrasias, metabolic acidosis and renal stones.	CI: Suprarenal gland failure, electrolyte imbalance, severe liver disease and sickle cell disease. P: Reduce dose if renal failure (liaise with renal physicians).
Hyperosmotics	Glycerol (1.0–1.5 g/kg p.o.) Mannitol (1.0–1.5 g/kg i.v.)	RAP	Hyperglycaemia (glycerol), pulmonary congestion, electrolyte imbalance, dehydration, headache, chest pain (mannitol), disorientation and coma	CI: Diabetes. P: Renal failure, elderly patients with renal or cardiovascular disease

MINIMALLY INVASIVE GLAUCOMA SURGERY

Background Minimally invasive glaucoma surgery (MIGS) uses an increasing array of implants, devices and techniques to lower IOP with less surgical time and complexity than traditional trabeculectomy or aqueous shunts. If IOP below or close to 10 mmHg is required, trabeculectomy remains the gold standard.

Indications

- As for traditional surgery – when medicines and/or laser fail to adequately control IOP
- To reduce medication burden – either for clinical need or patient preference.
- As a way to further supplement IOP reduction during cataract surgery.
- To mitigate or defer the need for more invasive procedures in patients who have clinical or other reasons that may compromise the safety of the surgery.

Classification This heterogeneous group of procedures can be classified by surgical approach, mechanism of IOP reduction or conjunctival involvement (**Table 8.2**). Conjunctival manipulation and bleb formation will affect success and increase risks of future surgery.

Cautions

- *Evidence*: The commercial availability of MIGS devices and techniques often precedes long-term evidence, so consider the options carefully and explain any uncertainty during consent.
- *Licensing*: Most devices are licensed for early primary open-angle disease, but may be effective in other open or even closed angle disease. Gonioscopic examination is vital prior to listing.
- *Endothelial cell count*: Known to reduce following intraocular procedures, but is related to the procedure duration and possibly also each device's characteristics.
- *View and positioning*: As well as lying flat, some MIGS procedures require neck rotation, so ask about neck flexibility when listing.

Table 8.2: Minimally invasive glaucoma surgery (MIGS) devices

Approach	Mechanism of reducing intraocular pressure	Device	Additional characteristics
Trabecular meshwork and canal manipulation[I]	Bypasses trabecular meshwork (TM) resistance by destruction of TM and juxta-TM tissue, accessing Schlemm's canal	Trabectome[G I]	Piezoelectric ablative probe
		Kahook Dual Blade[G I]	Parallel twin blades
		Canaloplasty iTrack[I] OMNI[G I]	LED-guided catheter fed through entire Schlemm's canal, used to stretch Schlemm's canal with viscoelastic injection, or to perform trabeculotomy (de-roof the canal)
Canal stent	Bypasses TM resistance by placing stent through TM into Schlemm's canal	iStent, iStent Inject/W (**Fig. 8.13**)[G I]	"Inject" has two stents in one injector, normally placed 2 clock hours apart
		Hydrus (**Fig. 8.14**)[G, I]	Longer stent, dilates ~2 clock hours of Schlemm's canal. Only the tip is visible in the AC
Supra-choroidal stent	Bypasses aqueous drainage resistance by placing stent from AC to suprachoroidal space	MINIject[G I]	Soft, flexible silicone implant with porous structure designed to prevent influx of scar tissue
Conjunctiva-involving	Bypasses aqueous drainage resistance by placing stent from AC to subconjunctival space. Subsequent aqueous drainage forms a drainage bleb	Xen[I]	Crosslinked porcine collagen, flexible, 8 mm injectable tube
		Preserflo microshunt (formerly Innfocus)[E]	Conjunctival peritomy prior to insertion, which also enables higher mitomycin dose
Cilio-ablative procedures	Endoscopic visualisation and laser destruction of ciliary processes. Subsequent reduction in aqueous production	Endo-cyclophoto-coagulation (ECP)[I]	This includes micropulse laser. As this procedure requires no incision into the eye, it can be performed in a clean but non-sterile environment

E – *ab externo*
G – requires use of surgical gonio lens
I – *ab interno*

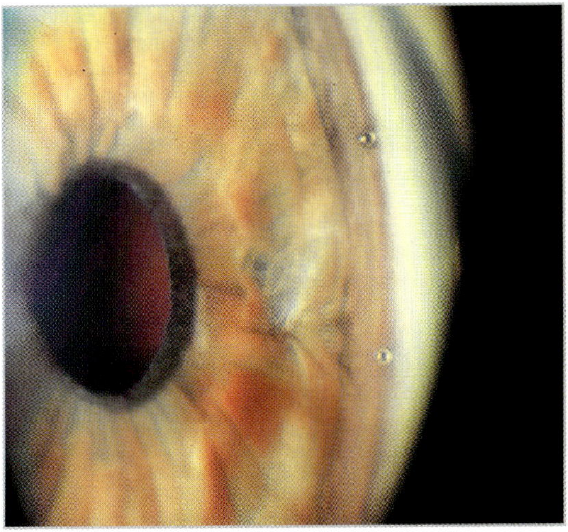

Fig. 8.13: Gonioscopic view of iStent inject microstent. The proprietary injector is supplied with two devices, placed at least 2 clock hours apart, within Schlemm's canal.

Fig. 8.14: Gonioscopic view of Hydrus microstent positioned within Schlemm's canal.

Follow-up Follow-up duration depends on the number of glaucoma medications stopped at the time of surgery, the risk of complications (**Table 8.3**) for each procedure/patient, and glaucoma severity. Check for stability of the wound and AC. If a device has been inserted, check the position. For bleb-dependent procedures, post-operative checks mirror those for trabeculectomy (p. 390).

Table 8.3: Minimally invasive glaucoma surgery (MIGS) complications

Complication	Cause	Management
Early		
Anterior chamber haemorrhage	Small amounts of haemorrhage are common, and even desirable for canal stents (shows access to episcleral veins)	For hyphaema >1 mm commence medical management of inflammation ± IOP, and same day discussion with surgical team
High IOP	May occur due to misplacement of device, blockage of drainage pathway, or discontinuation of glaucoma medications	Reintroduce topical medications. If IOP > 40 mmHg consider systemic acetazolamide and same day discussion with surgical team
Low IOP	Overdrainage, cyclodialysis cleft and ciliary body shutdown	If AC shallow, start G. atropine 1% o.d. Check for choroidal effusions. Ensure same week review by surgical team.
Endophthalmitis	Rare, and can present early in a similar way to post cataract surgery, or late due to a thinning, porous bleb	Treat as for postcataract surgery endophthalmitis (p. 456)
Late		
Some devices require multiple manipulations in theatre or outpatients (e.g. subconjunctival injection of antimetabolite), so record the sequence of events. Acute IOP rises can occur late, normally due to device blockage		

TRABECULECTOMY I: SURGICAL TECHNIQUE

Indications Progressive glaucomatous field and/or disc changes. Failure to achieve target IOP. Failure or inability to use regular medication.

Anaesthesia

- *General anaesthetic*: Children, anxious adults, complex/long procedures, high preoperative IOP (>30 mmHg).
- *Local anaesthetic*: Use low volumes of anaesthetics combined with hyaluronidase to prevent pressure elevations. Subconjunctival anaesthesia is feasible combined with intracameral anaesthetic.

Consent

- *Benefit*: Stabilise but not improve vision. Reduced dependence on medication.
- *Risk*: Blindness ('wipe-out' in advanced glaucoma, endophthalmitis and suprachoroidal haemorrhage); loss of one line of Snellen acuity is likely; 12–66% chance of cataract progression at 3 years (most in first year); long-term possibility of blebitis ± endophthalmitis and need for surgical bleb revision; problems wearing contact lenses. Failure to control IOP and continued dependence on medication (or need for further surgery) occurs in 10–30%.

Preoperative eyedrops

- *Steroids and NSAIDs*: Topical application 24–72 hours before surgery in patients with conjunctival hyperaemia, who require iris manipulation or if fibrinous uveitis is possible.
- *IOP-lowering agents*: Consider stopping aqueous suppressants in advance, with outpatient IOP monitoring.

Technique See **Box 8.4**.

Box 8.4: Trabeculectomy

- Superior limbus, under the lid, is the only acceptable site (document lid position preoperatively). Other sites have a markedly increased risk of endophthalmitis.
- Place a 7/0 corneal traction suture (semicircular needle).
- Use spring scissors to make a limbal conjunctival incision ('fornix-based flap'), at least 10 mm long.
- Posteriorly, dissect a 15 × 15 mm subconjunctival pocket.
- Lift conjunctiva and separate its attachments to muscle tendon.
- Create a 4 × 3 mm scleral pocket by lamellar dissection (50% thickness) **(Fig. 8.15)**.
- Cut side incisions to within 1 mm of the limbus **(Fig. 8.16)**.
- Soak 2–3 sponges with mitomycin C (MMC) (0.2–0.5 mg/mL). Other anti-scarring agents can also be considered, often in combination with MMC, e.g. subconjunctival, intracameral or intravitreal VEGF drugs, β-radiation, and less commonly subconjunctival 5-fluorouracil (5-FU; 50 mg/mL).
- Fold and insert sponges into the subconjunctival and scleral pockets. Treat as large an area as possible, but avoid and dry the conjunctival wound edges **(Fig. 8.17)**. After 3 minutes, remove sponges and irrigate with 20 mL of balanced saline solution (BSS).
- Preplace 10/0 Nylon sutures on the posterior corners of the scleral flap.
- Make an oblique paracentesis. Consider continuous AC infusion in 'high-risk' patients.
- Create a small (1 mm) limbal keratectomy with a punch, or blade and scissors, under the scleral flap **(Fig. 8.18)**.
- Create a peripheral iridectomy.
- Suture the flap watertight with a combination of permanent, releasable or adjustable sutures (especially important with MMC use) **(Fig. 8.19)**.
- Test outflow by injecting BSS into the paracentesis, before conjunctival closure. Rotate any 'permanent' scleral flap sutures.
- Close conjunctiva with 10/0 Nylon purse-string sutures at the corners, and mattress sutures through conjunctiva and limbus.
- Inject subconjunctival steroid and antibiotic, 180° away from the trabeculectomy site.
- Ensure careful postoperative management (see p. 390).

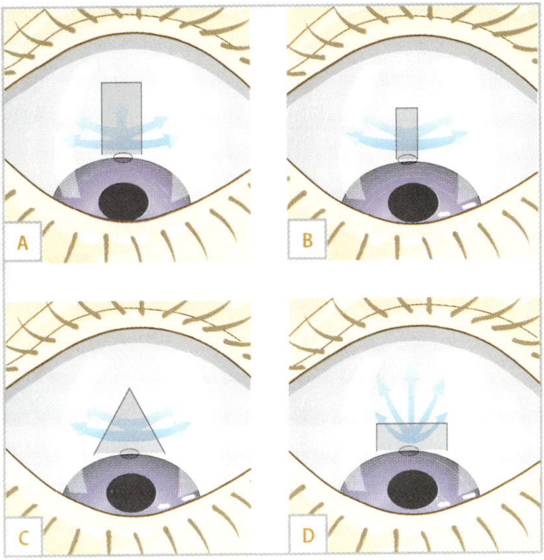

Fig. 8.15: Scleral flap design. Long, narrow, and triangular flaps (A to C) encourage aqueous flow laterally towards the limbus, increasing the risk of conjunctival thinning. A short and broad flap (D) is preferred, as it directs aqueous flow posteriorly, away from the limbal conjunctiva.

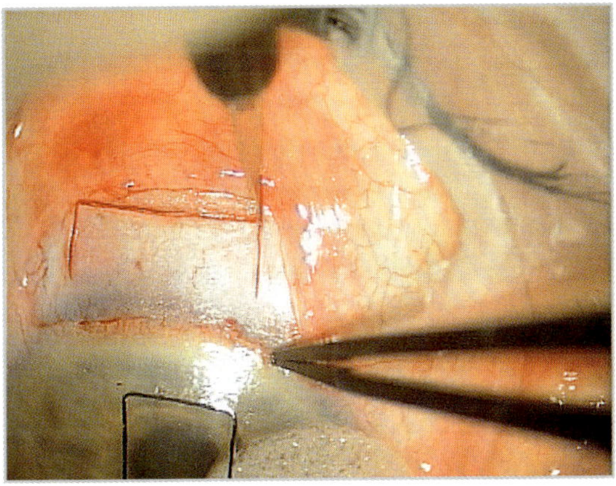

Fig. 8.16: Scleral flap. Limited side cuts help to prevent 'aqueous jets' at the limbus which can produce conjunctival thinning.

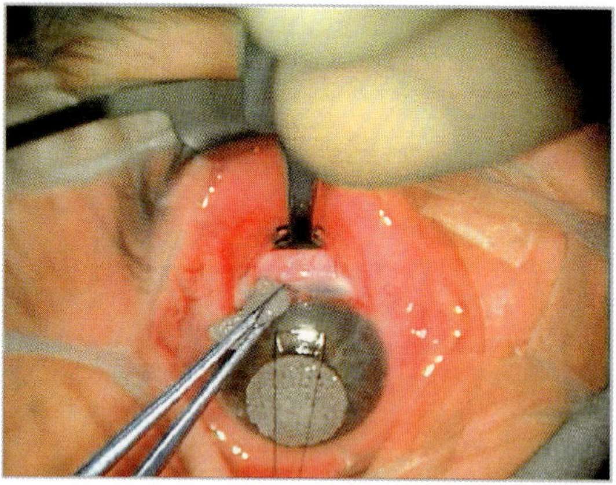

Fig. 8.17: Mitomycin-soaked sponge being inserted under the conjunctiva while protecting the conjunctival edge with a clamp.

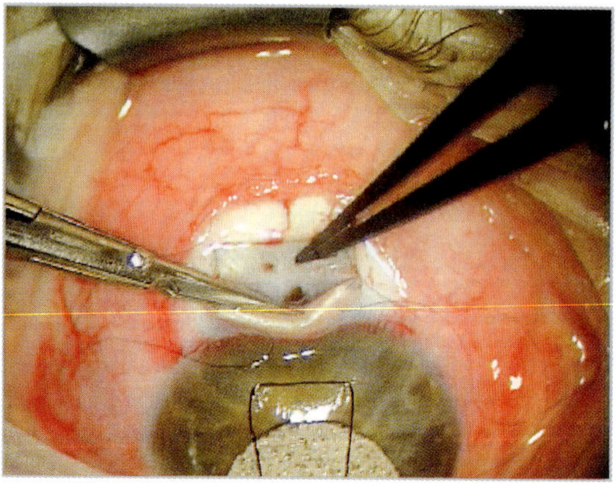

Fig. 8.18: Small sclerostomy with iris presenting prior to iridectomy. Note preplaced Nylon sutures.

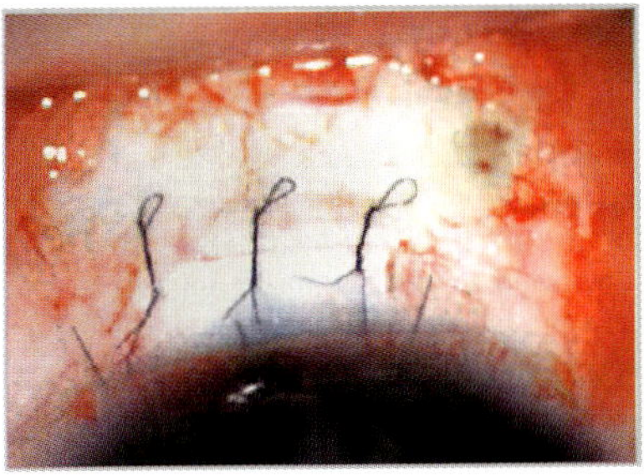

Fig. 8.19: Releasable and adjustable sutures tied with four throws. The apex of the loop extending into the cornea is buried in a shallow corneal groove.

TRABECULECTOMY II: POSTOPERATIVE CARE

Background Careful postoperative care is essential to the success of glaucoma surgery. Typically, topical therapy includes: preservative-free dexamethasone 0.1% 2-hourly for 4 weeks, tapering off over 12 weeks (or longer if required), topical antibiotics for 4 weeks and subconjunctival 5-fluorouracil (5-FU) ± Betnesol if the bleb is failing.

Signs of impending bleb failure Increased bleb vascularity, reduction of conjunctival microcysts, progressive IOP elevation or focal bleb encapsulation (**Fig. 8.20**).

Subconjunctival 5-FU Used to modify postoperative wound healing, following a needling or re-exploration procedure, or to prevent failure after cataract surgery. Use topical amethocaine and povidone-iodine 5%. Inject one-tenth of 1 mL of 50 mg/mL 5-FU in an insulin syringe (integral 29-gauge needle) posterior to the bleb. May be combined with 1–2 mg Betnesol. Stop before the injection meets the drainage area. Leave the needle in place for a few seconds (this helps to hydrate and seal the injection site). Irrigate any leakage first with tetracaine (to chelate the 5-FU) and then saline. A preceding injection of lignocaine/adrenaline may reduce pain and scarring.

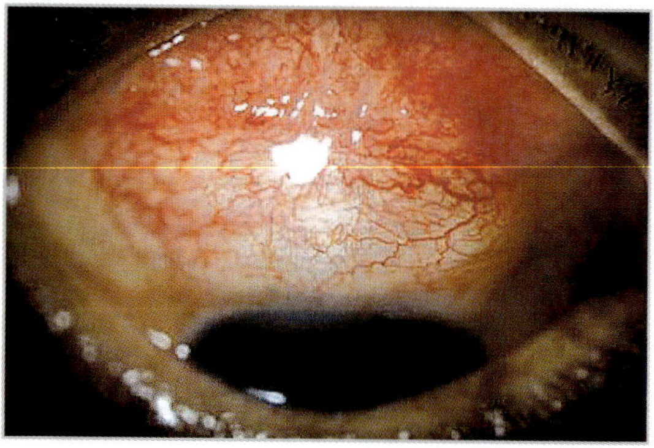

Fig. 8.20: Inflamed bleb with increased vascular diameter and tortuosity (cork-screw vessels). This appearance suggests a high risk of failure, particularly if persistent for >2 weeks. Indicates need for further therapy, e.g. subconjunctival 5-FU injection.

Post-trabeculectomy complications

- *Shallow/flat AC*: Differentiate high and low IOP. High IOP indicates aqueous misdirection (see below, and p. 371). Low IOP suggests over-drainage. Prevent by suturing the flap tight initially and avoiding early release of scleral flap sutures. Exclude conjunctival wound leaks. Dilate with G. atropine 1% and consider temporarily reducing steroid. Most cases settle without intervention. Hypotony maculopathy requires revision of flap. If there is lens–corneal touch, consider reforming the AC with gas or viscoelastic.
- *Choroidal effusion*: Treat with atropine. Drain effusions only if there is lens–corneal touch with corneal oedema, bleb failure with increasing IOP, marked anterior segment inflammation, or apposition of the effusions (kissing choroidals). Consider other causes of effusions such as scleritis and nanophthalmos.
- *Raised IOP*: Usually due to inadequate aqueous outflow. Treatment depends on the site of obstruction, which may occur in several sites at once:
  1. Aqueous misdirection (malignant glaucoma): Presents with a very shallow AC. Ensure the peripheral iridectomy is patent. Use atropine 1%, phenylephrine 10% (if no contraindication), and aqueous suppressants ± hyperosmotics. Vitrectomy may be necessary (see p. 371).
  2. Blockage of fistula: Causes include a tight scleral flap, fibrin and blood, and iris/ciliary body/vitreous incarceration in the sclerostomy. Manage with gentle massage at the posterior lip of the scleral flap. Remove releasable sutures, loosen adjustable sutures or perform argon laser suture lysis. Pilocarpine may help. Argon or YAG-laser obstructions in the sclerostomy.
  3. Cyst or capsule formation: Use intensive topical steroids and topical aqueous suppressants. Needling of an encapsulated bleb may only be of temporary benefit.

BLEB-RELATED INFECTION

Background Bleb-related infection is a potentially blinding, late complication of glaucoma filtering surgery. It refers to a spectrum of disease ranging from blebitis (isolated bleb infection) to bleb-related endophthalmitis (BRE). The organisms usually responsible for BRE (*Streptococcus* and *Haemophilus* species) are different to, and more virulent than, those of early postoperative endophthalmitis. Thin-walled, cystic, leaking blebs are at risk.

Early and aggressive antimicrobial therapy often permits retention of functional VA and a filtering bleb.

Symptoms Redness, photophobia, pain, reduced VA, and discharge.

Signs Bleb opalescence or mucopurulent infiltrate with surrounding conjunctival injection (white on red), ± bleb leak, intraocular inflammation and purulent discharge **(Fig. 8.21)**.

History and examination Ask about the duration and severity of symptoms (prodrome of a few days suggests blebitis; sudden onset with rapid progression suggests BRE), ocular trauma (accidental or iatrogenic, e.g. bleb needling), contact lens use, and risk factors such as blepharitis, trichiasis, and dry eyes. Record VA and test for the presence of a bleb leak using 2% fluorescein (Seidel's test).

Differential diagnosis Bleb leak alone may produce mild ocular discomfort and AC activity. Recent corticosteroid withdrawal or rapid tapering may result in rebound inflammation. In both these cases the bleb is clear, the AC reaction mild, and VA unchanged.

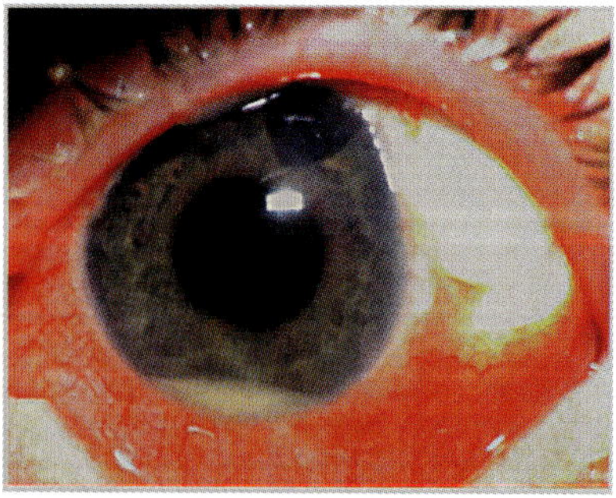

Fig. 8.21: Bleb-related endophthalmitis.

Investigations Blebitis associated with ≥1+ AC cells is considered as BRE, even in the absence of vitritis. BRE requires AC tap plus vitreous biopsy. A conjunctival swab is not indicated as cultures often correlate poorly with intraocular cultures. Perform a B-scan if vitritis cannot be excluded or the fundal view is inadequate.

Treatment

- Instil povidone-iodine 5% into the conjunctival sac.
- G. ofloxacin hourly and G. cefuroxime hourly (day and night) for at least 24 hours, reducing frequency as clinically indicated.
- Ciprofloxacin 750 mg b.d. p.o. and co-amoxiclav 625 mg t.d.s. p.o. (azithromycin 500 mg b.d. p.o. if penicillin allergy) for 7 days.
- Review patients with blebitis or bleb-related infection within 6 hours to exclude progression to BRE.
- Intravitreal vancomycin 2 mg and either amikacin 0.4 mg or ceftazidime 2 mg in cases of BRE.
- G. prednisolone 1% q.d.s. (once the course of infection is clear in blebitis).

Follow-up Following an episode of bleb-related infection, surgery is advisable but its risks and benefits must be evaluated for each patient. Surgical revision of the bleb usually involves bleb excision with conjunctival advancement. If present, scleral thinning or a defect must also be repaired with a scleral, Tenon's or Tutoplast graft to avoid the recurrence of cystic blebs. Treat chronic blepharitis, ocular surface, and lid disorders. Prophylactic topical antibiotics are not advised.

GLAUCOMA DRAINAGE IMPLANTS

Indications Uncontrolled IOP, especially after failed trabeculectomy, extensive conjunctival scarring, and as a primary procedure for certain secondary glaucomas.

Surgery A reservoir explantation is sutured to the sclera, usually superotemporally. This connects to the AC by a tube inserted through a tight stab incision (25-gauge) behind the limbus. This should lie just anterior to, and parallel with, the plane of the iris, touching neither the iris nor cornea. Before a fibrous capsule forms around the explant/plate, the tube provides too much flow if left unrestricted. Valved implants (such as the Ahmed shunt) do not usually need flow restriction, but the flow needs to be tested prior to insertion to ensure the valve is functioning. Non-valved devices (e.g. Baerveldt shunt, PAUL Glaucoma Implant) require flow restriction. Common techniques to reduce flow include an intraluminal stent suture (e.g. 3/0 Supramid or Ethilon for Baerveldt, 6/0 gauge for PAUL) and external ligation sutures (e.g. 6/0 Vicryl or 9/0 Nylon). The extra-cameral course of the tube is covered with donor sclera, cornea, Tutoplast (donor pericardium or fascia lata), sometimes an autologous scleral flap, or sits in an excavated scleral valley. Sulcus or pars plana tubes are sometimes used. The PAUL Glaucoma Implant has a smaller external diameter so may be advantageous if there are concerns over anatomical spacing or future corneal health.

Follow-up

- *Early complications*:
  1. Raised IOP: Manage medically and avoid early ligature or stent removal.
  2. Hypotony: Due to inadequate ligation or oversized entry site – both require surgery. Tube occlusion with iris indicates a precipitous IOP drop.
- *Late complications*:
  1. Hypotony when the ligature absorbs.
  2. Tube erosion **(Fig. 8.22)**.
  3. Iris or corneal contact.

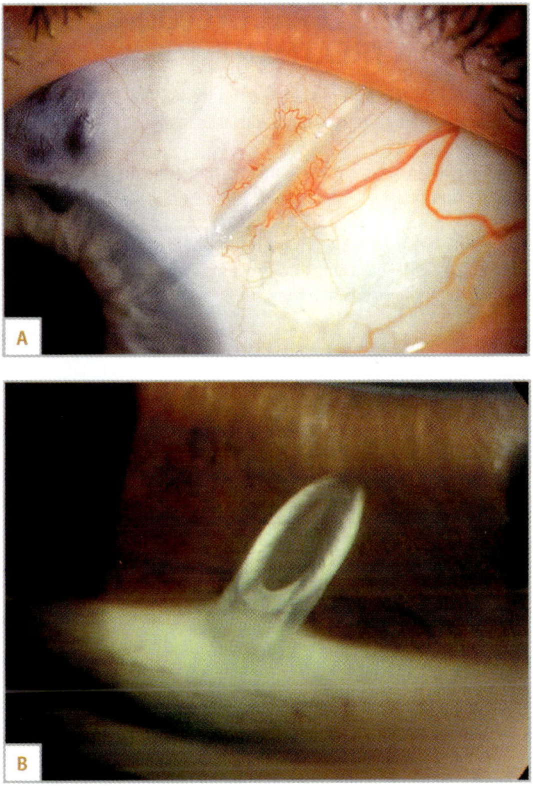

Fig. 8.22: Glaucoma drainage implants with the tube eroded through the conjunctiva (A) and in contact with the iris (B).

TRANS-SCLERAL CYCLODIODE LASER TREATMENT

Background Cyclodiode aims to reduce IOP by cyclodestructive trans-scleral diode laser.

Indications Advanced glaucoma with uncontrolled IOP, often with a poor visual prognosis.

Contraindications Exercise caution if there is low aqueous flow (e.g. uveitic glaucoma and previous cyclodestructive procedures): the risk is hypotony.

Technique See **Box 8.5**.

Follow-up The full effect takes 4–6 weeks. Continue glaucoma therapy until reviewed.

Box 8.5: Trans-scleral cyclodiode laser treatment

- Give a sub-Tenon's or peribulbar block.
- Avoid areas of subconjunctival haemorrhage (risk of conjunctival burns).
- Transilluminate the globe to locate the ciliary body, as its position may be highly variable, especially in eyes with congenital glaucoma or multiple previous operations.
- Use a diode laser and the appropriate probe. Position the heel of the probe at the anterior border of the ciliary body.
- Apply two rows of five burns (one slightly posterior to the other) per quadrant. Avoid the long ciliary nerves (3 and 9 o'clock positions).
- Standard settings are 1.5 Watts for 1.5 seconds. The number of burns may vary depending on different protocols. Reduce power if popping occurs. If painful despite the block, the same energy can be delivered with less powerful settings, e.g. 900 mW for 2,500 ms = 1,500 mW for 1,500 ms
- Prescribe G. prednisolone 1% 6–8 times daily.
- Prescribe strong analgesics, e.g. paracetamol or ibuprofen, as postoperative pain is common. If pain persists, NSAID drops may help, e.g. G. ketoralac 0.5% t.d.s. for 1 week.

OPTOMETRY AND GENERAL PRACTICE GUIDELINES

General comments

Cases of suspected open-angle glaucoma require routine referral for assessment by an ophthalmologist, or preferably a glaucoma specialist. Acute angle-closure and bleb-related infections are emergencies that require prompt action and immediate ophthalmology review.

Optometrists

Glaucoma is a progressive optic neuropathy in which the optic nerve head has characteristic changes, and there is typically a corresponding visual field loss. Intraocular pressure (IOP) and age are the major risk factors, but IOP on its own is not a good predictor of glaucoma (5% of the normal population have IOPs > 21 mmHg and about one-third of those with open-angle glaucoma have IOPs < 22 mmHg). Other risk factors are ethnicity (Afro-Caribbean) and family history (a first-degree relative with glaucoma).

Consider the vertical cup-to-disc ratio (CDR) in relation to the disc size. A large CDR may be normal if the disc is also large, as the same number of nerve fibres are distributed over a larger area (p. 346). Look for notches and variations from the normal distribution of rim thickness (see the ISNT rule, p. 755 and **Fig. 15.2**, p. 753). An IOP consistently >24 mmHg carries a 9% risk of progressing to glaucomatous optic neuropathy. A modest (20%) reduction of the IOP reduces this risk to 4%. Refer on a routine basis, or manage in line with local protocols.

General practice

The optometry guidelines also apply. Headaches and eye pain are not generally associated with glaucoma, unless the IOP is very high. If unable to assess disc and fields effectively, recommend review by an optometrist. β-blocker eye drops are contraindicated in people with asthma and chronic airways disease. Note that steroids, both systemic and topical (eye, nose and skin), have the potential to generate a steroid-induced increase in IOP. People using these agents regularly for >6 weeks should have their IOP monitored. In general, steroid eyedrops are prescribed by ophthalmologists for short- to medium-term use, but with some exceptions, including blind painful eyes, some chronic corneal diseases, and chronic uveitis.

The following guide to referral urgency is not prescriptive, as clinical situations vary.

Immediate

- Suspected blebitis p. 392
- Acute angle-closure p. 353
- IOP > 40 mmHg p. 353

Soon (within 1 month)

- Advanced glaucomatous disc damage (CDR > 0.8 and advanced field loss) p. 346
- IOP > 35 mmHg on any occasion p. 350

Routine

- IOP consistently in mid-20s with normal disc and fields p. 350
- Suspected glaucomatous optic disc changes (any IOP) p. 350
- Repeatable and suspected glaucomatous field loss (any IOP) p. 350
- Pigment dispersion syndrome p. 359
- Pseudoexfoliation syndrome p. 357
- Suspected narrow angles (asymptomatic) p. 353

UVEITIS

Sue L Lightman & Avi Gurbaxani

9

HISTORY AND EXAMINATION

Uveitis is an umbrella term for intraocular inflammation which has a varied clinical phenotype. The diagnosis is predominantly clinical, reliant upon meticulous history taking and examination. The aetiology may be primarily inflammatory, infective, or malignant, or, in about 40% of patients, it remains undetermined (organ-specific autoimmune disease), even after appropriate clinical assessment and investigation. The Standardisation of Uveitis Nomenclature (SUN) system classifies uveitis anatomically into anterior, intermediate, posterior, or panuveitis and by duration into acute (<3 months) or chronic (**Table 9.1**).

History A comprehensive ocular and systemic history is paramount. Note age, sex, country of origin and ethnicity. Ask about the duration and pattern of symptoms, which may be unilateral or bilateral, acute, recurrent, or chronic, and previous eye surgery or trauma. Document a full past and current medical problem list, Bacillus Calmette–Guérin (BCG) vaccination history, any prior, recent and/or concurrent infections, and all drugs and dosages. Personal details including foreign travel, occupation, pets, social and family circumstances, are all relevant. Additional questions such as pregnancy, pregnancy intention, breastfeeding, sexual history, and intravenous drug usage may also be appropriate. Enquire about skin, joint, respiratory, gastrointestinal, genitourinary, and neurological symptoms of associated systemic disease.

Examination

- *Slit-lamp examination*: note pattern of conjunctival/episcleral/scleral injection; corneal epithelial or stromal disease; size, appearance, and distribution of keratic precipitates (KPs); cells, flare, fibrin, hypopyon; iris atrophy/nodules; cataract; posterior and peripheral anterior synechiae; rubeosis; and IOP.
- *Dilated fundoscopy*: both slit lamp and indirect ophthalmoscope examination are mandatory in all patients to assess for: vitreous cells; 'snowballs'; 'snowbanking' (which is in the retinal periphery and may be missed on slit-lamp examination alone); disc oedema or hyperaemia; vasculitis

Table 9.1: The Standardisation of Uveitis Nomenclature (SUN) classification

Type	Primary site of inflammation*	Includes
Anterior uveitis	Anterior chamber	Iritis
		Iridocyclitis
		Anterior cyclitis
Intermediate uveitis	Vitreous	Pars planitis
		Posterior cyclitis
		Hyalitis
Posterior uveitis	Retina or choroid	Focal, multifocal or diffuse choroiditis
		Chorioretinitis
		Retinochoroiditis
		Retinitis
		Neuroretinitis
Panuveitis	Anterior chamber, vitreous and retina or choroid	

*As determined clinically.

(arterial, venous, or both); perivascular exudates; cystoid macular oedema; retinitis; choroiditis or choroidal infiltrates; chorioretinal scars; retinal detachment (rhegmatogenous, serous, and tractional).

- If the best-corrected VA is worse than 6/9, seek the cause.

ACUTE ANTERIOR UVEITIS

Background Acute anterior uveitis (AAU) is the most common form of acute uveitis, accounting for ~75% of all cases of intraocular inflammation. It is often recurrent, has numerous causes, and is associated with human leucocyte antigen-B27 (HLA-B27) in 60% of cases.

Symptoms Onset over hours or days of redness, pain, and photophobia. Usually unilateral, but it may be simultaneously or sequentially bilateral.

Signs

Ocular: Conjunctival (predominately perilimbal) injection and AC flare and cells are the hallmarks of AAU. Grade cells by the number observed in a 1 × 1 mm slit beam, from 1 (mild) to 5 (severe) (**Fig. 9.1**).

Grade flare as 0–4, with grade 4 representing fibrin deposition. The cornea may show epithelial or stromal changes consistent with herpes zoster virus or less commonly herpes simplex virus infection. Keratic precipitates (KPs) may be large and greasy looking (mutton fat) or fine and small (**Fig. 9.2**, p. 405).

Fibrin, hypopyon, iris abnormalities (posterior synechiae, peripheral anterior synechiae, atrophy and nodules), and raised or low IOP, are variable findings. Posterior segment signs are restricted to a few anterior vitreous cells (spillover) and cystoid

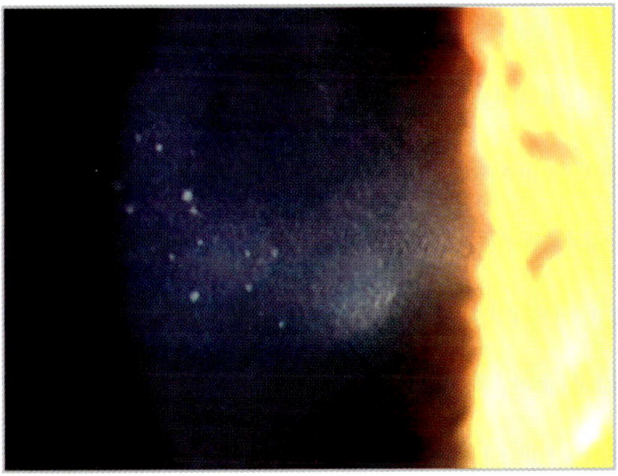

Fig. 9.1: Acute anterior uveitis. Anterior chamber cells with flare and keratic precipitates.

macular oedema (CMO). CMO is uncommon, but one of the most important causes of vision loss.

Systemic: Variable and dependent upon any associated disease.

History and examination Ask about the pattern of anterior uveitis (unilateral, bilateral and recurrent) and associated systemic disease, particularly back and joint pain (DUET and SENTINEL studies suggest 40% have sacroiliitis, so refer if low back pain or joint problems), skin lesions, and gastrointestinal and urinary tract symptoms linked with HLA-B27 disorders. Occupational and travel history may suggest brucellosis (abattoir workers and vets), leptospirosis (farmers and sewage workers), or Lyme disease (USA, Scandinavia, Eastern and Middle Europe). Record VA. The pattern of signs may suggest the aetiology:

- *Hypopyon*: HLA-B27, Behçet's disease and rarely fungal or bacterial endogenous endophthalmitis or malignancy
- *Large 'mutton fat' KPs*: sarcoidosis or TB.
- *Iris atrophy*: sectorial in herpetic infections.
- *Iris nodules*: sarcoidosis, syphilis or TB.
- *Complications of uveitis*: look for raised IOP (common in herpetic uveitis, Posner–Schlossman syndrome, and toxoplasma chorioretinitis), posterior synechiae, and CMO. Full and dilated examination is mandatory in the emergency department to exclude acute retinal necrosis (ARN) and other posterior segment disease.

Differential diagnosis

- *HLA-B27-positive AAU*: Systemic associations include ankylosing spondylitis, reactive arthritis, psoriatic arthritis, and inflammatory bowel disease.
- *Systemic disease*: Sarcoidosis and Behçet's disease.
- *Infection*: Herpetic (zoster and simplex), TB, syphilis, and other systemic infections.
- *Ocular syndromes*: Posner–Schlossman syndrome is an intermittent low-grade inflammation, with elevated IOP (often >40 mmHg), open-angle and no PS. Responds quickly to topical steroids and IOP-lowering medications including, if necessary, acetazolamide. Start with dexamethasone 0.1% q.d.s and refer to clinic (within 1 week if IOP ≥ 30 mmHg; 2–4 weeks if <30 mmHg).
- *Drug-induced*: Rifabutin, cidofovir, bisphosphonates and anti-cancer drugs.
- *Trauma*: Contusion and intraocular foreign body.

- Lens-induced
- Postoperative
- Masquerade syndromes
- Idiopathic

If the best-corrected VA is worse than 6/9, seek posterior segment disease; if the fundal view is inadequate to exclude intraocular infection, refer directly to a uveitis clinic.

Investigations Investigate in clinic, not in emergency department. Unilateral disease with unremarkable history and examination requires no investigation at first presentation. For recurrent, bilateral, or poorly responsive disease and no suggestive aetiology, restrict initial investigations to CXR, sACE, and syphilis serology. Confirmation of HLA-B27 status in a fit person may spare further investigation. Consider additional investigations, e.g. Lyme, Brucella, and Leptospira serology, but only if specifically suggested by the history and signs. If VA is worse than 6/9 and no cause is found, arrange OCT to exclude CMO. If there are symptoms of associated systemic disease, refer for appropriate medical evaluation.

Treatment Attacks of AAU typically last from several days to 6 weeks, but <3 months by definition.

- *Emergency department*: The majority of patients can be managed with intensive topical steroids, initially G. prednisolone 1% or G. dexamethasone 0.1% hourly for week 1, 2-hourly for week 2, 6 times daily week 3, q.d.s. week 4, then reduced every week by one drop/day, and cycloplegic/dilating drop (cyclopentolate 1% t.d.s). Add steroid ointment at night, if inflammation is more marked. Consider subconjunctival Mydricaine II (0.3 mL) to break new PS, if available, and subconjunctival dexamethasone or betamethasone (4 mg in 1 mL) for severe AAU (4+ cells or fibrin/hypopyon). Tissue plasminogen activator (TPA) is rarely required, but has a rapid effect in breaking down fibrin in cases with severe fibrinous response refractory to topical and subconjunctival steroids. Instil topical povidone-iodine 5% and anaesthetic then inject 12.5–25 μg in 0.1 mL directly into the AC using an insulin syringe and needle, either on the slit lamp or with the patient lying down. No paracentesis is required and the injection can be repeated if necessary. Instruct patients to return quickly if there is a deterioration of vision and persistent pain. Treat any associated IOP rise with topical anti-glaucoma drops (pp. 363 and 379). If an exact aetiology is determined, alternative or additional treatment may be required. Anterior uveitis following trauma is typically relatively mild and usually settles rapidly with less-intensive treatment, e.g. G. dexamethasone 0.1% q.d.s. tapered off over 2–3 weeks.

- *Clinic*: If the inflammation is settling, continue to slowly taper off topical steroids. Reintroduce hourly steroids and above regimen for exacerbations during the tapering period. Rarely, oral steroids are required for very severe cases resistant to subconjunctival and maximal topical treatment, or CMO unresponsive to local steroid injection.

Important: Diagnosing anterior uveitis mandates the exclusion of other features, especially posterior uveitis.

Follow-up See all children, patients with severe inflammation (fibrin and hypopyon), raised IOP, steroid responders, and CMO with reduced VA within 1 week. Otherwise, arrange clinic review within 7 weeks and then discharge those with uncomplicated and resolved AAU. Advise patients that recurrences are common and to attend the emergency department if they are symptomatic.

CHRONIC ANTERIOR UVEITIS

Background Anterior uveitis lasting >3 months. Not usually associated with HLA-B27.

Symptoms May be asymptomatic or present with only blurred vision.

Signs As for acute anterior uveitis (see previous section), but the eye may be white and there is a higher incidence of complications [posterior synechiae; peripheral anterior synechiae; raised IOP; cataract; cystoid macular oedema (CMO)].

Differential diagnosis

- *Systemic disease*: juvenile idiopathic arthritis and sarcoidosis.
- *Ocular syndromes*: Fuchs' heterochromic cyclitis.
- *Infective*: herpes zoster ophthalmicus (HZO); herpes simplex virus (HSV); cytomegalovirus and syphilis.
- *Chronic idiopathic anterior uveitis*: ~50% of cases.
- *Postoperative inflammation*: especially cataract surgery and intravitreal injections.

Clinical features May have anterior vitreous cells and CMO but no other posterior segment signs. Well-recognised types include:

- *Fuchs' heterochromic cyclitis (FHC)*: features include white eye; characteristic translucent round or stellate keratic

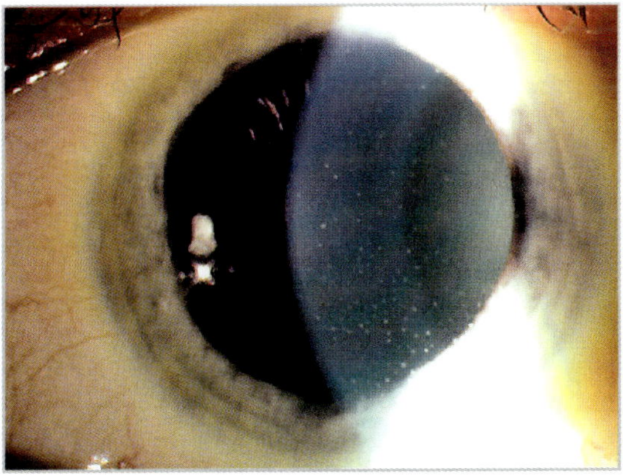

Fig. 9.2: Fuchs' heterochromic cyclitis with stellate keratic precipitates.

precipitates (KPs) scattered over the whole endothelium **(Fig. 9.2)**; heterochromia (variable); iris stromal atrophy, typically diffuse; posterior synechiae are absent; cataract is common; raised IOP (25%); vitreous cells and floaters may be considerable; CMO is rare.

- *Herpetic uveitis*: ask about vesicles of HSV or HZO rash. Look for corneal changes and sectoral iris atrophy (common). Assess for complications at each visit.
- *Cytomegalovirus*: features chronic low-grade inflammation, endothilitis and raised IOP.

Investigations Arrange macular OCT, CXR, sACE and syphilis serology if no suggestive aetiology. Normal sACE with no other suggestive symptoms makes sarcoidosis unlikely. Consider an AC tap for viral PCR.

Treatment

- *Emergency department*: Treat acute exacerbations and refer to clinic as for acute anterior uveitis (p. 403), but in addition to topical steroids and cycloplegics, add aciclovir 400 mg p.o. five times daily for 1 week. Topical antivirals are not effective except in the presence of epithelial disease.
- *Clinic*: Taper steroids slowly over months and attempt to stop. For steroid-responders, G. rimexolone 1% (Vexol) or loteprednol (Lotemax) may control inflammation without raising IOP: otherwise use G. dexamethasone 0.1% and a pressure-lowering eye drop, e.g. apraclonidine 0.5% t.d.s. Consider if oral aciclovir might reduce the frequency of relapses. FHC does not require topical steroids.

Follow-up Assess and manage any complications. Review several weeks after stopping topical steroids to exclude asymptomatic recurrence. For FHC with normal IOP arrange baseline disc imaging (photo or OCT) then annual optometry glaucoma screening. Monitor elevated IOP in clinic.

INTERMEDIATE UVEITIS

Background Intermediate uveitis is inflammation centred on the pars plana and peripheral retina. Pars planitis is defined as intermediate uveitis with 'snowbanking' and usually has no systemic association. There is no racial or gender bias, with onset typically in childhood or young adults. Pars planitis rarely presents after age of 40 years.

Symptoms Bilateral in >80%, although asymmetry is not uncommon and <20% present with unilateral disease. The history is frequently vague, but floaters from vitreous opacification or blurred vision from cystoid macular oedema (CMO) are common.

Signs The eye is white and the anterior segment usually quiet, or with slight flare, a few cells, and several small keratic precipitates (KPs). Vitreous signs predominate. Cells and opacities are variable and may aggregate to form 'snowballs' concentrated over the inferior peripheral retina **(Fig. 9.3)**. 'Snowbanking' describes a white plaque, typically overlying the inferior pars plana and retina, but it can encompass the entire peripheral fundus **(Fig. 9.4)**.

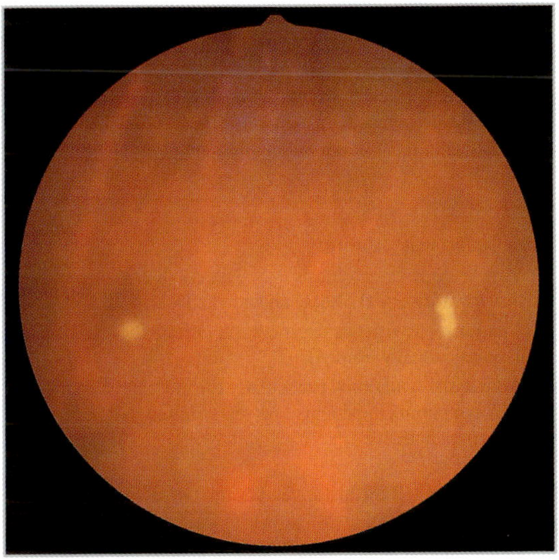

Fig. 9.3: Intermediate uveitis with 'snowballs'.

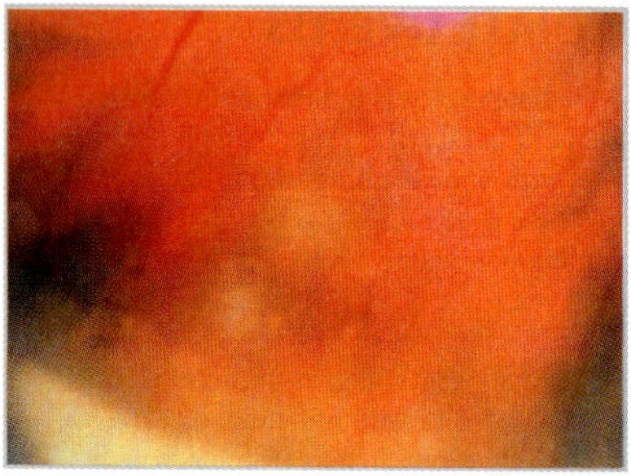

Fig. 9.4: Pars planitis with 'snowbank'.

CMO occurs in 25% and is the key threat to vision. Other findings include mild vasculitis and sheathing of peripheral retinal venules, diffuse retinal oedema, optic disc or peripapillary swelling, and neovascularisation of the disc or 'snowbank'.

History and examination The diagnosis is made by recognising vitreous signs, an absence of focal choroidal and retinal lesions, or the presence of systemic diseases associated with pars planitis (see differential diagnosis below). Retina/choroid scars are absent (their presence indicates posterior uveitis). Sarcoidosis and syphilis can be indistinguishable from idiopathic intermediate uveitis. A history of optic neuritis or other neurological features points to multiple sclerosis (MS). Record VA at each visit. Assess for complications: CMO, posterior synechiae, raised IOP, cataract, vitreous haemorrhage from posterior vitreous detachment (most common) or neovascularisation (less so), and epiretinal membrane.

Differential diagnosis

- *Idiopathic*: vast majority.
- *Systemic disease*: sarcoidosis, MS, Behçet's disease, syphilis, inflammatory bowel disease and amyloidosis.
- *Ocular disease*: vitreous degeneration (affects the middle-aged or elderly, usually women).
- *Masquerade syndromes*: particularly the initial presentation of B cell lymphoma in patients >60 years, although it may occur in younger patients.

Investigations If the history and examination are unremarkable, restrict investigations to OCT, CXR, sACE and syphilis serology, with other tests only as indicated.

Treatment It is important not to overtreat. The main indication is visual loss due to CMO, optic disc swelling or significant vitritis. Refer suspected systemic disease to a physician.

- *Emergency department*: Treat anterior uveitis with tapering topical steroids and cycloplegics (p. 403). If VA is reduced, arrange urgent clinic referral; otherwise, review within 8 weeks.
- *Clinic*: Select topical, periocular, intravitreal, and/or systemic steroids based on the pattern of disease, VA and presence of CMO or papillitis. In pars planitis, neovascularisation is secondary to inflammation, whereas in intermediate uveitis it may be secondary to inflammation, ischaemic retinal vasculitis, or both. Fluorescein angiography (ideally wide-field) helps to distinguish. Treat secondary neovascularisation with oral steroids (consider periocular injection in unilateral disease), and argon laser if driven by retinal ischaemia. Consider 2 weeks' oral prednisolone prior to panretinal photocoagulation, to dampen the inflammatory response.

Follow-up Most have a chronic course lasting several years, with subacute exacerbations and low-grade remissions requiring long-term, periodic follow-up. With adequate treatment VA prognosis is good.

POSTERIOR UVEITIS

Background Posterior uveitis may reduce vision in several ways:

- *Reversible*: cystoid macular oedema (CMO), retinal or disc neovascularisation, choroid neovascularisation, disc swelling, cataract, epiretinal membrane, vitreous debris and retinal detachment.
- *Irreversible*: macular ischaemia, optic atrophy, glaucoma and retinal scars.

Examination Identify anterior uveitis and its sequelae with slit-lamp examination (p. 401). Dilate and assess vitreous involvement. Use an indirect ophthalmoscope to look for peripheral vitreous condensations ('snowballs', **Fig. 9.3**, p. 407), 'snowbanking' (**Fig. 9.4**, p. 408), and any associated neovascularisation. Define the primary site of inflammation: choroiditis, chorioretinitis, retinitis, or retinochoroiditis. Establish the pattern of vascular involvement. Venous vasculitis is a common and non-specific sign; it may be ischaemic, and sheathing may persist after inflammation subsides. Arterial involvement is less common but associated with serious systemic diseases such as collagen/vascular disease (systemic lupus erythematosus, granulomatosis with polyangiitis and polyarteritis nodosa). A combination of arterial and venous vasculitis occurs in Behçet's disease, toxoplasmosis, syphilis, and acute retinal necrosis. Scars are associated with toxoplasmosis, sarcoidosis, presumed ocular histoplasmosis syndrome, punctuate inner choroidopathy, multifocal choroiditis, and Dalen–Fuchs' nodules such as in sympathetic ophthalmia and Vogt–Koyanagi–Harada syndrome. Determine the cause(s) of any visual loss. Exclude retinal detachment either as a cause of uveitis (masquerade) or as a complication of it.

Treatment

- *Emergency department*: Exclude infection (e.g. varicella-zoster virus, endogenous endophthalmitis), treat anterior uveitis (p. 401), and refer urgently to a uveitis clinic, the same day if vision is threatened.
- *Clinic*: Treat anterior uveitis accompanying posterior uveitis with topical steroids and mydriatics (p. 403). Regardless of the aetiology, the treatment of posterior uveitis is similar, but only after excluding infection and neoplasia (such as lymphoma). Treat only if the eye is being damaged or the vision threatened. The most common indications for treatment are vitritis and CMO (check OCT), but also retinitis, serous retinal detachment, papillitis, optic neuritis, and retinal neovascularisation. Control inflammation with the minimum

effective dose and duration of treatment. Consider: location and immediacy of the threat to vision; whether the disease is potentially reversible; if unilateral or bilateral; systemic factors including age, general health, and pregnancy; patient's compliance and preference. In general, use regional steroids if the patient is not a steroid-responder, particularly in unilateral disease. Otherwise, use oral steroids initially, adding mycophenolate or methotrexate if unable to induce remission or reduce the relapse rate. If the disease is still not controlled, consider intravitreal triamcinolone/Ozurdex if not a steroid-responder. If second-line drug addition fails or patient does not tolerate this, consider adding biologics particularly adalimumab (screen for latent TB and consider if needs MRI scan to exclude MS. **Box 9.1** lists recent key trials. For drug use in pregnancy, see page 840.

Corticosteroids are the mainstay of management.

- *Local administration*: topical steroids treat anterior uveitis and anterior vitreous cells but not posterior segment inflammation. In contrast, local steroid injections (periocular or intravitreal) are effective in non-infectious posterior uveitis and can be used when appropriate. The most common indications are unilateral or bilateral asymmetric disease, especially where high-dose systemic steroids are contraindicated, e.g. pregnancy, or while obtaining diabetic

Box 9.1: Key studies

- MUST: Compared an intravitreal 0.59 mg fluocinolone acetonide implant (Retisert) with systemic therapy for active intermediate or posterior uveitis. After 7 years, systemic therapy produced better vision due to less macular scarring than the implant.
- SYCAMORE: Compared adalimumab plus methotrexate to placebo plus methotrexate in children and adolescents with active juvenile idiopathic arthritis-associated uveitis. Adalimumab reduced the treatment failure rate and better controlled inflammation, but with a much higher incidence of adverse events and serious adverse events.
- POINT: Compared intravitreal triamcinolone, periocular triamcinolone and the dexamethasone implant, Ozurdex, for the treatment of macular oedema associated with active or inactive uveitis. At 3 months intravitreal triamcinolone and Ozurdex were superior to periocular triamcinolone, with modest increases in the risk of IOP elevation. This risk did not differ significantly between intravitreal treatments.
- MERIT: Compared intravitreal methotrexate, Ozurdex and ranibizumab for the treatment of residual macular oedema in previously inflamed eyes. At 12 weeks, Ozurdex was superior to methotrexate and ranibizumab. Ozurdex had a greater risk of IOP elevation, but pressures ≥30 mmHg were infrequent.

or hypertensive control. Periocular steroids are most useful in controlling vitritis and chronic CMO, but can take several weeks to work so avoid if there is an immediate threat to vision, and in steroid-responders. Posterior sub-Tenon's triamcinolone (4 mg in 0.1 mL) or orbital floor methylprednisolone (Depo-Medrone 4 mg in 0.1 mL) equally effective (see **Box 9.2**). These can be repeated after 6 weeks. Discontinue if there is no response after three 6-weekly injections. Intravitreal 700 μg dexamethasone implant (Ozurdex) is licensed for uveitis and can last for 4–6 months. In the 6 months after Ozurdex injection, cataract occurs in 15% and IOP-lowering medication may be required at up to

Box 9.2: Orbital floor injections

Orbital floor injections are favoured in some centres as they are believed to have a lower risk of globe perforation. Herniation of orbital fat following multiple orbital floor injections has been reported, but it is rare.

Technique:

- Check patient's name, date of birth, and side of injection.
- Use a 27-gauge 0.5" or 1" needle.
- Ask the patient to look straight ahead.
- Rotate the needle so the bevel faces the globe.
- Advance the needle directly posteriorly at the junction between the lateral third and medial two-thirds of the lower orbital rim. This can be transcutaneous or transconjunctival (following topical anaesthesia).
- Look for globe movement suggesting accidental contact by needle.
- Deposit the drug on the orbital floor.

Drugs:

- Triamcinolone 40 mg/mL – give 4 mg in 0.1 mL.
- Methylprednisolone acetate (Depo-Medrone) 40 mg/mL – give 4 mg in 0.1 mL.

Tips:

- A small amount of lidocaine can be used in the same syringe for additional anaesthesia. Slow injection also reduces pain.
- Do not ask the patient to look up as this will bring the optic nerve closer to the needle.
- Use a finger to displace the globe upwards to decrease the risk of inadvertent scleral engagement/globe perforation.

23% of visits. For the injection technique, see below. Review at 4 weeks when IOP often peaks, then monthly if indicated to 4 months. Patients requiring longer term local steroids can have intravitreal fluocinolone 0.19 mcg implant (Iluvien). Pre-treatment with Ozurdex, followed by Iluvien 4–6 weeks later, reduces the risk of recurrence. Iluvien lasts up to 3 years and can be repeated if required. IOP rise and cataract are known risks. If Ozurdex is unavailable, consider off-label intravitreal Triesence (preservative free triamcinolone) (Allergan) or (Kenalog 4 mg in 0.1 mL), given using the same technique as intravitreal antibiotics. Measure IOP 15–30 minutes after injection. The risk of raised IOP is ~30%, but may be up to 80% in patients under 30 years old. Triamcinolone injections can be repeated after 3–4 months, but control the IOP. All intravitreal injections carry a small risk of vitreous haemorrhage, retinal detachment and endophthalmitis.

- *Systemic steroids*: Use if the disease is bilateral, vision-threatening, or local steroids have failed, but discuss the risks versus benefits. If the vision is threatened that day or VA ≤6/60, a typical starting dose is prednisolone 80 mg o.d. (or 1–2 mg/kg) for 1 week, then, if responding, 60 mg o.d. 1 week, 40 mg o.d. 2 weeks, and thereafter guided by clinical effect. If VA is 6/12–6/18 and the visual threat is less severe, consider 40 mg o.d. (0.5–1 mg/kg) for 2 weeks then 30 mg o.d. 2 weeks, etc. The required duration of treatment varies. Aim to taper slowly, usually over months, to avoid reactivation. If unilateral reactivation occurs, consider local steroid injection to avoid increasing oral steroids. Some patients require long-term treatment for disease control.
  - *Side effects include*: Hypertension, diabetes, osteoporosis, cushingoid appearance and peptic ulceration. Cover with omeprazole 20 mg o.d., ranitidine 150 mg b.d., or similar. Review drug interactions in the British National Formulary or equivalent.
  - *Baseline tests*: Weight, BP, blood glucose, FBC, U&E, and CXR if history of TB or TB risk. Steroid-induced bone loss is worse at very high doses. Organise a bone scan if likely to be on steroids >3 months. Prescribe calcium supplements (Calcichew D3 Forte b.d.) for those with osteopenia, and 70 mg alendronate (Fosamax) once weekly for those with osteoporosis.
  - *Monitoring*: Measure weight, BP, and blood glucose at each visit. Check FBC (microcytic anaemia from gastrointestinal blood loss, neutrophilia and lymphopaenia), creatinine and U&E every 1–3 months. Advise patients to carry a steroid card and seek medical attention if they develop fever or lose their tablets.

Second-line agents Steroid-sparing agents are used to augment or help to reduce the steroid dose, e.g. when a steroid dose ≤ 7.5 mg daily produces frequent relapses. At all ages, balance the risk of lymphoma from second-line agents and try to avoid in unilateral disease. Some second-line agents may damage the fetus directly or via sperm mutations, so review contraceptive needs in men and women. These drugs should not be initiated or changed unless a senior clinician experienced in their use is involved.

- *Young healthy patients*: Mycophenolate (CellCept) is usually the first choice. Takes up to 6–8 weeks to work. Perform blood glucose, BP, FBC (bone marrow suppression), U&E (electrolyte imbalance) and LFT (liver damage) at baseline, then 6–8 weekly. Consider methotrexate (orally or subcutaneously) once weekly, given with folic acid orally (5 mg once weekly). Ciclosporin is an alternative but is used much less commonly now and some clinicians avoid it for long-term use. Tacrolimus has a similar mode of action to ciclosporin; it is more potent but has a high incidence of renal and CNS toxicity. Azathioprine can be used as either a second- or third-line drug. Consider adding biologics such as the anti-tumour necrosis factors (TNFs) infliximab or adalimumab. Due to toxicity, cyclophosphamide and chlorambucil are only rarely used except in severe vasculitis **(Table 9.2)**. Consider the need for contraceptives during treatment.
- *Patients of reproductive age*: Current Medicines and Healthcare products Regulatory Agency (MHRA) advice includes:
  - Insufficient evidence to completely exclude genotoxic risk, so use one form of highly reliable contraception during mycophenolate mofetil treatment and for 90 days after cessation. See also page 840.
  - Advice for use in females of reproductive age remains the same.
- *Older patients (>55–60 years)*: They are generally less tolerant of ciclosporin in the long term (nephrotoxicity and hypertension). Oral mycophenolate is increasingly used, or azathioprine. For azathioprine check thiopurine methyltransferase (TPMT). Allow 3–6 weeks for effect. Monitor FBC and LFTs 4–6 weekly.

Biologics Consider adalimumab if intolerant to second-line agents, or if they fail to reduce prednisolone dose to ≤7.5 mg daily. Screen for latent TB (CXR and Quantiferon gold test and/or Mantoux test), other infections suggested by history or examination, and MS (request MRI if intermediate uveitis co-exists).

Table 9.2: Immunosuppressive drugs used in the management of posterior uveitis

Name	Route	Expected onset	Monitor
Ciclosporin	Oral	2–6 weeks	FBC U&E LFTs
Tacrolimus	Oral	2–6 weeks	FBC U&E LFTs
Mycophenolate mofetil	Oral	4–6 weeks	FBC LFTs
Methotrexate	Oral or subcutaneous injection	6–8 weeks	FBC U&E LFTs
Azathioprine	Oral	4–6 weeks	FBC LFTs
Cyclophos-phamide	Oral or intravenous	2–6 weeks	FBC U&E LFTs
Infliximab	Intravenous infusion	2–12 weeks	FBC U&E LFTs Risk of TB reactivation. Risk of activating demyelinating disease
Adalimumab	Subcutaneous injection	2–12 weeks	FBC U&E LFTs Risk of TB reactivation. Risk of activating demyelinating disease

(FBC, full blood count; LFT, liver function test; U&E, urea and electrolytes)

Follow-up Varies, but generally see patients starting systemic treatment at 1–4 weeks to monitor disease, side effects, and compliance. As inflammation settles, increase progressively to 3-monthly review. Advise patients to attend if symptoms recur. Monitor closely if there is a relapse, if re-introducing high-dose steroids, or starting second-line or third-line agents.

SARCOIDOSIS

Background Systemic granulomatous disease most common in Asian and Afro-Caribbean patients. Multiple sites may be affected, but particularly the lungs, lymph nodes, skin, liver and eyes.

Symptoms Those of anterior, intermediate, or posterior uveitis (see previous sections). Systemic disease may be asymptomatic.

Signs These include: unilateral or bilateral acute or chronic anterior uveitis; intermediate uveitis; inferior 'snowballs' (**Fig. 9.3** p. 407); patchy periphlebitis and sheathing; venous occlusion and neovascularisation; small, round, usually inferior, chorioretinal lesions **(Fig. 9.5)**; optic nerve involvement (granulomas and papilloedema with CNS involvement); and secondary cataract/glaucoma. Look for iris infiltration with a velvety appearance and large, pink, peripheral nodules which tend to produce peripheral anterior synechiae.

History and examination Full uveitis history and examination (p. 399), plus assess for lung, skin, bone, joint, muscle, salivary gland and CNS involvement.

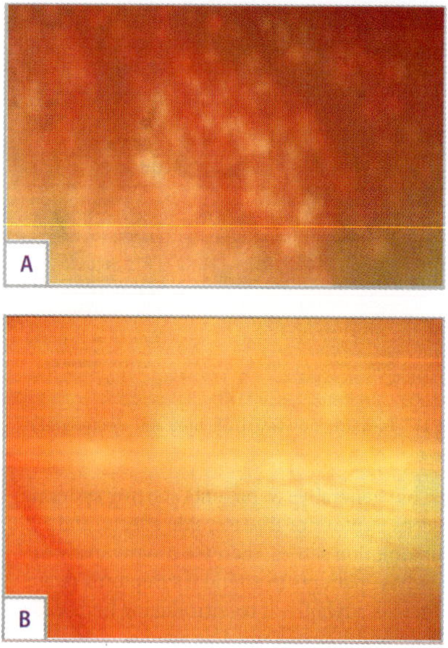

Fig. 9.5: Sarcoidosis with chorioretinal lesions (A) and severe retinal periphlebitis ('candlewax drippings') (B).

Differential diagnosis Depends on the pattern of ocular and systemic signs. Exclude TB (risk of reactivation with systemic steroids) and syphilis. Consider other causes of multifocal choroiditis (p. 428). Arteriolar involvement is rare and suggests Behçet's disease, toxoplasma chorioretinitis, syphilis, or acute retinal necrosis (ARN).

Investigations Arrange macular OCT, CXR, sACE, syphilis serology and Quantiferon Gold test or T-Spot TB test if there is a risk of TB (if unavailable then request Mantoux/Heaf via physicians). Biopsy conjunctival lesions if obvious clinically. Refer those with systemic symptoms to a physician. If sACE is normal and there are no systemic symptoms of sarcoidosis, sarcoidosis is very unlikely.

Treatment and follow-up Use topical, regional, or systemic steroids as appropriate (pp. 401–415). Neovascularisation may be secondary to ischaemia or inflammation, requiring panretinal photocoagulation laser or steroids, respectively, or sometimes both. Second-line drugs are less commonly required than in other sight-threatening uveitides. Relapses often follow remission and long-term follow-up is usually needed.

TUBERCULOSIS

Background At-risk groups include people from TB-endemic areas and the immunosuppressed, including human immunodeficiency virus (HIV). Ocular manifestations may be due to direct infection or a hypersensitivity response to TB elsewhere.

History Many patients are systemically well with latent TB. Pain, redness, blurred vision, and floaters are variable. Ask about Bacillus Calmette–Guérin (BCG) vaccination, previous TB or TB exposure, TB risk factors or treatment, and evidence of an old or active TB focus.

Examination Look for: conjunctival phlycten; nondescript anterior uveitis and associated iris nodules; variably sized keratic precipitates; choroidal granulomata (**Fig. 9.6**); multifocal or serpiginous-like choroiditis (lesions characteristically variable in size); subretinal abscess; retinitis; retinal vasculitis from infection (nonocclusive); or a hypersensitivity response with widespread peripheral retinal ischaemia ± new vessels elsewhere with associated vitreous haemorrhage.

Differential diagnosis The diagnosis is often presumptive but exclude other granulomatous disease, especially sarcoidosis (p. 416).

Investigations Request macular OCT, CXR, Quantiferon Gold test or T-Spot TB test (Heaf/Mantoux test by a physician if

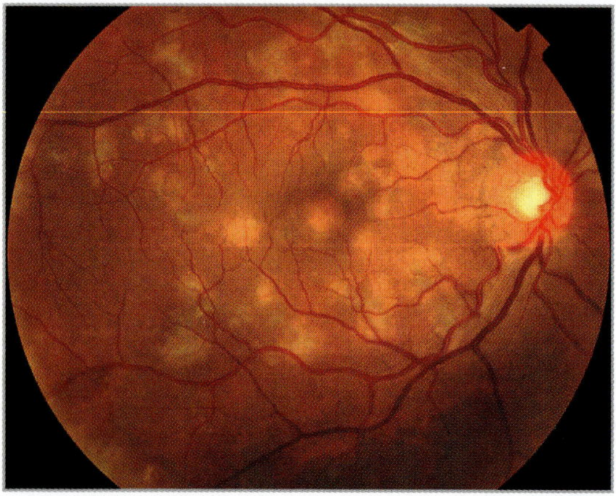

Fig. 9.6: TB choroidal granulomas.

not available), and sACE (overlap with sarcoidosis). Check for associated HIV infection (p. 448). Consider a positron emission tomography (PET) CT scan to look for systemic TB, via specialist physician referral.

Treatment and follow-up Manage in conjunction with a specialist physician. Consider TB chemotherapy, oral steroids for active inflammation, retinal laser for new vessels, and topical steroids for conjunctival phlycten and anterior uveitis. Adjust (double) steroid treatment for patients on rifampicin.

SYPHILIS

Background A sexually transmitted infection caused by the spirochaete *Treponema pallidum*. Mother-to-child transmission can cause congenital infection.

Classification and systemic features

- *Primary*: Chancre at the site of inoculation, usually but not always genital. Chancre is a painless slightly elevated ulcer with an indurated edge.
- *Secondary*: Lymphadenopathy, rash, mucous membrane lesions and meningitis. Neurovascular events may occur, including acute stroke.
- *Latent*: Untreated, most patients enter a latent phase with no clinical manifestations. May remain latent lifelong or progress to tertiary disease after several to many years.
- *Tertiary*: Cardiovascular disease (aortitis, aortic regurgitation and angina), neurosyphilis (myelopathy and mental changes) and systemic gummata (fibrous deposits).

Signs Ocular disease may occur at any stage. Primary infection may rarely present with a chancre on the eyelid. Signs of secondary and tertiary infection include oculomotor palsies, madarosis (loss of eyelashes), conjunctivitis, interstitial keratitis, episcleritis, scleritis, glaucoma, Argyll Robertson pupil (light-near dissociation), visual field loss, uveitis, chorioretinitis, retinitis, choroidal ischaemia, periarteritis, neuroretinitis and optic neuritis. Late changes may mimic retinitis pigmentosa, with paravascular retinal pigment, vascular attenuation and pale optic discs. Congenital syphilis classically produces interstitial keratitis and pigmentary retinopathy. May be associated with HIV and/or other sexually transmitted infections.

Investigations Request macular OCT, and venereal disease research laboratory (VDRL) or rapid plasma reagin (RPR) test. RPR measures antiphospholipid antibody levels and is not specific to syphilis. Never use VDRL as the sole screening test, as false positives occur in a variety of conditions including connective tissue diseases and pregnancy. The VDRL is valuable for monitoring response to treatment, with high titres in active disease that fall with effective therapy. A rising VDRL following successful treatment may suggest reinfection. Fluorescent treponemal antibody absorbed (FTA-ABS), microhaemagglutination-T. pallidum (MHA-TP), T. pallidum particle agglutination (TPPA), or the T. pallidum haemagglutination (TPHA) tests all measure specific antitreponemal antibody levels and usually remain positive for life, even after effective therapy. Many clinics now perform a syphilis immunoglobulin IgG/IgM as a cheaper screening test. If negative, then no action is needed. If positive, then the laboratory will proceed to a VDRL/TPHA. Other treponemal infections (including yaws, which is endemic in the Caribbean) give positive results, as occasionally do other spirochaetes (Lyme disease).

Management Refer to an infectious disease or genitourinary medicine consultant for evaluation and treatment. Treat primary, secondary and latent infection with sustained release intramuscular penicillin preparations. Treat tertiary disease, including CNS and eye, with high-dose penicillin. Treatment regimens for all stages of disease are covered in the British Association of Sexual Health Guidelines (www.bashh.org/resources/guidelines/).

BEHÇET'S DISEASE

Background A chronic systemic inflammatory disease most frequent in young men of Japanese, Arabic, Korean or Mediterranean origin (particularly Turkey and Greece). Major diagnostic criteria are:

- Recurrent oral ulcers
- Genital ulcers
- Skin lesions (erythema nodosum and pustules)
- Positive pathergy test
- Uveitis

Symptoms Pain and photophobia, or rapid-onset floaters and blurred vision.

Signs Transient hypopyon is common and may accompany anterior uveitis. Chronic panuveitis with severe acute recurrences is characteristic, as is an ischaemic vasculitis involving both arteries and veins. White necrotic retinitis may be accompanied by retinal infiltrates, oedema, and haemorrhage **(Fig. 9.7)**. Second eye involvement may be delayed by years.

Differential diagnosis Other causes of ischaemic vasculitis (collagen/vascular disorders) and syphilis.

Investigations None. Clinical diagnosis.

Treatment and follow-up Treat as for posterior uveitis (p. 410). Second-line agents are usually required from the outset if posterior segment disease is present. The long-term prognosis is guarded if there is ischaemic vasculitis. Introduce biologics early to reduce the frequency of attacks, visual loss and especially to protect the second eye. Recurrent posterior uveitis may result in retinal vascular attenuation and secondary optic atrophy. Lifelong follow-up is typical for posterior segment disease.

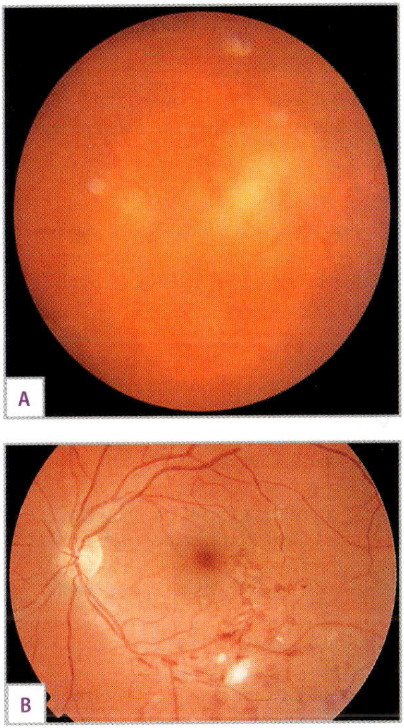

Fig. 9.7: Behçet's disease with active retinitis (A) and vascular occlusion (B).

VOGT–KOYANAGI–HARADA SYNDROME

Background A systemic disease with ocular and skin involvement. More common in Asian, Hispanic, and Japanese patients.

Symptoms Bilateral, synchronous or sequential blurred vision, with variable redness, pain, and photophobia. May have a prodrome of pyrexia, headache, malaise, and auditory or meningeal symptoms. Maybe drug-induced from microtubule affinity-regulating kinase (MARK) inhibitors.

Signs Serous retinal detachments overlying diffuse or multifocal choroiditis, with vitritis, disc oedema or hyperaemia (characteristic pink disc) (**Fig. 9.8**). Anterior uveitis is common. Cutaneous signs (alopecia, poliosis and vitiligo) may develop later. Check colour vision and exclude an RAPD.

Differential diagnosis Consider sympathetic ophthalmia, posterior scleritis, sarcoidosis, and masquerade syndromes. Acute multifocal posterior placoid pigment epitheliopathy (AMPPE) can rarely cause serous retinal detachment.

Investigations A clinical diagnosis. Fluorescein angiography shows pinpoint areas of enlarging hyperfluorescence with late staining of the disc and subretinal fluid. If a meningo-encephalitic picture occurs, request a neurology opinion, or if the eye lesions are atypical. B-scan ultrasound may help to exclude posterior scleritis. OCT shows serous retinal detachment, often septate, and a thickened choroid.

Treatment and follow-up For the treatment of posterior uveitis, see page 410. Second-line agents may be required to allow steroid dose reduction if inflammation is severe or prolonged. The length of treatment usually depends on the optic neuritis, as retinal detachments usually settle rapidly [leaving considerable retinal pigment epithelium (RPE) mottling or a 'sunset glow' fundus]. It is often possible to stop systemic treatment after 1 year. Recurrences are typically as an anterior uveitis only and respond to topical treatment alone.

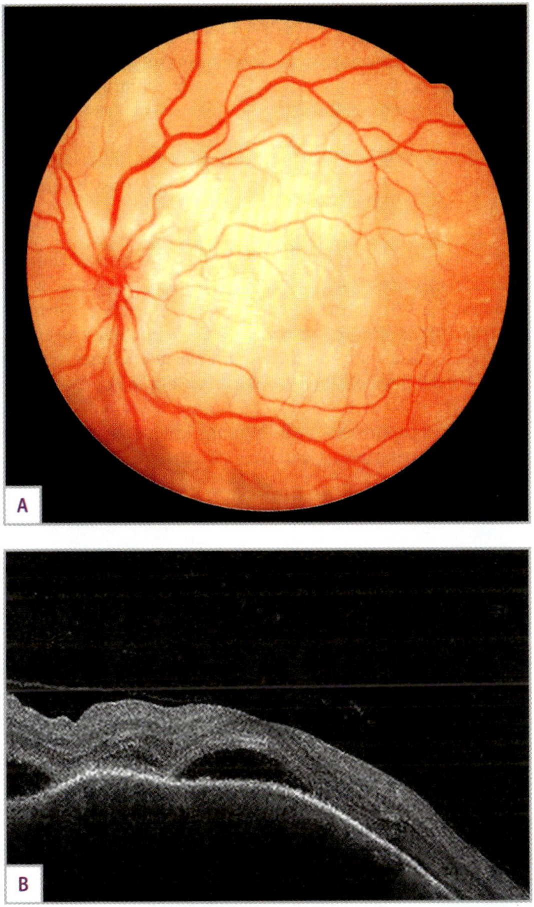

Fig. 9.8: Vogt–Koyanagi–Harada syndrome with swollen pink disc, serous detachments and choroidal lesions.

SYMPATHETIC OPHTHALMIA

Background Bilateral panuveitis following uniocular penetrating ocular injury, surgery, or non-penetrating cyclodestructive procedures.

Symptoms Bilateral subacute discomfort with redness and photophobia or visual loss, usually 1–12 months after the inciting event (range 5 days to 60+ years).

Signs Typically bilateral granulomatous panuveitis with diffuse choroidal involvement or multiple yellow-white Dalen–Fuchs' nodules (**Fig. 9.9**), often with papillitis or peripapillary oedema. There is a broad spectrum of disease activity that may appear confined to the anterior segment. Choroidal granulomas leave Dalen–Fuchs' nodules when quiescent (see **Fig. 9.9**).

Differential diagnosis Vogt–Koyanagi–Harada syndrome, phacoanaphylactic uveitis, and sarcoidosis.

Investigations A clinical diagnosis.

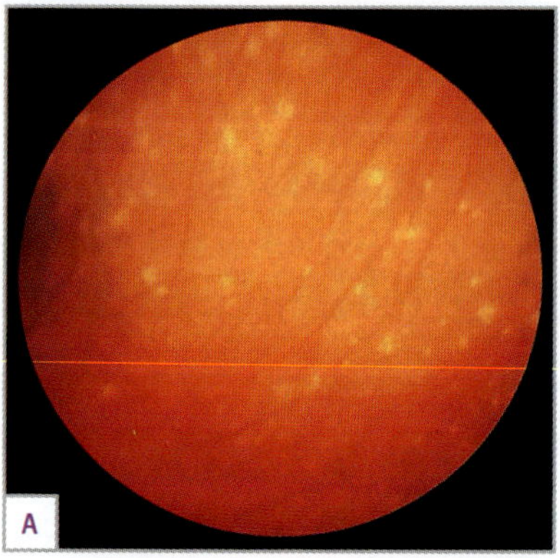

Fig. 9.9: (A) Sympathetic ophthalmia, (B) OCT of Dalen–Fuchs' nodules, which are healed inactive choroidal granulomas.

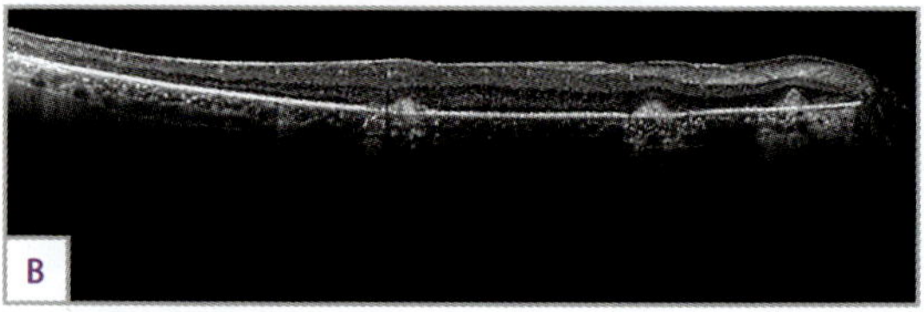

Treatment For the treatment of posterior uveitis, see page 410. There is no role for enucleation of the traumatised eye if there is visual potential. Use topical steroids alone for inflammation limited to the anterior chamber, if responds well, but systemic steroids are usually required, as may be second-line agents. Recurrences are likely, often with fresh choroidal granulomas or peripapillary oedema.

Follow-up It is unlikely that treatment can be stopped for at least 1 year. There is a reasonable long-term visual prognosis with adequate long-term immunosuppression, but a high risk of cataract and glaucoma.

WHITE DOT SYNDROMES

Background Incorporates several diseases characterised by white dots seen on fundus examination (**Table 9.3**).

Presumed ocular histoplasmosis syndrome

- Presumed ocular histoplasmosis syndrome (POHS) affects all ages with no gender bias.
- The characteristic triad is of peripapillary atrophy, multiple atrophic 'histo-spots' (**Fig. 9.10**), predominately around the posterior pole and often with internal pigment clumping, and serous or haemorrhagic disciform detachment due to choroidal neovascularisation (CNV), usually associated with a macular 'histo-spot'.
- Linear streaks of chorioretinal atrophy are sometimes seen.
- Vitreous cells are absent.
- Usually asymptomatic, until CNV develops.
- The diagnosis is clinical but request a fluorescence angiogram and/or OCT angiography if CNV is suspected.
- Consider intravitreal anti-VEGF treatment for active CNV.
- Provide an Amsler chart to monitor each eye.

Multifocal choroiditis and panuveitis

- Affects all ages.
- Acute, usually bilateral onset of AC and vitreous inflammation, with lesions of varying size and age in the periphery, posterior pole, or both. Acute lesions are pale yellow or grey (**Fig. 9.11**).
- Exclude sarcoidosis and miliary TB.
- Usually follows a relapsing–remitting course.
- VA is good unless cystoid macular oedema (CMO) or CNV occur. Request OCT, OCT angiography or fluorescein angiography as required.
- CMO may respond to systemic or local steroids, and CNV to anti-VEGF agents.

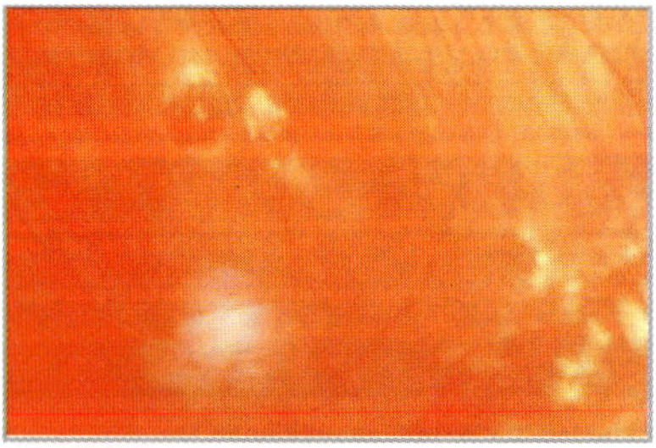

Fig. 9.10: Presumed ocular histoplasmosis.

Table 9.3: White dot syndromes

	Birdshot	AMPPE	MCP	Serpiginous	PIC	MEWDS	AZOOR
Average age (range)	53 (30–50)	20–50	45 (9–69)	20–60	32 (15–55)	10–50	37 (13–79)
Sex	F > M 3:2	M = F	F > M 3:1	M > F slightly	F > M 9:1	F > M 3:1	F > M 3:1
Onset	Insidious	Acute	Subacute	Acute or insidious	Acute or insidious	Acute	Acute
Laterality	Bilateral Symmetric	Bilateral Sequential	Bilateral Asymmetric	Bilateral Asymmetric	Bilateral	Unilateral Bilateral reported	Bilateral Unilateral 25%
Myopia	No	No	Yes	No	Yes	Yes	Yes
Viral prodrome	No	Yes	No	No	No	Yes, one-third	Yes, 20%
Inflammation	AC+, vitritis +	Vitritis +	AC ++, vitritis ++	–	–	Vitritis +	Vitritis +
Lesion size (μm)	500–1,500	<1500	50–350	Confluent	100–300	100–750	

Table 9.3: White dot syndromes—*Contd...*

	Birdshot	AMPPE	MCP	Serpiginous	PIC	MEWDS	AZOOR
Optic disc swelling	–	+	–	–	–	+	–
Enlarged blind spot	–	–	+	–	+	+	+
FFA	Can be normal, early hypo-fluorescence, subtle late stain, disc leakage, delayed AV transit time	Early blockage, late stain, ± delayed choroidal filling	Early hypofluorescence, late stain	Early hypo-fluorescence with poorly defined borders, late stain, leak at active border	Early hyper-fluorescence, variable late leakage/staining	Early wreath-like punctate hyper-fluorescence, late stain and disc leak	Normal in 50%. Hyper-fluorescence reflects RPE changes
ICG	Hypo-cyanescent spots, more than clinically visible	Hypo-cyanescent lesions	Multiple hypo-cyanescent lesions, confluence around optic disc, more than clinically visible	Early hypo-cyanescence ± late staining, more than clinically visible	Hypo-cyanescent spots, dilated choroidal capillaries, localised vessel wall hyper-cyanescent spots	Multiple hypo-fluorescent lesions, more than clinically visible; hypo-cyanescent annular ring around optic disc	Hypo-cyanescence of lesion and elsewhere

Table 9.3: White dot syndromes—*Contd...*

	Birdshot	AMPPE	MCP	Serpiginous	PIC	MEWDS	AZOOR
CNV	Uncommon	Rare	28%	35%	75%	Uncommon	Rare
CMO	Common	Uncommon	Common	Can occur	Uncommon	Uncommon	Uncommon
Prognosis	Preserved central vision until late, 13% VA ≤ 6/15	Good. Spontaneous resolution within 1–2 months. 25% VA ≤ 6/12	Guarded	Poor Mean VA 6/36	Guarded. 20% VA ≤ 6/60	Very good. Spontaneous resolution to normal VA and VF in weeks-months	Good. 85% VA ≥ 6/12
Recurrences	+	–	+	+ (progressive)	+	10–15%	25%

(AC, anterior chamber; AMPPE, acute multifocal posterior placoid pigment epitheliopathy; AV, arteriovenous; AZOOR, acute zonal occult outer retinopathy; CMO, cystoid macular oedema; CNV, choroidal neovascularisation; FFA, fundus fluorescein angiography; ICG, indocyanine green; MCP, multifocal choroiditis and panuveitis; MEWDS, multiple evanescent white dot syndrome; PIC, punctate inner choroidopathy; RPE, retinal pigment epithelium; VF, visual field)

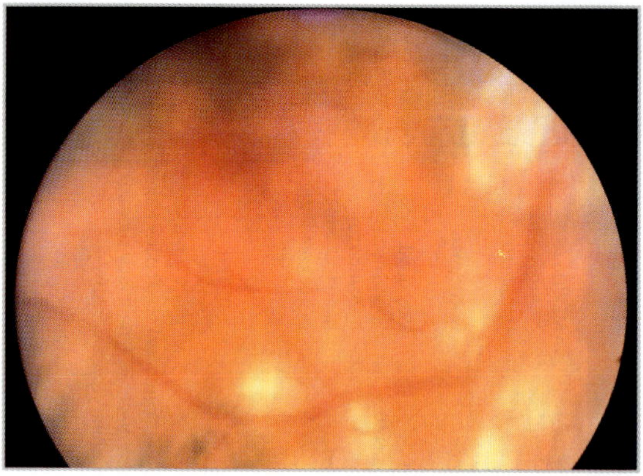

Fig. 9.11: Multifocal choroiditis.

Acute multifocal posterior placoid pigment epitheliopathy

- Primarily affects young adults of either gender.
- Causes acute, usually bilateral, blurred vision.
- One-third of cases are preceded by a viral prodrome.
- Cream-coloured, ill-defined lesions occur at the level of the choriocapillaris or retinal pigment epithelium (RPE), most commonly at the posterior pole.
- A mild vitritis occurs in 50% and AC cells in a minority.
- Severe hypertension may produce choroidal infarcts that mimic acute multifocal posterior placoid pigment epitheliopathy (AMPPE) so check BP.
- Request OCT. Fluorescein angiography shows early blockage of choroidal fluorescence with late staining (**Fig. 9.12**). Indocyanine green (ICG) angiography shows areas of choriocapillary hypoperfusion (**Fig. 11.10**, p. 506).
- The disease is usually self-limiting, but may recur.
- The benefit of systemic steroids is unproven, but they are often given if the presenting VA is reduced.
- Ask about severe headaches suggesting potentially fatal cerebral vasculitis (refer promptly to a neurologist).
- Few if any vitreous cells.
- Fluorescein angiography of acute lesions shows early hyperfluorescence and late staining.

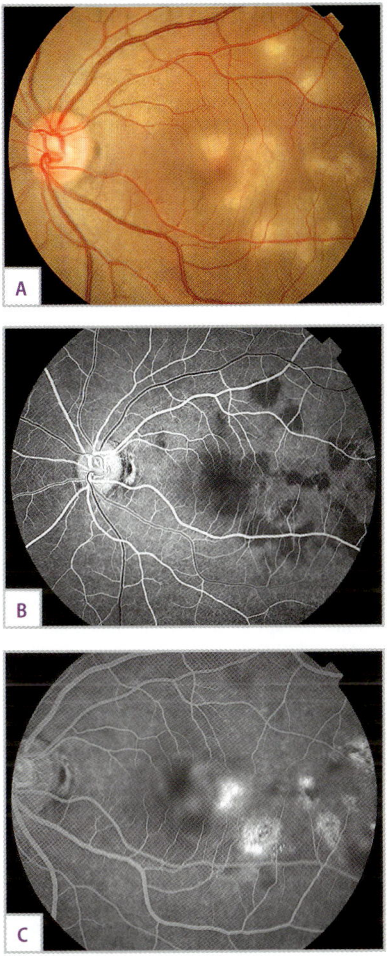

Fig. 9.12: (A) Creamy lesions due to AMPPE; (B) fundus fluorescein angiography (FFA) – early blockage; (C) FFA – late leakage.

- Recurrences are uncommon but can occur.
- There is a high risk of CNV which may respond to anti-VEGF agents. Suspect if there is retinal haemorrhage. Systemic or intravitreal steroids may also be useful.
- Provide an Amsler grid and instructions.

Punctate inner choroidopathy

- Usually affects young myopic females.
- Presents with bilateral acute blurring of vision or photopsia with small yellow or grey spots around the posterior pole within the arcades, at the level of the choroid or RPE (**Fig. 9.13**).

Birdshot chorioretinopathy

- Occurs in human leucocyte antigen-A29 (HLA-A29)-positive Caucasians aged 40–70 years but small proportion are HLA-A29 negative.
- Gradual bilateral onset of loss of night vision and colour vision.
- Oval, cream-coloured, ill-defined lesions occur around the posterior pole and mid-periphery (**Fig. 9.14**); may take years to appear. Choroidal neovascularisation may occur.
- Often associated with moderate vitritis, vasculitis, cystoid macular oedema (request OCT), and disc oedema.
- A chronic progressive course usually requires systemic steroids and second-line agents for visual loss from a variety of causes, including cystoid macular oedema.
- Loss of electroretinogram (ERG) retinal function precedes VA change and may be an indication to start or continue therapy. Long-term second-line therapy produces better functional outcome, visual fields and ERGs.

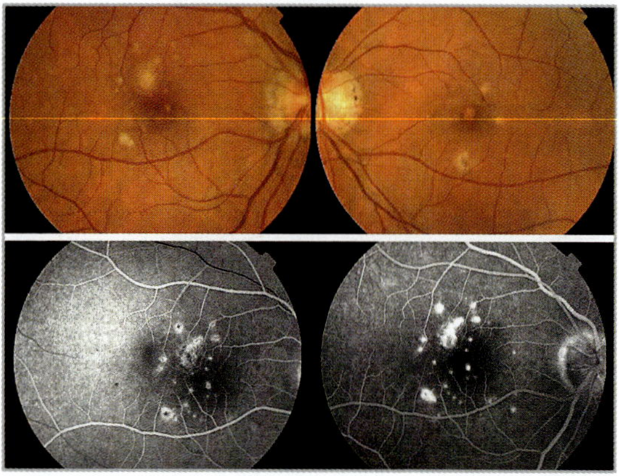

Fig. 9.13: Punctate inner choroidopathy.

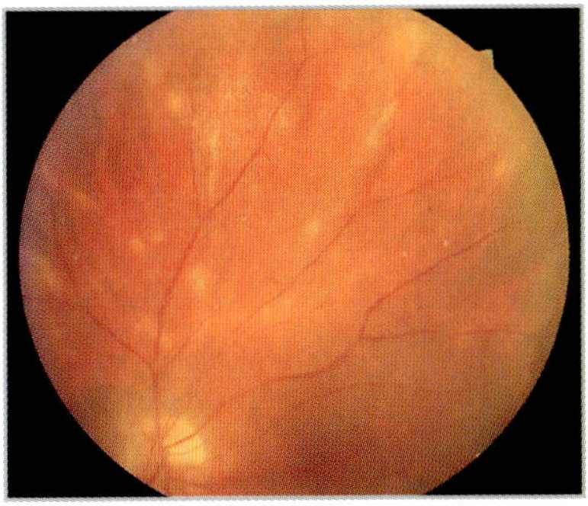

Fig. 9.14: Birdshot chorioretinopathy.

Multiple evanescent white dot syndrome

- Typically causes acute unilateral visual loss or paracentral scotoma in young adult females, often following a flu-like illness.
- Small white spots occur at the level of the RPE or retina (request OCT), mostly within and around the vascular arcades and disc, showing early hypofluorescence and late staining on fluorescein angiography. The macula has a granular appearance due to tiny punctate yellowish or orange spots (**Fig. 9.15**). ICG angiography typically shows multiple hypofluorescent areas in late films which are more extensive than the lesions seen clinically.
- Vitreous cells may be present, as may an RAPD, disc swelling, and blind spot enlargement.
- Resolves spontaneously over weeks to normal or near normal VA.
- The fundus changes also resolve, and may be absent unless examined acutely. ICG angiography may, however, be abnormal for several weeks before reverting to normal.
- Recurrences and choroidal neovascularisation are rare.
- No proven treatment. Consider oral steroids for co-existing inflammation and vision loss.

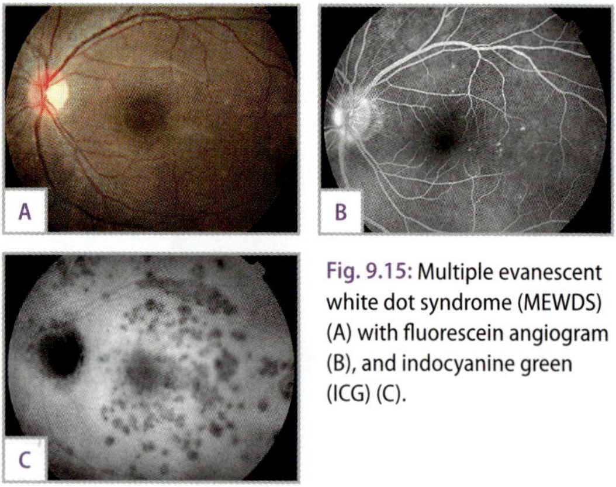

Fig. 9.15: Multiple evanescent white dot syndrome (MEWDS) (A) with fluorescein angiogram (B), and indocyanine green (ICG) (C).

AZOOR

- Rare. Affects mainly young females, although any age, sex and race can be affected.
- Presents with sudden onset of photopsias and visual field defects. Vision may uncommonly be affected.
- Fundus may look normal or have subtle pigmentary changes.
- Electroretinographic features are most commonly used to confirm the diagnosis – shows photoreceptor outer segment dysfunction.
- There is no proven useful treatment, although oral corticosteroids are often tried.
- Some patients may improve with time, but not all.

SERPIGINOUS CHOROIDOPATHY

- Rare, usually bilateral disease mostly affecting Caucasians of either gender. Also called geographic choroidopathy. Check Quantiferon gold or T-spot TB (or Mantoux via physicians if neither available), as 50% have active TB as an underlying cause.
- Presents typically as a middle-aged adult with active choroidal inflammation adjacent to previous scars (**Fig. 9.16**). May present at a younger age (>10 years).

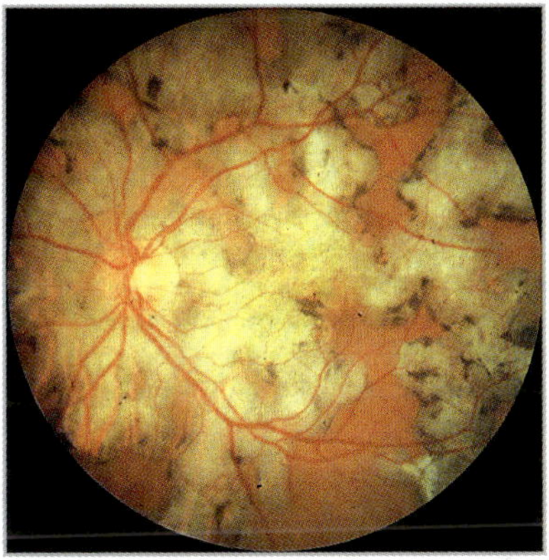

Fig. 9.16: Serpiginous choroidopathy.

TOXOPLASMOSIS

Background Usually a reactivation of healed early acquired or congenital toxoplasmosis, or less frequently, acute recently acquired infection.

Symptoms Blurred vision, or floaters due to vitritis.

Signs

- *Inactive disease*: characteristically, an atrophic chorioretinal scar of variable size with pigment clumping.
- *Active disease*: focal yellow-white area of active necrotising retinitis, with poorly demarcated edges, adjacent to the edge of an old inactive scar (**Fig. 9.17**), with associated vitritis. Localised arterial and venous vasculitis are common, and occlusion may occur. Anterior uveitis and ocular hypertension are frequent. Neuroretinitis, papillitis, retrobulbar neuritis, punctate outer retinal toxoplasmosis, massive granuloma, and diffuse unilateral toxoplasmosis are less frequent. VA is directly affected if there is involvement of the fovea, papillomacular bundle, or optic nerve, or indirectly as a consequence of cystoid macular oedema, serous retinal detachment, epiretinal membrane, vascular occlusion, ischaemia or neovascularisation. Choroidal

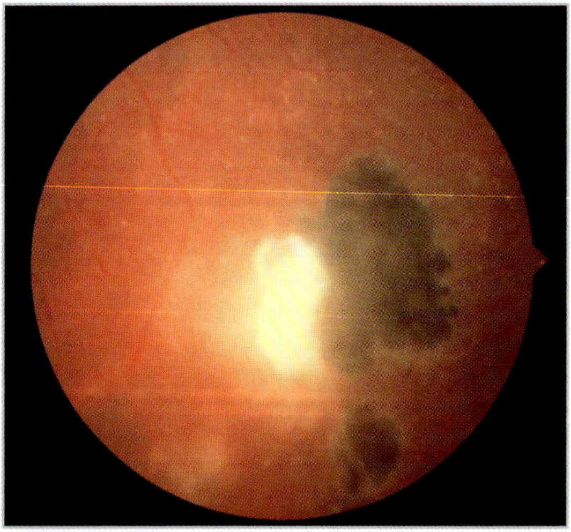

Fig. 9.17: Active toxoplasma chorioretinitis next to old scar.

neovascularisation, and tractional and rhegmatogenous retinal detachments can rarely occur. Recently acquired toxoplasma retinitis is not associated with chorioretinal scarring and is typically solitary, discrete, and unilateral. Bilateral disease activation is rare and usually indicates immunosuppression.

- Has a slow stepwise progression with spread from the peripapillary area towards the periphery.
- Active lesions show early blockage with late staining on fluorescein angiography.
- Often treated with systemic steroids and antibiotics for sight-threatening lesions, although not of proven benefit (**must never be treated with steroids alone**). Underlying TB needs urgent treatment so refer to physicians.
- CNV is sometimes treated with intravitreal anti-VEGF therapy, with steroid cover if there is inflammation.

History and examination Acute acquired infection is usually asymptomatic. Record VA, the degree of vitritis, and the location of the active retinitis. Look for inactive scars in the fellow eye.

Investigations None other than macular OCT required in typical recurrent disease. If recently acquired disease is suspected, the diagnosis is confirmed by high IgM antibody titre, which reverts to IgG after 3–9 months. When treatment is indicated, request baseline BP, capillary blood sugar, FBC, U&E, and LFT to monitor the side effects of antibiotics and steroids. Request CNS imaging in immunocompromised patients to exclude CNS involvement.

Treatment The disease is self-limiting and not all lesions require intervention. Treat the following lesions:

- Active lesions inside or straddling the temporal vascular arcades
- Threat to a major retinal vessel
- Within one-disc diameter of the optic disc or causing disc swelling
- Multifocal lesions
- Sufficient vitritis to obscure the macular view

Four commonly used oral antibiotic treatments are:

1. Azithromycin 500 mg o.d. as monotherapy or in combination with pyrimethamine 25 mg o.d., or
2. Pyrimethamine (50 mg loading dose, then 25 mg o.d.), folinic acid (15 mg twice weekly) to alleviate marrow toxicity, and sulphadiazine (500 mg q.d.s), or

Table 9.4: Risk of toxoplasma transmission to fetus		
Gestational age (weeks)	**Risk of vertical transmission to fetus**	**Risk of clinical manifestions**
13	6%	61%
26	40%	25%
36	72%	9%

3. Cotrimoxazole (Septrin) 960 mg b.d., or
4. Clindamycin 300–600 mg q.d.s.

Always combine antibiotics with systemic steroids, typically prednisolone 60 mg o.d. then tapered as inflammation subsides. Treatment length is guided by the clinical response but is usually 4–6 weeks. Do not give systemic steroids without antibiotics, and local steroid injections are contraindicated. Advise female patients with primary disease that there is a risk of passing the infection to the fetus (**Table 9.4**) for 6 months, so use appropriate contraception.

Follow-up If no treatment is required, review in 1 week initially and reassess. Review regularly on treatment with FBC at each visit. As inflammation subsides, the edges of active lesion harden off and are replaced by a chorioretinal scar, with clearing of vitritis. Overall, 30% retain 6/12 vision or better. Discharge when the retinitis is quiescent. Consider prophylactic long-term Septrin 960 mg three times per week for at least 1 year if reactivation is likely to involve significant visual loss.

ACUTE RETINAL NECROSIS

Background Most frequently caused by varicella zoster virus (VZV), but also reported with herpes simplex virus (HSV) I and II and rarely cytomegalovirus (CMV). Patients may be healthy or immunocompromised.

Symptoms Often there is no systemic disease, although some may have evidence of recent or concurrent VZV or HSV infection. Onset is typically unilateral with visual loss, often with ocular or periocular discomfort. Sequential bilateral involvement occurs in up to one-third of cases, usually within 3 months, but may be delayed for several years. Patients may get recurrent, isolated anterior uveitis in the longer term.

Signs Characterised by focal, well-demarcated, whitened areas of peripheral retinal necrosis outside the major vascular arcades (**Fig. 9.18**), which rapidly progress circumferentially to become confluent. These can be bilateral, especially in immunocompromised patients. Arterial or venous vascular occlusions are an important clinical feature. Optic nerve head swelling is common. Vitritis is always present and may obscure the fundal view. There is a high incidence of retinal breaks just anterior to normal retina several weeks after onset due to posterior vitreous detachment. Anterior uveitis is present in all patients, keratic precipitates may be large, and IOP is often elevated. Severely immunocompromised patients, particularly those with HIV infection, may have a more aggressive form (progressive outer retinal necrosis) but with virtually no inflammation.

Investigations diagnostic vitreous biopsy for PCR (VSV, HSV-I and -II, Epstein–Barr virus, and CMV DNA) in all patients.

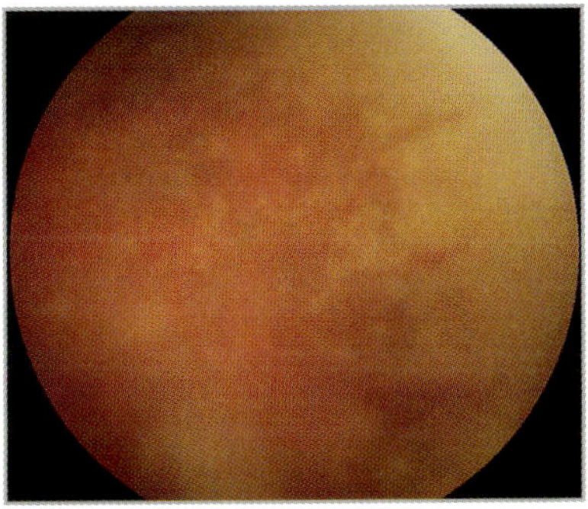

Fig. 9.18: Acute retinal necrosis.

Request baseline FBC, U&E, and LFTs. If bilateral at presentation, ask about sexual history/HIV risk and arrange testing as appropriate with infectious disease clinicians. Systemic VZV infection preceding acute retinal necrosis (ARN) indicates immunocompromise until proven otherwise.

Differential diagnosis

- *Behçet's disease*: features retinal necrosis and arterial and venous vasculitis, but also extraocular features.
- *Pars planitis*: may produce significant peripheral retinal whitening and vitritis, but onset is not acute and ischaemia is absent.
- *Syphilis*: may cause retinal whitening, arteritis, and vitritis, but is typically mid-peripheral.
- *Toxoplasmosis*: Can cause large peripheral white lesions (especially in older patients) and significant vitritis, but typically there is a chorioretinal scar.

Treatment Early initiation of antiviral therapy is important. Start with oral valaciclovir 2 g t.d.s. (if there is evidence of renal impairment use 1 g t.d.s.) for at least 2 weeks reducing to 1 g t.d.s. for at least 3 months, or intravenous aciclovir 10 mg/kg t.d.s. for at least 7 days followed by oral valaciclovir 1 g t.d.s. for at least 3 months. Both drugs can cause renal toxicity so monitor U&Es. As retinitis subsides, whitened necrotic retina is replaced by retinal pigment epithelium scarring and atrophy. Systemic steroids (1 mg/kg and rapidly tapered) are usually introduced with valaciclovir if significant vitritis limits the fundal view and/or for optic nerve involvement. Prophylactic laser retinopexy posterior to the margin of involved retina is not recommended. If immunosuppressed, avoid systemic steroids, arrange physician review, and consider continuous prophylactic treatment (valaciclovir 1 g t.d.s.). Give intravitreal foscarnet (2.4 mg in 0.1 mL) at the time of vitreous biopsy; can be repeated once or twice per week. Advise patients of the symptoms of retinal detachment.

Follow-up Usually for up to 2 years to assess for second eye involvement and rhegmatogenous retinal detachment (most commonly at 6–8 weeks after onset). Proliferative vitreoretinopathy is common when retinal detachment occurs and silicone oil is required.

CYTOMEGALOVIRUS RETINITIS

Background Usually occurs in association with severe immunocompromise, either malignancy, AIDS (CD4+ count almost always <50 cells/μL) or iatrogenic, including chemotherapy for malignancy or severe autoimmune disease. In the majority, the cause of the underlying immunosuppression is already established, but cytomegalovirus (CMV) retinitis is the presenting feature in 2% of undiagnosed AIDS patients.

Symptoms Visual loss or scotomas from posterior pole involvement. May be asymptomatic.

Signs Unilateral or bilateral at presentation. Full-thickness necrotising retinitis with haemorrhage, often with accompanying retinal vasculitis (**Fig. 9.19**). Slowly progressive (250–300 μm/week) and usually more rapid towards the retinal periphery than the posterior pole, so areas are characteristically sectorial. The edges of lesions are the most active, with expansion resembling a 'brush-fire'. Visual loss occurs when retinitis involves the optic nerve or macula, or from rhegmatogenous retinal detachment, serous macular detachment, or cystoid macular oedema (CMO).

Differential diagnosis Small focal areas of involvement may be mistaken for cotton-wool spots of HIV retinopathy (these wax and wane, whereas CMV retinitis is progressive without treatment), or other herpes virus retinitis. HIV retinopathy is rare in black patients.

Investigations Ask about immunosuppressive treatment, sexual history and HIV risk, and arrange testing as appropriate with an infectious disease clinician. Check macular OCT and VDRL. Arrange a vitreous biopsy for CMV PCR at the time of the first intravitreal injection.

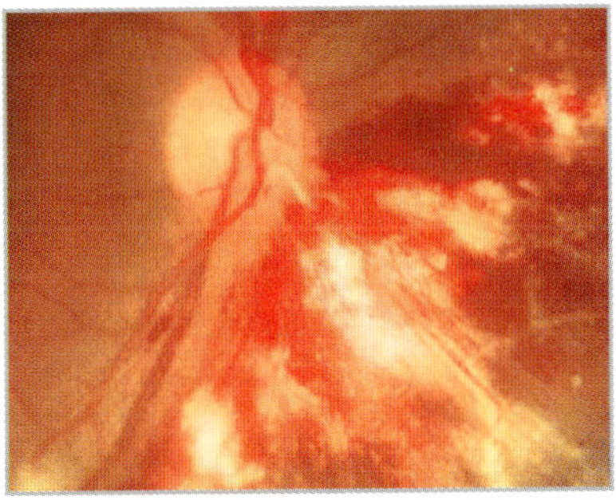

Fig. 9.19: Cytomegalovirus retinitis with severe haemorrhage and vasculitis.

Treatment Start treatment immediately and manage jointly with physicians. CMV retinitis drugs are virostatic and cannot prevent recurrence. Aim to induce remission with induction doses, then use maintenance therapy while monitoring for relapse. Start with valganciclovir 900 mg b.d. p.o. for 3 weeks followed by 900 mg o.d. Alternatives include i.v. ganciclovir induction 5 mg/kg b.d. for 2–3 weeks then 5 mg/kg o.d.; i.v. foscarnet initially 60 mg/kg every 8 hours for 2–3 weeks, alternatively initially 90 mg/kg every 12 hours for 2–3 weeks, then maintenance 60 mg/kg daily, then increased if tolerated to 90–120 mg/kg daily: if disease progresses on maintenance dose, repeat induction regimen. Consider starting with an intravitreal injection (ganciclovir 2 mg, foscarnet 2.4 mg) if the optic nerve or macula are threatened, or if systemic treatment is inadequate. Physicians can start antiretroviral therapy after 2 weeks of anti-CMV treatment, to avoid immune reconstitution inflammation. In others, titrate drug dosing and choice to encourage the immune recovery, such as non-HIV patients, needed for long-term CMV control.

Follow-up Watch for recurrence and second eye involvement. Within 2 weeks of induction therapy expect resolving retinal whitening and oedema, exudate, and haemorrhage, eventually leaving retinal atrophy and retinal pigment epithelium scarring. Reactivation may manifest as a smouldering border with a small area of retinal whitening, isolated changes in the whiteness of the border, or a recurrence of perivascular sheathing. Serial photographs are invaluable. Retinal detachment may occur, as may late-onset CMO that is very resistant to treatment.

MASQUERADE SYNDROMES

Background Masquerade syndromes are disorders that mimic intraocular inflammation but have an underlying cause that may be malignant, infective, or a miscellany of other causes. These include drug-induced, retained intraocular foreign body, Schwartz syndrome (rhegmatogenous retinal detachment and anterior chamber 'cells'), ghost-cell glaucoma following vitreous haemorrhage, ocular ischaemic syndrome, and retinitis pigmentosa. Many are apparent from the history and examination, their atypical clinical features, or failure to respond to steroids.

Lymphoma Always consider in patients over 60 years of age who present for the first time with intraocular inflammation resembling intermediate or posterior uveitis. Suspect if there is marked vitritis but good VA. Usually bilateral with both an AC reaction and vitritis (classically 'veils'), sometimes with subretinal or intraretinal infiltration. The majority have CNS non-Hodgkin's lymphoma but there can be systemic spread, although this tends initially to produce choroidal disease. The eye may be the only organ involved. If suspected, arrange CNS imaging, a vitreous biopsy for cytology if there is significant vitritis, and consider CSF cytology. Treatment comprises ocular and CNS irradiation and chemotherapy. Cystoid macular oedema is uncommon despite significant vitritis.

Leukaemia All forms of leukaemia may involve the eye. Manifestations include direct retinal and optic nerve infiltration, and serous retinal detachment overlying choroidal infiltrates. Subhyaloid haemorrhage, Roth's spots, vascular dilatation or tortuosity, and cotton wool spots are secondary to thrombocytopenia and anaemia. Anterior segment involvement is less common, but includes acute anterior uveitis with hypopyon (white eye), diffuse iris infiltration, or iris nodules. If suspected, check FBC and refer to a haematologist.

Retinoblastoma This may mimic a toxocara mass in the eye, but on ultrasound toxocara rarely calcifies.

Melanoma Choroidal melanomas may cause signs of both anterior and posterior segment inflammation. Amelanotic choroidal tumours may simulate an inflammatory mass. Ultrasound and fluorescein angiography help to establish the diagnosis. Iris tumours may be mistaken for inflammatory nodules. Diffuse iris melanomas may cause heterochromia.

Metastases Most commonly from lung and breast. Usually present as an isolated choroidal lesion which when flat may resemble an inflammatory focus, but patients can present with endophthalmitis. Anterior segment metastases are rare but may cause an anterior uveitis, pseudohypopyon, or iris nodules.

UVEITIS IN CHILDREN

Background Most types of uveitis can be seen in children and are managed in a similar way to adults depending on the anatomic location, severity, threat to vision, and complications. For example, children may get recurrent acute anterior uveitis associated with HLA-B27 and diseases such as ankylosing spondylitis. Although uncommon, Fuchs' heterochromic cyclitis has been reported in young children. Children may get sympathetic ophthalmia following trauma and disorders such as Vogt–Koyanagi–Harada syndrome. Infective disorders such as chickenpox can cause anterior uveitis alone and acute retinal necrosis, and metastatic endophthalmitis can occur from any septic site. Reactivation of toxoplasmic retinochoroiditis is uncommon in children. The most common cause of posterior uveitis in those under 16 years of age is pars planitis.

Juvenile idiopathic arthritis is associated with uveitis that is usually asymptomatic, so review all children at diagnosis. The risk of uveitis depends on the type of arthritis (systemic versus polyarticular versus pauciarticular). Uveitis in systemic disease is rare. Antinuclear antibody positive (ANA+ve) pauciarticular females aged <7 years are at highest risk. Review high-risk children (those aged <7 years who are ANA+ve, with pauci- or polyarticular arthritis) 3 monthly, medium-risk 6 monthly, and low-risk (systemic disease) yearly. The high-risk group becomes medium-risk after 4 years follow-up. The medium-risk group becomes low-risk after 4 years. All go to low risk after 7 years. The characteristic chronic anterior uveitis has a high ocular morbidity if not very well controlled; band keratopathy, posterior synechiae, cataract, glaucoma, cyclitic membranes, and macular oedema can all occur. The risk of uveitis is greatly reduced by early (prior to uveitis) systemic methotrexate, especially with adalimumab, to control joint inflammation. Topical steroids and mydriatics are used in children with anterior uveitis, but systemic treatment with methotrexate and other agents including biologics (not etanercept) may be required. Cataract is much more likely with topical and systemic steroids in children and early use of systemic non-steroidal treatment is advised. Raised IOP and glaucoma may occur due to steroid response, pupillary occlusion, and open-angle glaucoma from trabecular meshwork damage. Avoid using α-2-adrenergic agonists in children <12 years of age. For cataract surgery, the eye must be uninflamed for at least 3 months beforehand, with adequate systemic immunosuppression cover. An IOL insertion is preferable, but consider with caution.

UVEITIS IN PREGNANCY

Patients with uveitis who wish to get pregnant need to consider the risks and benefits of any systemic medication. Acetazolamide is commonly avoided. Prednisolone ≤ 15 mg daily is probably safe throughout pregnancy. There is less information on other immunosuppressive agents so avoid if possible, but azathioprine, ciclosporin, and biologics can be used in pregnancy at the lowest effective dose. Many of the drugs can be found in breast milk, and this information must be given to mothers wishing to breastfeed. For drug use in pregnancy, see Appendix 8 (p. 840).

Immune-mediated uveitis may get better during pregnancy, stay the same, or get worse. The same applies to postpartum uveitis. Periocular steroids may be used during pregnancy and breastfeeding, and can be given bilaterally if necessary. Although some drug is absorbed systemically by this route, the amount is extremely small and is not thought to harm the baby.

Patients with reactivation of toxoplasma retinochoroiditis present no infective risk to their babies, but consider which drugs can be used safely. Patients developing primary toxoplasma infection, even if apparently in the eye alone, must be made aware that this is a systemic infection which carries a serious risk of fetal involvement, the level of which depends on the stage of the pregnancy (**Table 9.4**, p. 440). Infected babies with no toxoplasma scars at birth can develop new lesions which may be sight-threatening up to the age of 12 years, so long term anti-toxoplasma treatment is required – drugs used may vary, so discuss with paediatrician.

HUMAN IMMUNODEFICIENCY VIRUS

Background The ocular manifestations of human immunodeficiency virus (HIV) vary with the level of immunocompromise, reflected in the presence of HIV virus in the blood (viral load) and CD4+ count. A CD4+ count >1,000 cells/mL is normal; <50 cells/μL is extremely low with a high risk of serious ocular infection, particularly cytomegalovirus (CMV) retinitis. Active antiretroviral therapy (AART) markedly improves CD4+ counts and reduces opportunistic infections, but lymphoma is more common.

History and examination Ask about systemic illnesses, infections, interventions, medications, and duration of HIV infection. A minimum routine examination includes VA, eyelids, conjunctival fornices (Kaposi's sarcoma), anterior segment, and dilated fundoscopy including peripheral retina. Examine specifically to exclude uveitis and CMV retinitis.

Clinical features HIV infection is associated with:

- *Blepharitis*: Often severe.
- *Molluscum contagiosum*: Usually extensive.
- Premature presbyopia
- *Conjunctival Kaposi's sarcoma*: Signifies AIDS.
- *Conjunctival squamous cell carcinoma*: More common in Africa.
- *Herpes zoster ophthalmicus*: A common presenting feature of AIDS in developing nations.
- *HIV retinopathy*: Cotton-wool spots and dot haemorrhages are common and inconsequential (**Fig. 9.20**).
- *Uveitis*: Can be of infective (consider TB, syphilis), inflammatory, or malignant aetiology. Improved immunity following AART may cause an immune recovery uveitis that is a leading cause of new visual loss. As the CD4+ count drops, infections become increasingly common, particularly toxoplasmosis, herpes simplex, and herpes zoster. HIV itself can cause a panuveitis. Lymphoma may cause a masquerade-type of uveitis that may have CNS or systemic involvement. Syphilitic uveitis can occur at any CD4+ count, and in the presence of HIV may indicate tertiary syphilis.
- *CMV, varicella-zoster, or herpes simplex retinitis (previously called progressive outer retinal necrosis, PORN)*: Both CMV retinitis and PORN can occur with little or no intraocular inflammation (a useful diagnostic clue). PORN (**Fig. 9.21**) tends to be more aggressive than acute retinal necrosis (ARN)

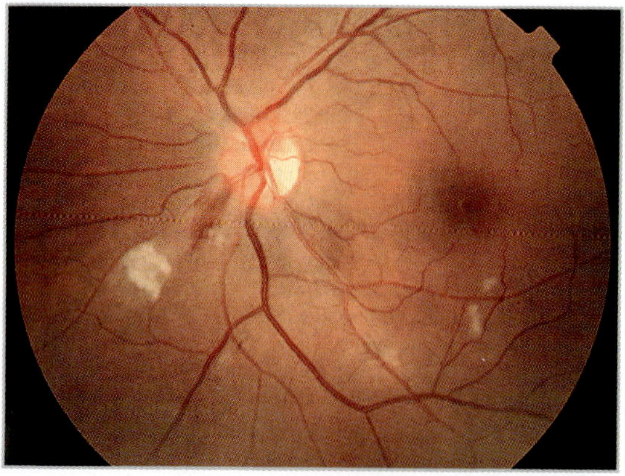

Fig. 9.20: human immunodeficiency virus (HIV) retinopathy.

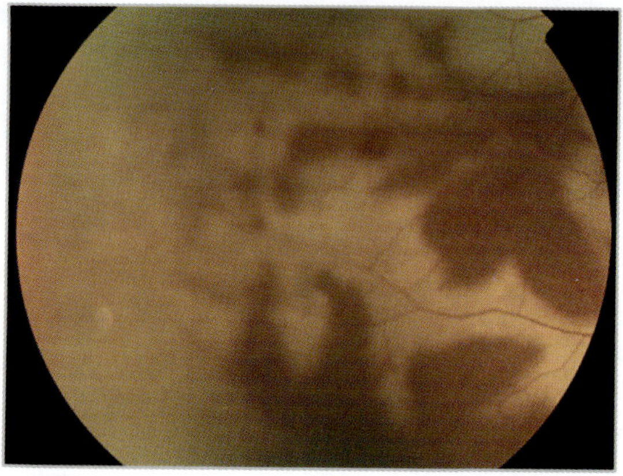

Fig. 9.21: Varicella-zoster retinitis (progressive outer retinal necrosis).

that can also occur in immunocompetent patients. Treatment requires combination anti-viral drugs.

- *Toxoplasmosis*: Retinal lesions may be bilateral and multifocal; 56% have CNS involvement.
- *Metastatic bacterial or fungal endophthalmitis*: Particularly following sepsis, surgery, or intravenous drugs use.

- *Tuberculosis*: Ocular manifestations include uveitis and optic nerve involvement. Choroidal granulomas indicate miliary TB.
- *Pneumocystis choroiditis*: Implies systemic infection requiring systemic treatment. No additional ocular treatment is required. Pneumocystis very rarely causes conjunctivitis, orbital masses, and optic neuropathy.
- *Retrobulbar neuritis*: Due to *Cryptococcus*, syphilis, histoplasmosis, or *Herpes zoster*.
- *Toxic optic neuropathy*: From drug therapy, especially dideoxyinosine, isoniazid and ethambutol.
- *Papillitis*: Secondary to CMV, syphilis, or toxoplasmosis.
- *Cortical visual loss*: Causes include non-Hodgkin's lymphoma, toxoplasmosis, and progressive multifocal leucoencephalopathy.
- *Cryptococcal meningitis*: May cause visual loss through raised intracranial pressure. Optic nerve sheath fenestration may help.
- *Reactive arthritis*: An acute non-purulent arthritis complicating an infection elsewhere in the body. Comprises a triad of urethritis, arthritis, and conjunctivitis, but uveitis can also occur. Treat conjunctivitis and uveitis with topical steroids and liaise with relevant specialties.

Follow-up In patients with CD4+ counts < 50 cells/µL, perform dilated fundoscopy every 6 weeks or earlier if they develop floaters, field loss, or blurred vision. The need for regular screening decreases with CD4+ counts > 150 cells/µL.

EPISCLERITIS

Background A self-limiting condition of unknown aetiology.

Clinical features Episcleritis is often mistaken for scleritis (next page). In episcleritis, congestion is limited to the radially orientated superficial episcleral vessels within Tenon's capsule (**Fig. 9.22**). In anterior scleritis, the irregular-crossing deep episcleral vessels on the scleral surface are also involved and there is accompanying scleral thickening. G. phenylephrine 2.5% blanches the superficial episcleral venous plexus only. Episcleritis typically presents more acutely, causes grittiness rather than pain, lacks corneal or intraocular involvement, and vision is unaffected.

Management Offer reassurance. Treatment is not routinely required as symptoms usually resolve. If frequently recurrent, oral NSAIDs such as flurbiprofen (Froben) 50 mg p.o. t.d.s. may help, but have side effects (gastric or duodenal ulceration, exacerbation of asthma). Topical steroids are sometimes useful, e.g. FML 0.1% q.d.s. or loteprednol etabonate (Lotemax) 0.5% q.d.s. for 2 weeks.

Follow-up Not required unless on topical steroids, but explain that recurrences are common.

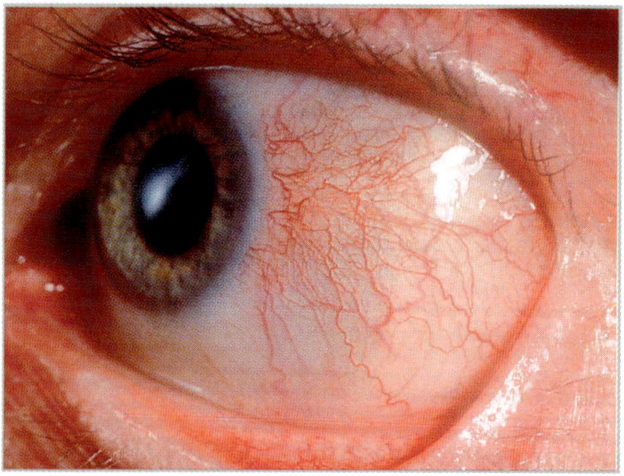

Fig. 9.22: Mild episcleritis.

SCLERITIS

Background Less common than episcleritis. Scleritis has frequent (~50%) systemic associations and can be vision-threatening. Systemic therapy is essential. Broadly classified into anterior and posterior scleritis.

Anterior scleritis Has a subacute onset of severe ocular and periocular pain, often worse at night, with redness, photophobia, and globe tenderness (**Fig. 9.23**). Deep episcleral vessels on the surface of the sclera are dilated, with vascular closure in necrotising disease. The sclera may have a bluish tint that is best appreciated with the naked eye and bright room light. Avascular

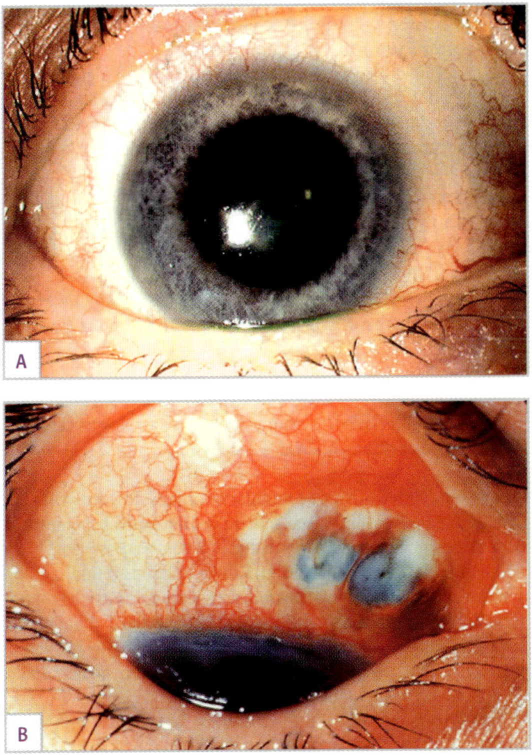

Fig. 9.23: Scleritis. Mild anterior diffuse scleritis (A) and necrotising anterior scleritis (B) with uveal tissue visible beneath thinned sclera.

areas are best seen with red-free (green) slit lamp light. May be diffuse, nodular, or necrotising.

- Diffuse:
  a. May involve small or large areas of sclera.
  b. The most common type of scleritis.
  c. Pain may be severe.
  d. Not usually sight-threatening and usually resolves.
- Nodular:
  a. Part of the inflamed sclera is raised in one or more nodules.
  b. May progress.
  c. Commonly recurs.
- Necrotising:
  a. Least frequent but the most severe type of anterior scleritis.
  b. Female preponderance.
  c. Associated with vascular closure and pale regions of scleral necrosis within areas of active scleritis.
  d. Scleromalacia perforans is a very rare form of necrotising anterior scleritis which occurs without inflammation, is asymptomatic, bilateral, and seen only in advanced rheumatoid arthritis (RA), usually in females. Perforation of the thinned and translucent sclera is unusual without trauma. There is no ocular treatment.
- Associations:
  a. Local: ocular surgery, infection (toxoplasmosis, acanthamoeba, fungal, herpes simplex virus, varicella-zoster virus, bacterial including TB), and masquerade syndrome (ocular surface carcinoma and intraocular tumour).
  b. Systemic (50%): most commonly RA but also other collagen/vascular disorders including granulomatosis with polyangiitis (GPA), systemic lupus erythematosus (SLE) and polyarteritis nodosa (PAN).

Posterior scleritis May be nodular or diffuse. Presents with pain and reduced vision. Rarely, there is conjunctival chemosis with some limitation of movement and proptosis. Posterior segment signs are variable and may include serous retinal detachment, swollen optic disc, subretinal mass, choroidal folds, and choroidal detachment. Approximately one-third of patients have associated anterior scleritis. Local associations are as for anterior scleritis. Systemic associations (30%) include RA, GPA, PAN, SLE, relapsing polychondritis, and neoplasia.

Differential diagnosis Episcleritis may overlay scleritis, so it is important not to miss the scleritis. For distinguishing features, see page 452.

Investigations There is a high incidence of systemic associations. If there is a suggestive history and general examination arrange urine dipstick for blood and protein, FBC, ESR, CRP, rheumatoid factor (RhF), ANA, U&E, LFTs, and antineutrophil cytoplasmic antibody (c-ANCA) (if this is positive suspect GPA). Discuss with physicians. In many cases, the diagnosis is already established. In patients with suspected posterior scleritis, B-scan ultrasonography is very useful in demonstrating either diffuse or nodular scleral thickening (>2 mm) with an adjacent echolucent area from oedema in Tenon's space (T sign). Fluorescein angiography in patients with serous retinal detachment typically shows multiple small foci of leakage at the level of the retinal pigment epithelium which may look similar to those in Vogt–Koyanagi–Harada syndrome.

Management

- *Emergency department*: Treat anterior non-necrotising scleritis and mild posterior scleritis with no visible posterior segment abnormalities with Froben 100 mg t.d.s. p.o. (combined with omeprazole 20 mg o.d. p.o. if there is a history or risk of either gastric or duodenal ulceration). Review in 1–2 weeks. Reduced pain indicates a good response, and treatment can then be tailed off, but warn of the risk of recurrence. If pain and inflammation persist, consider oral prednisolone 0.5–1 mg/kg o.d., then tapered off. Necrotising scleritis, and posterior scleritis associated with retinal or choroidal detachment, disc swelling, or subretinal mass lesion, requires same-day specialist review. If there is hypertension, protein or blood on urine dipstick, or associated systemic disease, then consult urgently with physicians; the associated systemic diseases can be life-threatening.
- *Clinic*: Use high-dose oral steroids (prednisolone 1 mg/kg) for necrotising anterior scleritis and for posterior scleritis with visual loss or threat. In severe cases consider admission and pulsed i.v. methylprednisolone 0.5–1.0 g for 1–3 days followed by oral steroids. Adjunct immunosuppressive therapy is often required for those with systemic disease or scleritis resistant to steroids alone. Cyclophosphamide may be necessary in very severe necrotising disease, as may occur in GPA. Surgical treatment may be required either for diagnostic (infection and masquerade syndrome) or therapeutic (cataract and corneal/scleral grafts) indications. Ideally, surgery is undertaken when scleritis has been controlled medically.

ENDOPHTHALMITIS

Background Endophthalmitis is vitreous and/or AC inflammation of presumed infective origin. Classified as exogenous (after surgery, keratitis, or trauma) or endogenous (also called metastatic endophthalmitis).

Exogenous postoperative endophthalmitis

Clinical features

- *Acute onset (0–17 days)*: ocular pain, reduced vision and headache with lid oedema, conjunctival hyperaemia, chemosis, purulent discharge, corneal oedema, AC reaction, hypopyon, and poor red reflex.
- *Delayed acute (18–60 days)*: due to less virulent organisms or from a suture track, wound dehiscence, or vitreous wick.
- *Chronic (>60 days)*: usually a capsular bag infection with a low-virulence organism (often *Propionibacterium acnes* or *Staphylococcus epidermidis*). Presents with reduced vision and minimal pain. May have signs of steroid-responsive anterior uveitis, capsular plaque, granulomatous uveitis, or localised vitritis. Hypopyon uveitis following YAG capsulotomy is a classic presentation. Endophthalmitis may occur years after trabeculectomy, especially if there is a thin bleb after use of mitomycin.

History and examination Assess severity, which relates to the speed of onset, presenting VA, RAPD, and fundal view. Measure the hypopyon height.

Differential diagnosis Assume all severe postoperative inflammation is infective endophthalmitis unless there is another obvious cause, especially in patients with no history of uveitis. If in doubt and VA is 6/12 or worse, admit for 6–12 hours of half-hourly, topical, preservative-free dexamethasone 0.1% and reassess 2-hourly.

Investigations Lid and conjunctival swabs are of no value. Take a corneal scrape if keratitis is present. Arrange aqueous and vitreous samples in all patients (including those with perception of light vision at presentation) (**Box 9.3**). If there is no fundal view, arrange ultrasound prior to sampling. If not immediately available, proceed with biopsy but arrange ultrasound at the first opportunity. Request baseline FBC, U&E, weight, blood sugar, and BP measurements before starting on systemic steroids.

Box 9.3: Aqueous and vitreous tap and intravitreal antibiotic injection

1. Contact the microbiology department to ensure Gram staining is done the same day.
2. Instil G. proxymetacaine then tetracaine (amethocaine), then povidone-iodine 5% into the conjunctival sac and on the lid margins. Allow ≥30 seconds dwell time for bacterial or fungal killing.
3. Administer subconjunctival or more usually subtenon anaesthesia (lidocaine 2%).
4. Prepare then draw up the required concentration of antibiotics, combined into a 1 mL syringe (change the needle, as this gets blunt going through the rubber bungs):
   a. Vancomycin: 2.0 mg in 0.1 mL.
   b. Amikacin: 0.4 mg in 0.1 mL (beware dilution errors).
   c. Amphotericin B: 5–10 µg in 0.1 mL only if fungi are suspected.
5. Scrub and don gloves. A drape and mask are not required. Insert the lid speculum but do not further manipulate the lashes. Wash away excess povidone-iodine with saline.
6. *Aqueous sampling* (may be done with patient at the slit lamp or lying down): Using a 1 mL syringe (not an insulin syringe) with an orange 25-gauge needle, aspirate 0.1–0.2 mL of aqueous via a limbal paracentesis. A larger needle may be used if a lot of pus is present. Place the needle into the sheath left resting on a flat surface, without touching the tip of the needle (be mindful of needle-stick). Label and leave to one side.
7. *Vitreous sampling* (do in a sterile environment with the patient lying flat): Use a 5 mL syringe and blue 23-gauge needle and insert 4 mm (phakic) or 3.5 mm (pseudophakic or aphakic eyes) behind the limbus into the mid-vitreous cavity. Aspirate 0.2–0.4 mL. If the tap is dry, carefully move the needle within the vitreous cavity. If still dry, try a 21-gauge needle. Place the sheath on the needle as above. Label and leave to one side.
8. Inject the 0.2 mL of combined intravitreal antibiotics in the 1 mL syringe in a sterile manner and through the same area as the vitreous sampling. As the eye can be very soft, counter pressure helps to get the needle through the sclera.
9. Plate out immediately, as per local protocol, for example:
   a. Blood agar: Place one drop from the syringe on an eccentric one-third of the plate and then streak with a loupe. Do not cut into the agar, as the organisms will not grow. Use a separate blood agar plate for aqueous and vitreous. Close with tape, and label.
   b. Robertson's cooked meat broth and brain heart infusion: Put one drop in each bottle (avoid touching the rim). Close, mix, and label.
10. Send specimens immediately to the microbiology department for Gram (±Giemsa) stain, and then culture. If the laboratory is closed, incubate the plates and transfer at the first opportunity, but this may reduce the yield so avoid if possible.

Treatment

- For children, discuss the drug dose and selection with a pharmacist. For adults, see **Figure 9.24**.
- Moxifloxacin may have an anti-biofilm effect on coagulase-negative staphylococci and a better spectrum of activity than ciprofloxacin, but use ciprofloxacin 750 mg b.d. 10 days if not available.
- Consider periocular steroids if systemic steroids are contraindicated.
- Chronic endophthalmitis usually responds to treatment, but some cases recur when treatment is stopped, as organisms may be sequestered behind the lens. Re-treat with intravitreal and systemic antibiotics but if inflammation recurs again then

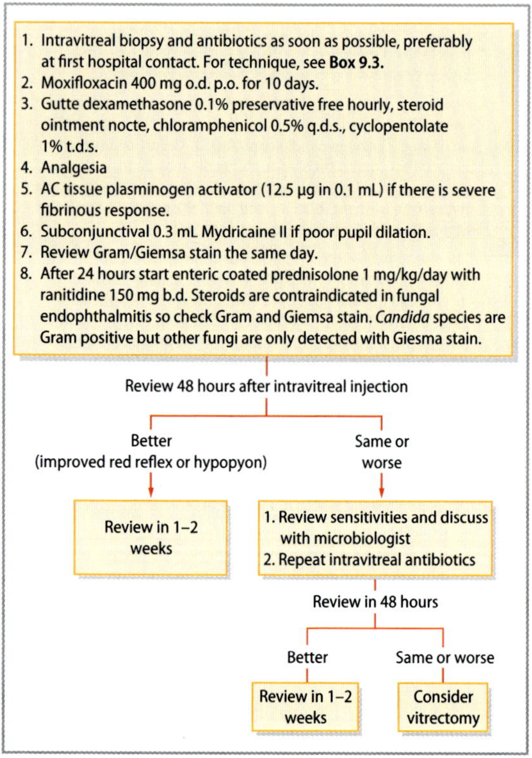

Fig. 9.24: Treatment of acute postoperative endophthalmitis.

arrange IOL and total capsule removal. Send samples at each stage for microbiology and histopathology. Avoid systemic steroids that may mask ongoing inflammation.
- The Endophthalmitis Vitrectomy Study (EVS) was a large randomised and controlled trial that suggested early vitrectomy with intravitreal antibiotics may improve the final VA for patients with perception of light vision. Recent local experience suggests that early vitrectomy results in a worse prognosis for those with PL vision, but many other centres follow the EVS recommendations.

Some reports advocate intravitreal ceftazidime 2 mg in 0.1 mL instead of amikacin for gram-negative cover, because of the risk of aminoglycoside retinal toxicity. Avoid combining vancomycin and ceftazidime in the same syringe. Other reports advocate adding intravitreal dexamethasone 0.4 mg to intravitreal antibiotics, but the evidence is not strong.

Follow-up Manage patients as daycases if they can cope; otherwise admit. If admitted, consider discharge when there is clinical improvement, typically after 48 hours, and then review within 2 weeks. If no improvement, reinject. If after a further 48 hours there is no improvement and hypopyon persists, seek a vitreoretinal opinion. Follow up all patients for 3–6 months, as they may require additional procedures, e.g. vitrectomy for vitreous debris. Final VA is <6/60 in 22–77%. Patients with an acute presentation, good presenting VA, and negative cultures tend to have a better prognosis.

Endogenous endophthalmitis

Endogenous endophthalmitis is haematogenous spread of infection to the eye. Most common in the elderly, debilitated, diabetics, those with indwelling foreign bodies (urinary or i.v. catheters and prosthetic heart valves), immunosuppressed (iatrogenic or disease) and intravenous drug users. Patients may or may not be acutely ill and can present with either a fulminating or low-grade endophthalmitis. Any systemic source of infection can be implicated. Manage in combination with a physician to identify the source, predisposing disease, and treatment options. Request blood cultures.
- *Endogenous bacterial endophthalmitis*: If the organism is not known obtain aqueous and vitreous taps (**Box 9.3**) and give oral and intravitreal antibiotics as described for exogenous infection.
- *Endogenous fungal endophthalmitis*: The majority are diagnosed on clinical grounds, most typically in i.v. drug users or following a septic or other hospital episode involving i.v. cannulation, or broad-spectrum antibiotics.

Collections of cells may be seen in the choroid, retina, or vitreous. These may form 'puff-balls' (*Candida* species) or hyphae (*Aspergillus* species). Fungal endophthalmitis is uncommon after intraocular surgery, but may occur secondary to penetrating injury, especially from wood and thorns, as well as from an endogenous source. *Candida* species are by far the most common (**Fig. 9.25**). Aspergillus and others are rare. The lesion site determines treatment:

- *Confined to choroid (outside the blood-ocular-barrier)*: Systemic medication as chosen by the physicians.
- *Flat lesions in the retina*: Either oral voriconazole – for adults ≤ 40 kg start with 200 mg b.d. for two doses then 100 mg b.d. increased if necessary to 150 mg b.d.; for adults > 40 kg start with 400 mg b.d. for two doses then 200 mg b.d. increased if necessary to 300 mg b.d., or oral fluconazole – start with 400 mg loading dose p.o. then 200 mg b.d. p.o. for 6 weeks (penetrates well into the eye).
- *In the vitreous*: Lesions extending into the vitreous require vitrectomy within 2 days (so no need to take samples in the emergency department). During vitrectomy administer either intravitreal voriconazole 50 μg in 0.1 mL, or intravitreal amphotericin B 5–10 μg in 0.05–0.1 mL. Patients are often systemically unwell, so liaise with infectious disease physicians.

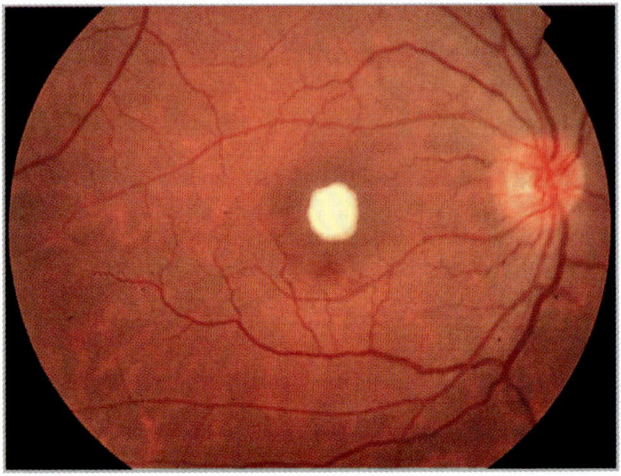

Fig. 9.25: *Candida* endophthalmitis extending from the retina into the vitreous.

OPTOMETRY AND GENERAL PRACTICE GUIDELINES

General comments

Accurate diagnosis and assessment of patients with uveitis requires slit-lamp examination. This is not usually available in general practice and topical steroids should not be initiated owing to their potential side effects including raised intraocular pressure, cataract, and exacerbation of dendritic corneal ulcers. All suspected intraocular inflammation should therefore be referred within 24 hours to an ophthalmologist.

Acute anterior uveitis accounts for 90% of all intraocular inflammation presenting to GPs, but it accounts for a minority of patients with a red eye.

General practice

Photophobia and pain are the predominant complaints in patients with uveitis, with conjunctival injection centred primarily around the cornea (circumcorneal injection and ciliary flush). It is usually possible to distinguish anterior uveitis from conjunctivitis from the history and lack of discharge.

Posterior uveitis is more difficult to diagnose from the history and is reliant upon proficient dilated fundoscopy. Acute onset of floaters, with or without blurred vision, are far more likely to be from posterior vitreous detachment than inflammation, but in either event urgent referral is required.

Optometrists

Optometrists who suspect anterior uveitis should take a careful history and look for anterior chamber cells. These are best seen against a dilated pupil, using a thin, maximally illuminated slit beam passed at 45° through the anterior chamber. Inflammatory cells can be seen to percolate upwards in the back of the anterior chamber, and downwards immediately behind the cornea (see **Fig. 9.1**, p. 401). Look for anterior vitreous activity using the same slit beam focussed behind the lens. For patients with suspected posterior uveitis, look for vitreous haze, macular oedema, and perivascular infiltrates. Pars planitis may be difficult to detect without indentation. Any anterior or posterior segment intraocular inflammation requires same-day review by an ophthalmologist.

OCULAR ONCOLOGY

10

Prithvi Mruthyunjaya, Mandeep S Sagoo & M Ashwin Reddy

CONJUNCTIVAL TUMOURS

Symptoms Usually asymptomatic, but non-specific symptoms include ocular irritation, redness and discharge. Vision loss may occur from tumour growth covering the cornea or inducing astigmatism.

History and examination Ask about sun exposure, viral infections, previous eye surgery, and immunosuppression (systemic and/or drug induced). Perform detailed anterior segment slit-lamp examination including the caruncle and conjunctival fornices by everting the upper eyelid. Lissamine green or Rose Bengal stain may identify atypical cells associated with a tumour. Palpate for enlarged preauricular or submandibular lymph nodes.

Differential diagnosis

- Nonpigmented tumours:
  1. *Papilloma* (**Fig. 10.1**):
     a. Benign

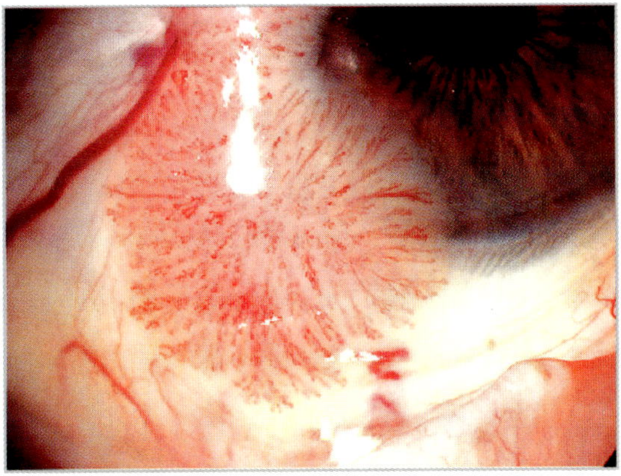

Fig. 10.1: Conjunctival papilloma.

b. Pink fibrovascular fronds (pedunculated or flat)
c. Viral aetiology
d. Symptomatic when large
e. Treat by oral cimetidine (beware of cardiotoxicity), delicate surgical excision, cryotherapy and topical therapy (interferon α-2B, 5-fluorouracil, or mitomycin C).

2. *Conjunctival intraepithelial neoplasia (CIN)* (**Fig. 10.2**):
   a. Benign (premalignant) but in the spectrum of ocular surface squamous neoplasia (OSSN).
   b. Histologic grades (mild, moderate and severe) are based on the degree and depth of conjunctival atypia which correlate with risk of progression to squamous cell carcinoma; determined after biopsy.
   c. Fleshy, thickened and vascularised lesion located at the interpalpebral limbus with occasional corneal extension.
   d. Anterior segment OCT demonstrates abrupt demarcation with hyperreflectivity of the epithelium and subepithelial layers.
   e. Treat by excisional biopsy with cryotherapy to margins or topical chemotherapy (interferon α-2b, 5-fluorouracil, or mitomycin C). May also use topical chemotherapy for residual or recurrent disease.
3. *Squamous cell carcinoma (SCC)* (**Fig. 10.3**):
   a. Part of the OSSN spectrum
   b. Malignant
   c. Fleshy, pink and elevated masses with feeder vessels; can extend widely across the conjunctiva and invade deep into the orbit or into the globe.

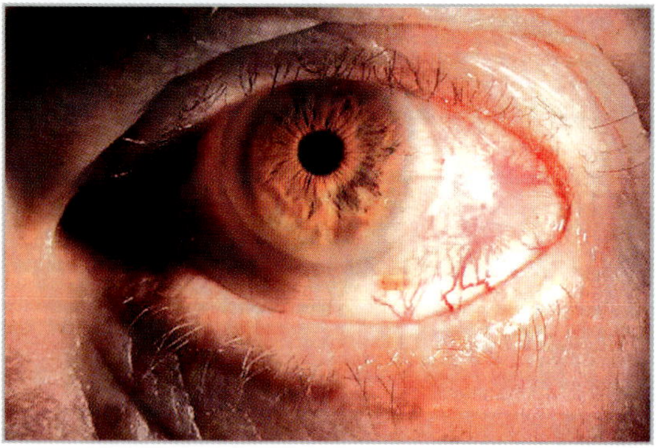

Fig. 10.2: Conjunctival intraepithelial neoplasia.

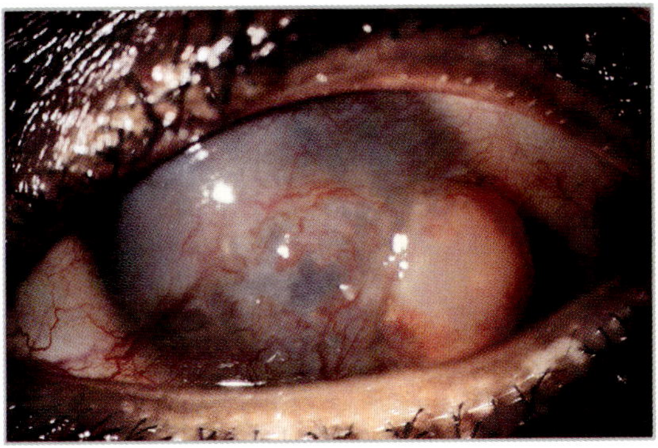

Fig. 10.3: Invasive squamous cell carcinoma.

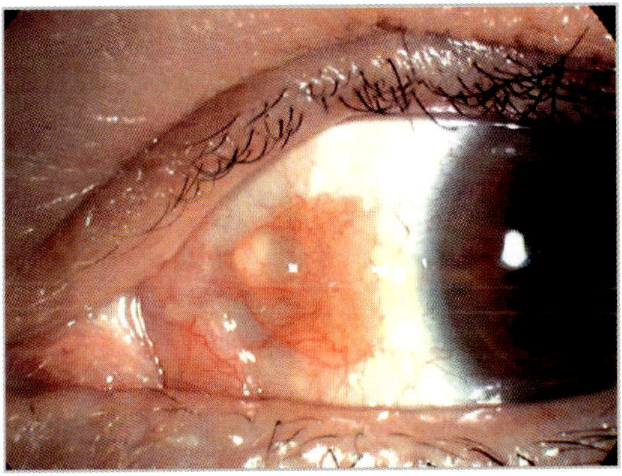

Fig. 10.4: Conjunctival naevus.

d. Manage by excision with adjuvant cryotherapy, topical therapy (interferon α-2b, mitomycin C, or 5-fluorouracil), or β-radiotherapy. Extensive local and regional recurrence may require enucleation or orbital exenteration.

- Pigmented tumours:
  1. *Naevus* (**Fig. 10.4**):
     a. Benign
     b. Circumscribed, light brown, generally flat lesion in the interpalpebral zone and often with intralesional cysts.

Growth seen in peripubescent children and during pregnancy.

c. Manage with photodocumentation and routine yearly observation if stable. Growing lesions and those that develop prominent feeder vessels can be biopsied to rule out malignant melanoma.

2. *Primary acquired melanosis (PAM)* (**Fig. 10.5**):
   a. Benign but premalignant if harbours atypical melanocytes.
   b. Diffuse, patchy, often punctate foci of increased conjunctival pigmentation. Sometimes extends to the eyelid skin and is occasionally non-pigmented. Acquired in middle-age and found in light-skinned patients. Usually unilateral.
   c. Histologic grades (mild, moderate and severe) are based on the degree and depth of conjunctival atypia which correlate with risk of progression to melanoma; determined after biopsy.
   d. Consider excisional biopsy for histological diagnosis. Adjuvant cryotherapy can be added. Review 6-monthly for life.
   e. May require adjuvant mitomycin eye drops in extensive involvement/incomplete excision.
   f. Dark-skinned patients may have diffuse complexion associated melanosis seen near the limbus, which is generally benign and does not require treatment or follow-up. Usually bilateral.

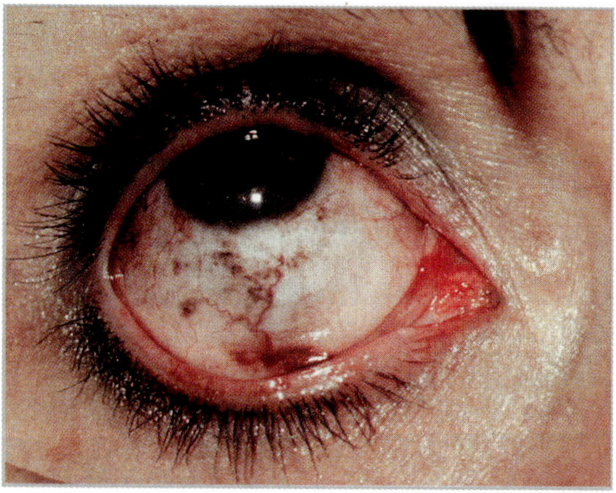

Fig. 10.5: Primary acquired melanosis.

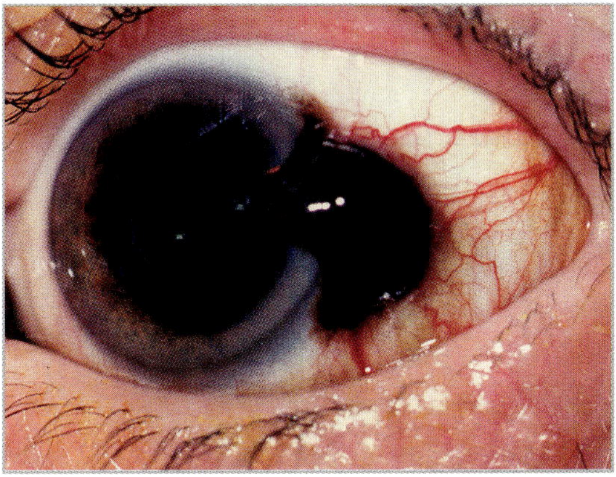

Fig. 10.6: Hyperpigmented conjunctival melanoma with feeder vessels.

3. *Malignant melanoma (MM)* (**Fig. 10.6**):
   a. Malignant
   b. May arise from a naevus, PAM, or *de novo*.
   c. Typically, darkly pigmented and focal, but variations include nonpigmented and diffuse forms. Feeder vessels may be present. Tumours arising in PAM may be multifocal and the eyelid skin may be affected.
   d. Manage by wide, *en bloc* excision with lamellar dissection of the cornea and sclera at the corneoscleral limbus. Adjuvant cryotherapy or β-radiotherapy may be applied to the tumour bed if there is doubt about the completeness of excision. May require adjuvant mitomycin drops.
   e. Review every 3–4 months to exclude new tumours arising in PAM and recurrences.
   f. Extensive or recurrent lesions may require orbital exenteration.
   g. Spread may occur to regional lymph nodes and is best managed by a combination of surgical excision of affected nodes and external beam radiotherapy. Metastatic disease can be fatal, but newer immunotherapy drugs may play a role.
4. *Ocular melanocytosis* (**Fig. 10.7**):
   a. Unilateral, congenital hyperpigmentation of the uveal tract extending to the episclera and presenting with increased iris pigmentation on the affected side, and slate-grey discolouration of the sclera.

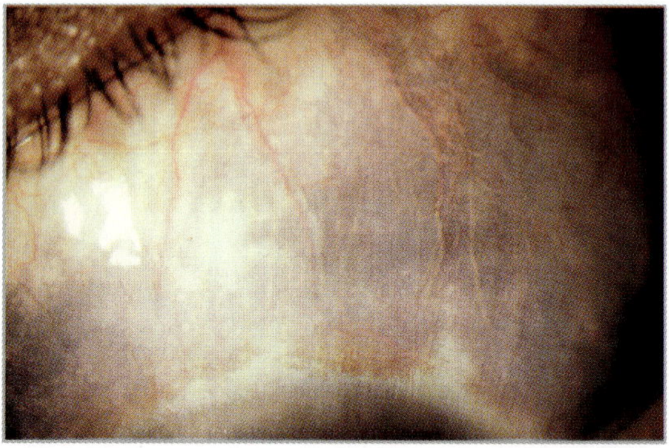

Fig. 10.7: Ocular melanocytosis.

   b. Termed oculodermal melanocytosis (naevus of Ota) if associated with ipsilateral periocular blue-grey skin discolouration, in V1 and V2 trigeminal distribution.
   c. Patients have an increased risk of developing ipsilateral malignant choroidal melanoma and, rarely, primary orbital melanoma, so arrange yearly dilated fundoscopy and ultrasound B scan.

- Vascular tumours:
  1. *Pyogenic granuloma* (**Fig. 10.8**):
     a. Benign fibrovascular tumour
     b. Neither an infection nor a granuloma
     c. Fleshy, thickened and red/pink-coloured lesions occurring near previous surgical sites
     d. May respond to topical steroid therapy but may require local surgical excision with careful wound closure.
  2. *Capillary haemangioma:*
     a. Benign
     b. Circumscribed, red lesion found in infants.
     c. May enlarge over time, but usually undergoes spontaneous involution.
     d. Typically managed by observation, but local excision or intralesional steroid treatment may be used.
     e. For skin and orbital involvement, see pages 48 (**Fig. 2.19**) and 118 (**Fig. 4.12**).
  3. *Kaposi's sarcoma:*
     a. Malignant
     b. Bright red, solitary or multifocal mass associated with haemorrhage

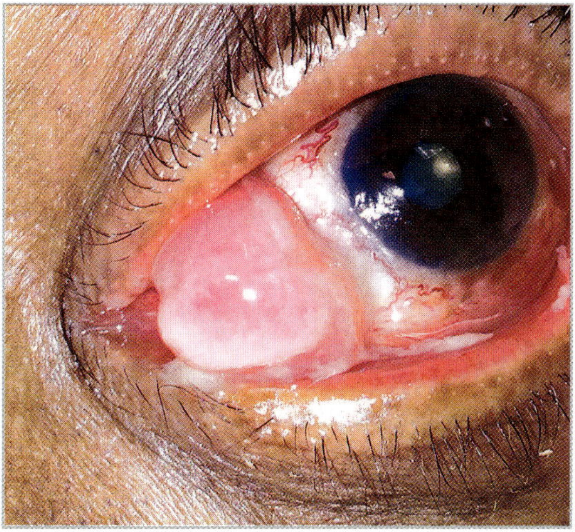

Fig. 10.8: Pyogenic granuloma.

c. May involve the eyelid skin (**Fig. 2.35,** p. 59).
d. A characteristic lesion in acquired AIDS.
e. Treatment options include observation, low-dose external beam radiotherapy and excision. Intralesional interferon α-2b chemotherapy is described. Generalised disease requires chemotherapy ± radiotherapy.

4. *Orbital varix and lymphangioma:* See **Figure 4.13**, page 120 and Figure 4.14, page 121.

- Lymphoma (**Fig. 10.9**):
  a. Malignant
  b. Fleshy lesions with deep pink 'salmon patch' appearance.
  c. Most are extranodal marginal zone B-cell lymphomas of mucosa-associated lymphoid tissue (MALT) type that develop *de novo* in conjunctiva. Bilateral presentation and orbital involvement are common. Some develop in association with systemic MALT lymphoma, or as an anterior extension of choroidal lymphoma.
  d. Evert the upper eyelids to identify forniceal lesions. Perform dilated fundoscopy to identify associated choroidal lymphoma, seen as pale to light pink choroidal elevation without vitritis. Orbital imaging (ultrasound and CT scan) may identify associated orbital lymphoma.

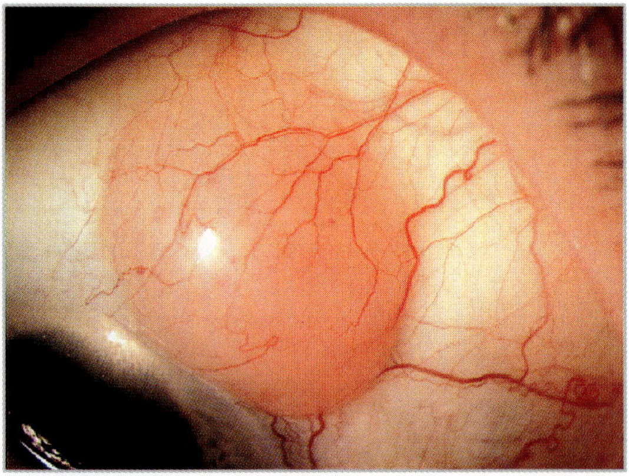

Fig. 10.9: Conjunctival lymphoma.

e. OCT shows normal overlying epithelium and subepithelial lobular hyper-reflectivity with some shadowing.
f. Diagnosed by incisional biopsy followed by systemic evaluation.
g. Disease localised to the conjunctiva and orbit is usually treated by external beam radiotherapy and the prognosis for the eye, vision, and life is generally good. Other modalities used include oral doxycycline and systemic rituximab. If associated with systemic lymphoma, chemotherapy protocols may be required.

Investigations Baseline and serial photographs are useful to detect or monitor change. Anterior segment OCT helps to identify epithelial involvement in OSSN and cystic structures in naevi. Histology is the gold standard for diagnosis. Orbital imaging and systemic evaluation, usually by a medical oncologist, may be needed to determine tumour extension.

Treatment

- *Surgical excision*: Generally, wide surgical margins are preferred, with primary closure or amniotic membrane grafts for large defects. Techniques such as absolute alcohol epithelial debridement and lamellar corneoscleral–conjunctival resection may be used.
- *Surgical debulking*: Needed when, in established cases, tumour overgrowth limits the use of adjuvant treatments such as topical agents or cryotherapy, and for symptomatic relief.

- *Cryotherapy*: With a double or triple freeze-thaw technique is an important tool for local tumour control during and after biopsy procedures.
- *Surface reconstruction*: With primary closure, amniotic membrane grafting or rarely conjunctival autografting.
- *Adjuvant treatments*: Diffuse disease is well managed by low dose of external beam radiotherapy for lymphoma. Other options include plaque radiotherapy or topical anticancer agents (interferon α-2B, 5-fluorouracil, or mitomycin C), in selected cases. May be combined with systemic treatments.
- *Orbital exenteration*: Reserved for extensive invasion by malignant tumours such as SCC or MM.

Follow-up After diagnosis and treatment, premalignant and malignant conjunctival tumours require close and thorough follow-up every 3–4 months to exclude progression or recurrence.

IRIS MELANOMA

Background Iris melanomas account for 5–10% of all uveal tract melanomas. They are usually well-differentiated and have a low rate of systemic metastasis. The mortality rate is around 5%, much lower than for ciliary body or choroidal melanomas. Distinguish from iris naevi.

Symptoms Typically asymptomatic. Visual changes occur with larger tumours that grow into the visual axis or induce a central cataract. There may be pain from elevated IOP associated with tumour pigment shedding, direct angle invasion, and anterior segment neovascularisation.

Signs Iris melanomas are raised, replace the iris stroma, have variable pigmentation (though classically dark brown, **Fig. 10.10**), and may have visible intrinsic tumour vessels, particularly with amelanotic tumours. They may arise from the pupillary margin but are more concerning when obscuring or involving the drainage angle. More commonly seen in the inferior iris. Pupil distortion, including a peaked pupil or uveal ectropion, is common. Other suspicious features include focal cataract in the region of the lesion, pigment seeding in adjacent or remote sites of the angle, tumour seeding or satellite lesions, and elevated IOP. Focal conjunctival and episcleral vascular dilation (sentinel vessels) are seen in the same quadrant as larger, more chronic malignant iris masses. Extraocular extension of a pigmented tumour through the sclera may occur.

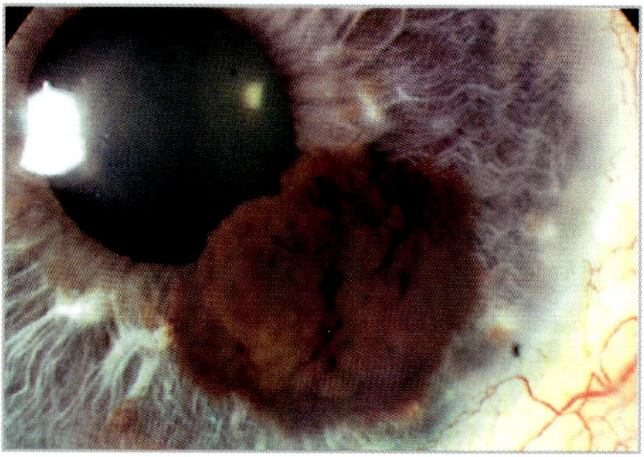

Fig. 10.10: Iris melanoma.

History and examination Ask about visual symptoms, ocular surgery, cancer, or constitutional symptoms. Detailed ocular examination includes IOP, gonioscopy to determine angle and/or anterior ciliary body involvement, lens examination, and dilated fundoscopy. Use transpupillary transillumination and ultrasound B scan and/or high-resolution ultrasound biomicroscopy (UBM) to determine the posterior extension of an iris tumour into the ciliary body. Ultrasound and UBM determine lesion size, location (relative to the posterior iris and ciliary body), and internal reflectivity (low for iris melanoma).

Differential diagnosis

- Hyperpigmented lesions:
  1. *Iris naevus* (**Fig. 10.11**):
     a. Asymptomatic
     b. Generally flat (<1 mm height) and pigmented
     c. Sporadic, often present after the second decade, and rarely grow.
     d. Iris infiltration, sectorial cataract, or pupil distortion increase the suspicion of malignancy.
     e. Small, focal and iris freckles may be associated with neurofibromatosis type I (Lisch nodules) and the iridocorneal–endothelial (ICE or 'Cogan-Reese') syndrome. Review stable lesions yearly, but more frequently if suspicious.
- Hypopigmented lesions:
  1. *Iris metastasis:*
     a. Pink- or yellow-coloured, rapidly growing, uni- or multifocal lesion, typically in the superior iris.

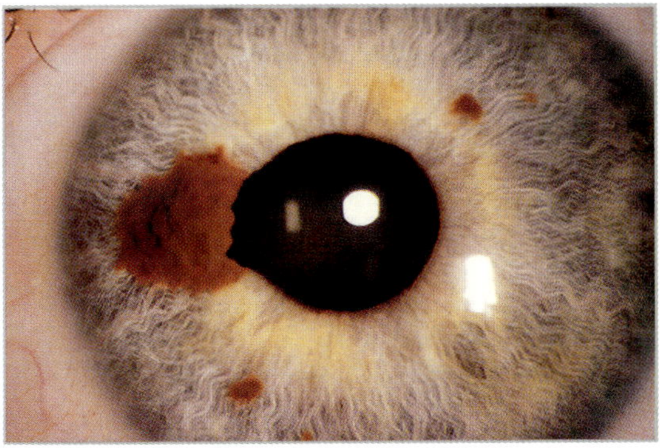

Fig. 10.11: Iris naevus.

b. Associated with pseudohypopyon, hyphaema and elevated IOP.
c. Many patients have a history of cancer (e.g. breast and lung), risk factors (e.g. smoking history, family history), or constitutional symptoms (e.g. weight loss and anorexia).
d. Requires full systemic oncology workup and iris tumour biopsy may be required to confirm the diagnosis. Iris metastasis may respond to systemic chemotherapy but may also require external beam radiation, plaque brachytherapy, proton radiation, or full surgical excision.

2. *Iris cyst:*
   a. Stromal cysts with a translucent appearance; pigment epithelial cysts produce a domed elevation of the overlying stroma and have a dark brown velvet appearance when visible.
   b. Absence of internal reflectivity on B scan or UBM.
3. *Inflammatory nodules:*
   a. Koeppe (peripupillary) and Busacca (mid-iris) nodules are small grey/yellow nodules seen in granulomatous uveitis, along with other signs of inflammation.

Investigations Request colour photography for documentation and follow-up, and ultrasound (UBM, A- and B-scan) to document size and internal reflectivity (usually low to moderate). Rarely, fluorescein angiography is needed. Incisional iris biopsy or fine-needle biopsy may confirm the diagnosis prior to definitive treatment, but can be difficult to interpret.

Treatment Occasionally, lesions may be observed closely if very small or if atypical/benign appearance.

Local treatments such as tumour resection by sector iridectomy or combined iridocyclectomy for combined iris and localised ciliary body tumours may be performed with tumour-free margins, although late locoregional seeding is reported.

Primary radiation therapy with a plaque (typically with the radioisotope ruthenium-106 in the UK) and/or proton beam therapy are the preferred options for iris melanomas. Enucleation is reserved for:

- Large iris masses infiltrating the angle and causing secondary glaucoma.
- Diffuse ('ring') iris melanomas with refractory elevated IOP.
- After failed local therapy.
- Blind, painful eye from melanoma-induced glaucoma.

Follow-up Examine 4–6 monthly for tumour recurrence, including gonioscopy and B scan/UBM. Generally, there is a low metastatic potential.

DIFFERENTIAL DIAGNOSIS OF FUNDUS TUMOURS

Choroidal naevus Typically asymptomatic, flat to very thin (<2 mm height), variably pigmented lesions with regular margins. Naevi with a low risk of malignant transformation to choroidal melanoma are typically small (<6 mm basal dimension), <1 mm height, and associated with drusen or retinal pigment epithelium (RPE) hyperpigmentation suggesting chronicity. Naevi with a high risk of malignant transformation typically have multiple risk factors as per **Table 10.1 (Fig. 10.12)**. Intermediate risk naevi may have one or two high-risk factors and are deemed suspicious for transformation into choroidal melanoma. The MOLES (mushroom shape, orange pigment, large size, enlargement and subretinal fluid) scoring system (**Table 10.2**) is an alternative scheme to decide which lesions are suspicious for melanoma. Each feature is given a score from 0 to 2. The total out of 10 is calculated with the following outcomes: 0/10 is a common naevus, 1/10 is a low-risk naevus, 2/10 is a high-risk naevus and 3/10 or more is likely to be a melanoma.

Photograph low-risk naevi for future comparison and arrange annual review by an ophthalmologist or optometrist. Photograph intermediate-risk naevi and review every 4–6 months by an ophthalmologist for at least 1 year, then yearly. Promptly refer progressing, intermediate and high-risk naevi (MOLES score ≥2) to an ocular oncology centre.

Choroidal melanoma See page 482.

Table 10.1: Clinical risk factors to predict malignant transformation of a choroidal naevus

Higher risk	Lower risk
Height >2.0 mm and/or the largest basal diameter > 5.0 mm	Abundant surface drusen
Presence of subretinal fluid	Chronic RPE atrophy or RPE metaplasia
Orange pigment (lipofuscin)	Hyper-reflective on ultrasound
Hollow acoustic signal on ultrasound	
Visual symptoms associated with tumour	
Documented growth	

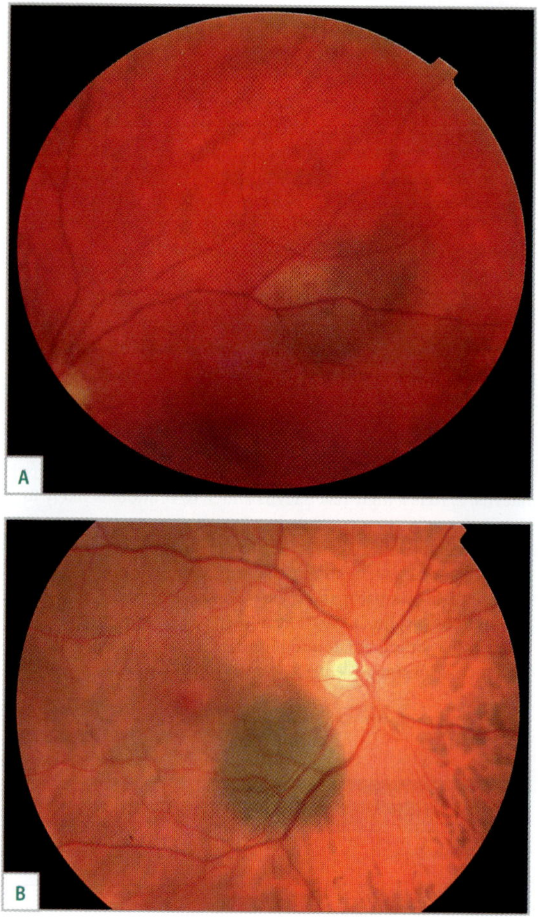

Fig. 10.12: High-risk (A) and low-risk (B) choroidal naevi.

Congenital hypertrophy of the retinal pigment epithelium (CHRPE) Asymptomatic, flat and dark black lesions with regular margins (**Fig. 10.13**). Focal areas of depigmentation (lacunae) suggest chronicity. Usually unilateral, unifocal and located in the peripheral retina. Can undergo physiologic growth and have a very rare risk of malignant transformation. Solitary peripheral lesions should be photographed then followed by an optometrist.

Table 10.2: The MOLES scoring system for melanocytic fundus lesions

Risk factor	Severity				MOLES score
Mushroom shape	0 Absent				0
	1 Incipient				1
	2 Definite				2
Orange pigment	0 Absent				0
	1 Trace				1
	2 Confluent				2
Large size		Thickness		Base diameter	
	0 Absent	<1 mm	and	<3 DD	0
	1 Borderline	1–2 mm	or	3–4 DD	1
	2 Present	>2 mm	or	>4 DD	2
Enlargement	0 None				0
	1 Possible				1
	2 Definite				2
Subretinal fluid	0 Absent				0
	1 Trace				1
	2 Significant				2
					Add up total score

(MOLES, mushroom shape, orange pigment, large size, enlargement and subretinal fluid)

Some patients may have small-medium sized, multifocal and bilateral CHRPE lesions. If these have a comma-shape or a depigmented tail, they may be associated with Gardner's syndrome (familial adenomatous polyposis and colon cancer) requiring systemic and genetic evaluation.

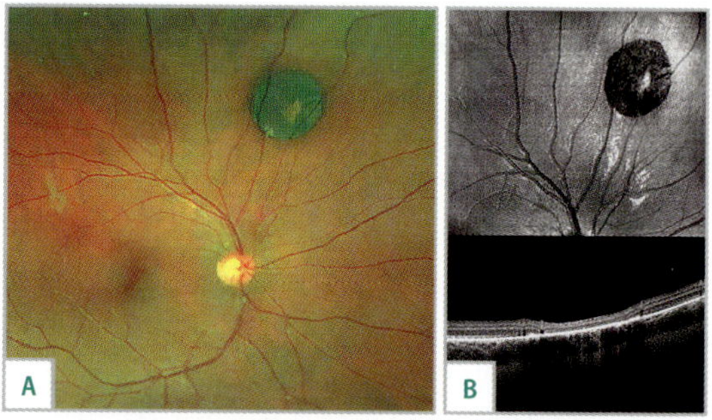

Fig. 10.13: Congenital hypertrophy of the retinal pigment epithelium (CHRPE).

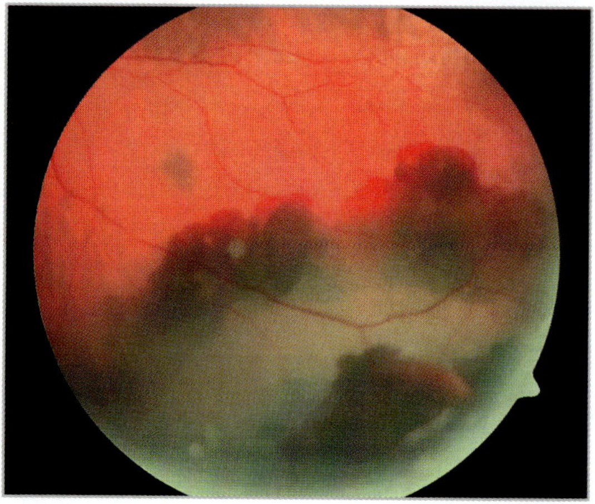

Fig. 10.14: Subretinal haemorrhage from choroidal neovascularisation.

Subretinal haemorrhage Peripheral, domed, disciform and subretinal haemorrhage may resemble choroidal melanoma due to the variable pigmentation of blood elements (**Fig. 10.14**). Commonly caused by non-macular subretinal choroidal neovascularisation (age-related, idiopathic polypoidal choroidal vasculopathy, high myopia, inflammatory and post-traumatic) or retinal artery macroaneurysms. Subretinal haemorrhage resolves over time with reduction in the height of the lesion (unlike malignant tumours), and develops variable pigmentation due to haemosiderin breakdown from dehaemoglobinised blood products.

Choroidal detachment Both serous or haemorrhagic choroidal detachments may mimic an intraocular tumour. History or examination findings may reveal hypotony, prior ocular surgery, intraocular inflammation (scleritis and posterior uveitis), carotid cavernous fistulae, or uveal effusion syndrome (**Fig. 12.11**, p. 655). B-scan ultrasound is helpful if the diagnosis is uncertain. Often resolve spontaneously.

Retinal capillary haemangioma A red nodular vascular tumour with dilated feeding arteriole and draining venule; may have secondary lipid exudates, subretinal fluid, or subretinal/preretinal fibrosis causing tractional retinal detachment (TRD) (**Fig. 10.15**). Arises in the first or second decade. Sporadic cases tend to be uniocular and unifocal with a less aggressive disease course. Inherited cases are associated with von Hippel–Lindau (VHL) syndrome, an autosomal dominant condition associated with cerebellar haemangioblastoma, phaeochromocytoma, and other visceral tumours. Use focal argon laser photocoagulation, verteporfin photodynamic therapy, or external cryotherapy to treat small tumours. Larger tumours require ruthenium-106 plaque brachytherapy. Vitreoretinal surgery may be needed to treat associated TRD. VHL can be confirmed with genetic testing and if positive requires systemic screening for non-ocular tumours and ocular screening with dilated fundoscopy yearly.

Choroidal haemangioma Circumscribed choroidal haemangiomas are low to medium elevated, orange-red coloured,

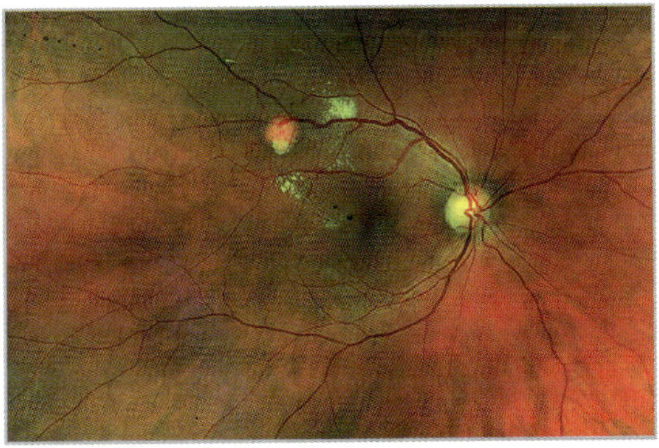

Fig. 10.15: Retinal capillary haemangioma.

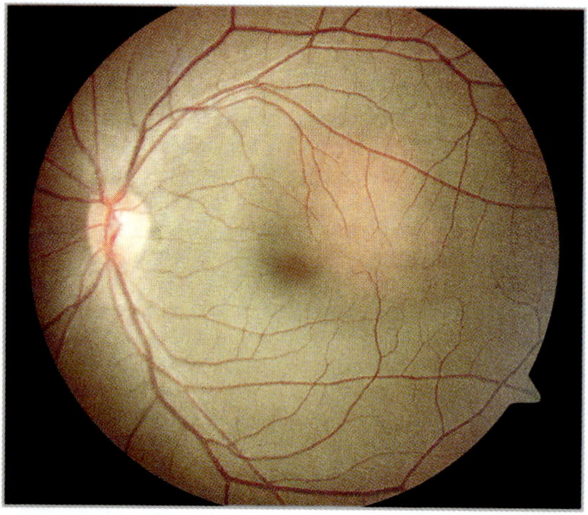

Fig. 10.16: Circumscribed choroidal haemangioma.

round lesions (**Fig. 10.16**). Associated with subretinal fluid or overlying intraretinal cysts and RPE hyperplasia in chronic cases. May be symptomatic, depending on their location, due to fluid exudation or refractive change. There is characteristic early choroidal flush on indocyanine green angiography, mild vascular leakage in late phase fluorescein angiography, and high internal reflectivity with ultrasonography. Treat small symptomatic lesions with fluid exudation with photodynamic therapy, or thermal laser for extramacular lesions. Larger tumours may require radiotherapy (plaque brachytherapy, proton beam or in some cases, external beam).

Diffuse choroidal haemangiomas produce an extensive 'tomato ketchup'-red choroidal appearance. Exudation may produce symptomatic exudative retinal detachments that may respond to external beam or plaque radiotherapy. Associated with Sturge–Weber syndrome with ipsilateral periocular cutaneous haemangiomas, glaucoma, and risk of expulsive choroidal haemorrhage during intraocular surgery if unsuspected.

Choroidal metastasis Elevated, generally amelanotic lesions with focal RPE hyperpigmentation ('leopard spot' pattern) which can be unilateral but commonly multifocal and bilateral (**Fig. 10.17**). Exudation may cause symptomatic exudative retinal detachment. Patients may have a history of cancer (e.g. breast and lung), risk factors (e.g. smoking and family

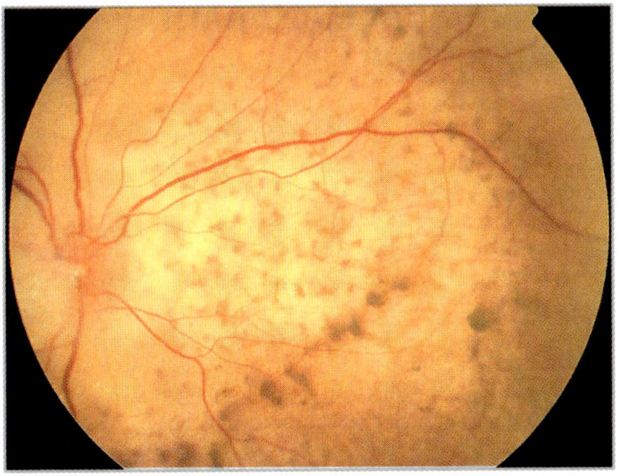

Fig. 10.17: Choroidal metastasis.

history), or constitutional symptoms (e.g. weight loss and anorexia). OCT demonstrates a thickened choroidal lesion with irregular undulating apical surface associated with subretinal fluid. High internal reflectivity on ultrasonography. Systemic oncology evaluation is required if the diagnosis is suspected, particularly in patients without known cancer. Treatment of the systemic primary tumour is usually coupled with external beam radiotherapy to the affected eye, or otherwise plaque radiotherapy, or verteporfin photodynamic therapy. Newer targeted systemic cancer therapies to treat the primary tumour may have a favourable effect on the choroidal lesions.

Lymphoma See page 445.

CHOROIDAL MALIGNANT MELANOMA

Background Choroidal malignant melanoma is the most common primary malignant intraocular tumour. Patients are commonly white, aged 55–75 years, and have no known family history. Local tumour control can be achieved in >90% of cases. However, systemic metastasis occurs in up to 40% within 5 years of ocular treatment. Tumours are unilateral and rarely metastasise to the orbit, brain or the fellow eye, but have a predisposition for the liver and less commonly the lungs.

Symptoms May present with vision loss, localised scotoma, metamorphopsia, and photopsia from the tumour and/or associated exudative retinal detachment. May be asymptomatic.

Signs Focal conjunctival and episcleral vascular dilation (sentinel vessels) are seen in the same quadrant as larger, more chronic anterior uveal melanomas. Trans-scleral extension of the pigmented tumour occurs rarely.

Posterior choroidal malignant melanomas are elevated, globular, tan to brown-coloured lesions (**Fig. 10.18**); occasionally they are pale (amelanotic melanoma) or minimally elevated while growing over a larger choroidal base (diffuse melanoma). Apical tumour growth through Bruchs' membrane results in the classic hyperpigmented 'mushroom' or 'collar-stud' appearance, but rarely in tumours <5 mm thick. Surface drusen and variable retinal pigment epithelium hypertrophy suggest chronicity and

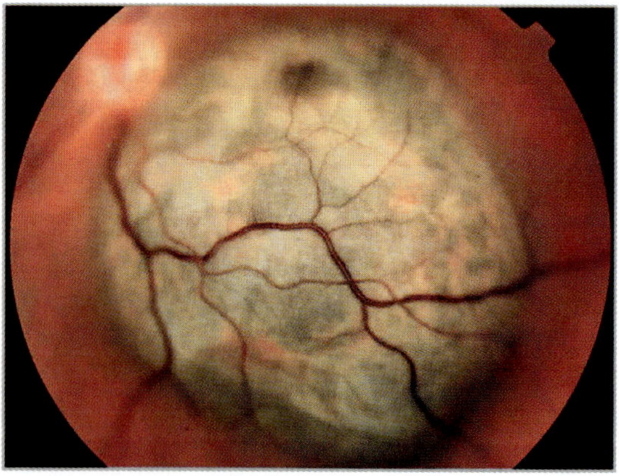

Fig. 10.18: Large choroidal malignant melanoma.

inactivity, while the presence of subretinal fluid, exudative retinal detachment, and overlying geographic orange lipofuscin pigment suggests tumour activity. Vitreous and subretinal haemorrhage may occur with larger tumours.

Classification Based on anatomic origin (ciliary body and/or choroid), histopathologic cell type, growth pattern (elevated versus diffuse), genetic patterns, posterior location (macular, juxtapapillary, or peripapillary), and, most commonly, tumour size, such as the COMS (collaborative ocular melanoma study) criteria:

- *Small*: thickness < 2.5 mm and basal diameter < 8 mm.
- *Medium*: thickness 2.5–10 mm and basal diameter 8–16 mm.
- *Large*: thickness > 10 mm and basal diameter > 16 mm.

History and examination Ask about visual symptoms, ocular surgery, cancer, and constitutional symptoms. Detailed serial ocular examination includes IOP, gonioscopy to assess for angle invasion in anterior choroid/ciliary body tumours, and dilated fundoscopy with precise tumour drawing. Transpupillary transillumination delineates the extent of ciliary body/anterior choroid involvement.

Differential diagnosis See page 475.

Investigations Arrange colour fundus photography for documentation and follow-up. Use ultrasonography to document size (height with longitudinal and transverse basal dimensions; note any extrascleral extension), and internal reflectivity (usually

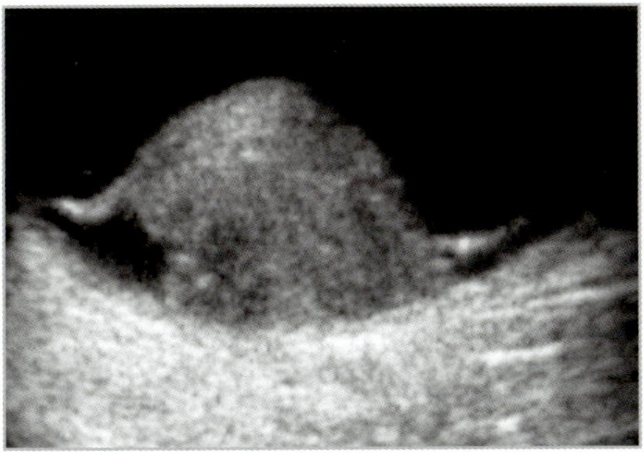

Fig. 10.19: B-mode ultrasound of choroidal melanoma associated with retinal detachment (Courtesy M Restori).

low to moderate) (**Fig. 10.19**). The absence of internal blood flow helps to rule out non-malignant disease such as disciform subretinal haemorrhage or nodular scleritis. Fluorescein angiography may show a prominent choroidal circulation pattern ('dual circulation') but is not diagnostic. Orbital imaging is rarely required. In most cases, a combination of clinical features and ancillary ophthalmic testing is sufficient to make the diagnosis. In cases of indeterminate lesions, careful serial follow-up to document growth or in some cases, intraoperative choroidal biopsy, may be used for confirmatory histologic diagnosis. Prior to treatment, investigate for systemic metastases with focal liver imaging (liver ultrasound or either CT or MRI of the abdomen), CXR, and positron emission tomography (PET) scan. If present, refer promptly to a medical oncologist. Genetic testing on ocular tumour specimens may help to identify a higher risk of systemic metastasis.

Treatment Refer to a designated treatment centre (in the UK: Moorfields Eye Hospital, London; Royal Hallamshire Hospital, Sheffield; St. Paul's Eye Unit, Liverpool; Gartnavel General Hospital, Glasgow). Treatment options are based on the results of metastatic work-up, fellow eye status, patient's age, preference and health status. These include:

- *Observation*: typically for small melanomas with chronic appearance.
- *Local therapy*:
  1. Episcleral plaque brachytherapy: typically, with ruthenium-106 for tumours up to 7 mm in height, and/or
  2. Local tumour resection: particularly for anterior, superonasal tumours with a small base and large height. Surgery requires specialised hypotensive anaesthesia.
  3. Transpupillary thermotherapy: rarely used as primary therapy, but may be effective for select small tumours.
  4. Proton beam radiotherapy: particularly for tumours adjacent to or surrounding the optic nerve, or larger tumours that cannot be treated with plaque radiotherapy.
  5. Stereotactic radiosurgery: can be used in specialised centres as an alternative to plaque brachytherapy or proton beam radiotherapy.
- *Enucleation*: typically for large tumours, recurrent tumours, blind, painful eyes with melanoma-induced neovascular glaucoma, or due to patient preference.

Follow-up Lifelong. After local therapy, ophthalmic examination with photodocumentation and ultrasound height assessment is performed initially every 4–6 months, then yearly if there is no growth. Advise patients to return immediately if their vision changes. Postenucleation sockets are followed if extraocular extension or orbital invasion is found. Requires twice-yearly focal liver imaging (ultrasound or MRI), by a melanoma oncologist or GP, to survey for metastatic disease for 5 years, which may reduce to annually from 5 to 10 years after treatment. Low-risk melanomas may not need any systemic staging or surveillance.

RETINOBLASTOMA

Background The most common malignant intraocular tumour in children. Cumulative incidence at 11 years old is 4.4/100,000 births in the UK. Most (82%) cases are diagnosed before the age of 3 years, with no sex or race predisposition. The majority of cases are unilateral.

Genetics Caused by a mutation in the *RB1* gene. A germline mutation is often associated with bilateral disease and autosomal dominant inheritance with almost complete penetrance (50% of offspring affected). Those with unilateral retinoblastoma are less likely to have a germline mutation or transmit the disease. Genetic testing is performed using tumour (two mutations are found) and white blood cells in the blood (one mutation if genetic retinoblastoma). Recent research has also included aqueous humor samples. 10% of cases have a family history (FH) of an inherited germline mutation; 75% of these develop bilateral tumours.

- 30% have a negative FH and develop bilateral tumours; >95% have new detectable germline mutations.
- 60% have a negative FH and develop unilateral tumours; <10% have new germline mutations.
- Siblings with negative FH have a small risk of disease, as some (<5%) carrier parents are unaffected due to germline mosaicism.

Clinical features: Classically presents with leucocoria (55%) from a large posterior retinal tumour mass (**Fig. 10.20**), but also secondary strabismus (25%) with decreased visual function (8%), and positive FH (10%). More advanced signs at presentation include preseptal/orbital cellulitis, elevated IOP (from secondary angle closure or direct tumour infiltration of the drainage angle), spontaneous hyphaema, conjunctival injection, buphthalmos, or AC invasion seen as white/yellow 'pseudo-hypopyon' tumour invasion or lesions on the iris surface. Extraocular, fungating tumours associated with extraocular extension are rare in high income countries.

On fundus examination, a white/light yellow solid retinal mass is characteristic, with four growth patterns:

1. *Endophytic:* into the vitreous cavity.
2. *Exophytic:* into the subretinal space.
3. *Combined:* endo- and exophytic.
4. *Diffuse:* minimally thickened and extensive tumour with retinal whitening.

Associated features may include exudative retinal detachment, engorged vessels on tumour surface that dive into the substance

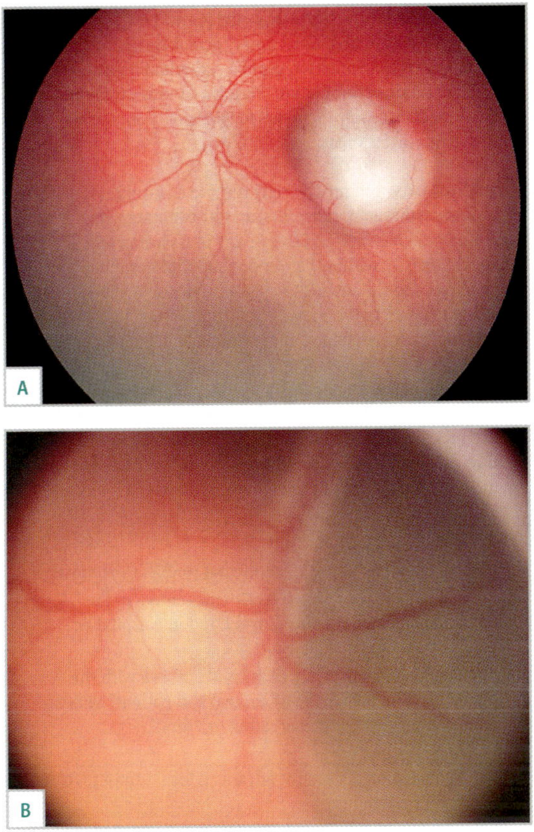

Fig. 10.20: Retinoblastoma.

of the tumour, tumour seeds (subretinal and/or vitreous), vitreous haemorrhage, vitreous opacity from vitreous seeding, or posterior uveitis.

Differential diagnosis A spontaneously regressed retinoblastoma (retinoma or retinocytoma) may be seen as a white, calcified retinal mass, often with chronic retinal pigment epithelium hyperpigmentation changes around the base. Coats' disease presents with non-calcified yellow subretinal exudates with retinal detachment and dilated, tortuous terminal bulb telangiectatic vessels.

History and examination Draw the family pedigree (p. 493) with specific questioning about family ocular cancer or prior enucleation. Perform anterior segment examination including IOP, and dilated fundus examination. Perform fundus examination of the immediate family members for signs of spontaneously regressed retinoblastomas.

Investigations Infants typically require examination under general anaesthesia. Arrange B-scan ultrasonography to document the presence and size of any mass lesion and any hyperechodensity within the tumour suggesting intralesional calcification and shadowing (a typical finding). A CT of the orbits was used to confirm the presence of intralesional calcification, extent of extraocular spread, and to exclude other diagnoses, but is in declining use due to anxiety surrounding the risk of secondary paediatric cancers. MRI is used to determine extraocular or intracranial spread. Genetic testing of blood or tumour cells is used to screen for germline mutations. Intraocular biopsies or other intraocular procedures must not be performed on eyes with suspected retinoblastoma.

Treatment

- *Casualty*: Refer to specialty clinic that week for diagnosis.
- *Clinic*: Refer to a designated treatment centre (in the UK: Retinoblastoma Unit at The Royal London Hospital or Birmingham Children's Hospital).
- *Treatment*: Customised for each child and eye with the primary goal of local tumour control and patient's survival. The secondary goal is preservation of vision.
  1. Local therapy:
     - Enucleation is used for advanced local tumours or after treatment failure.
     - Local and globe-sparing treatment options include external cryotherapy, transpupillary thermotherapy, local (sub-Tenon's or intracarotid artery) chemotherapy, or plaque radiotherapy.
     - Intra-arterial chemotherapy delivers chemotherapy into the ophthalmic artery and hence into the retinal tumour. It can be used as primary or salvage therapy in unilateral or bilateral cases at a specialised centre.
     - Intravitreal chemotherapy can be given for vitreous seeding using a special safety-enhanced technique to reduce the risk of extraocular seeding.
     - Intracameral chemotherapy has been described for salvage of eyes with AC seeding using a safety-enhanced technique.

2 Systemic chemotherapy:
- Multi-agent chemotherapy may be used alone or with local treatments as primary or salvage therapy.

3. External beam radiotherapy has now been abandoned due to long-term morbidity and mortality risks.

Follow-up Regular review including examination under anaesthesia for recurrence/new tumours to age 7 by a retinoblastoma centre, then yearly by a local ophthalmologist. Arrange prompt neuroimaging in older bilateral retinoblastoma patients with new-onset of CNS symptoms to look for ectopic intracranial retinoblastoma ('trilateral retinoblastoma'). The 5-year survival rate for retinoblastoma in the UK is >95%. The cumulative incidence of second primary neoplasms in heritable cases is ~1% per year (typically bone and soft-tissue sarcomas).

OPTOMETRY AND GENERAL PRACTICE GUIDELINES

General comments

Eye tumours are relatively rare. However, some eyelid tumours, particularly basal cell carcinomas, are common. Eyelid tumours are usually treated by oculoplastic surgeons rather than ocular oncologists and are covered in the oculoplastics chapter. The most common referral to most ocular oncology services is a choroidal naevus, to exclude (or treat) choroidal melanoma. Discriminating between naevi and melanomas can be difficult and many patients remain under regular review. The following factors suggest malignant potential: elevation, subretinal fluid, visual symptoms (blurred vision or distortion), orange pigment (lipofuscin), and most importantly, documented growth. Low-risk naevi do not routinely warrant hospital referral. The MOLES score (**Table 10.2**, p. 477) can be used to risk stratify lesions.

General practice

GPs and midwives assess newborns and infants at 6 weeks of age for a normal red reflex when using an ophthalmoscope. If abnormal, this may be a sign of congenital cataract or retinoblastoma, among other conditions. A white reflex necessitates an urgent review to a paediatric ophthalmologist usually within 2 weeks of referral. There is confusion surrounding an absent 'red' reflex, however, red reflexes are seen in white babies and loss of this reflex in one eye necessitates referral urgently. However, in non-white babies the normal reflex can be pink, orange or pale. To avoid unnecessary urgent referrals, the referrer should assess the parents to note what the reflex is in that ethnic group (Newborn and Infant Physical Examination screening guidelines).

In adults, GPs who are confident with an ophthalmoscope, fundal naevi may be a familiar finding, and assuming these are small, flat, discrete, and evenly pigmented, then arrange annual dilated optometry review, preferably by an optometrist with a fundus camera. If there are any worrying features refer to a general ophthalmologist.

Optometry

Benign-appearing naevi are common: carefully document the clinical features and size in disc diameters, and if possible, photograph the lesion. Arrange annual dilated fundus examination and ideally imaging, and explain to the patient that they should ensure that this occurs if they change optometrists. Inform the patient's GP. If there are visual symptoms, an increase in the size of the naevus or any suspicious features, then refer to a general ophthalmologist.

The following guide to referral urgency is not prescriptive, as clinical situations vary. See also the latest UK referral guidelines from Royal College of Ophthalmologists and the College of Optometrists.

Urgent

- Retinoblastoma p. 486
- Choroidal melanoma p. 482
- Choroidal metastasis p. 480
- Iris melanoma p. 472
- Malignant conjunctival tumours p. 463

Soon (within 1 month)

- High-risk choroidal naevi p. 475

Routine

- Intermediate-risk choroidal naevi p. 475
- Congenital hypertrophy of the retinal pigment epithelium (CHRPE) p. 476
- Retinal capillary haemangioma p. 479
- Choroidal haemangioma p. 479

MEDICAL RETINA

11

Timothy L Jackson, Catherine Egan, Andrew Webster, Adnan Tufail, Olivia Cundy & Chan Ning Lee

TAKING A FAMILY HISTORY FOR INHERITED DISEASE

Inherited retinal disorders cover a broad phenotypic spectrum, ranging from retinitis pigmentosa to macular degenerations. For an increasing number of these disorders the causative gene is known and testing is available. Patients need genetic counselling, with accurate information about the nature of their disorder, and the risks to their children and other relatives.

If inherited disease is suspected, take a detailed family history. Ask about consanguinity in the parents and patient. The former makes autosomal recessive inheritance more likely, the latter affects the risk to the patient's children. Examine family members where possible; carriers may show changes and others may have subclinical disease that helps to diagnose the proband (patient).

Draw a family tree as shown in **Figure 11.1**. Many inherited retinal diseases are Mendelian, but non-Mendelian complex disorders have genetic influences, and a family history is still relevant, e.g. type 2 diabetes mellitus. Inheritance may be obfuscated by non-penetrance (gene-carrier not showing the disease) or variable expressivity (gene-carriers showing a spectrum of disease severity). Look for the following patterns of inheritance.

Autosomal dominant

- Affected individuals generally have an affected parent.
- The disease does not usually skip a generation, unless there is non-penetrance.
- Affected individuals have a 50% risk of having affected offspring.
- Males and females are equally affected, and have an equal likelihood of transmitting the disorder to offspring.

Autosomal recessive

- Affected individuals are usually born to unaffected parents and offspring are rarely affected, unless there is consanguinity.
- There is a 25% risk to each subsequent child of parents with one affected child.
- Males and females are equally affected.

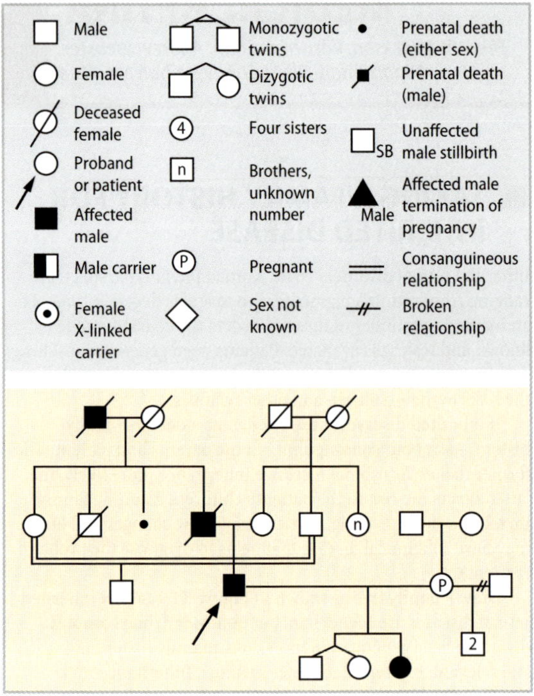

Fig. 11.1: Drawing a family tree. Example shows autosomal dominant inheritance.

X-linked recessive

- Affects males, or males are generally more severely affected than females.
- Affected males have unaffected sons, but all daughters are carriers.
- A female carrier has a 50% risk of her son being affected or her daughter being a carrier. Carriers may show abnormal signs, such as the tapetal retinal reflex that occurs in X-linked retinitis pigmentosa.
- Male-to-male transmission excludes X-linked inheritance.

Mitochondrial inheritance

- Mitochondrial DNA is derived exclusively from the ovum so inheritance is maternal.

- Therefore, male-to-child transmission excludes mitochondrial inheritance.
- Children of affected females all have the mutation, but may not be affected; non-penetrance and variable expressivity are common.

Simplex or sporadic

- A single-affected proband with no affected relatives is common. This is usually autosomal recessive inheritance.
- Consider X-linked disease in male probands.
- Consider autosomal dominant inheritance if family history is limited and when non-penetrance and/or variable expressivity might occur.
- Simplex cases may represent a *de novo* mutation. This is more likely in disorders that can affect survival such as retinoblastoma or von Hippel–Lindau disease, as they are less likely to be transmitted across generations.

FLUORESCEIN ANGIOGRAPHY

Background The fluorophore, sodium fluorescein, is injected into an antecubital vein and circulates to the eye. A fundus camera fitted with an illumination source and a barrier filter is then used to selectively photograph the retinal and choroidal circulation.

In health, fluorescein passes rapidly through the eye, but the inner and outer blood–retinal-barriers prevent penetration into the neurosensory retina. Retinal vessels are clearly visible, but an intact retinal pigment epithelium (RPE) reduces the apparent fluorescence of the choroid. Diseases that damage the ocular circulation, RPE, or blood–retinal barrier can all potentially be detected angiographically.

Indications Retinal and choroidal disease, including neovascularisation, inflammation and ischaemia; macular oedema; RPE disease; and iris angiography.

Method

1. Consider whether fundus fluorescein angiography (FFA) will alter management and whether it is the most appropriate investigation. Would clinical examination, OCT, OCT angiography (OCTA), autofluorescence (AF) imaging, or indocyanine green (ICG) angiography be better? Consider where the likely abnormality lies, and if standard or widefield FFA is best.
2. Avoid using topical fluorescein, e.g. for checking IOP, prior to FFA, as it reduces the contrast of the angiogram.
3. Exclude contraindications, e.g. fluorescein allergy and consider relative risks, e.g. severe renal failure. For use in pregnancy see below.
4. Explain the risks (below) and benefits. Obtain written consent.
5. Indicate to the photographer the area of interest, the eye from which to collect the initial images (the transit eye) and presumed diagnosis. Imaging peripheral retina requires a device capable of widefield angiography or a very skilled photographer.
6. Insert a 23-gauge cannula into an antecubital vein. Some clinicians prefer a Venflon for more secure access. If necessary, use a dorsal hand vein.
7. Inject 5 mL (2 mL with scanning laser ophthalmoscope systems) of 10% or 20% fluorescein over 4–6 seconds while looking for extravasation (swelling, pain, and resistance to injection), then turn off the lights. Consider oral fluorescein if intravenous (i.v.) administration is not possible, but image quality and transit phases are not as well-defined.
8. Retain i.v. access in case of anaphylaxis.

Adverse events While serious adverse events are rare, perform FFA in a facility with access to resuscitation equipment and care.

- *Yellowing of the skin and urine*: lasts 24 hours and occurs in all patients.
- *Nausea*: occurs in 2–3% (vomiting 1%) shortly after injection and resolves quickly. In those who experienced nausea with previous injections, consider warming the ampoule to body temperature, injecting more slowly, and giving promethazine (Phenergan) 30 mg p.o. 1 hour prior, or another antiemetic.
- *Extravasation (low risk)*: stop injecting, elevate the arm, and apply an icepack for 10 minutes. Extravasation rarely causes periphlebitis, skin necrosis, and granulomas, but pain is common and may last a few hours. Consider oral analgesia.
- *Vasovagal syncope (low risk)*: this is the most common cause of collapse. Patients have a transient reduction in pulse rate, BP and consciousness. Lay the patient supine with legs elevated above the heart level. Exclude other causes of collapse by history, examination, ECG, BP and blood glucose. Repeat observations in 1 hour, and discharge if well.
- *Skin rash and itch (3–5%)*: treat with oral antihistamines if itch alone or mild rash. Monitor for progression to anaphylaxis – auscultate the chest and check respiratory rate, pulse and BP. If there is facial or other soft-tissue swelling, difficulty with breathing or speech, secure a 20-gauge Venflon or larger, and monitor extremely closely for bronchospasm or shock. Liaise immediately with emergency physicians or anaesthetic team and be aware of any local anaphylaxis protocols.
- *Severe reactions (1:1,900–1:18,000)*: anaphylaxis; severe asthma/bronchospasm; cardiac arrhythmia; myocardial infarction; cardiac arrest; seizure.
- *Anaphylaxis*: signs include reduced consciousness, pallor, facial swelling, tachycardia, hypotension, and bronchospasm. Provide immediate emergency care as shown on page 824 or per local guidelines.
- *Death* (1:50,000–1:2,22,000).
- If an adverse event occurs provide the patient and GP with documentation of what occurred. If FFA is required in the future, this helps to understand the risk.

Pregnancy and breastfeeding OCT and OCTA obviate the need for FFA in most cases. Fluorescein crosses the placenta and can be found in breast milk, and is generally avoided, with risk profile detailed on page 840.

Renal failure FFA is possible. A small case series reported only a short-term alteration in renal function. Skin and urine yellowing takes longer to clear.

Reading and reporting fluorescein angiograms When asked to comment on angiograms, it is often better to start with a clear description, rather than a diagnosis. In general, most abnormalities are hyper- or hypofluorescent, and can be described with four terms: vascular filling defects, masking, leakage and window defects.

- Hypofluorescence:

1. *Vascular filling defect*: absent or obstructed retinal or choroidal vessels produce focal or diffuse hypofluorescence. Areas of capillary non-perfusion are suggested by leakage at the margin, staining of the large vessel walls passing through the area, and telangiectasia (tiny, saccular vessel dilatations) (**Fig. 11.2**).
2. *Masking*: most commonly occurs when retinal haemorrhage, exudates, or other opacities block underlying retinal or choroidal fluorescence. Fundus photographs or OCT may help to discriminate vascular filling defects from masking (**Fig. 11.3**).

- Hyperfluorescence:

1. *Leakage*: produces hyperfluorescence that increases in area and intensity as fluorescein accumulates in the extravascular space – compare an early image, shortly after the dye enters the retinal vessels, with a late image at 5–10 minutes (**Fig. 11.4**). If leaking fluorescein accumulates in a distinct anatomic space, such as under a pigment epithelial detachment (PED), then the area of leakage may be well-defined, but usually the margins of the area of leakage blur as fluorescein diffuses through tissue.

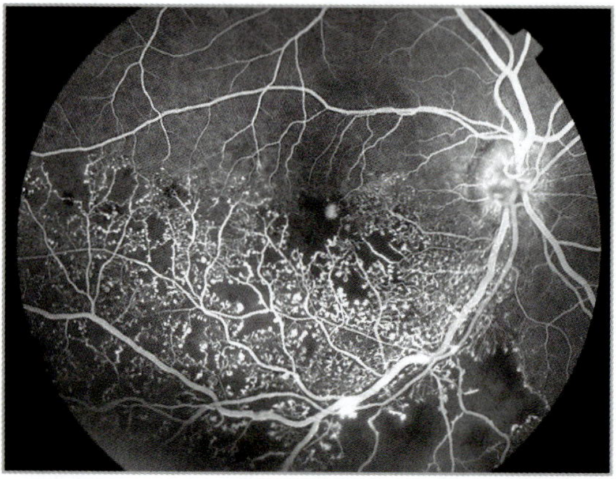

Fig. 11.2: Inferior retinal ischaemia from a branch of retinal vein occlusion.

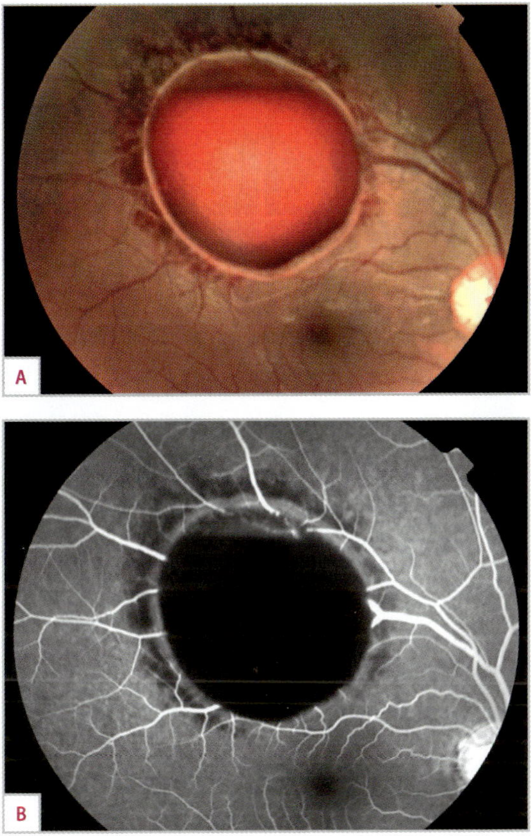

Fig. 11.3: Masking from a preretinal haemorrhage (Valsalva retinopathy).

2. *Window defect*: usually caused by focal RPE atrophy or a defect that increases the transmittance of choroidal fluorescence. Size remains the same as the RPE defect is constant, and early fluorescence fades as fluorescein leaves the choriocapillaris. Late staining of the sclera may leave some residual hyperfluorescence (**Fig. 11.5**).

A system for reporting angiograms is presented below:
1. Confirm patient's name, date of birth, date of investigation, VA, and diagnosis.

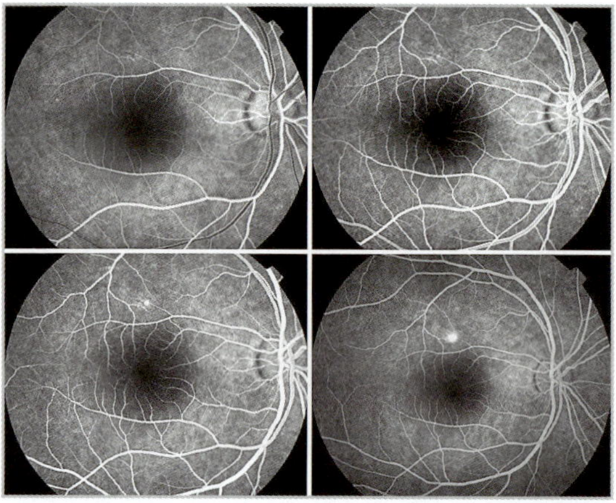

Fig. 11.4: Fluorescein leakage over time in central serous chorioretinopathy.

2. View the colour fundus photographs, OCT, OCTA and ICG alongside the FFA.
3. *Image quality*: note if poor and consider why, e.g. cataract.
4. Check the pre-injection image for AF from optic disc drusen.
5. *Timing*: Choroidal fluorescence appears at 10–15 seconds (arm to retina time), but varies between patients and injection techniques. It is initially lobular but should be uniform after an additional 5–10 seconds (choroidal transit time). Retinal filling usually follows the start of choroidal filling. From the start of retinal arterial filling to laminar flow in the veins takes ~15 seconds (retinal transit time), and is relatively constant between patients. Causes of apparently reduced choroidal or retinal flow include: arm tourniquet not released; low cardiac output in the elderly; pressure on the eye from holding eyelids open; ocular ischaemia from carotid or ophthalmic artery occlusion; giant cell arteritis; and retinal vessel occlusion (choroidal transit times intact).
6. *Vessel distribution and appearance*: Do all the quadrants fill evenly or is there topographical variation? Look for tortuosity, telangiectasia, macroaneurysms (large arterial dilatations that may leak fluorescein), and segmentation (focal narrowing or disruption of the blood column). Exclude disc and retinal new vessels that both produce very bright fluorescence, or other vascular changes such as diabetic IRMAs (IntraRetinal Microvascular Abnormalities). Look for patchy or diffuse areas of choroidal or retinal capillary non-perfusion. Vascular staining is seen with ischaemia, vasculitis and occlusion.

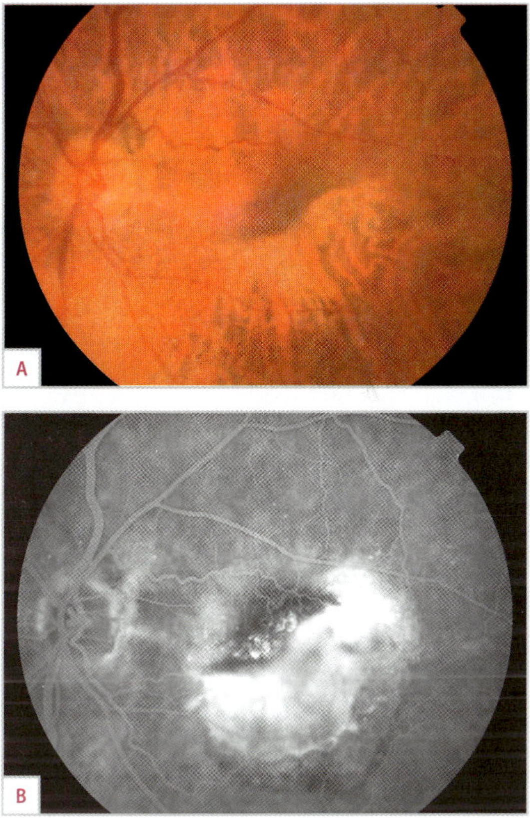

Fig. 11.5: Window defect from a retinal pigment epithelium tear.

7. *Macula*: inspect using digital enlargement, ± contrast enhancement.
   i. Measure the foveal avascular zone (FAZ). There is considerable variability in the size (650 μm average with 0–1,000 being compatible with normal VA in some patients) but >1,000 μm (two-thirds of a disc diameter) suggests ischaemia. Drop-out of the fine, lacy capillaries at the FAZ margin may give a 'moth-eaten' appearance (**Fig. 11.6**). Check for a corresponding reduction in VA, thinning of the inner retina on OCT, and corresponding OCTA changes. Ischaemia involving the papillomacular bundle has more effect on VA than other locations.

ii. Look for leak associated with macular oedema (hyperfluorescence that increases in size and intensity over time). Fluorescein may accumulate in cystic spaces and the radial arrangement of Henle's fibres sometimes produces a petaloid pattern (**Fig. 11.7**).
iii. Exclude choroidal neovascularisation (CNV), most commonly associated with age-related macular

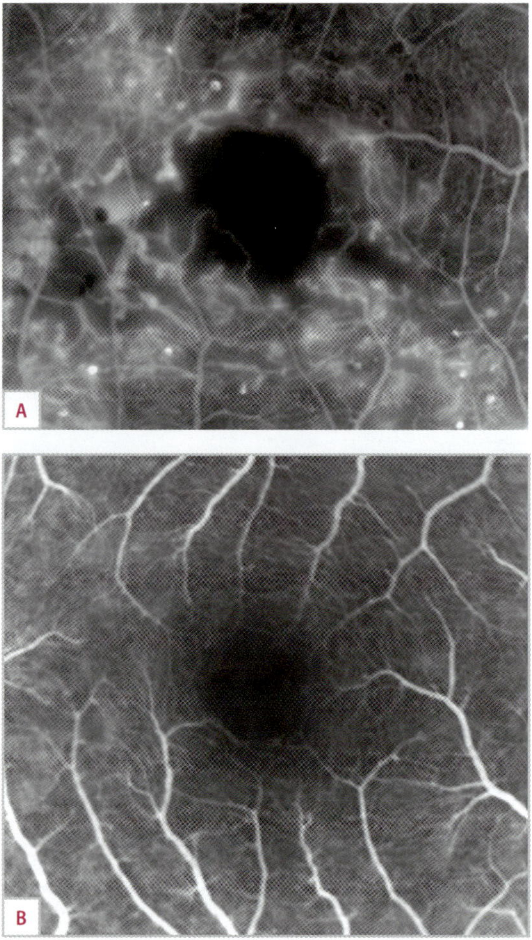

Fig. 11.6: Ischaemic foveal avascular zone (A) compared to normal (B).

degeneration (AMD) and myopia. Leakage occurs early from the choroidal circulation, forming a well-defined lacy network of new vessels (**Fig. 11.8**), or diffuse leakage.

8. Look for fluorescein leakage at the optic disc. A small crescent of late staining at the disc margin is normal, but more than this may suggest disc new vessels, inflammation or swelling (**Fig. 11.9**). Disc drusen autofluoresce but do not leak.

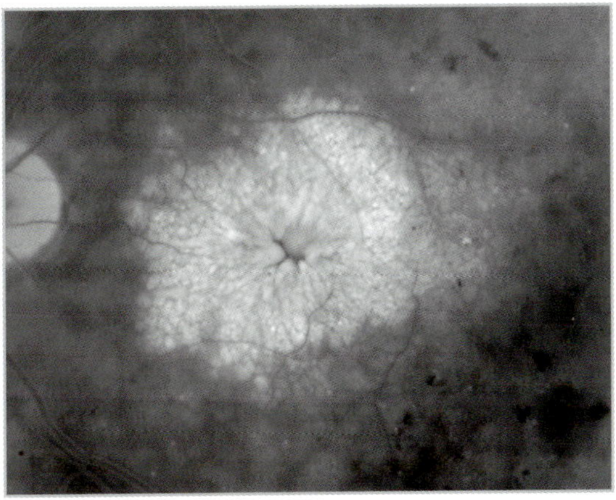

Fig. 11.7: Cystoid macular oedema.

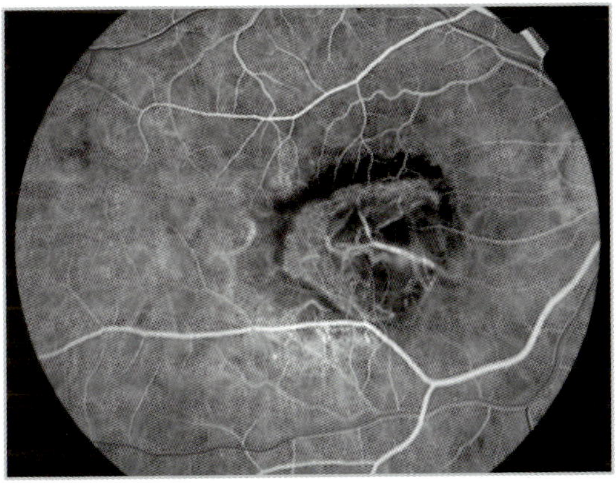

Fig. 11.8: Choroidal neovascularisation.

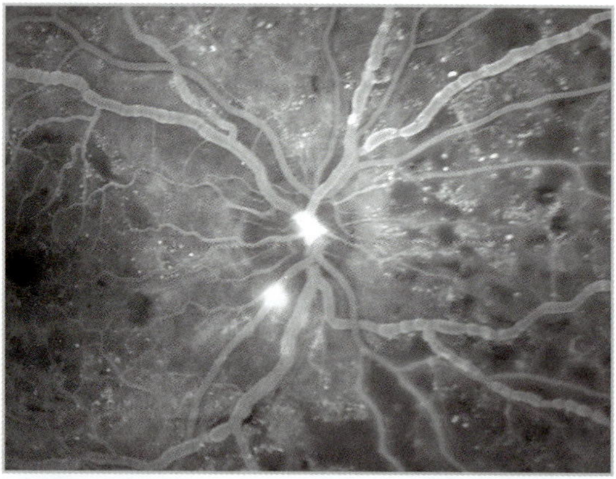

Fig. 11.9: Optic disc new vessels, retinal ischaemia, microaneurysms, and venous calibre segmentation (beading).

9. Conclude by addressing the clinical question that necessitated FFA.
10. Explain and ideally show the results to the patient.

INDOCYANINE GREEN ANGIOGRAPHY

Background Similar to fluorescein angiography except that the fluorophore dye, indocyanine green (ICG), absorbs and emits in near infrared, and is albumin-bound so that it does not leak freely from the choroidal capillaries. The use of infrared increases transmittance through the retinal pigment epithelium (RPE), haemorrhage, and exudates, relative to fluorescein angiography. ICG can, therefore, image choroidal disease and haemorrhagic neovascularisation. It is particularly helpful for polypoidal choroidal vasculopathy (PCV), and presumed inflammatory diseases like acute multifocal placoid pigment epitheliopathy (AMPPE) (**Fig. 11.10**), and multiple evanescent white dot syndrome (MEWDS). Can show increased choroidal vessel caliber in central serous chorioretinopathy.

Method

- ICG angiography can be performed at the same visit as fluorescein angiography, but ask if it will alter management or if other tests will suffice.
- Precautions and contraindications: allergy to ICG, sodium iodide, or iodine, hyperthyroidism and autonomic thyroid adenomas.
- Both ICG and shellfish contain iodine, so shellfish allergy is often considered a contraindication to ICG angiography. However, most seafood allergy is a reaction to fish protein, not iodine. Nonetheless, shellfish allergy is a relative contraindication as it may signal a general risk of allergies. Surface irritation following iodine eye drops may not necessarily indicate a true allergy and contraindication to ICG.
- Obtain written and informed consent. Explain the risk of dye extravasation, and rare (~0.5%) serious adverse reactions including anaphylaxis.
- Indicate to the photographer the area of interest and presumed diagnosis.
- Place an i.v. 23-gauge butterfly cannula or Venflon in the antecubital fossa.
- Dissolve 25 mg of ICG in 5 or 10 mL of the diluent provided (practice varies), and inject 5 mL (12.5 or 25 mg) or use premixed ICG, e.g. 25 mg in 5 mL.
- Inject as a rapid bolus but watch for extravasation.
- Request late photographs, as some abnormalities are not evident for 20–30 minutes, e.g. chorioretinal inflammatory disease and choroidal haemangioma.
- Retain i.v. access in case of anaphylaxis.

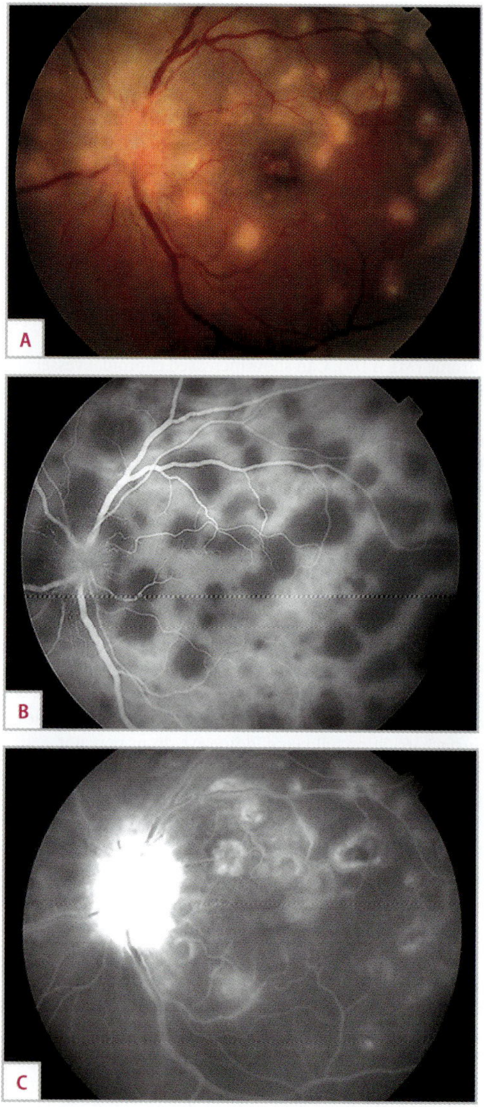

Fig. 11.10: (A) Acute multifocal placoid pigment epitheliopathy (AMPPE). Multiple areas of choriocapillary hypoperfusion are visible on the indocyanine green (B) but not the fluorescein angiogram (C).

Pregnancy and breastfeeding OCT and OCT angiography often obviate the need for ICG. However, there is evidence that ICG does not cross the placenta and the dye has been used in non-ocular investigations during pregnancy, but only consider after discussion with the patient. It is unknown whether the dye is found in breast milk. Despite low risks, on general principles, many minimise the use of ICG during pregnancy (see page 840).

OPTICAL COHERENCE TOMOGRAPHY

Background A superluminescent diode emits a near-infrared beam through the pupil, to the retina. A detector captures reflected light and uses interferometry to construct high-resolution, cross-sectional and three-dimensional (3D) images of the retina and vitreoretinal interface. Spectral domain (SD) OCT operates in the infrared range (~800 nm), whereas swept source (SS) OCT uses ~1,000 nm. Both use a Fourier transformation to analyse the depth information of the reflected signal. Many OCTs include angiography (OCTA) that generates motion-contrast images by measuring temporal changes in OCT signals from consecutive scans, distinguishing moving blood cells from static tissue. Unlike traditional angiography, OCTA does not involve a fluorophore injection, hence it cannot show vascular leakage, and the maximum retinal area that can be imaged is smaller, although emerging systems have wide field capabilities. However, it is quicker, safer and easier, and 3D depth-encoding means the superficial inner retinal, deep inner retinal and choroidal circulations can be viewed separately (normal outer retina is avascular).

Indications Most commonly used to diagnose and monitor disease of the macula, e.g. diabetic maculopathy and neovascular age-related macular degeneration (AMD) , vitreomacular interface, e.g. vitreomacular traction, macular hole, and epiretinal membrane, and optic nerve, e.g. glaucoma.

Reading a macular structural OCT

- Check the patient's name, date of birth, VA, and reason for OCT.
- Multimodal imaging helps, so review alongside the fundus examination, fundus photograph or angiogram.
- Scroll through the line scans to look for segmentation errors (inaccurate demarcation of the inner and outer retinal boundaries by the OCT software), as these determine macular thickness. If necessary, manually reposition the segmentation lines.
- Note image quality (reduced with media opacity).
- Select a good quality central (foveal) radial line scan and examine systematically from the inner retina out (**Fig. 11.11**).
- Look for vitreous opacities (e.g. asteroid, haemorrhage and inflammation) and examine the vitreomacular interface, noting vitreomacular adhesion/separation (the hyaloid face is often not visible if fully detached and hence anterior to the scan, or fully attached); vitreomacular traction;

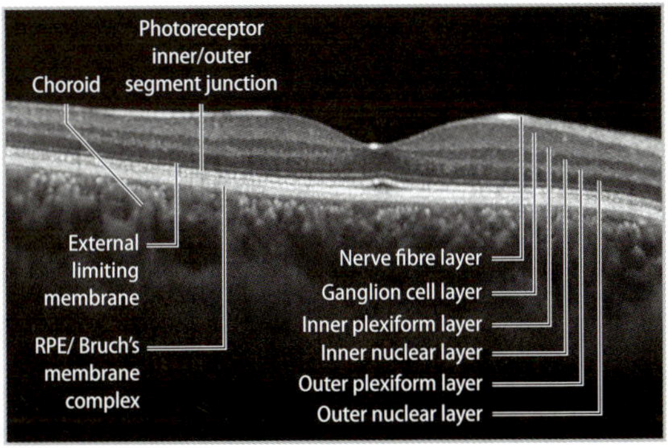

Fig. 11.11: Normal OCT. Abbreviation: RPE, retinal pigment epithelium.

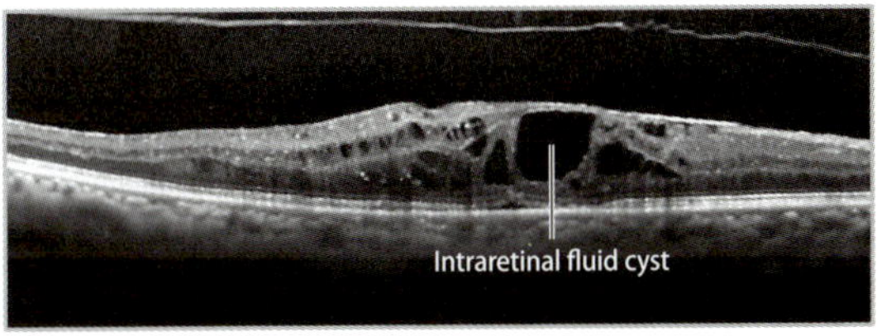

Fig. 11.12: Diabetic macular oedema. Note vitreomacular separation.

hyper-reflectivity of the inner retinal surface (common with epiretinal membrane).

- Note the presence, absence or shallowing of the normal foveal depression.
- Observe the retinal nerve fibre layer (RNFL). It is thicker and more visible on the nasal side of the fovea. If it is not discernable, consider optic nerve disease. Segmentation of the ganglion cell layer can help to identify glaucoma (p. 347) and established optic neuropathy (p. 752).
- Note inner versus outer retinal changes (or both) resulting in macular thinning [e.g. geographic atrophy (GA) causing outer retinal atrophy, or ischaemia causing inner retinal thinning]; thickening (**Fig. 11.12**), often with intraretinal fluid cysts (suggests disease activity with AMD and diabetic macular oedema); discontinuity of the ellipsoid zone (EZ, also referred to as the IS/OS line); loss of normal retinal layering; sub-retinal fluid (**Fig. 11.13**) such as from wet AMD or sub-RPE

fluid (usually hyporeflective); blood (often hyporeflective but can be variable); and fibrosis (hyper-reflective).

- Retinal new vessels lie anterior to the internal limiting membrane, differentiating it from other disease, e.g. intraretinal microvascular abnormality (IRMA).
- If relevant, use the digital callipers to measure the central retinal thickness (centred on the fovea), from the inner retinal surface to the RPE. Alternatively, view the topographic colour map with the nine Early Treatment Diabetic Retinopathy Study (ETDRS) sectors overlaid **(Fig. 11.14)**, and record the central subfield thickness (CST). For serial measurements ensure consistency. Consider measuring the maximum thickness, which may be extrafoveal. If relevant, measure the choroidal thickness at the foveal centre; enhanced depth imaging (EDI) OCT improves choroid visualisation.
- Scroll through the line scans looking for extrafoveal abnormalities.
- View the topographic colour map to look at the location and extent of any macular thickening, especially if planning focal macular laser.
- View the 3D reconstruction if there is complex vitreoretinal interface disease such as vitreomacular traction or tractional retinal detachment.
- Look for any disease specific features, e.g. drusen, choroidal neovascularisation (CNV) or pigment epithelial detachments (PEDs). Answer any disease-specific questions.
- Compare to any previous OCTs, and the fellow eye.
- Explain and ideally show the scan to the patient.

Reading optical coherence tomography angiography

- Check the patient's name, date of birth, side, VA, and reason for OCTA.
- Review alongside the fundus examination, photograph or conventional angiogram, ideally on dedicated viewing software that shows the OCTA, structural OCT, and B-scan with flow annotations and segmentation lines.

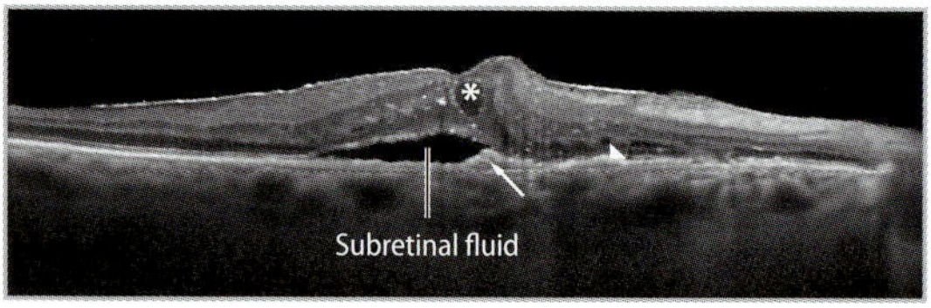

Fig. 11.13: Wet age-related macular degeneration showing intraretinal fluid (asterisk), drusen (arrowhead), pigment epithelial detachment (white arrow), and subretinal fluid.

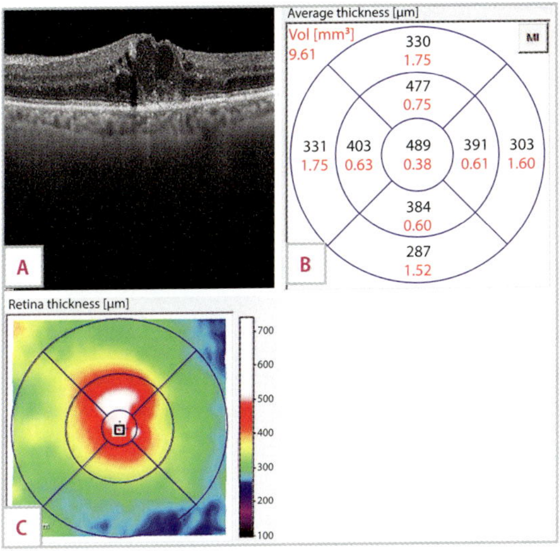

Fig. 11.14: OCT intraretinal fluid cysts (A), resulting in (B) increased central subfield thickness (489 μm) and macular volume (9.61 mm^2), seen as hot colours in the retinal thickness map (C).

- Note image quality and movement artefacts.
- Scroll through the B-scans and view the *en face* OCTA with the structural OCT to identify any "projection artefacts".
- Examine the default "slabs" in turn, from superficial to deep. The B-scan image shows two lines at the superficial and deep border of each "slab" area, shown on the *en face* view. Note the vascular pattern at each of the vascular layers; superficial and deep capillary plexus, and choriocapillaris (**Fig. 11.15**). Note any segmentation errors in these sub-slabs and interpret with caution if artifacts exist.
- Note any vascular metrics provided by the device, e.g. vessel density, flow area, FAZ area, non-perfused area and vessel length and tortuosity.
- Look for areas of vascular loss or neovascularisation. Retinal new vessels extend anterior to the internal limiting membrane, and CNV can be either Type I (sub-RPE) or Type II (subretinal). Check on the B-scan map that the high flow from outer retinal CNV is not projection artefact. Look for vessels in the usually avascular outer retinal slab.
- Compared to FFA, OCTA has a lower limit of flow detection that may not delineate lesions with slow flow rates, e.g. microaneursyms and polyps.

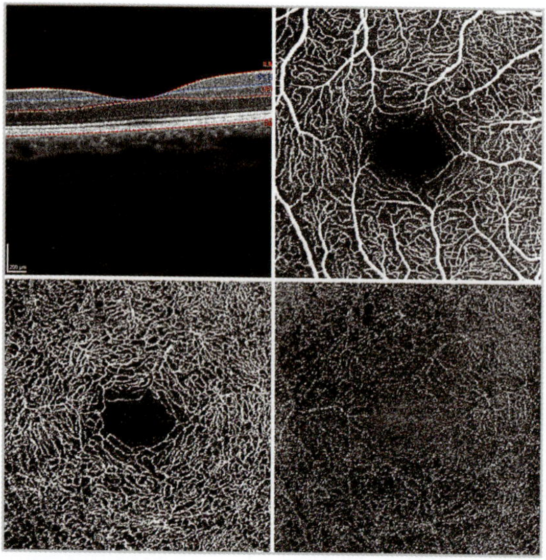

Fig. 11.15: Normal OCT angiography, showing superficial capillary plexus (top right), deep capillary plexus (lower left) and choriocapillaris.

BLUE LIGHT AUTOFLUORESCENCE IMAGING

Autofluorescence (AF) imaging evaluates the integrity and metabolism of the retinal pigment epithelium (RPE). It can use the same excitation and filters as fluorescein angiography, e.g. a 488-nm argon blue laser for excitation, combined with a barrier filter that cuts out light below 500 nm, placed in front of the detector (e.g. Heidelberg retinal angiograph). Emitted light above 500 nm is recorded as a series of images that are aligned and averaged to create the final image. The images detect the lipofuscin or melanolipofuscin within the RPE, which appears 'white'. Lipofuscin accumulation is driven by photoreceptor outer segment renewal, and is a balance between accumulation and clearance. Abnormal images can be hyperautofluorescent if there is RPE dysfunction, alteration of visual pigment or increased metabolic load, or hypoautofluorescent if there is RPE or photoreceptor loss, or masking, e.g. by normal macular pigments (lutein and zeaxanthin) in the central fovea. Levels of

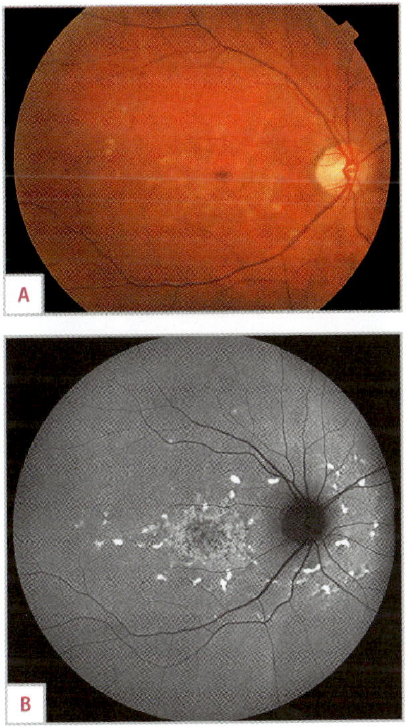

Fig. 11.16: Stargardt's macular dystrophy with autofluorescence showing bright flecks with sparing around the optic disc (Courtesy A Webster).

lipofuscin increase with age, but typically age-related drusen do not autofluoresce. In Stargardt's macular dystrophy, there are hyperautofluorescent posterior pole flecks, with sparing around the optic disc (**Fig. 11.16**). In Best's disease (see **Fig. 11.62**, p. 607) and in adult vitelliform macular dystrophy (**Fig. 11.63**, p. 608), lipofuscin accumulation within the vitelliform lesions produces hyperautofluorescence. In rod-cone dystrophy, there is often a parafoveal hyperautofluorescent "Robson's ring", with preserved macular function within the ring (**Fig. 11.17**). Hypoautofluorescence occurs with geographic

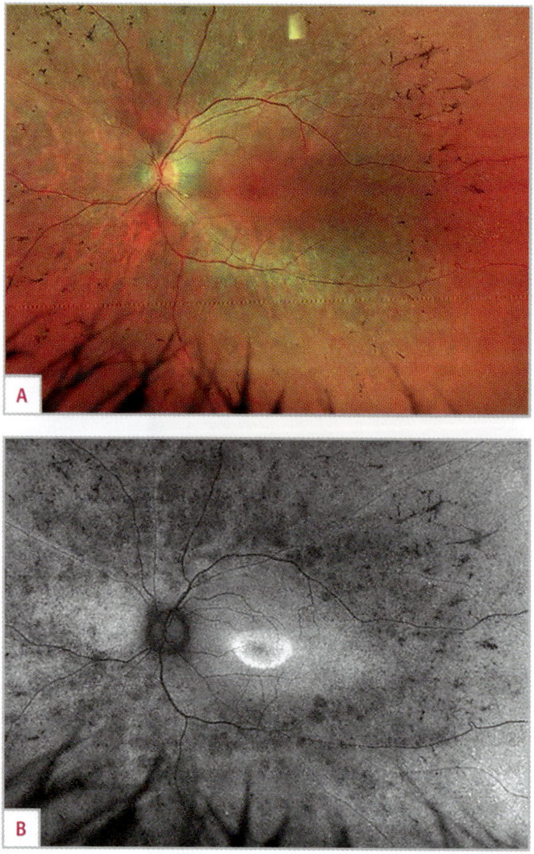

Fig. 11.17: Colour (A) and autofluorescence image (B) of a rod-cone dystrophy with a hyperautofluorescent Robson's ring.

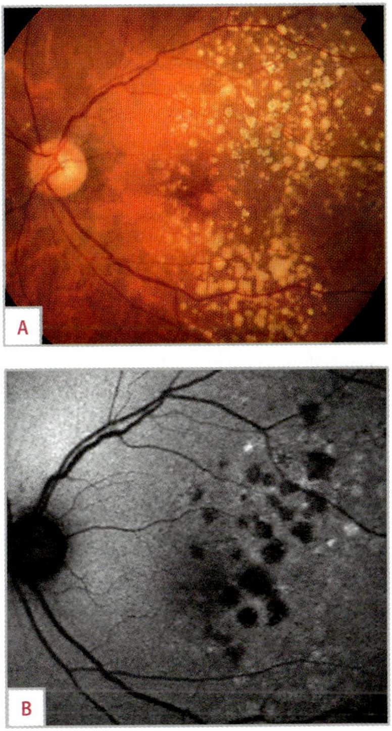

Fig. 11.18: Age-related drusen, with autofluorescence showing patches of atrophy due to loss of RPE and photoreceptors, with reduced autofluorescence between the drusen (Courtesy A Webster).

atrophy (GA) (**Fig. 11.18**), pre-retinal or retinal haemorrhage (due to masking) and over the optic disc and vessels due to the absence of lipofuscin. The margin of advancing GA may show hyperautofluorescence due to malfunction of the RPE cells and accumulation of lipofuscin.

ELECTROPHYSIOLOGY

Background Electrophysiology is an important diagnostic tool for many retinal and optic nerve diseases, and in non-organic visual loss. Full electrodiagnostic testing is expensive, so ensure it is clinically indicated. Provide staff with a clinical summary of ophthalmic, family, medical and surgical history, VA, refraction, examination, retinal imaging and differential diagnosis.

Pattern electroretinogram

1. *Indications*: disease of the macula, retinal ganglion cells or optic nerve.
2. *Method*: recording electrodes are placed on the cornea or conjunctiva and reference electrodes at the ipsilateral outer canthus. The standard stimulus is a high-contrast reversing checkerboard of low temporal frequency (2–4 reversals/sec), with a check size of approximately 40 minutes and a field size of 10 to 16 degrees. Defocus produces a poor waveform, so refractive correction is important.
3. *Key points*: the main measurements are a positive response peaking at ~50 ms (P50) followed by a negative response at ~95 ms (N95) (**Fig. 11.19**). P50 arises in part from the retinal ganglion cells and in part from other inner retinal neurones, but is driven by the macular photoreceptors and acts as an objective index of general macular function. N95 arises in the retinal ganglion cells. In the presence of an abnormal visually-evoked potential (VEP) (see below), an abnormal P50 implies the disease involves the macula and an abnormality confined to N95 localises disease to the optic nerve/retinal ganglion cells. The pattern electroretinogram (PERG) is used in association with the full-field electroretinogram (ERG) better to characterise retinal function.

Full-field electroretinogram

1. *Indications*: generalised retinal dysfunction.
2. *Method*: recording electrodes are placed on the ocular surface, reference electrodes at the outer canthus, and a ground electrode on the forehead. Stimulus protocols are designed to discriminate rod and cone function – the rod-specific response is obtained under dark adaptation (DA) using a dim white flash and consists of a positive-going b-wave arising in the on-bipolar cells of the inner nuclear layer. A bright white flash under DA then gives a mixed rod–cone response (dominated by rods) with a large negative-going a-wave, the first ~8 ms of which reflects photoreceptor function; the oscillatory potentials (small wavelets superimposed on the ascending limb of the b-wave) arise from the amacrine cells but have limited clinical value. After restoration of photopic

conditions, cone function is recorded using both a 30-Hz flicker stimulus and single white flashes, both superimposed upon a rod-saturating background.

3. *Key points*: rod–cone dystrophies (e.g. retinitis pigmentosa) show severely decreased rod b-wave amplitude with reduction in the mixed-response a-wave confirming photoreceptor disease. Cone ERGs are less severely affected but characteristically show both delay and amplitude reduction. A delay suggests generalised cone dysfunction. In cone–rod dystrophies, the cone ERGs are more affected than the rod ERGs. Inner retinal (post-transductional) dysfunction, such as X-linked retinoschisis or most forms of congenital stationary night blindness, shows an electronegative ERG in which the rod-specific ERG is subnormal, but there is preservation of the photoreceptor-derived mixed response a-wave with selective b-wave reduction such that the a-wave is larger than the b-wave. This is known as a 'negative' ERG because the waveform is dominated by the negative a-wave, and indicates dysfunction post-transduction.

Multifocal electroretinogram

1. *Indications*: assessing spatial function of central retinal cones.
2. *Method*: multiple hexagons which flash on and off are presented on a monitor according to a pseudorandom binary sequence. The ERG waveforms are produced by a cross-correlation technique that mathematically generates the individual responses to each of the individual hexagons.
3. *Key points*: highly dependent upon accurate fixation by the patient. May have some use in focal macular disease, i.e. where the PERG can be relatively normal.

Electro-oculogram

1. *Indications*: diagnosis of bestrophin mutations, e.g. Best's vitelliform macular dystrophy, autosomal recessive bestrophinopathy (ARB), autosomal dominant vitreoretinal choroidopathy (ADVIRC) and acute zonal occult outer retinopathy (AZOOR).
2. *Method*: electrodes are placed at the lateral and medial canthi with a ground on the forehead. The cornea is positive relative to the retina so when the patient looks left to right between two fixed targets, a potential difference is recorded between the inner and outer canthal electrodes. The amplitude of the potential reaches a minimum under DA (the dark trough) and a maximum during restoration of photopic conditions (the light peak). The ratio of the light peak to the dark trough is known as the Arden index, and is usually >180% in normals.
3. *Key points*: the response is generated by the interaction between the retinal pigment epithelium (RPE) and the retina.

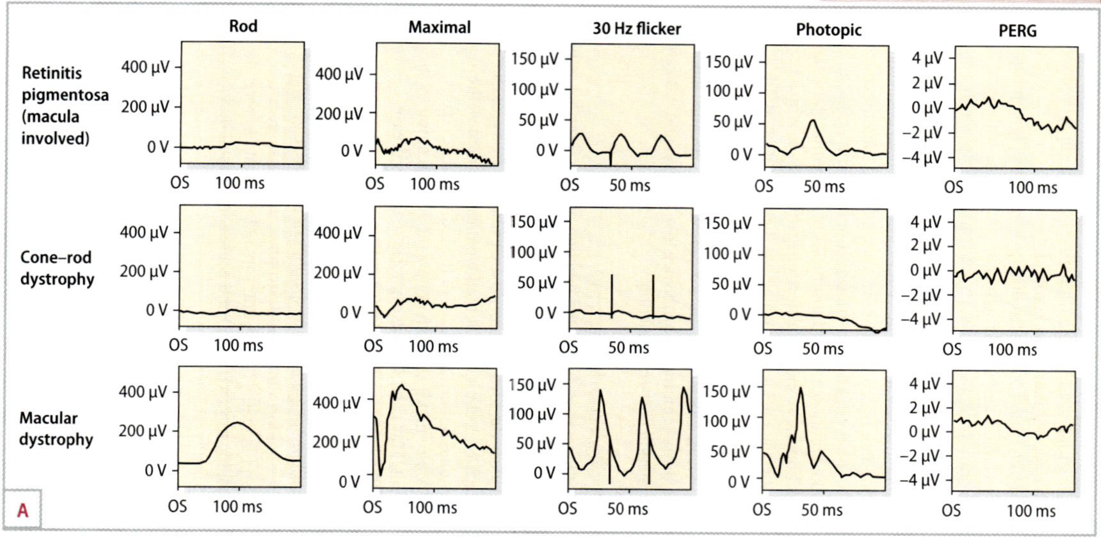

Fig. 11.19: Electroretinogram tracings. PERG, pattern electroretinogram.

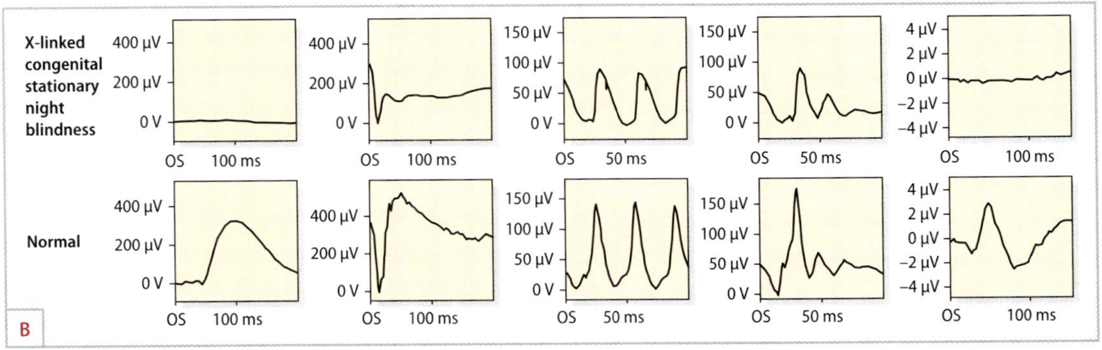

Fig. 11.19: *Continued*

The degree of electro-oculogram (EOG) light rise reduction is often related to the degree of rod ERG abnormality, but in Best's disease there is a normal ERG but severe reduction in the EOG light rise.

Visually-evoked potential

1. *Indications*: these include: optic nerve disease; albinism; to assess visual potential in patients with media opacity; estimation of visual function in conjunction with ERG in infants and children; non-organic vision loss.
2. *Method*: active electrodes are placed in the occipital areas. The reference may be mid-frontal, or the ipsilateral sylvian area. The stimulus is a flash and either pattern appearance or pattern reversal. The waveform is recorded monocularly. The normal pattern reversal response has a prominent major positive component at ~100 ms (P100).
3. *Key points*:
   a. *Demyelination*: shows a delayed reversal P100, with less effect on amplitude and waveform.
   b. *Non-arteritic anterior ischaemic optic neuropathy*: more commonly shows amplitude reduction with less effect on peak time.
   c. *Albinism*: associated with misrouting of fibres in the optic chiasm so that there is a contralateral predominance in pattern appearance VEP such that the largest and earliest response from both right and left eyes occurs over the contralateral hemisphere.
   d. *Media opacities*: flash VEP is usually minimally affected, and so may be useful in detecting underlying maculopathy or optic neuropathy.
   e. *Cautionary note*: macular disease also causes pattern VEP delay, and a delayed pattern VEP in itself should never be assumed to reflect isolated optic nerve disease unless there has been a measure of macular function obtained with multifocal electroretinogram (mfERG) or preferably PERG.

RETINAL LASER GUIDELINES

General points

- Confirm the eye, name and date of birth.
- Test the laser before bringing the patient into the room.
- There are many retinal laser lenses available, each producing a different retinal spot size. For example, selecting 100 μm on the laser produces the following spot size on the retina:
  - Volk Area Centralis: 100 μm (magnification factor ×1)
  - Volk TransEquator: 143 μm (×1.43)
  - Volk SuperQuad: 200 μm (×2)
- In general, macular laser requires smaller spots, shorter duration and lighter spots than peripheral laser.
- For macular treatment use a 100 μm retinal spot size, e.g. Area Centralis with laser set to 100 μm.
- For peripheral retinal laser use a TransEquator, QuadrAspheric, SuperQuad, or similar lens, and adjust the laser as needed to give a 400–500 μm retinal spot size.
- Identify the foveal centre using a fluorescein or OCT angiogram if available, or otherwise OCT and fundus photograph. Alternatively, use funduscopy and a fixation target prior to entering the laser room. Ensure that the patient understands not to subsequently look at the laser aiming beam during treatment, to avoid inadvertent foveal laser.
- Have the OCT and/or fluorescein angiogram visible to guide treatment. The fundus lenses invert the view so consider doing likewise to the OCT/angiogram to maintain alignment.
- Ensure the patient is comfortable, understands your instructions and is able to stay still for the duration of treatment. Explain how to signal pain or a need to pause treatment without moving their head/eye, e.g. a finger tap.
- Adjust the patient's seat and chin rest and your seat height, ensure you have elbow support, and reduce room light before applying the lens on the eye with a coupling agent (e.g. Viscotears). Avoid bubbles in the contact fluid. Place the slit-lamp column centrally and adjust illumination to give a comfortable 3D view of the retina. Adjust the patient's gaze for peripheral treatment.
- Modern multispot lasers use much shorter duration spots than 'standard' lasers, but require more power to achieve a similar fluence. They give faster treatment, less discomfort, and greater precision. However, the effective burn size is smaller so more burns and denser packing may be required to treat a similar area.

- Titrate power based on brightness of the laser spot, well clear of the foveal centre.
- Reduce power when treating pigmented fundi. Laser uptake may increase in the more peripheral retina, so titrate as needed.
- Treatment is more uncomfortable with standard laser, in the far periphery, the horizontal meridia, over previous laser scars or pigmentation, and in very lightly pigmented eyes.
- Shorter duration standard burns (0.05 seconds) are more comfortable. Longer burns (0.1–0.2 seconds) are more effective and less likely to rupture Bruch's membrane
- For subthreshold/micropulse laser select 200 ms, comprising 100 envelopes each with a duty cycle of 5% on and 95% off (for tissue cooling). Increase power until the spot is just visible, and then halve power. The evidence for the efficacy of subthreshold laser in common retinal diseases is evolving.
- Topical anaesthesia is usually adequate, but occasionally patients require peribulbar or sub-Tenon's anaesthetic for akinesia or analgesia, e.g. perifoveal treatment in a young, mobile patient. Macular treatments cannot be performed under general anaesthesia, but peripheral retinal laser can be performed using an indirect laser system.
- The laser wavelength varies with device. Those in the green spectrum are common, e.g. 532 nm. Green laser is attenuated by nuclear sclerosis and absorbed by luteal pigment, which intensifies foveal treatment (yellow laser may be preferable).
- For the treatment of retinal breaks (retinopexy), see page 634. Other common laser treatments are given below.

Macular grid laser

- *Indications*: Non-central macular oedema, particularly in diabetics, or following branch retinal vein occlusion.
- *Consent*: Benefit – improved visual prognosis; to avoid or reduce intravitreal injections in people unable or unwilling to have them. Risks – vary with the indication for treatment but may include: blindness from foveal burn; paracentral scotoma; altered colour vision; re-treatment; and subretinal neovascularisation.
- *Method*:
  1. See General Points, above.
  2. Select an Area Centralis lens (magnification factor × 1) or equivalent and set the laser to give a 100 μm retinal spot size (different lenses have different magnifications), and 0.05–0.1 seconds duration with standard lasers or 10 ms for multispot lasers. Although patterns can be used safely for macular treatments, single spot treatments are often

used. Some lasers adjust the true retinal spot size in the software interface, by inputting the lens type.

3. Test burn intensity and Bell's reflex (risk of foveal burn) using low-power burns (60 mW), near the temporal arcade.
4. Increase the power to give light-grey, just visible burns. More power is needed in areas of oedema. Typical power is 50–150 mW for a standard laser, 200–400 mW for multispot laser.
5. Avoid retinal haemorrhage, exudates, pigmentation, and scars. These produce variable laser absorption and more collateral damage. Avoid laser within the foveal avascular zone (FAZ).
6. Apply burns one burn width apart, over the area of oedema shown on the fluorescein angiogram or OCT. For diffuse leakage, use a grid pattern (**Fig. 11.20**). For circinate leakage, treat within the circinate. In modified grid laser, microaneurysms are targeted together with the grid coverage.
7. For more specific protocols see the sections on individual diseases.

- Follow-up: Usually 3–4 months.

Panretinal photocoagulation (PRP)

- *Indications*: Iris, angle, retinal, or optic disc neovascularisation secondary to retinal ischaemia, most commonly from proliferative diabetic retinopathy, following retinal vein occlusion or ocular ischaemic syndrome.

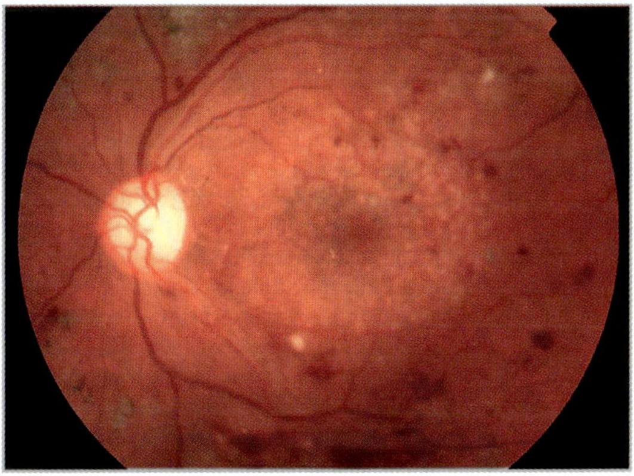

Fig. 11.20: Macular grid laser for diffuse macular oedema.

- *Consent*: Benefit – reduced risk of visual loss; reduced risk of blind painful eye from neovascular glaucoma if widespread retinal ischaemia. Risks – reduced vision including blindness from foveal burn; reduced night vision; macular oedema; glare; reduced accommodation; choroidal neovascularisation; re-treatment. Carefully explain that panretinal photocoagulation (PRP) aims to preserve not improve VA, and it can reduce peripheral vision which may affect a patient's legal entitlement to drive.
- *Method*:
  1. See General Points, above.
  2. Consider giving oral analgesics 30 minutes beforehand.
  3. Set laser to 250 μm with a SuperQuad lens or equivalent, to produce a 400–500 μm retinal spot size.
  4. Aim to produce a moderate-intensity, grey-white colour spot by slowly increasing the power.
  5. *Standard laser setting*: Select single shot (one shot each time the foot pedal is depressed) and 20–30 ms duration. Titrate the power (typically 100–300 mW) to desired spot intensity. Thereafter use repeat mode (shots continue whilst foot peddle is depressed), with ~300 ms interval between shots.
  6. *Multispot laser settings*: Select 20–30 ms with a distance between spots of 0.7–1.0 × spot size. Titrate power (typically 300–1200 mW) with single spots then try a 3 × 3 or 4 × 4 pattern.
  7. If possible start inferiorly, covering the retina with evenly spaced burns, about one burn width apart (**Fig. 11.21**). Spots that are too close risks a confluent lesion and vision loss, as lesion size increases long-term.
  8. Apply 2–3 treatment sessions of ~600–800 burns each, 1–2 weeks apart, aiming for a total of 1,600–2,000 burns. If there is iris neovascularisation, complete full treatment within days. Multispot lasers produce smaller burns closer together, hence a greater number of spots are usually applied (often 3,000+).
  9. Complete each quadrant in turn. This makes subsequent treatment easier and less painful.
  10. Many clinicians avoid any treatment within the temporal arcades during the initial treatments. Do not treat within two disc diameters of the foveal centre. Avoid treating larger retinal vessels or the posterior ciliary nerves directly. Angiography may guide how close temporally to treat.
  11. To preserve temporal visual field, avoid treating within 2–3 disc diameters nasal to the disc. Sometimes, this area is subsequently treated to control neovascularisation

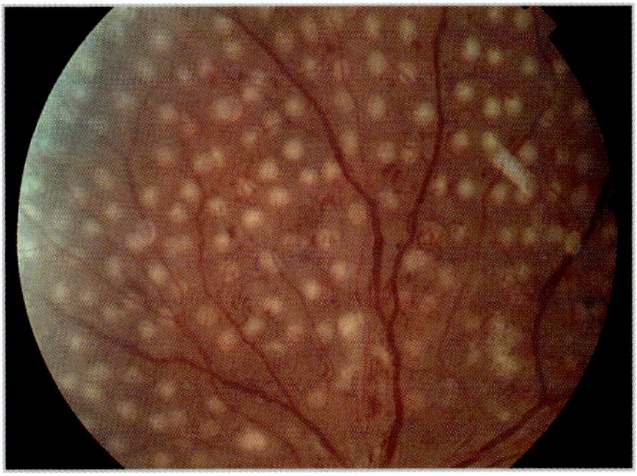

Fig. 11.21: Panretinal photocoagulation.

but intravitreal anti-vascular endothelial growth factor (VEGF) agents can be used as an adjunct or alternative to additional laser in select cases.

12. Neovascularisation that fails to regress may have further 'fill-in PRP', intravitreal anti-VEGF injections, or vitrectomy. Refractory cases may require peripheral treatment with an indirect laser, but SuperQuad and TransEquator lenses usually facilitate very peripheral coverage.

- *Causes of pain during PRP*:
  1. Inadequate anaesthesia (add topical anaesthetics and consider pre-treatment with oral analgesic, e.g. paracetamol 30 minutes before).
  2. High power or long duration burns (turn down power but retain visible spots; the short-duration burns from multispot devices usually hurt less).
  3. Large number of burns (consider splitting treatment over more than one session).
  4. Focused on the choroid rather than the retina.
  5. Treatment over the long posterior ciliary nerves on the horizontal meridian.
  6. Peripheral treatment.
  7. Variable ocular pigmentation or media opacity causing variable laser uptake.
  8. Accidental treatment of previous laser burns, hence 'fill-in' top-up laser can hurt.
  9. Poor communication with patient.

Occasionally, indirect PRP under a local anaesthetic block is necessary.

- *Follow-up*: From a few days to 2 weeks, until PRP completed, then 4–8 weeks depending on the underlying disease. Confirm that neovascularisation has stopped, with regression or fibrosis of the fine fronds of advancing new vessels. Larger new vessels often persist. Consider fundus photography or OCT angiography to document regression or reactivation of new vessels, if they are within the device's field of view.

Laser for macroaneurysm

- *Indications*: Macular oedema or exudates caused by a leaking retinal arteriolar macroaneurysm.
- *Consent*: Benefit – improve or stabilise vision. Risks – blindness from foveal burn; paracentral scotomas; altered colour vision; failure to prevent leakage; re-treatment; subretinal neovascularisation. Offer a guarded prognosis if there is chronic (>3 months) macular oedema suggested by cyst formation, subfoveal pigmentation, fibrosis or exudates.
- *Investigations*: Perform fluorescein angiography, as some macroaneurysms bleed then stop leaking.
- *Method*:
  1. See General Points, above.
  2. Set the laser to 200 μm and use an Area Centralis lens (200 μm retinal spot size). Start with 60 mW and increase the intensity to produce grey burns.
  3. Treat around the macroaneurysm with a single confluent line.
  5. Consider grid treatment (technique above) in areas of retinal telangiectasia with persistent oedema. Consider intravitreal anti-VEGF treatment for persisting oedema after closure of the aneurysm – although this is not a conventional indication.
- *Follow-up*: 2 weeks after first treatment for possible direct treatment to the macroaneurysm (optional visit), then 2–3 months to consider repeating the macular grid.

Photodynamic therapy (PDT)

- *Indications*: Polypoidal choroidal vasculopathy (PCV), central serous chorioretinopathy (using ½ dose or ½ fluence), some ocular tumours, e.g. choroidal haemangioma, metastases and, very rarely, predominantly classic choroidal neovascularisation (CNV).
- *Contraindications*: Porphyria, sensitivity to verteporfin, and pregnancy. Liver dysfunction is a relative contraindication.

- *Consent*: Benefit – stable or improved vision in 75–95% of PCV cases. Risks – transient or permanent loss of vision; submacular haemorrhage; acute vision loss occurs in 1–4% (less with reduced fluence PDT); photosensitivity (avoid sunlight for 48 hours, wear protective clothing and sunglasses); injection site complications; back pain; re-treatment; and multiple fluorescein angiograms.
- *Method for standard fluence PDT*:
  1. Dilute verteporfin (6 mg/m^2 body surface area) in 5% dextrose.
  2. Administer intravenously at 3 mL/min over 10 minutes, using a syringe pump and in-line filter.
  3. Laser spot size for CNV = greatest linear dimension of the lesion angiographically (including contiguous blood, blocked fluorescence, or RPE detachment) + 1,000 μm. This gives a 500 μm treatment margin around the lesion.
  4. At 15 minutes post infusion initiation, centre the aiming beam over the lesion and activate the laser. The laser is a non-thermal diode and produces red light (689 nm) at an intensity of 800 J/sec or 600 mW/cm^2 for 1 minute and 23 seconds.
  5. Can use bilateral treatment, and multiple spots in a single treatment to cover multifocal disease or large lesions, but ovoid spot overlap in the central macula.
  6. For central serous chorioretinopathy use reduced fluence (300 mW/cm^2) or reduce dose (3 mg/m^2 over 8 minutes, followed by ICG-guided PDT 10 minutes from the start of infusion).
- *Follow-up*: 10–12 weeks, or earlier if the patient has symptoms. Re-treatment may be required.

DIFFERENTIAL DIAGNOSIS

Rubeosis iridis

- Retinal ischaemia, e.g. diabetes (p. 557), retinal vein occlusion (p. 569) (**Fig. 11.22**), Eales' disease (p. 591).
- Ocular ischaemic syndrome (p. 583), e.g. atherosclerotic carotid artery disease.
- Intraocular inflammation, e.g. Fuchs' heterochromic iridocyclitis (p. 405).
- Intraocular tumour (p. 475), e.g. melanoma (p. 482).
- Iris ischaemia (p. 583) or anterior segment ischaemia (rare).
- Iris vasculitis (rare).

Retinal neovascularisation

- Diabetes mellitus (p. 557) (**Fig. 11.23**).
- Retinal vein occlusion (p. 569).
- Sickle cell retinopathy (p. 588).
- Ocular ischaemic syndrome (p. 583).
- Retinopathy of prematurity (p. 682).
- Inflammation (p. 399), e.g. vasculitis (p. 410), posterior uveitis (p. 410), pars planitis (p. 407).
- Radiation retinopathy.
- Hypertension (p. 579).
- Familial exudative vitreoretinopathy (p. 656).
- Norrie's disease (p. 686).

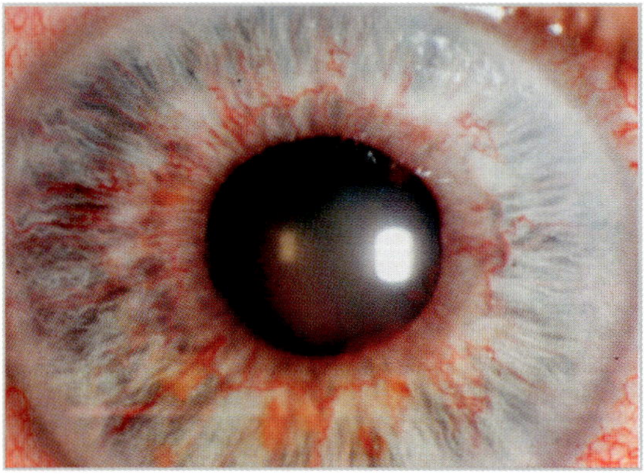

Fig. 11.22: Rubeosis iridis secondary to central retinal vein occlusion (Courtesy DH Verity).

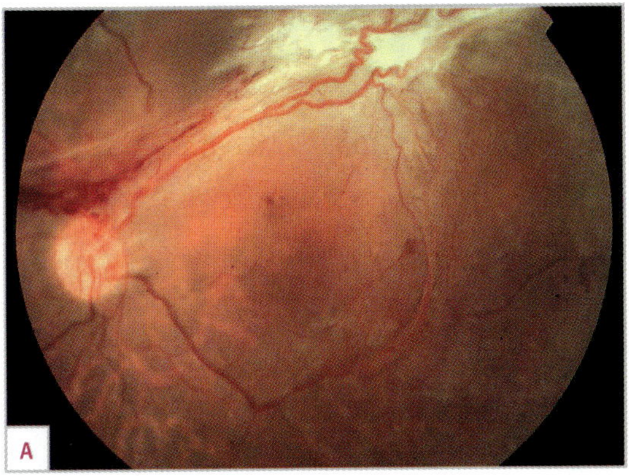

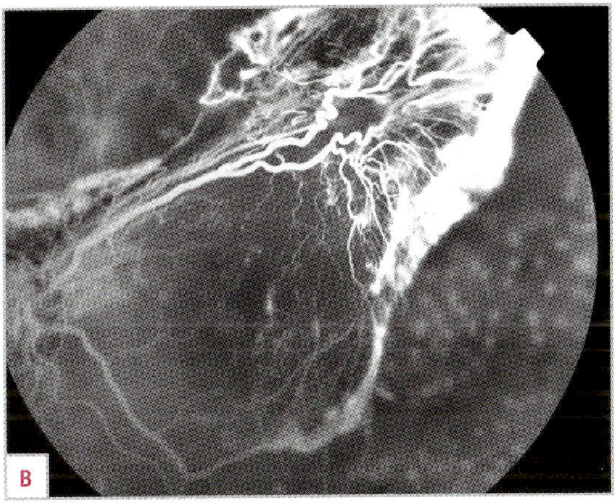

Fig. 11.23: Proliferative diabetic retinopathy.

- Eales' disease (p. 591).
- Hyperviscosity syndromes.
- Chronic retinal detachment (p. 636).
- Talc emboli (rare).

Intraretinal haemorrhage

- Diabetes mellitus (p. 557) (**Fig. 11.24**).
- Retinal vein occlusion (p. 569).
- Hypertension (p. 579).

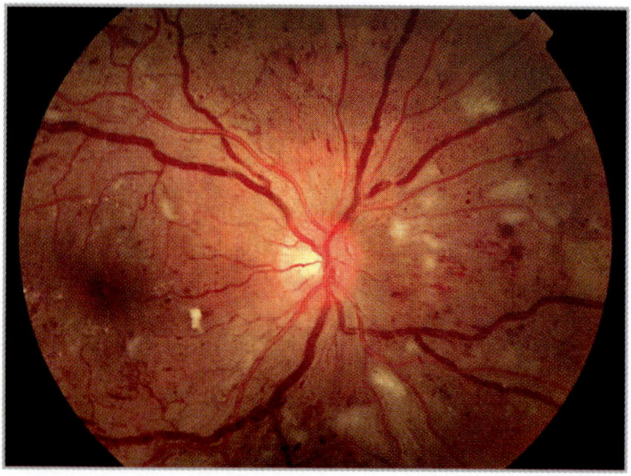

Fig. 11.24: Diabetic retinopathy.

- Subretinal disease, e.g. subretinal neovascularisation (p. 532), polypoidal choroidal vasculopathy (PCV) (p. 554), lacquer cracks in myopic degeneration (**Fig. 11.25**).
- Hyperviscosity syndrome, anaemia, blood malignancy.
- Associated with retinal ischaemia, e.g. sickle retinopathy (p. 588), Eales' disease (p. 591), ocular ischaemic syndrome (p. 583).
- Retinal arteriolar macroaneurysm (p. 581).
- Valsalva retinopathy (retinal haemorrhage caused by sudden increase in intra-abdominal pressure, e.g. coughing or vomiting, **Fig. 11.3**, p. 499).
- Retinal inflammation (p. 399), e.g. Behçet's disease (p. 422).
- Trauma (p. 661).
- Terson's syndrome (p. 651)
- Associated with infection, e.g. Roth's spots (p. 445).

Cotton wool spots (nerve fibre layer infarcts)

- Diabetes (p. 557).
- Retinal vein occlusion (p. 569).
- Hypertension (p. 579).
- Hyperviscosity syndrome, anaemia, haematologic malignancy.
- Sickle retinopathy (p. 588).
- Ocular ischaemic syndrome (p. 583), e.g. carotid stenosis.
- Infections including HIV microangiopathy (p. 449), bacteraemia (p. 459), fungaemia (p. 459), cat-scratch fever (p. 182).

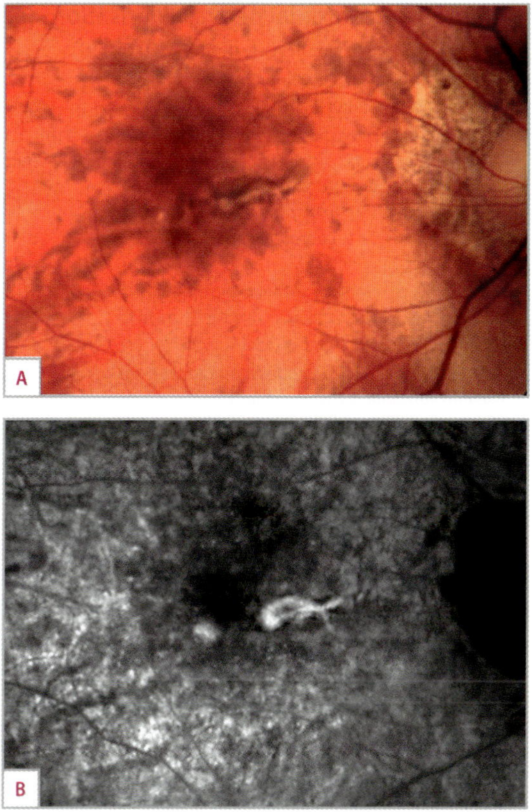

Fig. 11.25: Choroidal neovascularisation associated with a lacquer crack and high myopia.

- Drug reactions, e.g. interferon.
- Retinal arteriolar emboli (p. 576).
- Radiation retinopathy.
- Purtscher's retinopathy (thought to be due to fat microemboli from causes such as long bone fracture, compression fracture, surgery and pancreatitis).
- Other, e.g. SLE (p. 410), metastatic cancer (p. 480), Susac's syndrome (rare autoimmune microangiopathy associated with triad of CNS dysfunction, sensorineural hearing loss and branch retinal artery occlusion).

Subretinal choroidal neovascularisation

- Wet age-related macular degeneration (AMD) (p. 544).
- Polypoidal choroidal vasculopathy (p. 554).
- Myopic degeneration (**Fig. 11.25**).
- Postinflammatory or presumed postinflammatory (p. 410), e.g. presumed ocular histoplasmosis syndrome, punctate inner choroidopathy (p. 428), serpiginous retinopathy (p. 437), birdshot chorioretinopathy (p. 434).
- Trauma (p. 661), e.g. choroidal rupture (p. 662), photocoagulation (p. 524).
- Dystrophic, e.g. Sorsby's macular dystrophy (p. 611); Best's and adult-vitelliform macular dystrophy (p. 606).
- Optic nerve drusen (see **Fig. 15.19**, p. 777).
- Angioid streaks (p. 537) – most commonly from pseudoxanthoma elasticum (**Fig. 11.33**).

Retinal telangiectasia

- Diabetes (p. 557).
- Previous retinal vein occlusion (p. 569).
- Hypertension (p. 579).
- Sickle cell retinopathy (p. 588).
- Macular telangiectasia (MacTel, **Fig. 11.26**) and other idiopathic juxtafoveal telangiectasias (p. 585).
- Radiation retinopathy.
- Coats' disease (p. 679).
- Incontinentia pigmenti.
- Facioscapulohumeral muscular dystrophy (p. 816).

Retinal vascular tortuosity

- Retinal vein occlusion (p. 569).
- Epiretinal membrane (p. 643).
- Sickle cell disease (p. 588).
- Polycythaemia.
- Leukaemia.
- Dysproteinaemia.
- Hyperviscosity syndromes.
- Familial dysautonomia.
- Mucopolysaccharidosis VI.
- Fabry's disease.
- Eales' disease (p. 591).
- Racemose angioma (**Fig. 11.27**).
- Congenital

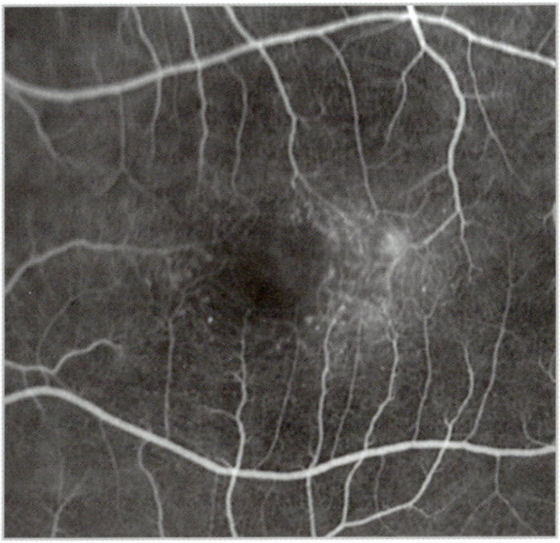

Fig. 11.26: MacTel (macular telangiectasia type 2).

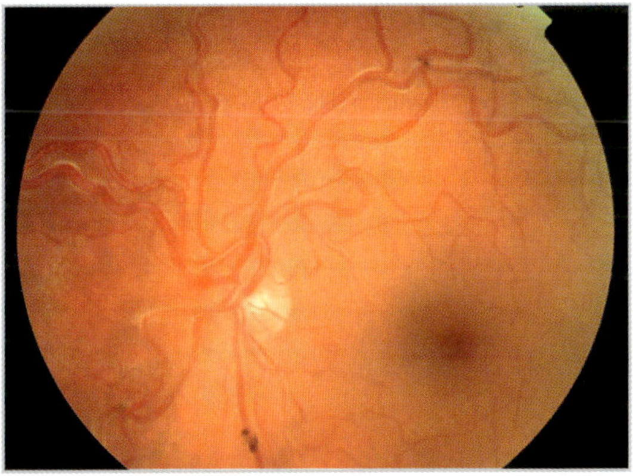

Fig. 11.27: Racemose angioma.

Retinal deposits

- *Exudates*: Diabetes (p. 557), hypertension (p. 579), macroaneurysm (p. 581), retinal vein occlusion (p. 569), vascular tumour (p. 479), and telangiectasia (Coats' disease) (p. 679).

- *Drusen*: AMD (p. 541, **Fig. 11.35**); basal laminar drusen (p. 542); dominant dystrophies (Doyne's macular dystrophy/ malattia leventinese; Sorsby's dystrophy; North Carolina macular dystrophy) (p. 611), and subretinal drusenoid deposits.
- *Crystals*: Macular telangiectasia type 2 (MacTel) (p. 585); talc emboli; tamoxifen; canthaxanthine; Bietti's crystalline retinopathy; West African crystalline maculopathy; oxalosis; cystinosis; chronic retinal detachment (p. 636).
- *White dots*: Multiple evanescent white dot syndrome (MEWDS) (p. 435); birdshot chorioretinopathy (p. 434); hereditary fundus albipunctatus (p. 598).
- *Flecks*: Stargardt's/fundus flavimaculatus (p. 610); pattern dystrophy (p. 609).
- *Yellow (vitelliform) lesions*: Best's macular dystrophy (p. 606); pattern dystrophy (adult vitelliform macular dystrophy form) (p. 609); pigment epithelial detachment (PED) from central serous chorioretinopathy (p. 594); AMD (p. 541); Vogt–Koyanagi–Harada's disease (p. 424) metastasis (p. 480).

Cherry-red spot at the macula

- Central retinal artery occlusion (**Fig. 11.28**) (p. 576).
- Sphingolipidoses, e.g. Tay-Sachs, Gaucher, and Niemann-Pick disease.
- Quinine toxicity.
- Traumatic retinal oedema (**Fig. 12.16**, p. 661).

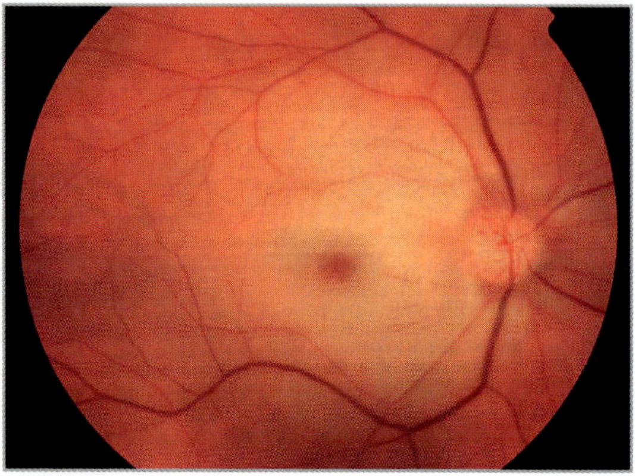

Fig. 11.28: Central retinal artery occlusion.

- Ocular ischaemic syndrome (p. 583).
- Macular hole with surrounding retinal detachment (**Fig. 12.10**, p. 649).

Macular oedema

- Diabetes mellitus (**Fig. 11.29**) (p. 560).
- Retinal vein occlusion (p. 569).
- Pseudophakic (Irvine–Gass syndrome) (p. 593).
- Subretinal neovascularisation, e.g. wet AMD (p. 541).
- Uveitis (p. 399).
- Posterior scleritis (p. 454).
- Hypertensive retinopathy (advanced) (p. 579).
- Epiretinal membrane (p. 643).
- Vitreomacular traction (p. 646).
- Choroidal ischaemia (p. 583).
- Retinitis pigmentosa (**Fig. 11.59**, p. 599).
- Optic disc pit (p. 653).
- Retinoschisis (p. 638).
- Vascular tumour (p. 479).
- Nicotinic acid (no leakage on fluorescein angiography).
- Sphingosine-1-phosphate (S1P) receptor modulators, e.g. fingolimod-associated macular edema (FAME) (p. 619)
- Macular telangiectasia (**Fig. 11.26**, p. 533) (p. 585).
- Ocular hypotony.
- Hereditary.
- Idiopathic.

Macular star

- Hypertension (**Fig. 11.30**) (p. 579).
- Retinal vein occlusion (p. 569).
- Papilloedema (p. 776).
- Inflammation (p. 399): Choroiditis (p. 428); posterior scleritis (p. 453); vasculitis; neuroretinitis (p. 441 and 443); toxoplasmosis (p. 438); chronic infection, e.g. syphilis (p. 420).
- Idiopathic.

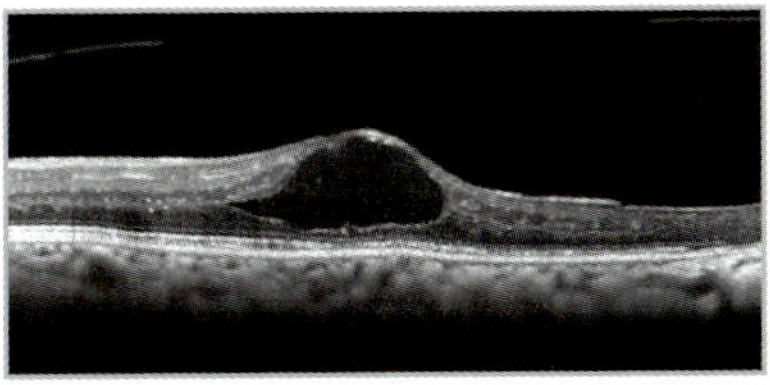

Fig. 11.29: Optical coherence tomography of diabetic macular oedema (Courtesy M Richardson).

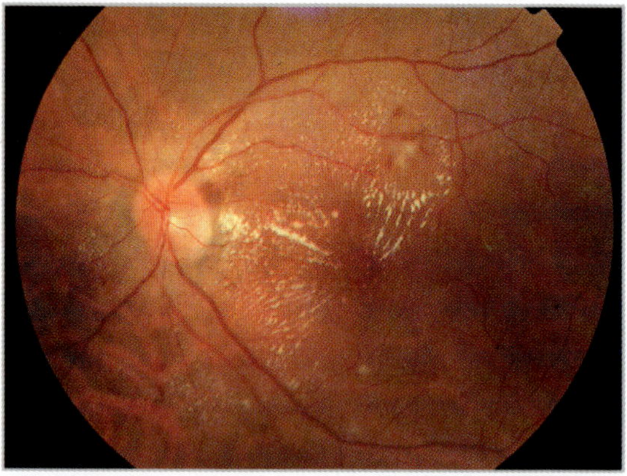

Fig. 11.30: Grade 3 hypertensive retinopathy with a macular star.

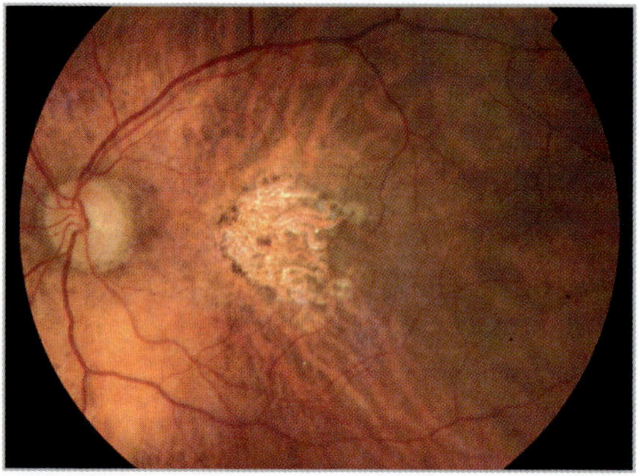

Fig. 11.31: Geographic atrophy from age-related macular degeneration.

Macular atrophy

- Geographic atrophy from late dry AMD (**Fig. 11.31**) (p. 543).
- Pathological myopia.
- Secondary to exudative process, e.g. after pigment epithelium detachment, subretinal haemorrhage, RPE rip, or active neovascularisation.
- Iatrogenic macular laser burn.
- Stargardt's disease (p. 610).

- Cone dystrophy (p. 602).
- Dominant retinal dystrophies, e.g. central areolar choroidal dystrophy (p. 611).
- A3243G mitochondrial mutation (maternally inherited diabetes and deafness) (p. 611).
- Best's vitelliform macular dystrophy (p. 606).
- Pattern dystrophy, e.g. adult vitelliform macular dystrophy (p. 609).
- X-linked retinoschisis (p. 656).
- North Carolina macular dystrophy (p. 611).
- Toxic, e.g. pentosan, chloroquine (p. 620).
- Infectious, e.g. onchocerciasis, late rubella.
- Solar retinopathy (p. 616).

Bull's eye maculopathy

- Macular, cone or cone/rod dystrophies (p. 598 and 602), e.g. Stargardt's disease (p. 610); PROM1 mutations; Bardet–Biedl syndrome (p. 599); Batten's disease (p. 600).
- Drug toxicity, e.g. chloroquine and hydroxychloroquine (**Fig. 11.32**) (p. 620).

Angioid streaks

- Pseudoxanthoma elasticum (**Fig. 11.33**).
- Paget's disease.

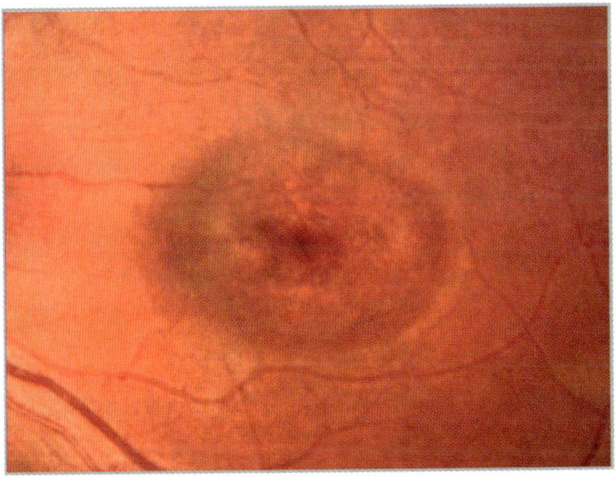

Fig. 11.32: Bull's eye maculopathy from hydroxychloroquine toxicity.

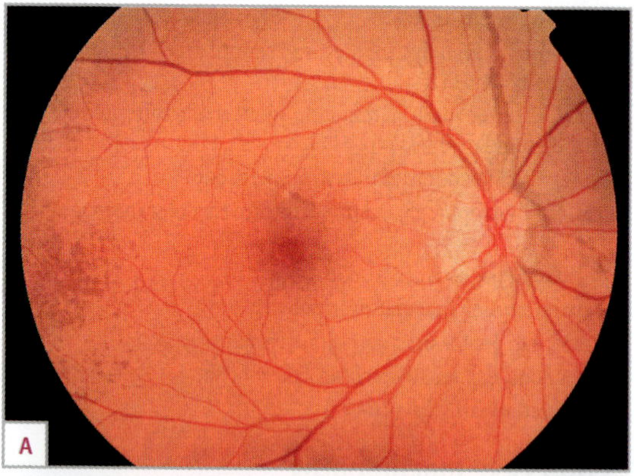

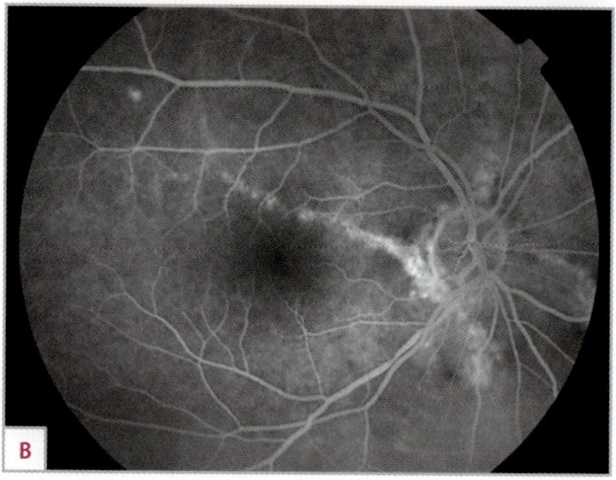

Fig. 11.33: Angioid streaks from pseudoxanthoma elasticum, with mottling temporal to the macula (peau d'orange).

- Haemoglobinopathies, e.g. Sickle cell disease (p. 588).
- Other rare associations, e.g. abetalipoproteinaemia (p. 599).

Choroidal folds

- Idiopathic chorioretinal folds or hypermetropia (**Fig. 11.34**).
- Hypotony.
- Retrobulbar mass lesions.
- Thyroid eye disease (p. 102).
- Scleritis (p. 453).

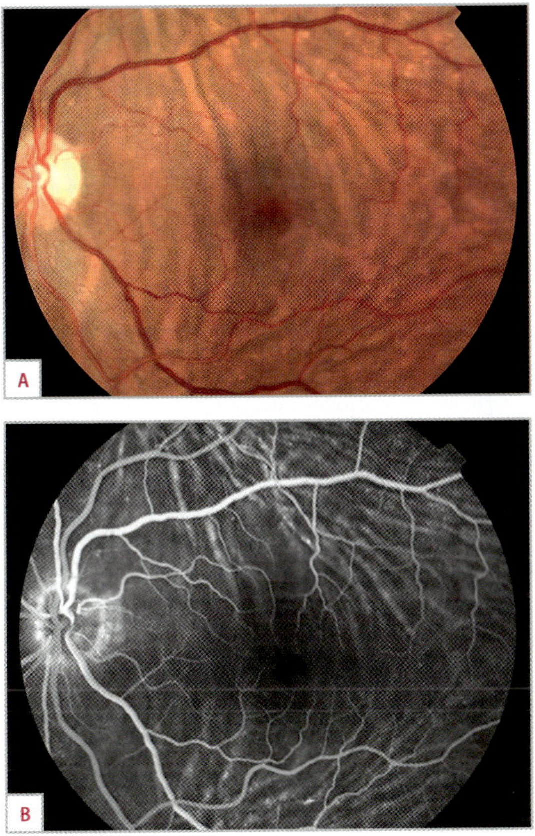

Fig. 11.34: Choroidal folds in a hypermetropic patient.

- Scleral buckle.
- Choroidal tumours (p. 482).
- Choroidal neovascularisation (p. 545).
- Focal chorioretinal scars.
- Optic nerve head diseases associated with swelling (p. 776).
- Papilloedema (p. 776).

Pigmentary retinopathy

See retinitis pigmentosa, page 598.

Vision loss with normal retina

- Exclude subtle abnormalities:
  1. Pale disc.
  2. Choroidal folds (**Fig. 11.34**).
  3. Retinal artery occlusion and emboli (p. 576).
  4. Angioid streaks (p. 537).
  5. Retinoschisis (p. 638).
  6. Albinism (p. 612).
  7. Macular atrophy (p. 536).
  8. Autoimmune phenomena.
  9. Old inflammatory lesions, including acute zonal occult outer retinopathy (AZOOR) (p. 436).
  10. History of malignancy – carcinoma-associated retinopathy (CAR) and melanoma-associated retinopathy (MAR).
- Amblyopia, which is common (p. 813)
- Optic nerve/visual pathway disease e.g. stroke, ischaemic optic neuropathy (p. 787-791), retrobulbar optic neuritis (p. 792), optic nerve trauma, infiltration and compression (p. 797), and nutritional (p. 799) and hereditary (p. 801) optic neuropathy.
- For transient vision loss (see p. 765).
- For medically unexplained vision loss (functional vision loss) see page 813 (adults) and p. 700 (children).

AGE-RELATED MACULAR DEGENERATION

Age-related macular degeneration (AMD) is a degenerative disorder and leading cause of severe sight impairment, affecting those ≥50 years (AREDS classification) or ≥55 years (Beckman classification).

Classification The underlying process is a 'dry' or non-exudative condition that can transition from early AMD to geographic atrophy (GA). This process may be complicated by exudative or 'wet' AMD in a minority of eyes. Exudative AMD can be non-neovascular, or neovascular AMD that features actively leaking choroidal neovascularisation (CNV). Classification systems vary, but generally a few (≤15) small drusen (<63 µm), and sub-retinal drusenoid deposits [reticular pseudodrusen, seen just above the retinal pigment epithelium (RPE)] do not define AMD but are part of a continuum. Early AMD has multiple small drusen, or a few intermediate drusen (63–124

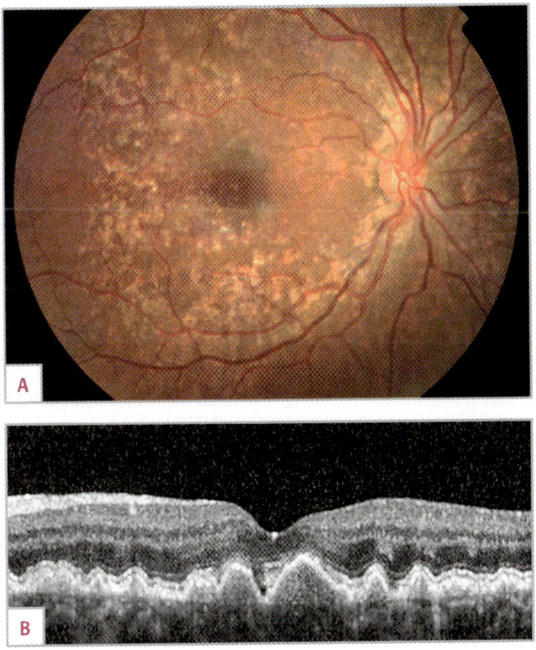

Fig. 11.35: (A) Retinal drusen (top). (B) optical coherence tomography of large central drusen in another patient (Courtesy R Leung).

μm), and/or pigmentary changes (macular hyperpigmentation or hypopigmentation). Intermediate AMD (**Fig. 11.35**) has extensive intermediate drusen, ≥1 large druse (≥125 μm, matching the size of a retinal vessel at the disc margin) or GA not involving the fovea. Advanced AMD has fovea-involving GA or CNV.

Early and intermediate age-related macular degeneration

Symptoms Usually asymptomatic, but a subgroup have issues with seeing in dim light or dark adaptation, prolonged after-images, or slight metamorphopsia may occur.

Differential diagnosis Inherited dominant drusen; basal laminar-type drusen/cuticular drusen (probably part of AMD spectrum); other causes of retinal flecks such as Stargardt's disease; pattern dystrophy; fundus albipunctate dystrophy; mesangiocapillary glomerulonephritis type II. Focal clumps of drusen may be secondary to any local disturbance of the RPE, e.g. naevus or pachychoroid.

Investigations Undertake OCT, and consider OCT angiography (OCTA) and/or fluorescein angiography if CNV is suspected. Consider fundus autofluorescence (AF) imaging if available, to help to define atrophy and exclude mimicking dystrophies.

Treatment

- *Stop smoking*: Current smokers are at higher risk of AMD than both past smokers and those who never smoked.
- *Dietary advice and antioxidant vitamin supplementation*: There is some evidence to support recommending a diet rich in lutein and zeaxanthin (green leafy vegetables ≥5 times weekly) or a 'Mediterranean diet', but no robust clinical trial data exist. In patients who have lost vision in one eye from neovascular AMD and have early AMD in the fellow eye, the Age-Related Eye Disease Study (AREDS) showed an antioxidant vitamin combination (500 mg vitamin C, 400 IU vitamin E, 15 mg β-carotene, 80 mg zinc, and 2 mg copper) has a ~25% protective effect to the fellow eye. Many ophthalmologists also place patients with bilateral intermediate and large drusen and no late AMD on AREDS vitamin supplementation, but the evidence is weaker. In smokers or ex-smokers use the AREDS2 formulation with β-carotene replaced by lutein and zeaxanthin that confers benefit, without increasing the risk of lung cancer associated with beta-carotene, or simply use AREDS2 for all. For a systematic review visit www.cochranelibrary.com.
- *Information*: Provide or refer to reliable AMD information, e.g. www.macularsociety.org; www.rcophth.ac.uk; and www.nhs.uk.

Follow-up Regular ophthalmic review is not required, but provide an Amsler grid and instructions to return urgently if the patient develops new macular symptoms suggesting CNV. Advise annual optometry review, ideally one with OCT.

Geographic atrophy

Symptoms GA produces a gradual loss of central vision or slight metamorphopsia. Extrafoveal GA may be asymptomatic.

Signs Sharply demarcated area(s) of GA that is pale relative to the surrounding retina, with increased visibility of underlying choroidal vessels (**Fig. 11.36**). Intermediate or large drusen are present in most eyes surrounding the GA, unless the atrophy is very extensive, when the drusen disappear.

Differential diagnosis Stargardt's disease, Best's macular dystrophy, rod–cone dystrophies, Sorsby's macular dystrophy, chronic central serous chorioretinopathy, basal laminar drusen, myopic macular degeneration, and drug toxicity, e.g. hydroxychloroquine.

Investigations OCT helps to exclude other diseases and shows atrophy of the outer retinal layers (**Fig. 11.37**), often labelled incomplete or complete RPE and outer retinal atrophy (iRORA/cRORA). The OCT near-infrared image (NIR) and AF help to quantify the GA area. Consider fluorescein angiography and/or OCTA if wet AMD is suspected.

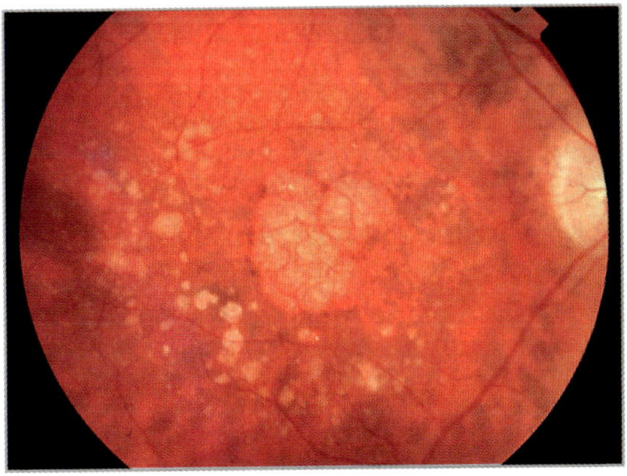

Fig. 11.36: Geographic atrophy.

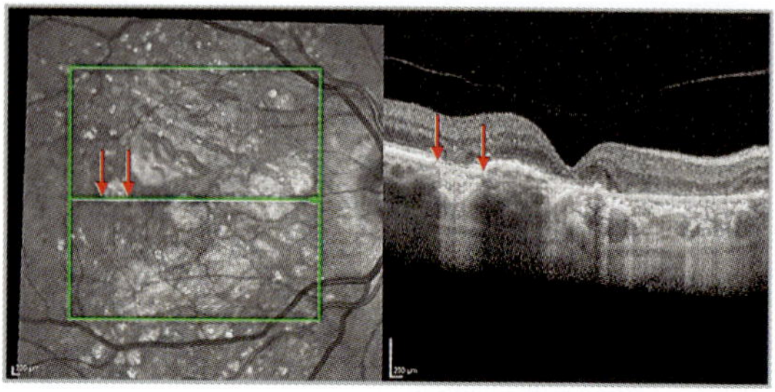

Fig. 11.37: The border of one area of geographic atrophy is shown by the red arrows on the near infrared image (left) and OCT, with associated hypertransmission of signal through to the choroid, seen as a white 'shadow'. A wider area of atrophy and hypertransmission is seen nasally along the same raster line (Courtesy R Leung).

Treatment See early AMD (above). Arrange low-vision aids if necessary. Explain that bilateral visual loss can be associated with visual hallucinations, ranging from simple flashes of lights or geometric patterns, to formed images of people or places (Charles Bonnet syndrome). Chronic intravitreal injections of pegcetacoplan and avacincaptad pegol target complement activation and both slowed GA enlargement in phase 3 studies, but neither showed an accompanying predefined vision benefit, with some concern they may promote conversion to wet AMD. Currently, they are licensed in the US but not in the EU. Consider AREDS vitamin supplements (see above), especially if there is wet AMD in one eye; some weak evidence (*post hoc* analyses) suggests AREDS supplements may reduce extrafoveal GA expansion.

Follow-up GA typically expands and this may reduce vision, but beware also the development of CNV, so provide an Amsler grid and instructions to return urgently if macular symptoms occur. Advise annual optometry review, ideally one with an OCT.

Neovascular age-related macular degeneration

Symptoms Typically, rapid (days or a few weeks) onset of visual loss, central blind spot or distortion. Uniocular, asymptomatic wet AMD may be picked up on routine eye testing, particularly if it involves the non-dominant eye.

Signs CNV may appear as a greenish-grey lesion, often with sensory retinal detachment. There may be surrounding drusen, pigment change, subretinal haemorrhage and exudates.

Differential diagnosis

- *Choroidal neovascularisation*: Other causes include myopia; central serous chorioretinopathy; angioid streaks; multifocal choroiditis; trauma; idiopathic; inherited dystrophies (Sorsby's).
- *Pigment epithelial detachment/serous detachments/vitelliform lesion*: Other causes include central serous chorioretinopathy; congenital optic nerve pit; genetic disorders (Best's disease or adult vitelliform dystrophy); macular hole with detachment; choroidal inflammatory disease; severe hypertension.
- *Age-related macular degeneration variants*: Polypoidal choroidal vasculopathy (PCV, p. 554); retinal angiomatous proliferation (RAP Stage I comprises intraretinal neovascularisation; progressing to Stage II, subretinal neovascularisation; then Stage III, CNV with a retinal-choroidal anastomosis).

Optical coherence tomography and OCT angiography

Perform OCT in all cases, and OCTA if necessary at baseline. On OCT, look for pigment epithelial detachment (PED), subretinal fluid (**Fig. 11.38**), intraretinal fluid and an outer retinal lesion

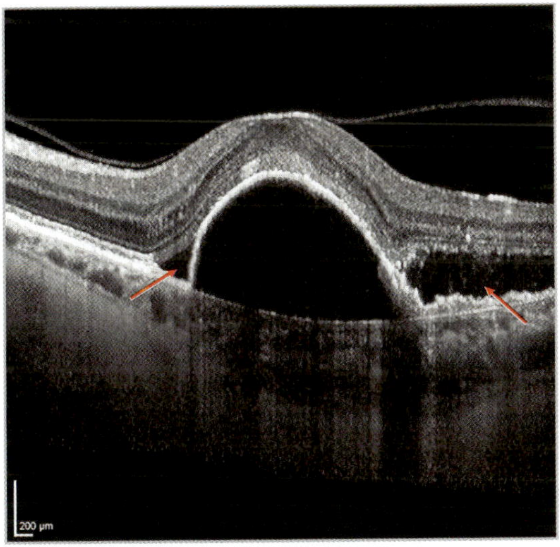

Fig. 11.38: OCT of a large central pigment epithelial detachment due to neovascular age-related macular degeneration, with bordering subretinal fluid shown by arrows (Courtesy R Leung).

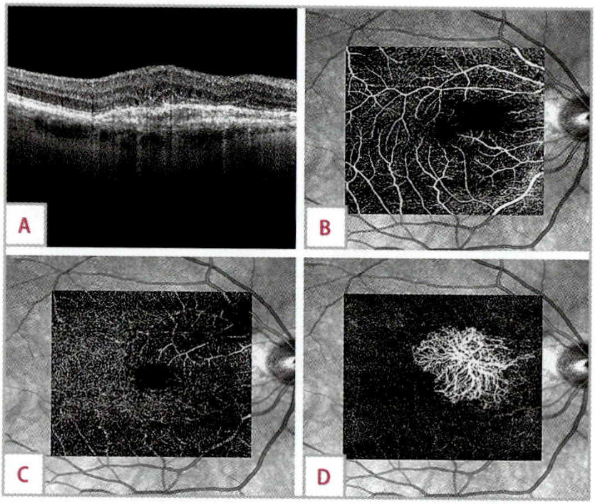

Fig. 11.39 Structural OCT with intraretinal fluid cysts (A). Superficial vascular complex (B), deep vascular complex (C) and avascular complex (D) seen on OCT angiogram, the latter with well-defined branching neovascularisation (Courtesy O Cundy).

compatible with CNV. On OCTA, CNV has vascular flow characteristics in the usually avascular outer retina slab avascular outer retina slab (**Fig. 11.39**).

Fluorescein angiography (FFA) Perform when angiography will not delay treatment, if it will exclude important differential diagnoses or if OCT ± OCTA are inconclusive. Consider indocyanine green (ICG) angiography, especially if PCV is suspected. When photodynamic therapy (PDT) was the standard of care for classic lesions (it is not now), FFA was also important to classify the disease as follows:

- *Classic CNV*: Early well-defined hyperfluorescence with late leak that obscures the boundaries (**Fig. 11.40**). May be 100% classic, predominantly classic (≥50% of lesion area), or minimally classic (<50%).
- *Occult CNV*: Hyperfluorescence is less well-defined (**Fig. 11.41**). Two commonly described subtypes are:
    1. *Fibrovascular PED*: An area of irregular RPE elevation that is less discrete than classic CNV in the transit phase and shows stippled hyperfluorescence in the mid-frames (1–2 minutes).
    2. *Late leakage of undetermined origin*: Pooling of dye and specked hyperfluorescence that occurs in the late frames.

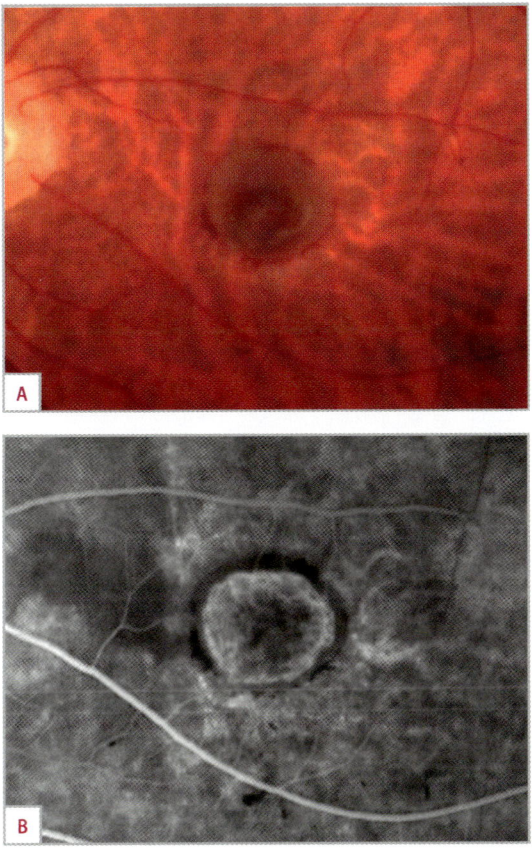

Fig. 11.40: Classic (100%) choroidal neovascularisation (A) and early angiogram (B).

- *Serous PED*: Sharply demarcated area of uniform hyperfluorescence that develops rapidly under the dome of the PED and persists late, with relatively sharp borders (**Fig. 11.42**). May be complicated by neovascularisation.
- *Disciform scar*: Late staining of fibrosis, with no leak beyond borders unless residual active membrane exists (**Fig. 11.43**).

Treatment See early AMD (p. 542) regarding AREDS vitamins, smoking advice and patient information. Arrange low vision aids

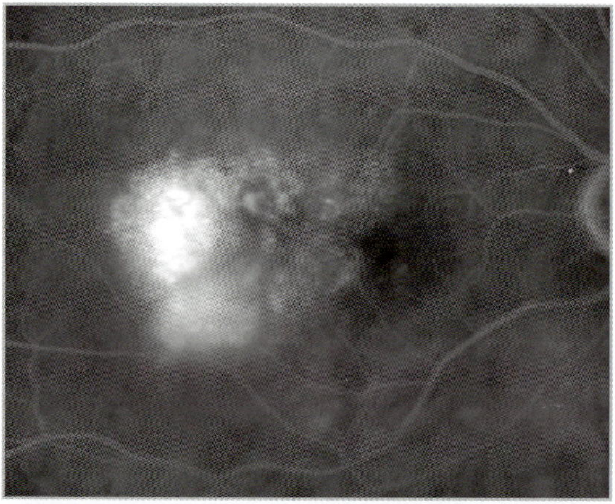

Fig. 11.41: Occult choroidal neovascular lesion.

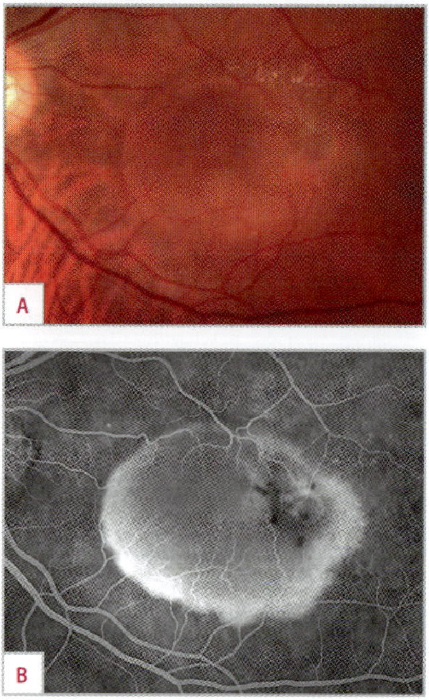

Fig. 11.42: Large pigment epithelial detachment, with associated superotemporal choroidal neovascularisation.

if necessary. If uniocular, warn of the fellow eye risk (10–15% per year) and provide an Amsler chart. Regular visits with VA, dilated fundus examination, OCT, and intravitreal anti-vascular endothelial growth factor (VEGF) drugs are the standard treatment, with significantly better vision versus natural history.

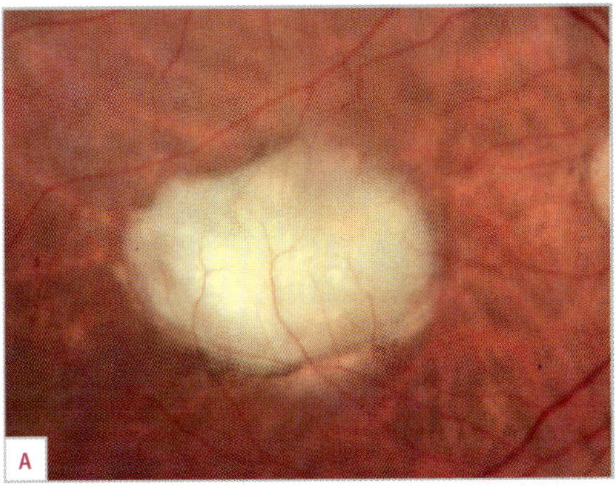

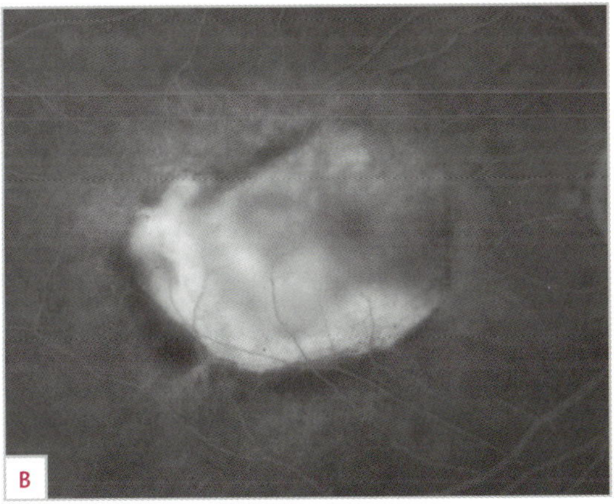

Fig. 11.43: Longstanding disciform scar, photograph (A) and fluorescein angiogram (B; Courtesy J Wong). OCT in another patient (C) shows a hyperintense area corresponding to subretinal disciform fibrosis, with overlying intraretinal fluid cysts (Courtesy O Cundy). *Continues overleaf*

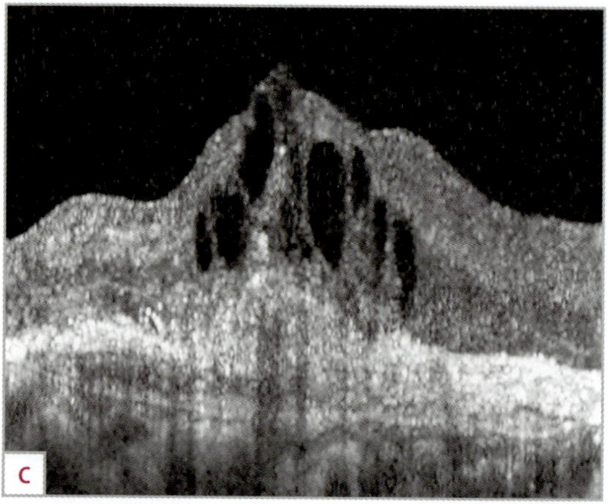

Fig. 11.43: *Continued*

Provide written information, collect written consent, help the patient decide which of the available drugs is best for them and revisit the options over time. See **Box 11.1** for the injection technique and risks.

The most commonly used drugs are detailed below, with dosing based mainly on their marketing authorisations, which often change over time, so check for updates, e.g. search ranibizumab Summary of Product Characteristics (SmPC), or visit www.medicines.org.uk/emc or www.ema.europa.eu.

- Ranibizumab 0.5 mg
    1. *Consent*: The MARINA study of monthly ranibizumab (Lucentis) for minimally classic or occult lesions showed 5% (treated) versus 38% (sham injection) moderate vision loss (>15 letters on ETDRS chart) at 1 year. The ANCHOR study of predominantly classic lesions showed 4% (treated) versus 36% (photodynamic therapy) moderate vision loss. The CATT trial found that regular monthly ranibizumab produces slightly better vision than monthly p.r.n. (2.2 letters difference at 2 years). Safety was generally favourable across all trials.
    2. *Follow-up*: Inject monthly until maximum stable VA is achieved and/or there are no signs of disease activity (haemorrhage or OCT fluid). Thereafter, two dosing regimens exist: (1) With p.r.n. dosing follow-up is typically at ~1-month intervals (but up to 3 months if very stable) with dosing at any visit where disease activity is present;

Box 11.1: Intravitreal injection (and anterior chamber paracentesis)

- *Consent*: Explain the procedure and the use of a covering drape. Risks include mild surface irritation (expected), conjunctival haemorrhage (common), vitreous floaters (common), corneal abrasion and pain, raised IOP, traumatic cataract, inflammation, retinal detachment (<1%), uveitis (<1%) and endophthalmitis (<0.1%). A theoretical small risk of stroke and myocardial infarction with anti-VEGF drugs is debated. Intravitreal steroids have a greater risk of cataract, raised IOP, and secondary glaucoma. For use in pregnancy see page 840. Explain that occasionally IOP-lowering medication is needed, or anterior chamber (AC) paracentesis (<1%).
- Confirm the patient's name and date of birth, laterality, drug selection, expiry date and any allergies including iodine. Before preparing for injection instil an anaesthetic eye drop and once this has worked, a drop of povidone iodine 5% (available in Minims), to maximise dwell time.
- For iodine allergy or sensitivity topical aqueous chlorhexidine 0.05% or 0.1% is available off-label for eye use. Avoid the chlorhexidine used to scrub, as it may contain alcohol and/or detergents.
- In sequence, use mask, sterile gloves, multiple anaesthetic drops, povidone iodine 5% to periocular skin, eyelid and conjunctival sac with a least 30 seconds' dwell time, dry the skin, drape then eyelid speculum.
- Use a filtered drawing-up needle to draw-up all the drugs into a 1-mL syringe, or select a preloaded syringe.
- Attach a 30-gauge needle, remove air bubbles and charge needle to the correct volume.
- Ask the patient to direct their gaze to expose the preferred injection site. Some advocate superior sites to avoid tear film debris and the risk of infection, but it depends on access.
- Instil an anaesthetic drop over the injection site, mark with a caliper (4 mm from the limbus if phakic, 3.5 mm if aphakic or pseudophakic), then add a final povidone iodine drop at the marked site (iodine will pool in the spot where the caliper pressed on the globe, confirming where to inject).
- Displace the conjunctiva slightly so that the conjunctival and scleral entries are not aligned, then aim the needle towards the optic disc to avoid the lens. Avoid contacting the eye lashes.
- Inject 0.05 mL (0.07 mL for Elyea HD) via the pars plana.
- Confirm hand motions or count fingers vision and if absent check for a central retinal artery occlusion (CRAO) with an indirect ophthalmoscope and 20D lens.
- Advise patients to immediately report any symptoms suggestive of endophthalmitis or retinal detachment.

Anterior chamber paracentesis

- Loss of vision and a collapsed central retinal artery at the disc indicates CRAO from raised IOP. AC paracentesis aims to remove fluid and promptly normalise IOP.

Box 11.1: *Continued*

- Maintain sterility.
- Request a pair of toothed forceps (e.g. St Martins) and an insulin syringe with inbuilt needle (use a 1-mL syringe with a short 30-gauge needle otherwise). Fully remove the plunger from the barrel. Partly remove the needle cap and use this to bend the needle ~45°, bevel up.
- Recheck the vision and if it is improving recheck the central retinal artery, as CRAO sometimes settles, often via a phase of pulsatile opening/collapse. If abandoning AC paracentesis, check IOP and if high give stat topical therapy, e.g. apraclonidine 1% plus Cosopt. If >35 mmHg add crushed acetazolamide 250 mg. Confirm IOP has settled before discharge.
- Secure the globe with the forceps.
- Insert the needle at the limbus aiming about ~30° tangential to the pupil centre. Keep flat in the iris plane but anterior to it, to avoid contact, noting the AC shallows as aqueous exits.
- As soon as the needle enters the AC look for aqueous filling the barrel, and then stop advancing. Maintain position until 0.05 mL fills the barrel, then withdraw the needle from the eye.
- Check IOP.
- Prescribe G. chloramphenicol q.d.s. for 1 week.
- Follow-up as usual, but in the absence of an obvious cause (e.g. mistakenly increased injection volume, pre-existing high IOP, ocular ischaemic syndrome) consider if any investigations are needed to exclude a compromised retinal artery (p. 583), e.g. digital ophthalmodynamometry (p. 570) at the next visit.

(2) With treat-and-extend (T&E) an injection is given at each visit but the visit interval is varied, e.g. increase by 1–2 weeks each visit without activity, up to 3 months, but reduce the interval (minimum 1 month) if fluid recurs. Many practitioners favour T&E, as this seems to have good real-world outcomes.

- Aflibercept 2 mg
  1. *Consent*: The VIEW trials showed that aflibercept (Eylea) given as three 1-monthly loading doses and then 2-monthly was non-inferior to monthly ranibizumab at 1 year. Risks were similar to ranibizumab.
  2. *Follow-up*: Inject monthly for 3 months then move to 2-monthly dosing. Based on visual and/or anatomic outcomes, maintain 2-monthly dosing or T&E, increasing in 2- or 4-weekly increments to maintain stable visual/anatomic outcomes (maximum interval 4 months). If deteriorating, shorten the dosing interval to a minimum of 1 month.

- Aflibercept 8 mg
  1. Eylea HD uses a higher concentration (114.3 mg/mL) and injection volume (0.07 mL), to deliver an 8 mg dose.
  2. *Consent*: The PULSAR trial showed that aflibercept 8 mg dosed variably up to 4-monthly was non-inferior to 2-monthly aflibercept 2 mg, with similar risks.
  3. *Follow-up*: Inject monthly for 3 months then T&E in up to 4-week increments to maintain stable visual/anatomic outcomes. The maximum interval is 5 months and the minimum 2 months.
- Bevacizumab 1.25 mg
  1. *Consent*: CATT found similar efficacy to ranibizumab. A 2019 Cochrane review reported similar vision outcomes to ranibizumab, and no significant difference in serious ocular adverse events at 1 year. Versus ranibizumab there was a trend for more serious adverse events due to mostly extraocular causes at year 1 (18% vs. 16%), that was significant at year 2 (36% vs. 30%). At year 2, there were more gastrointestinal adverse events but no significant difference in stroke, myocardial infarction, or transient ischaemic attack, and all-cause mortality was similar (6% vs. 5%). Explain possible concerns about inflammation/infection outbreaks related to third party 'compounding' of bevacizumab vials into aliquots designed for eye use and that treatment is off-label, or use bevacizumab licensed for neovascular AMD (Lytenava).
  2. *Follow-up*: Retreat and review as for ranibizumab.
- Faricimab 6 mg
  1. *Consent*: Faricimab is a bispecific molecule targeting VEGF and angiopoietin-2. At 1 year, the TENAYA and LUCERNE studies found faricimab 6 mg (Vabysmo) dosed variably up to 4-monthly was non-inferior to aflibercept 2 mg dosed 2-monthly, with similar safety.
  2. *Follow-up*: Inject monthly until disease is controlled, typically about 3 doses, then T&E in up to 4-week increments and 8-week reductions based on visual/anatomic outcomes. The maximum interval is 4 months and the minimum 21 days.

POLYPOIDAL CHOROIDAL VASCULOPATHY

Background Polypoidal choroidal vasculopathy (PCV), also called idiopathic polypoidal choroidal vasculopathy (IPCV) or aneurysmal type-1 neovascularisation, may complicate age-related macular degeneration (AMD), or occur independently.

Clinical features Originally described in hypertensive, black women aged 40–60 years with exudative retinal elevation, orange/red nodules due to haemorrhagic pigment epithelial detachments (PEDs), and hard exudates. Also more common in East Asians versus white populations. Unlike typical wet AMD, it often occurs beyond the arcades or near the optic disc. It may have a similar presentation to central serous chorioretinopathy.

Investigations Optical coherence tomography (OCT) features (**Fig. 11.44**) may suggest the presence of polypoidal lesions that are mainly below the retinal pigment epithelium (RPE), with multilobulated PEDs, some of which may have an internal reflective ovoid structure assumed to represent the polyp. A shallow double layer sign (separation of RPE and Bruch's membrane) can represent the branching vascular network. If the clinical and OCT features suggest PCV, perform indocyanine green (ICG) angiography, which shows characteristic collections of dilated choroidal vessels with terminal dilatations (polyps) that leak in the later frames (**Fig. 11.45**), best defined on SLO video angiography, if available.

Treatment The EVEREST II study in Asian participants showed ranibizumab p.r.n. plus photodynamic therapy (PDT) produced superior vision and polyp resolution versus ranibizumab p.r.n. monotherapy. Hence, treat with intravitreal

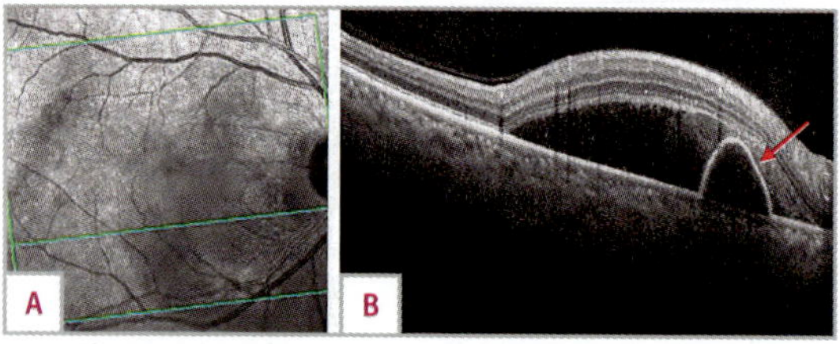

Fig. 11.44: OCT of polypoidal choroidal vasculopathy with non-central subretinal fluid and red arrow showing serous pigment epithelial elevation (Courtesy O Cundy).

anti-vascular endothelial growth factor (VEGF) drugs as for neovascular AMD (p. 544), often with a treat-and-extend regimen, aiming to eliminate fluid and reduce PED height, but also consider PDT laser to help close the polyp. EVEREST II and PLANET studies found that achieving a dry retina on OCT is associated with better vision, and may be a more important anatomic endpoint than polyp closure on ICG angiography.

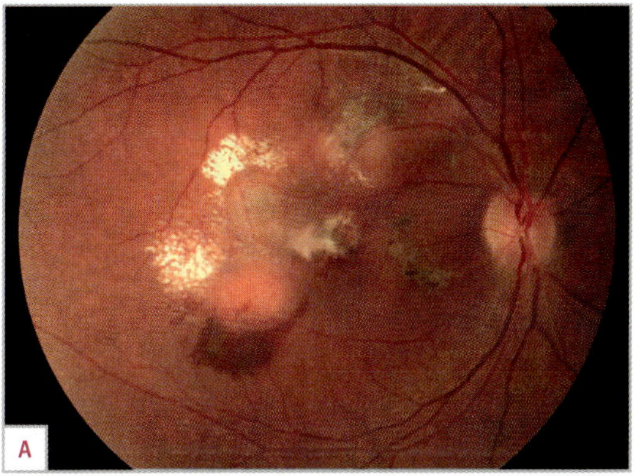

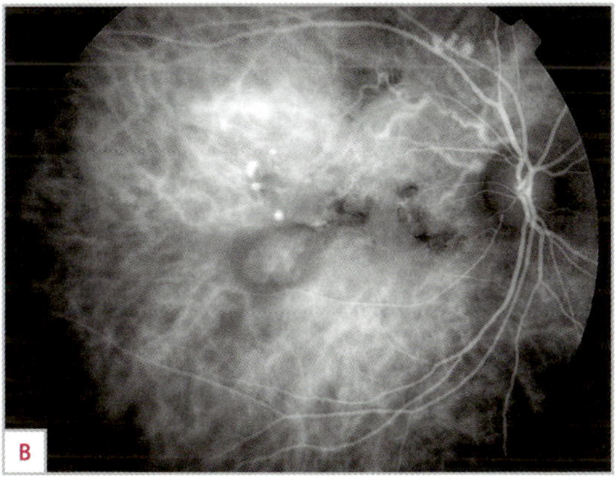

Fig. 11.45: Polypoidal choroidal vasculopathy. The fundus shows haemorrhagic pigment epithelial detachment, hard exudates, and serous retinal elevation (A). Indocyanine green angiography (B) shows saccular vessel dilatations and leakage, not easily seen with fluorescein angiography (C). *Continues opposite*

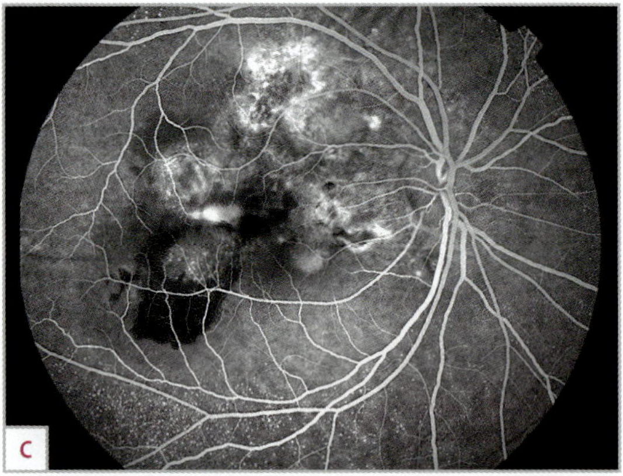

Fig. 11.45: *Continued*

Less commonly, extrafoveal lesions are treated with focal laser to leaking dilatations (e.g. 200 mW, 200 micron spot size, 0.2 seconds, to give a moderate white reaction), although the evidence for this is less than for than PDT and anti-VEGF drugs. It may not be possible to treat all lesions with PDT (or laser) due to haemorrhage. PCV may resolve spontaneously (~20%).

Follow-up As for neovascular AMD. If OCT leakage persists, consider repeat ICG 6 weeks after PDT to check polyp closure.

DIABETIC RETINOPATHY AND MACULOPATHY

Background People with diabetes can lose vision from macular oedema, macular ischaemia, vitreous haemorrhage, tractional retinal detachment and neovascular glaucoma. The ophthalmologist has several tasks: confirm the diagnosis; classify its severity and monitor accordingly; encourage tight diabetic control and monitoring; liaise with diabetic screening services and physicians; explain the clinical evidence (**Box 11.2**) and help patients to select which treatment is the best for them; treat with retinal laser, intravitreal therapy or surgery as required; and treat associated eye disease such as cataract and neovascular glaucoma. Patients are often systemically unwell and managing multiple medical appointments.

Box 11.2: Key diabetic studies

- *Diabetic Retinopathy Study (DRS)*: Defined high-risk proliferative diabetic retinopathy (PDR, p. 558) and risk of severe visual loss with different levels of retinopathy. Established that panretinal photocoagulation (PRP) laser more than halves the risk of severe visual loss in high-risk PDR.
- *Wisconsin Epidemiologic Study of Diabetic Retinopathy (WESDR)*: This population-based study showed that glycosylated haemoglobin levels and duration of diabetes are risk factors for retinopathy progression.
- *Early Treatment Diabetic Retinopathy Study (ETDRS)*: Showed that macular laser approximately halves the risk of moderate visual loss from macular oedema.
- *Diabetes Control and Complications Trial (DCCT)*: Demonstrated that intensive insulin treatment reduced the risk of sustained progression of retinopathy in type 1 diabetes mellitus (T1DM).
- *United Kingdom Prospective Diabetes Study (UKPDS)*: Showed that tight BP and glycaemic control in T2DM reduced retinopathy progression and visual loss.
- *RISE and RIDE, and RESOLVE*: Showed intravitreal ranibizumab was superior to sham, for the treatment of diabetic macular oedema (DMO).
- *Diabetic Retinopathy Clinical Research Network (DRCR.net)*: Compared ranibizumab plus laser, ranibizumab plus deferred laser (after ≥24 weeks) if needed, triamcinolone plus laser, and laser alone for DMO. Monthly ranibizumab (± baseline laser) was superior to laser or triamcinolone.
- *READ2 and RESTORE*: Compared ranibizumab, laser, and ranibizumab plus laser, for DMO. Ranibizumab was visually superior to laser alone. Combined treatment had similar visual outcomes with fewer injections.
- *VISTA and VIVID*: Compared intravitreal aflibercept versus laser for DMO. VA gains were significantly better with aflibercept.

Box 11.2: *Continued*

- *DRCR.net Protocol T*: Compared aflibercept, ranibizumab and bevacizumab for DMO. At year 1 aflibercept had greater VA gains than ranibizumab and bevacizumab for those with poor initial VA (<69 letters; ~6/15), but this advantage was only significant versus bevacizumab at year 2. Year 1 safety was similar, but ranibizumab had more arteriothrombotic events than aflibercept at year 2. The bevacizumab group required significantly more injections than the aflibercept group at year 1, but only by 9.7 versus 9.2.
- *DRCR.net Protocol S*: Compared ranibizumab and PRP for PDR. At 2 years, ranibizumab was non-inferior to PRP for VA, with less visual field loss, fewer vitrectomies, and less DMO. At 5 years, the benefit of anti-VEGF reduced, the 34% loss to follow-up makes anti-VEGF monotherapy risky (given the potential impact of uncontrolled PDR) and it was not cost-effective unless DMO was present.
- *CLARITY*: Compared aflibercept and PRP for PDR. At 12 months, VA was significantly better with aflibercept, with less binocular visual field loss.
- *YOSEMITE and RHINE*: Compared the bispecific drug faricimab (anti-VEGF and Ang-2) with extended dosing if the macula remained dry, versus mandated 2-monthly aflibercept, for DMO. Faricimab provided non-inferior VA despite fewer injections.
- *DRCR.net Protocol V*: Compared observation versus laser versus intravitreal aflibercept, for eyes with centre-involving DMO but good VA (6/7.5 or better). The VA at 2 years was similar with 8- to 16-weekly observation (versus aflibercept), with 34% needing rescue aflibercept.

Classification of retinopathy

There are multiple diabetic retinopathy severity scales, often designed to predict the risk of progression and vision loss. The ETDRS system (below) is the most common internationally, and England also uses the Diabetic Eye Screening Programme (DESP) system, ranging from R0 to R3.

- *No diabetic retinopathy, DESP severity grade R0*
- *Mild non-proliferative diabetic retinopathy (NPDR), R1*: At least one microaneurysm.
- *Moderate NPDR, R2L (low risk)*: Intraretinal haemorrhages or microaneurysms < ETDRS standard photograph 2a (**Fig. 11.46**) and/or cotton wool spots, venous beading, intraretinal microvascular abnormalities (IRMA) less than severe criteria.
- *Severe NPDR, R2H (high risk)*: Relies on the 4–2–1 rule, which requires one of the following:
  1. Multiple blot haemorrhages or microaneurysms in all four quadrants.
  2. Venous beading ≥ ETDRS photograph 6a (**Fig. 11.46**) in two quadrants.

3. IRMA ≥ ETDRS photograph 8a (**Fig. 11.46**) in one quadrant.

- *Very severe NPDR, R2H*: At least two of the criteria for severe NPDR.
- *Non-high risk PDR, R3A*: New vessels on the disc (NVD) or elsewhere (NVE), but criteria not met for high-risk PDR below.

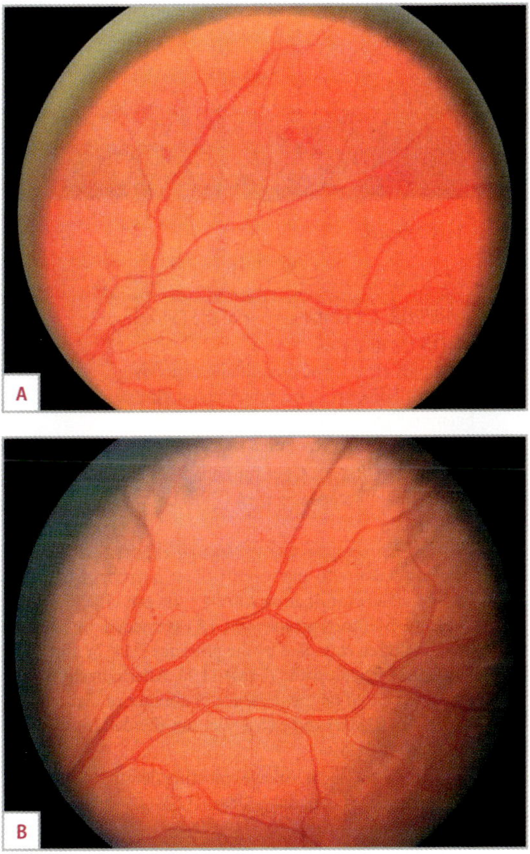

Fig. 11.46: Early Treatment Diabetic Retinopathy Study standard photograph, 2a (retinal haemorrhages, A), 6a (venous beading, B) and 8a (IRMAs, C) (Courtesy ETDRS Research Group). *Continues overleaf*

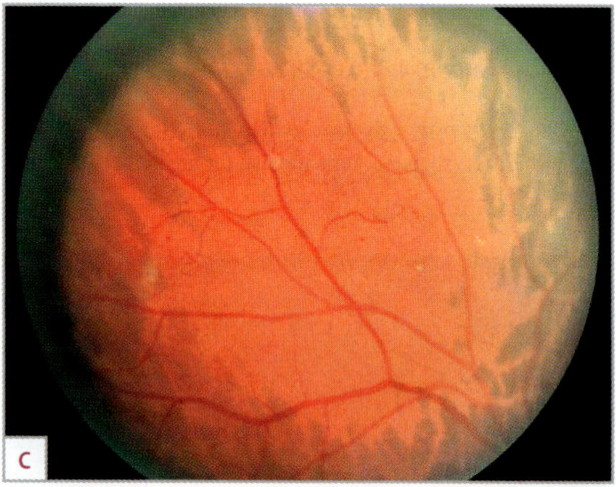

Fig. 11.46: *Continued*

- *High-risk PDR, R3A*: At least one of the following:
  1. NVD >1/3 disc area.
  2. NVD plus vitreous or preretinal haemorrhage.
  3. NVE >1/2 disc area plus preretinal or vitreous haemorrhage.
- *Advanced PDR, R3A*: Tractional retinal detachment (TRD).
- *Stable treated PDR, R3S*: Once retinopathy is stable and treated with panretinal photocoagulation (PRP) laser.

Classification of maculopathy Macular exudates or thickening can occur with any severity of retinopathy. Treatment is guided by fundus examination and OCT at each visit, and fluorescein and OCT angiography (OCTA) as needed. In England, maculopathy is often classified by the presence (M1) or absence (M0) of referable maculopathy **(Table 11.1)**. Alternatively, it can be classified based on the presence or absence of diabetic macular oedema (DMO) and ischaemia, sub-divided into:

- Centre-involving DMO
- Extra-foveal DMO (focal leakage) meeting definition of clinically significant macular oedema (CSMO):
  - Hard exudates located within 500 μm of the fovea with adjacent retinal thickening.
  - Retinal thickening at least one disc area in size, part of which is located within one disc diameter of the fovea.

- Non-clinically significant diabetic maculopathy, i.e. macular exudates with no DMO, or DMO that is neither centre-involving nor meeting the definition of CSMO.
- Ischaemic maculopathy.
- Mixed (DMO and ischaemia).

National Diabetic Eye Screening Programme (DESP)

Most UK patients are monitored by community photographic screening services that use the classification shown in **Table 11.1**, e.g. an eye with PRP but no maculopathy might be R3s, M0, P1, although the P grading is now often omitted.

History Ask about the duration and type of diabetes, blood glucose control (HbA1c), smoking and associated disease, especially hypertension, hyperlipidaemia, and renal disease. Identify if the patient is under a photographic screening service, and the clinicians monitoring their diabetes. If diabetes is only suspected, ask about polyuria, polydipsia and weight loss.

Table 11.1: English National Diabetic Eye Screening Programme (DESP) grading criteria. *Continues opposite*

Grading	Diabetic retinopathy	Features
R0	None	No retinopathy
R1	Background or mild non-proliferative	≥1 microaneurysm, retinal haemorrhage, or venous loops. Exudates and/or cotton wool spots may be present, but are not essential
R2	Pre-proliferative or moderate to severe non-proliferative	*Low risk (R2L)*: Venous beading in one quadrant, or >20 blot haemorrhages or microaneurysms in each of 1–3 quadrants, or Any IRMA less than standard photograph 8a (Fig. 11.45C) *High risk (R2H)*: >20 intraretinal haemorrhages or microaneursyms, in each of 4 quadrants, or Venous beading in ≥2 quadrants, or Moderate IRMA equal to or worse than standard photograph 8a in ≥1 quadrant

Table 11.1: *Continued*

Grading	Diabetic retinopathy	Features
R3A or R3S	Proliferative	*Active (R3A)*: NVD, NVE, or New preretinal or vitreous haemorrhage, or New preretinal fibrosis, or New TRD, or Reactivation of previously stable R3s *Stable (R3S)*: PRP with inactive proliferative retinopathy or stable appearing fibrosis
M0	No or non-referable maculopathy	No maculopathy or maculopathy without M1 features
M1	Maculopathy requiring referral to surveillance OCT clinic	Exudate or thickening within 1 disc diameter (DD) of the fovea, or Microaneurysms or haemorrhage within 1 DD if VA 6/12 or worse (unless there is another known cause for reduced VA), or Macular exudates ≥½ disc area (macular defined as a radius that measures from the temporal edge of the optic disc to the foveal centre)
P0	No macular or peripheral laser	No laser scars present
P1	Macular or peripheral laser	Laser scars present
U	Ungradable	Poor image quality

Examination Examine the iris at high magnification for neovascularisation (NVI), ideally before dilating. If present, or if IOP is elevated, perform gonioscopy to look for angle neovascularisation (NVA). Perform careful dilated fundus examination looking for atypical features. Exclude associated disease, especially posterior subcapsular cataracts. Classify retinopathy severity and any DMO.

Differential diagnosis

- *Non-proliferative diabetic retinopathy*: Central or branch retinal vein occlusion; ocular ischaemic syndrome; hypertensive retinopathy; radiation retinopathy; leukaemia; anaemia; and HIV microangiopathy.
- *Proliferative diabetic retinopathy*: Retinal artery or vein occlusion; sickle cell retinopathy; ocular ischaemic syndrome; sarcoidosis; Eales' disease; tuberculosis; embolisation from i.v. drug use.
- *Diabetic macular oedema*: See page 535.

Investigations For suspected diabetes, work-up varies from random or fasting glucose, to HbA1c, glucose tolerance test, and diabetologist review. Normal fasting glucose is <6.0 mmol/L; prediabetes 6.0–6.9 mmol/L; ≥7.0 mmol/L suggests diabetes, but repeat if there are no diabetic symptoms. For HbA1c, prediabetes is 42–47 mmol/mol (6.0–6.5%); ≥48 mmol/mol (6.5%) is diabetic. The definition of "good control" varies, but is ~60–70 mmol/mol (7.6–8.6%). Arrange OCT (**Fig. 11.29**, p. 535), and OCTA if available. Record if DMO involves the foveal centre and central subfield thickness (the central 1 mm circle of the ETDRS overlay on the colour map, **Fig. 11.14**, p. 511). Consider fluorescein angiography or OCTA to identify suspected macular ischaemia, and widefield angiography for peripheral ischaemia. For interpretation of fluorescein angiograms see page 498, OCT page 508, and OCTA page 510. Autofluorescence and OCT infrared images can help to locate previous laser treatment. Obtain widefield colour images, if available.

Management Correspond with all relevant health workers to ensure glucose, BP, and general health are well managed. Encourage smokers to stop and explain that poor glucose control threatens vision. Ocular management depends on the findings, but consider earlier review if there is poor diabetic or BP control, pregnancy, or recent marked improvement in diabetic control (can transiently worsen retinopathy):

- Non-proliferative diabetic retinopathy.
    1. *Absent or mild*: Refer to diabetic eye screening programme for 1–2 yearly review (1% risk of high-risk PDR in 1 year based on screening programme data, but probably less after a thorough peripheral retinal examination).
    2. *Moderate*: If there are no IRMAs consider referral to a local screening programme. If IRMAs are less than **Figure 11.46** (8a) review 6–9 monthly, if not see 4–6 monthly (4% risk of high-risk PDR in 1 year).
    3. *Severe*: Review 4–6 monthly (8% risk of high-risk PDR in 1 year).

4. *Very severe*: Review 3–4 monthly (17% risk of high-risk PDR in 1 year). Consider PRP in older T2DM patients, if poor compliance with follow-up, or significant systemic illnesses.

- Proliferative retinopathy.
  1. National Institute for Health and Care Excellence (NICE) recommends:
     - Detail the risks and benefits of PRP, anti-VEGF therapy, and observation, to help patients to choose the best option for them, but explain that PRP is the usual treatment. Aim to start PRP within 4 weeks and complete by 8 weeks.
     - For high-risk PDR or difficulty attending appointments, offer to start PRP the same day.
     - Offer anti-VEGF treatment if PDR remains active after complete PRP, or if cataract or vitreous haemorrhage prevent PRP.
  2. Pregnancy often requires PRP, as anti-VEGF therapy is usually avoided (p. 840)
  3. The DRCR.net Protocol S recruited eyes without prior PRP, using ranibizumab 4-weekly to week 12, then reviewed participants 4-weekly and re-treated if there was persisting neovascularisation. From week 24, subjects were injected 4-weekly unless neovascularisation resolved, or was stable after two consecutive injections. Injections could be resumed if neovascularisation worsened. PRP was considered for treatment failure with anti-VEGF. But for the reasons given in **Box 11.2**, ranibizumab tends not be the first-line treatment for PDR.
  4. Iris new vessels (NVI): Offer same day PRP and consider intravitreal anti-VEGF injections, dosed as above.
  5. Check for high IOP and manage as appropriate.
- Coexisting DMO: Consider macular laser or anti-VEGF drugs, but the latter may also help control PDR. PRP may improve or worsen DMO (worsening is usually temporary and is less common with modern lasers), so consider treatment timing, including fellow eye VA and patient's preference.
- Vitreous haemorrhage: Treat mild vitreous haemorrhage as high-risk PDR. If the haemorrhage obscures the fundal view, perform B-scan ultrasound to exclude retinal detachment. Examine monthly for NVI or raised IOP. Apply PRP as haemorrhage clears and the view improves. Arrange vitreoretinal review if the haemorrhage persists for 1 month (p. 641). Consider early referral for rubeosis, or if the other eye has poor VA.
- Tractional retinal detachment: If TRD inv olves or threatens the fovea arrange vitreoretinal review (p. 642). If not, review

every 2–3 months once PRP laser is complete and if the TRD remains stable.

- Maculopathy.
  1. Systemic disease control is very important. If there is a short term, bilateral, unexpected worsening of DMO consider systemic causes, like not using medications, onset of renal disease, sleep apnoea, infections and surgery – liaise with the relevant clinical team, GP and endocrinology team to steadily improve blood glucose and BP control.
  2. If 'non-clinically significant' DMO review in 4–6 months. Refer to GP/endocrinology.
  3. Treat non-centre-involving DMO meeting criteria of CSMO with 'modified ETDRS' macular laser or observe and/or improve systemic control. For laser settings, see page 522. Review in 3–4 months. If good VA and stable OCT after monitoring, consider discharge to a community eye screening programme that has OCT.
  4. For centre-involving DMO:
     - Undertake VA, dilated fundus examination and OCT at each visit.
     - Observe if VA >78 ETDRS letters (Snellen 6/8.3) and <250 μm thickening on OCT, but if symptomatic or worsening consider anti-VEGF injections if available, or laser for extra-foveal component.
     - NICE guidance (TA274, TA346, TA799 and TA820) supports ranibizumab, aflibercept, faricimab and brolucizumab treatment for vision loss due to DMO if it is ≥400 μm (usually measured in the central 1 mm subfield), but brolucizumab has not been widely adopted, likely due to concern about retinal vasculitis and occlusion. Provide written information and collect written consent: **Box 11.1** (p. 551) details the risks and injection technique and **Box 11.2** the benefits. Dosing regimens vary, based around each drug's marketing authorisation. Evidence, licensing and commissioning is evolving, so check local and national guidelines. Help patients decide which of the available anti-VEGF drugs is best for them:

       Ranibizumab 0.5 mg: Inject monthly until maximum VA is achieved and/or the OCT is dry. Thereafter use either a monitor-and-extend (varying interval and treating as needed) or treat-and-extend (T&E) regimen (inject each visit but vary interval). The interval depends on disease activity, e.g. increase the follow-up interval by up to 1 month each time the OCT remains dry, up to a maximum of 4 months, but inject and reduce the interval if fluid recurs. Studies indicate DMO ≥ 250 μm with VA < 78 ETDRS letters also benefits, but funding is not available in many countries.

Bevacizumab 1.25 mg: Explain bevacizumab is off-label for DMO and the DRCR.net Protocol T results (**Box 11.2**). Dose as for ranibizumab.

Aflibercept 2 mg: Inject monthly for 5 months then 2-monthly to 1 year. Thereafter T&E in 2-week increments to maintain stable visual and/or anatomic outcomes up to 4 months maximum. Reduce the interval if OCT fluid recurs, to 1 month minimum.

Aflibercept 8 mg: Eylea HD uses a higher concentration (114.3 mg/mL) and injection volume (0.07 mL vs. usual 0.05 mL), to deliver an 8-mg dose. Inject monthly for 3 months then T&E in up to 4-week increments to maintain stable visual/anatomic outcomes. The maximum interval is 5 months and the minimum 2 months.

Faricimab 6 mg: Inject monthly until disease is controlled, typically about 3 doses, then T&E in up to 4-week increments and 8-week reductions based on visual/anatomic outcomes. The maximum interval is 4 months and the minimum 21 days

- If poorly responsive despite 3–6 injections consider: swapping or stopping anti-VEGF drugs; other causes of persisting fluid, e.g. vitreomacular traction and epiretinal membrane; long-acting dexamethasone (Ozurdex) implant (TA824) and even longer-acting fluocinolone acetonide implant (Iluvien; TA953), but explain the materially increased risk of cataract and raised IOP with steroids (look for existing evidence of a steroid-induced IOP rise, e.g. after cataract surgery). For Ozurdex injection technique see **Box 11.3**, (p. 572)
- Offer modified ETDRS macular laser to the area of OCT thickening if anti-VEGF injections are unavailable, declined or contraindicated, e.g. pregnancy (p. 840), especially if foveal fluid has spread from a non-central focus of leakage.

Diabetic retinopathy and cataract surgery

- Preoperative.
    - Request OCT to look for DMO. Aim to operate early, before DMO or high-risk PDR develop.
    - If possible, treat DMO and wait until resolved before operating. If not, consider anti-VEGF or steroid implant at surgery.

- Treat high-risk PDR/NVI preoperatively if possible. If not, perform intraoperative indirect PRP.
- If there is no fundus view, perform B-scan ultrasound and refer any TRD or vitreous haemorrhage for combined phacovitrectomy.
- Explain that there is a guarded prognosis if a dense cataract prevents a good macular view, or if there is advanced diabetic retinopathy or DMO that cannot be treated preoperatively.
- Some (but not all) studies found that topical non-steroidal anti-inflammatory drugs (NSAIDs) reduce OCT-defined postoperative macular oedema with a greater chance of visual improvement. There are no good comparative studies between different NSAIDS, but most of the larger studies in diabetic eyes combine nepafenac and steroid. Consider nepafenac 0.1% or 0.3% t.d.s. 24 hours preoperatively, 30–120 minutes before surgery, and for up to 60 days after; consider 30 days if low-risk (e.g. no prior, preoperative or postoperative DMO). Omit the immediately preoperative dose if using topical NSAIDs alongside mydriatics, which is probably a good precaution anyway. Use topical NSAIDS only with caution in eyes with corneal disorders and avoid NSAIDs and Maxitrol. An EU study has also shown some benefit of subconjunctival steroid depot at the end of cataract surgery.

- Intraoperative.
  - Use a large-diameter optic, acrylic intraocular lens (to maximise retinal view postoperatively).
  - If intraoperative PRP is required, perform after crystalline lens removal and before intraocular lens insertion.
- Postoperative.
  - *Macular oedema*: If perioperative DMO is present, consider it due to diabetes and treat as above. DMO that develops after 1 week but before 6 months is often pseudophakic and may resolve spontaneously or with NSAID and steroid eye drops (p. 593; Irvine–Gass syndrome). Fluorescein angiography may help distinguish.
  - *Progression of retinopathy*: increase the frequency of review in eyes with severe NPDR or worse, as there is an increased risk of progression. Promptly treat high-risk PDR that occurs in the postoperative period.

Diabetic retinopathy and pregnancy

- Pregnancy can worsen diabetic retinopathy.
- Ideally, review preconception to assess baseline retinopathy.

- Minimum review is in the first trimester, and then at 28th week if no retinopathy is present, but an additional screen is recommended at 16–20 weeks, if even minimal retinopathy is present.
- Review more frequently if there is severe retinopathy/ maculopathy or poor diabetic control. Continue close monitoring until 6 months postpartum.
- Avoid fluorescein angiography if possible, but if needed discuss the relevant evidence (p. 840).
- Anti-VEGF injections are often considered contraindicated, but see see page 840.
- Treat by laser as required.

CENTRAL RETINAL VEIN OCCLUSION

Background Central retinal vein occlusion (CRVO) typically occurs in patients over 45 years secondary to retinal vein thrombosis. Risk factors include diabetes, hypertension, hyperlipidaemia, and glaucoma. CRVO in those under 45 years may suggest a clotting disorder.

Clinical features CRVO produces uniocular, painless vision loss. Signs include: retinal haemorrhages in four quadrants (**Fig. 11.47**); dilated tortuous retinal veins; optic disc swelling;

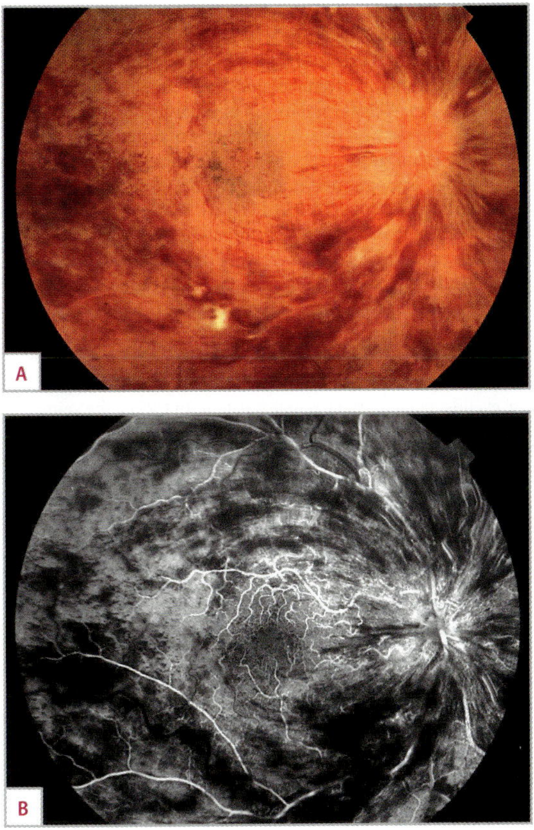

Fig. 11.47: Central retinal vein occlusion.

macular oedema; cotton wool spots; later neovascularisation of the iris, angle, retina, or disc. Disc collateral vessels are a sign of resolution.

Classification

- Non-ischaemic.
- Ischaemic.
  1. Clinical examination: RAPD, VA ~6/60, multiple cotton wool spots, dense mid-retinal haemorrhages, 'blood and thunder fundus'.
  2. Fluorescein angiogram: more than 10 disc areas of ischaemia.

History and examination Ask about glaucoma, systemic hypertension, raised lipids, diabetes or symptoms of diabetes (polyuria, polydipsia and weight loss). If younger than 45 years, ask about features of thrombophilia: deep vein thrombosis; pulmonary embolus; thrombosis in unusual sites, e.g. axillary vein; multiple miscarriages; family history of thrombosis <45 years. Examine for new vessels in the angle (undilated gonioscopy), iris, optic nerve, and retina. Examine both eyes for features of glaucoma (p. 350 and 361). Consider digital *ophthalmodynamometry* to check for raised central retinal vein pressure, although this is rarely necessary as other clinical features usually make the diagnosis. Lightly press on the upper lid whilst viewing the proximal retinal arteries (avoid pressing too hard, which may exacerbate vein occlusion). In normal eyes, the central retinal vein spontaneously pulses or can be made to pulsate or collapse with minimal ocular pressure through the eyelids, but the artery remains patent. In CRVO, the vein and artery pulsate together or, in extreme cases, the artery compresses more easily than the vein. The latter may also suggest reduced arterial pressure and ocular ischaemia, so compare with the fellow eye, assuming that is normal. Ocular ischaemia may present with VA loss due to cilioretinal hypoperfusion.

Differential diagnosis Consider ocular ischaemic syndrome (p. 583); diabetic retinopathy (p. 557); optic disc swelling for other reasons (p. 776); blood malignancy; rarer causes of cotton wool spots (p. 530) and retinal haemorrhages (p. 529).

Investigations Check BP, HbA1c, FBC, erythrocyte sedimentation rate (ESR), lipids (thyroid function if abnormal), and plasma protein electrophoresis. Consider thrombophilia screen, CRP, sACE, anticardiolipin antibody, lupus anticoagulant, autoantibodies, and CXR, only as indicated. Arrange OCT angiography if macular ischaemia is suspected, fluorescein angiography if unavailable or vasculitis suspected, and widefield angiography if peripheral ischaemia suspected.

Treatment Liaise with the patient and physicians regarding low-dose aspirin (if systemic cardiovascular risk warrants it), managing hypertension and discontinuation of oral contraceptives. Arrange panretinal photocoagulation (PRP) for neovascularisation.

- *Treat glaucoma*. For neovascular glaucoma consider intravitreal anti-VEGF drugs whilst laser takes effect, if the angle is partially open, but despite this, glaucoma surgery/cyclodiode may prove necessary (p. 361).
- *Anti-VEGF therapy*: Most patients with fovea-involving macular oedema require regular VA, dilated fundus examination, OCT, and intravitreal anti-VEGF injections. Provide written information and collect written consent (for risks and injection technique, see **Box 11.1**, p. 551). Help the patient choose the best available drug for them:
    - *Ranibizumab 0.5 mg*: The CRUISE trial compared monthly intravitreal 0.5 mg ranibizumab for 6 months then p.r.n. to sham, with 48% gaining ≥15 letters at 6 months, versus 17% in the sham group. NICE guidance (TA283) supports the use of ranibizumab for CRVO macular oedema. Start with monthly dosing then use a monitor-and-extend or treat-and-extend (T&E) regimen as for diabetic macular oedema (p. 565).
    - *Aflibercept 2 mg*: The COPERNICUS and GALILEO trials compared monthly intravitreal aflibercept 2 mg for 6 months then p.r.n., to sham, with 56–60% gaining ≥15 letters at 6 months, versus 12–22% in the sham group. NICE (TA305) supports the use of aflibercept for CRVO macular oedema. Commence with monthly dosing until maximum VA and/or no OCT fluid. Thereafter T&E, increasing or decreasing the dosing interval to maintain VA and dry OCT, e.g. by 2 weeks each visit. The specified minimum interval is 1 month; the best maximum is not known, but ~3 months is reasonable.
    - *Bevacizumab 1.25 mg*: The SCORE2 study compared monthly bevacizumab and aflibercept over 6 months. Bevacizumab mean VA gain was very similar to aflibercept (18.6 vs. 18.9 letters respectively), with 61% versus 65% gaining ≥15 letters. Dose as for either aflibercept or ranibizumab, but explain that bevacizumab is off-label for CRVO.
    - *Faricimab 6 mg*: The BALATON (branch retinal vein occlusion) and COMINO (hemi and CRVO) trials compared

faricimab 6 mg and aflibercept 2 mg, both dosed monthly for 6 doses. At the 6-month primary endpoint faricimab was non-inferior to aflibercept. Subsequently, the faricimab groups moved to T&E at up to 16-week intervals. NICE supports the use of faricimab for branch and CRVO (TA1004). Inject monthly until disease is controlled, typically about 3 doses, then T&E in up to 4-week increments and 8-week reductions based on visual/anatomic outcomes. The maximum interval is 4 months and the minimum 21 days.

- See www.nice.org.uk, www.rcophth.ac.uk and www.medicines.org.uk for latest UK guidance, patient information and marketing authorisations.
- Consider dexamethasone implant (Ozurdex) for a suboptimal response to anti-VEGF drugs.

Dexamethasone implant (Ozurdex) The GENEVA studies reported that 21% of cases improved ≥15 letters by month 1, versus 7% of the sham group, with a significant difference lasting 2 months. Cataract progression occurred in 7%, elevated IOP in 25% and 1% required surgical or laser treatment of IOP, so liaise with glaucoma specialists if there is preexisting ocular hypertension, glaucoma or known steroid response (look to see if IOP rose with any post-operative steroid eye drops). NICE guidance (TA229) supports the use of Ozurdex for CRVO.

See **Box 11.3** for technique. See 1 month after injection, then 2-monthly.

Box 11.3: Ozurdex injection.

- Confirm the patient's name and date of birth, laterality, drug selection, implant integrity, expiry date and any allergies including iodine. Before preparing for injection, instil an anaesthetic eye drop and once this has worked, a drop of povidone iodine 5% (available in Minims), to maximise dwell time.
- For iodine allergy or sensitivity topical aqueous chlorhexidine 0.05% or 0.1% is available off-label for eye use. Avoid the chlorhexidine used to scrub, as it may contain alcohol and/or detergents.
- In order, use mask, sterile gloves, multiple anaesthetic drops, povidone iodine 5% to periocular skin and conjunctival sac with a least 30 seconds' dwell time, dry eye, drape then eyelid speculum.
- Remove the Ozurdex applicator cap. Pull out the safety tab without twisting or flexing.

Box 11.3: *Continud*

- Place an anaesthetic drop over the injection site, mark with a caliper (4 mm from the limbus if phakic, 3.5 mm if aphakic or pseudophakic), then a final povidone iodine drop at the marked site, which will pool where the caliper pressed the globe (confirming where to inject).
- Consider securing the globe with a toothed forceps, e.g. St Martins.
- With the bevel facing away from the sclera and aiming circumferentially (parallel with the limbus), advance the applicator needle 1 mm within the sclera, then angle and advance into the vitreous cavity. Do not advance beyond the point where the sleeve touches the conjunctiva.
- Slowly depress the actuator button until a click is heard.
- Remove the needle using the same angles, in reverse.
- Confirm hand motions or count fingers vision and if absent check for a central retinal artery occlusion with an indirect ophthalmoscope and 20D lens. If the central retinal artery is collapsed perform anterior chamber paracentesis (Box 11.1 p. 551).
- Some clinicians check IOP within 30 minutes.
- Detail the symptoms of endophthalmitis and retinal detachment, but explain the patient may see the implant.
- Consider G. chloramphenicol q.d.s for 4 days.

Follow-up Monthly for 3 months, then up to 3-monthly if stable, for 2 years; monthly if there is active neovascularisation; and as above if injecting. Check VA, IOP, iris (to exclude rubeosis), dilated fundoscopy and OCT at each visit.

BRANCH RETINAL VEIN OCCLUSION

Background Branch retinal vein occlusion (BRVO) occurs 2–3 times more commonly than central retinal vein occlusion (CRVO), but has similar risk factors. The main sequelae are macular oedema and vitreous haemorrhage from disc or retinal new vessels. BRVO affecting the entire superior or inferior retina (hemicentral RVO) has a higher risk of rubeosis and disc new vessels and behaves more like CRVO.

Symptoms Usually painless loss of vision in one eye, but may be asymptomatic.

Signs Same as CRVO (see p. 569) except for branch distribution (**Fig. 11.48**). Rubeosis is less common; macular oedema, disc and retinal new vessels, more so.

Classification

- *Ischaemic*: >5 disc areas of ischaemia on fluorescein angiography.
- *Non-ischaemic*: <5 disc areas on angiography.
  - With macular oedema.
  - With macular ischaemia.

History and examination Similar to CRVO. Fully exclude systemic causes in patients with multiple BRVOs.

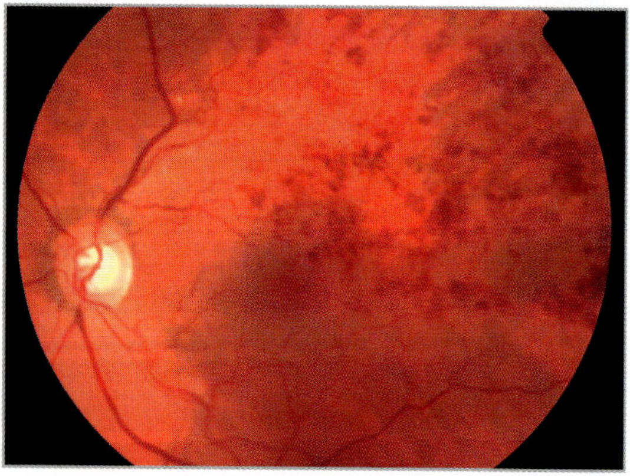

Fig. 11.48: Branch retinal vein occlusion.

Investigations Same as for CRVO.

Treatment Treat neovascularisation with scatter retinal laser to areas of ischaemia, as shown angiographically. If macular oedema reduces VA consider grid laser to areas of thickening (but avoiding the FAZ) and/or intravitreal anti-VEGF therapy and/or Ozurdex therapy. The BRAVO study reported that after 6 consecutive monthly ranibizumab injections BRVO eyes with macular oedema gained 18.3 ETDRS letters, versus 7.3 with sham. The VIBRANT study found that 53% of eyes treated with monthly aflibercept gained ≥15 letters versus 28% with macular laser. The MARVEL study found similar VA gains comparing baseline then monthly p.r.n. bevacizumab (+15.6 letters) and ranibizumab (+18.1 letters) at 6 months. In the GENEVA study eyes treated with one Ozurdex injection gained ~8 letters within 1 month versus ~4 letters for sham, with a peak gain of 10 letters at month 2, and a significant difference out to 6 months. Injections may be the best option if fluid is centred on the fovea, and use anti-VEGF drugs if there is neovascularisation. Macular laser may provide more durable treatment for non-central leakage that has spread to involve the fovea (for technique, see p. 277). Ozurdex lasts longer than anti-VEGF drugs, but is more likely to raise IOP and cause cataract. NICE guidance supports the use of both Ozurdex (TA229) and ranibizumab (TA283) for BRVO macular oedema if macular laser has failed or macular haemorrhage precludes laser. NICE TA409 and TA1004 support the use of aflibercept and faricimab respectively (without restriction to previously failed treatment or macular haemorrhage). For consent, dosing, injection technique and faricimab, see CRVO (p. 569).

Follow-up As for CRVO (p. 569).

CENTRAL RETINAL ARTERY OCCLUSION

Background Most commonly caused by atheroma, but also heart and carotid emboli, severely raised IOP, arteritis, or rarely vasospasm (retinal migraine).

Symptoms Sudden, painless, unilateral, and often severe visual loss.

Signs Acute changes include retinal opacification, whitening, and oedema; cherry-red spot at the macula; RAPD; intra-arteriolar blood column segmentation (box-carring); possible cilioretinal artery sparing. An example is shown on page 534. Disc pallor occurs later.

History and examination Ask about transient ischaemic attacks, cerebrovascular accidents, symptoms of giant cell arteritis (p. 789), or amaurosis fugax (retinal emboli causing transient uniocular visual obscuration lasting a few minutes). Auscultate the carotids for bruits using the stethoscope bell, check heart sounds for a valvular murmur, and radial pulse for atrial fibrillation. Look for intra-arteriolar calcific, cholesterol, or fibrinoplatelet emboli.

Differential diagnosis See the differential diagnosis of cherry-red spot at the macula (p. 534). Also consider giant cell arteritis, intraocular gentamicin toxicity, and acute ophthalmic artery occlusion.

Investigations Arrange BP; urgent ESR and CRP; blood sugar and/or HbA1c; FBC; lipids; ECG; carotid artery Doppler; cardiac examination (±echocardiogram) for embolic source; OCT; and fluorescein angiography. Acutely, the inner retinal layers are hyper-reflective and oedematous on OCT, becoming atrophic over ~1 month. In younger patients; those without known cardiovascular risk factors; if history or results suggest autoimmune disease or hypercoagulopathy (prior vascular occlusions); and for raised inflammatory markers, consider any or all of: ANA; rheumatoid factor; serum protein and haemoglobin electrophoresis; thrombophilia screen; and temporal artery biopsy. Investigations other than basic blood tests may be best undertaken by a physician, or stroke team urgently if acute.

A meta-analysis of all treatments for central retinal artery occlusion did not find a benefit for any of the published local ocular treatments. Most published guidance suggests early/urgent referral to a stroke pathway with appropriate treatment, potentially including systemic thrombolytics, although the evidence is evolving and should be reviewed. Similar to the guidance for stroke, there may be longer windows for visual recovery than previous recommendations have suggested.

Treatment Consider starting aspirin 75 mg o.d. p.o. while awaiting stroke workup, if no contraindications. Although the evidence is weak, if there is recent onset (with ~24 hours) and a visible embolus, attempt to dislodge by:

- Firm ocular massage through closed eyelids for 15 minutes.
- Stat crushed acetazolamide 500 mg p.o., G. iopidine, and G. β-blocker.
- Offer anterior chamber paracentesis (**Box 11.1**, p. 551) aiming to drain at least 0.1 mL, but explain that the benefits are uncertain.

Follow-up Review initially in 2–4 weeks. Examine for iris neovascularisation. Review investigations and liaise with the relevant clinicians – ask them if anti-platelet and/or anticoagulation are indicated, to avoid recurrence or vascular events elsewhere. Advise immediate ophthalmic review if visual obscuration occurs in either eye. Local policies for carotid endarterectomy vary and depend on the degree of carotid occlusion, so discuss with a vascular surgeon, particularly if >60% stenosis.

BRANCH RETINAL ARTERY OCCLUSION

Symptoms Unilateral, painless and sudden visual field loss.

Signs Retinal swelling similar to central retinal artery occlusion (CRAO, page 576), except for branch distribution (**Fig. 11.49**). Emboli may be present.

Classification

- Single episode.
- Multiple episodes: Consider systemic disease and urgent medical review.

History, examination and investigations See CRAO. Cilioretinal vascular stasis may occur in the presence of central retinal vein occlusion and is often missed.

Treatment and follow-up See CRAO. About 80% of symptomatic cases achieve a VA of 6/12 or better.

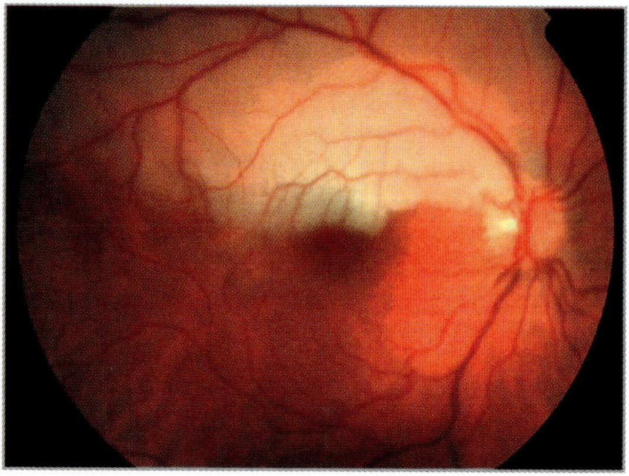

Fig. 11.49: Branch retinal artery occlusion.

HYPERTENSIVE RETINOPATHY

Symptoms Usually asymptomatic, but may have visual loss if there is optic disc swelling or macular oedema.

Signs of essential hypertension include venous deflection and narrowing at arteriovenous crossings (AV nipping); arteriolar narrowing and sclerosis producing an altered light reflex (so-called copper and silver wiring); cotton wool spots; lipid exudates with a macular star if severe (**Fig. 11.30**, p. 536); macular oedema; retinal haemorrhage; macroaneurysms; vitreous haemorrhage; retinal vascular occlusions; neovascularisation. Accelerated hypertension affects the choroidal circulation and may cause exudative retinal detachment, focal choroidal infarctions that can produce acute, yellow, retinal pigment epithelium spots and later hyperpigmentation (Elschnig's spots), and optic disc swelling.

Classification

- *Grade 0*: normal.
- *Grade 1*: barely detectable arteriolar narrowing.
- *Grade 2*: obvious widespread plus focal arteriolar narrowing, arteriovenous crossing changes.
- *Grade 3*: retinal haemorrhages or exudates.
- *Grade 4*: disc swelling.

A newer classification may better link to prognosis:

- *Mild*: Arteriolar narrowing, arteriovenous nipping or focal arteriolar narrowing
- *Moderate*: Microaneurysms, haemorrhages, hard or soft exudates
- *Severe*: Optic disc swelling

History and examination Ask about known hypertension, diabetes, radiotherapy, or other systemic disease. Measure BP.

Differential diagnosis Exclude other causes of macular oedema (p. 535), vascular tortuosity (p. 532), macular star (p. 535), optic disc swelling (p. 776), and retinal haemorrhage (p. 529), in particular diabetic retinopathy, retinal vein occlusion and sickle cell disease.

Investigations OCT may show macular oedema, exudates, retinal nerve fibre layer infarcts, and sometimes subretinal fluid. OCT angiography may reveal retinal and choroidal ischaemia, an enlarged foveal avascular zone (FAZ), vascular tortuosity and reduced vascular density. Widefield imaging (e.g. Optos) helps to survey the retina and assess change. If there is disc swelling, arrange optic disc cube OCT (to objectively measure change), and visual field testing (enlarged blind spot ± generalised constriction).

Treatment Control of hypertension by a physician.

Follow-up Consider seeing 4-6 months after BP is controlled, to confirm improvement (some vascular changes can persist) and exclude other causes of non-resolving retinopathy. Manage any associated disease as required e.g. retinal vein occlusion (p. 569) or leaking macroaneurysm (p. 581).

RETINAL ARTERIAL MACROANEURYSM

Background An acquired dilation of the retinal arterioles, most common in late-middle-aged women. Associated with hypertension, embolic disease, and hyperlipidaemia, with a rare association between multiple macroaneursyms and sarcoidosis.

Symptoms Blurred vision if the macula is involved.

Signs Arteriolar aneurysm, often with a large haemorrhage, exudation, and surrounding retinal oedema. Usually an isolated finding, but bilateral in 10%.

Differential diagnosis Consider diabetic retinopathy; retinal telangiectasia; choroidal tumour; retinal capillary haemangioma; cavernous haemangioma; haemorrhagic wet age-related macular degeneration; polypoidal choroidal vasculopathy; Coats' disease and idiopathic retinal vasculitis, aneurysms and neuroretinitis (IRVAN).

Investigations Perform OCT, which shows focal thickening corresponding to the dilated lumen of the macroaneurysm, often with neighbouring retinal oedema (**Fig. 11.50**). OCT angiography shows a hyper-reflective vascular dilation, most often in the inner retina. Consider fluorescein angiography, which shows early arterial filling and late staining of the macroaneurysm, if not masked by haemorrhage (**Fig. 11.51**). Dilated leaking capillaries sometimes surround the aneurysm. Indocyanine green angiography may show flow in cases with haemorrhagic masking on fluorescein angiography. Look for predisposing causes on imaging, such as arteriolar emboli and inflammation, e.g. sarcoidosis. Check BP, lipids and glucose.

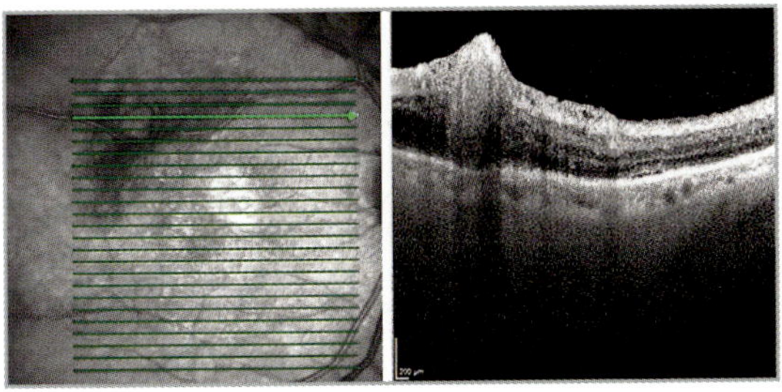

Fig. 11.50: OCT of retinal macroaneurysm.

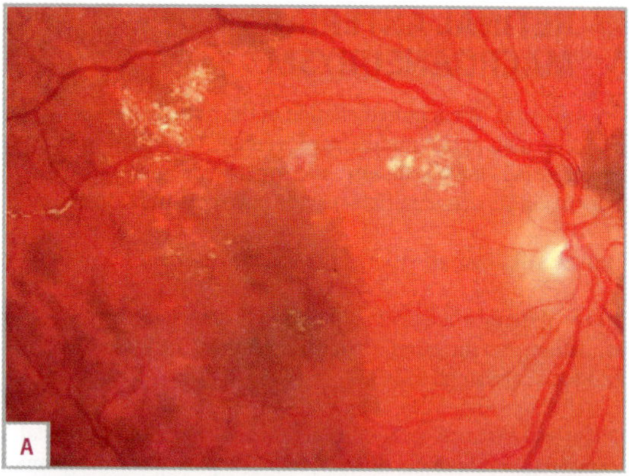

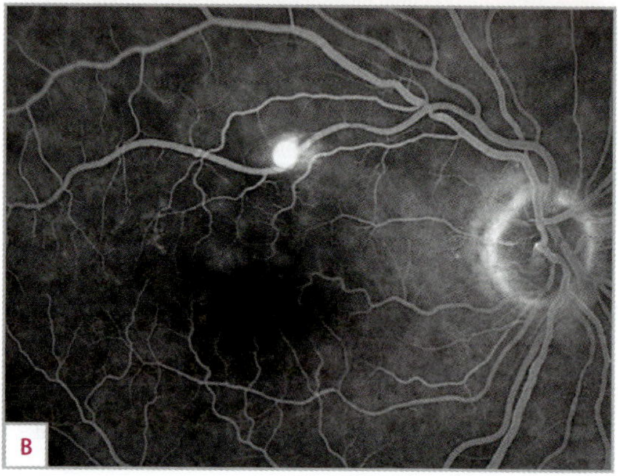

Fig. 11.51: Macroaneurysm with exudates (A), and hyperfluorescence on fluorescein angiography (B).

Treatment Many macroaneurysms thrombose and spontaneously involute, so treatment is often not needed. Laser photocoagulation may help for severe or persistent macular leakage and flow confirmed on angiography, but the evidence is uncertain and there are risks. The laser technique is described on page 526. For persistent macular oedema despite macroaneurysm closure consider grid laser or intravitreal anti-VEGF drugs (unproven).

OCULAR ISCHAEMIC SYNDROME

Background Ocular ischaemia is most commonly secondary to carotid artery atherosclerosis, usually in patients aged >50 years. Less common causes include ophthalmic artery occlusion, carotid aneurysm, giant cell arteritis, and vasospasm.

Symptoms Visual loss (sometimes precipitated by bright light), pain (~40%), and transient visual obscuration (10% have coexisting carotid emboli).

Signs

- Reduced VA.
- *Anterior segment*: Iris rubeosis, elevated IOP, anterior chamber flare or cells, and cataract.
- *Posterior segment*: Common features are retinal arterial attenuation, venous dilatation, retinal haemorrhages, disc neovascularisation, and cherry-red spot at the macula. Others include retinal neovascularisation, microaneurysms, cotton wool spots, vitreous haemorrhage, and spontaneous arterial pulsations (spontaneous venous pulsations are normal).

History Ask about cardiovascular risk factors and features of giant cell arteritis (p. 789) or other vasculitidies.

Examination Check temporal arteritis, BP and blood glucose or HbA1c. Perform digital ophthalmodynamometry (p. 570) to look for reduced perfusion pressure.

Differential diagnosis Consider the causes of iris rubeosis (p. 528), retinal haemorrhages (p. 529), retinal neovascularisation (p. 528) and cherry-red spot at the macula (p. 534). In particular, exclude retinal vein or artery occlusion, diabetic retinopathy, and giant cell arteritis.

Investigations Fluorescein angiography shows patchy choroidal filling and usually (~95% sensitivity) demonstrates increased retinal and choroidal transit times (normal values, p. 500), with vascular staining and macular oedema in some cases. Carotid artery ultrasound usually shows >90% obstruction. Consider MR and/or CT angiography if ultrasound is negative or ophthalmic artery stenosis suspected.

Management Discuss >60% carotid stenosis with a vascular surgeon, or as advised by local policy. Note IOP may rise if subsequent endarterectomy improves ciliary body perfusion. Ask the patient's GP to manage any cardiovascular risk factors.

Consider panretinal photocoagulation for disc, retinal, or iris new vessels. Inflammation is typically just mild flare and does not require treatment, but consider topical steroids if there are cells or discomfort. In eyes with visual potential, consider brimonidine as a first-line treatment of raised IOP due to its possible neuroprotective effect. If topical therapy fails, consider cyclodiode.

JUXTAFOVEAL TELANGIECTASIA

Background Typically presents aged 40–60 years with irregular, saccular dilatations of the parafoveal capillaries, and very occasionally capillary obliteration. Also called parafoveal telangiectasia.

Classification Classified into four groups (**Table 11.2**). Group 2 is now more often called macular telangiectasia (MacTel), and is the most common and is characterised by 'right-angle' capillaries, opaque (greyish) perifoveal retina, inner retinal crystals, and intraretinal retinal pigment epithelium migration. It is thought to be caused by Müller cell neurodegeneration.

Table 11.2: Classification of juxtafoveal telangiectasia

Group	Description	Usual site of perifoveal telangiectasia	Typical clinical features
1A	Unilateral congenital	Temporal	Visible telangiectasia on clinical examination; macular oedema and exudates may significantly reduce VA
1B	Unilateral idiopathic	Limited to edge of the foveal avascular zone	Limited leakage with good VA
2	Bilateral acquired	Temporal or more extensive	Greying of parafoveal nerve fibre layer, macular crystals and intraretinal pigment, subretinal neovascularisation, significant leak on fluorescein angiography; more than expected on clinical examination. VA mildly reduced in early disease but patient very symptomatic with reading
3	Bilateral idiopathic with capillary obliteration	Entire perifoveal region	Enlarged foveal avascular zone with severe visual loss

Examination Undertake a full dilated ocular examination including retinal periphery. Late complications include subretinal neovascularisation, full-thickness macular holes and macular atrophy (<5% of cases). Check BP.

Differential diagnosis See page 532.

Investigations

- *Optical coherence tomography (OCT):* Group 1 has increased central macular thickness. Group 2 (MacTel) has relatively thin maculas for the degree of angiographic leakage (**Fig. 11.52**); loss of the inner/outer segment band or ellipsoid layer, especially in the temporal macula in early disease; subfoveal cysts with relatively good VA; and rarely, subretinal neovascularisation.
- *Autofluorescence*: Abnormal in MacTel only. Abnormal distribution of macular pigment appears as a loss of the usual central macular dark spot.
- *OCT angiography*: MacTel starts temporally with reduced vascular density and deep plexus telangiectasia. Changes expand to involve all the perifoveal network and the superficial plexus. May show retinal-choroidal anastomoses that co-localise with outer retinal hyper-reflective lesions, often underlying the most affected areas.
- *Fluorescein angiography*: Features include telangiectatic vessels, outer retinal hyperfluorescence and RPE hyperpigmentation that may mask choroidal fluorescence. An example is shown on page 533 (**Fig. 11.26**). Subretinal

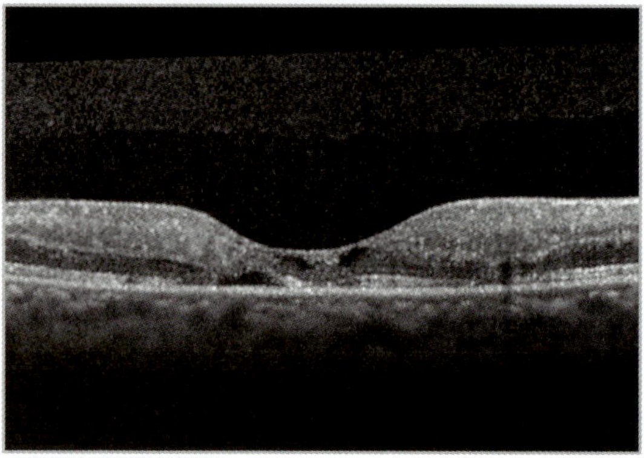

Fig. 11.52: Macular telangiectasia OCT.

neovascularisation sometimes occurs in MacTel, defining neovascular vs non-neovascular MacTel.

- *Fasting blood glucose*: Reported association with diabetes and the features may appear similar.
- *Electrophysiology*: Normal examination except for central hexagon on multifocal ERG, with abnormally low amplitude.

Treatment Laser is unproven; consider only for visually significant exudates and oedema that can be treated without applying laser to the foveal avascular zone (most likely to help Group 1 disease). Intravitreal anti-VEGF therapy is unproven for VA loss from fluid leakage, but is effective for neovascular MacTel. The FDA has approved ciliary neurotrophic factor delivered by an encapsulated cell implant. An international study website has further information (www.lmri.net).

SICKLE CELL RETINOPATHY

Background Different mutations in the β-haemoglobin gene produce either HbC or HbS, and subsequently homozygous HbSS (sickle cell disease), HbSC (sickle cell haemoglobin C disease), and HbAS (sickle trait). HbSC has the highest risk of eye disease.

Clinical features

- *Conjunctiva*: Dark-red, comma-shaped vessels particularly in the inferior bulbar conjunctiva.
- *Iris*: Focal iris atrophy and neovascularisation.
- *Angle*: Sickled red blood cells in the AC can elevate IOP. Many clinicians avoid or minimise the use of mannitol or acetazolamide in sickle patients, particularly those with intraocular haemorrhage, as this may theoretically increase sickling via dehydration and acidosis. Despite the theoretical risk, there are very few clinical reports of acetazolamide producing a sickle crisis.
- *Retina*:
  1. Angioid streaks.
  2. Focal collections of superficial or retinal haemorrhages that are initially bright red but degrade to form a 'salmon-patch haemorrhage'. Residual haemosiderin may produce refractile bodies (iridescent spots) and secondary retinal pigment epithelium (RPE) migration may leave intraretinal pigment (black sunburst) (**Fig. 11.53**).

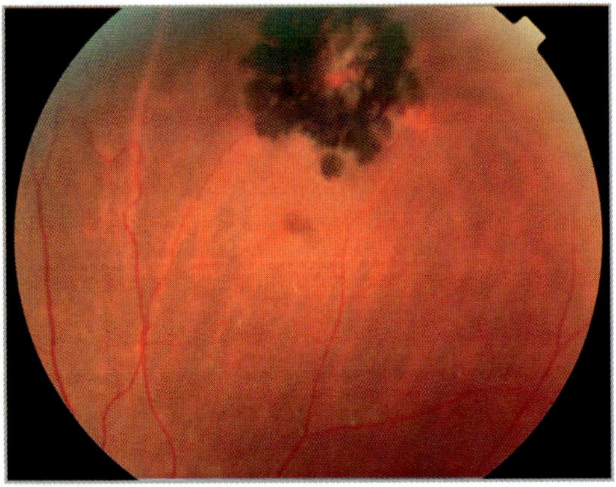

Fig. 11.53: Black sunburst (intraretinal pigment) in sickle cell retinopathy.

3. *Vessels*: Look for increased tortuosity, silver wiring, central and branch retinal artery occlusion, microhaemorrhages, peripheral ischaemia and vascular loops, enlargement of the foveal avascular zone (FAZ), macular ischaemia and thinning. Vaso-occlusion of the choroid may produce secondary RPE and outer retinal damage. Retinopathy is classified as:
   - Stage I: peripheral ischaemia.
   - Stage II: peripheral anastomoses that do not leak fluorescein.
   - Stage III: sea fan peripheral neovascularisation that leaks fluorescein (**Fig. 11.54**).

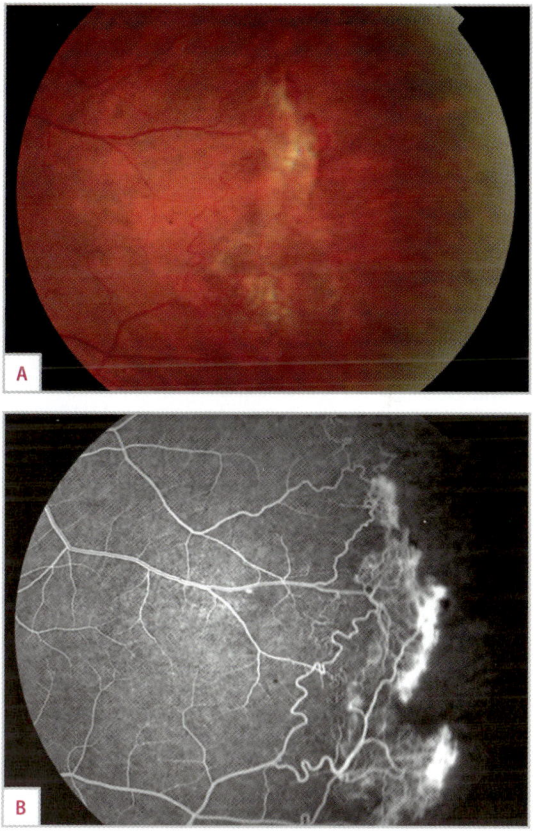

Fig. 11.54: Stage III sickle cell retinopathy.

- Stage IV: vitreous haemorrhage.
- Stage V: tractional and/or rhegmatogenous retinal detachment.

Differential diagnosis For causes of retinal neovascularisation, see page 528.

Investigations Test sickle status, if this is not known. OCT typically shows neuroretinal thinning, particular temporally. OCT angiography may show reduced vessel density, enlarged FAZ and capillary drop-out. Fluorescein angiography is not mandated, but if available widefield angiography may show peripheral leakage and ischaemia.

Treatment Although some clinicians advocate scatter laser photocoagulation (0.2 seconds, 500 μm spot size, grey-white burns, one burn width apart) in the area of non-perfusion for problematic stage III disease, this is rarely required, as many sea fans autoinfarct.

Follow-up The value of regular review in those who are asymptomatic is doubtful. Vitreous haemorrhage requires 2–4 weekly retinal ultrasounds if the fundal view cannot exclude retinal detachment. Refer for possible vitrectomy if there is non-clearing vitreous haemorrhage (within 3–6 months), tractional macular elevation (within 1 month), or rhegmatogenous retinal detachment (same day). Liaise with haematology, especially if there is progressive capillary ischaemia, which may require systemic investigations or treatment changes. For patients receiving treatment for transfusion-related iron overload, consider desferrioxamine toxicity (p. 620).

EALES' DISEASE

Background Rare, idiopathic, occlusive, peripheral vasculitis typically affecting healthy adults aged 20–30 years. More common in India and the Middle East. May be associated with prior TB infection and tuberculoprotein hypersensitivity.

Clinical features Common retinal features are vascular sheathing (venous > arterial), haemorrhage, peripheral ischaemia (collaterals, neovascularisation, vascular tortuosity, sclerosed vessels), and vitreous haemorrhage (**Fig. 11.55**).

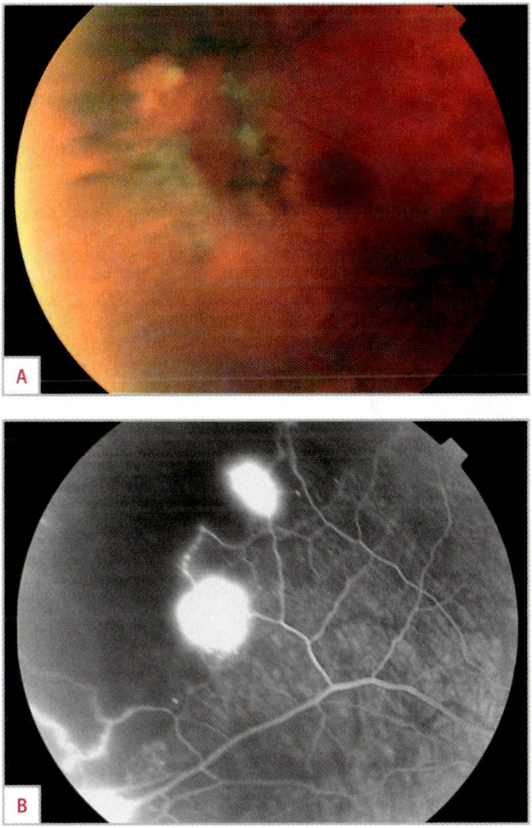

Fig. 11.55: Eales' disease (A), with peripheral ischaemia and leakage on fluorescein angiography (B).

Rubeotic glaucoma, disc new vessels, macular oedema, branch retinal vein occlusion (BRVO), macular holes, and tractional or rhegmatogenous retinal detachment may occur. Vitritis and anterior uveitis are mild or absent. Usually bilateral but often asymmetric at presentation.

Differential diagnosis Consider diabetic retinopathy, sickle cell retinopathy, isolated BRVO, sarcoidosis, tuberculosis, collagen vascular diseases and Coats' disease.

Investigations Fluorescein angiography shows ischaemia, vascular staining and leakage. Other tests are chosen as indicated to exclude other disease, e.g. glucose or HbA1c, sickle testing, ANA, sACE, CXR and TB tests.

Treatment Scatter photocoagulation in areas of ischaemia may lead to regression of neovascularisation. Refer non-clearing vitreous haemorrhage or retinal detachment for possible vitrectomy. Refer for antituberculosis treatment, if suspected or confirmed.

PSEUDOPHAKIC MACULAR OEDEMA (IRVINE–GASS SYNDROME)

Background Macular oedema occurring most commonly 1–12 months after cataract extraction, but can occur after other intraocular procedures. Thought to be caused by inflammation, although anterior chamber activity is typically mild or absent. Risk factors include cataract surgery complicated by vitreous loss (10–20% vs. 1%), epiretinal membrane, diabetes, retinitis pigmentosa and history of retinal vein occlusion, uveitis, retinal detachment repair or fellow eye Irvine–Gass syndrome.

Symptoms Initially good VA, then gradual central blurring.

Signs Macular oedema, often cystic.

History and examination Exclude diabetes, uveitis, retained vitreous lens material, vitreous traction, epiretinal membrane and retinitis pigmentosa as contributory factors. Examine the operation note and eye for signs of surgical complications, e.g. sulcus lens.

Investigations OCT shows macular oedema, and excludes vitreomacular traction or epiretinal membranes. Consider fluorescein angiography, which classically shows optic nerve and petalloid macular leakage (**Fig. 11.7**, p. 503).

Management Prescribe G. ketorolac 0.5% or other topical NSAIDs and G. dexamethasone 0.1%, both q.d.s. for 2 months, then taper over 1 month. Reinstate if the oedema recurs, which is common. Consider second-line therapies: acetazolamide (e.g. 250 mg sustained release b.d. p.o.), subtenons or intraocular steroids (e.g. 700 μg dexamethasone implant) if fluid persists but note the cautions and risks. A small subgroup analysis of the PROMETHEUS study suggested a benefit from anti-VEGF drugs, but confirmatory studies are needed. Surgically relieve any anterior or posterior chamber vitreous traction. Consider prophylactic pre- and postoperative NSAID drops and subconjunctival steroid for fellow eye surgery following incident cases and for patients with diabetic retinopathy (dosing given on p. 566), but a 2016 Cochrane review found no high-quality evidence of better VA or less Irvine–Gass syndrome following prophylactic NSAIDs for routine cataract cases.

Follow-up Two-monthly while on treatment.

CENTRAL SEROUS CHORIORETINOPATHY

Background Focal choroidal hyperpermeability with overlying retinal pigment epithelium (RPE) barrier compromise causes fluid to collect in the subretinal space. Central serous chorioretinopathy (CSCR) is also known as central serous retinopathy (CSR). The typical patient is male, 30–60 years old, with a type A personality, although some studies dispute the latter. CSCR may be part of the pachychoroid spectrum, a group of conditions with thick choroid, including pachychoroid pigment epitheliopathy (see below), focal choroidal excavation [an 'inverse pigment epithelial detachment (PED)' with focal choroidal depression], peripapillary pachychoroid syndrome (around the optic disc), pachychoroid with drusen (macula-sparing yellow-white sub-RPE deposits called pachydrusen). Some studies report a familial predisposition and potential genes defects in GATA binding protein, cadherin, and mineralocorticoid receptors.

Symptoms Blurred central vision, slow recovery from bright light, scotoma and distortion. Most often presents unilaterally, but is bilateral in up to half of those aged over 50 years.

Classification Acute, chronic, recurrent, multifocal and bullous.

History Ask about previous episodes, refractive change (increased hyperopia from retinal elevation) and risk factors

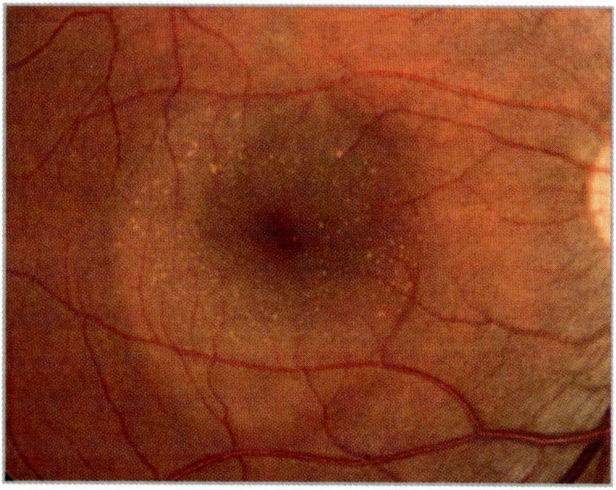

Fig. 11.56: Central serous chorioretinopathy.

(pregnancy; topical, local or systemic corticosteroid use; hypertension; emotional stress; allergic respiratory disease; Cushing's symptoms or signs; possible association with *Helicobacter pylori*).

Signs Neurosensory retinal detachment, often but not always in the macular area (**Fig. 11.56**), sometimes with PED. Detachment may be difficult to detect. Chronic disease may have poor VA. Choroidal neovascularisation (CNV) occurs in 3–4%. Previous episodes often leave focal RPE mottling and hyper /hypopigmentation, in either eye.

Differential diagnosis Consider polypoidal choroidal vasculopathy (PCV); optic disc pit; choroidal melanoma or other tumour; dome-maculopathy (especially in myopes); rhegmatogenous retinal detachment; age-related macular degeneration with CNV and/or PED; choroidal inflammation or ischaemia (Vogt–Koyanagi–Harada disease, white dot syndromes); posterior scleritis; choroidal haemangioma; choroidal lymphoma, paraproteinaemias and leukemia; malignant hypertension; pregnancy-induced hypertension; uveal effusion syndrome; vitelliform lesions; and drug-induced, in particular mitogen activated protein kinase (MEK) inhibitor-associated serous retinopathy (MEKAR) caused by drugs used to treat melanoma and ovarian cancer.

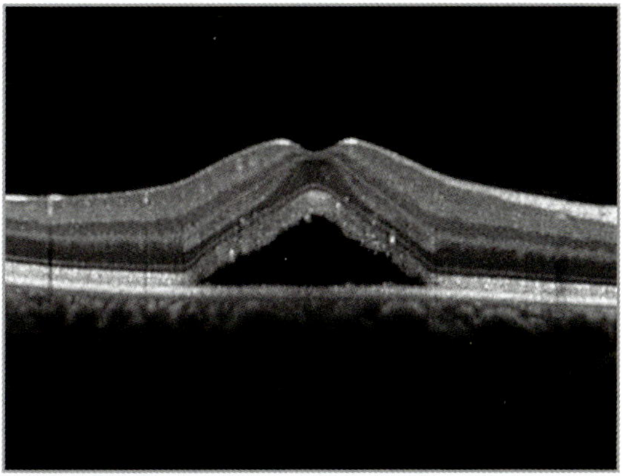

Fig. 11.57: Central serous chorioretinopathy OCT with subretinal fluid and large choroidal 'pachyvessels' (Courtesy M Richardson).

Investigations OCT shows subretinal fluid with a dome of elevated retina (**Fig. 11.57**), sometimes with multiple small PEDs and double-layer sign (formed by shallow separation of RPE from its underlying basement membrane). Enhanced depth imaging (EDI) OCT often shows a central choroid >300 μm thick (pachychoroid) in one or both eyes. The fellow eye may show a forme fruste termed 'pachychoroid pigment epitheliopathy', with reduced fundus tessellation, varied RPE changes including small

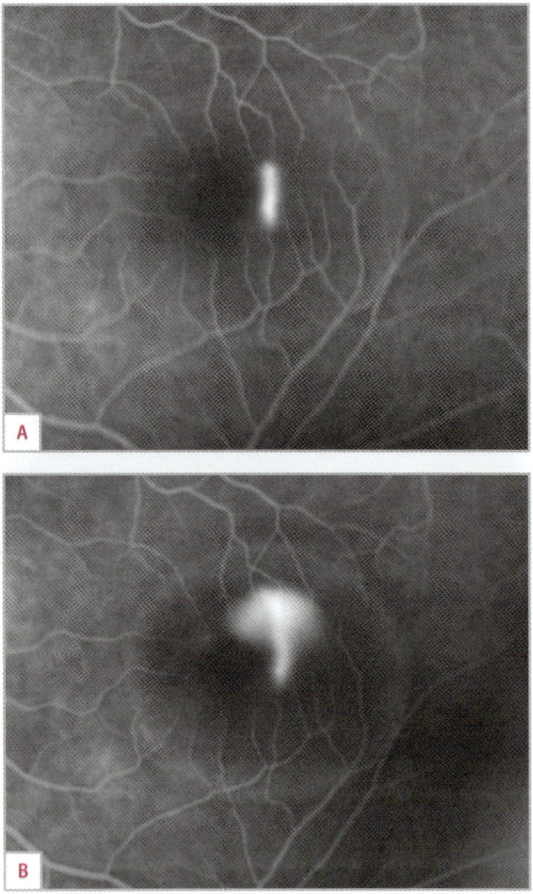

Fig. 11.58: Central serous chorioretinopathy with a 'smoke-stack' seen in an early (A) and later (B) fluorescein angiogram.

'bumps', and PEDs. Fundus autofluorescence and the OCT near infrared image may show mottled RPE changes from previous lesions in either eye. OCT angiography is sensitive at detecting associated CNV. If the diagnosis is uncertain arrange fluorescein angiography that may show a 'smoke-stack' (**Fig. 11.58**) or more commonly 'ink-blot' leakage in the acute phase (**Fig. 11.4**, p. 500). Chronic disease shows diffuse hyperfluorescence. ICG is helpful in detecting choroidal hyperpermeability, guiding the photodynamic therapy (PDT) treatment area, and may show mid-phase hyperfluorescent plaques. Autorefract. If Cushing's syndrome is suspected, check optic nerves and visual fields to exclude pituitary compression, and refer to an endocrinologist. Consider further specific investigations based on the differential diagnosis list above.

Treatment Most acute cases resolve spontaneously within 3–6 months, so observe. Approximately 85% of acute cases achieve 6/6 VA, but 30–50% recur. Recurrent or chronic cases have a worse prognosis, but 30% of chronic cases fully resolve within a year. Advise against corticosteroid use if possible. The PLACE randomised controlled trial (RCT) found that half-dose PDT was superior to high density sub-threshold micropulse laser. The VICI RCT found that the mineralocorticoid antagonist eplerenone offered no benefit over placebo, and the SPECTRA RCT found it inferior to half-dose PDT. Therefore, if fluid persists >6 months, offer half-dose (3 mg/m^2) PDT, but avoid if there is RPE atrophy. Plan the treatment to cover areas of leakage on angiography/OCT. Argon laser treatment of a single leaking focus that is well clear of the fovea reduces the interval to recovery, but does not change the long-term visual prognosis. Intravitreal anti-VEGF treatment is effective for secondary CNV, but lacks strong evidence of benefit for primary disease.

Follow-up 3–6 monthly until resolved.

RETINITIS PIGMENTOSA

Background Retinitis pigmentosa (rod-cone dystrophy, RP) is a group of progressive, degenerative retinal disorders characterised first by rod, then cone dysfunction. They have heterogeneous clinical features, mode of inheritance and causative genes. Key features are night blindness (nyctalopia), progressive visual field loss, neurosensory retinal pigmentation, and disc pallor.

Classification

- By inheritance:
  1. Autosomal recessive (AR): 60% of cases.
  2. Autosomal dominant (AD): 10–25% of cases.
  3. X-linked (XL): 5–18% of cases.
- By phenotype, e.g. sector RP, paravenous, adult, child onset.
- By causative gene: e.g. rhodopsin, CRB1.

History Ask about: nyctalopia; VA; glare; field loss; visual requirements (driving); consanguinity; associated systemic syndromes, especially congenital deafness (Usher's), anosmia (Refsum's), and polydactyly (Bardet–Biedl).

Examination Note any associated changes: myopia; cataract; glaucoma; vitreous cells; macular oedema; cellophane maculopathy; peripheral telangiectasia. Localised loss of the red fundus colour occurs in early disease. Bone-spicules occur later, and are intraretinal, versus causes affecting the retinal pigment epithelium (RPE). Note their topographical distribution or photograph. Advanced disease shows retinal vessel attenuation, RPE atrophy, and may show disc pallor (**Fig. 11.59**).

Examine family members to determine the inheritance pattern. Draw a family pedigree (**Fig. 11.1**, p. 494). Consider AR inheritance if both parents are normal and more than one sibling is affected (particularly a female), or there is consanguinity. X-linked female carriers may show bone-spicules, altered (tapetal) retinal reflex, and electroretinogram (ERG) changes. Isolated cases (simplex or sporadic RP) occur in ~40%, but many are probably unconfirmed AR.

Differential diagnosis Consider glaucoma with normal RPE pigmentary changes; normal reticular changes; syphilis; rubella; drug toxicity; cancer-associated retinopathy; autoimmune retinopathy; 'bear-track' RPE hypertrophy; diffuse unilateral subacute neuroretinitis; female choroideremia carriers. White RPE changes can occur or even predominate (retinitis punctata albescens). Fundus albipunctatus is a distinct and stationary

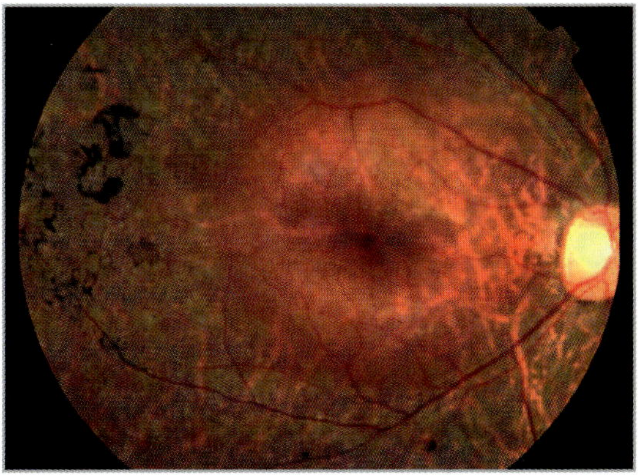

Fig. 11.59: Retinitis pigmentosa.

(non-progressive) disorder with nyctalopia and small punctate white dots throughout the fundus.

Syndromic and metabolic disorders with pigmentary retinopathy include:

- *Usher's syndrome*: Always AR. Rod-cone dystrophy with neurosensory hearing loss. There are three subtypes based on hearing loss: Type I – profound congenital hearing loss, no speech, hearing aids unhelpful, sign-communication necessary, vestibular dysfunction delays motor developmental milestones, five causative genes; Type II – partial congenital deafness usually presenting before 5 years, with symptoms of RP occurring in adulthood. Hearing aids helpful, sign-communication unnecessary, abnormal articulation, three causative genes. Type III – normal hearing at birth with progressive loss of hearing in adulthood, highly variable, normal speech, one causative gene.
- *Bardet–Biedl syndrome*: AR, usually cone–rod dystrophy (rarely rod-cone). VA is affected early. Highly variable syndrome which includes some of, polydactyly (always post-axial; lesser digit side of hand or foot; involvement of 0–4 limbs), hypogonadism (hypotestosteronism in males, late or irregular periods in females), obesity, cognitive impairment, and congenital renal disease. More than 20 causative genes identified so far.
- *Bassen–Kornzweig syndrome (abetalipoproteinaemia, acanthocytosis)*: presents in infancy due to altered fat and vitamin A metabolism with strabismus, neuromuscular disturbance, ataxia, and fat intolerance. Retinal dysfunction and degeneration can be severe if the systemic disorder

is unrecognised or untreated. Angioid streaks and neovascularisation are late complications.

- *Batten's disease (juvenile neuronal ceroid lipofuscinosis)*: AR due to *CLN3* gene mutation, with lipopigment accumulation in neural tissue. Presents aged 5–10 years with progressive central vision loss. Bull's eye maculopathy is often the presenting feature. 'Negative' ERG. Progresses to include mental deterioration, ataxia, seizures, and early death.
- *Gyrate atrophy*: AR disorder due to ornithine metabolism deficiency (mutation of gene encoding ornithine amino transferase). There is nyctalopia and progressive loss of peripheral vision through adulthood. The fundus shows distinctive scalloped atrophy of the anterior retina. High serum ornithine is diagnostic. Some mutations respond to vitamin B6 supplementation, but otherwise a low-arginine diet is required.
- *Homocystinuria*: an AR deficiency of homocysteine breakdown with myopia, ectopia lentis, glaucoma, optic atrophy, CNS and vascular disease.
- *Kearns–Sayre syndrome*: A mitochondrial DNA deletion with progressive external ophthalmoplegia before age of 20 years, short stature, heart block, neuromuscular weakness, ataxia, deafness, cognitive deficiency, diabetes, and hypoparathyroidism. Regular cardiac review is recommended.
- *Oxalosis*: a metabolic AR disorder that produces oxalate deposition with optic atrophy, RPE changes, retinal vascular obstruction, renal, bone, and vascular disease.
- *Refsum's disease*: AR – the rod-cone dystrophy is usually the presenting feature, but the syndromic nature of the disorder is often initially missed. Ask about anosmia (usually the first neurological symptom) and symptoms of sensory and motor polyneuropathy. Examine for malformation of the 4th digit of hands and feet (variable) and poorly dilating pupils. Refer to a neurologist if suspected. Elevated serum phytanic acid confirms the diagnosis. Requires a specialised diet to delay neurological manifestations.

Investigations

- *Electroretinography*: usually shows a markedly reduced or extinguished response (**Fig. 11.19**, p. 518). Scotopic amplitudes ≥100 mV suggest a better prognosis.
- *Visual field test*: initial field loss is variable, but classically bilateral, symmetric, and midperipheral, with central vision preserved until late.
- *Estermann driving fields*: for legal requirements, see page 825.
- *Fluorescein angiography*: avoid if possible, as extremely uncomfortable and some concern may add to retinal damage.

- *Optical coherence tomography*: may show macular oedema.
- *Fundus autofluorescence*: quantifies macular atrophy if it is clinically uncertain, and may show a Robson's ring of hyperautofluorescence surrounding the fovea (see **Fig. 11.17**, p. 514), with macular function preserved within the ring.
- *Syphilis serology*: in doubtful cases.
- *Genetic testing*: improved sequencing technology has made genetic testing more accessible in many countries. Requires informed consent. Provide genetic counselling with an experienced clinician prior to testing, and if not available refer to a subspecialist unit. A molecular diagnosis informs prognosis and helps to direct patients to relevant emerging treatments.

Management RP requires specialised support. Advise drivers of their obligation to inform the licensing authority. Consider:

- Low-vision aids and sunglasses.
- Assistive technology: smart phones, tablet computers, and applications such as Seeing AI, 'Be My Eyes', Envision, and Synaptic.
- Registration as sight impaired or severely sight impaired.
- Cataract surgery: Use low illumination and an IOL with a low risk of posterior capsular opacification and phimosis.
- Try G. dorzolamide t.d.s. (or brinzolomide) for macular oedema. Consider a 4-week trial of oral acetazolamide 250 mg o.d or b.d. if absent or incomplete response, with U&E 4-monthly to exclude or treat hypokalaemia.
- Counselling, once the diagnosis and likely inheritance pattern have been established. Misinformation may profoundly affect work and family planning, so involve experienced staff.
- Provide contact details of support groups, e.g. Retina UK, RNIB. For patient information see www.rcophth.ac.uk.
- Voretigene neparvovec (Luxturna) is an adeno-associated virus vector-based gene therapy licensed for the treatment of biallelic RPE65 mutation, which can cause RP and Leber's congenital amaurosis. It is delivered by vitrectomy and subretinal injection.

CONE DYSTROPHY

Classification

- *Stationary*: may show only subtle alteration in colour vision or anomalous trichromacy. Vision may be better in the dark (hemeralopia). Examination shows nystagmus and a normal fundus. Macular atrophy can occur in adulthood without worsening of function, but significant congenital visual impairment occurs in rod monochromacy (achromatopsia), with VA typically ~6/60. More than 15 genes identified so far; gene-replacement may be available in the future. Consider X-linked blue-cone monochromatism in males with myopia and some preservation of blue-yellow axis. Consider 'cone dystrophy with supernormal rod ERG' (KCNV2 retinopathy) in those with both nyctalopia and hemeralopia, nystagmus and a normal fundus.
- *Progressive*: includes autosomal recessive disorders due to ABCA4 (which causes Stargardt's disease) and other rarer genes. If family history suggests autosomal dominant inheritance then consider retinopathy due to gain-of-function mutations in GUCY2D and GUCA1A.
- *Systemic disease*: may coexist with several systemic or metabolic diseases, in particular Bardet–Biedl syndrome (p. 599).
- *Toxic*: consider also chloroquine or hydroxychloroquine toxicity.

History and examination Ask about VA, colour vision, and problems with bright light. Some forms show Mendelian inheritance (usually autosomal recessive), so examine family members and draw a family pedigree (**Fig 11.1**, p. 494). Check colour vision with Ishihara plates, Hardy-Rand-Rittler plates (allows rapid determination of colour defect) and, if time allows, consider the Farnsworth–Munsell 100-hue test. Funduscopy may be normal, but the characteristic finding is macular atrophy or bull's eye maculopathy (p. 537).

Investigations Electrophysiology shows cone dysfunction with absent or mild rod involvement. Autofluorescence imaging is the most sensitive method of recording the degree of retinal involvement, and gives a clue of the causative gene. Consider genetic testing.

Management See retinitis pigmentosa management (previous page). Augmented technology may be particularly helpful, e.g. real-time magnification and increased contrast using GiveVision, EnSight, or OxSight. Offer counselling with senior staff, low-vision aids, corrective or plano sunglasses (~5% transmission) or tinted contact lenses, and registration as sight impaired or severely sight impaired, as appropriate. Trials are ongoing for ABCA4-cone dystrophy including gene-replacement and small drug modifiers of the visual-cycle. Gene-replacement trials are ongoing for CNGB3 and CNGA3 achromatopsia. As yet there are no treatments for the primary disorders.

Follow-up Agree the interval with the patient, e.g. as needed with more frequent low vision assessment, or yearly.

CHOROIDEREMIA

Background X-linked chorioretinal degeneration due to mutations in geranylgeranyl transferase Rab escort protein 1 (REP1).

Symptoms Night blindness (nyctalopia) and visual field loss in young males. Loss of central vision and profound blindness after 50 years in males. Nyctalopia and variable visual loss in adult female carriers.

Signs Midperipheral atrophy of the RPE and choriocapillaris, with choroidal depigmentation and resulting prominence of the choroidal vessels and sclera (**Fig. 11.60**). Retinal blood vessels are less attenuated than in retinitis pigmentosa.

History and examination Examine family members and draw a family pedigree (**Fig. 11.1**, p. 494). Female carriers are generally asymptomatic, but almost invariably show regional irregular fundal pigmentation and patchy RPE atrophy in later life.

Differential diagnosis Consider retinitis pigmentosa, gyrate atrophy, albinism, Bothnia dystrophy, and thioridazine retinopathy.

Investigations Arrange Estermann driving fields if relevant. Fluorescein angiography is rarely needed, but shows reduced background fluorescence and prominent choroidal vessels

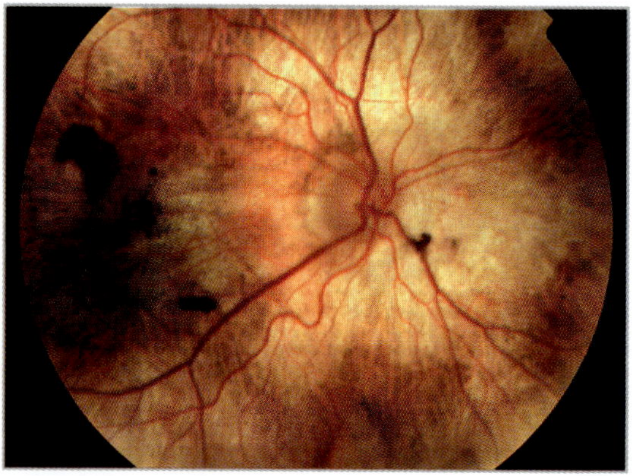

Fig. 11.60: Choroideremia.

caused by retinal pigment epithelium and choriocapillaris atrophy. Electrophysiology may initially be normal, but marked abnormalities usually develop. Consider genetic confirmation through sequencing of the *REP1* gene (technically easier in affected hemizygous males than in heterozygous female carriers).

Management Offer genetic counselling with an experienced clinician, annual review, low-vision aids and registration as sight impaired or severely sight impaired.

BEST'S DISEASE

Background Autosomal dominant macular dystrophy due to mutations in the *BEST1* gene. Also called Best's vitelliform macular dystrophy. A milder form, adult-onset vitelliform macular dystrophy (adult Best's), is often grouped with the pattern dystrophies (p. 609) and is not always due to mutations in BEST1. Autosomal recessive bestrophinopathy is a rare subtype of bestrophinopathy caused by biallelic mutations of the *BEST1* gene. It is characterised by multifocal subretinal deposits accompanied by macular oedema or subretinal fluid, hyperopia and narrow iridocorneal angle.

Symptoms May be asymptomatic, or present in childhood or teens with poor central acuity. Adult-onset vitelliform macular dystrophy typically presents aged 30–50 years with mild or absent symptoms, mild-moderate VA loss, and relatively subtle macular changes.

Signs The macula may appear normal, or show variable amounts of yellow deposition which can initially appear as an 'egg-yolk' (vitelliform) lesion (**Fig. 11.61**). Atrophy and scarring appear later. Hyperopia is common. Choroidal neovascularisation (CNV) sometimes occurs.

History and examination Examine family members and draw a family pedigree (**Fig. 11.1**, p. 494). Inheritance has variable penetrance, so affected relatives may be asymptomatic

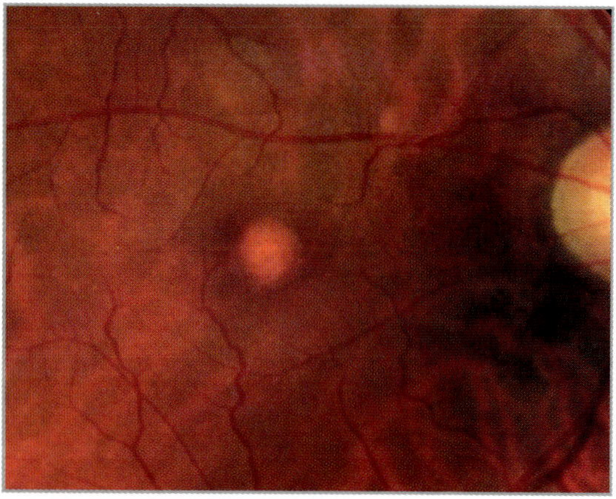

Fig. 11.61: Best's disease.

and have subtle signs. A recessive form exists, with more widespread funduscopic and electrophysiological abnormalities, due to distinct mutations in *BEST1* (inherited from each parent).

Differential diagnosis Consider central serous chorioretinopathy, pigment epithelial detachment (PED), toxoplasma and other causes of macular atrophy (p. 536). Consider also other vitelliform maculopathies such as pattern dystrophy due to *PRPH2* gene defect. In the elderly, tractional, paraneoplastic, toxic, and degenerative disorders may produce vitelliform lesions.

Investigations Reduced light-induced rise of the electro-oculogram (EOG), with normal full-field electroretinogram (ERG), is diagnostic. Fluorescein angiography shows hypofluorescence initially (blockage from vitelliform material), and hyperfluorescence if retinal pigment epithelium (RPE) atrophy occurs. Testing for the affected Bestrophin gene is available. Fundus autofluorescence shows hyperautofluorescence of the deposit (**Fig. 11.62**). Adult-onset vitelliform macular dystrophy may show subtle hyperautofluoresence and foveal OCT changes that can look similar to drusen (**Fig. 11.63**).

Management Offer genetic counselling with a senior clinician and annual review. Treat CNV with intravitreal anti-VEGF agents.

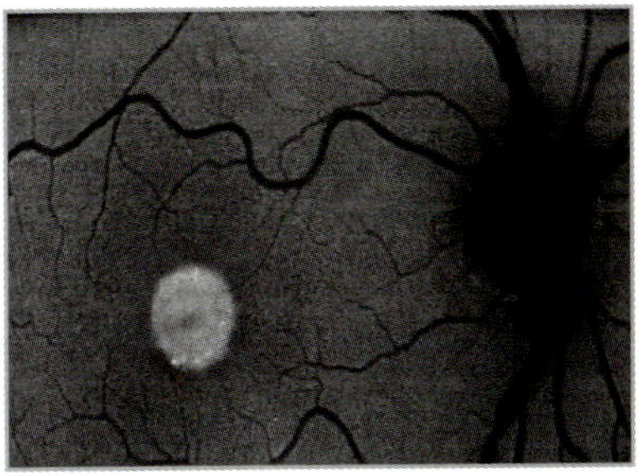

Fig. 11.62: Best's disease fundus autofluorescence (Courtesy S Mann).

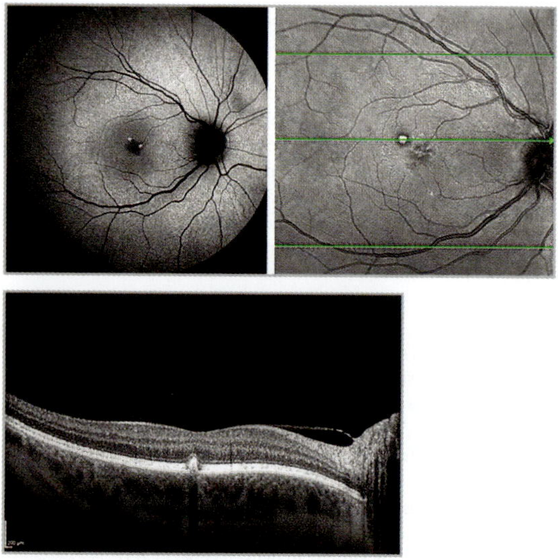

Fig. 11.63. Adult vitelliform macular dystrophy with central hyperautofluorescence on fundus autofluorescence (top left) due to accumulation of lipofuscin within the retinal pigment epithelium, and a focal foveal change on the near infrared image (top right) and OCT (Courtesy S Mann).

PATTERN DYSTROPHY

Background An autosomal dominant macular disease. Shows overlap with adult-onset vitelliform macular dystrophy (p. 606).

Symptoms May have paracentral distortion, loss of VA or be asymptomatic.

Signs The macula may show a pale subretinal or pigmented deposit at the fovea or in a linear distribution (**Fig. 11.64**). With time, central atrophy may occur. Choroidal neovascularisation (CNV) is rare.

History and examination Examine family members and draw a family pedigree (**Fig. 11.1**, p. 494). Although autosomal dominant, there is variable expression and incomplete penetrance, so affected relatives may be asymptomatic and signs subtle.

Differential diagnosis Consider central serous chorioretinopathy, age-related macular degeneration, Best's disease and other inherited conditions, e.g. maternally inherited diabetes and deafness (MIDD).

Investigations Autofluorescence imaging shows hyperautofluorescence of the fundal lesions. Genetic testing is possible (*RDS/PRPH2* and *IMPG1* genes).

Management Offer genetic counselling with a senior clinician and annual review. Currently, no treatment exists.

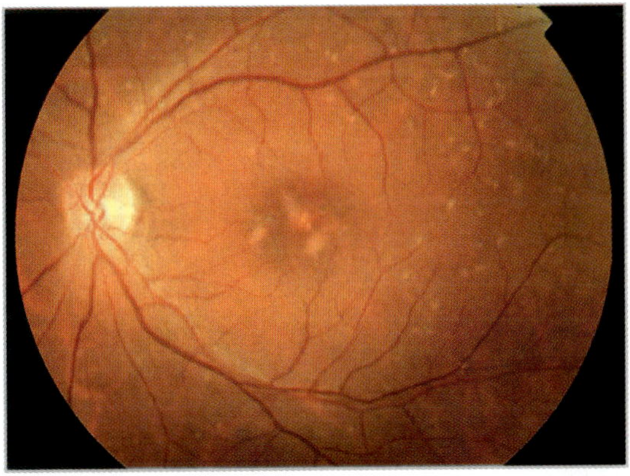

Fig. 11.64: Pattern dystrophy.

STARGARDT'S DISEASE

Background A common autosomal recessive disease with yellow retinal pigment epithelium (RPE) flecks plus macular atrophy due to mutations in the *ABCA4* gene. The carrier rate is high (1 in 50) so the children of affected individuals may be affected (pseudodominance ~1%). Also known as 'fundus flavimaculatus'.

Symptoms Poor central vision in childhood or teens is most common, but may present later.

Signs May be normal initially, but the macula develops atrophy, surrounded by yellow flecks (**Fig. 11.65**). Retinitis pigmentosa-like pigmentation can occur. The peripheral visual field is full.

Differential diagnosis Exclude other causes of macular atrophy (p. 536), especially cone dystrophy. The yellow flecks have a more patterned appearance than drusen.

Investigations The pattern electroretinogram (ERG) is always abnormal. In more severe cases the cone, or both the cone and rod responses, are affected (type II and III, respectively). Fluorescein angiography classically shows a dark choroid with hyperfluorescent flecks, but not always. Fundus autofluorescence helps to quantify RPE damage (**Fig. 11.16**, p. 513); the yellow flecks are hyperautofluorescent. Genetic testing of *ABCA4* has high sensitivity.

Management Offer counselling with senior staff, registration as sight impaired or severely sight impaired, low-vision aids, and annual review. There is no treatment.

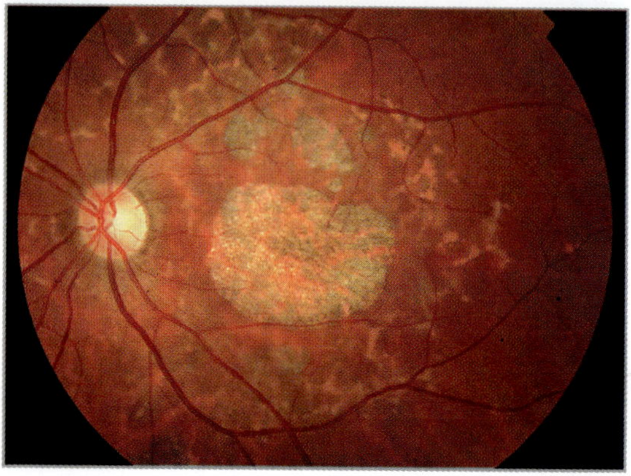

Fig. 11.65: Stargardt's disease.

OTHER MACULAR DYSTROPHIES

Retinal degeneration slow (RDS)/Peripherin-2 (PRPH2) dystrophy (central areolar choroidal dystrophy) The most common autosomal dominant macular dystrophy in the UK. Presents in early adulthood with slowly developing bull's eye lesions. The peripheral retina and full-field electroretinogram are usually normal. Genetic testing for specific missense changes in *RDS/PRPH2* is diagnostic.

Sorsby's macular dystrophy Autosomal dominant. Presents in the 5th decade with choroidal neovascularisation; a minority present later with macular atrophy. Nyctalopia is a common early symptom. The causative gene is *TIMP3*, due to a few specific alleles. Genetic testing is sensitive and specific.

Dominant drusen (Doyne's honeycomb choroiditis, Malattia Leventinese) Autosomal dominant. Variable onset of reduced VA due to deposition of macular drusen. Peripapillary deposit is a common and pathognomonic feature. A specific missense mutation in *EFEMP1* (fibulin-3) is diagnostic.

North Carolina macular dystrophy [MCDR1, central areolar pigment epithelial dystrophy (CAPED)]: Rare, autosomal dominant, non-progressive disorder with variable lesions at the macula, from well-defined atrophy to subtle hard drusen. Genetic testing is available for the causative *PRDM13* mutation at the *MCDR1* locus of chromosome 6. The *MCDR3* locus of chromosome 5 is also implicated.

Maternally inherited diabetes and deafness (MIDD) A m.3243A>G mitochondrial mutation. Can cause macular dystrophy, typically with mid-macular, circumferential atrophy. The phenotype is highly variable and comprises neurosensory deafness and adult-onset diabetes mellitus. The same mutation can rarely cause more severe disease termed mitochondrial encephalomyopathy, lactic acidosis and stroke-like episodes (MELAS).

ALBINISM

Background A genetic disorder of melanin production.

Classification
- Ocular.
- Oculocutaneous:
  1. Tyrosinase-negative.
  2. Tyrosinase-positive.

Symptoms Photophobia and blurred central vision.

Signs Complete absence of skin and hair pigment suggests tyrosinase-negative oculocutaneous albinism. Otherwise, pigmentation is variable and in some, lightest after birth. Skin and hair pigmentation is normal in ocular albinism. Features include foveal hypoplasia and reduced VA, nystagmus, strabismus, refractive errors, iris transillumination and pale fundus.

History and examination Examine family members and draw a family tree (**Fig. 11.1**, p. 494). Ocular albinism is commonly X-linked, but sometimes autosomal recessive. Female carriers may show mild iris and characteristic fundus changes (**Fig. 11.66**). Oculocutaneous cases are usually autosomal recessive. In tyrosinase-positive patients ask about recurrent infections (Chediak–Higashi syndrome) and bleeding/bruising problems (Hermansky–Pudlak syndrome).

Investigations Consider electrophysiology (p. 516), tyrosinase testing, FBC, and coagulation. Misrouting of fibres in the optic chiasm is detectable with visually-evoked potentials. Optical coherence tomography may show absence of the foveal depression.

Management Arrange genetic counselling with an experienced clinician, and low-vision aids if required. Patients have an increased risk of basal and squamous cell carcinomas, so refer to dermatology if suspected. Refer patients with immunocompromise or bleeding diathesis to haematology.

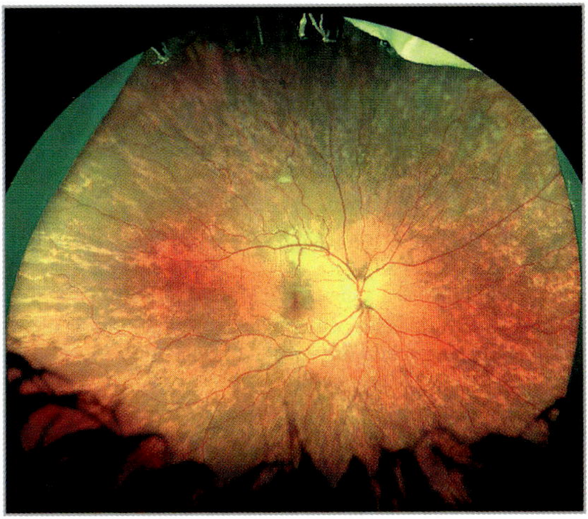

Fig. 11.66: Wide angle pseudo-colour image (Optos) of X-linked ocular albinism female carrier (heterozygous mutation in GPR143).

SYPHILIS

Background A sexually transmitted infection caused by the spirochaete *Treponema pallidum*. Mother-to-child transmission can also result in congenital infection.

Classification and systemic features

- *Primary*: Genital ulcer (chancre).
- *Secondary*: Lymphadenopathy, rash, mucous membrane lesions and meningitis.
- *Latent*: No clinical manifestation. May last for many years.
- *Tertiary*: Cardiovascular disease (aortitis, aortic regurgitation, angina), neurosyphilis (myelopathy, mental changes) and systemic gummata (fibrous deposits).

Signs Ocular disease may occur at any stage. Primary infection may rarely present with a chancre on the eyelid. Signs of secondary and tertiary infection include oculomotor palsies, madarosis (loss of eyelashes), conjunctivitis, interstitial keratitis, episcleritis, scleritis, glaucoma, Argyll Robertson pupil (light-near dissociation), field loss, uveitis, chorioretinitis, retinitis, choroidal ischaemia, periarteritis, neuroretinitis and optic neuritis. Late changes may mimic retinitis pigmentosa with paravascular retinal pigment, vascular attenuation, and pale discs. Congenital syphilis classically produces interstitial keratitis and pigmentary retinopathy.

Investigations

- *Optical coherence tomography and fundus autofluorescence*: OCT changes often involve the outer retina, with ellipsoid defects, retinal pigment epithelium nodularity and thickened placoid chorioretinal lesions. Acutely, autofluorescence typically shows hyperautofluorescense, that can resolve or become hypoautofluoresent, if retinal pigment epithelium atrophy emerges. The acute appearance can mimic AZOOR.
- *Venereal Disease Research Laboratory (VDRL) and RPR*: these react with IgM and IgG antibodies after ~6 weeks seroconversion. Termed 'non-treponemal tests' as they are not specific to syphilis and can be positive with tuberculosis, rickettsial diseases, endocarditis and pregnancy; hence only use for initial screening. Valuable for monitoring treatment as the titres are high in active disease and fall with effective therapy.
- *FTA-ABS, MHA-TP or TPHA*: these tests measure specific antitreponemal antibody levels and usually remain positive for life, even after effective therapy. Other treponemes (including yaws) give positive results, as occasionally do other spirochaetes (Lyme disease).

Management Refer to an infectious disease or genitourinary medicine consultant for evaluation and treatment. Treat primary, secondary and latent infection with sustained release intramuscular penicillin. Treat tertiary disease, including central nervous system and eye, with high-dose parenteral therapy under specialised care. A Jarisch–Herxheimer reaction with marked inflammatory response may follow the first penicillin dose and may lead to ocular inflammation. In many countries, syphilis is a notifiable disease. In at-risk individuals, consider referral for HIV testing, which may coexist. Topical steroids may be required for ocular inflammation. Only consider systemic steroids after full investigation and treatment of any underlying infection.

SOLAR RETINOPATHY

Background Foveal phototoxicity secondary to sun-gazing.

History Ask about predisposing factors, such as recreational drug use, mydriatic or photosensitising medications (e.g. tetracycline), use of condensing lenses (e.g. telescopes), and viewing a solar eclipse.

Symptoms Blurred vision, scotoma, chromatopsia, metamorphopsia and afterimage.

Signs VA is usually 6/12 to 6/60 acutely, with reduced near acuity and Amsler grid changes. Funduscopy reveals a uni- or bilateral yellowish foveal lesion, sometimes with a grey annulus (**Fig. 11.67**). This fades over a week, leaving a small, well-defined, deep red spot which persists for life, or rarely mild retinal pigment epithelium changes. Recovery of VA is usual.

Differential diagnosis Consider micromacular hole, poppers maculopathy, Best's disease, cone dystrophy, light-damage from an operating microscope, central serous chorioretinopathy, age-related macular degeneration, and toxic retinopathy. For other causes of macular atrophy, see page 536.

Investigations OCT typically shows subfoveal outer retinal disturbance with discontinuity of the inner/outer segment line (**Fig. 11.68**). Fluorescein angiography is often normal.

Treatment There is no proven treatment.

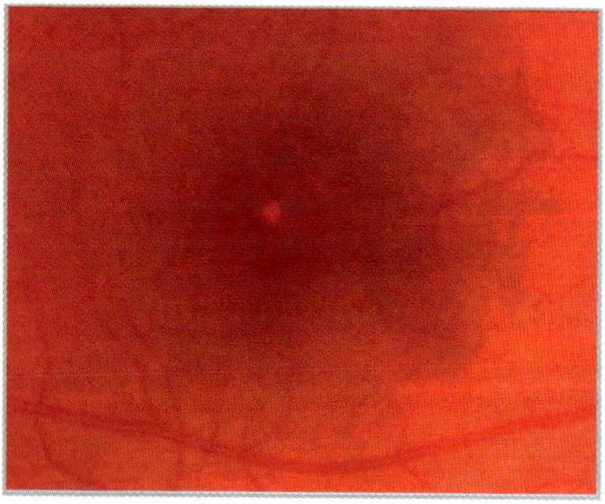

Fig. 11.67: Solar retinopathy.

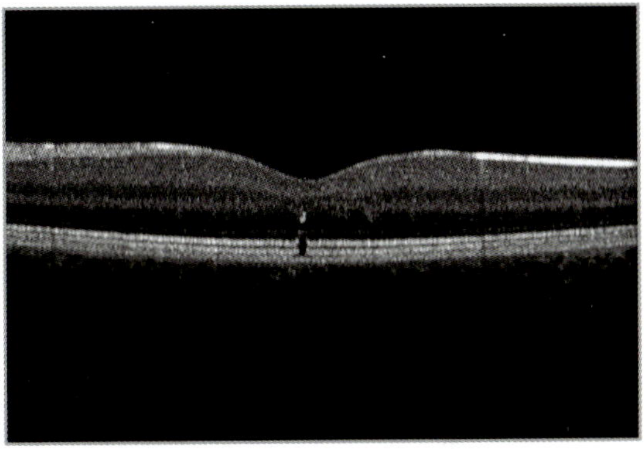

Fig. 11.68: OCT of solar retinopathy, showing damage to the photoreceptor inner/outer segment line (Courtesy A Simpson).

POPPERS MACULOPATHY

Background Foveal damage due to inhaled recreational use of poppers (alkyl nitrite compounds), often by gay men or at night clubs.

History Ask about the frequency, duration and timing of drug use. Exclude sun gazing.

Symptoms Blurred vision, chromatopsia, and metamorphopsia.

Signs VA ~6/9 to 6/18. Ishihara colour plates may be normal or slightly reduced. Funduscopy typically shows a uni- or bilateral, small, yellow foveal spot, with loss of the foveal reflex. Subtle retinal pigment epithelium changes may occur subsequently. VA can recover fully or partially.

Differential diagnosis Consider solar retinopathy, micromacular hole, central serous chorioretinopathy, Best's disease, macular dystrophy, age-related macular degeneration, and toxic retinopathy.

Investigations OCT shows subfoveal outer retinal disturbance of the inner/outer segment line (**Fig. 11.69**).

Treatment There is no proven treatment. Avoid poppers.

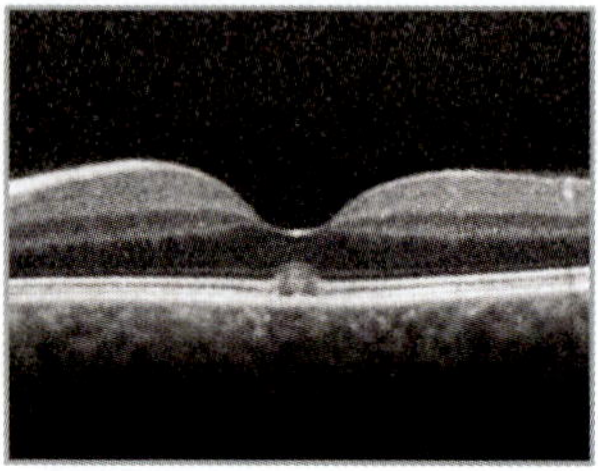

Fig. 11.69: OCT of poppers maculopathy.

FINGOLIMOD-ASSOCIATED MACULAR OEDEMA

Background Fingolimod, siponimod, ozanimod, etrasimod and ponesimod are oral sphingosine-1-phosphate (S1P) receptor modulators used as immunomodulating treatment for relapsing-remitting MS and/or inflammatory bowel disease. Fingolimod-associated macular edema (FAME) occurs in ~0.4% of patients, usually within 3–4 months of starting fingolimod, and rarely after 6 months. The manufacturers of fingolimod and siponimod advise ophthalmic review 3–4 months after starting treatment; plus regular monitoring in those at risk of macular oedema, e.g. diabetes, uveitis and retinal disease. The manufacturers of etrasimod and ponesimod advise eye examination before starting treatment; plus periodically thereafter for at-risk patients. The manufacturer of ozanimod advises both pre-treatment and periodic eye examination, but only for at-risk patients.

Symptoms Blurred vision and metamorphopsia occur, but can be asymptomatic.

Signs VA is typically 6/9 to 6/24. Macular oedema may be subtle, so request OCT.

Differential diagnosis Degenerative microcysts occur in 4–5% of MS patients, usually in the inner retina; VA is typically unaffected. If VA is reduced look for optic disc palor and reduced colour vision, from prior optic neuritis.

Investigations OCT shows foveal or parafoveal cysts, and/or subretinal fluid. Only consider fluorescein angiography if other causes of macular oedema (p. 535) need to be excluded.

Treatment Interrupt treatment if macular odema occurs; ~80% of FAME cases resolve, usually within 3–6 months. If not, try G. dexamethasone 0.1% and G. ketorolac 0.5%, both q.d.s.

Follow-up Monitor FAME until resolution. Discharge screening patients without FAME with an Amsler chart and advice to present if there is any change in vision, and suggest annual review by an optician with OCT capability.

TOXIC RETINOPATHIES

Chloroquine and hydroxychloroquine

Background Retinopathy occurs in ~7.5% of patients taking long-term hydroxychloroquine, increasing to 20–50% after 20 years of treatment. Chloroquine is thought to be higher-risk.

Symptoms Blurred vision, abnormal colour vision and scotomas.

Signs
- *Reversible*: Whorl-like corneal epithelial changes (verticillata) and abnormal foveal reflex.
- *Irreversible*: Fine granular macula appearance (**Fig. 11.70**). Bull's eye maculopathy is the only sign associated with impaired VA and central visual field disturbance.

History and examination Ask about the dose and duration of treatment, tamoxifen use, and renal impairment. Test near and distance VA, macular function (Amsler grid), and colour vision (Ishihara and red pin desaturation). Examine the cornea on a slit lamp for verticillata and perform dilated funduscopy.

Screening and investigations See **Flowchart 11.1** including the legend, and **Figure 11.71**.

Differential diagnosis
- *Granular macular changes*: age-related macular degeneration (AMD).
- *Bull's eye maculopathy*: retinal dystrophies such as cone dystrophy, Stargardt's disease, and benign concentric annular macular dystrophy can usually by differentiated by drug and family history and electrodiagnostic testing. Consider also AMD, and lipofuscinosis (usually presents in childhood).

Treatment Stop medication if toxicity develops and liaise with the prescribing physician.

Desferrioxamine (Deferoxamine)

Symptoms Decreased vision, scotomata, nyctalopia, photopsia, metamorphopsia, and hearing loss. Acute toxicity has been reported 7–10 days post i.v. infusion, but may also occur subacutely with chronic treatment.

Signs May be absent in early disease despite positive symptoms.

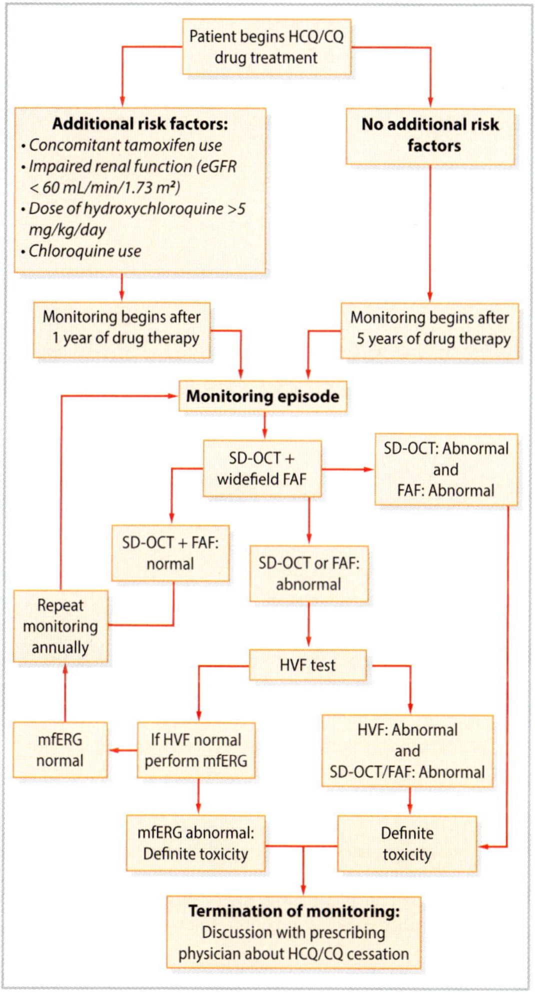

Flowchart 11.1: Hydroxychloroquine (HCQ) and chloroquine (CQ) screening algorithm, based on the Royal College of Ophthalmologists' 2020 guidelines. Use widefield fundus autofluorescence (FAF) if available, photomontage otherwise, and swept source or spectral-domain optical coherence tomography (SD-OCT). For parafoveal disease (2–6° eccentricity) use a 10-2 Humphrey visual field (HVF), or 30-2 HVF if pericentral (≥7 degrees; outside the macula). eGFR, estimated glomerular filtration rate; mfERG, multifocal electroretinogram.

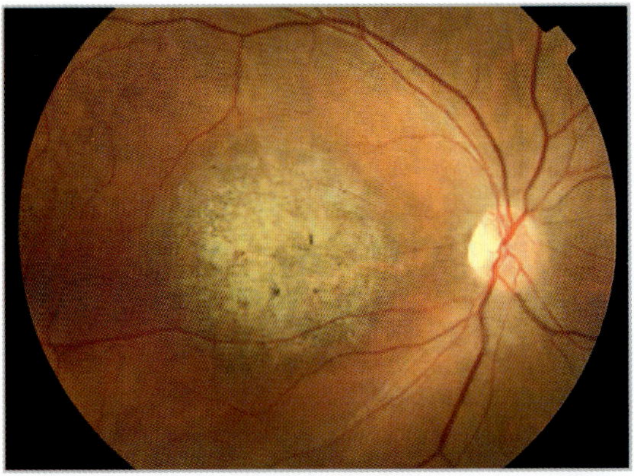

Fig. 11.70: Chloroquine retinopathy.

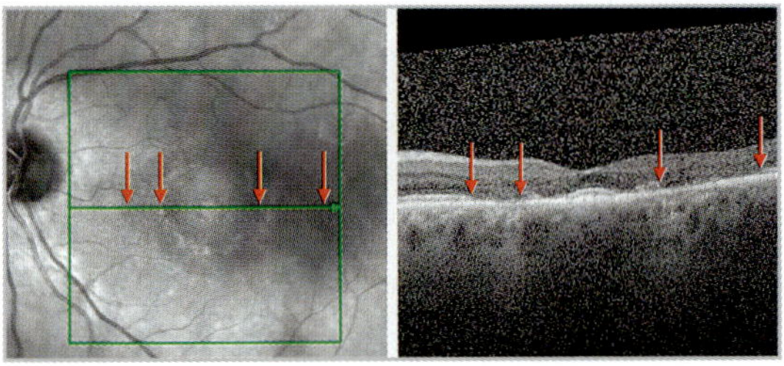

Fig. 11.71: Hydroxychloroquine toxicity seen with near infrared (left) and OCT (right). There is a bull's eye maculopathy, with an annular ellipsoid defect (red arrows).

Signs are usually bilateral, including irregular outer retina/retinal pigment epithelium (RPE) pigmentation, RPE hypopigmentation, and granularity (late phase). May involve just the macula or the entire retina. Disc swelling and optic atrophy are reported.

Investigations Arrange visual fields, fundus autofluorescence (FAF) and OCT. Fluorescein angiography shows a variable mottled appearance with blocked fluorescence in the transit phase and late hyperfluorescence, even in the presence of a normal-appearing retina. Electroretinogram, electro-oculogram, and visually-evoked potential may all be affected.

Treatment Careful monitoring may be required prior to and after starting desferrioxamine. If toxicity occurs, discontinue treatment if possible.

Follow-up Visual recovery is possible over 3–4 months. Damage may be more common in the presence of an abnormal blood-retinal-barrier, e.g. diabetes mellitus.

Phenothiazines (thioridazine and chlorpromazine)

Symptoms Blurred vision, abnormal colour vision (brownish tinge), nyctalopia, typically 2–8 weeks after excessive ingestion. The chronic form leads to progressive vision loss and nyctalopia.

Signs

- *Thioridazine*: The fundus may be normal initially, and then develop fine to coarse pigmentary retinopathy, usually uniformly in the macula to midperipheral retina (**Fig. 11.72**). Late stages show nummular areas of atrophy and severe diffuse outer retinal degeneration.
- *Chlorpromazine*: Mild pigmentary retinal changes, cataract and corneal deposits.

Differential diagnosis

- *Late atrophy*: Gyrate atrophy, high myopia, Bietti's crystalline dystrophy, syphilis, didanosine (HIV drug) toxicity and choroideremia.
- *Pigmentary retinopathy*: Retinitis pigmentosa.

Investigations Fluorescein angiography and/or FAF may help to detect mild RPE abnormalities. The EOG is abnormal.

Treatment Discontinue medication but liaise with psychiatrists.

Follow-up If the thioridazine dosage exceeds 800 mg/day or chlorpromazine dosage exceeds 2,400 mg/day, review 6-monthly, otherwise screening is not required.

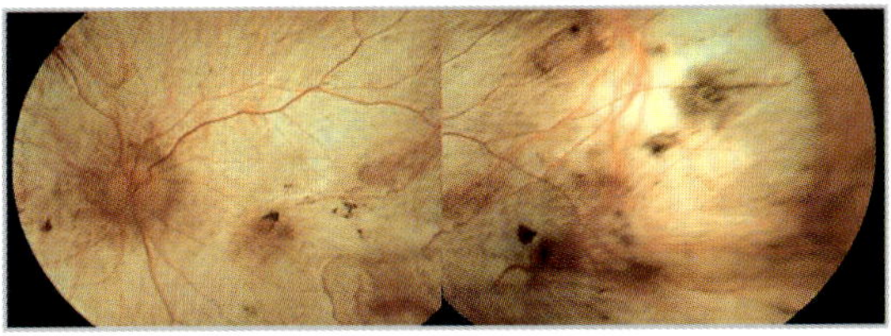

Fig. 11.72: Thioridazine toxicity.

OPTOMETRY AND GENERAL PRACTICE GUIDELINES

General comments

The most urgent retinal referral is central retinal artery occlusion. It is sometimes possible to dislodge the embolus, but as the period of retinal ischaemia extends, the visual prognosis declines. Visual symptoms are often acute and severe, with patients classically describing a curtain coming over their vision. There may be a history of cardiovascular risk factors. Also consider retinal detachment (p. 636).

Any history of acutely blurred or distorted central vision is worrying. Wet (neovascular) age-related macular degeneration (AMD) often produces distortion occurring over days or weeks, whereas dry AMD has a more insidious onset. Wet AMD requires rapid referral, whereas dry AMD does not.

Beware of the absence of acute symptoms in those with good vision in the fellow eye; they may be unaware of monocular blurred vision. Conversely, patients may experience a chronic decline in monocular vision as an acute symptom, when for some reason the better eye is covered. A careful history may help.

Optometrists

Dilate and carefully examine patients with suspected AMD. Macular elevation or haemorrhage may suggest wet AMD, so refer urgently to hospital. In younger patients consider central serous chorioretinopathy. This causes retinal elevation (sometimes subtle) with a small hypermetropic shift. If available, optical coherence tomography is very helpful at excluding multiple macular diseases.

General practice

Dilated funduscopy by an optometrist will uncover many retinal diseases and is a useful means of triage for all but the most urgent referrals. An optometrist with optical coherence tomography (OCT) is particularly helpful, as it can detect many of the most important macular diseases. Monitor cardiovascular risk factors in patients diagnosed with retinal artery or vein occlusion. Studies show that smokers are more likely to get sight-threatening AMD. Diabetics with poor glucose control, raised lipids and hypertension are more likely to lose vision from diabetic eye disease, so manage each carefully. Encourage near relatives to accompany patients referred to hospital with suspected inherited retinal disease, for dilated fundus examination, e.g. retinitis pigmentosa.

The following guidelines for hospital referral urgency are not prescriptive, as clinical situations vary. In particular, macular disease with an uncertain diagnosis should be referred urgently.

Immediate

- Acute central retinal artery occlusion, or branch retinal artery occlusion with macular involvement p. 576
- Macular-on retinal detachment (nil by mouth) p. 636

Same day

- Macular-off retinal detachment (nil by mouth) p. 636
- Branch retinal artery occlusion not involving the macula p. 578
- Retinal breaks p. 630

Urgent (within 1 week)

- Neovascular (wet) age-related macular degeneration p. 544
- Proliferative diabetic retinopathy p. 557
- Toxic maculopathy p. 620
- Branch retinal vein occlusion p. 574
- Central retinal vein occlusion p. 569

Soon (within 1 month)

- Severe non-proliferative diabetic retinopathy p. 557
- Pseudophakic macular oedema p. 593
- Central serous chorioretinopathy p. 594
- Retinal macroaneurysm p. 581
- Fingolimod-associated macular oedema (FAME) p. 619

Routine

- Mild-to-moderate non-proliferative diabetic retinopathy p. 557
- Hypertensive retinopathy (treat hypertension first) p. 579
- Retinitis pigmentosa or other pigmentary retinopathy p. 598
- Best's disease p. 606
- Stargardt's disease p. 610
- Choroideremia p. 604
- Flat choroidal naevus p. 475
- Macular telangiectasia p. 585
- Dry age-related macular degeneration p. 541
- Macular atrophy p. 536

SURGICAL RETINA

Timothy L Jackson & Lyndon da Cruz

12

INDIRECT OPHTHALMOSCOPY

Indirect ophthalmoscopy takes time to master.

1. Explain the procedure to the patient.
2. Ensure the patient is lying supine on a single pillow, eyes well dilated. Provide enough space to move to either side and behind the patient's head. Instill local anaesthetic eye drops in both eyes. Dim the room lights.
3. Put on the indirect headpiece and adjust the tension band so that it will not move when your head is tilted. Adjust the interpupillary distance to give a single image at about 30–40 cm away.
4. View the red reflex then interpose a 20D lens into the light path. Some lenses have a white circular marking on the metal frame that should face the patient. When learning, and for difficult examinations, e.g. children or those with small pupils, a 28D lens is easier to use but provides lower magnification. Move the lens sideways and anteroposteriorly until the fundal details appear.
5. To increase patient's compliance and comfort, start with a peripheral fundal examination using a dim light – avoid bright illumination of the posterior pole.
6. Develop a routine for peripheral fundal examination, e.g. start at 6 o'clock and move clockwise 360°; this makes it easier to remember the position of retinal features. Ask the patient to look in the appropriate direction, e.g. towards their feet for inferior peripheral examination. Tilting your head to the side facilitates a more peripheral view.
7. Two indenters are commonly used: Socket and T-bar. Use a cotton-bud or large paper-clip if neither are available. Gently indent the patient's eyelids immediately above the upper tarsus, or below the lower tarsus, until a retinal elevation is visible. Move the indent back and forward, and view the retina as it rolls over the apex of the indent. This dynamic examination may open small breaks and the tangential view may reveal small operculated tears. It is sometimes necessary to gently indent directly onto the anaesthetised conjunctival surface to view the retina at 3 and 9 o'clock.
8. Draw the findings. The image is inverted, so it is helpful to draw the disc and fovea then rotate the paper 180°, and draw as seen. Some surgeons use colour to show the attached (red) and detached (blue) retina (see **Fig. 12.6**, p. 637).

POSTERIOR VITREOUS DETACHMENT

Background Spontaneous posterior vitreous detachment (PVD) is extremely common, but PVD may also follow eye surgery, trauma, uveitis, or laser. In the majority of cases, it causes no serious problem. Sometimes it causes troublesome floaters, or retinal tears that can lead to retinal detachment.

Symptoms Photopsia (flashes of light) in the temporal field and floaters are common. Vitreous haemorrhage or floaters may reduce VA.

Examination Maximally dilate both eyes. PVD can be difficult to detect but biomicroscopy may show a '*Weiss ring*' of thickened vitreous cortex avulsed from the optic disc **(Fig. 12.1)**. The space behind a PVD is usually optically clear, unlike the condensed vitreous. The detached vitreous face is sometimes visible without a lens, using a slit beam focussed in the mid-vitreous cavity. This fine and crumpled membrane slopes away when viewed top to bottom, and swirls with eye movement. In eyes with no previous intraocular surgery check for *Shafer's sign*. Use a bright, thin slit beam focussed into the anterior vitreous (no lens) with the slit lamp on high magnification; ask the patient to look up-down-straight ahead. If fine, pigmented cells (tobacco dust) are visible the test is positive **(Fig. 12.2)**. Repeat looking left-right-straight ahead. The test may help to exclude a break; only 8% of eyes with

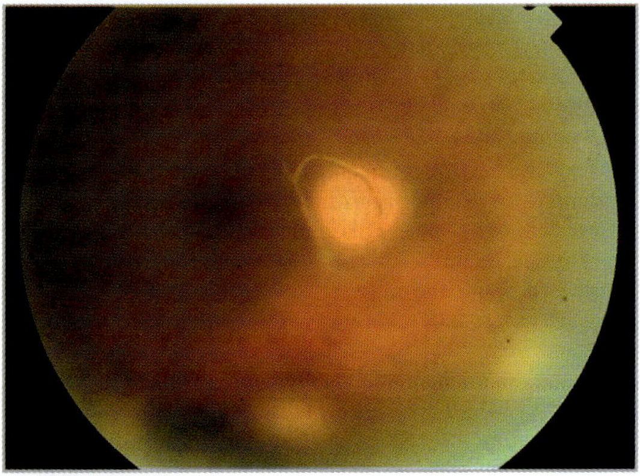

Fig. 12.1: Weiss ring.

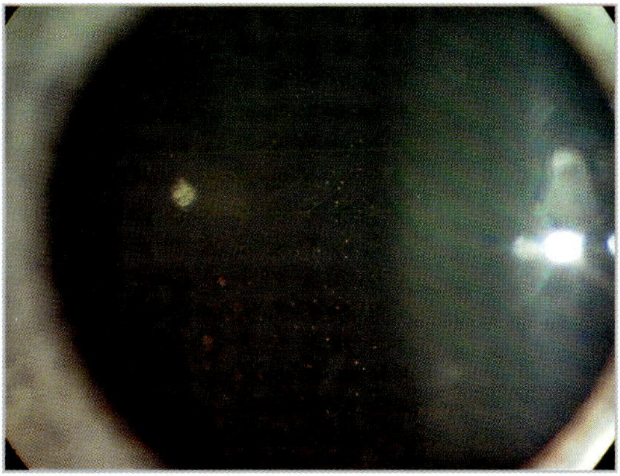

Fig. 12.2: Anterior vitreous pigment cells (tobacco dust).

retinal breaks are Shafer negative. If positive, arrange urgent vitreoretinal review, even if no break is found.

Document 360° indented, indirect ophthalmoscopy. If indentation is not possible, or the view is insufficient, consider using a 3-mirror, TransEquator or SuperQuad lens with viscous coupling gel e.g. Viscotears.

Investigations Consider widefield imaging if available, e.g. Optos. Ultrasound if the fundal view is inadequate to exclude a retinal break. Repeat in 1–2 weeks if the view remains poor.

Management PVD does not usually require treatment. Photopsia usually stops soon after the onset of the PVD, but floaters often last longer. Advise patients that floaters will tend to become less troublesome and may ultimately disappear. Very occasionally, persistent floaters are treated with vitrectomy ('floaterectomy'). YAG laser distruption of floaters is described (vitreolysis), but is not a common practice.

Follow-up Discharge, but document that a *retinal detachment warning* was given: if the patient notices any sudden change or worsening of floaters, flashes, vision decline or any visual field defect they should return immediately. Provide written information.

RETINAL DEGENERATIONS AND TEARS

Peripheral retinal degenerations

Background There are several peripheral vitreoretinal degenerations. Some predispose to retinal detachment (RD). More common in myopes but can occur in emmetropic and hypermetropic eyes.

Classification

- *Lattice:* Retinal thinning associated with overlying vitreous liquefaction, retinal vascular sclerosis, and abnormally strong vitreoretinal adhesion **(Fig. 12.3)**.
- *Nonlattice:* Several peripheral degenerations such as white – with/without-pressure, snail-track, microcystoid, reticular (mid-peripheral), and paving stone.

Management

- *Lattice:* The three common situations are lattice alone, atrophic round holes in lattice, and lattice-associated retinal tears. Retinopexy may be appropriate for some cases but not others, to reduce the risk of RD (**Table 12.1** p. 633).
- *Non-lattice:* Prophylactic treatment is not usually required.
- Provide all patients with an RD warning (RDW; p. 629).

Retinal breaks

Background Full-thickness defects usually occurring following posterior vitreous detachment (PVD). Their configuration influences the likelihood of subsequent RD.

Symptoms, signs, and investigations Similar to PVD, except Shafer's sign is usually positive (p. 628). Consider widefield imaging, if available, e.g. Optos.

Management See **Table 12.1**. This outline will be modified by the break size and position (large, superior defects are greatest risk), other ocular disease or risk factors such as high myopia, patient/clinician preference, and increased pigmentation under the break, indicating retinal pigment epithelial (RPE) hyperplasia and chronicity. Provide an RDW.

Retinopexy Two options exist – laser or cryotherapy **(Fig. 12.4)**. If possible, select laser as it is less destructive. Laser safety training is usually mandatory. For techniques, see **Boxes 12.1** and **12.2** (p. 634).

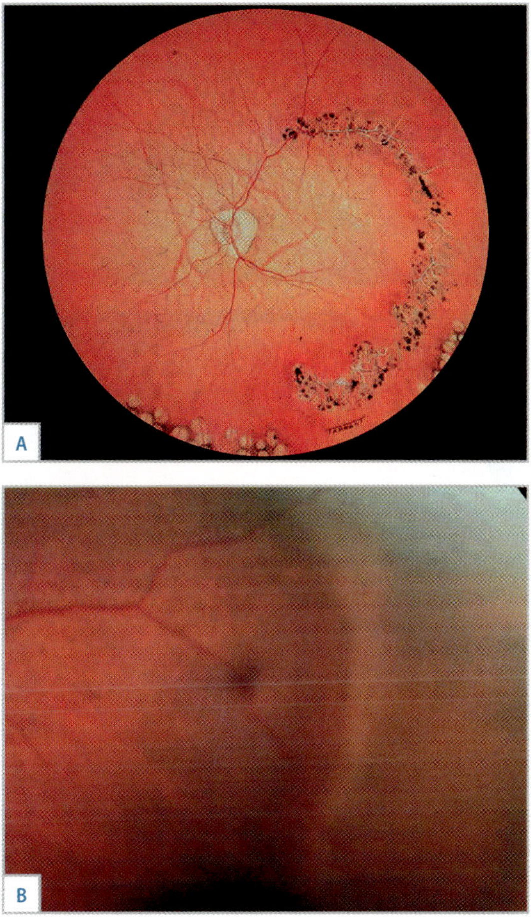

Fig. 12.3: (A) Lattice degeneration temporally, with paving stone degeneration more peripherally, and inferiorly. (B) White-without-pressure. (C) Microcystoid degeneration, just posterior to the ora. (D) Reticular degeneration (Courtesy P Leaver/PM Sullivan. Artwork, T Tarrant). *Continues overleaf*

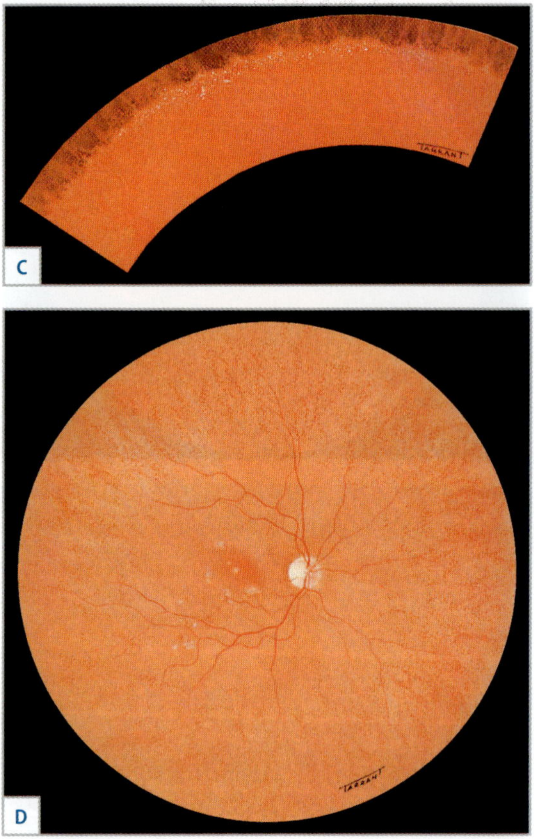

Fig. 12.3: *Continued*

Consent

- *Benefit:* Reduced risk of RD and vision loss.
- *Risk:* Failure to prevent RD, retreatment, visual field defect, accidental foveal burn and vision loss, subsequent distortion from epiretinal membranes (can also occur with untreated retinal breaks), mild surface discomfort or more significant pain if corneal abrasion occurs.

Table 12.1: Treatment of retinal tears and lattice

Group	PVD	Incomplete or no PVD	Risk factors such as fellow eye RD	Subretinal fluid*
Lattice degeneration	–	–	±	Not applicable
Round holes in lattice	–	–	±	+
Fully operculated round holes	–	–	±	+
Acute flap-shaped tears with or without lattice	+	++	++	++

*Obtain a same-day vitreoretinal opinion unless chronic, as surgery may be indicated.
Abbreviations: ++, treat virtually all; +, treat most; ±, variable or contentious; –, seldom treat; PVD, posterior vitreous detachment

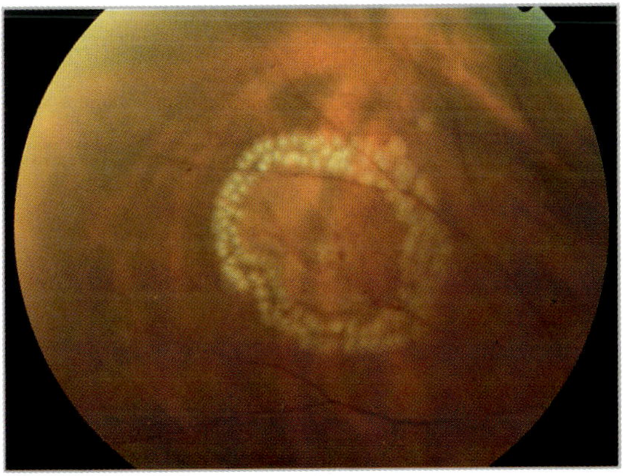

Fig. 12.4: Retinal U-tear with a thin collar of subretinal fluid and fresh laser retinopexy.

Box 12.1: Laser retinopexy

1. Obtain written consent. Warn the patient that they will see bright flashes of light, their vision may temporarily dim, and they may feel the laser pulse, but to try not to move. Confirm patient name, date of birth and mark the eye needing treatment
2. Connect the argon laser to either the slit lamp or indirect output
3. Once warmed up, fire a test shot against a nonreflective object
4. Ensure patient is maximally dilated, in a darkened room, with topical anaesthesia in both eyes. Others in the room require protective goggles

   Slit lamp: select the contact lens that gives the best view, typically TransEquator or SuperQuad, or three-mirror otherwise. Noncontact lenses (e.g. 90D) may be used, but require more power and do not stabilise the eye. Select 200 µm spot size; 0.1 seconds (20 ms for multispot lasers)

   Indirect ophthalmoscope with 20D lens: good for peripheral breaks and allows indentation. Spot size varies with focusing
5. Adjust the aiming beam brightness
6. Confirm landmarks to prevent accidental macular burns
7. Laser power will vary with media clarity, fundus pigmentation, and machine. Start low and gradually increase to produce a definite white spot
8. Encircle the break and any subretinal fluid with 2–3 rows of semiconfluent spots **(Fig. 12.4)**
9. Occasionally periocular local anaesthesia is needed if patients cannot tolerate laser treatment

Box 12.2: Cryotherapy

1. Explain the procedure and obtain written consent. Confirm patient's name, date of birth and mark the eye needing treatment.
2. Anaesthetic requirements vary from topical, subconjunctival injection at the cryo-site (most common), to subtenons. Fellow eye topical anaesthesia may help to keep lids open.
3. Some machines require gas purging, e.g. set the temperature to –25°C, depress foot pedal for 10 seconds, wait 1 minute, and repeat.
4. Cryoprobes are notoriously unreliable, so check. Set the treatment temperature (typically –85°C), dip into sterile water, depress the foot pedal for 10 seconds, lift out. A 5-mm ice-ball should form. Release pedal. Within 2 seconds it should be possible to free the ice-ball from the tip.

Box 12.2: *Continued*

5. The handle is usually marked to manually orient the probe, as the tip is not visible during treatment
6. *Beware:* It is possible to indent the break with the probe handle whilst the tip is accidentally treating the macula. Avoid treating the ciliary body (painful)
7. View the fundus with the indirect ophthalmoscope and a 20D lens
8. Indent the break with the probe tip, and plan treatment
9. The break margin requires treatment but not the central defect
10. Larger breaks may require treatment in more than one site, but avoid unnecessary treatment to reduce discomfort and the risk of epiretinal membranes
11. Depress the foot pedal until the treatment area freezes, then release
12. Wait until fully thawed before moving the probe to another site to avoid scleral/choroidal damage
13. Wait for 1 minute after the last treatment before turning off machine. This allows gas to escape
14. Provide analgesia

Follow-up Two weeks. If RPE hyperpigmentation fully encircles the break and there is no subretinal fluid outside the pigmented area, discharge with an RDW for annual dilated optometry review, ideally one with OCT (to exclude epiretinal membrane) and widefield imaging (to exclude new breaks). Otherwise, top-up retinopexy. Review those presenting with subretinal fluid within 2–3 days, then weekly until sufficient RPE reaction occurs.

RHEGMATOGENOUS RETINAL DETACHMENT

Background Usually occurs secondary to retinal tears (rhegma). These are most commonly caused by posterior vitreous detachment (PVD), p. 628, when the posterior vitreous face separates from the internal limiting membrane and vitreoretinal adhesion tears the retina. Syneretic vitreous fluid passes through these tears, detaching the retina from the retinal pigment epithelium (RPE). Retinal detachments (RDs) are more common in high myopes and tears are more common at sites of lattice degeneration (p. 630).

Symptoms Photopsia in the temporal field, floaters, visual field loss, with reduced VA if there is vitreous haemorrhage or macular detachment.

Signs Bullous RD is easily detected **(Fig. 12.5)**, but the only sign of shallow elevation may be loss of choroidal markings and subtle elevation on binocular examination. RD may be associated with an RAPD, low IOP, vitreous haemorrhage, and tobacco dust (p. 628). Chronic RDs often have thinned retina and RPE pigmentation at their edge ('high-water mark'; **Fig. 12.17**, p. 662), and may have retinal cysts, retinal telangiectasia, retinal scarring [proliferative vitreoretinopathy (PVR)], choroidal detachment, mild anterior uveitis, and low or high IOP.

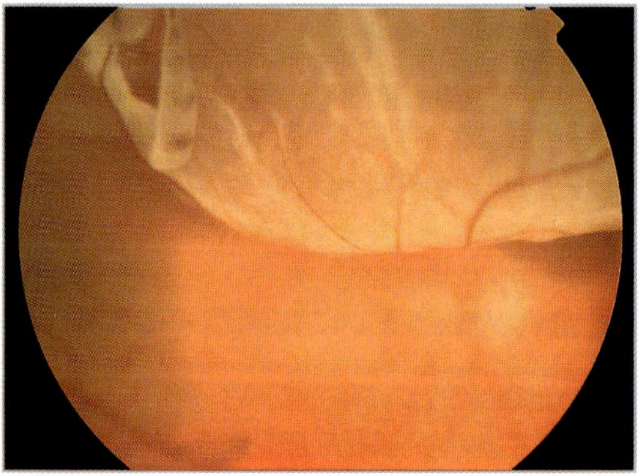

Fig. 12.5: Right superior bullous retinal detachment with a superotemporal U-tear.

Examination Record VA, RAPD, lens status (clear, cataractous, pseudophakic or aphakic), and PVD presence or absence. Draw the extent of the RD noting macular involvement, breaks, and lattice degeneration. Check the periphery of both eyes using an indirect ophthalmoscope, 20D lens (or equivalent), and 360° indentation, or TransEquator or SuperQuad otherwise. Finding breaks can be difficult, but their position may be suggested by Lincoff's rules in phakic patients **(Fig. 12.6)**. Trauma may cause tears at the anterior retinal border that are hard to detect (see retinal dialysis; p. 662). Grade any PVR as A (increased vitreous haze and pigment), B (inner retinal fibrosis), and C (full-thickness retinal folds), and note if anterior (A) or posterior (P), and the extent in clock hours, e.g. PVR CA2, CP6.

Investigations Consider widefield imaging if available, e.g. Optos. Perform same-day ultrasound if there is significant media opacity. OCT can show foveal attachment if uncertain and secondary epiretinal membrane.

Differential diagnosis Consider PVD, serous RD (no breaks with shifting subretinal fluid), and tractional RD (usually caused by fibrosis from severe diabetic retinopathy or PVR).

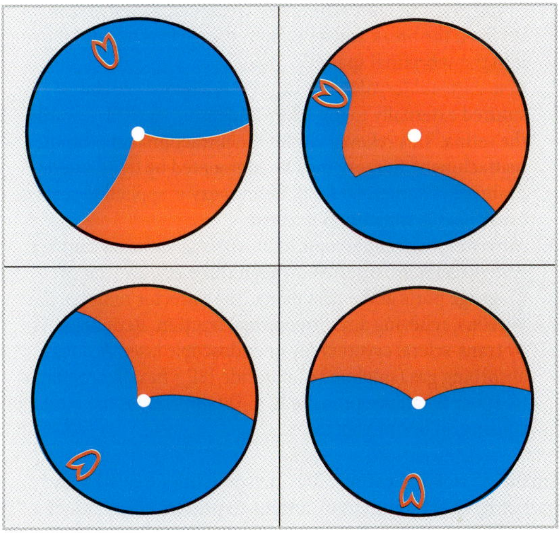

Fig. 12.6: Lincoff's rules. The location of the break is suggested by the configuration of the retinal detachment. Detached retina is shown in blue.

Retinoschisis occurs secondary to an intraretinal split that produces an appearance similar to RD. It is often bilateral and symmetric, is more common in hypermetropes, uncommon in myopes, tends not to produce a 'high-water mark', and unlike RD produces an absolute rather than partial scotoma (test during fundus examination by moving a small square of slit-lamp light between normal and schitic retina). The elevated inner retinal layer appears thin and atrophic. Outer leaf breaks may be visible as holes in the outer retinal layer. With appropriate eye gaze OCT may reach peripherally enough to show an intraretinal cleft, versus the subretinal fluid from RD. Retinoschisis does not require treatment but advise annual dilated optician examination with widefield imaging, if available, and provide a retinal detachment warning (RDW, p. 629). Retinoschisis may occasionally be associated with, or lead to, RD.

Management Request a same-day vitreoretinal opinion. Aim to repair most sight-threatening macula-on RDs within 24 hours and macula-off RDs less urgently, but as soon as possible. Three surgical options exist:

1. *Pneumatic retinopexy:* Suitable only for a minority of straightforward cases with superior breaks. A vitreous injection of expansile gas produces a flotation force that tamponades retinal breaks and flattens the retina. Cryotherapy or laser retinopexy creates an adhesive scar between the break and RPE, preventing vitreous fluid moving into the subretinal space.
2. *Conventional (cryobuckle) surgery:* A silicone explant is sutured externally to the sclera, indenting the RPE towards the retina. This relieves vitreoretinal traction and promotes reattachment. Surgery may be augmented by trans-scleral drainage of subretinal fluid. Retinopexy is applied to seal the break. Gas is sometimes injected.
3. *Vitrectomy:* An endoscopic light, vitreous infusion cannula, and vitrector are inserted through three 20-, 23-, 25- or 27-gauge ports at the pars plana. The vitrector removes the vitreous, relieving any vitreoretinal traction. Retinopexy is by trans-scleral cryotherapy or endoscopic laser. A slowly absorbing gas (sulphur hexafluoride [SF_6], hexafluoroethane [C_2F_6] or octafluoropropane [C_3F_8]) tamponades the retina, or silicone oil in complex cases.

Small, inferior and chronic RDs are sometimes treated with barrier laser to their margin, aiming to prevent enlargement and avoid surgery. Occasionally, surgery is not advised if a late-presenting RD has a low chance of reattachment and visual recovery.

Consent A large UK database study reported 86% reattachment of primary RDs with one operation. The final reattachment rate is >95% with two or more operations. The VA following macula-off RD varies widely, but some reduction is to be expected. Macula-on RDs usually retain good acuity although epiretinal membranes occur in 4–8% of cases. Severe loss of vision can rarely occur from haemorrhage and endophthalmitis. Prophylactic retinopexy may be required in the fellow eye (see **Table 12.1**, p. 633).

- *Pneumatic retinopexy:* Lower success rate than other options but a simpler procedure. The consequences of gas injection are similar to vitrectomy.
- *Cryobuckle:* Risks include diplopia (~3%); myopic shift; postoperative discomfort (common). The buckle may need to be removed if it becomes infected, extrudes or causes complications.
- *Vitrectomy:* Markedly impaired vision until gas absorbs in about 1 week (air), 2 weeks (SF_6), 1 month (C_2F_6) or 2 months (C_3F_8). Patients must not fly or ascend mountains during this period as gas expansion may dangerously elevate IOP. Patients should advise anaesthetists that they have gas in their eye, as inhaled nitrous oxide may also elevate IOP. Most patients require ~7 days of head posturing to float the gas bubble onto the breaks. Postoperative IOP elevation is common and may require treatment. Silicone oil is removed later if the retina is secure, typically at 3–6 months. Silicone may lead to chronic IOP elevation and corneal changes. See the general risks of vitrectomy below.
- *General risks of vitrectomy (for any indication):* Progressive nuclear sclerosis (81% at 6 months, 98% at 1 year); iatrogenic retinal breaks (~5%) that require retinopexy/gas injection and may lead to RD; redness and mild to moderate pain (expected); high or low IOP (common); vitreous haemorrhage (often clears); macular oedema; choroidal haemorrhage (<1%) and endophthalmitis (<1%).

For patient information see https://www.moorfields.nhs.uk/condition/retinal-detachment.

Postoperative care Patients are usually treated as day cases and otherwise discharged on the first postoperative day. The RPE pump usually removes any shallow residual subretinal fluid within a few days of cryobuckle. All patients require an RDW (p. 629) and G. chloramphenicol 0.5% q.d.s. 2 weeks, G. atropine 1% b.d. 2 weeks, and G. dexamethasone 0.1% q.d.s. 2 weeks, then tail off over 3 weeks.

- *Pneumatic retinopexy:* Check for inferior secondary retinal breaks caused by gas-induced vitreous traction, and raised

IOP. Advice is as for vitrectomy, but with more frequent early follow-up, e.g. day 1, 3 and 7.

- *Cryobuckle:* Check there is an adequate indent directly under the breaks and consider anterior segment ischaemia (uncommon) if there is raised IOP, anterior uveitis, and pain. Routine follow-up is day 1–7, 14, 30, then optometrist yearly.
- *Vitrectomy:* The vitreous gas fill should be at least 70%, especially if there are inferior breaks. Advise on head posturing, e.g. right cheek to pillow for a right eye RD with nasal breaks. Posture 50 minutes per hour for 7 days and be active for the 10 minutes rest period to avoid deep vein thrombosis and musculoskeletal discomfort. Transient, fine and crystal-like lines on the posterior lens surface are common ('gas cataract'). Inadvertent lens touch by endoscopic instrumentation produces a focal, linear opacity, often at the 2 or 10 o'clock position. Measure IOP:
- If <25 mmHg, discharge and review in 7–14 days.
- If >25 mmHg add G. β-blocker b.d. (unless contraindicated) and review in 7–14 days.
- If >30 mmHg add G. β-blocker b.d., G. apraclonidine 0.5% t.d.s., acetazolamide 250 mg s.r. b.d. p.o. and review in 5–7 days.

If >35 mmHg, give stat acetazolamide 500 mg p.o., G. β-blocker, G. apraclonidine and recheck IOP in 2 hours. Send home when IOP < 30 mmHg on G. β-blocker b.d., G. apraclonidine 0.5% t.d.s., and acetazolamide 250 mg s.r. b.d. p.o. Review in 5–7 days. If IOP fails to respond, consider gas overfill (look for absent gas-fluid meniscus inferiorly). Remove or replace gas if necessary.

For routine vitrectomy see day 1–7, 10–14, 30, 60–90.

On discharge document RDW and advise optometrist yearly, ideally one with OCT (to exclude secondary epiretinal membrane) and widefield imaging (to exclude new breaks or RD).

DIABETIC VITREORETINAL SURGERY

Diabetic vitrectomy may be indicated for nonclearing or recurrent vitreous haemorrhage, tractional retinal detachment (TRD) involving or threatening the fovea, combined rhegmatogenous and TRD, and aggressive progressing proliferative diabetic retinopathy (PDR) not controlled by panretinal photocoagulation (PRP) or anti-VEGF therapy.

Persistent vitreous haemorrhage

Background The abnormal and fragile new vessels that define PDR may bleed into the vitreous cavity, reducing VA, and preventing treatment with PRP. As 20% of haemorrhages clear within 1 year, surgical timing is crucial: Operate too early and expose some patients to unnecessary surgical risks; operate late and delay PRP and visual recovery.

Diabetic Retinopathy Vitrectomy Study (DRVS) For type 1 diabetes mellitus (T1DM), early vitrectomy (1–6 vs 12 months) increased the chance of VA ≥6/12 at 2 years. Not significant for type 2 diabetes mellitus (T2DM), but none had intraoperative PRP and 30% had lensectomy. Surgical techniques have improved, so the threshold for vitrectomy has reduced.

History Determine age, T1DM or T2DM, diabetic and BP control, duration of visual loss, total number of PRP burns, use of anticoagulants and antiplatelet drugs, and surgical risk factors.

Examination Note VA, IOP, iris rubeosis, lens status, RAPD, density of vitreous haemorrhage, retinopathy and the presence and severity of fellow eye disease.

Investigations If the fundal view is inadequate, arrange ultrasound to determine the presence of posterior vitreous detachment (PVD) or RD. If presenting acutely repeat in 2 weeks. Repeat every 1–2 months if the fundal view remains inadequate.

Treatment Vitrectomy timing:

- *T1DM:* Within 3 months.
- *T2DM:* Within 4–6 months.

Consider earlier surgery if there is rubeosis, raised IOP, incomplete PRP, or poor fellow eye VA. Simultaneous vitrectomy and cataract surgery is often required but avoid cataract surgery if possible, as diabetics may get posterior synechiae from increased postoperative inflammation after combined surgery, a poor red reflex makes capsulorhexis difficult, and biometry may be more reliable after the haemorrhage is cleared.

Consent

- *Benefit:* Improve and stabilise vision. VA ≥ 6/12 in 36% of T1DM, 16% of T2DM.
- *Risk:* Rapid visual loss including no light perception (NLP). Haemorrhage may recur but usually resolves more quickly in vitrectomised eyes. See general risks of vitrectomy (p. 639) and PRP (p. 523) as endoscopic PRP (endolaser) is often required.

Recurrent vitreous haemorrhage

May occur despite adequate PRP, if inactive new vessels have ongoing vitreous traction. Vitrectomy can relieve vascular traction if haemorrhages are frequent and slow to clear.

Tractional retinal detachment

Background Proliferative fibrovascular membranes may cause TRDs. Consider surgery if OCT shows they involve or are expanding to threaten the fovea.

Examination Note VA, IOP, rubeosis, RAPD, lens status, presence of PVD, extent of PRP and membranes, retinal breaks, and fellow eye disease.

Treatment Vitrectomy and membrane removal by delamination (horizontal dissection between the membrane and retina), segmentation (vertical membrane division to relieve tangential traction), or *en bloc*. Endolaser PRP is often performed.

Consent

- *Benefit:* Improve or stabilise vision in ~75%. VA ≥ 6/60 in 50–60%. Complete retinal reattachment, 80–85% (in one operation).
- *Risk:* See general risks of vitrectomy (p. 639) and PRP (p. 523). Retinal breaks during membrane dissection cause RD in 5–15%. Intraoperative gas injection may be used to reduce this risk. Recurrent vitreous haemorrhage occurs in ~10%.

EPIRETINAL MEMBRANE

Background A thin pre-retinal membrane formed by fibroblastic cells. Most often idiopathic, but may be secondary to intraocular surgery, retinal breaks, inflammation, diabetes, vitreous haemorrhage, retinal vein occlusion, trauma, or any other disease that stimulates fibrosis. It has been linked to retinal laser and cryotherapy. Sometimes called cellophane maculopathy, premacular membrane, or preretinal gliosis. Macular pucker occurs when epiretinal membrane (ERM) contraction causes visible retinal folds.

Symptoms Many patients are asymptomatic, but the most common symptoms are blur and distortion (metamorphopsia). VA reduction is often mild (≥6/9 in two-thirds of cases) and nonprogressive, but may not capture the symptomatic impact of distortion.

Signs Typically, cellophane-like, preretinal membrane causing fine wrinkles of the macula **(Fig. 12.7)**. Thicker membranes are often associated with other diseases such as retinal vein occlusion. Bilateral in 25%. Retinal pigment epithelium changes and macular oedema may occur, and may indicate a worse surgical prognosis.

History and examination Assess subjective severity and visual requirements. Record: near and distance VA, Amsler

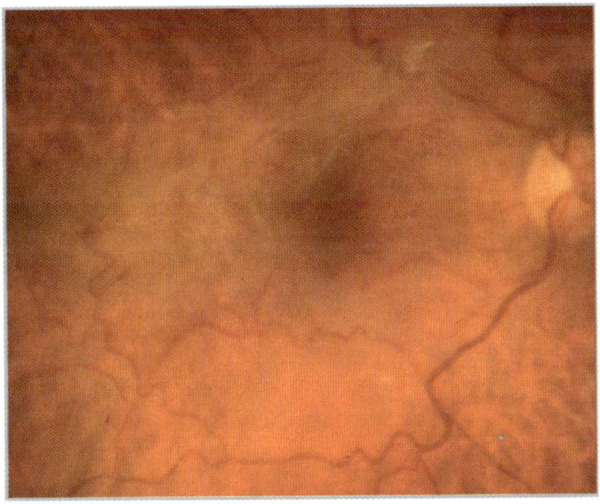

Fig. 12.7: Epiretinal membrane (Courtesy M Michaelides).

grid, lens status, vitreous attachment, retinal periphery and fellow eye disease. Try and establish the dominant eye ('which eye would you use to look through a telescope'). Symptoms in the dominant eye are typically more problematic, and more likely to need surgery.

Investigations OCT usually shows macular thickening (**Fig. 12.8**), and sometimes coexisting vitreomacular traction. If the inner segment/outer segment line (see **Fig. 11.11**, p. 509) is intact, VA is often preserved. Fluorescein angiography is not routinely required, but may show vessel distortion and leakage and is mostly used to identify associated disease such as retinal vein occlusion and diabetes, that may have ischaemia. *Macular epiretinal proliferation* describes a tissue more intimately integrated with the retinal surface; it is less likely to show pucker or a gap between it and the retina, but more likely to appear as a macular pseudohole (p. 648).

Management

- *Casualty:* Routine vitreoretinal referral after excluding retinal breaks.
- *Clinic:* Discuss vitrectomy and membrane peel. The aim is to reduce distortion and improve VA. Exclude associated disease such as diabetes, retinal vein occlusion and age-related macular degeneration as these can damage vision independently of the ERMs and may alter the surgical prognosis.

Consent VA improves ≥2 lines in 74%, with 24% unchanged and 2% worse. Most patients report some improvement in metamorphopsia, but few achieve entirely normal vision. Without surgery, VA is often stable. Occasionally (<1%) the membrane separates spontaneously and VA improves. Explain the general risks of vitrectomy (p. 639). Complications occur in

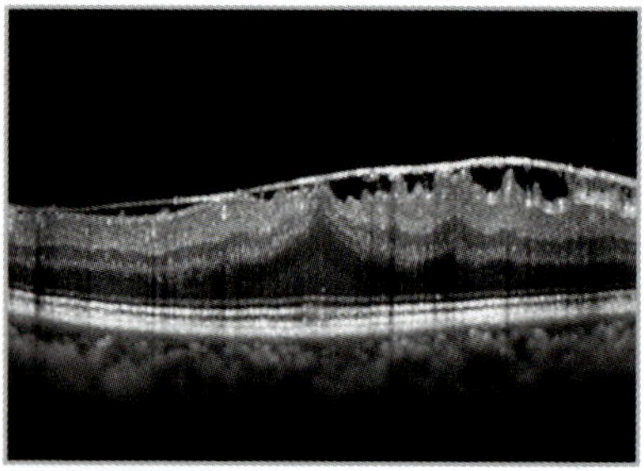

Fig. 12.8: Epiretinal membrane, causing inner retinal corrugations (pucker).

~8% of cases. Explain that it may take 6–8 weeks, or longer, for the vision to improve and that it may initially be worse.

Follow-up

- *No surgery:* Discharge for annual optometrist review, ideally one with OCT, requesting re-referal if there is deteriorating vision. Provide an Amsler chart.
- *Postoperative:* G. chloramphenicol 0.5% q.d.s. 2 weeks, G. atropine 1% b.d. 2 weeks, G. dexamethasone 0.1% q.d.s. 2 weeks then tail off over 3 weeks. Review subjective change in distortion, near and distance VA, lens opacity, residual membrane or wrinkling, and retinal periphery at day 1–7, 10, 30 and 90, then discharge for annual optometrist review, ideally one with OCT. Membranes recur in 7%, but rarely require further surgery.

VITREOMACULAR TRACTION SYNDROME

Background Incomplete vitreous detachment with residual macular attachment leads to vitreomacular traction (VMT), with resulting foveal distortion and thickening. Often associated with epiretinal membrane.

Symptoms Blurred vision, metamorphopsia, micropsia, monocular diplopia, or an incidental finding. VA loss may not fully capture the impact of metamorphopsia.

History and examination Determine the duration and exact nature of symptoms and test with an Amsler grid. Macular signs may be subtle **(Fig. 12.9)**. Exclude peripheral breaks that may be associated with epiretinal membranes.

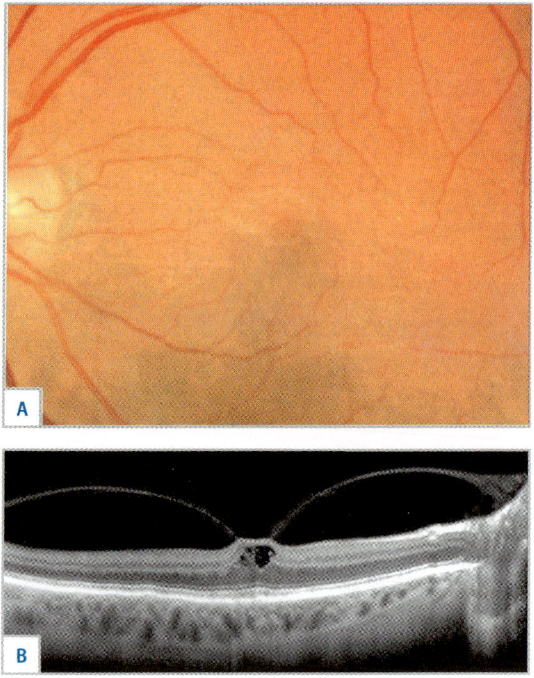

Fig. 12.9: Vitreomacular traction syndrome seen in (A) Colour photograph and (B) On OCT.

Differential diagnosis Consider full- or partial-thickness macular hole (p. 648) and epiretinal membrane (p. 643); both may co-exist, and other causes of macular oedema (p. 535).

Investigations Obtain OCT, which typically shows foveal vitreous attachment, foveal elevation, and macular cysts **(Fig. 12.9)**. Fluorescein angiography is not required.

Management With observation, 6% of VMT releases over 2 years. Vitrectomy reduces retinal thickening in most cases and VA improves two lines or more in 33%, but 21% have stable or decreased VA. Vitrectomy can precipitate macular hole formation, particularly with 'impending macular holes' (VMT with only a thin roof of inner retinal tissue remaining). Explain the general risks of vitrectomy (p. 639).

Follow-up For observation, see every 4–6 months but provide an Amsler chart and advise to present if there is loss of vision. If VMT resolves discharge for annual optician review, ideally one with OCT. If not, consider vitrectomy. Following vitrectomy, review as for epiretinal membrane (p. 645).

MACULAR HOLE

Background A full-thickness retinal defect centred on the fovea. Most common in women in their 50s and 60s. Usually idiopathic, but may occur in high myopes, or following trauma or prolonged cystoid macular oedema.

Symptoms Reduced VA, distortion or incidental finding (more common if the nondominant eye is affected).

Signs

- *Stage I:* Yellow spot, loss of normal foveolar depression, pseudocysts and vitreofeveolar traction.
- *Stage II:* Similar to stage I but with a small round or curvilinear full-thickness retinal defect <300 μm.
- *Stage III:* Full-thickness macular hole (FTMH). A prefoveal operculum is common.
- *Stage IV:* FTMH with complete posterior vitreous detachment.

An alternative OCT classification system (International Vitreomacular Traction Study Group) considers aetiology (primary or secondary), vitreomacular adhesion (VMA present or absent), and apical hole size: small ≤250 μm; medium >250 to ≤400 μm; large >400 μm (**Fig. 12.10**). Some advocate using 500 μm as the cut-off for large holes.

Associated findings include a grey cuff of subretinal fluid surrounding the hole, fine yellow-white deposits in the base of the hole, underlying retinal pigment epithelium (RPE) atrophy and occasionally retinal detachment in high myopes. VA is typically 6/24–6/60. Approximately 30% also have an epiretinal membrane (p. 643).

History and examination Record duration and severity of symptoms, near and distance VA, lens and refractive status, vitreous attachment, stage and size of hole, and check retinal periphery.

Differential diagnosis Partial-thickness (lamellar) holes tend not to have a cuff of fluid around the hole or RPE changes, but they may progress to FTMHs. Pseudoholes occur when epiretinal membrane, macular epiretinal proliferation, or macular cysts create the false appearance of a FTMH.

Investigations OCT confirms FTMH and excludes lamellar or pseudohole. May show co-existing epiretinal membrane (p. 643), epiretinal proliferation (p. 644) or vitreomacular traction (p. 646). The 4-year risk of fellow eye involvement is 46% if it has focal

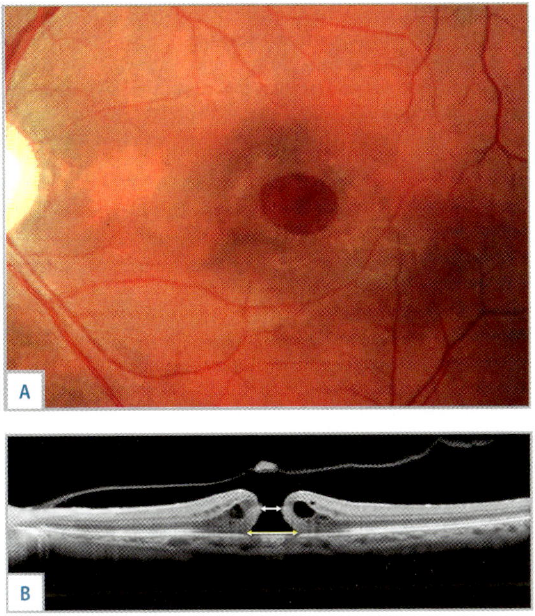

Fig. 12.10: Macular holes. (A) Large full-thickness macular hole; (B) Stage III macular hole with a prefoveal operculum. There is vitreomacular separation, but vitreous attachment at the optic disc. Find the line scan with the widest diameter, then use the caliper function to measure the minimum linear diameter (shown in white), usually parallel to the RPE. Yellow shows the basal diameter.

foveal VMA on OCT, or 6% without. Repeat OCT postoperatively, once the gas has cleared.

Management

- *Casualty:* Routine vitreoretinal clinic referral for longstanding cases, but recent onset FTMHs have better results if surgery is expedited.
- *Clinic:* Discuss the natural history and treatment options. Spontaneous FTMH closure occurs in only 12%. Studies suggest stage I holes do not benefit from vitrectomy and gas injection, but vitrectomy is advisable for most stage II–IV holes of up to 12 months duration, with an ~80–90% anatomic closure rate. Small holes of short duration are the

most likely to close. The surgical closure rate reduces to 47% for holes present longer than 1 year, but surgery may still be appropriate. To maximise gas tamponade many, but not all surgeons, recommend face-down posturing for 45–50 minutes in every hour, for 5–7 days. Almost all peel the internal limiting membrane (ILM), and some create an ILM flap to cover large holes.

Consent Following vitrectomy, 70% get two lines VA improvement, 10% no change, and 10% lose VA. Explain the risks of vitrectomy (p. 639). Failed primary surgery may warrant reoperation.

Follow-up

- *No surgery:* Discharge with an Amsler chart for annual optometrist review, ideally one with OCT to monitor for fellow eye FTMH.
- *After vitrectomy:* G. chloramphenicol 0.5% q.d.s. 2 weeks; G. atropine 1% b.d. 2 weeks; G. dexamethasone 0.1% q.d.s. 2 weeks then tail off over 3 weeks. Perform OCT when the gas has absorbed sufficiently to visualise the macula. Inspect for raised IOP, retinal breaks, visual and anatomic outcome, and cataract, at day 1–7, 30 and 90, then discharge for annual optometrist review, ideally one with OCT. Provide an Amsler chart.

VITREOUS HAEMORRHAGE

Background Vitreous haemorrhage is a sign, not a diagnosis, so it is important to determine the cause.

History Ask about floaters, photopsia, duration of reduced VA, diabetes, sickle cell disease, cardiovascular risk factors (risk of retinal vein occlusion), anticoagulants/antiplatelet drugs, eye or head trauma, intracranial haemorrhage, headache, and previous eye disease or surgery.

Examination Note VA, rubeosis, anterior chamber red blood cells, IOP, whether phakic, pseudophakic, or aphakic, other evidence of previous eye surgery, posterior vitreous detachment (PVD), haemorrhage location and density. Fundoscopy may be easier using a 28D lens. Dilate and examine the fellow eye, as this may assist diagnosis, e.g. diabetic retinopathy and wet age-related macular degeneration (AMD). Grade the haemorrhage: I, macula and optic disc easily visible; II, disc and macula visible but one or both obscured; III, only periphery visible; IV, no fundal view.

Differential diagnosis Consider PVD, proliferative diabetic retinopathy, retinal tears, wet AMD with breakthrough bleeding, neovascularisation from central or branch retinal vein occlusion, sickle cell retinopathy, Valsalva bleed, macroaneurysm and trauma. Intracranial haemorrhage may be associated with retinal or vitreous haemorrhage (*Terson's syndrome*), particularly in patients with raised intracranial pressure and coma. Vitreous haemorrhage alone seldom produces an RAPD or NPL.

Investigations Widefield imaging, e.g. Optos, may assist examination and monitor change, but acquire B-scan ultrasound if the fundal view is insufficient, looking for retinal breaks, retinal or vitreous detachment, and macular elevation (AMD disciform lesions).

Management See PVD (p. 628), retinal tears (p. 630), nonclearing diabetic vitreous haemorrhage (p. 641), retinal vein occlusion (p. 574), neovascular AMD (p. 544), sickle cell retinopathy (p. 588), and trauma (p. 661).

Follow-up In those not undergoing vitrectomy to clear the haemorrhage, repeat the examination, widefield imaging, or ultrasound examination at 2 weeks, then at intervals until the fundal view is sufficient. The interval depends on the cause: PVD-related haemorrhage carries a high risk of retinal tears and requires frequent imaging (~2 weekly), whereas diabetic vitreous haemorrhage is less likely to be associated with rhegmatogenous retinal detachment. Watch for raised IOP and ghost cell glaucoma. Haemorrhage tends to clear more quickly in those with anterior chamber red blood cells, aphakia, and previous vitrectomy. Haemorrhage from AMD or central retinal vein occlusion carries a poor prognosis.

OPTIC DISC PIT

Background A typically small congenital defect of the optic disc that can lead to egress of vitreous or cerebrospinal fluid into and under the neuroretina. Inferotemporal and unilateral in the majority of cases.

History Often asymptomatic, but if there is neuroretinal fluid that reaches the fovea then blurred or distorted vision usually results. Ask about current or former high myopia, diabetes, affected and fellow eye disease.

Examination Often visible with high magnification slit-lamp disc examination. Check IOP and look for retinal haemorrhage and exudate, macular or peripapillary laser burns, drusen and fellow eye macular or optic disc abnormalities.

Differential diagnosis Consider titled optic discs and other congenital disc anomalies such as disc coloboma. If present, consider other causes of macular oedema (p. 535), in particular myopic maculoschisis, epiretinal membrane, vitreomacular traction, diabetes, choroidal neovascularization, and hypotony.

Investigations Undertake autorefraction or focimetry, or request former refraction if pseudophakic. The pit may be visible on disc cube optical coherence tomography (OCT). Fluid is often absent, but macular OCT may show sub or intraretinal fluid that can create a schitic appearance. Discontinuity between central macular fluid and disc margin suggests another cause. Perform OCT or fluorescein angiography if neovascularization or diabetic maculopathy are suspected. Visual field tests may show an enlarged blind spot or field defect.

Management Provide an Amsler chart and instructions. Treatment is only required if vision is affected or threatened by macular fluid, but the evidence base is weak. Laser demarcation near the disc margin aims to wall off fluid, but some reports show no benefit. Case series suggest vitrectomy and gas tamponade often helps, possibly by relieving vitreous traction. May be combined with internal limiting membrane (ILM) peel, laser demarcation, fenestration of the inner retina to let fluid exit into the vitreous, and plugging the pit with ILM or amniotic membrane.

Follow-up If there is no fluid, discharge to an optician with OCT capability. Otherwise monitor up to 2–3 monthly if fluid is expanding or near the fovea.

UVEAL EFFUSION SYNDROME

Background Idiopathic choroidal effusions, thought to be secondary to reduced trans-scleral outflow, occur typically in middle-aged men. A rare disease, but hypermetropic or nanophthalmic eyes are predisposed.

Clinical features Spontaneous onset of choroidal effusions **(Fig. 12.11A)** with shifting subretinal fluid, often with a chronic relapsing-remitting course. Pain, hypotony and vitritis are absent. Macular involvement may reduce VA.

Differential diagnosis

- *Rhegmatogenous retinal detachment (RD)*: Look for retinal breaks, vitreous pigment, and an absence of shifting subretinal fluid.
- *Serous RD:* Shifting subretinal fluid may also occur, but look for signs suggesting other causes, e.g. scleritis, retinal vasculitis, vitritis, or disc swelling.
- *Central serous chorioretinopathy*: See page 594.
- *Ocular hypotony:* Choroidal effusions settle as the IOP normalises.
- *Choroidal neoplasm:* Visible on examination or with ultrasound.

Investigation Use B-scan ultrasound to look for scleritis and choroidal mass, and measure scleral thickness which can be increased in uveal effusion syndrome ($\leq$ 2 mm is normal posteriorly, neighbouring the optic nerve). Measure axial length and refraction. Fundus autofluorescence shows the 'leopard spot' pattern characteristic of chronic disease **(Fig. 12.11B)**. Fluorescein angiography and OCT may rule out other diseases.

Treatment Partial or full-thickness sclerectomy. Some authors advocate oral steroids to treat cases without nanophthalmos or abnormal sclera, but the evidence is limited

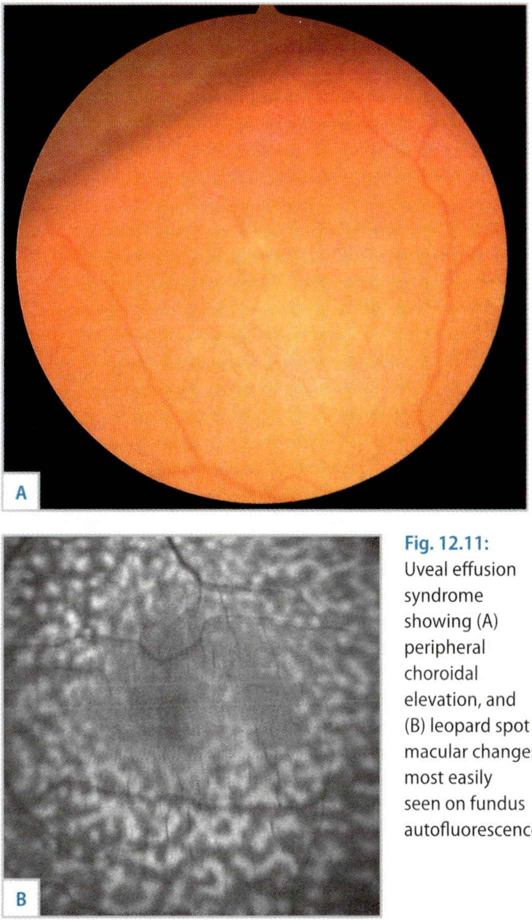

Fig. 12.11: Uveal effusion syndrome showing (A) peripheral choroidal elevation, and (B) leopard spot macular changes most easily seen on fundus autofluorescence.

HEREDITARY VITREORETINAL DEGENERATIONS

If a hereditary degeneration is suspected, draw a family tree (**Fig. 11.1**, p. 494) and ask to examine the relatives. Genetic testing is available for the conditions listed below. Arrange genetic counselling with an experienced clinician.

Stickler's syndrome

An autosomal dominant vitreoretinal degeneration, also known as hereditary progressive arthro-ophthalmopathy. Caused by a mutation of the gene (most often *COL2A1*) coding type II or XI collagen (*COL11A1*), and classified as type 1 or 2, respectively. Type 3 (*COL11A2)* involves collagen type XI, but typically spares the eye. Type 4 (*COL9A1* and *COL9A2*) has ocular features similar to type 1, but lacks the typical systemic abnormalities of hearing (sensorineural and conductive deafness), face (cleft palate and flat midface), joints (premature arthropathy and laxity), and bones (spondyloepiphyseal dysplasia). Ocular involvement includes congenital high myopia (average −5.00D), angle anomalies and glaucoma, presenile wedge-shaped cataracts, and congenital vitreous abnormalities (type 1 membranous, or type 2 beaded condensations). Patients are at very high risk of retinal detachment (RD), irrespective of whether they exhibit typical paravascular pigmented lattice (**Fig. 12.12**). Some clinicians arrange regular review so that prophylactic retinopexy can be applied as required.

Familial exudative vitreoretinopathy

Familial exudative vitreoretinopathy (FEVR) is usually autosomal dominant (chromosome 11), but occasionally X-linked recessive or sporadic. The fundus appearance is similar to retinopathy of prematurity **(Fig. 12.13)**. Three stages are based on the severity of the retinal features: (1) peripheral nonperfusion, especially temporally; (2) localised tractional RD, exudation, and neovascularisation, and (3) more extensive tractional, exudative and rhegmatogenous RD. Fluorescein angiography shows areas of nonperfusion and leakage. Widefield optical coherence tomography (OCT) angiography can also be helpful. Most cases are mild but often progressive, so observe. Some require panretinal photocoagulation (PRP) to the avascular peripheral retina to reduce the ischaemic stimulus, or RD surgery.

Juvenile X-linked retinoschisis

An X-linked retinal dystrophy with secondary vitreous changes and variable phenotypic expression. Caused by a defect in the gene coding a protein (retinoschisin) thought to influence

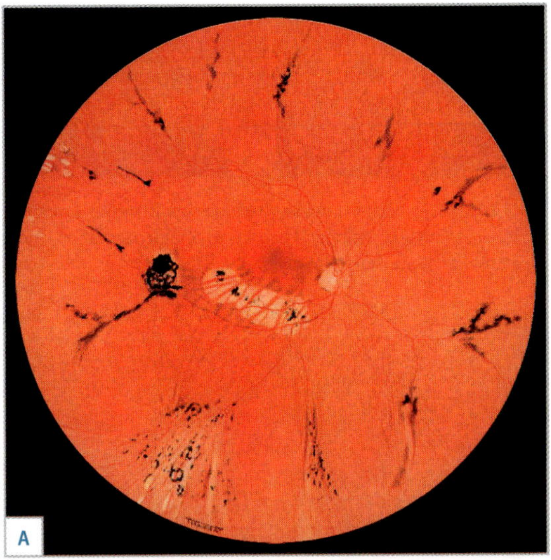

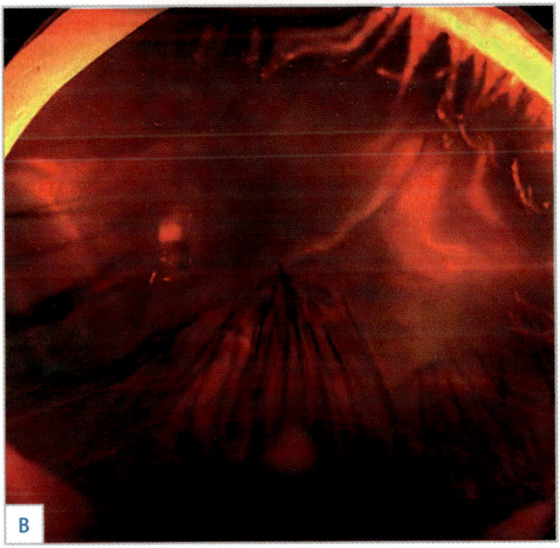

Fig. 12.12: (A) Stickler's syndrome (Courtesy P Leaver/PM Sullivan, artwork T Tarrant); (B) Type 1 membranous vitreous due to *COL2A1* defect (Courtesy R Henderson).

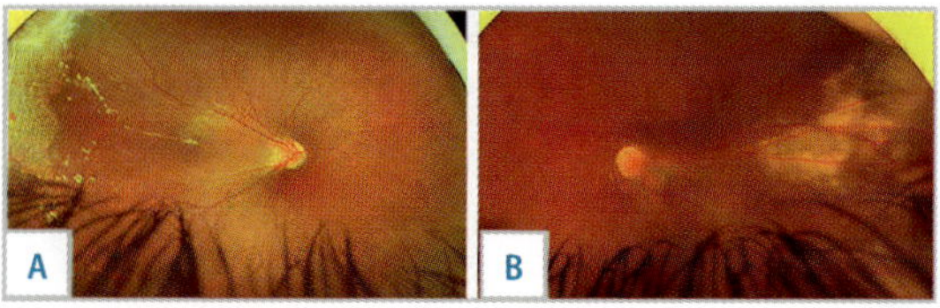

Fig. 12.13: (A) Familial exudative vitreoretinopathy, with temporal vessel dragging and peripheral panretinal photocoagulation, and (B) exudation (Courtesy R Henderson).

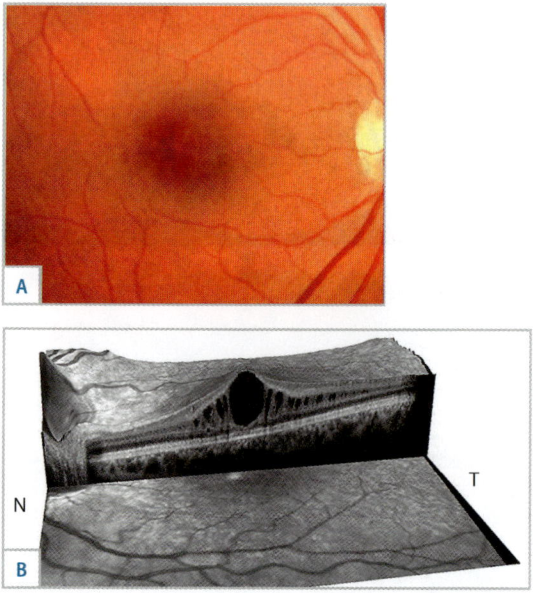

Fig. 12.14: Juvenile X-linked retinoschisis fundus photograph (A), and optical coherence tomography (B; Courtesy R Henderson).

cellular adhesion. Presents in childhood with reduced VA and cystic foveal cavities that coalesce to produce schisis of the nerve fibre layer **(Fig. 12.14A)**. May have peripheral retinoschisis, neovascularisation, vitreous haemorrhage or RD. Electroretinography shows reduced B wave amplitude ('negative ERG', p. 517), and OCT shows schitic separation of the retinal layers, sometimes in more than one plane **(Fig. 12.14B)**. Vitreous haemorrhage can occur and may need vitrectomy. Other treatments may include amblyopia therapy, PRP for new vessels, and RD surgery.

MARFAN'S SYNDROME

Background An autosomal dominant connective tissue disorder.

Systemic features Tall thin stature, long limbs and fingers (arachnodactyly), joint laxity, scoliosis, pectus excavatum, high-arched palate, aortic dilatation, mitral valve prolapse, and hernias.

Ocular features Myopia, corneal abnormalities (including keratoconus), angle anomalies, ectopia lentis **(Fig. 12.15)**, and retinal detachment.

Differential diagnosis of ectopia lentis

- *Trauma*
- *Homocystinuria:* An inborn error of metabolism with marfanoid appearance, fair complexion, osteoporosis, mental deficiency, circulatory insufficiency and thromboembolic events (sometimes precipitated by general anaesthesia). Heterozygotes have hyperhomocysteinaemia with an increased risk of premature (<50 years) retinal vein, and retinal artery occlusion.
- *Weill–Marchesani syndrome:* Short stature, reduced joint mobility, myopia, microspherophakia, and pupil block from displaced lenses.
- *Other causes:* Sulphite oxidase deficiency, hyperlysinaemia, Ehlers–Danlos syndrome, pseudoexfoliation syndrome, high

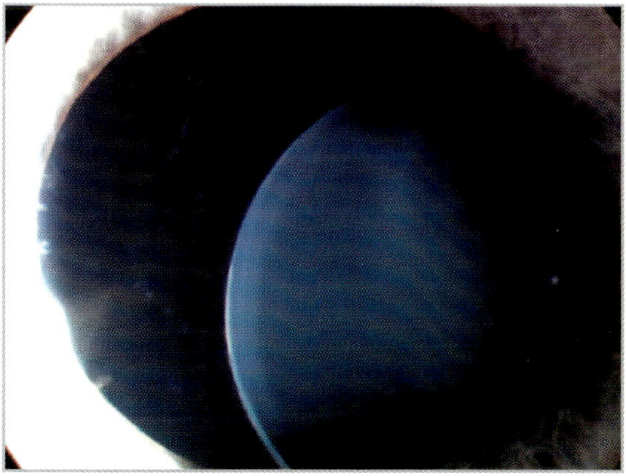

Fig. 12.15: Ectopia lentis in Marfan's syndrome.

myopia, congenital glaucoma, retinitis pigmentosa, aniridia, hypermature cataract and intraocular tumour.

Investigations Genetic testing of the affected fibrillin gene is available (*FBN1* on chromosome 15).

Management Arrange genetic counselling with an experienced clinician and cardiology review. Lens instability may lead to prolapse into the anterior chamber with pupil block, elevated IOP, and corneal decompensation requiring emergency lens removal. Zonular deficiency makes routine cataract surgery difficult, so consider vitreolensectomy with an anterior chamber lens, iris fixated lens, posterior chamber scleral fixated lens, or aphakia and contact lens correction.

POSTERIOR SEGMENT TRAUMA

Blunt or penetrating ocular trauma can produce various injuries due to ocular penetration, tissue compression, shearing, and tensile strain. If the injury results from an alleged assault or workplace injury, make detailed notes documenting the timing and circumstances of injury. Measure or preferably photograph all injuries, and consider an orbital X-ray. Label injuries correctly: cut (clean edges); laceration (ragged wound); penetration (full-thickness defect) and perforation (entry and exit wound). Consider tetanus prophylaxis and extraocular injury. For eyelid injury (see p. 66); cornea (p. 267); angle recession (p. 367) and optic neuropathy (p. 796). Exclude the following posterior segment injuries.

Commotio retinae

Photoreceptor damage produces a white retinal sheen immediately after injury **(Fig. 12.16)**. Often associated with retinal haemorrhage. VA is unaffected unless the macula is involved. No treatment is required. Provide a retinal detachment warning (RDW; p. 629) and review in 1–2 weeks.

Retinal breaks

More common in the inferotemporal and superonasal quadrants. Look for Shafer's sign (p. 628). Some traumatic breaks do not require retinopexy as the healing response produces a chorioretinal adhesion, but request a same-day vitreoretinal

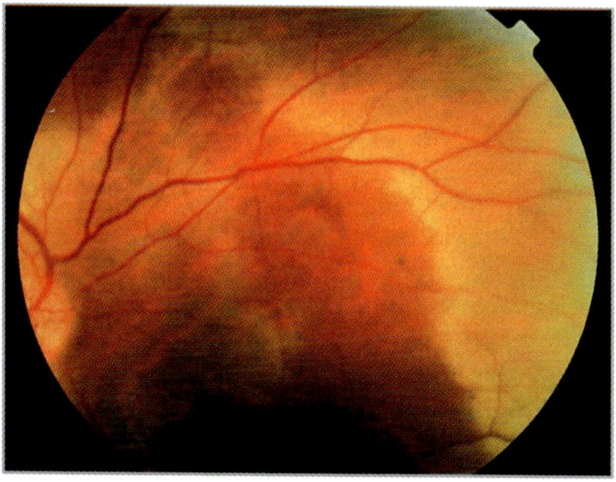

Fig. 12.16: Retinal commotio.

opinion. Provide a RDW and review in 1 week. Head injury without direct ocular trauma seldom produces retinal breaks.

Retinal dialysis

These very peripheral retinal tears have vitreous bridging over the tear, may progress to retinal detachment (RD), and are easily missed. Perform indented fundoscopy or three-mirror examination unless an open-globe injury is suspected. Arrange same-day vitreoretinal review for possible retinopexy, but surgery is usually required (cryobuckle) if RD is present, in which case keep nil by mouth (**Fig. 12.17**).

Choroidal rupture

Rupture and retraction of the choroid–Bruch's–RPE complex allows the underlying sclera to be seen as a white streak (**Fig. 12.18**). Alternatively, it may be obscured by subretinal haemorrhage. If there is subfoveal haemorrhage, discuss urgently with a vitreoretinal surgeon, as some advocate drainage. Otherwise, manage conservatively with review in 2–3 weeks.

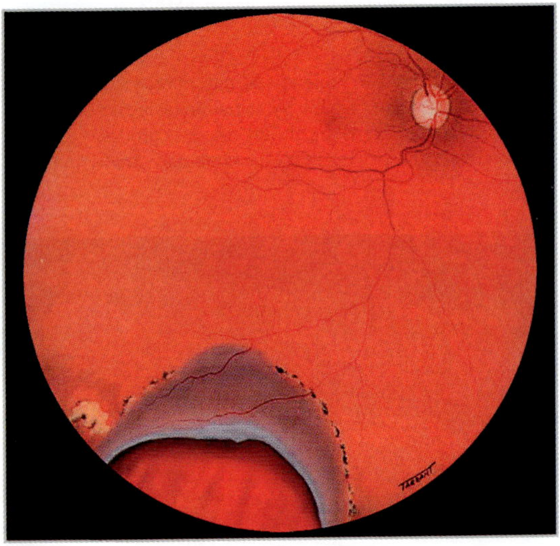

Fig. 12.17: Retinal dialysis with subretinal fluid and a 'high-water mark' (HWM) indicating long duration. The HWM provides neuroretinal adhesion similar to retinopexy, but posteriorly the subretinal fluid has broken through the HWM, with risk of an expanding retinal detachment (Courtesy P Leaver/PM Sullivan; artwork T Tarrant).

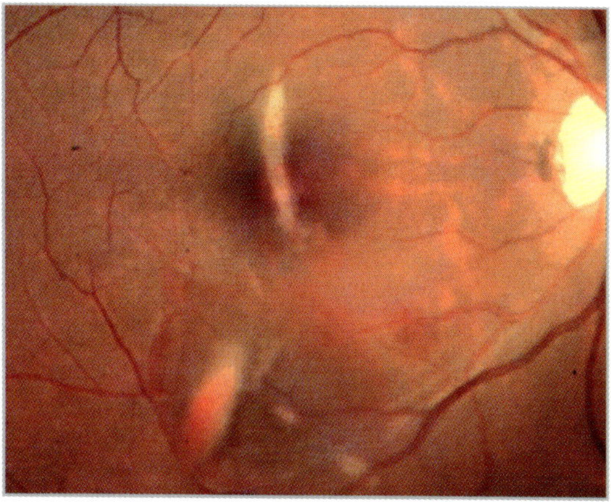

Fig. 12.18: Choroidal rupture with foveal involvement.

Ruptured globe

Ruptured sclera is easily missed if haemorrhagic chemosis obscures the view or the injury is posterior. Ask about the mechanism of injury, and previous eye disease or surgery. Record VA and gently examine for hypotony, deep or collapsed anterior chamber, hyphaema, corneal or lens injury, uveal or vitreous prolapse, vitreous haemorrhage, and reduced ocular motility. Normal IOP does not exclude open-globe injury, but normal fundal examination makes posterior scleral rupture from blunt trauma unlikely. If intraocular haemorrhage obscures the view and the index of suspicion is low, an ultrasound scan (USS) may help to rule out lens dislocation, RD, vitreous haemorrhage, and posterior scleral rupture. Avoid USS if penetration is thought likely, as transducer pressure during examination may extrude intraocular tissue (consider CT instead). Request plain X-rays if a metal orbital or intraocular foreign body (IOFB) is possible, but if revealed, use CT to localise. MRI is unsafe with metal FBs. Examination under anaesthesia with conjunctival recession is sometimes required, so keep nil by mouth except for prophylactic moxifloxacin 400 mg o.d. p.o. Guard the eye with a plastic shield preoperatively, and consider an anti-emetic. For repair of open-globe injuries see **Box 12.3**.

Box 12.3: Primary repair of ruptured globe

1. Explain the procedure and the uncertain, usually guarded prognosis. Subsequent surgery is often required to improve vision (or remove the eye). Primary evisceration or enucleation is rarely necessary and only after review by two consultants and careful discussion with the patient
2. Warn the anaesthetist that surgery sometimes takes several hours. General anaesthesia is usually better than local
3. Gently insert a lid speculum
4. Perform a 360° conjunctival peritomy and carefully examine the sclera back to the four vortex veins. Blunt injury often produces rupture at the limbus, under the recti, or through old surgical wounds. This tends to be limited to one wound, but may be extensive
5. Consider slinging the recti with 2/0 silk sutures to help position the eye. Recti may need to be temporarily disinserted to access underlying wounds. Measure the muscle's distance from the limbus before removing and pre-place a double-armed 5/0 Vicryl suture at the anterior muscle border. Reattach after scleral repair
6. Gently lift prolapsed, nonviable uveal tissue, vitreous, or blood with a dry cellulose sponge and trim flush with the sclera using fine scissors. Avoid excessive vitreous traction. Alternatively, use a vitrector at high cut rate, e.g. 300 cuts/minute
7. Remove any intraocular foreign bodies visible at the wound opening
8. Close corneal wounds with interrupted, simple, 10/0 Nylon sutures. Bury knots. It can be difficult to rotate sutures in hypotonous eyes, so consider starting the first bite within the wound margin so that the knot ties within the wound. Close sclera with 8/0 Nylon sutures, conjunctiva with 7/0 Vicryl
9. It may not be possible to suture very posterior wounds, but these often seal spontaneously after 10 days
10. Cadaveric sclera is occasionally required to replace missing tissue. Silicone explants or a pericardial scleral patch can be used if none is available
11. Once closed, re-inflate the eye with intraocular saline and revise any leaking wounds. Cyanoacrylate glue can seal small leaks; dry tissue before applying
12. Once the globe is secure, examine for conjunctival foreign bodies and eyelid injury
13. Gently inject subconjunctival antibiotic away from the wound

Follow-up: See day 1 postoperatively to exclude endophthalmitis, RD, and hypotony. Later complications include phthisis, proliferative vitreoretinopathy (PVR) with RD, tissue downgrowth and sympathetic ophthalmia. Prescribe G. dexamethasone 0.1% 1-hourly by day, Oc. betamethasone nocte, G. ofloxacin 2-hourly, and G. atropine 1% o.d. Continue oral antibiotics for 10 days. Review in 1 week. Explain the symptoms of RD (p. 629) and sympathetic ophthalmia (p. 426). Do not enucleate seeing eyes (even faint perception of light) in an attempt to prevent sympathetic ophthalmia in the undamaged eye, as the visual prognosis is hard to predict in the injured eye, and enucleation is not proven to reduce the fellow eye risk.

Intraocular foreign body

IOFB is most commonly caused by metal hammering metal. Signs are similar to open-globe injuries (see 'Ruptured globe' above) but endophthalmitis is more common (~10% and often associated with wood or vegetable matter from 'strimming' injuries). The decision whether to remove the IOFB as a primary procedure or subsequently depends on its size and material, visual potential, surgeon, and patient preference. Discuss with a vitreoretinal surgeon. Endophthalmitis, organic or reactive metal IOFBs (iron/copper) usually require primary removal. Surgery usually involves a three-port pars plana vitrectomy with removal through a sclerotomy. Sometimes a magnet is used to retrieve ferrous IOFBs via a sclerotomy, with or without vitrectomy. Document the IOFB size and send for culture. Pre- and postoperative management is similar to ruptured globe, but explain the guarded prognosis and general risks of vitrectomy (p. 639). Gas tamponade may be required, so flying may be contraindicated for several weeks.

OPTOMETRY AND GENERAL PRACTICE GUIDELINES

General comments

Many patients have a few long-standing vitreous floaters or the occasional flash of light (photopsia), and do not require ophthalmology review. Clues to more significant vitreoretinal traction are a sudden increase in the number or appearance of the floaters, especially the onset of many tiny black dots that can indicate a vitreous haemorrhage. Any change in the nature of the photopsia, especially flashes of light in the temporal field, or new onset of photopsia, are potentially significant. Risk factors for retinal detachment (RD) include high myopia, trauma, and previous RD in either eye. In the context of photopsia and floaters, a field defect suggests RD and blurred vision suggests macular detachment or vitreous haemorrhage. Any of these features warrant same-day ophthalmology review. The most common differential of photopsia is migraine, but the photopsias of migraine are usually sustained over a few minutes then abate, unlikely the instantaneous but recurrent flashes of vitreoretinal traction. Give any patient with flashes or floaters a RD warning (p. 629).

Optometrists

Acute onset or suddenly changed symptoms of flashes and/or floaters in one eye should be managed as an RD until proven otherwise. Same-day ophthalmology review is often required regardless of findings, so dilated fundoscopy by an optometrist may not therefore be required, unless experienced and confident to do so. Anxious patients can be reassured that >90% of cases will not have RD or tears.

Long-standing floaters, or the occasional flash of light, should be investigated by the optometrist. Maximal dilation is necessary to view the extreme periphery, therefore use a combination of tropicamide 1%, and phenylephrine 2.5% (after excluding narrow angles, drop allergies, a history of unstable cardiac disease or iris clip intraocular lenses). Warn not to drive until the drops have worn off. If available, wide-angle fundus imaging is often helpful. Refer abnormalities as detailed below.

General practice

The optometry guidelines also apply, except that many GPs will not feel as confident with ophthalmoscopy. If so, then refer chronic mild floaters for routine hospital review. If there are any acute symptoms or features suggesting significant vitreoretinal traction (see general comments, above), arrange same-day ophthalmology review.

No referral is required for posterior vitreous detachment (PVD) or lattice degeneration if these occur in isolation (after excluding retinal breaks or RD). The following guide to hospital referral urgency is not prescriptive, as clinical situations vary.

Immediate

- Macular-on RD (nil by mouth) p. 636

Same day

- Macular-off RD (nil by mouth) p. 636
- Posterior vitreous detachment with flashes and floaters p. 628
- Positive Shafer's sign (pigment cells in vitreous) p. 628
- Vitreous haemorrhage p. 651
- Retinal tears p. 630

Routine

- Lattice degeneration with atrophic round holes, but no tears p. 630
- Epiretinal membrane p. 643

Urgent (within 2 weeks)

- Macular hole present ≤ 2 months p. 648

Soon (within 1 month)

- Macular hole present >2 months p. 648

PAEDIATRICS 13

Gillian GW Adams, Lucy Barker & Adam Bates

HISTORY AND EXAMINATION

Basics Before each consultation read the notes and decide what questions to prioritise: perform the key parts of the examination first in uncooperative children. Be flexible; for example, it may sometimes be better to examine a child before taking a history. Children (and their carers) are often anxious and it helps to perform the examination in a child-friendly setting. Speak and move gently, and explain what you are going to do. Consider examining the child's carer or toy first and warn that drops sting. Fundoscopy, retinoscopy and portable slit-lamp examination can sometimes be carried out with the child asleep. Copy correspondence to the GP and all clinicians and carers involved in the child's care.

History Note the presenting complaint and birth, family, social and drug/allergy history. If relevant, draw a tree (**Fig. 11.1**, p. 494). Ask if the child attends any other clinics. Ask about hearing and normal developmental milestones. Consider prenatal methadone exposure in childhood nystagmus without obvious aetiology.

Vision assessment Vision develops throughout infancy and does not reach normal adult levels until age ~2 years. It may not be possible to accurately assess the VA of each eye separately until age of 3–4 years.

Perform an age-appropriate vision test. A logMAR test is preferable. Check the suspected worst eye first. Observe the child's response to occlusion. If an eye is densely amblyopic, covering the good eye causes distress.

In an infant with suspected blindness, test the blink response to threat and bright light and see if the child fixes and follows a silent stimulus. Do a spinning baby test. The normal response is tonic deviation of the eyes in the direction of rotation with reflex saccadic movement in the opposite direction. Severe visual impairment due to higher visual pathway damage produces prolonged nystagmus on cessation of rotation (normally only 1–2 beats). Oculomotor apraxia produces tonic deviation without saccades, and characteristic head thrusts are used to break fixation.

Examination Observe the child's visual attention, alertness, and the presence of any facial abnormality or head posture. Significant field defects can usually be detected by holding an interesting target straight ahead and then moving a toy in the periphery to see if the child looks towards it.

With a torch, examine the conjunctiva, corneal clarity, and pupil reactions. Examine the anterior segment in more detail with a portable slit lamp or direct ophthalmoscope using plus lenses. Infants can be examined on the normal slit lamp by one adult holding them in a prone position while a second extends their neck, so they can then be 'flown' into the chin rest.

Look for nystagmus and examine ocular movements. If a squint is suspected, perform cover–uncover, and alternate cover tests to look for manifest and latent deviations, respectively. Examine the pupillary response to light and exclude exclude an RAPD.

Perform cycloplegic refraction and fundal examination to exclude refractive errors, media opacities, and fundus abnormalities. Document if examination is difficult or incomplete. Use G. cyclopentolate 0.5% under 6 months of age and 1% if older. Adding G. phenylephrine 2.5% or G. tropicamide 0.5–1% (as for cyclopentolate) can help to dilate dark or poorly dilating eyes. Rarely, it may be necessary to use G. atropine 1% b.d. for 3 days prior to examination.

Using a 'non-stinging' anaesthetic eye drops (e.g. proxymetacaine) before dilating drops may reduce discomfort, lacrimation and future anxiety about eyedrops.

Check the red reflex then start fundoscopy using an indirect ophthalmoscope and a 28-D or 30-D lens (or equivalent), and then a direct ophthalmoscope or higher magnification lens for a more detailed disc examination. Reduced illumination improves cooperation.

If glaucoma is suspected in younger children who cannot be checked with applanation tonometry, then check the IOP with an ICare tonometer (or similar).

If cooperation is lost

- *Casualty*: in an emergency situation, it is important to obtain as full an examination as possible. Record any relevant tests that were not completed. Explain to the carer what needs to be done and why. Swaddle the child in a blanket then complete the fundus and anterior segment examination.
- *Clinic*: consider ending the consultation and re-booking. Rarely, examination under anaesthetic is required.

PRESCRIBING GLASSES

Background Most infants have 1–3 dioptres (D) of hypermetropia, with varying degrees of astigmatism. Hypermetropia of under 5 D usually emmetropises by the age of 6–7 years. There is some evidence that fully correcting hypermetropia in a child may reduce emmetropisation, so small degrees are not usually corrected and large degrees are usually under-corrected. Anisometropia is a risk factor for the development of amblyopia.

The following are only guidelines for the prescription of glasses in children, as situations vary.

Hypermetropia If a child has >4 D of hypermetropia, correct two-thirds of the spherical equivalent, with full correction of any astigmatism. Correcting hypermetropia may improve reading in some children with normal distance of VA. Fully correct hypermetropia if the child has a convergent squint.

Myopia Correct myopia if there is reduced vision, which is likely with −0.5 D or more. Correcting even small degrees of myopia in a child with intermittent exotropia may substantially improve control of the squint.

Anisometropia Fully correct >1 D of anisometropia after the age of 3 years. Correct higher degrees at younger ages. If there is one nearly emmetropic eye and the fellow is amblyopic and hypermetropic, fully correct the amblyopic eye. If both eyes are hypermetropic with similar vision, give an equal correction to each eye, maintaining the interocular difference, e.g. for +6 D OD and +3 D OS subtract 2 D in both eyes to give final refraction of +4 D OD and +1 D OS.

Astigmatism Correct ≥1.50 D of astigmatism. Consider correcting smaller degrees in older children if it improves their VA. Astigmatism is often overestimated in children, secondary to off-axis retinoscopy.

Bifocals Bifocals may be a useful alternative to surgery in children with convergence excess esotropia, and also for children with poor accommodation, e.g. Down's syndrome.

MYOPIA CONTROL

The incidence of myopia is increasing worldwide alongside the associated morbidities of retinal disease (detachment and maculopathy), glaucoma and cataract. Interventions to reduce childhood myopia progression include:

Environmental Increase time outside and avoid excessive near-work activities, e.g. reduced 'screen time'.

Spectacle correction Avoid over-correcting myopic prescription.

Myopia management spectacles and contact lenses Peripheral defocus spectacle lenses and overnight orthokeratology contact lenses can reduce the rate of myopia progression. Neither of these is currently available in the National Health Service (NHS).

Pharmacological Nightly atropine drops of varying concentration (0.01–1%) have been reported to slow myopia progression. The only long-term study reported progression of myopia after stopping atropine, suggesting that myopia retardation requires long-term management. Low-dose atropine is not currently provided by the NHS. It is not commercially available and has to be compounded; it may affect pupil size and accommodation, depending on concentration.

LEUCOCORIA

Leucocoria is a white pupil (**Fig. 13.1**). It is a serious sign that requires urgent referral and assessment. The most common causes include:

- *Infantile cataract*: Page 674
- *Coats' disease*: Page 679
- *Persistent fetal vasculature*: Page 680
- *Toxocariasis*: Page 681
- *Retinoblastoma:* Page 486
- *Familial exudative vitreoretinopathy:* Page 656

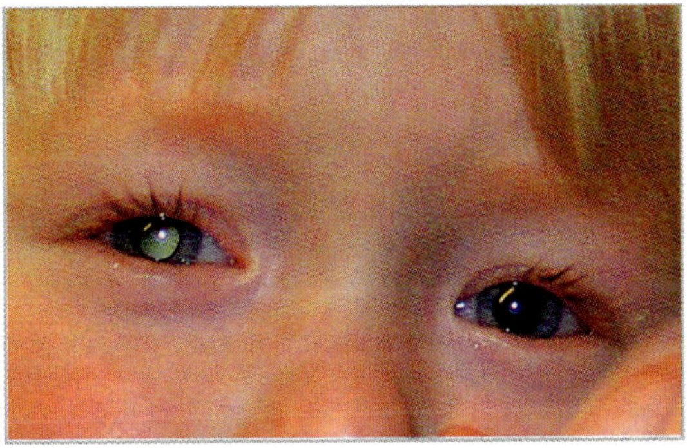

Fig. 13.1: Leucocoria in the right eye due to congenital cataract.

INFANTILE CATARACT

Background Bilateral or unilateral lens opacity is historically termed 'congenital cataract' if presumed present at birth. The cumulative UK incidence by 1 year is 2.5 cases per 10,000 births. It is bilateral in 66%, with 55% being isolated cataract and 45% associated with other ocular or systemic disorders. Inherited cataract (usually autosomal dominant) accounts for 56% of bilateral lens opacities. Associated ocular anomalies are more common with unilateral cataract, particularly persistent fetal vasculature (PFV, also known as persistent hyperplastic primary vitreous or PHPV), while systemic disease usually produces bilateral cataract, with prenatal infection and Down's syndrome the most common. Genetic testing improves the diagnostic yield and may identify treatable conditions such as cerebrotendinous xanthomatosis but is unlikely to benefit those with uniocular cataract associated with PFV.

History and examination Ask the parents about the pregnancy and family history. Check for an RAPD. A portable slit lamp makes cataract assessment easier and helps to exclude associated anterior segment dysgenesis. The quality of the retinal image on direct or indirect ophthalmoscopy is another measure of severity; if the posterior pole cannot be easily seen visual deprivation is expected. Common cataract morphologies are nuclear (**Fig. 13.2**), lamellar (**Fig. 13.3**), anterior polar, posterior subcapsular, posterior with lenticonus (**Fig. 13.4**), and total lens involvement. Examine the parents for unrecognised cataract.

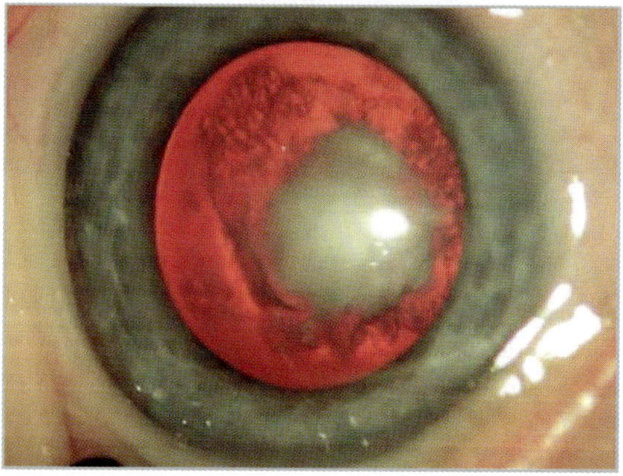

Fig. 13.2: Congenital nuclear cataract.

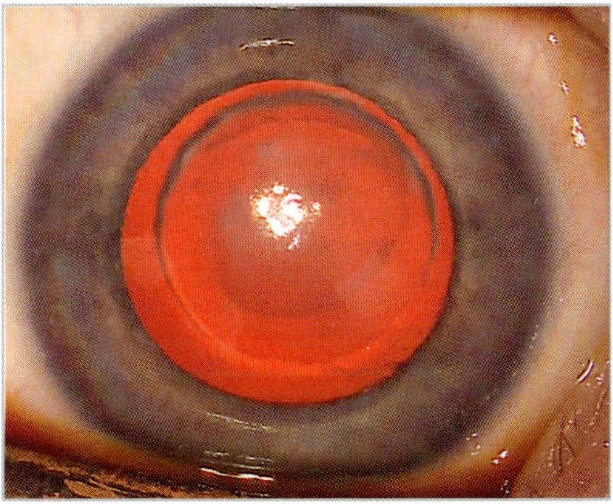

Fig. 13.3: Congenital lamellar cataract.

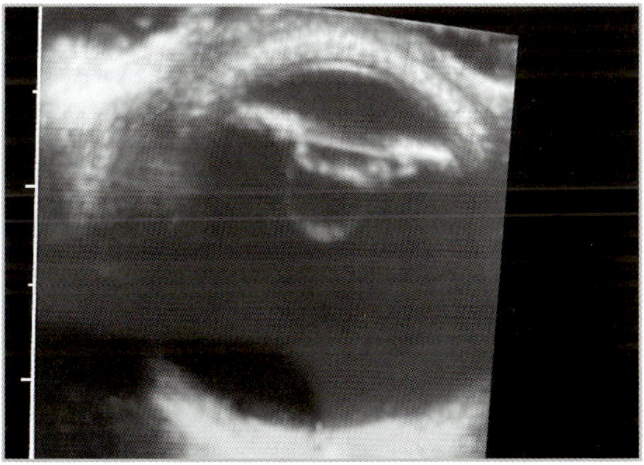

Fig. 13.4: B-scan ultrasound showing congenital cataract and posterior lenticonus.

Other signs include delayed visual development, strabismus and nystagmus.

Differential diagnosis Consider other causes of leucocoria (p. 673).

Investigations Perform B-scan ultrasonography (**Fig. 13.4**) to assess posterior structures and the globe size (including interocular asymmetry), and biometry if required. Request paediatric assessment to exclude systemic causes and associations and to ensure safety for urgent general anaesthesia. If additional clinical signs are present, consider TORCH (toxoplasmosis, rubella, cytomegalovirus, herpes simplex, and HIV) screen (maternal infection), urinary reducing sugars (galactosaemia), and urinary amino acids (Lowe's syndrome). Refer to a paediatric genetic clinic for testing. Offer next generation sequencing (tests 115 known genes) to all bilateral cases. Consider electrodiagnostic testing, if retinal dysfunction is suspected.

Treatment

- *Casualty*: Refer newborns to a specialty clinic the same week, as visually significant unilateral or bilateral cataracts are ideally removed within 6–10 weeks of birth, to avoid deprivational amblyopia.
- *Clinic*: The decision to operate is made by the parents, after discussion with a surgeon experienced in infant cataract surgery. Bilateral cataracts detected early are treated by lensectomy and anterior vitrectomy, with the resulting aphakia treated with glasses or contact lenses. Unilateral cataract is managed the same way but with a contact lens, rather than glasses, postoperatively. Intraocular lens implants are used from 12 months of age, in association with primary posterior capsulorhexis and anterior vitrectomy. Earlier implantation is not advised because of the increased complication rate. The lens power depends on the age of the child, with infants and younger children left hyperopic to allow for later 'myopic shift' as the eye grows.

Consent Discuss the usual risks of adult cataract surgery (p. 285), but warn the parents that paediatric cataract surgery has higher risks and less predictable vision outcomes (**Box 13.1**). Median logMAR VA for uniocular surgery is 0.7 (6/30) at 5 years and 0.34 (6/13) with both eyes open for bilateral surgery. Considerable parental input is required after surgery. The major complications are glaucoma, amblyopia and strabismus. Aphakic glaucoma is a significant risk; up to 50% for children undergoing very early surgery. Surgery is therefore usually deferred until >6 weeks of life, when risk reduces (to 20% by the age of 5 years). By the age of 10 years, 40% are reported to have known or suspected glaucoma. Strabismus and amblyopia occur in virtually all cases of unilateral cataract, whether treated or not. In children undergoing lens implantation, 40% require re-operation for

Box 13.1: Key studies

1. *Infant Aphakia Treatment Study (IATS)*: Recruited infants undergoing cataract surgery aged 28–210 days old. At 4.5 years, there was no VA benefit to intraocular lens (IOL) implantation compared to aphakia with contact lens correction, but a significantly increased rate of adverse events and a 3.5-fold increase in additional intraocular operations. Recommended leaving infants under 7 months of age aphakic.
2. *Intraocular Lens Under 2 Years (IOLu2) study*: Showed no better vision or incidence of glaucoma with primary IOL implantation in children <2 years of age, but a significantly higher rate of re-operation. The routine use of IOLs in this age was not recommended.

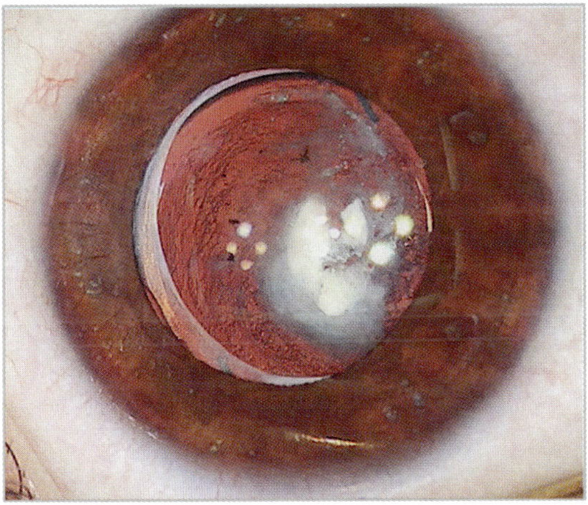

Fig. 13.5: Significant visual axis opacification in paediatric pseudophakia (Courtesy IC Lloyd).

visual axis opacification; the risk is highest with implantation before age of 2 years (**Fig. 13.5**). After unilateral surgery, failure to patch the non-affected eye is the leading cause of poor vision.

Follow-up See at 1 day, then 1 and 4 weeks after surgery, then long-term to monitor for complications. Prescribe topical antibiotic/steroid (e.g. G. maxitrol 2-hourly for 7 days then q.d.s. for 3 weeks) and mydriatic (G. cyclopentolate 0.5–1% depending on age) for 4 weeks after surgery. For babies, consider temporary +20 D glasses until sutures dissolve at about 4 weeks, then refract and prescribe contact lenses or glasses initially for near vision (give the retinoscopy with no subtraction for working distance). Regularly update refraction and alter spectacles or contact lenses accordingly, with single vision lenses until age ~3 years, then bifocal or varifocal correction from ~4 years of age. Check IOP at every visit (iCare is helpful). Increased corneal thickness may give falsely elevated IOP readings. Rarely, examination under anaesthesia may be required. Patching is required for amblyopia. If no surgery is undertaken, review in clinic until age ~5 years to ensure that the good eye develops normally, and to monitor the cataractous eye.

COATS' DISEASE

The main features are unilateral, idiopathic retinal telangiectasia with intra- and subretinal exudation and retinal detachment (**Fig. 13.6**). Apparently bilateral Coats' disease is usually familial exudative vitreoretinopathy or another disease. Coats' disease typically presents in boys at a median age of 5 years, but there is a large range from neonate to adult, with severity inversely related to the age of presentation. There is no racial predisposition, and it is non-heritable in >95% of cases. Telangiectasias are temporal or inferior in the majority of cases, and anterior to the equator in half. B-scan ultrasound aids diagnosis. OCT angiography or fluorescein angiography, especially widefield, may help to identify the telangiectasia. Treatment is cryotherapy to telangiectatic vessels if there is exudative detachment or laser photocoagulation if less exudation. Use VEGF injections if there is macular involvement; and can be combined with sub-Tenon's steroid. Consider vitrectomy in severe cases where laser and cryotherapy have failed. If there is macular involvement or extensive exudation the visual prognosis is poor, even after treatment.

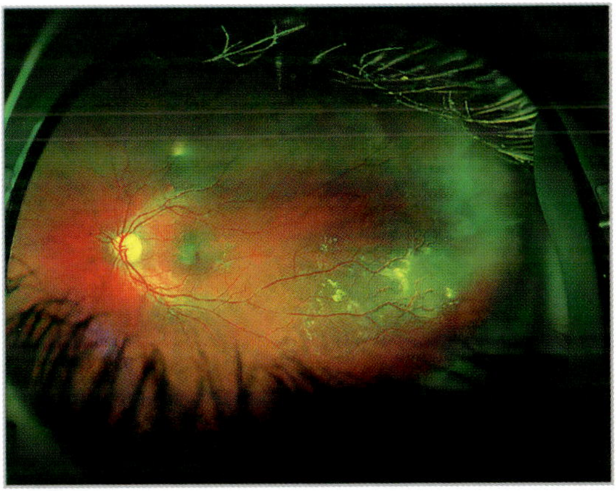

Fig. 13.6: Coats' disease (Courtesy C Wong).

PERSISTENT FETAL VASCULATURE (PERSISTENT HYPERPLASTIC PRIMARY VITREOUS)

Persistent fetal vasculature (PFV) occurs when the primary vitreous fails to regress. It may be anterior or posterior. The most common type is anterior with a micro-ophthalmic eye and a vascularised retrolental mass. Cataract develops early. In the posterior form the lens is usually clear and there is a retinal fold or detachment. It is unilateral in >95% cases with no racial/sex predisposition and is non-heritable in >95%. Observe for angle closure glaucoma secondary to progressive anterior chamber shallowing or direct fibrovascular angle invasion. Exclude other causes of leucocoria (p. 673). Secondary tractional retinal detachment (usually tent-like or sickle-shaped) occurs in a minority. Surgery is rarely required; usually only if anterior chamber shallowing causes glaucoma. The final vision is related to the extent of posterior involvement, development of glaucoma, or phthisis.

Persistent hyaloid artery can be a less severe variant of PFV. This occasionally runs from the disc to the lens; more commonly an anterior remnant gives a Mittendorf dot on the posterior lens surface, or a posterior remnant gives a Bergmeister's papilla over the disc (**Fig. 13.7**).

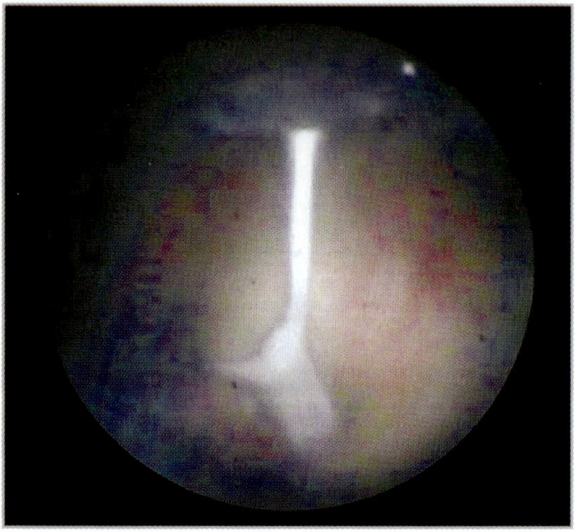

Fig. 13.7: Persistent fetal vasculature (Courtesy C Wong).

TOXOCARIASIS

Ocular toxocariasis is caused by infection with the nematode *Toxocara canis*, which is commonly found in dogs and is excreted in their faeces. If faecally contaminated matter is ingested, the ova develop into larvae in the gut and then travel to other organs. Ocular infection is always unilateral and presents in the age range 2–10 years as a severe endophthalmitis, or in a slightly older child with posterior or peripheral granuloma formation (**Fig. 13.8**). Vitreous activity is very variable, and macular dragging or retinal detachment may occur. The eosinophil count may be raised on FBC or aqueous examination. Immunodiagnostic tests are only about 50% sensitive. Treat with local or systemic corticosteroids and albendazole (10 mg/kg of body weight/day in two divided doses). Titrate the duration of treatment to the response.

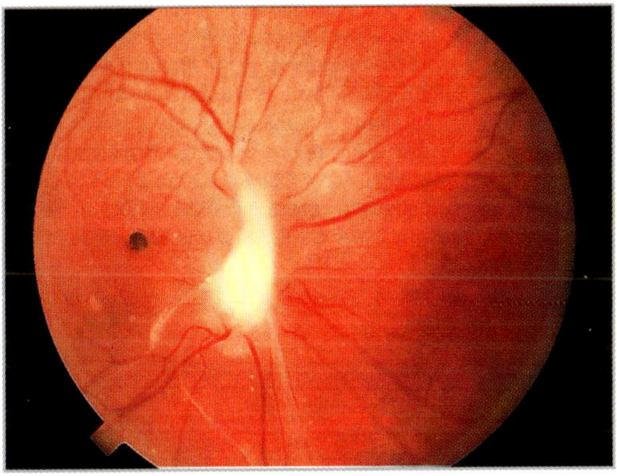

Fig. 13.8: Toxocara (Courtesy C Pavesio).

RETINOPATHY OF PREMATURITY

Background Retinopathy of prematurity (ROP) is a proliferative retinopathy developing in immature retinal vessels. It remains an important cause of visual loss in premature babies (the major cause is cerebral visual impairment), especially in those born at 23–26 weeks' gestation. Despite a reducing incidence, >50% of babies <1,000 g birthweight develop some ROP. Most ROP regresses – in the UK, only ~4% of screened babies require treatment.

Classification The international classification of ROP (ICROP) details location, severity or stage, extent and plus disease. Normal vascularisation proceeds centrifugally from the optic disc to the ora serrata, reaching the nasal ora at ~36 weeks' gestation and the temporal ora at term; thus, any baby born prematurely will have immature retinal vascularisation, increasing with decreasing gestation.

- *Location*: Described as three concentric zones centred on the optic disc (**Fig. 13.9**). Zone I extends 30° from the optic disc to a radius of twice the distance from the disc to the fovea. To define the temporal edge of zone I clinically, view the posterior pole with a 28D lens and align one edge of the lens with the nasal side of the disc: the temporal lens edge then aligns with the temporal zone edge. Zone II surrounds zone I, up to the nasal ora. Posterior zone II extends from the zones I and II border anteriorly by 2 disc diameters. Zone III is the residual

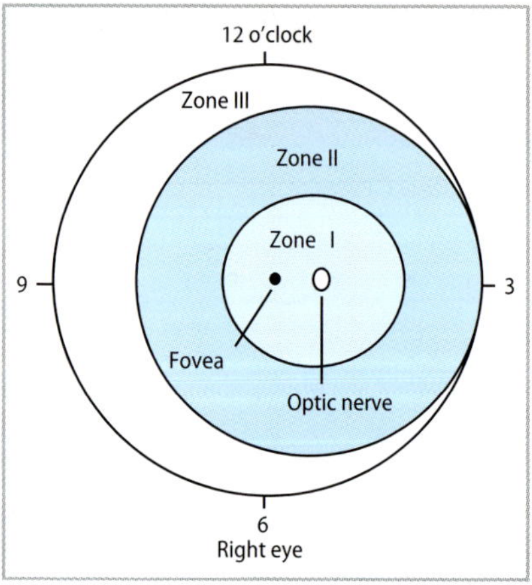

Fig. 13.9: Retinopathy of prematurity, zones I to III.

retina anterior to zone II. The term 'notch' describes the ROP extension into a more posterior zone.

- *Stage*: Stage 1 is a thin white demarcation line at the junction of anterior avascular and posterior vascularised retina (**Fig. 13.10**). Stage 2 has a ridge at the avascular/vascular junction. Also included in this stage is 'popcorn' or small retinal tufts of new vessels posterior to the ridge. Stage 3 has neovascularisation extending from the ridge into the vitreous. Stage 4, with partial retinal detachment, is subdivided into 4A

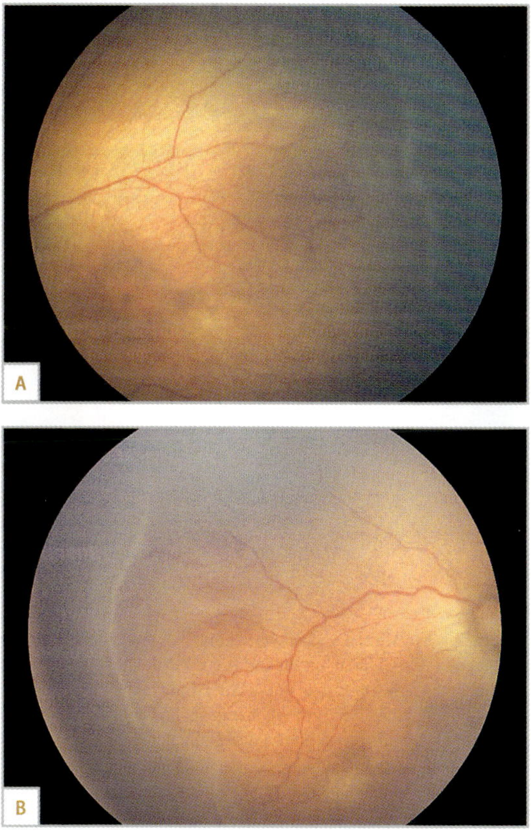

Fig. 13.10: Stages 1 to 4 retinopathy of prematurity, in panel A to D respectively. *Continues overleaf*

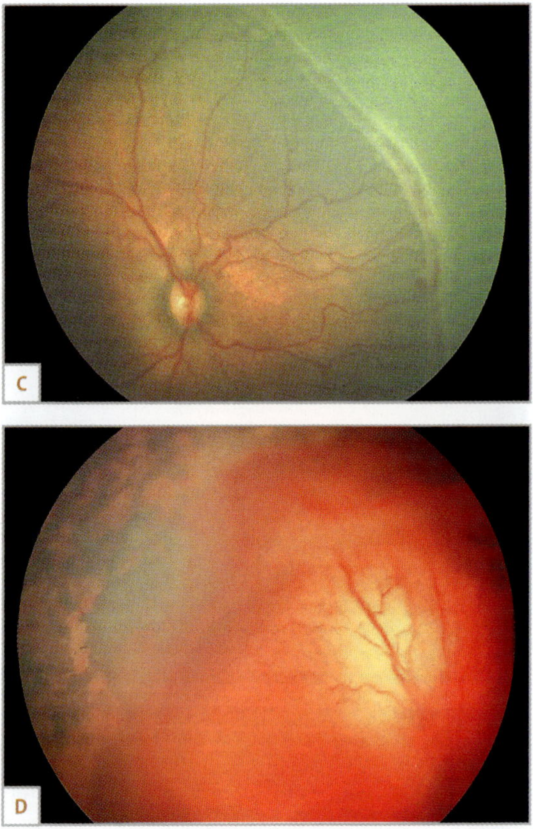

Fig. 13.10: *Continued*

which is extrafoveal and 4B which involves the fovea. Stage 5 has total retinal detachment and is subdivided into A (optic disc visible), B (optic disc not visible) and C (optic disc not visible with anterior segment changes). The most posterior disease (including by a notch) determines staging.

- *Extent*: Recorded by the number of clock hours of retina involved.
- *Plus disease*: It is a marker of severity in active ROP and includes engorgement and tortuosity of the posterior pole vessels, iris vessel engorgement, poor pupil dilatation, and vitreous haze. The presence of plus disease is shown by the

addition of a plus sign (+) to the staging. Plus disease involves two or more quadrants of vessel change. Plus disease in one quadrant is regarded as pre-plus disease. Pre-plus disease is between normal posterior pole vessels and frank plus disease (**Fig. 13.11**). Assess plus and pre-plus disease on the zone I vessels. There is a spectrum of vascular change, from normal to pre-plus, to plus disease.

Extremely immature babies, 25 weeks' gestation or less, may have a different morphology to typical ROP.

Screening guidelines Gestation is often recorded in weeks + days, e.g. 30+6. The UK guidelines were updated in 2022 to screen all babies <31 weeks' gestation (up to and including 30+6) or <1,501 g birth weight. In 2024, the UK screening guidelines were updated again and reported that all infants <31 weeks' gestational age (up to and including 30+6) or <1,501 g birthweight should be examined to screen for the presence of ROP (one criterion to be met for inclusion) and in addition infants born between 31+0 weeks' and 31+6 weeks' gestational age should be considered for screening for the presence of ROP.

For infants born <32+0, perform the first ROP screen between 31+0 and 31+6 post-menstrual age or 4 weeks completed post-natal age, whichever is later. For infants born at or after 32+0, perform the first screen at 36 weeks post-menstrual age or 4 weeks completed post-natal age, whichever is sooner. Examine every 1–2 weeks until vascularisation progresses into zone III. Severe ROP (stage 3 and above) develops between 33 and 43 weeks' gestation.

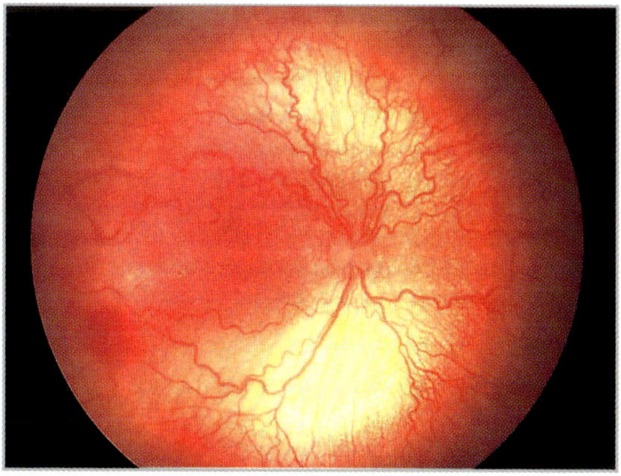

Fig. 13.11: Plus disease.

History A separate eye record within the neonatal paper or electronic notes helps to identify significant disease progression. Document gestational age at birth, birthweight, current gestational age at each examination, and significant medical problems.

Examination Dilate with G. phenylephrine 2.5% and G. cyclopentolate 0.5%, each applied twice, starting 30 minutes before examination. Use an indirect ophthalmoscope and a wide-angle indirect lens (e.g. 28 D or 30 D). If a lid speculum or indentation is required, instill topical anaesthetic. If available, undertake photographic widefield imaging, using topical anaesthetic and a lid speculum. Screening stresses the baby, so have a neonatal nurse to assist when examining any infant in an incubator or on oxygen.

Differential diagnosis The cicatricial form of ROP may appear similar to familial exudative vitreoretinopathy, Norrie's disease (abnormally vascularised retinal detachment ± hearing loss and developmental delay), and congenital retinal folds.

Referral-warranted ROP This describes ROP that either requires treatment or is at high risk of requiring treatment. It comprises any ROP in zone I, any plus disease or any stage 3 of ROP.

Management Treat any of the following:

- Threshold disease:
  - Stage 3 ROP involving at least five contiguous or eight cumulative clock hours in zone I or II, with plus disease, (children are now treated before this 'threshold').
- Type 1 pre-threshold disease:
  - Zone I involvement of any stage with plus disease
  - Zone I stage 3 with or without plus
  - Zone II stage 2 or 3 with plus disease
- Aggressive posterior ROP (A-ROP): A deceptively featureless form of ROP that progresses rapidly to stage 5, skipping stages 1–3. It usually occurs in zone I but can occur in posterior zone II (**Fig. 13.12**). There is plus disease with flat brush-like neovascularisation at a poorly defined vascular/avascular border.

Closely monitor

- Type 2 pre-threshold disease:
  - Zone I stage 1 or 2 disease without plus
  - Zone II stage 3 without plus

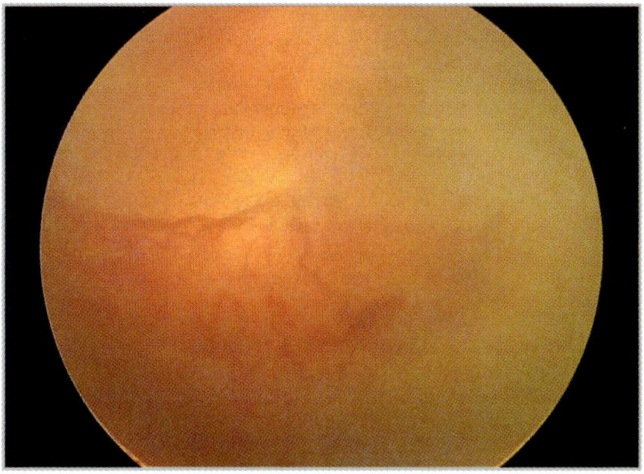

Fig. 13.12: Aggressive posterior retinopathy of prematurity (A-ROP) with stage 4 disease superiorly.

Treatment Treat A-ROP, zone I and posterior zone II disease with an intravitreal anti-VEGF injection such as ranibizumab or bevacizumab (avoid if any signs of periocular infection). Treat zone II disease with transpupillary laser. ROP disease is usually symmetrical with both eyes requiring treatment. Even if only one eye reaches treatment criteria, it is usual to treat both eyes.

Transpupillary diode laser: Apply burns confluently to all avascular retina up to and just anterior to the ridge. Prescribe G. cyclopentolate 0.5% q.d.s. for 5–7 days and prednisolone 0.5% and neomycin q.d.s. for 1-week post-treatment. Review in 1 week. Re-treatment may be required in up to 14% of babies and, if required, is usually at 2 weeks after the initial treatment. The majority have a favourable outcome (an essentially normal posterior pole).

An intravitreal injection of bevacizumab (0.625 mg in 0.025 mL per eye) has shown better results than laser for zone 1 stage 3 plus disease (**Box 13.2**). Smaller doses may also be effective. Ranibizumab (0.2 mg in 0.02 mL per eye) is licensed for ROP treatment in the UK/EU and aflibercept (0.4 mg in 0.01 mL per eye) in the US. The long-term systemic effects of anti-VEGF drugs are unclear. If considering anti-VEGF therapy either as monotherapy or as an adjunct to laser, detailed parental consent is important. When treating both eyes, treat each eye as a separate sterile procedure. Prescribe G. chloramphenicol q.d.s. for 1 week postinjection. Review 24–48 hours and 5–7 days after treatment. After anti-VEGF treatment, follow-up to 69 weeks

Box 13.2: Key studies

1. *Early Treatment for Retinopathy of Prematurity (ET-ROP) study*: Compared treatment of pre-threshold ROP versus treatment of threshold disease. Early treatment had better long-term VA and retinal structure.
2. *Intravitreal Bevacizumab for Stage 3+ Retinopathy of Prematurity (BEAT-ROP)*: Compared retinal laser to intravitreal bevacizumab for stage 3+ ROP. Bevacizumab showed a significant benefit for zone I disease but not zone II disease.
3. *Ranibizumab versus laser therapy for the treatment of very low birthweight infants with retinopathy of prematurity (RAINBOW) (with an extension study)*: Compared laser to 0.1 mg or 0.2 mg ranibizumab. Reported fewer unfavourable outcomes with ranibizumab, particularly the 0.2 mg dose.

postmenstrual age, due to risk of late recurrence of disease. Monitor also for peripheral avascular retina (PAR). Time to recurrence varies with different anti-VEGF drugs, but is shortest with ranibizumab. Treat recurrence with laser therapy.

Consider vitreoretinal surgery for stage 4 ROP but, in the UK, this is currently not recommended for stage 5.

Follow-up Review all infants with stage 3 ROP or worse long-term. Issues include subnormal vision, myopia, strabismus, and visual field loss. Cerebral visual impairment due to white matter damage may also occur with or without ROP treatment.

CONJUNCTIVITIS OF THE NEWBORN (OPHTHALMIA NEONATORUM)

Background Defined as conjunctivitis in neonates aged <4 weeks. The infection may be acquired during delivery (if the mother has vaginal infection or if born in an unhygienic environment) or from postnatal caregivers. Causes include *Chlamydia trachomatis, Staphylococcus aureus, Streptococcus viridans,* enterococci, *Neisseria gonorrhoeae* and herpes simplex virus (HSV). Gram-positive cocci are the most common pathogens.

Signs Look for injected conjunctiva, lid swelling and discharge. Skin vesicles and keratitis occur with HSV. *N. gonorrhoeae* can cause corneal ulceration and perforation within 24 hours. The causative organism cannot be accurately diagnosed from the clinical presentation, but gonococcal conjunctivitis tends to be more severe with earlier onset, usually 2–5 days after birth, while chlamydial infection has a creamy white discharge, a velvety conjunctival appearance, and presents 5–12 days after delivery. Staphylococcal infection often produces a yellow discharge.

Differential diagnosis Conjunctivitis secondary to nasolacrimal duct obstruction. Test for mucopurulent reflux on lacrimal sac massage.

Investigations Arrange an urgent Gram stain to identify any gram-negative diplococci (*N. gonorrhoeae*) and take swabs for bacteria and *Chlamydia*. If HSV is suspected, take a swab for viral polymerase chain reaction (PCR). A special *Chlamydia* swab is required, taken before any fluorescein eye drops, with the specimen obtained from the everted lid to include conjunctival cells and not just exudate. Warn parents that the conjunctiva is friable and may bleed after taking the chlamydial swab. If the infant has chlamydial or gonococcal infection, both the mother, father and any sexual partners require treatment and contact tracing.

Treatment If there is mild-to-moderate conjunctivitis without a history of maternal vaginal infection, treat empirically with lid hygiene and broad-spectrum topical antibiotic (e.g. azithromycin b.d. for 3 days) until the microbiology results are available. For more significant discharge/conjunctivitis, treat empirically for both *N. gonorrhoeae* and *C. trachomatis* but amend as swab results dictate.

- *N. gonorrhoeae*: If only conjunctivitis, admit for intravenous (i.v.) cefotaxime 100 mg/kg as a single dose. For disseminated gonococcal disease use i.v. cefotaxime 50 mg/kg t.d.s. for 7 days (or 14 days if meningitis is suspected or proven). Chlamydial coinfection may occur.

- *C. trachomatis*: Prescribe erythromycin syrup 12.5 mg/kg/day q.d.s. for 14 days. A second course may be required.
- *Herpes simplex virus:* Prescribe i.v. aciclovir 20 mg/kg t.d.s. for 14 days, and for at least 21 days if there is CNS involvement. Confirm cerebrospinal fluid is negative for HSV before stopping treatment.

Follow-up Review in clinic once weekly until improving. If infection recurs, reconsider *Chlamydia* even if initial testing was negative. Observe for chlamydial pneumonitis (cough, nasal discharge and tachypnoea).

ANTERIOR SEGMENT DYSGENESIS

Background Anterior segment dysgenesis (ASD) describes a heterogeneous group of rare disorders characterised by variable maldevelopment of anterior segment structures including the cornea, iris and drainage angle (**Table 13.1**). Occasionally associated with systemic abnormalities. Glaucoma is common and often difficult to manage. Goniotomy or trabeculotomy may be required for infantile glaucoma, and trabeculectomy with antimetabolites or drainage tubes for juvenile glaucoma. Several genes have been implicated. Draw the family pedigree (**Fig. 11.1**, p. 494), examine family members, and arrange review with an experienced clinician for genetic testing and counselling. Regularly review refraction, cornea, lens, IOP, optic nerve and field tests as required.

Aniridia Characterised by bilateral complete or partial iris hypoplasia with associated foveal hypoplasia, resulting in photophobia, reduced VA (6/36–6/60) and nystagmus (**Fig. 13.13**). Presents in early infancy. Frequently associated with later onset cataract and glaucoma (up to 50%). Corneal opacification and vascularisation (secondary to limbal stem-cell deficiency) often occur in adulthood but may occur in children, necessitating limbal stem-cell transplantation and corneal grafting. Aniridia may occur as an isolated abnormality without systemic involvement, or as part of a systemic condition such as the Wilms' tumour–aniridia–genital anomalies–retardation (WAGR) syndrome [*PAX6* and adjacent Wilms' tumour (WT), WT-1 locus] or Gillespie syndrome (cerebellar ataxia, mental retardation and aniridia; ITPR1, or PAX6 in atypical cases). Aniridia may be familial or sporadic; both are caused by mutations or deletions of the *PAX6* gene on 11p. Test children with sporadic aniridia for deletion of the Wilms' tumour suppressor (*WTS*) gene. Those with WTS deletion are at high risk of Wilms' tumour and need regular abdominal ultrasound. Children with familial aniridia are not at significantly increased risk of Wilms' tumour and do not need ultrasound screening. Correct any refractive errors with tinted spectacles. Artificial iris implants have been used in certain cases but with a risk of secondary glaucoma or corneal decompensation (**Fig. 13.14**).

Sclerocornea Describes opaque scleral tissue with fine vascular arcades extending into the peripheral cornea. There is a spectrum of severity from complete corneal opacification to a poorly defined limbus (**Figs. 13.15 and 13.16**). Most (90%) are bilateral, but often asymmetrical. Disease can be genetic (dominant or recessive) or sporadic and non-progressive. May be associated with: cornea plana; microphthalmos;

Table 13.1: Anterior segment dysgenesis

Signs	Posterior embryotoxon	Axenfeld's anomaly	Rieger's anomaly	Peters' anomaly type 1	Peters' anomaly type 2	Posterior keratoconus
Prominent Schwalbe's line	√	√	√			
Iris strands to Schwalbe's line		√	√			
Hypoplasia of the anterior iris stroma			√			
Strands from iris collarette to edge of posterior corneal depression				√	√	
Posterior corneal depression with variable overlying haze				√	√	√
Central corneal opacity				√	√	
Adherence between iris and cornea					√	
Abnormal lens position/clarity					√	
Glaucoma (%)	0	0*	60	50–70	0	

* Called Axenfeld's syndrome if glaucoma is present.

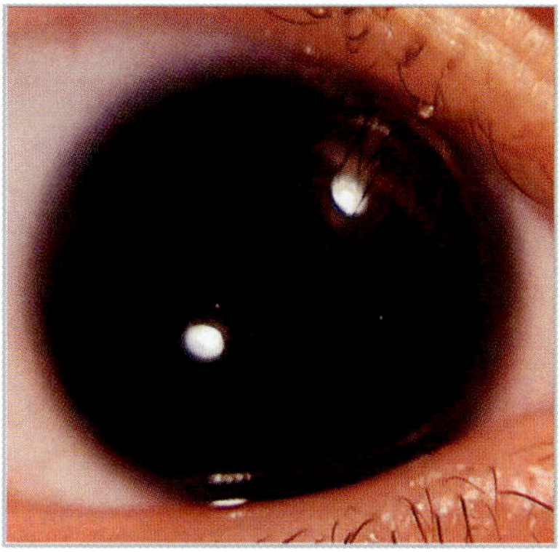

Fig. 13.13: Complete aniridia (Courtesy A Martins).

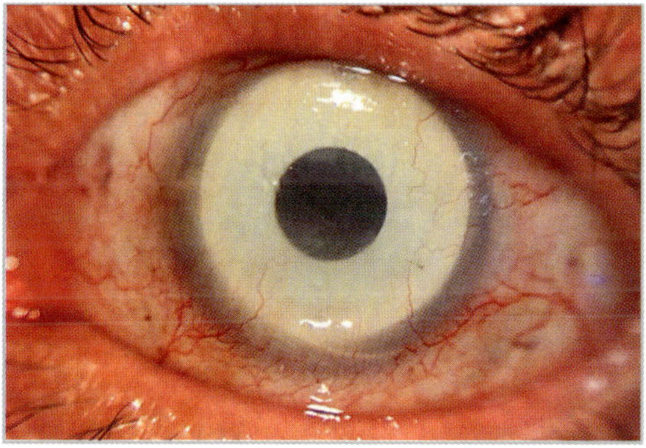

Fig. 13.14: Aniridia with stem-cell deficiency, corneal vascularisation and Morcher intraocular lens (Courtesy A Martins).

iridocorneal synechiae; persistent pupillary membrane; angle and iris dysgenesis; congenital glaucoma; coloboma; posterior embryotoxon; mental deficiency; deafness; and craniofacial, digital and skin abnormalities. The differential diagnosis includes interstitial keratitis (p. 223) and arcus juvenilis. Treatment includes correcting refractive errors ± optical iridectomy in partial cases, and corneal graft surgery in selected cases. The visual prognosis after penetrating keratoplasty is poor with a high rate of graft rejection.

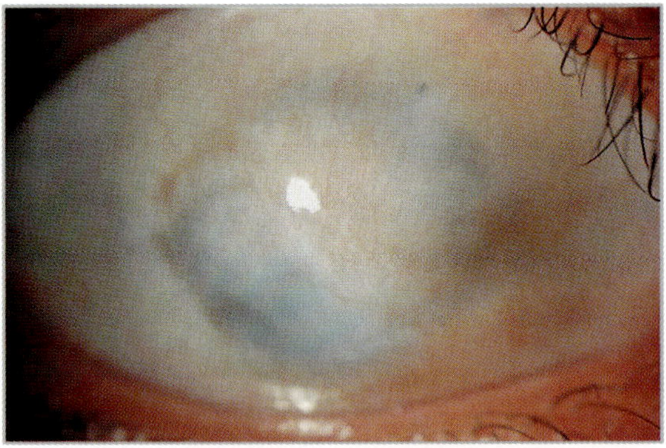

Fig. 13.15: Total sclerocornea (Courtesy F Larkin).

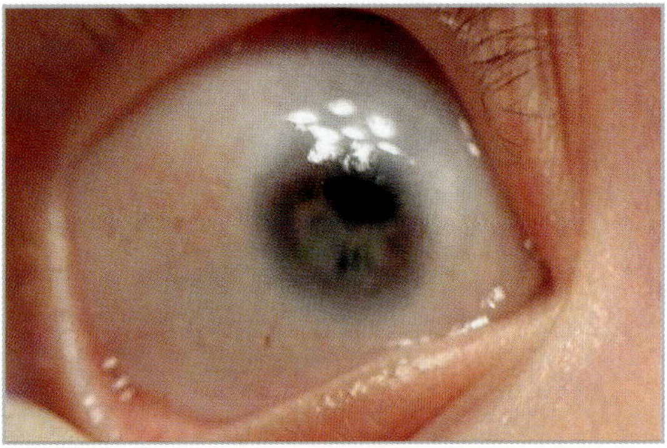

Fig. 13.16: Partial sclerocornea (Courtesy F Larkin).

Posterior embryotoxon Anterior displacement and enlargement of Schwalbe's line is seen as an irregular circumferential ridge on the posterior corneal surface, just inside the limbus. Present in 10–15% of normal eyes. May be associated with primary congenital glaucoma, Alagille's syndrome, megalocornea, aniridia, corectopia and Noonan's syndrome.

Axenfeld anomaly Posterior embryotoxon with attached iris strands. Called Axenfeld's syndrome if glaucoma is present.

Rieger's anomaly Axenfeld anomaly with hypoplasia and distortion of the iris stroma. May have corectopia or polycoria.

Glaucoma occurs due to incomplete development of aqueous outflow pathways. Associated with oculodigital dysplasia, osteogenesis imperfecta and Down's, Ehlers Danlos', Noonan's syndrome, and Rieger and Franceschetti's syndrome. It is also called Rieger's syndrome (or Axenfeld–Rieger syndrome) if there are skeletal abnormalities such as maxillary hypoplasia, abnormal dentition, micrognathia, hypertelorism, and other limb or spinal malformations.

Peters' anomaly Congenital central corneal opacity (**Figs. 13.17** and **13.18**) with iridocorneal ± lenticulocorneal adhesions. Bilateral in 80%, with glaucoma in 50–70%. Usually sporadic, but when familial, autosomal recessive inheritance is the most common. Management may involve corneal grafting, with an excellent prognosis.

- *Type I*: Central corneal opacity with iridocorneal adhesions.
- *Type II*: Central corneal opacity with lenticulocorneal adhesions. May be associated with abnormal lens position, cataract, microcornea, microphthalmos, cornea plana, sclerocornea, coloboma, aniridia and dysgenesis of the angle and iris.

Posterior keratoconus May represent a mild variant of Peters' anomaly.

Iridocorneal endothelial (ICE) syndrome Abnormal epithelioid endothelium migrates across the angle and iris. Contraction of this tissue then causes high peripheral anterior synechiae (**Fig. 13.19**), pupillary abnormalities (**Fig. 13.20**)

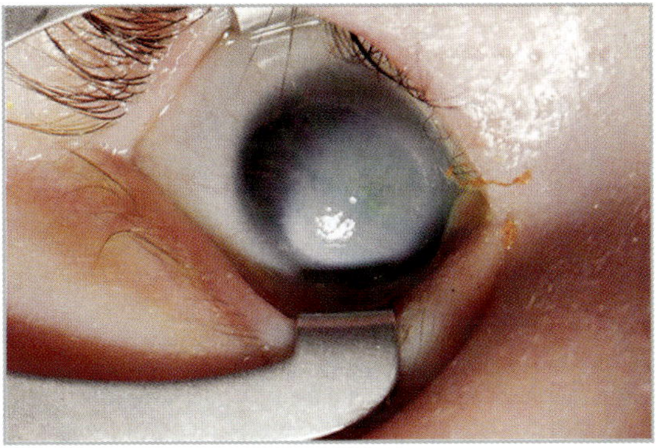

Fig. 13.17: Type I Peters' anomaly (Courtesy F Larkin).

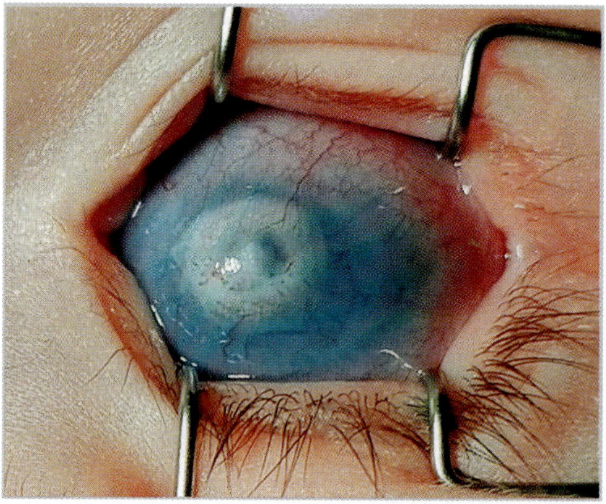

Fig. 13.18: Type II Peters' anomaly, with no discernible lens (Courtesy W Moore).

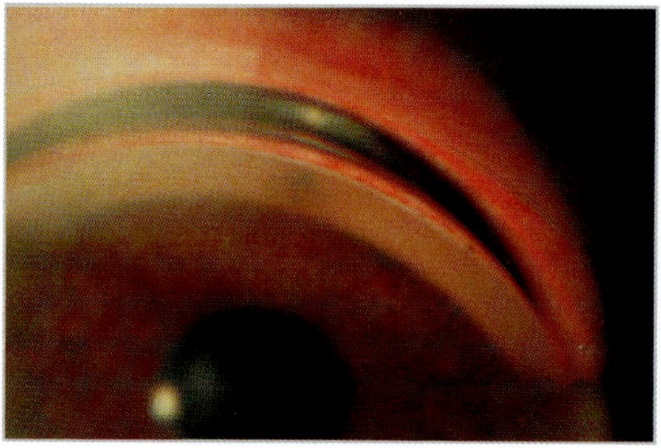

Fig. 13.19: Gonioscopy of iridocorneal endothelial (ICE) syndrome, Cogan Reece type. Note multiple iris papillae with flat iris and high insertion into angle (Courtesy A Martins).

and secondary glaucoma. Usually unilateral, progressive, and diagnosed in young adults to middle-aged patients, rather than childhood. It is not inherited, and is more common in women. May be linked to HSV or Epstein–Barr virus. Descemet's membrane has a beaten-metal appearance and there may be

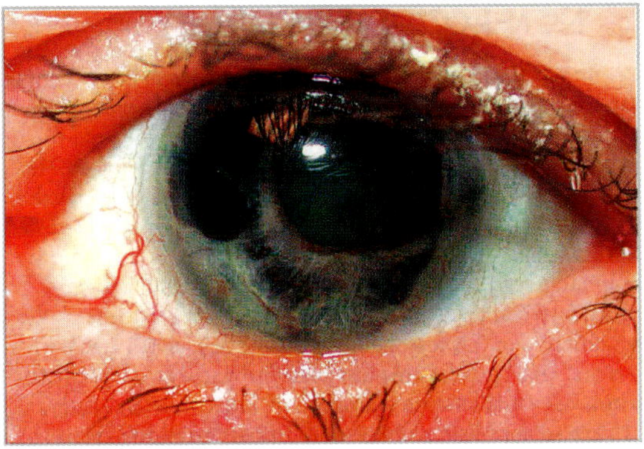

Fig. 13.20: Iridocorneal endothelial (ICE) syndrome, with essential iris atrophy (Courtesy PT Khaw).

microcystic corneal oedema. The iris has stromal thinning, full-thickness holes, 'naevi', and broad, tenting peripheral anterior synechiae, depending upon the subcategory. IOP may be raised and the disc cupped. Perform gonioscopy at presentation, and treat elevated IOP (topical antihypertensives) and epithelial oedema (G. sodium chloride 5% q.d.s.). May need corneal grafting eventually. Variations include:

- *Chandler's syndrome*: Mild iris thinning and pupil distortion. Most common subtype, ~50% cases.
- *Cogan–Reese syndrome*: Pigmented iris nodules. Iris atrophy is less common.
- *Essential iris atrophy*: Marked iris thinning, iris holes, and pupil distortion.

NON-ACCIDENTAL INJURY

Background Ophthalmic signs of non-accidental injury (NAI) can be varied and include periorbital and conjunctival injuries, damage to the anterior segment and lens, and vitreoretinal injuries. The most common is retinal haemorrhage (**Fig. 13.21**), usually in children below 1 year of age and in ~80% associated with subdural haemorrhage. Retinal haemorrhages can be caused by trauma, both accidental and non-accidental (including birth trauma), or non-traumatic conditions, including infection, raised intracranial pressure, blood disorders, and rare metabolic conditions. For this reason, never assume deliberate harm has, or has not, taken place. Care must be co-ordinated by the paediatric team. Relevant literature is available at: https://www.rcophth.ac.uk/resources-listing/abusive-head-trauma-and-the-eye-in-infancy.

History and examination As legal proceedings are likely, make clear, timed and dated entries in the records. Document laterality, location (posterior pole, periphery), layer (pre-retinal, intraretinal, subretinal) and severity [few, many, too numerous to count (TNTC)] of the retinal haemorrhages. Download and use the Royal College of Ophthalmologists' record sheet, if possible. Also document any facial bruising and non-retinal trauma, e.g. subconjunctival haemorrhages.

Signs The morphology of retinal haemorrhage is determined by the anatomy of the layer it occurs in, rather than by the

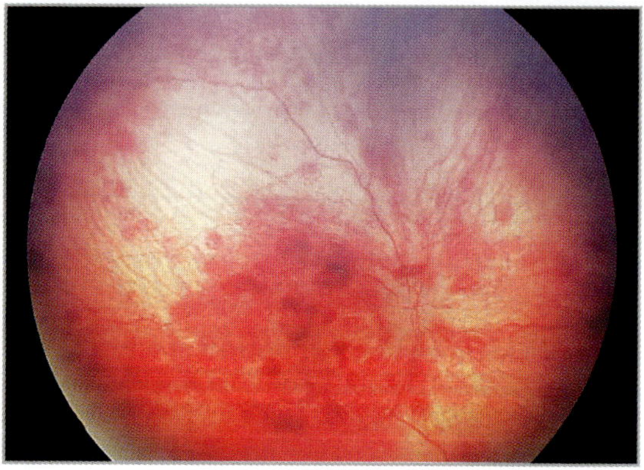

Fig. 13.21: Retinal haemorrhages in non-accidental injury.

cause, so the appearance does not establish the cause. Although perimacular folds and traumatic retinoschisis are usually only seen in cases of inflicted injury, they have rarely been described as occurring accidentally.

Timing Superficial retinal haemorrhage normally clears by a week, deeper intraretinal haemorrhages by 4 weeks, and preretinal and vitreous haemorrhages take longer, however, all timings are approximate.

Management

- *Casualty*: Refer immediately to a consultant ophthalmologist, and designated paediatrician or nurse. They will undertake further management and contact social services, if necessary. Consultant examination should occur as soon as possible and within 48 hours.
- *Clinic*: Arrange follow-up at 1 week to review any retinal haemorrhage and again clearly describe its morphology. Review until the retinal haemorrhages clear. Some children are left significantly visually impaired from associated damage to the visual pathways, and need long-term follow-up. Electrodiagnostic testing may be useful in these children. Surgery is rarely required but may have to be considered for non-clearing vitreous haemorrhage to prevent deprivational amblyopia.

REDUCED VISION WITH AN OTHERWISE NORMAL EXAMINATION

Background Reduced vision for age with an apparently normal examination may be due to ophthalmic or neurological disease. In the older child, it may be functional. Some children will have subtle abnormalities on detailed examinations that explain their reduced vision.

History Ask about prematurity, consanguinity, family history of ophthalmic disease, photophobia, night blindness and evidence of visual field loss.

Examination Perform a full ophthalmic examination. In particular, look for nystagmus, which can be easily overlooked when of small amplitude. Check for iris transillumination which suggests albinism. Optic nerve abnormalities such as hypoplasia and atrophy can be subtle and difficult to identify; examine carefully with a direct ophthalmoscope. Check for an RAPD or sluggish pupillary reactions. Small babies usually have small pupils, which may make pupil testing difficult. In older children, perform an Ishihara test to check colour vision. A careful examination should exclude albinism and optic nerve hypoplasia. Most retinal dystrophies have fundal abnormalities present by the time visual symptoms occur but, in some cases, especially in infants, the early fundus appearance can be normal.

Investigation Undertake macular and optic nerve OCTs (handheld for small children). Perform electrodiagnostic tests if there is no obvious cause for visual loss. Consider paediatric neurological referral and neuroimaging.

Differential diagnosis Depends on the age at presentation.

- Infants (0–12 months):
    1. *Cerebral visual impairment*: Reduced vision due to damage to the cerebral visual pathways. Most patients have associated neurological deficits. The most common cause is hypoxic/ischaemic damage, but also intracranial infection, bleeding or hydrocephalus. Electrodiagnostic tests show post-retinal dysfunction.
    2. *Delayed visual maturation (DVM)*: Presents as reduced visual function in a child <16 weeks old, but vision improves with time. There are three categories: visual problem only (type 1); as part of generalised developmental delay or with fits (type 2); in association

with other ocular disease, particularly albinism (type 3). Electrodiagnostic tests are normal for age. Associated with an increased incidence of reading problems even after VA improves. Only consider DVM once other causes are excluded.

3. *Retinal dystrophies*: May be present in infancy or childhood. Most are progressive but some are stationary. They may involve either the rod or cone systems or inner retina. Nystagmus is common in early-onset forms. Electrophysiology is essential for diagnosis. Associated with high refractive error. Stationary dystrophies presenting in infancy include congenital stationary night blindness (CSNB), and the achromatopsias. *Leber's congenital amaurosis* is an autosomal recessive, severe, early-onset rod–cone dystrophy. Affected infants have roving eye movements or nystagmus, high hyperopia, and poor pupillary light responses. Eye-poking is common. The initial fundus examination is usually normal, but later in childhood a pigmentary retinopathy with optic disc pallor and retinal arteriolar narrowing develops. The electroretinogram (ERG) is severely abnormal or undetectable.
4. *Optic nerve hypoplasia*: May be unilateral or bilateral and of variable severity. The disc is very small and often appears grey. There may be a 'double-ring sign' with the true edge of the optic nerve surrounded by the scleral opening, which may be pigmented. There may be a history of maternal alcohol/drug ingestion. Bilateral cases may be associated with intracranial anomalies, for example, septo-optic dysplasia (absence of the septum pellucidum and agenesis of the corpus callosum) and pituitary stalk abnormalities. Endocrine abnormalities are common. Arrange neuroimaging and paediatric endocrinology referral.

- Children (age >1 year):
  1. *Neurological disease*: While rare, consider neurological diseases including Batten's (p. 600) disease and chiasmal tumours which, in the early stages, may have few ophthalmic signs Batten's disease has an electronegative response on the photopic ERG (p. 517); chiasmal disease shows post-retinal dysfunction with hemisphere asymmetry on electrodiagnostic testing.
  2. *Retinal dystrophies*: These include CSNB, retinitis pigmentosa, and progressive cone dystrophy. ERGs are abnormal and can distinguish between the different dystrophies.

3. *Inherited macular dystrophies:* Stargardt's disease (p. 610) and X-linked retinoschisis (p. 656) have fundal abnormalities that may be subtle or absent in early disease.
4. *Inherited optic neuropathies:* Dominant optic atrophy may be subtle and difficult to detect. If possible, look for a yellow/blue colour defect, and a central field defect. *Leber's hereditary optic neuropathy* (p. 801) typically presents in males aged 15–35 years and is caused by a mitochondrial DNA defect, hence maternal inheritance. It presents with painless, central vision loss in the first eye, followed by second eye involvement over weeks to months. VA deteriorates slowly, often to 6/60, with colour vision affected early. The optic disc may be normal or hyperaemic with peripapillary telangiectasia in the early stages, but becomes atrophic later.
5. *Functional visual loss:* Most commonly presents over the age of 8 years, with a female preponderance. It is usually bilateral but can be unilateral. Check vision with neutralising lenses and look for spiral visual fields. Examine pupils for for an RAPD. Orthoptic testing is often helpful. Do not diagnose this condition unless good vision can be demonstrated or appropriate electrodiagnostic testing and/or imaging have been undertaken. It may be associated with psychological difficulties, so consider psychology referral. See also Medically Unexplained Visual Loss, page 813.

Management Establish the diagnosis and arrange genetic referral if appropriate. Involve paediatric and family support early. Provide spectacle correction, low-vision aids, and educational support as appropriate. If photophobia is prominent, tinted spectacles or tinted contact lenses may help. Gene therapy is now available for Leber congenital amaurosis. Idebenone has been used to treat Leber's hereditary optic neuropathy, but the National Health Services England concluded that there is not enough evidence to make the treatment available; it is accepted for restricted use in Scotland.

OPTOMETRY AND GENERAL PRACTICE GUIDELINES

If there is any doubt about the appropriate referral for a child with an eye problem, ask a paediatric ophthalmologist for advice or discuss with the local hospital eye service. The following guidelines for urgency of hospital referral are not prescriptive, as clinical situations vary.

Same day

- Suspected non-accidental injury (consult local guidelines first) (p. 698)
- Papilloedema with neurological signs or systemically unwell (refer to accident and emergency) (p. 776)
- Neonatal conjunctivitis (p. 689)

Urgent (within 1 week)

- Optic disc swelling with headache (p. 776)
- Sudden onset of double vision (p. 7 and 8)
- Sudden onset of squint with restricted eye movements (p. 7 and 8)
- Absent red reflex, or suspected cataract at the 6–8-week postnatal check (p. 674)
- Leucocoria (p. 673)
- Abnormalities detected at the postnatal check, e.g. anophthalmos, microphthalmos, or colobomas (p. 100)
- Complete ptosis (p. 39)

Soon (within 1 month)

- Juvenile arthritis (p. 447)
- Severe allergic eye disease (p. 159)
- Staphylococcal keratoconjunctivitis (p. 150)
- Children with significantly reduced vision bilaterally (p. 669)

Routine

- Chalazion (p. 42)
- Squint (p. 747)
- Allergic eye disease (p. 159)
- Watery eyes (p. 71)
- Recurrent conjunctivitis (p. 150)

STRABISMUS

Gillian GW Adams & Naz Raoof

14

ANATOMY AND PHYSIOLOGY

Extraocular muscles The actions of the extraocular muscles are summarised in **Table 14.1**. They are examined in nine positions of gaze. This includes moving from the primary position (looking straight ahead) into the eight other cardinal positions, as illustrated in **Table 14.2**, which also shows the muscle pairs that move the eyes into these positions. Remember SIN RAD: Superior muscles (superior rectus, superior oblique) INtort; Recti (superior rectus, inferior rectus) ADduct.

Binocular vision The ability to use both eyes simultaneously so that each eye contributes to a common vision perception. Classified as three grades:

1. *Simultaneous perception:* The ability to simultaneously perceive two images, one formed on each retina.
2. *Fusion:* Sensory fusion is the ability to fuse these two images and perceive them as one. Bagolini glasses and the Worth four dot test can be used to confirm sensory fusion. Motor fusion is the ability to maintain sensory fusion through a range of eye movements – essential to join diplopia (double vision) because it allows similar retinal images to fall on corresponding retinal points in each eye. The prism fusion range is used to quantify motor fusion.

Table 14.1: Actions of the extraocular muscles

Muscle	Primary action	Secondary action	Tertiary action
Medial rectus	Adduction		
Lateral rectus	Abduction		
Superior rectus	Elevation	Intorsion	Adduction
Inferior rectus	Depression	Extorsion	Adduction
Superior oblique	Intorsion	Depression	Abduction
Inferior oblique	Extorsion	Elevation	Abduction

Table 14.2: Actions of the extraocular muscles examined in the nine cardinal positions of gaze

		RSR, RIO LSR, LIO ↑		
RSR, LIO ←	Dextroelevation	Direct elevation	Laevoelevation	→ LSR, RIO
RLR, LMR ←	Dextroversion	Primary position	Laevoversion	→ LLR, RMR
RIR, LSO ←	Dextrodepression	Direct depression	Laevodepression	→ LIR, RSO
		↓ RIR, RSO LIR, LSO		

Abbreviations: R, right; L, left; S, superior; I, inferior; R, rectus; O, oblique

3. *Stereopsis*: The perception of depth based on binocular image disparity.

Binocular single vision (BSV) The ability to use the foveae and other corresponding retinal points in both eyes to perceive a single image with stereopsis. Two types exist:
1. *Normal retinal correspondence (NRC):* The visual directions of both foveae are the same. The temporal retina of one eye corresponds with and has a common visual direction with the nasal retina of the other eye.
2. *Abnormal retinal correspondence (ARC):* A sensory adaptation in the presence of a constant manifest squint, i.e. a 'second-best' form of binocular vision. The fovea of the fixing eye corresponds with a nonfoveal area of the deviating eye, e.g. in a manifest left convergent strabismus the fovea of the right eye corresponds with an area of nasal retina in the left eye; all retinal areas (nasal and temporal) similarly adapt when both eyes are open. The angle of anomaly refers to the difference between the subjective and objective angles of deviation.

Suppression The cortical inhibition of the visual sensation from one eye, when both eyes are open. Suppression occurs to avoid diplopia or visual confusion. Suppression areas (scotomata) may vary in position, size, and density. Prisms can be used to measure their size and the Sbiza bar to measure their density.

HISTORY AND EXAMINATION

Background Eyes that are correctly aligned are described as orthophoric or 'straight'. A manifest deviation or heterotropia is when one or other visual axis is not aligned – esotropia if convergent, exotropia if divergent, hypertropia if up, and hypotropia if down. In heterophoria (latent deviation) both eyes are directed towards the fixation point but deviate on dissociation – esophoria (latent convergence), exophoria (latent divergence) or hyperphoria/hypophoria (latent vertical deviations). A constant deviation typically refers to a deviation that is present for near and distance, whereas an intermittent deviation is only present at one distance, e.g. near fixation, or certain conditions, e.g. without spectacles. A concomitant deviation occurs when the angle of deviation is the same in all directions of gaze, whichever eye is fixing, unlike an incomitant deviation where the angle between the two eyes is different in different gaze positions, or with asymmetrical accommodative effort.

History Ask about the presenting complaint and its duration. If diplopia is a symptom, ask whether it is monocular or binocular (only present with both eyes open), constant or intermittent, the position of gaze in which it occurs, and whether it produces vertical, horizontal or tilted images. Does it stop the patient from doing anything? Is the deviation socially embarrassing? Older children and adults may be distressed by even small squints. Check medications and allergies. In children, take a birth history, ask about any family history of amblyopia, strabismus, or refractive error, and make a brief developmental assessment if appropriate. Ask about any previous ophthalmic treatment including spectacles, prisms, occlusion therapy, and surgery. If in doubt about a prior eye position or abnormal head posture (AHP), ask to see old photographs or smartphone videos. Ask adults about their occupation and if they drive. Advise drivers to cease driving if they have diplopia, and to inform the Driver and Vehicle Licensing Agency (DVLA), or equivalent drivers' licensing authority outside UK. UK Group 1 drivers (car or motorbike) may be allowed to resume driving if their diplopia is controlled (p. 825).

General examination and cover testing

- Measure VA and record refraction.
- Observe any AHP, including head-tilt, face turn, or chin elevation or depression. Deafness, torticollis, and cervical spine abnormalities may also cause an AHP.
- Observe ocular posture including an obvious manifest squint, wide epicanthic folds (pseudosquint), spectacles, and any spectacle prisms ('stick-on' Fresnel or incorporated prisms).

- Using a pen torch at 33 cm, observe the corneal reflections (CRs). Look for symmetry or asymmetry. Small manifest deviations may not be obvious by CRs. Note – CRs are central or slightly nasal in most people. Not all abnormal-appearing CRs are due to strabismus, e.g. high refractive errors can produce a pseudosquint – a pseudoesotropia in high myopia.
- Perform cover test (CT) at near (33 cm) to a light and then an accommodative target (e.g. reduced Snellen letter at VA of worst eye, or pictures/toys for children). CT involves two manoeuvres:
  a. *Cover-uncover test:* To detect manifest strabismus. Cover one eye and look at the other. Movement inwards to take up fixation indicates an exotropia (XT). Movement outwards indicates an esotropia (ET). If the eye is slow to fix the target, this may indicate poor VA or amblyopia. Note any manifest or manifest latent nystagmus (MLN) – horizontal jerky, often very fine nystagmus with fast phase towards the uncovered eye. Note any movement of the covered eye, particularly dissociated vertical deviation (DVD) associated with infantile esotropia (p. 714).
  b. *Alternating cover test:* To detect latent strabismus. Alternately occlude left and right eye for 1–2 seconds each. Do not allow both eyes to view in between covering as fusion may occur. A latent deviation sometimes becomes temporarily manifest after fusion is disrupted by testing. Note how fast the eyes resume BSV once testing is complete (rapid or slow recovery), indicating how well the deviation is compensated.
- Move the target occasionally to check fixation.
- Perform CT at distance to a suitably sized chart letter or picture/toy.
- Repeat CT with/without glasses, and then with/without AHP.

Eye movements (cranial nerves III, IV and VI)

- If suggested by the history, check for monocular diplopia by occluding each eye separately. Note VA. If not already known, clarify if diplopia is horizontal, vertical, or tilted.
- Observe any head-tilt, proptosis, ptosis, or lid retraction.
- Ask the patient to follow a light held at 50 cm and report if they see diplopia. Go from primary position and back again in the other eight cardinal positions of gaze (p. 706). Ensure the CRs are always visible; the patient or examiner may need to lift the lids, particularly in down gaze. Check for lid-lag on downwards smooth pursuit and any narrowing (Duane's syndrome) or widening (aberrant IIIrd nerve regeneration or Brown's syndrome) of the palpebral aperture on adduction; observe any pupillary changes, e.g. constriction of the pupil

in adduction or other gaze position may occur with aberrant IIIrd nerve regeneration.

- If diplopia occurs in any position, check which image disappears when an eye is covered; the more peripheral image comes from the eye with the paretic muscle(s).
- If the CT shows a hypertropia/hyperphoria in the primary position (step 1) then do a CT in right and left gaze to see where the height is greatest (step 2). If greater in right gaze, then repeat the CT up and down to the right. If the deviation is greater down to the right, a left IVth nerve palsy is suspected. Finally, compare CT (eyes in primary position, fixing at 3 metres) with the head-tilted right and left, to see if the height differs (step 3). If the deviation is greater on head-tilt left, a left IVth nerve palsy is likely. However, the head-tilt test is not always reliable and other causes of hypertropia should not be ignored, e.g. thyroid eye disease (TED). *Park's three-step test* refers to steps 1, 2, and 3 combined. Step 3 is also called the *Bielschowsky head-tilt test*. However, the diagnostic importance of testing in all nine positions cannot be over-emphasised. Vertical deviations can be associated with bilateral (often asymmetrical) muscle under- or over-actions.
- Examine saccades in suspected supranuclear lesions to help to differentiate newly acquired palsies from mechanical strabismus (normal in the latter). Position a target to the right and left of the patient's eyes, within the visual field; instruct the patient to look from one target to the other as quickly as possible, without moving their head. Repeat the test in the vertical plane. Compare the vertical and horizontal velocity of the excursion, as well as the velocity in each eye; e.g. a reduced excursion of the adducting eye on horizontal saccades may indicate an internuclear ophthalmoplegia (same side). Cerebellar disease and multiple sclerosis (MS) may produce hypermetric saccades (eyes overshoot the target). Myasthenia gravis and Parkinson's disease may produce hypometric saccades (eyes undershoot the target).
- Test convergence to a detailed target. Note the distance at which binocular convergence fails and observe normal pupillary constriction.
- If required perform Doll's head manoeuvre to differentiate supranuclear from nonsupranuclear lesions (e.g. Steele Richardson Olszewski syndrome). Ask the patient to fixate a target in the distance. Inform the patient that you are going to gently move the head right, left, up and down. Look for the normal compensatory ocular rotations, e.g. eyes move left if the head is turned to the right. If these movements are present, it suggests the lesion is above the motor nucleus (supranuclear).

- Test optokinetic nystagmus with an OKN drum rotated slowly in front of the patient, both horizontally and vertically, and in both directions. Horizontal asymmetry may indicate a parietal lesion. Convergence retraction nystagmus with a downward moving drum (producing upwards refixation saccades) suggests Parinaud's syndrome.

AMBLYOPIA

Background Amblyopia is a condition of reduced visual function, usually in one eye but sometimes in both, that is not improved by correcting any refractive error or pathological obstacle to vision, e.g. cataract.

Causes are form deprivation and abnormal binocular interaction producing degraded retinal images in the sensitive or critical period of visual system development, particularly in the first 2–3 years of life, decreasing with age, up to 7 years of age. During this sensitive period amblyopia can develop as well as respond to treatment.

Classification

- *Strabismic amblyopia:* From a constant, unilateral, manifest strabismus.
- *Anisometropic amblyopia:* More than 1 D interocular difference.
- *Ametropic amblyopia:* Bilateral moderate to high refractive errors.
- *Meridional amblyopia:* Astigmatism >1.5 D.
- *Stimulus deprivation amblyopia:* Lack of adequate visual stimulus in early life, e.g. cataract; ptosis.

History Take a full ophthalmic history noting any previous eye surgery, squint, refractive error, and relevant birth history such as prematurity. Review previous VA if available and note poor compliance with glasses or occlusion.

Examination Crowded or logMAR-based VA tests increase the sensitivity to detect amblyopia. If vision testing is unreliable or unachievable, compare fix and follow responses. Suspect amblyopia with constant unilateral strabismus; suspect equal vision (good or bad) with alternating strabismus. Refract and examine the ocular media and fundus. Assess motor fusion with the Sbisa bar placed over the better eye. Record the filter at which diplopia is appreciated. Readily appreciated diplopia indicates weak fusion or less dense suppression.

Treatment Prescribe the full spectacle correction to be worn full-time (**Box 14.1**). Allow up to 16 weeks for 'spectacle adaptation' then start occlusion if:

- Visual acuity is stable at worse than 6/9.5 (0.2 logMAR).
- There is more than one logMAR (0.1) line interocular VA difference.
- VA cannot be reliably tested and there is fixation preference.

Box 14.1: Key studies

PEDiatric eye Investigator Group (PEDIG) studies: Multiple publications on strabismus, amblyopia and other childhood eye disorders. Studies of amblyopia reported:

- Refractive correction alone improves vision in anisometropic and strabismic amblyopia so dispense spectacles before occlusion therapy
- Two hours of occlusion as effective as 6 hours
- Atropine is an effective treatment and can be used at the weekend only (versus daily)
- Dichoptic video game treatment not superior to conventional treatment
- Dichoptic virtual reality (VR) headset (Luminopia one) 1 hour/day and glasses superior to glasses wearing alone

Occlusion normally starts with 2 hours/day part-time total (light and form deprivation) using an adhesive patch. Increase to 4 hours and, if necessary, continue to double hours if VA fails to improve. If the logMAR VA is worse than 0.6, start with 6 hours/day.

Penalisation is the optical reduction of form vision in the nonamblyopic eye, usually with G. atropine 1% twice a week to the better eye. It compares well to occlusion, and is acceptable to carers, but there is a slower improvement.

In children <2.5 years consider using less occlusion, because of the risk of occlusion amblyopia, and monitor closely. If using optical penalisation, reduce the frequency of installation of drops.

Binocular (dichoptic) therapy for amblyopia provides treatment whilst using both eyes. It gives simultaneous stimulation of both eyes, most often presenting high contract images to the amblyopic eye and low contrast or degraded images to the normal eye, whilst the child is watching a video. The child needs to have straight eyes or a micro strabismus. It can be undertaken using anaglyphic glasses or more engagingly via a VR headset. It is currently not used in the National Health Service.

Stimulus deprivation amblyopia (e.g. cataract) requires a more intensive regimen regardless of age.

The key to success is compliance.

Amblyopia treatment can sometimes continue after the usual 7–8 years cut-off, if there is good motor fusion, otherwise occlusion risks causing troublesome diplopia in children >6 years with strabismus. The presence of motor fusion is key to this decision. If motor fusion is poor or absent, warn parents to stop occlusion if diplopia occurs.

Follow-up Review regularly. Continue with the dose of occlusion that works for that patient, aiming to achieve 6/9.5 or better, or less than one-line interocular difference. Once therapy has ceased, observe for visual regression for 1 year, and continue follow-up until the age of 7 years. If VA drops more than one line, re-commence occlusion.

ESOTROPIA

Background Esotropia (ET) is a manifest convergent squint. The following relates to concomitant esotropia (angle of deviation the same in all positions of gaze and regardless of which eye is fixing). For incomitant strabismus, see page 725.

Classification

- *Primary esotropia:*
  1. Constant (present for near and distance).
     a. *Constant esotropia:* With an accommodative element – esotropia at near and distance with hypermetropic correction. Increases without glasses. Formerly called partially accommodative esotropia.
     b. *Infantile esotropia:* Onset of constant esotropia before 6 months of age in a neurologically normal child. Associated with manifest latent nystagmus (MLN) (p. 708), and dissociated vertical deviation (DVD) where on cover test either eye elevates or extorts under cover.
     c. *Early-onset convergent squint:* In children with neurological problems, e.g. ex-premature babies with periventricular leukomalacia or those with cerebral palsy.
     d. *Late-onset esotropia:* A sudden-onset esotropia usually in a child >5 years, often with diplopia.
  2. Intermittent (present for near or distance but not both, or only present when control is dissociated, e.g. illness/tiredness).
     a. *Fully accommodative esotropia:* Binocular single single vision (BSV) with hypermetropic correction for near and distance. Becomes esotropic for near and distance on accommodation without hypermetropic correction.
     b. *Convergence excess esotropia:* Binocular single vision at distance and near when fixing a light; esotropia at near with an accommodative target. Usually associated with hypermetropia but sometimes emmetropia and rarely myopia. Associated with a high accommodative convergence/accommodation (AC/A) ratio.
     c. *Near esotropia:* Binocular single vision at distance; esotropia at near with both a light and accommodative target. Normal AC/A ratio.
     d. *Distance esotropia:* Binocular single vision at near; esotropia at distance. No limitation of abduction, unlike a lateral rectus palsy which can appear similar. Often associated with myopia and ageing; if not, consider neurological disease.
     e. *Cyclic esotropia:* Varies between straight and large-angle esotropia in rhythmic cycles, usually every

48 hours. Onset usually <5 years of age. Assess patients on alternate days to confirm the diagnosis. Rarely, it may occur in adults with a secondary squint. Can become a constant esotropia over time.

- *Consecutive esotropia:* Esotropia in a previously divergent eye. It may be constant or intermittent. Usually, it follows surgical overcorrection.
- *Secondary esotropia:* Constant deviation secondary to visual loss or impairment occurring usually before 2 years of age.

History Ask about the nature of any double vision (rare in children), family history of strabismus, febrile illness (may precede accommodative esotropia), developmental delay, history of occlusion, spectacles, strabismus surgery, and birth history.

Examination Check VA, cover test with light and accommodative targets (near and distance, with and without spectacles), alternate cover test, and eye movements. 'V' patterns are common (p. 727). Refract (with cycloplegia in children). Check stereopsis, fusion, prism cover test (PCT), AC/A ratio, synoptophore, and postoperative diplopia test, as required.

Treatment More than one treatment option often applies.

- *Optical correction:* Fully correct any hypermetropia (minus working distance) and treat amblyopia if appropriate. If myopic, reducing the myopic correction may help to maintain BSV, but retain good VA to prevent amblyopia. Only in children <3 years might a low myopic correction be postponed. Executive bifocals (+3D add) can help convergence excess esotropia—wean off as the condition stabilises, e.g. postoperatively.
- *Amblyopia therapy:* If <8 years.
- *Observe:* Consecutive esotropia following exotropia surgery usually settles in a few months; correcting previously uncorrected low hypermetropia or prisms may help. If the deviation is not improving, particularly in younger children who are at risk of amblyopia (usually <8 years) and loss of stereopsis, do not allow consecutive esotropia to persist for >6 weeks without intervention (consider botulinum toxin or further surgery). In children <8 years, monitor for amblyopia if suppression occurs.
- *Botulinum toxin:* Injected into an extraocular muscle to weaken its action and thereby temporarily alter eye position. Useful in assessing: The risk of postoperative diplopia in 'cosmetic' cases not expected to achieve BSV; diagnostically in cases with weak potential BSV to see if BSV can be restored; where several previous squint procedures make surgery

unpredictable; in sudden onset esotropia where it can give long-term benefit.

- *Prisms:* May help small-angle deviations, especially distance esotropia.
- *Surgery:* Performed to improve the appearance of the eyes and, where possible, to restore BSV. In general, if surgery aims to restore binocular function it is performed once hypermetropia is satisfactorily corrected and amblyopia treated. The timing of alignment surgery depends largely on patient (or parent) preference.

1. *Constant esotropia with an accommodative element*: Operate if cosmetically unsatisfactory with glasses. Consider medial rectus recession (MR–) with lateral rectus resection (LR+) or plication (where muscle is folded over to shorten it but not resected) if the deviation is a similar size near and distance, or bilateral MR (bimedial) recessions if the deviation is larger at near **(Fig. 14.1)**. Undercorrect, as residual convergence tends to reduce over time – in the absence of BSV there is a high risk of consecutive exotropia.
2. *Infantile esotropia:* Requires early surgery, preferably before the age of 1 year, for any chance of binocular vision, but most

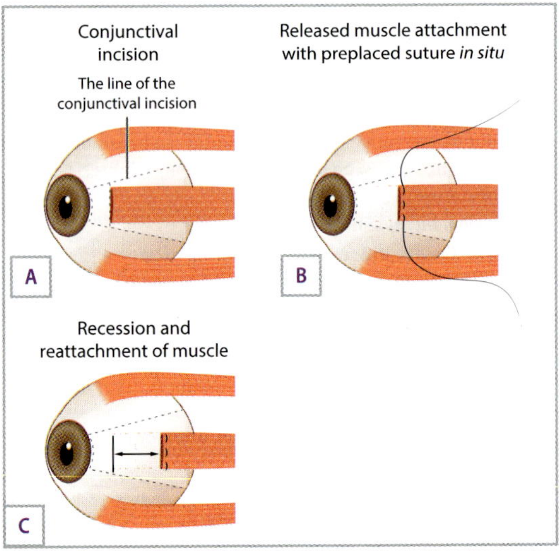

Fig. 14.1: Strabismus surgery – recession (Courtesy by C Roberts).

patients suppress and there is a risk of consecutive exotropia in later life. Surgery may involve bimedial recessions, or medial rectus recession/lateral rectus resection/plication. Patients usually need more than one procedure; however, multiple procedures increase the risk of consecutive exotropia as many patients continue to suppress. For cosmetically poor DVD consider bilateral inferior oblique anterior positioning or bilateral superior recti recessions (with Faden procedure for worse eye, if asymmetrical). Consider botulinum toxin to reduce the angle of squint prior to surgery.

3. *Early onset convergent squint:* Can be either be managed with unilateral medial rectus recession and lateral rectus resection, or bimedial recessions. Patients are more likely to become consecutively divergent in later life.
4. *Late-onset esotropia:* Botulinum toxin or surgery if BSV not restored by glasses.
5. *Convergence excess esotropia:* Notoriously difficult to manage. Start with bimedial recessions, with further surgery including Faden procedures or supramaximal medial rectus recessions.
6. *Near esotropia:* Normally undertake bimedial recessions.
7. *Distance esotropia:* If not controlled with prisms, usually requires bilateral lateral rectus resections/plication **(Figs. 14.2 and 14.3)** or medial rectus recessions using adjustable sutures.

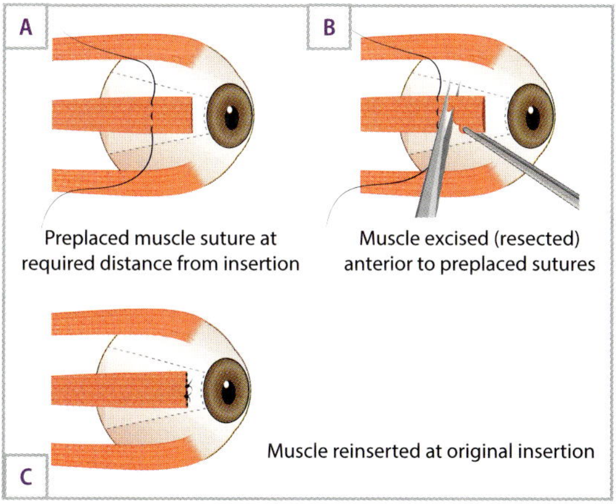

Fig. 14.2: Strabismus surgery – resection (Courtesy by C Roberts).

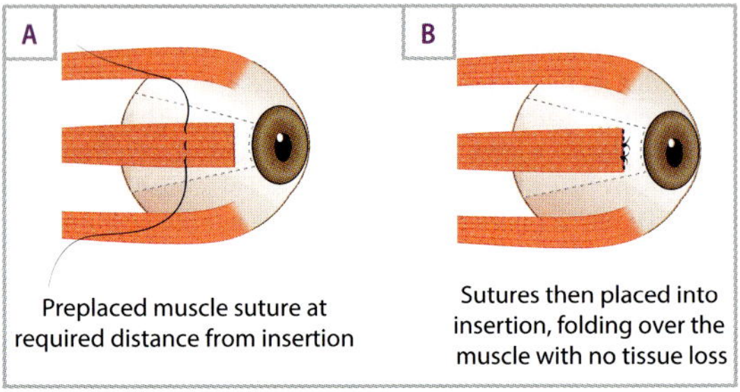

Fig. 14.3: Strabismus surgery – plication.

8. *Cyclic esotropia:* Consider medial rectus recession with lateral rectus resection as the deviation is usually a similar size near and distance. Plan surgery based on the maximum angle present on a squinting day.

EXOTROPIA

Background Exotropia is a manifest divergent squint. The following relates to concomitant exotropia (angle of deviation the same in all positions of gaze and regardless of which eye is fixing). For incomitant strabismus, see page 725.

Classification

- *Primary exotropia:*
  1. Constant (present for near and distance).
     a. *Early-onset exotropia:* Typically associated with dissociated vertical deviation (p. 714) and manifest latent nystagmus (p. 708). Much less common than early-onset esotropia and found particularly in Asian or African populations.
     b. *Constant primary exotropia:* Rare. Exclude an underlying neurological or developmental problem, as well as secondary exotropia or decompensating intermittent exotropia.
  2. Intermittent (present for near or distance but not both, or only present when control is dissociated, e.g. illness/tiredness).
     a. *Distance exotropia:* Binocular single vision at near; constant exotropia at distance. Diplopia is very rare as suppression normally occurs on divergence. Subdivided into two types – true distance exotropia and simulated distance exotropia (see differential diagnosis below).
     b. *Near exotropia:* Binocular single vision (BSV) for distance; exotropia for near. It is more common in adults than children, e.g. near exophoria decompensated by presbyopic correction.
     c. *Nonspecific exotropia:* Intermittent exotropia can present in any age group, and for either near or distance fixation.
- *Consecutive exotropia:* Usually follows surgery for esotropia after a variable period of time. Usually constant but can be intermittent.
- *Secondary exotropia:* Constant, secondary to visual impairment, and usually >2 years of age.

Symptoms Ask about diplopia (rare except in near exotropia and occasionally in consecutive exotropia) and previous eye treatment or surgery. Intermittent exotropia commonly presents in toddlers or infants; ask about closure of one eye in bright sunlight.

Signs VA is reduced in secondary exotropia. Amblyopia is common in consecutive exotropia, but rare in intermittent exotropia.

Examination Perform a cover test for near and distance, with and without spectacles. Perform the alternate cover test; a slowly recovering latent deviation may decompensate (become manifest) later in the examination. Examine eye movements. Intermittent exotropia may have a 'V' exo or 'X' pattern (p. 727) and slight limitations of adduction. Consecutive exotropias may have limitation of adduction from previous squint surgery. Reduced convergence can be associated with near exotropia. If VA is reduced, carefully exclude intraocular disease. Obtain refraction.

Investigations The accommodative convergence/accommodation (AC/A) ratio is often high (>5:1) in simulated distance exotropia, normal (3–4:1) in true distance exotropia, and low in near exotropia (<3:1). Consider postoperative diplopia testing if there is no BSV, e.g. consecutive or secondary exotropia.

Differential diagnosis Distinguish true from simulated distance exotropia. Simulated distance exotropia can be controlled by a high AC/A ratio and/or fusional convergence. Use +3 spectacle lenses to abolish accommodation for near and disrupt fusion by occluding one eye for >45 minutes then measure the maximum true near angle.

Treatment

- *Amblyopia therapy:* Treat amblyopia in children <8 years.
- *Optical correction/therapy:* Give the full myopic correction (minus working distance). Consider minus lenses or reduced hyperopic correction in children to stimulate accommodative convergence to help control intermittent distance exotropia, or to improve the cosmetic appearance in consecutive exotropia, but avoid asthenopia and retain 6/6 VA. Consider the effect of the full hypermetropic correction, which may increase the angle of squint, when planning surgery.
- *Orthoptic exercises*: Have a role in intermittent deviations <20 prism dioptres, and can be useful postoperatively, e.g. convergence exercises, stereograms. For near exotropia, treat any convergence insufficiency with exercises.
- *Botulinum toxin:* Useful diagnostically where the quality of BSV is poor, or where there is a risk of postoperative diplopia.
- *Surgery:* Small to moderate-sized distance exotropia often remains stable but consider surgery if control deteriorates or for cosmesis. Grading systems (e.g. Newcastle system)

can be used to assess both the home and clinical effects of exotropia and are useful in planning the timing of surgery. Undertake lateral rectus recession (LR–) and medial rectus resection (MR+) in simulated distance exotropia and other exodeviations, if the angle of deviation is similar for near and distance; or bilateral lateral rectus recessions in true distance exotropia or other exodeviations if the angle is much greater at distance. Surgery is often the treatment choice to improve appearance in consecutive and secondary exotropia. Warn patients that surgery aims for an early postoperative esotropia, as the eyes drift outwards over a few months. Diplopia may occur during this period. Consecutive exotropia usually requires exploration with medial rectus advancement and lateral rectus recession but may recur; consider adjustable sutures in patients >10 years old.

MICROTROPIA

Background Optimal binocular single vision exists with bifoveal fusion. A microtropia is a small-angle squint (<10 prism dioptres) with subnormal stereopsis. There is foveal (central) suppression with peripheral binocular vision and reduced 3D vision. Motor fusion is present, but the range may be reduced. Microtropia is commonly associated with anisometropia and amblyopia in the deviating eye. Can also occur after surgical or optical treatment for a larger-angle squint and can be present with other strabismus, e.g. a fully accommodative microtropia.

Classification

- *Microtropia with identity:* No manifest deviation on cover test because the eccentric point of fixation coincides with the angle of squint and is used for monocular and binocular fixation.
- *Microtropia without identity:* A minimal flick deviation is seen on cover testing. Usually, but not always, an esotropia.

History and examination Take a full history, perform cover testing, examine eye movements, and refract. Anisometropia is common.

Investigations Assess fusion, stereopsis, and measure any deviation with a prism cover test (PCT). The simultaneous PCT, rarely used in practice, measures the manifest component of the deviation where there is an associated heterophoria. The 4-dioptre prism test (base out for suspected microesotropia) usually shows no movement when the prism is placed in front of the deviating eye due to central suppression.

Treatment Fully correct refractive error. Consider amblyopia therapy (p. 711), but if motor fusion is absent or poor there is a risk of intractable diplopia in patients >6 years. Treatment is unlikely to produce bifoveal fixation. Treat decompensated microtropias as for concomitant strabismus (p. 714 and 719).

ACCOMMODATION AND CONVERGENCE DISORDERS

Classification

- Isolated primary convergence insufficiency (CI)
- Primary CI with secondary accommodative insufficiency (AI)
- CI secondary to vertical deviation or decompensating near heterophoria (convergence weakness exophoria)
- Primary AI
- Near reflex palsy (variably involving convergence, accommodation and pupil)
- Accommodative fatigue
- *Accommodative inertia:* Slowness in changing focus between near and distance or *vice versa.*
- *Spasm of the near reflex:* Presents with diplopia, miosis and pseudomyopia. Treat with cycloplegic drops, usually G. atropine 1% b.d., near reading glasses, and sometimes psychological support.

Accommodation and convergence weakness

History Can present at any age. Symptoms are associated with close work and include blurred vision, difficulty in changing focus, horizontal diplopia, headaches, eye strain and nausea. Check medications that may contribute to reduced accommodative responses, particularly antidepressants, muscle relaxants, antihistamines, and some antihypertensives.

Examination Assess ocular motility, as decompensating vertical deviations may be unable to converge. Check the near pupil response. In patients with near reflex palsy or marked AI or CI the pupils may fail to constrict, or conversely dilate, on attempted near fixation. Consider neurological assessment in convergence and accommodation paralysis.

Investigations Test the near point of convergence (NPC). The patient follows a small-detailed target as it is slowly moved to within 8–10 cm of the nose on an RAF rule. Test three times. CI is diagnosed if this is not achieved, or if only with effort. Check accommodation under emmetropic conditions using the RAF rule; bring the target progressively nearer until blurred. Alternatively, use increasing plus and then minus lenses to determine the accommodative facility. Reduced accommodation is commonly associated with CI. Examine the prism fusion range (often reduced).

Treatment Leave asymptomatic adults without treatment. Consider treating asymptomatic children if they have any other binocular imbalance. Treat with orthoptic exercises (pen and jump convergence, dot cards, stereograms, and voluntary convergence). Consider prisms if symptoms persist despite exercises. Convex lenses may be needed in those with AI. Botulinum toxin may provide some temporary relief in gross CI. Surgery is usually unhelpful, as CI recurs, however plication of the inferior part of both medial recti is reported to help.

INCOMITANT STRABISMUS

Background Incomitant strabismus occurs when the angle of deviation differs depending upon the direction of gaze or according to which eye is fixing. It is associated mostly with defective eye movements, particularly neurogenic or mechanical lesions such as IIIrd nerve palsy or thyroid eye disease, and less commonly with asymmetrical accommodative effort such as anisometropia.

History Establish when symptoms occurred (acute, chronic, or congenital). Vague symptoms imply a long-standing deviation. Ask about diplopia (monocular or binocular; intermittent or constant; position of gaze when it occurs; vertical, horizontal, or tilted images), trauma, hypertension, diabetes, thyroid conditions and previous eye surgery or treatment. Neck ache may occur with recently acquired abnormal head posture (AHP). Long-standing AHP may be asymptomatic.

Examinations Note any AHP, nystagmus, lid malposition, and pupil reactions. Check spectacles for prisms. Perform cover test with and without any AHP. In paralytic strabismus the secondary deviation of the unaffected eye when fixing with the affected eye will be larger than the primary deviation when fixing with the normal eye, based on Hering's law of equal innervation. Examine ocular movements and perform cover tests in the nine cardinal positions to establish overactions, underactions, and where the deviation is greatest. Compare subjective diplopia with objective findings. Check for bilateral asymmetric underactions. Examine ductions (movements tested monocularly with fellow eye covered) to differentiate underactions versus (mechanical) limitations.

Investigations

- Note the angle of deviation in primary position, fixing right and left eyes, and relevant positions of gaze with the prism cover test. Look for binocular single vision (BSV), stereopsis, and sensory and motor fusion. Patients with severe head injuries may lose motor fusion with intractable diplopia.
- *Synoptophore:* Useful if BSV is not present in free space and for measuring torsion.
- *Hess chart:* Based on simultaneous perception. Compare the patient's results with the 'normal' grid on the chart. Different size fields show incomitance. Observe the deviation in the primary position. The smaller field indicates the primarily affected eye (primary deviation), the larger field shows the secondary deviation. The greatest inward displacement compared to the normal field shows the primarily affected

muscle(s), or in mechanical limitations the greatest restriction of movement. In the larger field, the greatest outwards displacement from normal indicates the main overacting muscle(s) – the contralateral synergist according to Hering's law. Longstanding deviations may be more concomitant and identifying the primarily affected muscle can be difficult. In mechanical strabismus, the outer field of the Hess chart tends to be compressed. A sloping field indicates an 'A' or 'V' pattern and not torsion.

- *The field of BSV chart:* Usually plotted on a perimeter – shows the size, position, and usefulness of the area of BSV.
- Imaging and other investigations may be required depending on the cause. See the appropriate sections for details (p. 736, IIIrd nerve palsy; p. 739, IVth nerve palsy; p. 742, VIth nerve palsy; p. 735, thyroid eye disease)

Treatment Initial management of acquired incomitance includes advice about the use of an AHP, stick-on prisms, or occlusion.

- *Prisms:* Usually placed on one eye – the paralytic eye or the eye with the worse VA. It can be tilted to join both vertical and horizontal diplopia. It can also be placed on the top segment (or bifocal segment) of spectacles as required. Aim to join diplopia in the primary position and depression at least. Diplopia on extremes of gaze may not be correctable with prisms as this may lead to overcorrection in another position of gaze. Monitor patients, reducing prism strength as they recover or stabilise. Long-term prisms can be incorporated into glasses for small deviations.
- *Occlusion (graded frosting, foils, frosted tape, or lenses)*: Used for large deviations or large incomitance, unsatisfactorily controlled with prisms, or lack of fusion.
- *Orthoptic exercises*: Have a limited role except for associated convergence insufficiency.
- *Amblyopia therapy*: Treat amblyopia if age <8 years (p. 711).
- *Surgery*: For acquired incomitance, surgery is indicated for symptomatic deviations such as unsatisfactory control with prism/large AHP, and when the deviation is stable for at least 6 months. The type and number of operations depends on clinical findings. For neurogenic strabismus, weaken the overacting muscle(s). For mechanical strabismus, weaken the tight muscle(s).

ALPHABET PATTERNS

Background Alphabet pattern refers to a change in the angle of horizontal strabismus in up-/down-gaze.

Classification

- *'V'*: A relative divergence of >15 prism dioptres on up-gaze compared to down-gaze. The normal physiological 'V' pattern measures <15 prism dioptres.
- *'A'*: A relative divergence of ≥10 prism dioptres or more on down-gaze compared to up-gaze.
- *'X'*: Relative increase in elevation and depression, usually in an exodeviation.
- *'Y'*: Relative exodeviation on up-gaze. Down-gaze and primary positions have similar deviations.
- *'λ'*: Relative exodeviation on depression. Up-gaze and primary positions have similar deviations.

Aetiology The main causes are bilateral oblique and vertical rectus muscle dysfunction, e.g. inferior rectus overactions producing adduction on depression ('V' pattern). Conversely, inferior recti underactions produce an 'A' pattern. Super oblique underaction can produce a 'V' pattern, and overaction an 'A' pattern. High medial recti insertions can produce a 'V' eso pattern and low lateral recti insertions a 'V' exo pattern. Children with craniofacial abnormalities have a high incidence of 'A'/'V' patterns.

Symptoms Possible diplopia where the deviation is greatest.

Signs Chin elevation or depression to achieve binocular single vision. May have vertical deviation in primary position if vertical recti/oblique actions are asymmetrical.

Examination Cover test for near, distance, depression, and elevation by moving the head up and down. Look for bilateral asymmetrical muscle dysfunctions during eye movement testing.

Investigations Hess chart – slanting sides indicate an 'A' or 'V' pattern.

Treatment Usually surgical. Weaken oblique overactions. Recess or disinsert inferior obliques for a 'V' pattern. Use superior oblique posterior tenotomies for 'A' patterns. Weakening the obliques may cause a relative esodeviation. Where no oblique

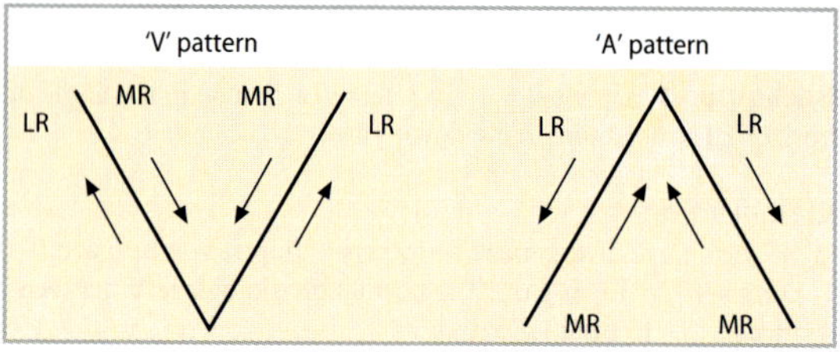

Fig. 14.4: Transposition of horizontal recti in 'A' and 'V' patterns. The arrows indicate the direction of muscle transposition.

overactions occur, transposing the horizontal recti by a half or full muscle width, as shown in **Figure 14.4**, can reduce 'A' or 'V' patterns. This can be combined with horizontal recti recession/ resection.

DUANE'S SYNDROME

Background Duane's syndrome is a spectrum of congenital motility disorders with anomalous innervation of the lateral rectus muscle, together with retraction of the globe, and narrowing of the palpebral fissure on adduction. There is hypoplasia of the VIth nerve nucleus and/or absence of the VIth nerve, with the lateral rectus innervated by a branch of the IIIrd nerve. Secondary myogenic factors are also involved.

The condition usually presents in childhood, but mild cases are sometimes found incidentally in adults. The left eye and females are more commonly affected. May be bilateral, although sometimes very asymmetric. Systemic abnormalities may coexist, including hearing defects, ear malformations, Goldenhar's syndrome, Klippel–Feil syndrome, or spinal abnormalities.

Classification

- The underlying pathophysiology is similar in all types, but they differ in the degrees of abnormality of the lateral and medial rectus innervations **(Table 14.3)**.
- Alternatively, Duane's syndrome is sometimes referred to as typical (mainly limited abduction), or atypical (mainly limited adduction).

History and examination Check for anisometropia and amblyopia. Observe any abnormal head posture (AHP) – usually a face-turn to the affected side in types 1 and 3 and to the opposite side in type 2. Most patients have fusion and stereopsis, often maintained by the AHP. Diplopia is rare.

- *Cover test:*
  1. *Types 1 and 3:* Orthophoria/esophoria/esotropia
  2. *Types 2 and 3:* Exophoria/exotropia
- *Ocular movements:* Lids show narrowing of the palpebral fissure (sometimes subtle) with retraction of the globe on attempted adduction **(Fig. 14.5)**. The palpebral fissure often widens on abduction. Upshoot or downshoot of the eye may occur on adduction. Retraction on adduction is often best observed from the side.

Table 14.3: Classification of Duane's syndrome

	Abduction	Adduction
Type 1	Limited or absent	Normal or slight limitation
Type 2	Normal or slight limitation	Limitation or absent
Type 3	Marked limitation or absent	Marked limitation or absent

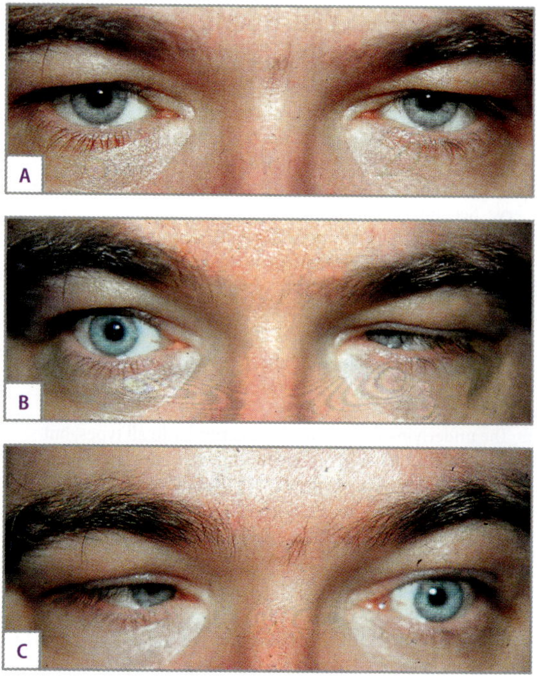

Fig. 14.5: Bilateral type 1 Duane's syndrome.

Treatment Treat associated refractive error, and amblyopia if <8 years (p. 711). Prisms and botulinum toxin have a limited role.

Surgery also has a limited role and patients/carers must understand that normal eye movements cannot be restored. Indications include a large primary position deviation, noticeable AHP, marked globe retraction or up-/downshoots, and large decompensating phorias.

- *Type 1:* Ipsilateral/bilateral medial rectus recession(s). With large deviation and no abduction beyond midline: Nishida procedure or vertical muscle transposition (superior rectus and inferior rectus moved to lateral rectus) or move superior rectus only with Faden sutures to alter muscle vector path. If large angle, consider combining with medial rectus recession but there is a risk of over correction, so usually only recess 3–4 mm.

- *Type 2:* Ipsilateral/bilateral lateral rectus recessions. Nasal transposition of lateral rectus.
- *With globe retraction*: Ipsilateral medial and lateral rectus recessions.
- *With up/downshoots*: Lateral rectus recession and splitting.

BROWN'S SYNDROME

Background A condition with limited elevation in adduction due to mechanical restriction rather than inferior oblique paresis. Commonly congenital but can be acquired. Usually constant but there is a rare intermittent variant often associated with a 'clicking' sensation. Congenital cases were previously thought to be due to a short superior oblique tendon sheath, but are now considered to be caused by anomalies of the tendon–trochlear complex. Causes of acquired Brown's syndrome include trauma of the trochlear region, sinus surgery, inflammatory conditions, and following superior oblique surgery.

History and examination

- *Congenital cases:* Parents may not notice reduced elevation but instead the overaction of the contralateral eye on elevation. Acquired cases usually complain of diplopia.
- *Abnormal head posture:* If present, this is usually a chin elevation, but there may be a head-tilt to the affected side ± face turn away from the affected side.
- *Cover test:* Often straight in the primary position with binocular single vision (BSV) or less commonly, hypotropia in the affected eye/hypertropia in the unaffected eye.
- *Ocular movements:* Features include limited elevation in adduction, usually good elevation in abduction **(Fig. 14.6)**, overaction of the contralateral superior rectus, and no/minimal ipsilateral superior oblique overaction **(Fig. 14.7)**. A 'V' pattern (p. 727) is often present. There may be down-drift in adduction and widening of the palpebral fissure in adduction. There is resistance to passive elevation of the eye in adduction (positive forced-duction test). Check for an audible/palpable click on elevation. Diplopia, if present, is usually on elevation.

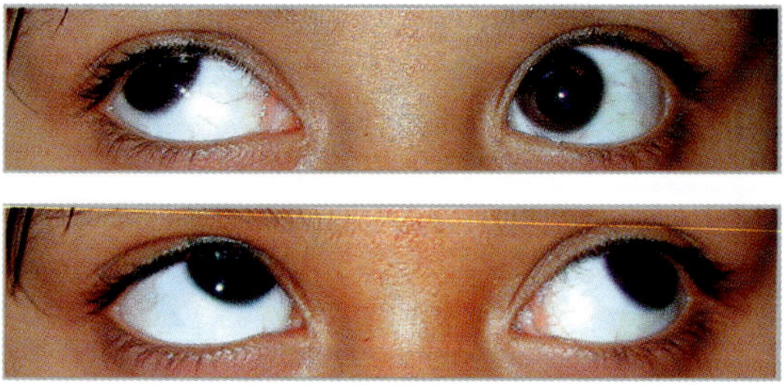

Fig. 14.6: Left Brown's syndrome.

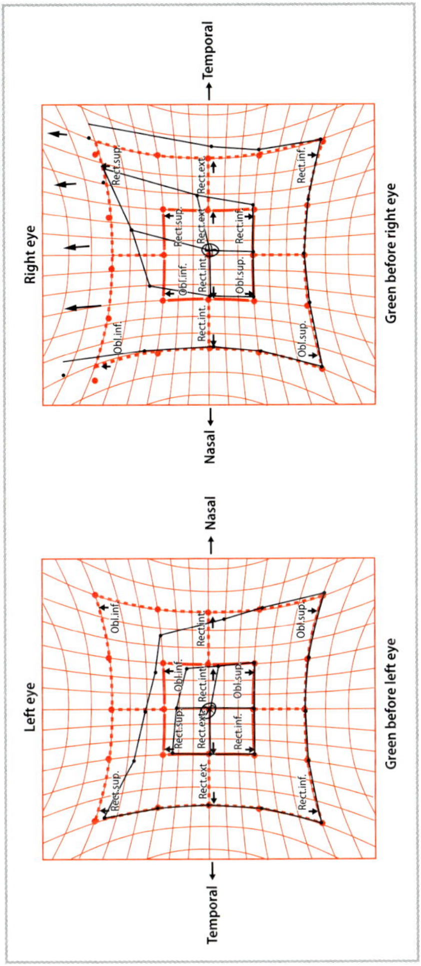

Fig. 14.7: Hess chart of a typical left Brown's syndrome. Note there is no deviation in the primary position; the smaller left field shows the greatest constriction in the field of action of the left inferior oblique muscle (the primary defect). The greatest outwards displacement in the right field is in the field of action of the superior rectus (the contralateral synergist).

Treatment

- Treat any refractive error and amblyopia. Most patients do not require surgery as BSV is present in primary position and down-gaze. Also, spontaneous improvement often occurs in congenital cases, particularly in cases with a click/discomfort on elevation in adduction.

- If associated with an acquired inflammatory condition, peritrochlear steroid injections can help.
- Surgery is indicated if there is significant hypotropia in the primary position or marked abnormal head posture. Surgical options include superior oblique tenotomy/tenectomy (be aware of the risk of palsy requiring further treatment), silicone band, or suture spacer on the tendon. Traumatic cases often have a poor surgical outcome.

■ THYROID EYE DISEASE

Background Patients with thyroid eye disease (TED) may experience diplopia due to inflammatory change that is then followed by extraocular muscle fibrosis. For other aspects of TED see page 102.

History Diplopia is commonly intermittent, vertical, and in either up-gaze or primary position. It may be worse in the morning (fusion interrupted overnight) and evening (from decompensation).

Examination Note any abnormal head posture (commonly chin elevation to maintain binocular single vision because of limited elevation), perform cover test, and examine eye movements. A tight inferior rectus is most common (restricted elevation, maximum in abduction, hypodeviation, and possible excyclotorsion) followed by medial rectus (restricted abduction and esodeviation) and then superior rectus (limited depression maximum in abduction). Hypo- and esodeviations often coexist. Look for bilateral signs that may be asymmetric. An 'A' esodeviation (p. 727) is common, especially following orbital decompression. The superior oblique muscles are also enlarged and incyclotorsion may occur after surgery to release the inferior recti.

Investigations Compare the Hess chart to ocular motility but the Hess chart is unreliable in bilaterally restricted eye movements. Be aware that patients with moderately limited elevation may guess the upper points when plotting the Hess chart (using visual fields, or moving head). Consider testing the field of binocular single vision and monocular eye movements (uniocular fixation).

Management Stop smoking as this worsens TED. Consider selenium 100 μg b.d. for 6 months in mild TED. Prisms often help diplopia in the primary position. Patients often have increased vertical fusion ranges and need prisms of smaller strength than the angle of deviation. Occlusion of one eye may be necessary for very large incomitant deviations. Await stability of eye movements and thyroid condition for at least 6 months before undertaking corrective surgery. Both horizontal and vertical surgery may be required. Use recessions not resections, preferably with adjustable sutures. Recess the inferior rectus for hypotropia or restricted elevation. Recess the medial rectus for esotropia. Bilateral surgery is common, e.g. bilateral inferior recti recessions for bilateral limited elevation. Four muscles can be recessed at one operation (two in each eye); usually, one eye has the medial and inferior recti on adjustable sutures. Undercorrect if using adjustable sutures to allow for postoperative drift.

THIRD NERVE PALSY

Background Can be congenital, but most often acquired. Signs and symptoms vary depending on the lesion site. Urgently exclude posterior communicating artery aneurysm in cases of painful, unilateral IIIrd nerve palsy, and strongly consider brain CT or MRI with angiography and emergency neurology referral. Microvascular, pupil-sparing IIIrd nerve palsies are commonly associated with diabetes and hypertension. Other causes of IIIrd nerve palsy include trauma, neoplasm, infection, migraine, congenital cases and giant cell arteritis (rare).

Signs A total IIIrd nerve palsy affects all extraocular muscles except the superior oblique and lateral rectus, which act unopposed to give exotropia and hypotropia ('down and out') plus a dilated pupil with paralysis of accommodation. The extent to which the IIIrd nerve is affected can depend on various factors, including aetiology, e.g. pupil-sparing IIIrd nerve palsies are commonly ischaemic (microvascular). Superior division involvement produces ptosis and superior rectus underaction.

There may be aberrant regeneration if the affected nerve fibres are misdirected during recovery, producing retraction of the upper lid on attempted adduction ± depression, adduction on attempted elevation (and rarely depression), pupil constriction on attempted adduction ± depression, and retraction of the globe on attempted elevation ± depression. Aberrant regeneration is rare with microvascular causes.

History Ask about the duration of onset, diabetes, hypertension, headache, trauma, features of giant cell arteritis (p. 789), myasthenia gravis (can mimic a IIIrd nerve palsy), and MS.

Examination Check BP, other cranial nerves including visual fields, and fundus for retinopathy and optic disc swelling. Examine the temporal arteries if aged >50 years. Exclude proptosis, lid fatigue with sustained up-gaze, and Cogan's lid twitch (overshoot of lid when going from sustained down-gaze to primary position). Check eye movements and cover test.

Investigation

- *Orthoptic testing.*
- *Pupil-sparing:* Fasting glucose and/or glycated haemoglobin (HbA1c). Check ESR and CRP if age >50 years, and CT or MRI with angiography if age <50 years and no diabetes or hypertension. Closely observe patients who do not undergo neuroimaging for any signs of progression, e.g. worsening eye movements, ptosis or pupil involvement.

- *Pupil or other cranial nerves involved, or optic disc swelling:* Urgent CT or MRI brain/orbits with angiography and emergency neurology referral.
- *Myasthenia suspected:* Check acetylcholine receptor antibodies and anti-MuSK antibodies. Try 'ice-pack test': An ice pack applied to lid for 10 minutes improves neuromuscular transmission and improves function (ptosis and eye movements). Tensilon testing is rarely used. Single fibre electromyelogram testing can be arranged via a neurologist.
- *Congenital cases:* Work-up for a possible neurological aetiology.
- *Hess chart:* See **Figure 14.8.**

Treatment

- Treat amblyopia in children <8 years old (p. 711). Prisms may help in isolated muscle cases.
- Surgery only achieves a limited area of binocular single vision at best. The main aim is to improve the appearance. Residual diplopia can be treated with an occlusive contact lens.

1. *Exotropia with hypotropia:* Large lateral rectus recession, and resection of medial rectus with supraplacement of the insertions. Consider recessions of contralateral synergists.
2. *Mainly exotropia:* Large lateral rectus recession and resection of medial rectus with temporary traction sutures. Nasal transposition of the vertical rectus muscles or nasal transposition of split lateral rectus muscle if not previously operated. Periosteal fixation of both medial and lateral rectus muscles with temporary skin traction sutures is effective in those with no adduction beyond the midline.
3. *Superior division:* Knapp (vertical transposition of medial and lateral recti) procedure for hypotropia.
4. *Inferior division:* Inverse Knapp for hypertropia on depression.

Follow-up Review isolated pupil-sparing cases within 1 week, then monthly. Expect improvement in presumed microvascular cases and arrange CT or MRI if not evident in 6–12 weeks, or if any aberrant regeneration occurs.

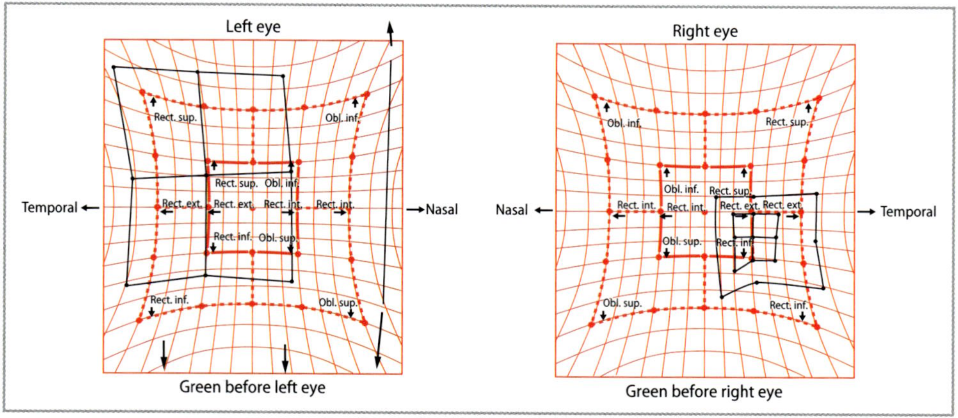

Fig. 14.8: Hess chart of a total right IIIrd nerve palsy. This shows the primary deviation with the right eye exotropic and hypotropic (right lateral rectus and superior oblique functioning). The right affected eye has the smaller field and is markedly constricted in the fields of action of the affected muscles (right superior, medial and inferior recti and inferior oblique). The large left field shows the secondary deviation and overactions of the contralateral synergists (Sherrington's law).

FOURTH NERVE PALSY

Background May be uni- or bilateral, congenital (abnormal superior oblique tendon/trochlea) or acquired (head trauma; trochlear/orbital injury; ENT surgery; sinus infections; or vascular). May also be idiopathic or associated with hypertension and diabetes, or more rarely demyelination, giant cell arteritis, tumours, and aneurysms.

Symptoms Vertical diplopia ± torsional and horizontal components.

Signs A left superior oblique palsy may have a head-tilt ± slight face turn to right, with chin depression. Cover testing shows left hyperdeviation, greater for near, with slight esodeviation. Excyclotorsion may be present. Hyperdeviation and diplopia increase in dextrodepression but this is less common in congenital cases. Torsional diplopia is maximum on laevodepression. The Bielschowsky head-tilt test (p. 709) may be positive – an increased hyperdeviation on head-tilt left – but not all practitioners feel it is reliable.

History and examination Diplopia is a presenting sign in acquired cases – usually vertical, more marked on depression and to one side; diplopia may also have horizontal and tilted components. In congenital cases, diplopia is less common as a presenting symptom. Such cases may present at any age because of signs of decompensation, or abnormal head posture (AHP) noticed by others.

Investigations

- *Full orthoptic testing:* Including vertical fusion range.
- *Synoptophore*
- *Hess chart:* See **Figure 14.9**.
- *Blood tests:* Fasting glucose, or HbA1c. ESR and CRP if age >50 years.
- *CT or MRI:* If age <50 years and no diabetes or hypertension, or if failure to improve after 6 weeks. Image urgently via neurologists if there are other signs, including cranial nerve palsies, unless there is evidence that the nerve palsy is long-standing or from childhood, e.g. photos demonstrating a childhood AHP.

Differential diagnosis

- *Congenital versus acquired:* Acquired cases are more likely to experience diplopia, especially with subjective torsion, have

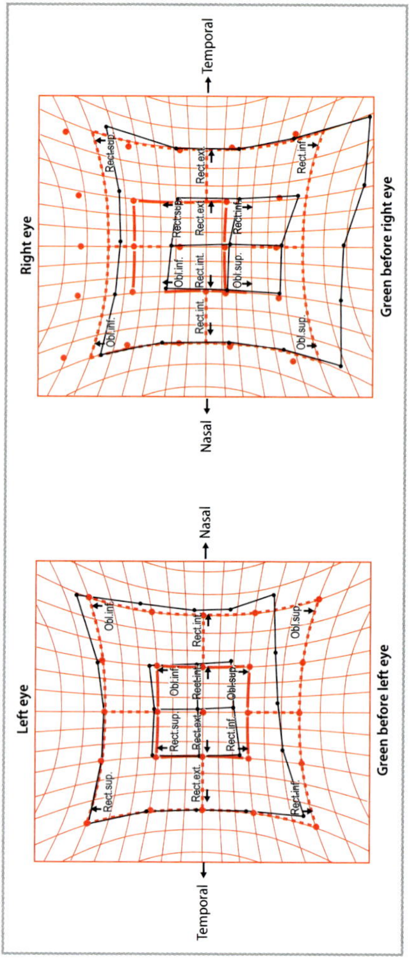

Fig. 14.9: Hess chart showing a left IVth nerve palsy. This shows the primary deviation of a small left hypertropia. The smaller left field shows greatest constriction in the field of action of the superior oblique. The left field also shows a small overaction of the unopposed ipsilateral antagonist – left inferior oblique. The right field shows the larger secondary deviation – right hypotropia (Hering's law) and the greatest enlargement is in the field of action of the right inferior rectus (contralateral synergist – Sherrington's law), and a slight underaction of the right superior rectus (secondary inhibitional palsy of contralateral antagonist).

BSV, and normal (6 dioptres) vertical fusion range. Congenital cases may have contralateral facial hypoplasia, a large vertical fusion range (but not always), and often have a long-standing AHP visible in old photographs.

- *Unilateral versus bilateral:* Assume bilateral until proven otherwise. Bilaterality is suggested by a 'V' esodeviation (p. 727), a right over left in laevodepression and left over right in dextrodepression (may be very asymmetrical), and ≥10 degrees of excyclotorsion on the synoptophore in depression.

- *Other diseases:* Consider myasthenia gravis, skew deviation, and orbital disease.

Treatment

- *Medical:* Prisms (and/or AHP) may control small deviations. Joining the vertical diplopia often allows patients to then fuse a remaining slight horizontal deviation, if present. Prisms cannot join torsional diplopia. Treat any amblyopia in children <8 years old (p. 711).
- *Surgery:* Options for hyperdeviation include –
    1. Ipsilateral inferior oblique weakening if <15 prism dioptres in primary position.
    2. Superior oblique tendon tuck if superior oblique underaction exceeds inferior oblique overaction, particularly in congenital cases.
    3. Ipsilateral superior rectus recession.
    4. Contralateral inferior rectus recession.

For bilateral acquired cases perform bilateral Harado-Ito procedure to correct torsion first.

Follow-up

- Review every 1–2 months to monitor stability/recovery.
- Unilateral cases of vascular origin usually recover within 6 months. Congenital cases, as the deviations tend to be larger, often require surgery as do large unrecovered vascular or more frequently bilateral traumatic superior oblique palsies. Manage small unrecovered deviations with vertical/horizontal diplopia by long-term spectacle prisms.

SIXTH NERVE PALSY

Background Several possible causes include –

- *Adults:* Microvascular (particularly if aged >50 years, hypertensive, or diabetic), MS, neoplasm, head trauma, infection (bacterial or viral), raised intracranial pressure, giant cell arteritis and idiopathic.
- *Children:* Similar to adults except microvascular causes are unlikely. Transient VIth nerve palsies may occur in neonates. 'Benign VIth nerve palsy of childhood' may occur 1–3 weeks after a febrile viral illness and may recur throughout childhood.

Symptoms Horizontal diplopia, greater looking to the affected side and in the distance. Diplopia may be constant in a total VIth nerve palsy.

Signs Look for a head turn to the same side, limited abduction, and esodeviation most easily detected with cover test and a distant target, comparing findings in extreme left and right gaze. Nuclear lesions are accompanied by a gaze palsy to the same side because of involvement of the conjugate gaze mechanism. Pontine lesions may be accompanied by a VIIth nerve palsy, and cavernous sinus disease is often accompanied by IIIrd, IVth and trigeminal division of Vth nerve palsies. Look for bilaterality.

History and examination As for IIIrd nerve palsy (p. 736).

Investigations

- *Orthoptic testing:* A prism cover test in right and left gaze at distance quantifies incomitance and is useful diagnostically and preoperatively. There is usually motor fusion and stereopsis at near.
- *Hess chart:* See **Figure 14.10**.
- *Blood tests:* Fasting glucose, or HbA1c. ESR and CRP if >50 years old.
- *MRI and CT:* Request neuroimaging of brain and orbits if age <50 years and no diabetes or hypertension, or if failure to improve after 6 weeks. Image urgently via a neurologist if there are other signs, including other cranial nerve palsies or papilloedema.

Management Most microvascular palsies and childhood postviral palsies resolve spontaneously, so offer prisms or, for large very incomitant deviations, occlusion. If stable and symptomatic after >6 months, consider surgery. The selected operation depends on the abduction status (check

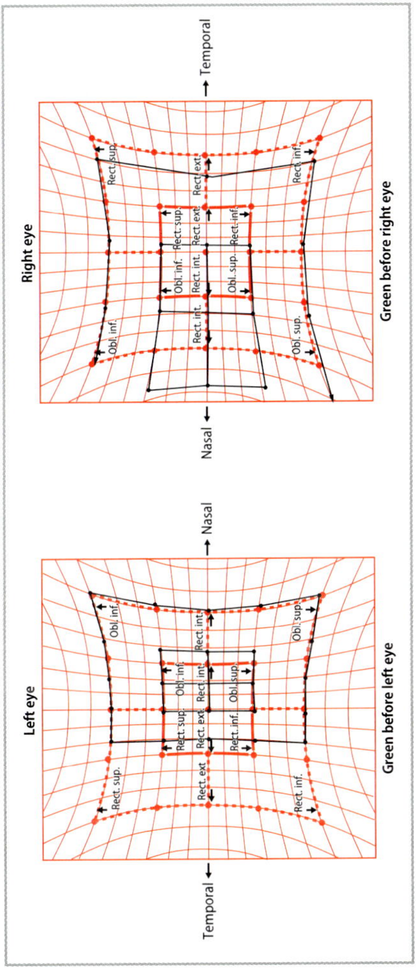

Fig. 14.10: Hess chart of a left lateral rectus palsy. The left smaller field in the affected eye shows a small esotropia in the primary position; there is greatest constriction in the field of action of the left lateral rectus. The right field shows a larger secondary esotropia in the primary position (Hering's law); the greatest enlargement is in the field of action of the right medial rectus (contralateral synergist—Sherrington's law).

with diagnostic botulinum toxin to medial rectus). If there is abduction beyond the midline, the palsy is incomplete, so perform medial rectus recession and lateral rectus resection. If not, the palsy is complete, so undertake Nishida procedure or transposition of one or both vertical recti to the lateral rectus border, and botulinum toxin to the ipsilateral medial rectus.

Medial rectus recession may be needed as a second operation, but beware of the risk of anterior segment ischaemia. Treat bilateral palsies like unilateral ones, but these often need second-stage surgery.

Follow-up Monitor for stability or recovery. Review every 1–2 months. Unilateral cases of vascular origin usually recover within 6 months. If recovery does not take place, manage smaller unrecovered deviations by long-term spectacles prisms. Larger/very incomitant deviations may require surgery.

OPTOMETRY AND GENERAL PRACTICE GUIDELINES

General comments

All children under the age of 5 years old with suspected strabismus and amblyopia should be assessed by an orthoptist. However, those older than 5 years may be seen initially by a community optometrist. The risk of amblyopia and strabismus is increased in children with a family history of squint, amblyopia or a high refractive error (particularly hypermetropia), and children born prematurely or with developmental delay/ neurological conditions.

Optometrists

Preschool children who are found to have abnormal amounts of hypermetropia (> +3.5 D), or anisometropia (>1.0 D), or astigmatism (>1.5 D) are at risk of developing strabismus and amblyopia. To prevent this, a spectacle correction is required. If in doubt about management, discuss with a Hospital Eye Service.

General practice

Never delay referral for suspected squint as it is very rare for a child to 'grow out of it', particularly as some squints may have a sight or life-threatening aetiology. Squint or limited eye movements due to trauma, even when the eye does not appear inflamed, should be seen the same day. Childhood refractive errors (without squint) are usually treated by an optometrist experienced in refracting children.

The following guide to referral urgency is not prescriptive, as clinical situations vary.

Same day

- IIIrd nerve palsy with pupil involvement p. 736
- Orbital blowout fractures p. 127
- VIth nerve palsy with papilloedema (refer to neurology) p. 742
- Squint with other neurological symptoms or signs p. 8

Urgent (within 1 week)

- Sudden onset of squint with diplopia in an otherwise well child >5 years old p. 7
- Sudden onset of double vision p. 7

Routine

- Disorders of accommodation and convergence p. 723
- Childhood squints with full ocular movements p. 707

- Adults, without diplopia, requesting squint surgery for cosmetic improvement p. 661, 665
- Long-standing squints with increasing angle of deviation p. 661, 665
- Amblyopia p. 711
- Suspected squint p. 707
- Refractive errors (see comments above) p. 711

NEURO-OPHTHALMOLOGY 15

Fion Bremner, Neringa Jurkute & Emanuel De Carvalho

HISTORY AND EXAMINATION

History Ask about past medical history, drug history, family history, and occupation. Smoking, alcohol and recreational drugs usage and diet may be particularly important. The history is guided by the presenting complaint. The following symptoms and signs are relatively common and are dealt with elsewhere:

- *Transient visual loss*: Page 765
- *Headache*: Page 782
- *Anisocoria*: Page 763
- *Diplopia*: Pages 7 and 8
- *Ptosis*: Page 39

Examination Basic neuro-ophthalmic examination includes near and distance VA, colour vision, confrontation field tests, pupil tests, cover tests, eye movements, cranial nerves, fundoscopy including optic disc examination, and other tests as indicated. Full neurological examination may be required.

- *Cover test and eye movements:* See pages 707 and 708.
- *Pupils*:
  1. Observe: look for anisocoria, ptosis and iris abnormality (at the slit-lamp check for heterochromia, rubeosis, posterior synechiae, coloboma, irregular shape and iris lesions).
  2. Check the near response using a target that is a strong stimulus to accommodation (e.g. text/image on a fixation target, some patients find it easier to converge on their own finger).
  3. Test pupillary constriction to light: dim the lights and ask the patient to look at a distance target. Check the direct response (pupil constriction in the same eye) and consensual response (fellow eye constriction). Use a very bright light such as an indirect ophthalmoscope.
  4. Look for an RAPD using the swinging light test. Ask the patient to fix on a distant object. Shine light in one eye for 2–3 seconds, then move to the other for the same interval. Repeat as required but do not spend longer on one eye than the other as this may bleach the retina and create an artificial RAPD. If the left optic nerve is damaged, shining the light in the right eye will produce a normal efferent

response in the right and left pupil. Moving the light to the left eye then causes a paradoxical dilatation of both pupils as the stimulus intensity is effectively diminished (left RAPD). Extensive retinal disease can also cause an RAPD (pre-retinal disease does not). Only one functioning pupil is required to test for an RAPD; for example, despite a fixed left dilated pupil the test can be carried out as above by observing just the right pupil. Remember that in bilateral symmetrical optic nerve disease the pupil deficit will be balanced with no RAPD. If the iris is dark and the pupil is difficult to observe ask a colleague to shine another torch tangentially across the anterior chamber. This illuminates the iris and increases pupil visibility, but causes minimal constriction. Consider asking the patient which eye the light seems brighter/dimmer, or using neutral density filters to quantify very subtle RAPDs.

- *Confrontation visual field testing*:
  1. Establish the VA and explain that you are testing peripheral vision.
  2. Ask the patient to cover one eye with the palm of their hand: 'Look at my nose: are any parts of my face missing or blurred? Can you see both my eyes?'
  3. Hold up both your palms, one in each hemifield and ask, 'Is each hand equally clear, are there any differences' or 'does each hand look the same?'
  4. Now ask the patient to fix on your eye. Always begin by testing for a defect to hand movements. Advance your hand, with fingers moving, from the periphery towards fixation, asking the patient to report when they see movement. A patient will not be able to count fingers in a visual field region in which he or she cannot detect hand movements.
  5. Ask the patient to fixate on your eye and hold up a finger in one quadrant; ask how many fingers can be seen. Repeat in each quadrant, presenting 1, 2, or whole hand (3 or 4 is too difficult). This identifies areas where vision is better than hand movements. Remember, finger counting is the best possible peripheral VA.
  6. In visual field areas where finger-counting vision has been established look for red desaturation using a red target such as a 4-mm hat pin (a red bottle top may also be used but it is too large for the blind spot or small scotomas). Compare subjective colour intensity in four quadrants while the patient fixes your eye. Simultaneously holding two red pins either side of the vertical midline (in each eye separately) may help to detect bitemporal red desaturation from pituitary tumours, or a relative homonymous hemianopia.

7. Test the mid-peripheral and central field with the red target: 'Tell me when you first see the red colour, rather than the pin, and tell me if it then disappears or the colour changes at any point.' Move obliquely in each quadrant from periphery to fixation, equidistant between you and the patient. Compare to your own monocular visual field. Look for scotomas.
8. Consider comparing the blind spot size with your own using the red target.
9. It is possible to ascertain the isopter to a small white target such as a 4-mm white hat pin. Failure to detect the white target indicates greater severity of loss than is revealed by the 'red desaturation' technique. Similarly, the white target can also be used to plot scotomas and the blind spot.
10. Test the fellow eye.
11. If any defect is detected, sketch the visual fields and arrange quantitative perimetry. If the vision is very poor or the patient finds the tests difficult then confrontation fields may be more valuable than automated perimetry. Document the left eye visual field on the left side of the page; the right visual field on the right side of the page (all visual fields are plotted as if the subject is looking at the page, opposite to VA convention).
12. For the interpretation of common field defects, see page 770.

- *Colour vision*: Optic nerve damage can cause colour desaturation and poor colour discrimination before significant VA loss. Test for red desaturation by asking the patient to report any difference in the appearance of a red target viewed with each eye in turn, or in different regions of the visual field of the same eye. *Ishihara plates* test colour discrimination and help to determine the cause of visual loss (i.e. refractive, lenticular, retinal, optic nerve and post-chiasmal):

1. Patients should wear reading correction if required.
2. Cover one eye and ask the patient to read through the book. Allow 2 or 3 seconds per plate only.
3. Patients with VA better than 6/60 can usually complete the test, but do not proceed if they cannot see the first (control) plate, which does not require colour vision. Test patients before examining them with bright lights (e.g. fundal examination or RAPD check) or allow them time to recover after such examination. Patients who have had dilating drops can still perform the test but may need to use a +1.00 or +2.00 lens. Consider testing red desaturation instead if VA is very poor (see below).
4. Score the number of plates read out of 13, 17, or 21 depending on which book is used (1/17 or 'control only' if only the control plate was read). Record the reading distance and any refractive correction.

5. The 'hidden number' plates can only be seen by some patients with congenital anomalous colour vision (Daltonism). Do not include these when testing for acquired visual loss unless the patient has Daltonism. The Ishihara book comes with instructions on how to interpret performance on the missed plates in cases of Daltonism. 'Transformation number' plates will be misread. The missed and misread numbers should be the same using each eye.
6. Ask patients who cannot identify numerals (e.g. small children) to trace the outline of the numbers with their finger or trace the wiggly line across the page in the colour plates at the end of the book.

- *Cranial nerves*:

I. Rarely formally tested; ask about sense of smell and if food tastes different. Anterior cranial fossa masses can present with anosmia and visual failure.

II. Test VA, pupil reactions, visual field and colour vision.

III, IV and VI. See page 708.

V. Warn the patient then test corneal sensation by lightly touching a wisp of cotton-wool on the peripheral cornea. Sensation may be decreased in contact lens wearers, recurrent herpetic keratitis, or if anaesthetic drops have been instilled to check IOP. Check facial sensation to light touch. It is important to understand the distribution of the three divisions and peripheral branches of the trigeminal nerve. Test for dissociated loss to pain using pin-prick sensation. Ask the patient to clench their teeth together and feel for contraction of the masseter and temporalis muscles. Ask the patient to open the mouth against the resistance of your hand and look for jaw deviation towards the weaker side.

VII. Ask the patient to show their teeth (smile), purse lips, blow out cheeks against the resistance of your fingers, raise eyebrows (forehead wrinkling is spared in central/upper motor neurone lesions) and screw up eyes (assess Bell's phenomenon). Look for loss or asymmetry of nasolabial folds. Assess for lagophthalmos and corneal exposure by asking the patient to close their eyes lightly.

VIII. Ask about hearing loss and vertigo. Cover one ear and whisper a number in the other for the patient to repeat. To test more formally, check that a 256 Hz or 512 Hz tuning fork held on the midline forehead (Weber's test) is heard equally in both ears, and that air conduction persists after audible bone conduction (with the tuning fork held on mastoid) ceases (Rinné's test).

IX and X. Ask the patient to open their mouth and say 'Ahhh!'. Look for symmetrical midline elevation of the uvula, or deviation away from the affected side. Ask about any choking or problems swallowing. If concerned test the gag reflex with a tongue depressor or similar.

XI. Ask the patient to lift both shoulders and press down to check power. Ask the patient to turn the chin towards one shoulder and press against this action with your palm. With the other hand, feel the muscle bulk of the contracting sternocleidomastoid.

XII. Observe the patient's tongue when it is in their mouth for fasciculations or wasting. Ask the patient to stick out their tongue (deviates to the weaker side) and then return it into the mouth (deviates to the stronger side). Testing both movements is helpful where there is coincident facial weakness.

- *Cerebellar tests*:
  1. Listen to the patient's speech, which may be slurred or interrupted and staccato. Ask them to say 'British constitution', 'Baby hippopotamus', or 'West Register Street'.
  2. Test for dysdiadochokinesis. Ask the patient to place one hand palm down on the other and then rapidly turn it palm up and palm down again, repeating this about 10 times. Compare with the other side. This is often a little asymmetrical in people who are strongly right or left handed.
  3. Ask the patient to touch their nose and then touch your finger held about 50 cm in front of them, then to touch their nose again. Repeat this, moving your own finger further away to make the patient stretch to reach it. In cerebellar disease past-pointing occurs and an intention tremor appears or increases as the target is approached.
  4. Examine gait, which in cerebellar disease will be broad-based. If uncertain, ask the patient to walk 'heel-toe' (as if on a tight rope), which exaggerates minor degrees of gait ataxia.
  5. If gait is unsteady, perform Romberg's test of dorsal column function (proprioception). Ask the patient to stand still with feet together and eyes open. If the patient cannot do this, abandon the test. See how steady the patient is for 15 seconds, then ask the patient to close their eyes. In cerebellar disease, there should be little difference in balance whether the eyes are closed or open, while in dorsal column disease, the patient will become more unsteady when the eyes are shut. Do not let the patient fall!
  6. If the patient has binocular double vision, consider patching one eye for steps 3 to 5.

INVESTIGATIONS

Optical coherence tomography

Optic nerve head Image the optic nerve head (ONH) using radial scans centred on the optic nerve and three-dimensional (3D) volumetric cube scans obtained by raster scanning (**Fig. 15.1**). Proper positioning is essential to avoid inaccurate measurements. The contour of the ONH is defined by the interface between the low backscattering (dark) vitreous and the highly backscattering (bright) retinal nerve fibre layer (RNFL). OCT images are often axially stretched to better show the neurosensory retinal layers (see **Fig. 11.11**, p. 508), exaggerating the optic disc cup depth.

Enhanced depth imaging (EDI) OCT improves visualisation of deeper ONH structures, back to the lamina cribrosa (**Fig. 15.1**). EDI-OCT's diagnostic accuracy surpasses ultrasound, and is useful for papilloedema, pseudo-papilloedema, optic nerve sheath meningioma, optic nerve hypoplasia, myelinated nerve fibres, optic disc melanoma and melanocytoma.

Retinal nerve fibre layer Circumpapillary RNFL density can show both atrophy and swelling on the ONH (**Figs. 15.2** and **15.3**).

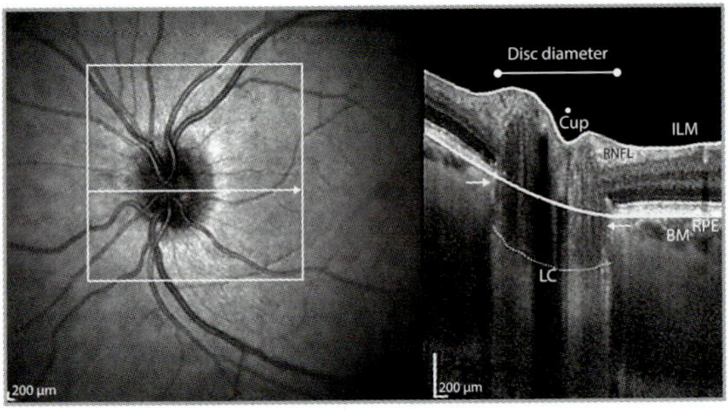

Fig. 15.1: Enhanced depth imaging-optical coherence tomography (EDI-OCT) of a normal optic nerve head. The device delineates the internal limiting membrane (ILM) and Bruch's membrane (BM), top and bottom. The retinal pigment epithelium (RPE) is a bright layer, abruptly terminating at the disc margin (arrow), defining the disc diameter. The retinal nerve fibre layer (RNFL) thickness increases as it approaches the optic disc, then blends with the optic nerve head and decreases in reflectance due to the loss of perpendicular orientation relative to the incident OCT beam. The optic disc cup is seen as a surface depression (asterisk). The lamina cribrosa (LC) appears posteriorly.

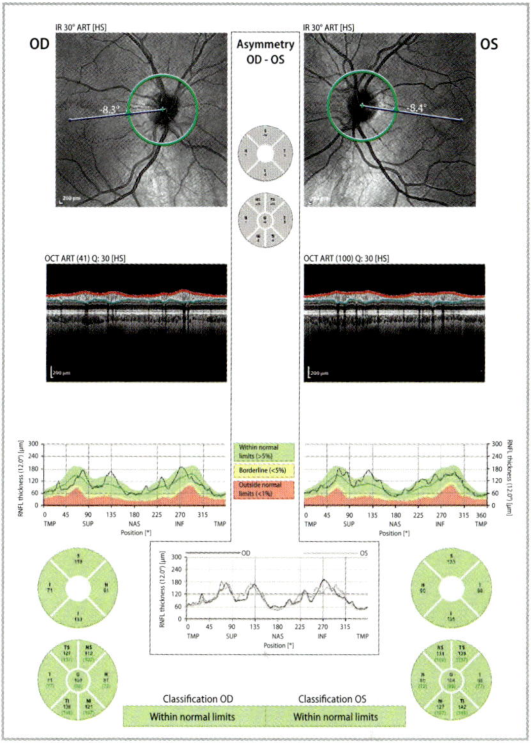

Fig. 15.2: Normal spectral-domain OCT retinal nerve fibre layer (RNFL) report. The RNFL thickness falls within the normal range in all segments (temporal = T; superior = S; nasal = N and inferior = I).

Measurements are typically extracted from a circle scan centred on the ONH with a 3.4-mm diameter. Misplacement during repetitive scanning can cause variable measurements. Consider 3D cube scanning, which allows repositioning of the circle for consistency. The RNFL's anterior boundary is at the vitreoretinal interface, and the posterior boundary at the interface between the RNFL and ganglion cell layer (GCL). RNFL segmentation is more sensitive to OCT image quality variations than total retinal thickness measurements. ONH atrophy is associated with reduced RNFL thickness, with normal ~105 µm at age of 18 years, decreasing to ~85–95 µm by the age of 80 years.

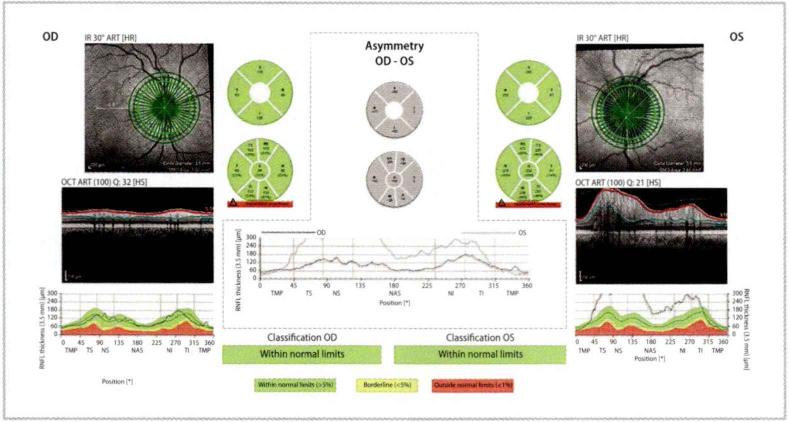

Fig. 15.3: Spectral-domain OCT retinal nerve fibre layer measurement showing left optic disc oedema.

Spectralis spectral domain OCT displays average RNFL thickness in four quadrants (temporal, superior, nasal and inferior) and sectoral thickness in up to 16 equal sectors. The ISNT rule is followed, where the inferior quadrant usually has the thickest RNFL, followed by superior, nasal, and temporal quadrants (in **Fig. 15.2**, the green 'doughnut' shows the thickness values for each quadrant). Cirrus high definition (HD)-OCT generates a deviation map comparing RNFL measurements to an age-matched normative database, highlighting locations under the lower 95% of the normal range. Other devices display RNFL thickness as colour-coded maps, useful for assessing small, localised thinning outside the sampling location. See also page 347.

Macula Consider macular OCT to segment and quantify the GCL layer and inner plexiform layer (IPL) for suspected afferent visual dysfunction (**Fig. 15.4**). Ganglion cell thinning with subtle inner nuclear layer (INL) changes suggests retrograde trans-synaptic degeneration secondary to afferent visual pathway damage. The inner retinal complex (RNFL, GCL, IPL and INL) can be segmented by different methods:

- Cirrus HD uses an ellipse centred on the fovea, measuring the combined GCL and IPL.
- RTVue captures a 7 mm^2 area centred 1 mm temporal to the fovea.

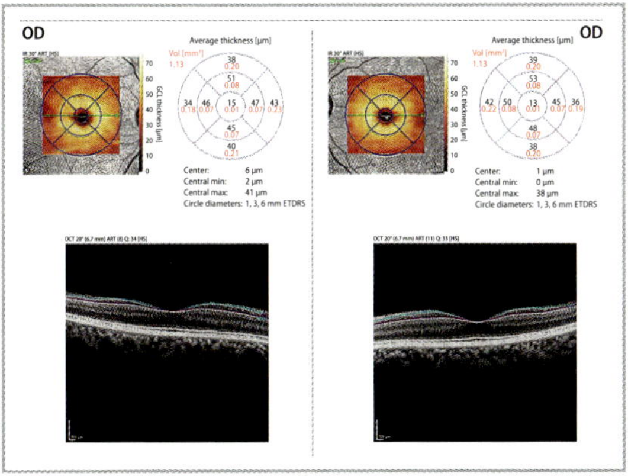

Fig. 15.4: Normal Spectralis OCT display of software of serial macular ganglion cell density analysis (1, 3 and 6 mm volume scan).

- Spectralis provides automated segmentation of perifoveal volumetric macular scans.

Macular ganglion cell-inner plexiform layer (mGCIPL) assessment is sensitive to afferent visual pathway dysfunction and useful for diagnosing and monitoring acute and chronic optic neuropathies. Ganglion cell loss often correlates with visual field loss patterns, as seen in chiasmal compression and non-arteritic ischaemic optic neuropathies (**Fig. 15.5**). Serial mGCIPL monitoring is less prone to artefacts than serial perimetric visual field tests.

Be aware that automated OCT segmentation of RNFL and mGCIPL can have errors. Diseased eyes with poor image quality may have segmentation errors requiring manual segmentation, and in patients with poor vision the foveal centre may be incorrectly identified, requiring manual repositioning. If uncertain, the most central foveal measurements may be the more reliable. Repeatability of automated segmentation measurements varies across OCT devices and protocols. Consistent methodology and OCT modality are crucial for monitoring.

Optical coherence tomography angiography

In addition to retinal imaging (p. 510), OCT angiography (OCTA) can image the ONH vascular network (**Fig. 15.6**). It shows the peripapillary radial capillary network (not visible with fluorescein angiography) that is particularly susceptible to IOP fluctuations and correlates with RNFL thickness. In glaucomatous optic neuropathy, reduced perfusion, vessel density and pre-laminar ONH blood flow correlate with RNFL, GCL, visual field mean deviation and visual field index. Reduced perfusion is also seen in demyelinating optic neuritis and ischaemic optic neuropathies. Partial recovery of peripapillary vascular flow is associated with visual recovery in non-arteritic anterior ischaemic optic neuropathies. Focal non-perfusion and superficial peripapillary capillary dilation are potential diagnostic signs for arteritic anterior ischaemic optic neuropathy. Established cases of Leber's hereditary optic neuropathy and autosomal dominant optic atrophy show reduced peripapillary perfusion.

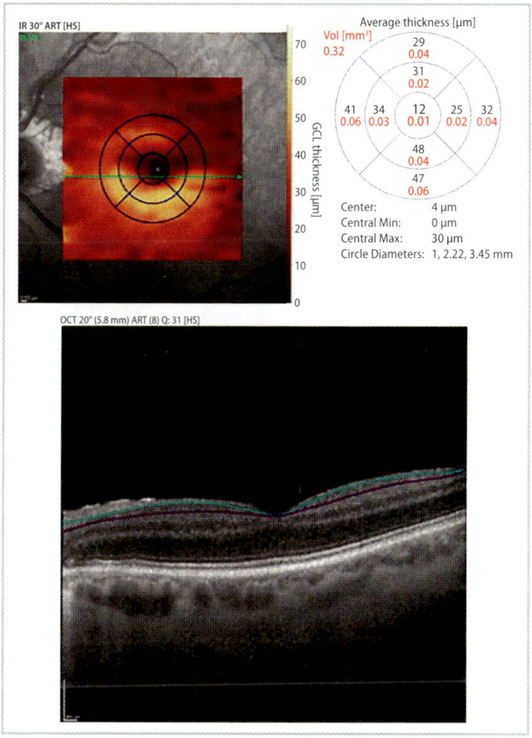

Fig. 15.5: Spectralis OCT display of macular ganglion cell (mGCL) density showing established left optic neuropathy secondary to non-arteritic anterior ischaemic optic neuropathy. There is clinically significant, superior paramacular ganglion cell thinning corresponding to an inferior arcuate inferior visual field deficit on automated 24-2 perimetry *Continues overleaf*

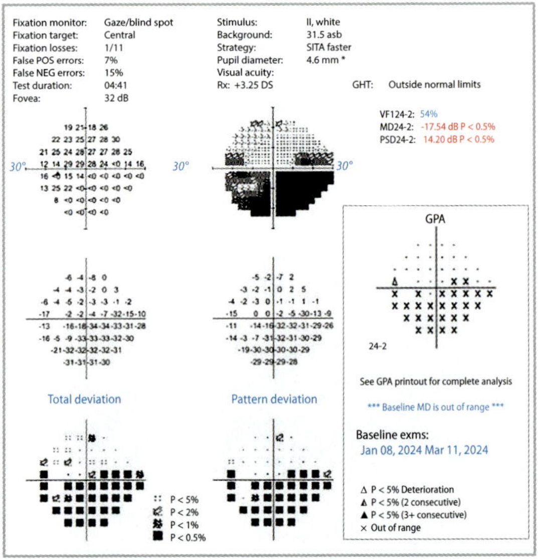

Fig. 15.5: *Continued*

Computed tomography

See page 96.

Magnetic resonance imaging

Useful for imaging the anterior and posterior visual pathways (including optic nerve, chiasm, optic tracts, optic radiation and visual cortex), brain, soft tissue or vascular masses, and non-organic, non-metallic foreign bodies (FB). It does not show bone or calcium well. It is more expensive and less readily available than CT, and less useful for some orbital disease (p. 97). Contraindications include possible metal FB and some pacemakers (many modern devices are safe but must be recalibrated immediately after MRI). Patients with clipped intracranial aneurysms need documentation to show that their clip is not ferromagnetic. Claustrophobic patients may not tolerate conventional MRI. Avoid gadolinium enhancement unless it is known that renal function is normal.

- Commonly used sequences:
  a. *T_1 image*: Best for structural definition of anatomy. Water (vitreous and CSF) appears black (hypointense), fat

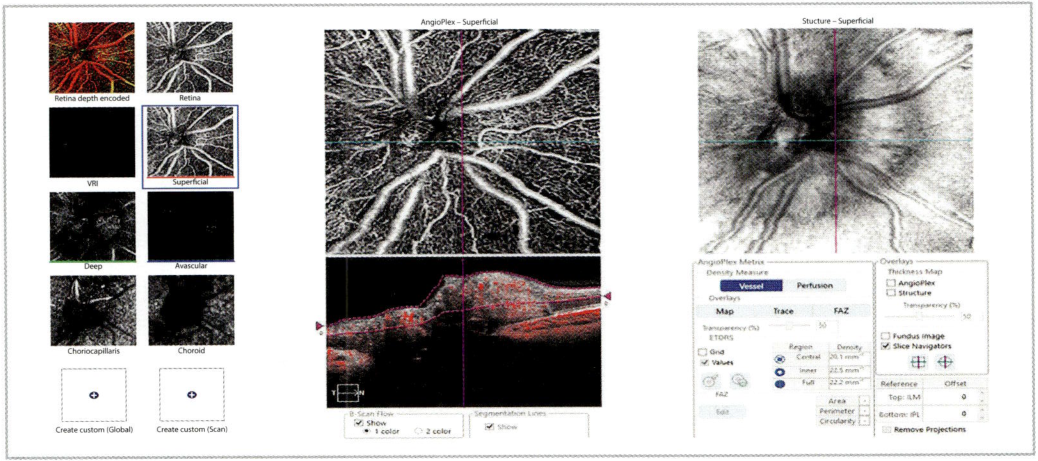

Fig. 15.6: Cirrus angioplex OCT angiography display of a normal circumpapillary optic nerve head vascular plexus.

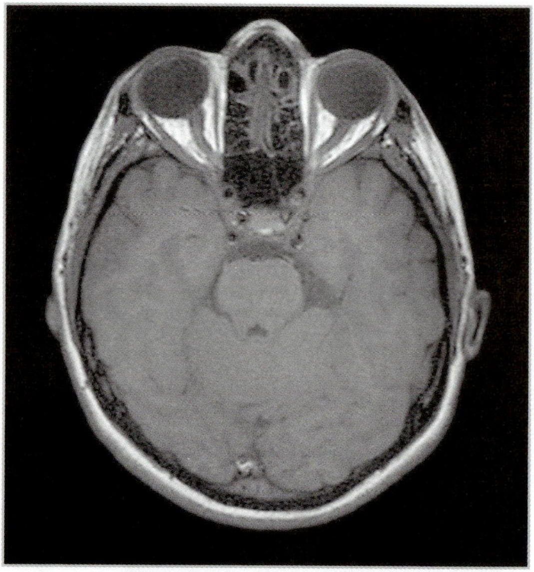

Fig. 15.7: Normal T_1-axial magnetic resonance imaging.

is hyperintense, which aids definition of orbital soft-tissue anatomy, (**Fig. 15.7**) but hinders interpretation of gadolinium enhancement.

b. *T_2 image*: Best for identifying diseased tissue. Water appears white, so oedema shows as a high signal; fat is also hyperintense (**Fig. 15.8**).
c. *Fat suppression*: Suppression of high signal from orbital fat allows clear definition of the optic nerve and extraocular muscles in T_2 weighted images and interpretation of gadolinium enhancement in T_1 weighted images (**Fig. 15.9**).
d. *Fluid-attenuated inversion recovery sequence (FLAIR)*: CSF appears dark, making it easier to detect small T_2 hyperintense lesions (e.g. MS plaques) adjacent to the lateral ventricles.
e. *Short tau inversion recovery sequence (STIR)*: Ideal for imaging the intraorbital optic nerve as orbital fat is suppressed but water (inflammatory oedema) can still be seen as high signal. Similar to T_2-weighted images with fat suppression.
f. *Susceptibility weighted imaging (SWI)*: Exquisitely sensitive to venous blood, haemorrhage and iron

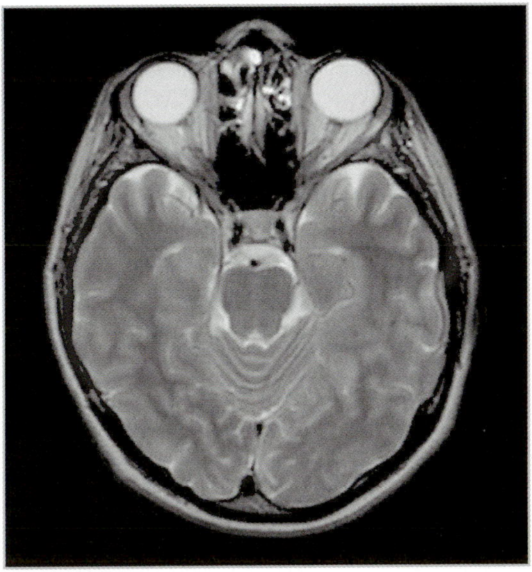

Fig. 15.8: Normal T_2 axial magnetic resonance imaging.

deposition. Particularly good at detecting conditions with haemosiderin deposition in the brain, such as cavernoma and amyloid angiopathy.

g. *Diffusion weighted imaging (DWI)*: Measures the diffusion of water molecules. It can identify acute arterial infarction within minutes.
h. *Gadolinium contrast*: Useful when looking for lesions with disrupted blood–tissue barrier. Consider if suspected meningioma, acoustic neuroma, lymphoma, metastatic disease, optic neuropathy (e.g. sarcoid), or active MS plaques. Contrast enhancement can be seen on T_1-weighted images but not on T_2 images. Fat saturation is essential in contrast-enhanced imaging of the orbit.

- Common examples:
  a. *Optic nerve disease*: Judge size on coronal sections. Acute optic neuritis shows high signal on T_2 imaging and gadolinium enhancement on fat saturated T_1 imaging. In the acute phase, anterior ischaemic optic neuropathy shows no abnormality. Both show high signal chronically due to Wallerian degeneration.
  b. *Vascular imaging*: Blood flow in arteries and veins produces a 'flow void' on MRI, appearing as low signal

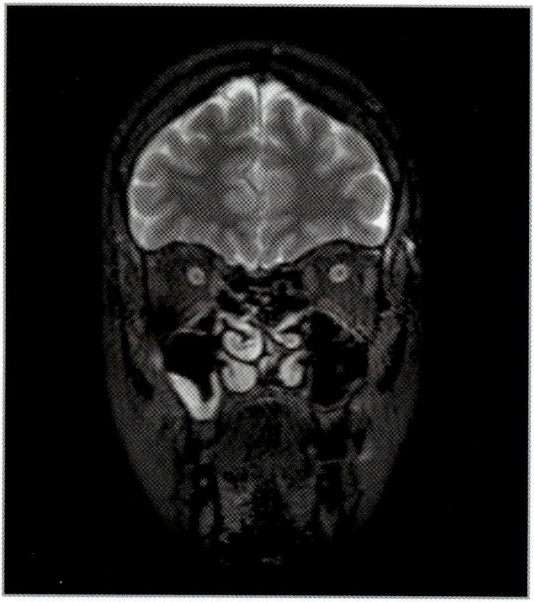

Fig. 15.9: Normal T_2 coronal magnetic resonance imaging with fat suppression.

in most of the above-mentioned sequences. Lack of flow void implies complete or partial occlusion. Consider axial T_2 cuts where carotid artery dissection is suspected. MR venography (MRV) and MR arteriography (MRA) can confirm blood flow without contrast injection, but may fail to detect very slow flow. MRA and CT arteriography (CTA) will, in expert hands, exclude intracranial arterial aneurysms of >3 mm but have not yet completely replaced intra-arterial catheter angiography, e.g. in acute, painful IIIrd nerve palsy with pupillary involvement. The gold standards for detecting vascular lesions of all kinds are contrast enhanced MRA, MRV, CTA and CTV.

c. *Stroke*: Immediate non-contrast CT is preferred to exclude clinically significant acute haemorrhage especially if thrombolysis is an option. SWI-MRI can also detect acute intracerebral haemorrhage. DWI and FLAIR on MRI imaging are the most sensitive techniques for detecting early ischaemic cerebrovascular accidents and are positive within minutes of onset, including small brainstem infarcts that are not well imaged using CT.

ANISOCORIA

History Ask who first noticed the anisocoria (difference in pupil size) and attempt to establish the duration. Review of old photos may help. Magnification of photographic images may be required to assess pupil size. Exclude a history of neck or chest surgery/injury, limb weakness, difficulty focusing, diplopia and ptosis.

Examination Identify which pupil is abnormal by examining first in the dark, then in the light. Greater anisocoria in the dark indicates impaired dilatation (sympathetic dysfunction): greater anisocoria in the light indicates impaired constriction (parasympathetic dysfunction). Physiological anisocoria is usually ≤1 mm, or slightly greater in the dark. Examine the pupils (p. 747), and iris on the slit lamp.

Differential diagnosis of an abnormally large pupil

Consider Adie's pupil (below), IIIrd nerve palsy, dilating drops or chemical dilation (e.g. after using antiperspirant wipes with glycopyrronium), traumatic mydriasis, iris rubeosis, Urrets–Zavalia's syndrome (iris atrophy following intraocular surgery), and physiological anisocoria.

- *Adie's tonic pupil*: Presumed post-viral denervation of the sphincter pupillae and ciliary muscle produces anisocoria and difficulty focussing. Owing to aberrant re-innervation, accommodation recovers but is slower than normal, whereas some fibres are re-routed from the ciliary muscle to the sphincter pupillae. Signs thereafter include light-near dissociation (reduced or absent constriction to light but extensive and characteristically 'slow' constriction on attempted near vision), and segmental sphincter palsy on slit-lamp examination which gives rise to an irregular pupil shape and so-called vermiform movements of the iris. There may be an asymptomatic peripheral neuropathy giving absent tendon reflexes (if so, the condition is known as Holmes–Adie syndrome). Slow constriction and re-dilation associated with looking at a near target or into the distance respectively ('tonic' pupil behaviour) differentiates it from Argyll Robertson pupils. Exclude ptosis and diplopia (IIIrd nerve palsy). Whereas normal pupils do not usually constrict to G. pilocarpine 0.125%, Adie's pupil does (denervation hypersensitivity), but this test has only moderate sensitivity and specificity, and has similar results with both pre- and postganglionic lesions. Clinical examination is usually all that is required to make the diagnosis of Adie's pupil, and further investigations are not normally required. Arrange routine referral to a neuro-ophthalmologist. Long-term follow-up is not required. It is often bilateral but asymmetric. The affected pupils may eventually become small.

Differential diagnosis of an abnormally small pupil

Consider Horner's syndrome (below), pilocarpine drops, uveitis/ posterior synechiae, and physiological anisocoria.

- *Horner's syndrome*: Sympathetic denervation produces miosis and mild ptosis. It may be central, pre- or postganglionic. Central causes include stroke (Wallenberg's syndrome) and syringomyelia. Preganglionic causes include apical lung and breast malignancy, sympathetic chain schwannoma, cervical spine damage (e.g. C8 or T1 disc prolapse), and neck tumours or trauma. Postganglionic causes include internal carotid artery dissection, cavernous sinus disease (especially if a VIth nerve palsy coexists), and cluster headache. The diagnosis of Horner's syndrome (regardless of lesion location) is confirmed by administration of 0.5% (or 1%) apraclonidine drops. Apraclonidine is an α2-adrenergic agonist which dilates a Horner pupil after 40–60 minutes and reverses the ptosis, whereas it mioses a normal pupil (leading in many cases to a reversal of the anisocoria in cases of unilateral Horner's syndrome). Preganglionic causes produce ipsilateral anhydrosis of the face (ptosis, miosis and anhydrosis). Investigations depend on the likely cause, but if painful and acute request urgent T_2-weighted MRI axial scans to exclude carotid dissection or contrast-enhanced arteriography (CT or MRI). This is associated with a high risk of embolic stroke within 10 days and anticoagulation is indicated. Congenital Horner's syndrome typically has iris heterochromia and is seen on old photographs. Importantly, iris heterochromia can occur if Horner's syndrome is acquired within the first year of life. Acquired childhood cases require investigation to exclude neoplasia, particularly cervicothoracic neuroblastoma, though most are benign.

TRANSIENT VISUAL LOSS

Background Transient visual loss has numerous causes. A careful history is crucial.

History Ask about: duration; whether one or both eyes are affected; total blackness (arterial occlusion) or just blurred; patchy grey blobs (spasm of choroidal vessels); cardiovascular risk factors; transient ischaemic attacks (TIAs) or strokes; known carotid disease; headache; migrainous aura; dizziness, hearing, or speech problems; loss of balance; haloes; eye pain; improves with blinking (tear film), abnormal clotting or deep thromboses (DVTs); scalp tenderness and jaw claudication (if over 50 years). Specific precipitants may suggest the diagnosis:

- *Bright light*: chronic retinal ischaemia due to carotid insufficiency.
- *Eye movements*: space occupying orbital lesion or optic nerve tumour.
- *Prolonged reading or evening onset*: intermittent angle-closure glaucoma, or accommodative spasm in young patients.
- *Exercise*: pigment dispersion syndrome, or Uhtoff's phenomenon following demyelinating optic neuritis.
- *Standing up*: usually indicates reduced perfusion pressure including postural hypotension, carotid insufficiency, and giant cell arteritis (precedes nerve infarction). Also occurs in angle-closure where reduced perfusion is secondary to IOP. Papilloedema may produce brief (seconds only) monocular or bilateral obscurations with either standing up or stooping forwards.

Examination Check BP in both arms (sitting and standing if appropriate); radial pulse; cardiac and carotid auscultation; temporal artery palpation (in patients over 50 years of age); VA; confrontation visual fields; colour vision; RAPD; corneal clarity (oedema or endothelial pigment); iris rubeosis; gonioscopy (is angle closeable?); IOP; dilated fundoscopy (especially retinal vessels for emboli, venous dilation, retinal haemorrhages and optic disc for swelling); assess central retinal artery perfusion pressure (p. 570); and other tests as indicated.

Differential diagnosis See **Table 15.1**.
The following are the more common or serious causes:

1. *Carotid or cardiac emboli:* See below.
2. *Carotid dissection:* May have neck pain and Horner's syndrome.

Table 15.1: Causes of transient visual loss

Visual loss lasting < 1 minute		Visual loss lasting 5–30 minutes	
Monocular	**Binocular**	**Monocular**	**Binocular**
• Carotid insufficiency • Giant cell arteritis • Papilloedema	• Bilateral carotid insufficiency • Bilateral papilloedema • Vertebrobasilar insufficiency • Cardiac dysrhythmia • Postural hypotension • Occipital epilepsy	• Retinal arterial embolus • Retinal vasospasm • Choroidal vasospasm (controversial) • Angle-closure glaucoma • Pigment dispersion syndrome	• Migraine • Occipital embolus

3. *Migraine:* usually hemianopic, although patients may report this as being monocular, positive features, with zig-zags typical (p. 785).
4. *Giant cell arteritis:* Page 789.
5. *Vertebrobasilar ischaemia:* Page 809.
6. *Intermittent angle-closure glaucoma:* Page 353.
7. *Occipital embolus:* may cause hemianopic loss or transient blindness.
8. *Retinal arterial embolus:* typically, a curtain descent to a blackout (p. 576).
9. *Retinal vasospasm:* more likely a whiteout.
10. *Choroidal vasospasm:* vision disappears and reappears in patches.
11. *Cardiac dysrhythmia and Stokes Adams' attacks:* blindness may precede loss of consciousness or occur in isolation.
12. *Occipital epilepsy:* usually hemianopic with positive symptoms such as coloured circles rather than zig-zags. Lasts seconds vs many minutes in migraine.

Management Investigation and treatment depend on the likely cause. In the case of transient monocular blindness, emboli usually arise from the aorta, carotids, or heart valves. Most commonly they are cholesterol, platelet-fibrin, or calcific, but septic, amniotic fluid, air, fat or talc (i.v. drug users) may rarely occur in specific situations. If likely, start oral aspirin 75 mg o.d. and check BP, FBC, ESR, glucose, and lipids as a minimum. Arrange carotid Doppler, echocardiogram and review by a stroke physician or TIA clinic within 48 hours. Warn patients that intervention may be indicated if investigations reveal internal carotid artery stenosis or valvular heart disease. A statin is likely to be indicated. Posterior circulation transient blindness or transient hemianopia suggest a cardiac source, especially atrial fibrillation or a paroxysmal dysrhythmia.

NYSTAGMUS

Background Nystagmus is a rhythmic, often rapid, involuntary eye movement. Patients may or may not be experiencing the movement of the image on the retina caused by nystagmus as oscillopsia (movement of the visual image). Oscillopsia is uncommon in congenital nystagmus which includes most causes of pendular nystagmus due to low vision from birth (e.g. albinism and Leber's congenital amaurosis), and congenital motor nystagmus (also known as the 'infantile nystagmus syndrome'). The latter is usually horizontal in all directions of gaze, uniplanar, and often accompanied by an abnormal head posture to achieve best vision, usually with a head turn to match gaze direction to the null position of the nystagmus (the eye position that minimises the nystagmus); OCT often reveals foveal hypoplasia.

Examination Observe and document whether the nystagmus is pendular or jerk, vertical or horizontal, and the direction of the fast phase. Is it present in primary position? Direct ophthalmoscope magnification can reveal low-amplitude nystagmus in the primary position. Is it always horizontal and uniplanar with a null point (e.g. congenital motor nystagmus)? Is the direction of the fast phase always in the direction of gaze (gaze evoked) or not (vestibular and congenital)? Is there a torsional component? Examine the eyes in primary position for several minutes. Does the nystagmus change direction in a regular cycle (periodic alternating nystagmus)? Look for the following patterns.

Gaze evoked nystagmus A jerk nystagmus in which the fast phase occurs in the same direction as the patient's gaze, but is absent in the primary position. Seen in cerebellar and brainstem disease and with some drugs (anticonvulsants and sedatives). A few beats of nystagmus at the extremes of gaze may be normal. Does not cause oscillopsia.

Acquired pendular nystagmus May occur with severe visual loss, brainstem strokes, and MS. Consider gabapentin (100 mg t.d.s. increasing slowly to 300 mg t.d.s.) or baclofen (5 mg daily increasing to a maximum of 10 mg t.d.s.). Often associated with oscillopsia.

Downbeat nystagmus Often most obvious on downwards and lateral gaze; the direction of the fast phase is downwards. The amplitude varies with position, usually maximal with the patient prone. Seen with Arnold–Chiari malformations, cerebellar degenerations, and some drugs. Often associated with oscillopsia.

Upbeat nystagmus Seen with intrinsic brainstem disease. Up- and downbeat nystagmus is present in primary position, and this distinguishes these disorders from vertical gaze evoked nystagmus. Often associated with oscillopsia.

Convergence-retraction nystagmus Test with an optokinetic (OKN) drum rotating the stripes downwards to induce attempted up saccades. The saccadic impulse manifests as convergence and retraction (co-contraction of all the horizontal recti) rather than up saccades, and is typically seen in Parinaud's syndrome. Also called 'dorsal midbrain syndrome'. Causes include pinealoma, head trauma, arteriovenous malformation, MS, and basilar artery cerebrovascular accident (CVA). Parinaud's syndrome may have light-near dissociation of pupils, lid retraction, and spasm/paresis of convergence/accommodation. It is not a true nystagmus.

See–saw nystagmus One eye elevates and intorts while the other depresses and extorts then *vice versa*. Occurs with suprasellar lesions. May have a fast phase or be a variant of pendular nystagmus. Often associated with oscillopsia.

Periodic alternating nystagmus Horizontal jerk nystagmus that changes direction every few minutes. Often associated with oscillopsia. May be congenital or occur in a variety of vestibulocerebellar diseases and occasionally following severe bilateral visual loss. Consider gabapentin (100 mg t.d.s. increasing slowly to 300 mg t.d.s.) or baclofen (5 mg daily increasing to a maximum of 10 mg t.d.s.). Try baclofen first.

Peripheral vestibular nystagmus Unidirectional, uniplanar with a torsional element, and the greatest amplitude with gaze in the direction of the fast component. Associated with paroxysmal vertigo, tinnitus, and hearing loss. Occurs in acute labyrinthitis, Ménière's disease, and benign positional vertigo.

Central vestibular nystagmus Chronic jerk nystagmus, uni- or bidirectional, that varies with the direction of gaze. Often but not always torsional. Pure torsional nystagmus is of central vestibular origin. Vertigo, deafness and tinnitus are less of a feature than in peripheral vestibular nystagmus. It is caused by a variety of brain stem diseases, e.g. MS, CVA and tumour.

VISUAL FIELD DEFECTS

Background The accurate delineation of visual field defects is critical to the diagnosis of visual pathway lesions. Visual field defects are frequently asymptomatic and may be detected on routine screening (usually by an optometrist), or when field tests are performed for some other reason. Their pattern relates to lesion location (**Fig. 15.10**). An awareness of the various artifactually produced field defects is important.

Symptoms Patients are less likely to notice field defects from optic nerve or visual pathway lesions if these spare the central field. Retinal lesions often produce positive scotomas with patients aware of photopsia within the visual field defect.

History Ask when and how the field defect was first noticed. Sudden onset or gradual? Any recovery? Ask about cardiovascular risk factors, photopsia, pain, headache and other neurological symptoms, and symptoms of pituitary disease

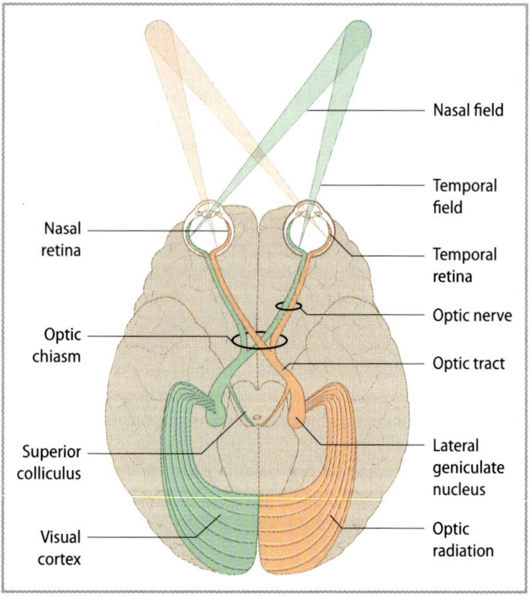

Fig. 15.10: Visual pathways.

(amenorrhoea, hypothyroidism, loss of libido, headache and acromegaly).

Examination Check BP, cranial nerves, VA, colour vision, RAPD, formal fields, eye movements, IOP, drainage angle and dilated fundoscopy. Exclude ptosis and disc cupping, pallor, or swelling. Many field defects are relative, and not absolute. Consider Amsler grid testing with different colour grids for subtle scotoma detection.

Differential diagnosis Abnormal visual fields may be caused by retinal disease e.g. retinal detachment or vein occlusion. Cataract may cause a globally decreased field but not focal defects. A homonymous hemianopia should not cause a decreased VA although patients may miss the letters on one side of the chart. Glaucoma can cause a range of field defects but confirm that the field defect corresponds to the sectoral neuroretinal rim thinning; colour vision is relatively well preserved until late in the disease, unlike optic nerve disease.

- *Right homonymous hemianopia* (**Fig. 15.11**): Consider a left postchiasmal lesion such as occipital lobe cerebrovascular accident or tumour. The more congruous the field defect, the nearer to the occipital lobe, but a large lesion affecting both temporal and parietal lobes (the entire optic radiation) is also possible.
- *Left superior homonymous quadrantanopia* (**Fig. 15.12**): Probably right inferior occipital cortex but consider a right temporal lobe lesion. Inferior homonymous quadrantanopia may be caused by a parietal lobe lesion. The defect may be relative or absolute. The vertical meridian will be absolutely respected but usually not the horizontal meridian.

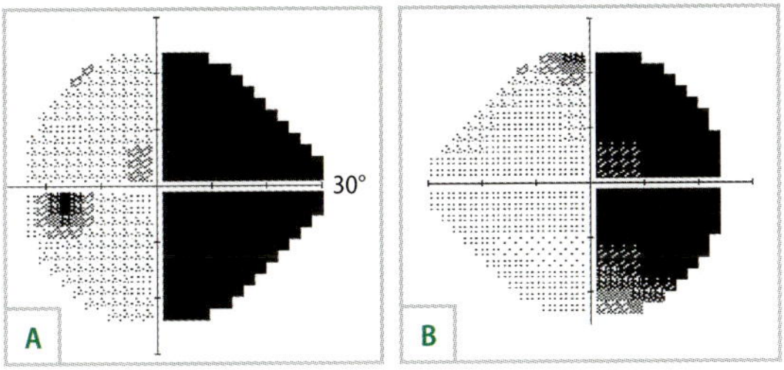

Fig. 15.11: Right homonymous hemianopia. (A) left eye; (B) right eye.

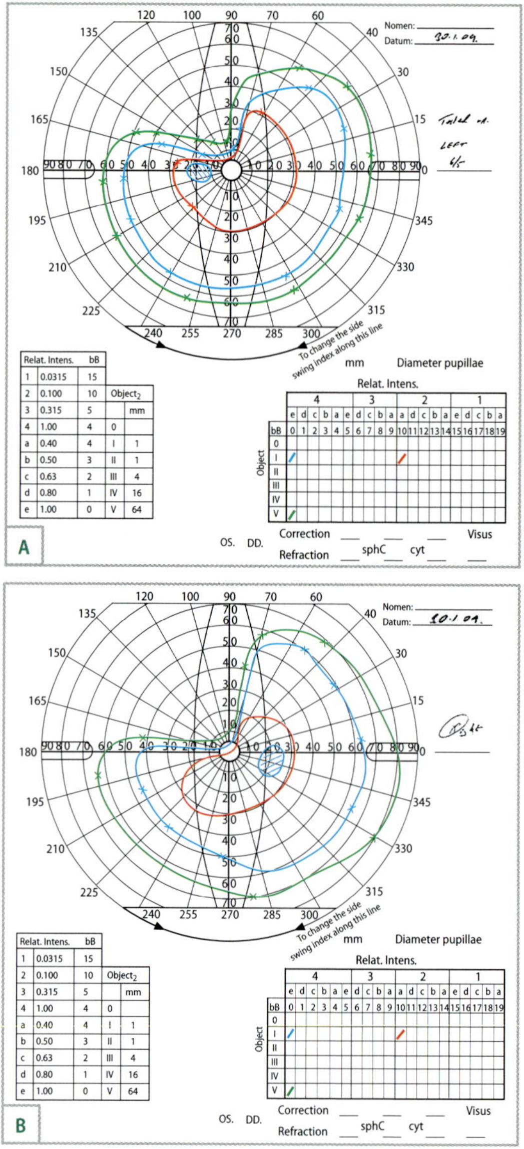

Fig. 15.12: Left superior homonymous quadrantanopia (Goldmann perimeter).

- *Bitemporal superior quadrantanopia* (**Fig. 15.13**): Typically caused by pituitary tumours but will be relative; the defect will respect the vertical meridian but not the horizontal meridian. As the defect progresses, the bitemporal hemianopia becomes more complete but usually asymmetric and eventually with optic atrophy on one or other side. A craniopharyngioma may cause a bilateral inferotemporal quadrantanopia but is more likely to give rise to a combination of optic nerve, chiasm and tract deficits.
- *Complete bitemporal hemianopia* (**Fig. 15.14**): May occur with compressive lesions of the chiasm, but such a clear-cut deficit is typically only seen in cases of traumatic chiasmal transection.
- *Central scotoma* (**Fig. 15.15**): The most common cause is age-related macular degeneration. In optic nerve disease, it is typical to observe central or cecocentral symmetrical scotoma. Such optic neuropathy may be associated with toxic/

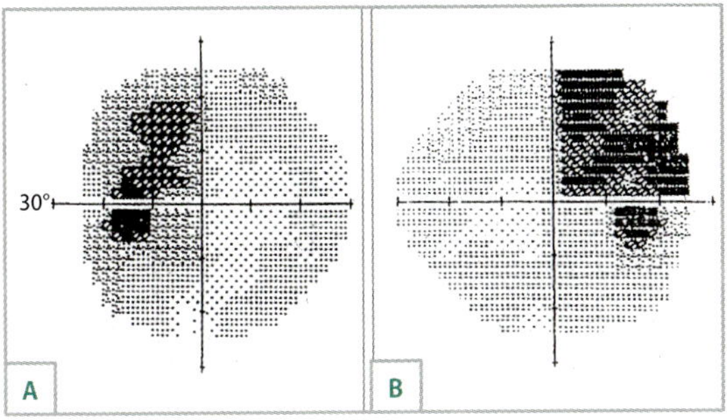

Fig. 15.13: Bitemporal superior quadrantanopia.

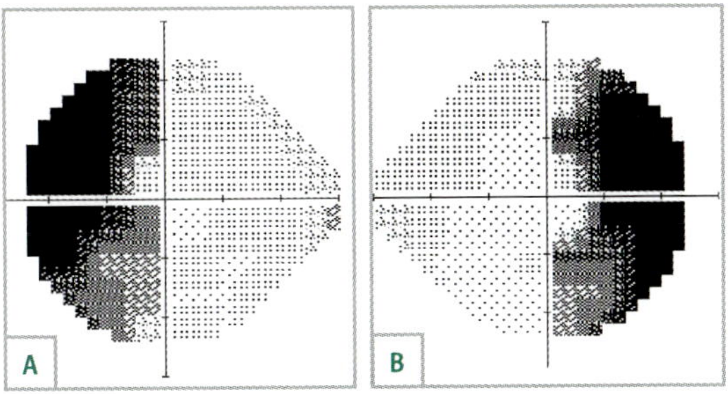

Fig. 15.14: Complete bitemporal hemianopia.

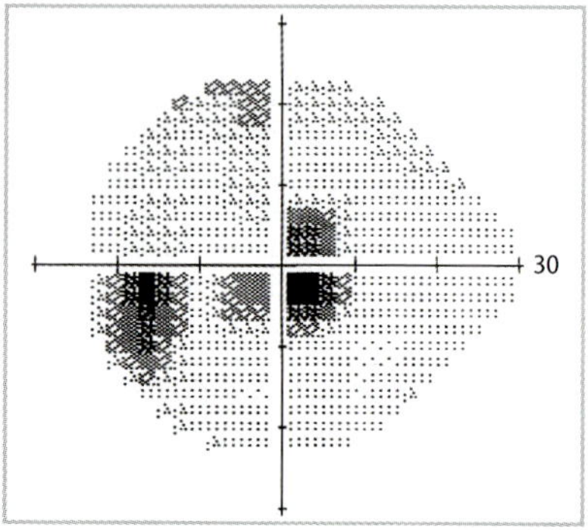

Fig. 15.15: Central scotoma.

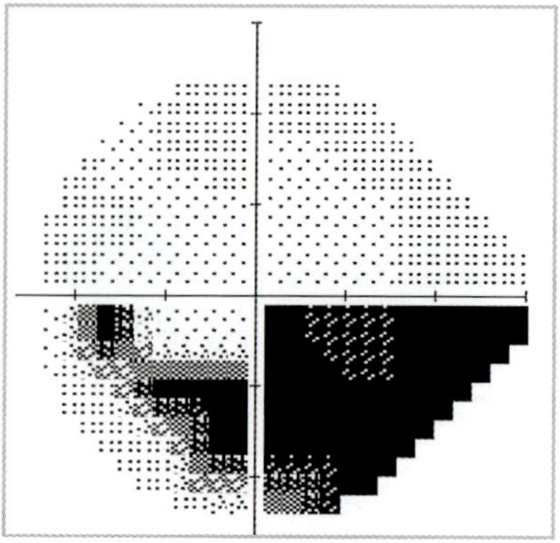

Fig. 15.16: Inferior altitudinal hemianopia in the left eye.

nutritional, or an inherited condition. Of note, cone dystrophy can produce a similar picture.

- *Inferior altitudinal hemianopia in the left eye* (**Fig. 15.16**): Typically seen with non-arteritic anterior ischaemic optic neuropathy but also normal pressure glaucoma (usually bilateral and with arcuate defects in the lower field also), hemicentral vein occlusion, branch retinal artery occlusion, ptosis (less severe), sector panretinal photocoagulation (PRP) laser, and superior retinal detachment.
- *Concentric peripheral field loss* (**Fig. 15.17**): May be seen in retinitis pigmentosa, autoimmune/paraneoplastic retinopathy, atrophic papilloedema (e.g. idiopathic intracranial hypertension), end-stage glaucoma, PRP, central retinal artery occlusion with cilioretinal artery sparing (usually unilateral), optic neuropathies, and vigabatrin toxicity.

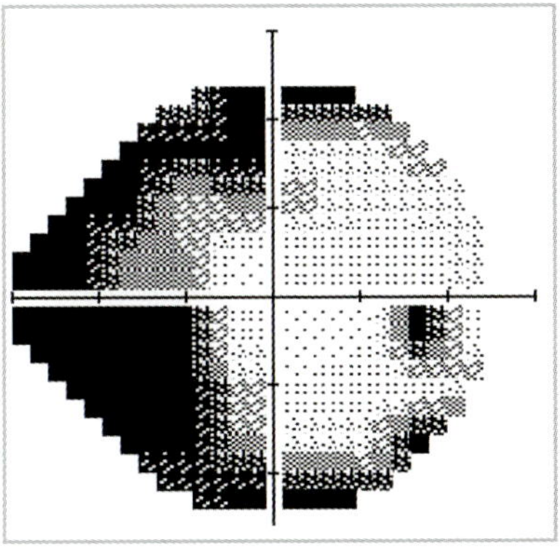

Fig. 15.17: Concentric peripheral field loss.

Investigations Most afferent visual system deficits affect the central 10° of the visual field. Central full-threshold static field testing is therefore suitable for most indications, including subtle chiasmal lesions. Review the reliability indices. Manual or automated kinetic perimetry may be preferable for medically unexplained visual loss, patients who cannot adequately perform a static test, and conditions such as idiopathic intracranial hypertension and vigabatrin-associated visual field loss where peripheral loss may be outside the area tested by central field testing alone. Full-field tests are also useful for patients with very large central scotomas (e.g. severe optic neuritis) who may see nothing on a Humphrey, but the remaining peripheral field can still be used to assess progression or improvement.

Management Depends on the cause of the field loss. Consider eligibility to drive (p. 825) and test binocular Esterman field if in doubt.

OPTIC DISC SWELLING

Background By convention papilloedema refers exclusively to optic disc swelling caused by raised intracranial pressure (ICP). There are many other causes of disc swelling, and disc elevation that mimics true swelling.

History Take a full systemic, neurologic, and ophthalmic history. Headache from raised ICP may be stereotypic (p. 783).

Examination Check BP, cranial nerves (raised ICP may cause a VIth nerve palsy), VA, colour vision, pupils, refraction, dilated fundoscopy, and general examination as indicated by the history. The observation of spontaneous pulsation (SVP) of the central retinal vein excludes raised ICP (but only at the time the observation is made) but the converse is not true, as absent SVPs may be normal. Severe papilloedema causes blurring of the disc margin and nerve fibre layer thickening that obscures disc vessels. The normal optic disc cup is absent except in early/mild papilloedema. Flame haemorrhages at the optic disc may occur, particularly in acute anterior ischaemic optic neuropathy (AION) and also acutely in raised ICP (**Fig. 15.18**). In central retinal vein occlusion (CRVO), there will be haemorrhages on the disc but also throughout the retina.

Differential diagnosis Consider: raised ICP; meningitis; posterior uveitis (panuveitis); infiltration or inflammation e.g. leukaemia; sarcoid; demyelinating optic neuritis; posterior scleritis; compressive optic neuropathy e.g. thyroid eye disease

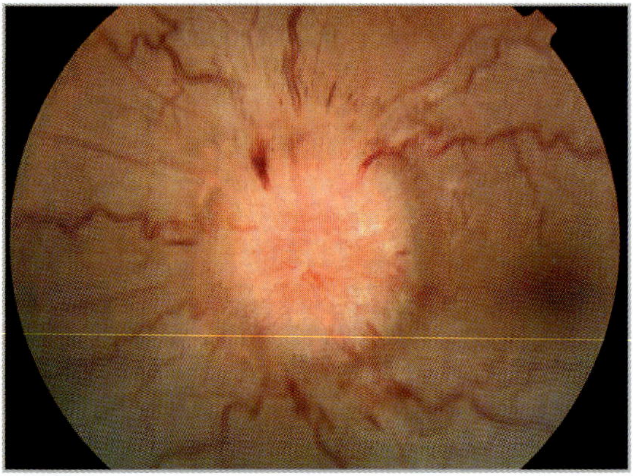

Fig. 15.18: Papilloedema.

or sheath meningioma; malignant hypertension; diabetic papillopathy; AION; CRVO; Leber's hereditary optic neuropathy; carbon dioxide retention; hypoparathyroidism; and uraemia.

Optic disc swelling may be simulated (pseudopapilloedema) by small, crowded hypermetropic discs, tilted discs, and disc drusen. In these conditions, the disc is elevated but there is no swelling of the nerve fibre layer and no vessel obscuration.

Optic disc drusen (**Fig. 15.19**) are calcified deposits in the optic nerve head which may be clearly visible but if buried may simulate disc swelling. They are sometimes associated with

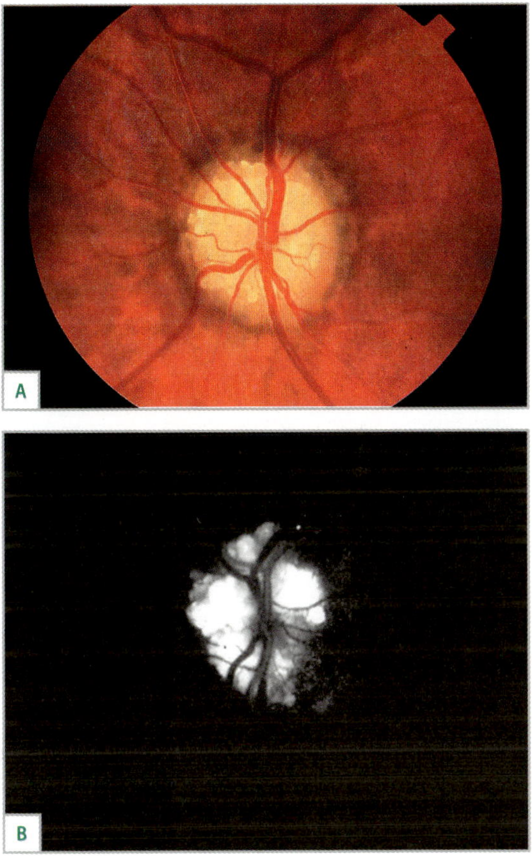

Fig. 15.19: Optic disc drusen shown on (A) colour imaging and (B) autofluorescence.

arcuate field loss. Drusen involute in later life. No treatment is available.

Investigations Arrange formal perimetry. If papilloedema is suspected, request neuroimaging and liaise urgently with neurology. If imaging shows no cause for raised ICP, lumbar puncture may be required to measure ICP. Photograph the optic discs. Consider fundus photographs using angiography filters or OCT to show drusen autofluorescence, or alternatively disc drusen are detected using ultrasound examination (calcium also shows on CT). Enhanced depth imaging (EDI) of the optic disc using OCT can image individual drusen directly.

Management Treat the underlying cause. If pseudopapilloedema is confirmed, no further action is required, but if in doubt repeat VA, colour vision, visual fields, disc photography and disc OCT after several months to check there has been no change, as this suggests another diagnosis.

IDIOPATHIC INTRACRANIAL HYPERTENSION

Background A condition with raised intracranial pressure (ICP) but no mass lesion or hydrocephalus. Previously referred to as pseudotumour cerebri and benign intracranial hypertension. The syndrome known as 'idiopathic intracranial hypertension' (IIH) occurs most commonly in women of child-bearing age with a history of recent substantial weight gain. The same clinical picture may also be associated with prolonged therapy with tetracyclines (e.g. minocycline for acne), anabolic steroids, danazol, exogenous growth hormone, hypervitaminosis A, isotretinoin, tretinoin, nalidixic acid, lithium, ciclosporin, pregnancy (probably related to weight gain), several endocrine disorders, iron-deficiency anaemia, polycystic ovaries syndrome, chronic meningitis (especially in sarcoidosis), and vasculitis rarely. Dural sinus thrombosis is another cause of raised intracranial pressure, especially in association with prothrombotic conditions such as Behçet's disease, pregnancy, antiphospholipid syndrome, protein S deficiency, protein C deficiency, oral contraceptive pill use, and Factor V Leiden mutation. In cases of dural sinus thrombosis onset of ICP is more likely to be subacute. Also consider the obstructive sleep apnoea syndrome, especially in obese males.

Symptoms These include headache (94%), unilateral or bilateral transient visual obscurations lasting seconds (68%), pulsatile tinnitus (58%), photopsia (54%), retrobulbar pain (44%), diplopia (38%), and loss of vision (26%). Headache may be throbbing, wake the patient from sleep, and be exacerbated by recumbent posture and Valsalva. It may improve on rising in the morning, but get worse during the day.

Signs The patient will be overweight but recent weight gain and the demographic of premenopausal female are more significant than even severe obesity without these features. There is bilateral papilloedema and there may be a unilateral or bilateral VIth nerve palsy. Visual fields show enlarged blind spots but may also be severely constricted or lead to other types of visual field defects.

History and examination Take a full medical history and record medications, particularly those for acne. Check for neck stiffness, temperature, BP, VA, colour vision, confrontation visual fields, and IOP. Exclude vitritis and scleritis. Perform a full neurological examination and measure weight and height to determine body mass index (BMI). Patients have a surprisingly high incidence of functional visual loss, which should be considered carefully before any surgical intervention.

Differential diagnosis Consider any cause of papilloedema or disc swelling (p. 776). Exclude intracranial space occupying lesions (SOL), meningitis, malignant hypertension, and dural sinus thrombosis.

Investigations Any patient presenting with headache and bilateral disc swelling needs urgent neuroimaging to exclude imminent coning. In IIH MRI will not show hydrocephalus or a mass lesion, but there is usually evidence of chronic raised ICP (dilated optic nerve sheaths and so called 'empty sella', which is herniation of the arachnoid into the pituitary fossa). Dural sinus occlusion (by thrombosis or small SOL) is usually visible on brain MRI, but contrast-enhanced MR or CT venography may clarify. Dural sinus stenosis may be seen due to a small tumour compressing a venous sinus—usually the torcula or transverse sinus—but is also seen in otherwise typical IIH. This finding raises the possibility that intracranial venous hypertension is at least a contributory cause of raised ICP in IIH as in cases of dural sinus thrombosis, compression or arterial fistula. Once normal imaging has been established (other than changes due to raised ICP) arrange neuro-ophthalmological referral for lumbar puncture and perimetry. The CSF constituents are normal and lumbar CSF pressure is raised (usually >25 cmH_2O). Request FBC, ESR, autoantibody screen, syphilis serology, U&E, calcium, phosphate, and glucose (should all be normal). Disc cube OCT enables quantitative monitoring of optic disc swelling, but ganglion cell layer thickness (macular thickness with segmentation) may be more useful as an early warning of permanent loss.

Treatment

- Lumbar puncture is a useful holding move. Neurosurgical referral for immediate insertion of a lumbar drain is preferred in severe cases with impending visual loss.
- Weight loss: refer to a dietician and/or obesity specialist. Bariatric surgery is increasingly being recommended where vision is threatened.
- Cease any drug thought to have precipitated the condition.
- Acetazolamide 250 mg p.o. (usually up to a total dose of 1 g/day or sometimes 2 g/day) if not contraindicated (warn about possible side effects; sustained release preparations are more expensive but may be better tolerated). Higher doses may be required. May promote nephrolithiasis (of calcific stones). The use of other diuretics is controversial but bendroflumethiazide

(a carbonic anhydrase inhibitor) 2.5–10 mg o.d. is effective. Topiramate (50–200 mg daily in divided doses) is also prescribed because of its carbonic anhydrase inhibitor activity and it may also help in coexisting migraine.

- Where vision is threatened despite medical management consider a CSF diversion procedure (lumboperitoneal or ventriculoperitoneal shunt). In cases where there is transverse dural sinus stenosis, and a pressure gradient can be demonstrated across the narrowing on angiographic manometry, venous sinus stenting may be indicated. These procedures should be rarely recommended to treat headache alone where there is no risk to vision, unless there is no evidence of any cause for headache other than raised ICP. Optic nerve sheath fenestration is sometimes recommended for visual failure, but will usually not help headache.
- The use of corticosteroids is controversial.

Follow-up Once the diagnosis is confirmed, see at 2–4 weeks with repeat field test, then less often if responding. The condition usually resolves spontaneously following cessation of the drug which initiated it, or after weight loss. As it may be multifactorial, it is important to address all risk factors at the same time (e.g. weight management, iron deficiency management, sleep apnoea, etc.). Ideally, co-manage with neurology and a headache specialist.

HEADACHE AND FACIAL PAIN

Background Headache is one of the most common of all symptoms. Patients seen in eye clinics usually have headaches localised to one or both eyes, associated visual symptoms, or concern that eye-strain is causing the headaches. Headache may be a manifestation of eye disease, or systemic disease.

History Ask about the mode of onset and duration of the headache, how often it occurs, the site, and relieving or exacerbating factors. The pain itself may have a throbbing quality, be constant or paroxysmal. Associated features may include: blurred vision; double vision (binocular or monocular); field defect; scintillating scotoma; nausea; photophobia; phonophobia; autonomic symptoms such as lacrimation, nasal congestion or Horner's syndrome; scalp tenderness; jaw claudication; anisocoria; or tinnitus.

Examination Check BP (ensure the cuff pressure is high enough to occlude the radial pulse to ensure correct systolic measurement in patients with possible malignant hypertension), cranial nerves, VA, colour vision, pupils, confrontation fields, IOP, drainage angles, and fundoscopy (exclude disc swelling and retinal or subhyaloid haemorrhage). Exclude strabismus by cover/uncover and alternate cover test. Palpate the temporal arteries in those over 50 years. Check autorefraction versus focimetry. Consider full refraction and orthoptic review.

Differential diagnosis

- *Chronic daily headache*: Symptoms vary but pain is 24 hours a day and not relieved by analgesics. Analgesic overuse is common, although patients will usually report that the analgesics have no effect. May follow local trauma. Insomnia usually coexists.
- *Tension headache*: A common and benign headache that feels like a tight band across the forehead, around the head, or sometimes at the back of the head and involving the muscles in the back of the neck. A form of chronic daily headache rather than due to muscle tension.
- *Atypical facial pain*: Has similar characteristics to chronic daily headache with unremitting pain, but it is unilateral and usually localised to the cheek. Many causes of ocular and periorbital pain have identical characteristics. May be precipitated by local trauma, including eye surgery. Exclude local causes and treat as for chronic daily headache.
- *Herpes zoster ophthalmicus-associated pain*: Characteristic pain precedes the appearance of a V1 rash. Postherpetic neuralgia occurs in 10% of cases. For managements, see page 241.

- *Trigeminal neuralgia*: Must be lancinating (flashes of pain), most commonly in V3 territory, but can affect the brow or cheek. Patients are aware of triggers such as touch, cold, or chewing. Responds to carbamazepine or gabapentin. Refer to a neurologist.
- *Other neuralgic facial pain*: Damage to the sensory nerves emerging from the orbit may result in neuralgic pain, particularly with a history of trauma or surgery, with sensory disturbance in the distribution of the affected nerve. Tapping the nerve produces pain: local anaesthetic relieves it. Refer to a pain specialist.
- *Ocular causes*: Significantly raised IOP (almost always >35 mmHg) produces ache around the eye. Uncorrected refractive error usually produces ache between the eyebrows. Scleritis causes a deep boring pain which may wake the patient from sleep.
- *Giant cell arteritis*: Must be considered. See page 789.
- *Raised intracranial pressure*: Produces headache (sometimes with nausea and vomiting), often worse on waking, coughing, and bending over. A pulsatile tinnitus is often present. Look for absent spontaneous venous pulsations. Check eye movements, pupil size, and reaction. A VIth cranial nerve palsy may be a false localising sign. Full neurological examination is essential. Drowsiness and/or unilateral dilated pupil are serious signs suggesting coning and the need for urgent neurosurgical intervention to prevent death: contact a neurologist immediately.
- *Low pressure headache*: Most commonly seen following lumbar puncture, but chronic CSF leak may occur for a variety of reasons. The headache is relieved by lying flat.
- *Sinus infection*: Typically causes pyrexia, unilateral tenderness over the affected sinus (usually ethmoid), and pain worse on bending forward. Foul nasal discharge and loss of sense of taste/smell may occur with nasal obstruction. Optic neuropathy can occur with severe infection or an expanding mucocoele. Imaging (plain films are useful) shows opacification of the affected sinus, however incidental maxillary sinus disease is common. Opacification of the sphenoid sinus implies a genuine pathological process.
- *Malignant hypertension*: Produces headache ± blurred vision. Look for retinopathy (p. 579). Can cause confusion and fits.
- *Subarachnoid haemorrhage*: Causes sudden severe headache onset of severe headache 'like being hit over the head with a hammer'. Neck stiffness, decreased consciousness, or other neurological signs may be present. A diagnostic finding is subhyaloid haemorrhage. Lay the patient flat and do not allow the patient to sit up even to go to the toilet if this diagnosis is

likely. Needs immediate admission and investigation. Painful IIIrd nerve palsy with pupil involvement may indicate an expanding posterior communicating artery aneurysm and imminent rupture. Anterior communicating artery aneurysm may affect the optic nerve in a similar fashion.

- *Meningitis*: Features include photophobia, neck stiffness, possible decreased consciousness or neurological signs, and pyrexia. Purpuric or petechial rash suggests meningococcal meningitis. Test passive neck flexion looking for stiffness ± pain (but may be normal in children). If passive straight leg raise causes pain, suspect meningism (or nerve root entrapment). Meningococcal meningitis can kill within hours; if suspected, give intravenous benzylpenicillin immediately (300 mg in infants, 600 mg child 1–9 years, 1,200 mg >10 years).
- *Migraine*: In facial migraine, the pain is centred on the face, but retains the typical time course and associated autonomic features of classical migraine (see next page).
- *Cluster headache*: Features paroxysmal attacks of severe pain, red watering eye, transient or permanent postganglionic Horner's syndrome, and nasal stuffiness/rhinorrhoea. Patients pace around rather than lie still as with migraine. Usually lasts ~30 minutes, occasionally longer. Characteristically, a daily headache for several weeks, usually occurring at the same clock hour (usually at night) that then disappears for months or years. Usually affects middle-aged men, and may be precipitated by alcohol. Refer to a neurologist.
- *SUNCT syndrome*: Causes short-lasting unilateral neuralgiform headache attacks with conjunctival injection and tearing. Severe orbital, periorbital, forehead, or temple pain lasts from 5 seconds to a few minutes. Occurs from once daily to >60 times per hour. As with cluster headache, the dysautonomic features are an essential element.
- *Midfacial segment pain*: Features bilateral facial pain around the eyes, over the frontal or maxillary sinuses, or orbits. Sinus tenderness or hyperaesthesia over the sinuses may occur, as may pain on bending. Patients may complain of their eyes puffing up and nose feeling blocked, and have often had sinus surgery with no lasting relief of symptoms.

MIGRAINE

Background Migraine affects 15% of people, women more than men, with peak prevalence aged 35–45 years.

Symptoms Visual aura may be hemianopic or affect the entire visual field. A slowly enlarging scotoma with a shimmering border evolves over a period of minutes, but usually resolves completely within 30 minutes. Zig-zag lines (fortification spectra/teichopsia) are pathognomonic. Vision recovers fully within 1 hour. Headache may occur about 30 minutes after the visual aura has resolved. Headache is typically unilateral, throbbing, and associated with nausea, photophobia, and phonophobia. It is usually exacerbated by movement and therefore relieved by lying down in a dark and quiet room. Nonvisual aura (vertigo and paraesthesia), migraine without aura (common migraine), and aura without headache (acephalgic migraine) can all occur. Many patients identify a prodromal period of 1–2 days prior to the onset of the headache. Yawning is common in this period.

History Ask patients about the nature of the attack, or past history of typical migraine headache in their early twenties. This may not be present in elderly patients presenting with aura without headache. If the visual aura is always restricted to the same hemifield this may very rarely be due to an occipital lobe lesion (such as an arteriovenous malformation, AVM).

Examination Ocular examination is normal. Field tests may be abnormal during an attack. Occasionally, persistent defects are seen, usually homonymous hemianopic scotomas. A IIIrd, IVth or VIth nerve palsy (ophthalmoplegic migraine) occurs in children more frequently than adults, usually lasting for days or weeks, often following a prodrome of migrainous headache—the pathogenetic mechanism, and indeed the relationship to migraine itself, is uncertain, but the terminology persists for now. The occurrence of retinal migraine is also controversial, and such cases are most likely due to vasospasm. Perform dilated fundoscopy to exclude a retinal tear, embolus, or haemorrhage. Check BP, VA, colour vision, confrontation fields, and optic discs.

Differential diagnosis Consider other causes of transient visual loss that could be associated with positive or negative symptoms. If monocular (and therefore not migraine), this should include vasospasm, thromboembolism, narrrow-angle glaucoma, retinal tear or detachment. If binocular (hemianopic or total), then consider thromboembolism, occipital epilepsy, and occipital lobe AVM or tumour (rare).

Investigations Not required unless atypical. Acephalgic migraine in older patients is not equivalent to a transient ischaemic attack and does not require referral.

Treatment Reassure the patient. Advise to stop driving during an attack. Paracetamol or aspirin (more effective in acute migraine), and an antiemetic relieve headache and nausea if taken early. Avoid precipitating factors such as red wine or cheese if any can be identified.

Follow-up Refer to the GP or a neurologist, particularly if the headache is disabling and frequent (more than twice per month), needing prophylactic treatment to prevent headache (e.g. propranolol, pizotifen, or amitriptyline), or atypical features are present requiring investigation. Specific antimigraine agents are available for acute attacks but are best prescribed in neurology or general practice.

NON-ARTERITIC ANTERIOR ISCHAEMIC OPTIC NEUROPATHY

Background Anterior ischaemic optic neuropathy (AION) is caused by infarction of the optic nerve head. It may be non-arteritic (described below), or arteritic (giant cell arteritis, GCA, see next section).

AION risk is increased if male, systemic arteriopathy, aged 40–60 years, or disc vessel crowding (disc without a cup, small hypermetropic discs and disc drusen). Occasionally precipitated by severe hypovolaemia or anaemia, e.g. cardiac surgery, spinal surgery. Excluding an arteritic cause is key but GCA is rare under 65 years; other types of vasculitis may occur in younger age groups but this and thrombophilia are rare causes of AION.

Symptoms Typically sudden, painless, non-progressive partial monocular vision loss. Sometimes asymptomatic.

Signs Optic disc swelling that may be sectoral, with flame haemorrhages and occasionally a macular star. Long-standing cases show sectoral disc atrophy corresponding to the field defect.

History and examination Ask about the speed of visual loss and any recovery. Importantly, exclude symptoms of GCA (p. 789). Record: refractive error; VA (typically 6/12–6/60); Ishihara plates (reduced); RAPD (expected); confrontation fields (typically, unilateral altitudinal visual field defect); and dilated peripheral fundoscopy (exclude peripheral haemorrhage, vitritis and periphlebitis). Draw or photograph the optic disc. Confirm pulsatile, nontender, temporal arteries, full eye movements, and no lid-lag or proptosis.

Differential diagnosis Similar to GCA (p. 789). Consider posterior ischaemic optic neuropathy following face-down spinal surgery, radiotherapy, and hypotension/hypovolaemia/haemodialysis. This produces no disc swelling, is often bilateral, with worse VA, and a poor prognosis. There is no proven treatment.

Investigations Check visual field, BP; fasting blood glucose or HbA1c; lipids; FBC; ESR and CRP (mandatory in over 50s) ± temporal artery ultrasound or biopsy (**Box 15.1**, p. 590). If disc drusen are suspected, consider ultrasound or disc imaging for autofluorescence (**Fig. 15.19**, p. 777).

Treatment

- *Casualty*: Review all vascular risk factors. Exclude GCA and if in doubt discuss with a senior colleague. Request review at 6 weeks.
- *Clinic*: Recheck clinical findings, particularly fields. Early stepwise progression occurs but is unusual. Neuroimaging is not required unless findings are atypical. Expect three lines of VA improvement in 30%. The affected eye has a higher risk or recurrence within the first few weeks while disc swelling persists, but AION is unlikely (5%) to recur after nerve fibre atrophy relieves disc vessel congestion. Studies suggest a 15–50% risk of fellow eye involvement. Review in 6 months then discharge if stable.

GIANT CELL ARTERITIS (TEMPORAL ARTERITIS)

Background Occlusive arterial inflammation causes optic disc ischaemia and sudden, usually total, unilateral visual loss. It is an ophthalmic emergency, as the second eye may develop irreversible visual loss within hours. Patients are usually elderly. Associated with polymyalgia rheumatica.

Symptoms These include new headache, scalp tenderness, loss of appetite, weight loss, limb girdle pain (worse in the morning, relieved by movement), and ischaemic jaw pain on chewing. Prodromal episodic transient visual loss, often on standing due to poor perfusion, occurs in 10%. Ophthalmoplegia may occur with transient diplopia in ~6%.

Signs Common features include thickened temporal arteries which may be nonpulsatile and tender, RAPD, and pale disc swelling ± flame haemorrhages. VA is usually count fingers or worse. Central retinal artery occlusion and retinal cotton-wool spots may occur. Optic nerve ischaemia may be retrobulbar, in which case the RAPD is the only acute sign. Choroidal hypoperfusion may also be present.

History and examination Ask about polymyalgia rheumatica (particularly stiffness of shoulders on waking) and steroid contraindications or recent withdrawal. Record: temporal artery findings; VA; Ishihara plates; confrontation fields; eye movements; proptosis; RAPD; dilated fundoscopy; disc appearance; and any vitritis. Measure BP and BM before starting steroids. Palpate superficial temporal, facial and occipital arteries. An involved artery may be thickened and pulseless.

Differential diagnosis Disc infarction is sectoral in non-arteritic anterior ischaemic optic neuropathy (AION, previous section), but total in giant cell arteritis (GCA). Disc infarction makes the diagnosis of GCA relatively easy, but it can be more difficult in those presenting with headache only, ophthalmoplegia, postural transient monocular visual loss, posterior nerve ischaemia (no disc swelling) or choroidal ischaemia.

Investigations ESR > 47 and CRP > 25 = 97% probability of GCA if the clinical features fit. Normal ESR is ≤ age/2 in men; (age +10)/2 in women. Thrombocythaemia is common. Numerous other causes of raised ESR include infections that may worsen with steroids. Arrange temporal artery ultrasound or biopsy (see **Box 15.1**) if available, but do not delay treatment. Choroidal hypoperfusion on fluorescein angiography suggests GCA. Duplex ultrasound of the superficial cranial vessels is an increasingly available alternative to biopsy, but is negative soon after starting corticosteroids.

Treatment Give stat methylprednisolone 1 g in 500 mL normal saline over 30 minutes, and oral ranitidine 150 mg b.d. Substitute oral prednisolone 1 mg/kg body weight if arranging intravenous (i.v.) treatment will cause delay. Admit if elderly or cardiac disease. Expect a dramatic improvement in systemic symptoms within 24 hours. Continue i.v. steroids for 3 days then switch to oral prednisolone 100 mg daily. Osteoporosis prophylaxis is mandatory as treatment will be required for many months. For this and other aspects of long-term steroid use, see page 413. In 2018, the National Institute for Health and Care Excellence (NICE) recommended co-management with rheumatology, and tocilizumab for steroid-resistant and relapsing GCA. Aortitis is a potentially very serious feature of GCA (dissection can occur)

Box 15.1: Temporal artery biopsy (See Fig. 15.20)

May be positive after months of steroids, but aim to do within a week. If negative it does not exclude GCA, as skip lesions occur.

1. Consent:

   Benefit: Confirms diagnosis in ~35%.

   Risk: Bleeding, infection and scar. Scalp necrosis is very rare. Repeat biopsy is sometimes required. Damage to the facial nerve is theoretically possible but very rare. Stroke has been reported but is extremely rare.

2. Mark tender areas of the artery to biopsy, with a surgical pen. If not obvious, mark the frontal branch.
3. Infiltrate with lidocaine 2% with adrenaline (≤10 mL).
4. Open skin with a No. 15 blade directly over the artery. Control bleeding with cautery.
5. Blunt dissect with blunt-nosed scissors, down to temporal fascia.
6. Identify and bluntly dissect around the artery. Before removing, tie two pairs of 4/0 Vicryl suture around either end, at least 3 cm apart. Avoid crush artefact. Ensure haemostasis.
7. Close with Vicryl (4/0 subcutaneous tissues; 7/0 skin). Let skin sutures dissolve or remove at 1 week.
8. Apply a compression bandage for 24 hours. Avoid excessive compression over the auricular cartilage (risk of ischaemia).

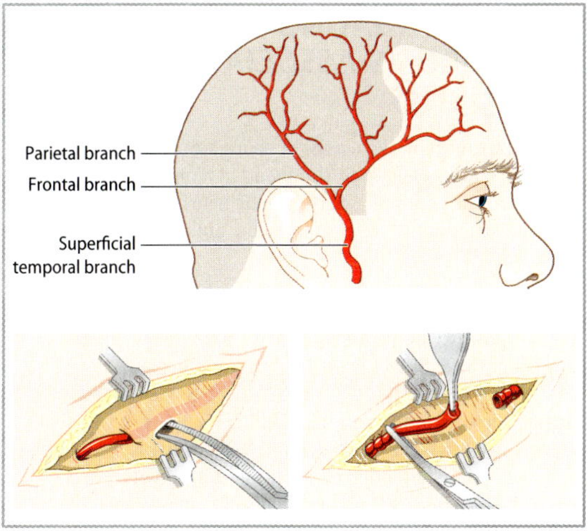

Fig. 15.20: Temporal artery anatomy and biopsy.

and should be excluded with MRI, CT or positron emission tomography (PET) chest scan.

Follow-up Review at 1 week then monthly with repeat ESR. Taper steroids only when the patient is asymptomatic and the ESR has fallen substantially. Patients are usually under joint care with a rheumatologist.

DEMYELINATING (MULTIPLE SCLEROSIS-ASSOCIATED) OPTIC NEURITIS

Background Typically occurs in young women (average age of 31 years) who spent their childhood in temperate latitudes. Associated with multiple sclerosis optic neuritis (MS-ON). One of the most common causes of subacute unilateral visual loss in young adults.

Symptoms Headache and/or pain on eye movements (92%) then progressive, uniocular loss of vision over days. Photopsia may occur (brief flashes provoked by eye movement).

Signs These include optic disc swelling (50%) or retrobulbar neuritis, reduced Ishihara plates and VA (≤6/60 in 35%), diffuse field loss in 48% (although classically a central scotoma) and uveitis in 3%. An RAPD is always present, unless bilateral.

History and examination Ask about symptoms of demyelination: episodes of paraesthesia or sensory loss; transient weakness with onset over days and resolution over weeks; bladder dysfunction; vertigo; diplopia; Lhermitte's symptom (electric sensation down the spine and into the limbs on neck flexion), and Uhthoff's symptom (see below). Record: BP; cranial nerves; saccades; cerebellar signs; proptosis; VA; Ishihara plates; confrontation fields; ocular inflammation and dilated fundoscopy.

Differential diagnosis Question the diagnosis if any of the following are present: age >60 years or born and raised in tropical latitudes; severe pain interrupting sleep; very rapid and severe visual loss (<48 hours, worse than CF vision); simultaneous bilateral involvement; pain >2 weeks; optic disc haemorrhage; family history of Leber's hereditary optic neuropathy (LHON); and known sarcoidosis, collagen vascular disease or cancer. Consider the following alternatives:

- *Orbital*: thyroid eye disease (not usually painful) and myositis (painful but causes ophthalmoplegia; visual loss is rare). Any other orbital inflammatory disorder involving the optic nerve (perineuritis).
- *Ocular*: posterior uveitis, neuroretinitis, central serous chorioretinopathy, and scleritis.
- *Optic neuropathy*: compressive (optic nerve, orbital, or intracranial tumours are rarely painful); paranasal mucocoele (usually painful and subacute onset; may closely mimic MS-ON); inflammatory (sarcoid, autoimmune disease); ischaemic

(arteritic or non-arteritic: do not usually produce retro-orbital pain); nutritional (B_{12}, folate, alcohol—always bilateral and symmetrical); hereditary (LHON); and infective causes (uveitis will be present; syphilis; viral; e.g. herpes zoster; and fungal, e.g. *Cryptococcus*).

- *Systemic disease*: severe hypertension, raised intracranial pressure (occasionally causes unilateral disc swelling), acute disseminated encephalomyelitis, and neuromyelitis optica spectrum disease (NMOSD), when bilateral visual loss and involvement of intracranial optic nerve including chiasmitis are more common.

Investigations If the clinical picture is typical of MS-ON and if spontaneous recovery has occurred, no investigations are necessary. Refer the patient to a neurologist for discussion. Investigate all atypical cases: In the acute-phase MRI, short tau inversion recovery (STIR) orbital sequences show high signal/swelling of the optic nerve. T_1 orbital scan with fat suppression shows gadolinium enhancement of the optic nerve. In the chronic phase, there is no enhancement but a high T_2 signal. Also in the chronic phase, with good recovery of acuity, the typical visually evoked potential (VEP) finding is a substantial delay with preserved amplitude; this is unusual in any other cause of optic neuropathy. Consider: FBC, syphilis serology, sACE, ANA, ESR, antineutrophil cytoplasmic antibodies (ANCA), B_{12}, folate, CXR, and lumbar puncture. Exclude vitamin D deficiency as this is a risk factor for MS. Cases not associated with MS may have antibodies to aquaporin-4 or myelin oligodendrocyte glycoprotein. The risk of conversion from a demyelinating Clinically Isolated Syndrome (CIS) to MS can be stratified with brain MRI (**Box 15.2**).

Treatment

- *Casualty*: Refer to clinic within 1 week. Offer analgesia but if pain is severe (e.g. through the night) reconsider the diagnosis.
- *Clinic*: Expect 93% to improve by 5 weeks; 70% recover near-normal vision, but this may take 1 year. May recur (19% at 5 years), or affect the other eye within months (17%).

A short course of high-dose methylprednisolone 500 mg o.d. for 5 days speeds recovery in acute MS-ON but does not alter the eventual outcome. Episodes are typically treated if the initial VA loss is marked (e.g. worse than 6/60). MS is defined by the appearance of T_2 lesions on MRI which are disseminated in both time (new lesions on follow-up) and space (at least 2–4 characteristic locations in brain and spinal cord). Evidence is building that immunomodulatory disease-modifying therapies

Box 15.2: Optic Neuritis Treatment Trial

- Intravenous (i.v.) methylprednisolone 1 g daily for 3 days hastened visual recovery and reduced the risk of a second, MS-defining relapse at 2, but not 5 years. Alternatively, consider 1,250 mg methylprednisolone o.d. p.o for 3 days.
- Neither oral nor i.v. treatment offered any long-term visual benefit.
- Some inflammatory optic neuropathies (e.g. sarcoid and autoimmune disorders, neuromyelitis optica spectrum disease) may require steroids to prevent severe visual loss, and patients may be dependent on steroids or other immunosuppression to avoid relapses. The conclusions of the ONTT (Optic Neuritis Treatment Trial) do not apply to such patients.
- 72% of patients with abnormal baseline MRIs developed clinical definite MS after 15 years versus 25% with normal baseline MRIs.

(DMT) reduce the rate and severity of relapses by reducing disease activity.

In children, bilateral optic neuritis may follow viral infection or immunisations. The risk of MS is low. Treat with i.v. methylprednisolone 15 mg/kg for 3 days if there is significant vision loss.

Follow-up Most patients with optic neuritis require MRI and specialist neurology review. The DMT fingolimod occasionally causes macular oedema so request baseline VA by the prescribing neurologist, then ophthalmic screening at 3–4 months, as detailed on page 619.

Other ocular features of multiple sclerosis

- *Uhthoff's phenomenon*: transiently decreased vision with exertion or in hot conditions.
- *Intermediate uveitis*: sheathing of retinal venules, peripheral snowbanks and snowballs may be seen on dilated fundoscopy.
- *Cranial nerve palsy*: commonly VIth, but any may be affected.
- *Internuclear ophthalmoplegia*: the ipsilateral eye fails to adduct or adducts slowly, while the contralateral eye has horizontal nystagmus on abduction.
- *Wall-eyed bilateral internuclear ophthalmoplegia (WEBINO)*: both eyes have no adduction. Prisms or surgery may reduce diplopia.
- *One-and-a-half syndrome*: one eye has no voluntary horizontal movements and the other can only abduct. If supranuclear,

the palsy is overcome by dolls-head movements. Other supranuclear gaze palsies may occur.

- *Cerebellar disease*: broken (saccadic) pursuit, dysmetric saccades and gaze-evoked nystagmus are common.
- *Acquired pendular nystagmus*: associated with reduced acuity; the amplitude may differ greatly in the two eyes.

TRAUMATIC OPTIC NEUROPATHY

Background Caused by direct head, face, or orbital trauma. Rarely surgically induced. May be unilateral or bilateral. So-called 'indirect' injury to the optic nerve occurs following a blow to the brow which can be relatively minor with no other injuries, no fractures, and no loss of consciousness.

Symptoms Sudden loss of vision at the time of injury. May progress initially as soft-tissue swelling compresses the nerve or if there is a haematoma.

Signs RAPD, VA decreased (6/6 to NPL), variable field loss, and decreased colour vision. The optic nerve may initially appear swollen or avulsed but is usually normal, with later atrophy.

Examination Record Glasgow Coma scale and ensure extraocular injuries are treated. Exclude eyelid, orbital, anterior and posterior segment injuries (pp. 66, 127, 237 and 661 respectively). Check VA, RAPD, Ishihara colour vision, confrontation fields, eye movements, IOP, and dilated fundoscopy, noting disc, or retinal abnormalities. Generally avoid dilating patients requiring neuro-observation, but balance with the risk of missing posterior segment injury (consider dilating only the eye with suspected injury).

Differential diagnosis Consider occipital infarct, vitreous haemorrhage, retinal detachment, retinal commotio, globe rupture, traumatic cataract and lens dislocation.

Investigations Arrange an urgent CT scan of the brain and orbits looking for a displaced orbital fracture, and orbital or intracranial haemorrhage, particularly if the patient has a decreased Glasgow coma scale. Liaise with other specialties as required. Arrange field testing if general health permits.

Treatment About 30% improve spontaneously. High-dose steroids have been advocated but there is no evidence that they influence the outcome. Consider immediate lateral cantholysis if the orbit is tense and retrobulbar haemorrhage is suspected. Surgical decompression is rarely indicated unless there is evidence of optic nerve compression by a haematoma or bone fragment.

Follow-up Review with regular field tests for the first year. Check eligibility drive (p. 825).

COMPRESSIVE, INFILTRATIVE AND INFLAMMATORY OPTIC NEUROPATHY

Background A wide range of orbital and systemic conditions may rarely involve the optic nerve.

Symptoms Visual loss over hours to weeks, severe periocular pain, pain on eye movements, or headache may occur. May be unilateral or bilateral. Compressive lesions usually cause gradual, painless, monocular loss of visual field or VA that may go unnoticed for months.

Signs Findings include reduced VA and colour vision, RAPD (if unilateral or asymmetric), visual field loss, optic nerve swelling, or atrophy (or both—Foster–Kennedy's syndrome). Examination may be normal.

History and examination Record the duration of symptoms and speed of visual loss. Ask about any obscurations on sustained eccentric gaze. Take a complete history and systems review. Look for typical features of demyelinating optic neuropathy (p. 792). Record VA, Ishihara colour vision, RAPD, IOP, eye movements, and dilated fundus examination. Exclude vitritis and thyroid eye disease. Check orbital signs, cranial nerves, and confrontation visual fields. Look for optic disc venous collaterals suggesting optic nerve sheath meningioma. Physician review is advisable.

Differential diagnosis Consider neoplasm (leukaemia, lymphoma and secondaries); syphilis; sarcoid; TB; autoimmune disease; collagen vascular disease; vasculitides; sinus disease/mucocoele; HIV; thyroid eye disease; pituitary tumour; craniopharyngioma; fibrous dysplasia; Paget's disease; sphenoid wing meningioma; frontal lobe tumour; optic nerve glioma or meningioma; nasopharyngeal carcinoma; ophthalmic or carotid artery aneurysm; and other optic neuropathies (demyelinating, traumatic, nutritional, toxic and radiation).

Investigations Initially request FBC and film, ESR, CRP, U&E, LFT, glucose, ANA, sACE, *Treponema pallidum* haemagglutination assay (TPHA), antineutrophil cytoplasmic antibody (ANCA), protein electrophoresis, CXR, MRI of brain and orbits, and formal perimetry (Goldmann or Humphrey). Consider Mantoux and HIV testing if the history is suggestive, and Lyme serology in endemic areas. Consider lumbar puncture.

Treatment This should not usually be started until a diagnosis is established, but if an inflammatory cause is suspected do not delay treatment beyond a few days. Consider admission for investigation. Discuss systemic steroids with a neuro-ophthalmologist in severe or rapidly progressive cases, but beware of TB.

- *Casualty*: If visual loss is progressing rapidly, arrange admission for investigations; otherwise, arrange an early clinic appointment.
- *Clinic*: Review results of imaging. Treatment depends on the diagnosis. If a suprasellar tumour is present, involve an endocrinologist.

Follow-up Long-term management of the underlying aetiology by a neuro-ophthalmologist and appropriate multidisciplinary team is usually required.

NUTRITIONAL AND TOXIC OPTIC NEUROPATHY

Background In developed nations, this condition typically affects male alcoholic smokers, but also those with poor diet, B_{12} deficiency, or on certain drugs, e.g. ethambutol and isoniazid.

Symptoms Painless, bilateral, central scotoma or reduced vision occurring over days to weeks.

Signs Sluggish pupil reactions (but usually no RAPD because eyes are affected equally), decreased colour vision and VA, and field defects. Optic discs usually appear normal, but are occasionally mildly swollen and may appear atrophic later.

History and examination Ask about alcohol intake, smoking, methanol abuse, dietary intake (vegan?), medications, any overdoses (quinine), pernicious anaemia, stomach resection or other causes of malabsorption. Record VA, Ishihara colour vision, confrontation visual fields, and dilated fundal appearance. Exclude proptosis and dysmotility.

Differential diagnosis Consider other optic neuropathies (compressive, demyelinating, traumatic, infiltrative, inflammatory and radiation) and quinine overdose.

Investigations Arrange an MRI scan to exclude a compressive lesion. Check serum B_{12}, folate, syphilis serology, FBC and film, and LFTs to detect undeclared alcohol abuse. Investigate for infiltrative, inflammatory, or inherited optic neuropathy if indicated. Request Humphrey 24-2 visual field test (colour perimetry may reveal larger central scotomas).

Treatment

- *Casualty*: Advise to stop smoking and drinking alcohol and improve diet, if appropriate, and offer referral to alcohol or smokers' support services. Prescribe multivitamins. Refer to neuro-ophthalmology clinic within 1 month.
- *Clinic*: Confirm the diagnosis, check results, and repeat VA, colour vision, visual fields, and dilated fundoscopy. In tobacco amblyopia or if B_{12} deficient use intramuscular hydroxocobalamin 1 mg daily for 2 weeks, then 1 mg twice weekly until no further improvement, then 1 mg every 2 months for 6 months. Do not use cyanocobalamin.

Follow-up Review initially in a few weeks to confirm the diagnosis then 3–6 monthly. A slow recovery is expected if smoking stops. The role of vitamins is uncertain but advisable.

HEREDITARY OPTIC NEUROPATHY

Background Mitochondrial diseases caused by mutations in mitochondrial DNA (mtDNA) or nuclear DNA (nDNA) encoding mitochondrial proteins are one of the most common causes of clinically heterogeneous inherited neurological disorders, where optic atrophy is the major neuro-ophthalmic feature. Hereditary optic neuropathies are an important cause of blindness in both paediatric and adult populations, with an estimated prevalence of 1 in 10,000 in the UK. They can present as isolated optic neuropathy or be accompanied by systemic abnormalities ('plus' phenotype).

The two classical inherited optic neuropathies are Leber's hereditary optic neuropathy (LHON), caused by a number of specific mtDNA variants, and autosomal dominant optic atrophy, which in the majority of patients is due to pathogenic mutations within the nuclear gene *OPA1*.

Examine carefully for other manifestations of mitochondrial disease, especially retinopathy (p. 598) and progressive external ophthalmoplegia (p. 816).

Clinical features

- *OPA1-associated dominant optic atrophy (OPA1-DOA)*: The most common inherited optic neuropathy with UK prevalence ~1 in 25,000. Has an insidious childhood onset with subnormal vision often detected during preschool screening or due to difficulty following classes. Features bilateral and symmetrical visual loss, central/caecocentral field defects, and impaired colour vision. Characteristically, it has incomplete penetrance, giving variable severity, from subclinical carriers to severely affected individuals, even within the same family.
- *Leber's hereditary optic neuropathy*: The most common primary mtDNA genetic disorder, with Northern Europe prevalence ~1 in 40,000. Affects any age, but typically those 15–35 years. The lifetime risk of visual loss is 50% among males carriers versus 10% for females. Typically presents with rapidly progressive, uniocular, painless, severe (worse than 6/60) central vision loss with dense central or caecocentral scotoma, followed by stabilised vison loss. Fellow eye involvement occurs within 3 months. The optic disc usually has a hyperaemic appearance with peripapillary retinal nerve fibre layer swelling and telangiectatic microangiopathy, but in about 20% can appear normal. The central retinal vessels look tortuous, but there is no vascular or optic disc leakage on fluorescein angiography. There is rapid retinal ganglion cell axonal loss starting within the papillomacular bundle, which results in temporal atrophy of the optic nerve head.

More diffuse pallor and progressive cupping can occur later in some cases. The majority of patients are legally blind. Spontaneous visual recovery, which is invariably incomplete, can sometimes occur, normally in the first year following disease onset. The likelihood of a clinically significant vision improvement depends on the primary mtDNA mutation, with reported rates of 4–25% for the m.11778G>A mutation, 15–25% for the m.3460G>A, and 37–58% for m.14484T>C, the latter carrying the best prognosis. A number of LHON-like phenotypes caused by nDNA pathogenic biallelic variants (autosomal recessive) are reported.

- *Wolfram's syndrome*: A rare autosomal recessive inherited progressive neurodegenerative disease historically known as DIDMOAD (diabetes insipidus, diabetes mellitus, optic atrophy, and sensorineural deafness) with a UK prevalence of ~1 in 7,70,000. There are two types: the most common is caused by *WFS1* variants, the rarer type by *CISD2* variants. Importantly, variants in *WFS1* may lead to autosomal recessive or autosomal dominant disease. The later has a pathognomonic lamination of the outer plexiform layer on OCT, featuring an innermost highly-reflective lamina, non-reflective cleft-like middle lamina and outermost highly-reflective lamina resembling Henle's fibre layer.

Differential diagnosis Consider other causes of bilateral symmetrical optic neuropathy (mostly nutritional or toxic). It is very unlikely for bilateral central scotomas to be compressive in aetiology. MS and normal tension glaucoma may cause progressive bilateral optic atrophy, but they tend not to show the initial temporal predilection and have more variable visual field defect patterns.

Draw the family pedigree and establish the inheritance pattern (p.494).

Investigations Request macula and optic nerve OCT; widefield photography, e.g. Optos; visual electrophysiology including full field electroretinogram (some cases have outer retinal involvement); and brain and orbit MRI. Consider investigating other causes of optic neuropathy if in any doubt about the diagnosis.

Request genetic testing. Reaching a confirmed molecular diagnosis can be challenging as pathogenic variants have been identified in both mtDNA and nDNA, with maternal, autosomal dominant, recessive, and X-linked inheritance observed. There are a limited but expanding number of testable genes. If LHON is suspected, request the three most common variants as ~90% of LHON carriers have one of three mtDNA point mutations (m.3460G>A, m.11778G>A and m.14484T>C). If results are negative, request whole mtDNA sequencing, as there are rare mtDNA variants known to cause LHON. If results still remain negative, request optic atrophy panel/whole exome sequencing or whole genome sequencing. Genetic testing fails to identify pathogenic variants in roughly 50% of cases.

Management Establishing a molecular diagnosis allows a better prediction of visual outcomes, and may prompt screening of extraocular features. Consider:

- *Lifestyle management*: Advise on quitting smoking and avoid high alcohol consumption.
- *Arrange genetic counselling*: This can calculate the risk of passing the condition to children, enable prenatal diagnostics and selective *in vitro* fertilisation.
- Refer for mitochondrial replacement therapy (for known pathogenic mtDNA variants only).
- Sight-impaired registration
- Low-vision aid clinic
- Neurologist/mitochondrial specialist referral for muscle biopsy for further mitochondrial disease confirmation, if other neurological features are present.
- *Limited pharmacological treatments for the mitochondrial optic neuropathies:* Idebenone, a synthetic hydrosoluble analogue of CoQ10, is the only treatment approved by the European Medicines Agency for LHON. In the UK, idebenone is approved and funded in Northern Ireland, Scotland, and Wales, but not England. Idebenone appears to be efficacious in improving visual function or stabilising vision in individuals with LHON up to 5 years from onset. Benefit was demonstrated in a LHON gene therapy trial, with several genetic therapies under development for DOA.

Follow-up Annual review once the diagnosis is established.

RADIATION OPTIC NEUROPATHY

Background Radiation to the anterior visual pathways can cause an optic neuropathy months or years after the treatment, but usually within 1–3 years. It is bilateral in 75% of patients. The cumulative radiation dose is usually >2,400 cGy with 75% receiving >5,000 cGy. Chemotherapy and diabetes increase the risk. The mechanism is likely to be microvascular. An optic neuropathy might also occur secondary to extensive inflammation and tumour necrosis following the radiation. In such cases, the onset is usually within a few weeks of commencing the radiotherapy.

Clinical features Rapid, progressive, painless and visual loss that stabilises after a few months (<6/60 in 85%, 45% become no perception of light NPL). There is decreased colour vision, field loss, and a RAPD. The disc is initially normal, then becomes atrophic. If the eye has been irradiated, cataracts and radiation retinopathy that mimics diabetic retinopathy, are typical, and disc swelling may occur.

Differential diagnosis Consider recurrence of the primary disease, radiation-induced malignancy, raised intracranial pressure, venous sinus thrombosis, postchiasmal radiation damage, and other optic neuropathies (compressive, demyelinating, traumatic, infiltrative, inflammatory and nutritional).

Investigations T_1- and T_2-weighted MRI is normal, but optic nerves enhance with contrast for the first few weeks. Arrange a Humphrey 24–2 field test.

Treatment
- *Casualty*: Refer to clinic within 1 month.
- *Clinic*: Arrange imaging and exclude other diagnoses. Arrange low-vision aids, and certificate of visual impairment as appropriate. There is no proven treatment although high dose-steroids in the acute stage, hyperbaric oxygen therapy and Avastin injections are sometimes used.

Follow-up Review every 2–3 months until the vision stabilises, then annually.

OPTIC NERVE TUMOURS

Background Optic nerve glioma typically develops early in life and 90% are diagnosed by the age of 20 years. Optic nerve sheath meningioma is unilateral in 95% with a peak incidence in the third to sixth decades and a 4:1 female preponderance. Rarely, malignant glioma causes visual loss over several weeks in adults.

Symptoms Gradual painless loss of vision often described as fogging or dimming. Gaze-evoked amaurosis occurs with optic nerve sheath meningiomas. Sudden visual loss occurs rarely when the tumour bleeds into itself. Children may present with strabismus.

Signs Features include loss of colour vision and VA, any type of visual field loss, disc swelling, optic atrophy or optic disc venous collateral vessels, particularly with meningiomas. Proptosis and limitation of eye movements may occur from a splinting effect of a large tumour. Tumours may compress the eye and induce choroidal folds and hyperopia. Signs are usually unilateral, rarely bilateral, but glioma of the chiasm causes bilateral signs. Malignant glioma may present with a retinal vein occlusion progressing to a retinal artery occlusion.

History and examination Record the duration and progression of symptoms, VA, colour vision, confrontation visual fields, RAPD, eye movements, measure proptosis, dilate and examine the optic discs and fundi. Exclude vitritis.

Differential diagnosis Consider optic neuropathy (traumatic, compressive, demyelinating, infiltrative, inflammatory, radiation, nutritional and toxic) and normal pressure glaucoma.

Investigations Arrange Humphrey 24–2 field test and imaging:

- *Glioma*: CT or MRI shows enlargement (classically fusiform) of the nerve with minimal contrast enhancement (**Fig. 15.21**).
- *Meningioma*: Fat suppression T_1 weighted MRI characteristically shows bright enhancement with gadolinium (**Fig. 15.22**). CT may show calcification. Diffuse optic nerve thickening of the optic nerve/sheath complex is typical with a 'tram-track' sign of enlarged nerve sheath demonstrated either as calcification on CT or gadolinium enhancement on MRI.

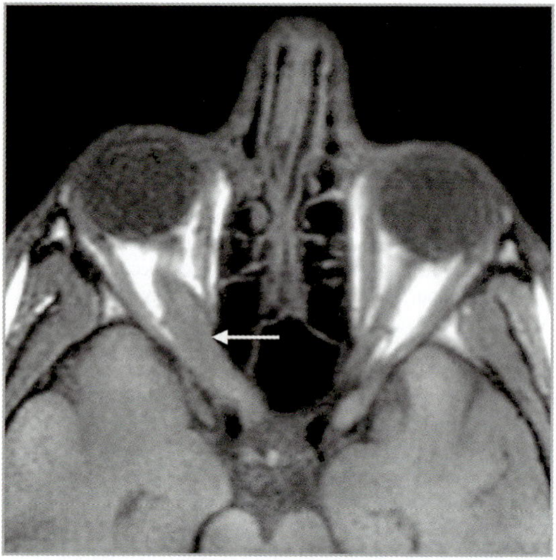

Fig. 15.21: Right optic nerve glioma (T_1 weighted MRI).

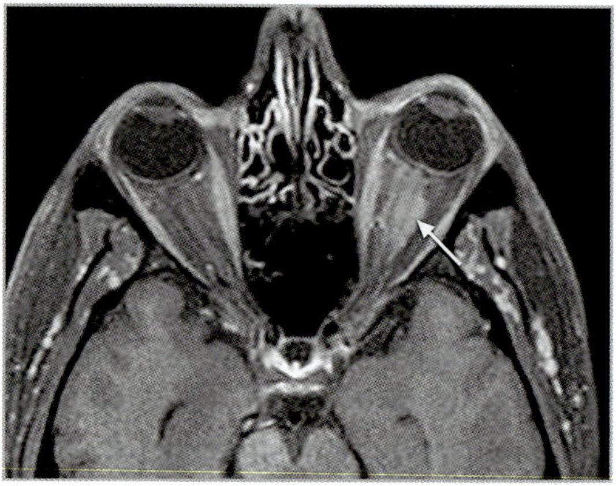

Fig. 15.22: Left optic nerve meningioma (Gadolinium-enhanced, fat-suppression T_1 weighted MRI).

Treatment

- *Casualty*: if available, order a contrast enhanced MRI or high-resolution orbital CT scan and arrange neuro-ophthalmic follow-up in 4–6 weeks.
- *Clinic*:
  1. *Glioma:*
     a. Children generally follow a benign course so observe, but exclude neurofibromatosis type 1 (29% have NF-1). Tumours are usually only treated if there is hypothalamic involvement or progressive visual loss. Avoid radiotherapy as chemotherapy is much safer. Surgical excision is usually reserved for blind eyes with unacceptable proptosis.
     b. Adult gliomas may be highly aggressive, often presenting with bilateral simultaneous visual loss from chiasmal involvement. There may be pain, and most die within 12 months despite treatment.
  2. *Meningioma*: Treat with stereotactic fractionated conformal radiotherapy in selected cases, which should stabilise or improve vision. Surgery may be required if intracranial extension threatens vision from the other eye.

Follow-up Lifelong annual review is required in case of progression, which may necessitate treatment.

CEREBROVASCULAR DISEASE

Background Disease of the carotid artery can cause monocular visual symptoms. Vertebrobasilar thromboembolism can result in recurrent episodes of bilateral, simultaneous and transient visual loss. Occlusion may be due to cardiac emboli and typically affects elderly arteriopaths.

History Record the duration of visual loss and speed of onset. Ask about scintillations, zig-zags (migraine), coloured circles (occipital epilepsy), hemianopia, haloes and postural hypotension. Assess cardiovascular risk factors including smoking and diabetes.

Examination Record VA, Ishihara colour vision, confrontation visual fields, RAPD, dilate and check fundus for emboli, disc swelling, and hypertensive changes. Listen for a heart murmur, carotid bruit, and examine the peripheral pulse rate and rhythm, BP lying and standing and in both arms, cranial nerves, and cerebellar function.

Clinical features Consider the following manifestations of cerebrovascular disease and whether urgent onward referral is required.

- *Carotid territory*:
  1. *Transient monocular visual loss*: See page 765.
  2. *Ocular ischaemic syndrome*: See page 583.
  3. *Carotid dissection*: There may be a history of trauma which may be minor. Features include pain in the neck, jaw or throbbing headache, ipsilateral Horner's syndrome (32%), transient visual loss, transient ischaemic attacks (TIAs) (30%), or embolic cerebrovascular accidents (CVAs) (46%). Arrange axial MRI of the neck ± MR or CT angiography. Anticoagulate for 3 months. Associated with Ehlers–Danlos and Marfan's syndromes, pseudoxanthoma elasticum, and medial cystic necrosis.
  4. *Takayasu's disease*: A rare vasculitis which affects large vessels such as the aorta and carotids. May present to eye clinics with ocular ischaemic syndrome.
  5. *Moya Moya*: If carotid occlusion occurs early in life (radiotherapy and idiopathic) collateral vessels develop and ischaemic complications of the abnormal vasculature develop in later life.
  6. *Giant internal carotid aneurysm*: If supraclinoid may cause retro-orbital pain and compressive optic neuropathy; if in the cavernous sinus may affect the IIIrd, IVth, Vth (V1 and V2) and VIth nerves. Rupture is rare and as the aneurysms are extradural rupture is less likely to be fatal than an

intradural berry aneurysm. May require endovascular embolisation if visual loss progresses.

7. *Carotid cavernous fistula*: See page 811.
8. *Vasculitis*: See page 789.

- *Vertebrobasilar territory*:
  1. *Occipital stroke*: Produces a congruous homonymous hemianopia of sudden onset, often with macular sparing. Usually, ischaemic rather than haemorrhagic. Bilateral lesions from 'top of the basilar' artery occlusion result in cortical blindness.
  2. *Anton's syndrome*: Patients with bilateral cortical blindness and damage to the visual association areas may deny blindness and claim to see normally. Extrastriate strokes may produce selective disorders of submodalities of vision such as colour (cerebral achromatopsia), spatial vision (visual disorientation or Balint's syndrome), or face recognition (prosopagnosia).
  3. *Vertebrobasilar dissection*: Features include bilateral transient visual obscurations lasting 1–5 minutes, transient vertigo, hearing abnormalities, dysarthria, diplopia, unilateral limb numbness or weakness, perioral numbness or tingling, reduced coordination and gait instability and sudden loss of consciousness. Eye examination is usually normal, but may have abnormal eye movements, nystagmus, and other cerebellar or brainstem signs during an episode. Patients with marked stenosis of the vertebrobasilar circulation and inadequate circle of Willis may precipitate symptoms by postural changes. Imaging confirmation may be problematic. Anticoagulation is advised.
  4. *Basilar artery thrombosis*: May begin with focal brainstem signs, then lead to death. Refer urgently.
  5. *Transient homonymous hemianopia*: May be considered a type of TIA caused by emboli, usually lasting a few minutes, but may last several hours. Consider migraine as an alternative explanation. Patients often report that loss of vision was monocular in the eye with the temporal field loss.
  6. *Transient binocular visual loss*: Consider basilar artery embolism or a drop in perfusion, e.g. postural hypotension, presyncope or heart block.
- *Dural sinus thrombosis*:
  1. Intracranial venous hypertension produces a pseudotumor cerebri syndrome involving headache of subacute onset, papilloedema, and visual obscurations. Extension of the thrombus to cortical veins may give rise to venous infarction and consequent focal signs.

Differential diagnosis For causes of persistent or transient monocular or binocular visual loss/disturbance (see **Table 15.1**, page 766).

Investigations Request Humphrey 24–2 field test and other tests as detailed below.

Management

- *Casualty*: For presumed atherosclerotic disease start aspirin 75 mg o.d. if not contraindicated. Advise smokers to stop. Check FBC, ESR, CRP, lipids, fasting glucose, and refer to clinic soon or to a neurologist. For suspected acute occipital infarction refer to local hyperacute stroke unit (HASU) to immediately exclude haemorrhagic stroke, or to consider thrombolysis according to local guidelines.
- *Clinic*: Confirm the diagnosis, check results, and refer to stroke assessment clinic for further management. Most vascular syndromes affecting vision (central retinal artery occlusion, transient monocular vision loss, etc.), other than acute stroke, need work up by a TIA clinic. TIA clinic waiting times should only be days, with ready access to investigations such as MR or CT angiography, echocardiography including transoesophageal echo, ECG, and 24-hour ECG. Do not refer anterior ischaemic optic neuropathy (AION) or central retinal vein occlusion (CRVO) to a stroke clinic. AION is never embolic and CRVO needs thrombophilia work-up in selected cases (p. 570).

Follow-up Check visual fields and VA remain stable and exclude disc swelling. Follow for about 1 year then discharge if there are no new symptoms.

CAROTID CAVERNOUS FISTULA

Background Occurs when the arterial circulation connects directly to the venous circulation in the cavernous sinus. May follow blunt head trauma (80%) or occur spontaneously, especially in hypertensive patients. May be high-flow (direct, rupture of the intracavernous carotid artery) or low-flow (indirect, rupture of a small dural artery in the wall of the cavernous sinus).

Symptoms Direct lesions produce a sudden onset of a whooshing noise in the head. Vision may be blurred with minor ocular discomfort. The indirect type is less severe, slower onset, and tinnitus may be absent.

Signs Patients are apyrexial, usually with unilateral proptosis. Eye movements are limited by a combination of nerve palsy and swelling of the extraocular muscles. There is conjunctival chemosis (**Fig. 15.23**) with engorged vessels that become arterialised, with a spiral appearance near the limbus. Other features include exposure keratopathy, IOP with increased pulse pressure, poorly reactive mid-dilated pupil, and congested

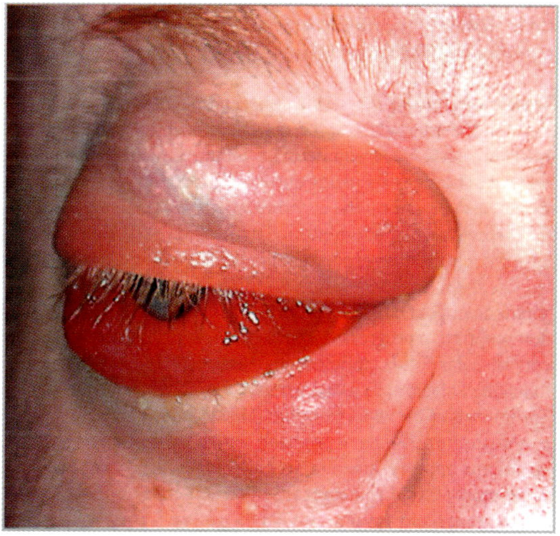

Fig. 15.23: Carotid cavernous fistula.

retinal veins. Superior ophthalmic vein occlusion and optic disc swelling may occur. Glaucoma is the principal cause of optic neuropathy.

History and examination Document any history of head trauma, hypertension, previous thyroid problems, or diplopia. Lid retraction is absent. Record temperature, proptosis, eye movements, VA, confrontation fields, corneal exposure, IOP, and RAPD. Listen for an orbital bruit with the stethoscope bell over the globe, forehead, and temple.

Differential diagnosis Consider severe scleritis, cavernous sinus thrombosis, and orbital disease including thyroid, cellulitis, abscess, neoplasia, and inflammatory lesions (idiopathic, myositis and granulomatosis with polyangiitis).

Investigations Request FBC, ESR, glucose, and renal function. For dysthyroid eye disease request thyroid antibodies and thyroid function tests. Arrange urgent orbital ultrasound or CT to look for dilation of the superior ophthalmic vein and enlarged extraocular muscles. Ultrasound shows dynamic features such as pulsatile and reversed flow in the superior ophthalmic vein. Vascular sequence CT/MRI of the orbit seldom adds much, but may show increased fat vascular markings, cavernous sinus distension, and evidence of cortical venous drainage. Confirmation of the nature of the fistula prior to endovascular treatment requires catheter angiography.

Treatment Admit. Prescribe topical lubricants and treat elevated IOP topically ± oral acetazolamide. Record daily VA, Ishihara plates, fields, and IOP. Life-threatening nose bleeds may occur, occasionally requiring emergency carotid ligation. Some fistulas also drain into the cerebral venous system and predispose to cerebral vascular accidents due to cortical vein thrombosis.

Direct carotid cavernous fistulas usually require embolisation to close them, with 85% success. Indirect fistulas often close spontaneously and may be observed if the vision is not deteriorating; if progressive visual loss occurs then consider endovascular fistula embolisation. Some fistulas close following angiography alone without attempted embolisation. Thrombosis of the superior ophthalmic vein may cause a paradoxical worsening of proptosis for a few weeks before symptoms improve. Stereotactic radiosurgery has been used occasionally. Avoid glaucoma filtration surgery as suprachoroidal haemorrhage may result.

Follow-up Until resolution occurs.

MEDICALLY UNEXPLAINED VISUAL LOSS

Background There are four types of medically unexplained visual loss:

1. Undiagnosed organic disease
2. Malingerers with a secondary gain
3. Psychosomatic visual loss, often due to serious emotional stress. Patients genuinely believe they have lost vision. Also called functional, or nonorganic loss.
4. Munchausen's syndrome and Munchausen's by proxy

For children with reduced vision but an otherwise normal examination, see also page 700.

Clinical features Malingerers typically have unilateral blurred vision. Functional loss is bilateral in 70%. VA is typically 6/12 to NPL. Examination is normal, although note any evidence of self-harm or eye rubbing.

History and examination A full history is essential. Ask if there is any ongoing litigation or compensation claim or any stressful event, e.g. divorce and bereavement. Observe behaviour. Is navigation consistent with VA? Test VA at 6 and 2 metres to see if the Snellen fraction is similar. Are near VA and Ishihara plates consistent with distance VA?

In moderate visual loss place a +1 dioptre lens in one side of a trial frame, and cover fellow eye. Explain that you are adding a stronger (-1 dioptre) lens to see if a spherical equivalent of zero improves vision. If the subjective vision is NPL use an optokinetic (OKN) drum to elicit nystagmus or move a mirror in front of the patient who will track their reflection unless genuinely NPL. Check for an afferent pupil defect: an NPL eye should have an amaurotic pupil (on stimulating the blind eye the pupil light reflex—both direct and consensual—is absent). The only exception to this is bilateral loss due to cortical blindness. In cases of moderate to severe monocular visual loss, place a 4D base down prism in front of the 'good eye' and ask the patient under binocular viewing conditions if they see one or two targets: true visual loss will elicit the response 'one', whereas the patient with functional visual loss will answer 'two'.

Differential diagnosis Exclude the following by thorough history and examination: tear film abnormality; keratoconus; refractive error; presbyopia; intermediate uveitis; central serous chorioretinopathy; macular dystrophy; central retinal artery occlusion; drug toxicity (e.g. quinine); amblyopia; optic nerve/chiasm disease, especially retrobulbar neuritis; traumatic optic neuropathy; and cortical blindness.

Investigations Non-physiological perimetry results are common (**Fig. 15.24**), but tired patients may also show this. Hospital refraction is advisable. Electrodiagnostic testing is very useful to confirm the integrity of the visual pathways, particularly pattern appearance visually evoked potentials. Brain and orbit MRI are sometimes required. Arrange macular OCT and autofluorescence. Fluorescein angiography is occasionally helpful.

Treatment

- *Casualty*: For suspected functional disease explain that the eye findings are not typical of the proposed injury mechanism, and that there is no objective evidence of irreversible visual loss. Offer reassurance that there is nothing seriously wrong and that stress is a likely explanation. Tell them their vision should improve and this will be confirmed via a routine clinic appointment with a senior colleague. Consider an earlier appointment if the diagnosis is uncertain.
- *Clinic*: Confirm the diagnosis. Functional loss does not exclude eye disease.

Follow-up Review until the patient, family, GP and other involved parties understand the nature of the visual loss

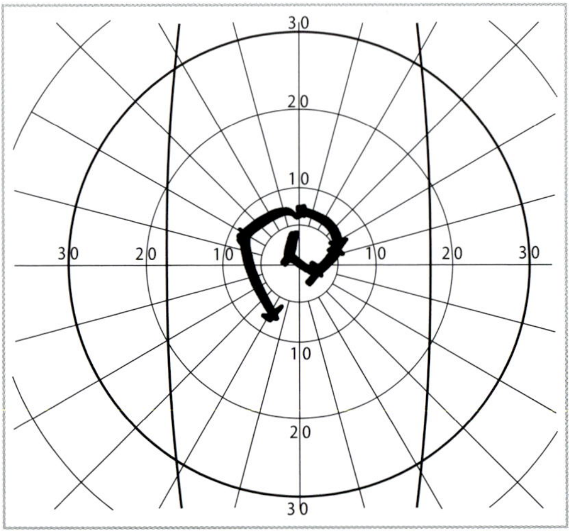

Fig. 15.24: Spiral field on a Goldmann field test.

and that further investigations/opinions will not be helpful. Most children and adolescents recover with reassurance. Adults tend not to improve as quickly if the secondary gain or psychological illness persists. Liaise with the patient's GP about psychological assessment if appropriate. Patients tend not to have an identifiable psychiatric syndrome such as depression and drug treatment is rarely recommended. Progressive worsening of vision from visit to visit is unusual and should prompt reassessment of the diagnosis.

SYSTEMIC DISEASE ASSOCIATIONS

Chronic progressive external ophthalmoplegia (CPEO)

Most cases presenting as CPEO are sporadic mitochondrial DNA deletions and not inherited. Cases with other features may be maternally inherited (e.g. mitochondrial DNA point mutations) or in an autosomal fashion (mutations in nuclear DNA coding mitochondrial proteins, e.g. polymerase gamma). CPEO is a feature of many different mitochondrial myopathies. Presents with bilateral ptosis with ophthalmoplegia later. May have generalised muscle weakness. Usually symmetrical so no diplopia, except for reading. Consider prisms on reading glasses, ptosis props, or cautious lid-raising surgery. For Kearns–Sayre's syndrome (CPEO with pigmentary retinopathy), see page 600.

Progressive supranuclear palsy Sporadic condition. Also known as Steele–Richardson–Olszewski's syndrome. Loss of downwards saccades occurs first, then up saccades, and eventually complete ophthalmoplegia. Paucity of blinking and apraxia of lid opening are typical. There is progressive dementia, rigidity of neck and trunk muscles, and failure of postural reflexes leading to falls. MRI shows midbrain atrophy. The differential includes Parkinsonism, diffuse Lewy body disease, and multisystem atrophy. Avoid bifocals or varifocals.

Myotonic dystrophy type 1 Autosomal dominant due to a cytosine-thymine-guanine (CTG) trinucleotide repeat on chromosome 19. Shows genetic anticipation: this means that trinucleotide repeat sequences become ever longer with each generation and this typically results in progressively more serious disease with each generation.

- *Systemic features*: frontal balding, sunken temples, long face, peripheral weakness and wasting of muscles with myotonia, testicular atrophy, cardiac conduction defects, nocturnal hypoventilation, diabetes ± mild intellectual impairment.
- *Ocular features*: bilateral ptosis ± orbicularis weakness, slow saccades, varying degrees of ophthalmoparesis (rarely significant), cataracts in almost all patients (coloured crystals) and retinal pattern dystrophy.

Myotonic dystrophy type 2 Myotonic dystrophy type 2 is due to a CCTG tetranucleotide repeat on chromosome 3. The phenotype is similar to type 1 except that the myopathy is proximal and anticipation does not occur.

Facioscapulohumeral muscular dystrophy Inherited muscular dystrophy featuring progressive muscle weakness of the face, scapula and upper arm. Adult-onset disease may be relatively mild, but infantile-onset disease is more often associated with hearing loss, spinal deformities, cardiac and respiratory problems, and lower limb weakness with reduced mobility. Ocular features include retinopathy and poor lid closure with risk of exposure keratopathy.

Sturge–Weber syndrome Sporadic condition.

- *Systemic features*: naevus (port wine stain, **Fig. 2.20** p. 49) ± epilepsy, hemiplegia, and intracranial calcification on skull X-ray.
- *Ocular features*: homonymous field defect, glaucoma, and diffuse choroidal haemangioma. Consider in cases of unilateral glaucoma as patients may have covered the naevus with make-up.

Tuberous sclerosis Autosomal dominant disease due to mutations of the *TSC1* gene on chromosome 9, or *TSC2* on chromosome 16, with multiple hamartomas affecting many systems.

- *Systemic features*: ash leaf spot, shagreen patch, adenoma sebaceum over nasolabial folds, subungual fibromas, epilepsy, periventricular astrocytic hamartomas, and mental retardation may occur.
- *Ocular features*: retinal hamartomas (50%) may be flat, translucent lesions or multinodular 'mulberry' lesions (astrocytic hamartomas) – these are benign and rarely enlarge; optic nerve hamartoma; and hypopigmented iris patches.

Neurofibromatosis type I Dominantly inherited due to mutations in the neurofibromin 1 (*NF1*) gene, a tumour suppressor gene located on chromosome 17.

- *Systemic features*: 6+ café au lait spots; neurofibromas; axillary freckling; phaeochromocytomas; meningioma; multiple tumours of the brain, spinal cord and peripheral nerves.
- *Ocular features*: optic nerve glioma (15%; only 1% progress and need treatment); >1 Lisch nodule (iris hamartomas present in 90% of those aged >6 years); congenital glaucoma; upper eyelid plexiform neurofibroma (± ipsilateral glaucoma); retinal hamartoma; choroidal hamartomas; thickened corneal nerves; pulsatile proptosis (absent greater wing of sphenoid). OCT near infrared imaging may show a choroidal lesion.

Neurofibromatosis type II Dominantly inherited due to mutations in the neurofibromin 2 (*NF2*) gene, a tumour suppressor gene located on chromosome 22.

- *Systemic features*: bilateral vestibular schwannomas; meningioma (4%); other central nervous system tumours; café au lait spots (60%).

- *Ocular features*: early-onset cortical or posterior subcapsular cataracts (81%); retinal hamartomas (combined hamartomas of retina and retinal pigment epithelium, 22%); optic nerve sheath tumours; Lisch nodules are rare.

Von Hippel–Lindau (VHL) syndrome Dominantly inherited due to mutation in the VHL tumour suppressor gene on chromosome 3.

- *Systemic features*: Cerebellar, brainstem or spinal haemangioblastomas (25%); phaeochromocytomas and renal cell carcinoma. Regular imaging is required to look for tumour development.
- *Ocular features*: Retinal capillary angiomas characterised by a large feeder artery and dilated draining vein. Leakage may cause decreased vision, exudate deposition or serous retinal detachment. Treatment is with extensive laser photocoagulation or cryotherapy.

Wyburn–Mason syndrome Sporadic. Features retinal racemous angioma associated with intracranial arteriovenous malformation (**Fig 11.27**, p. 533). Request brain MRI.

Ataxia telangiectasia (Louis–Bar syndrome) Autosomal recessive due to mutations in the ataxia telangiectasia mutated (ATM) gene on chromosome 11. The gene codes for a kinase involved in DNA repair and tumour suppression. The most common progressive ataxia of childhood. Thymic hypoplasia and a defective immune system result in recurrent infections. Conjunctival telangiectasia is common.

OPTOMETRY AND GENERAL PRACTICE GUIDELINES

General comments

Many neuro-ophthalmic symptoms are non-specific, and it is not always clear if they should be managed by a GP, neurologist, ophthalmologist, or other specialist. Thus, transient loss of vision might reflect systemic disturbance such as hypoglycaemia or hypotension, carotid emboli, or raised intraocular pressure (IOP).

Headache can be caused by several eye conditions and the following questions may help:

- Is the headache precipitated by visual tasks? This may suggest refractive error or ocular muscle imbalance.
- Is headache associated with a red eye? This may suggest uveitis, scleritis, or acute angle-closure glaucoma. Mild or moderately raised IOP does not usually cause headache or a red eye.
- Is headache associated with blurred vision? Consider high IOP, uveitis, raised intracranial pressure, optic neuritis, and migraine. A careful history can usually distinguish migrainous phosphenes from those associated with retinal detachment (p. 785).

General practice

Although rare in general practice, always consider giant cell arteritis in those aged over 50 years with jaw claudication and temporal tenderness, especially those with polymyalgia rheumatica; an ESR and/or CRP is helpful. Assessment of refraction, anterior chamber depth (to rule out angle-closure glaucoma), IOP, dilated fundoscopy including optic discs, ocular muscle balance and visual field tests can usually be undertaken via an optometrist and will help to exclude many eye conditions associated with headache. Note that patients with good visual acuity but hemianopia (as may occur after a stroke) can be registered as sight impaired by an ophthalmologist and this may confer some benefits.

Optometrists

An asymptomatic visual field defect picked up on routine screening should usually be repeated. Many defects will disappear as the patient learns how to perform the test. If a superior field defect is present, exclude ptosis. Tape the drooping lid up while the test is repeated. Exclude obvious optic disc and retinal disease with dilated fundal examination. Homonymous visual field defects (p. 770) suggest postchiasmal lesions and require relatively urgent medical assessment. For glaucomatous field defects, see page 348.

The following guide to referral urgency is not prescriptive, as clinical situations vary.

Immediate

- Giant cell arteritis p. 789

Same day

- Acute IIIrd nerve palsy (consider referral to a neurologist or neurosurgeon) p. 736
- Transient visual loss without features of migraine p. 765
- Optic disc swelling with headache or transient visual loss p. 776
- Anisocoria or Horner's syndrome with head or neck pain. Consider carotid artery dissection. p. 763
- Sudden-onset visual field defect. Consider:
  1. Retinal detachment p. 636
  2. Retinal artery occlusion p. 576
  3. Retinal vein occlusion p. 569
  4. Ischaemic optic neuropathy p. 787
  5. Stroke (refer to neurology) p. 808

Urgent (within 1 week)

Sudden onset of symptomatic (oscillopsia) nystagmus. Consider ENT referral if deafness, vertigo or tinnitus are prominent. Also consider neurology referral. p. 768

Soon (within 1 month)

- Optic disc swelling with no headache, no eye pain and normal vision p. 776
- Asymptomatic, non-specific visual field defect detected by optometrist screening p. 770

Routine

- Anisocoria with normal vision and no pain p. 763
- Unilateral twitching of facial muscles. This can be hemifacial spasm (a neurovascular compression syndrome) or facial myokymia (which occurs in MS). If isolated to an eyelid then labelled lid myokymia which is invariably benign p. 60
- Bilateral involuntary eye closure (blepharospasm) p. 60
- Asymptomatic nystagmus (no oscillopsia), or longstanding nystagmus p. 768

APPENDIX 1

CARDIORESPIRATORY ARREST

Act quickly 'time is (cardiac) muscle'.

Confirm diagnosis Unconscious or unresponsive patient, and not breathing normally (ignore occasional gasps). Ensure personal safety.

Treatment Call for help, ask a colleague to call the resuscitation team and collect an automated external defibrillator (AED) if one is available. Perform in-hospital resuscitation algorithm (**Fig. A1.1**) while waiting for a defibrillator and further support. Compress 5–6 cm at rate of 100–120/min, allowing the chest to completely recoil after each compression. Minimise any interruptions to chest compression (hands-off time). After 30 compressions, provide two rescue breaths. Alternate between providing 30 compressions and 2 rescue breaths. Use airway adjuncts and ventilate to produce visible chest lifting. Add supplementary oxygen as soon as possible. Continue cardiopulmonary resuscitation until AED present and follow audio-visual commands. Once resuscitation team arrives, follow Advanced Life Support (ALS) algorithm (**Fig. A1.2**).

- Emphasize minimally interrupted high quality chest compressions throughout any ALS intervention.
- Epinephrine (adrenaline) dose is 1 mg i.v. after the third shock and repeated every 3–5 minutes for ventricular fibrillation/ pulseless ventricular tachycardia (VF/pVT). Also give amiodarone 300 mg i.v. for VF/pVT after the third shock. Give a further dose of amiodarone 150 mg i.v. for VF/pVT after the fifth shock. Continue CPR whilst giving all drugs.
- For pulseless electrical activity (PEA) and asystole, give adrenaline 1 mg i.v. as soon as intravenous access is achieved and repeat every 3–5 minutes.
- Consider thrombolytic drug therapy when pulmonary embolus is the suspected or confirmed cause of cardiac arrest.

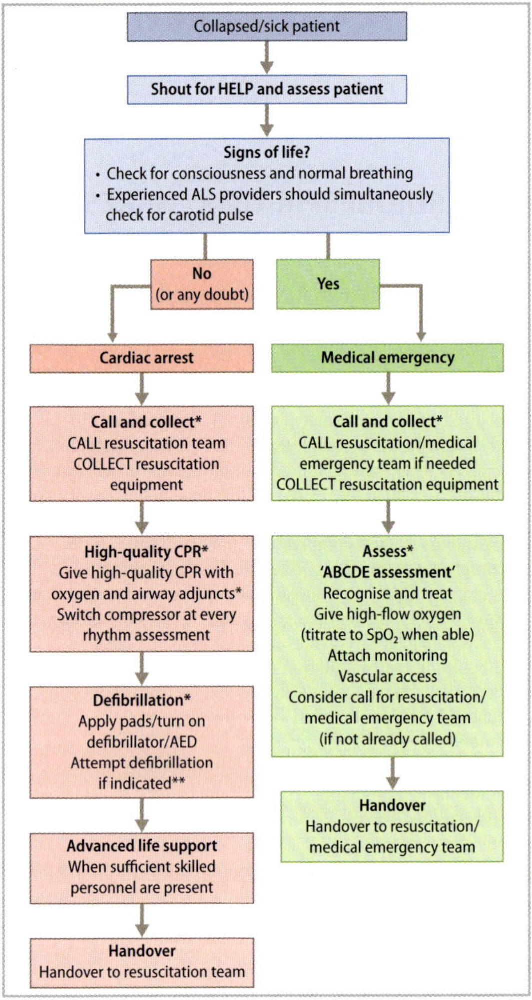

* Undertake actions concurrently if sufficient staff available.
** Use a manual defibrillator if trained and device available.

Fig. A1.1: Adult in-hospital resuscitation algorithm (2021 Guidelines, Resuscitation Council, UK). Reproduced with the kind permission of the Resuscitation Council (UK).
Abbreviations: ABCDE, airway, breathing, circulation, disability, exposure; AED, automated external defibrillator; ALS, advanced life support; CPR, cardiopulmonary resuscitation.

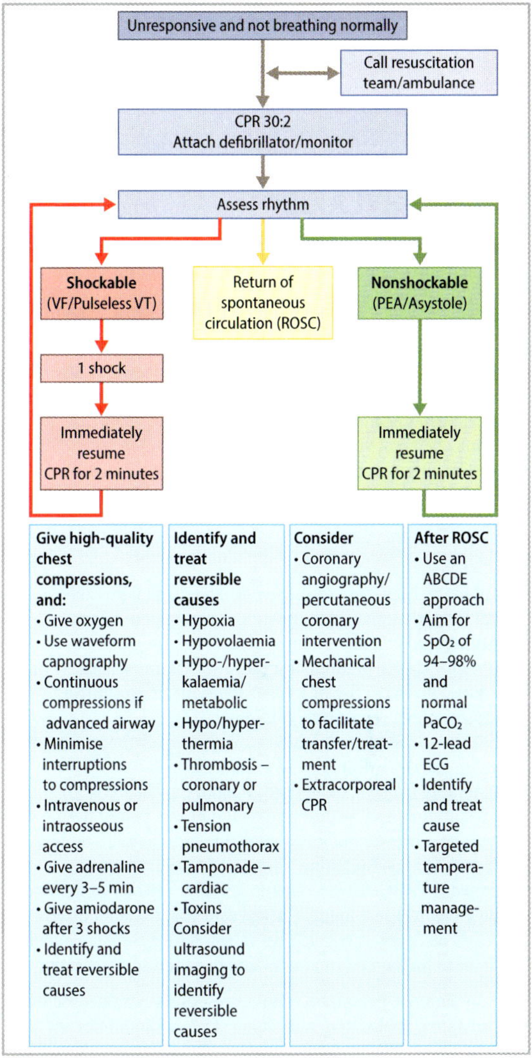

Fig. A1.2: Adult advanced life support (ALS) algorithm (2021 Guidelines, Resuscitation Council, UK). Reproduced with the kind permission of the Resuscitation Council (UK).
Abbreviations: ABCDE, airway, breathing, circulation, disability, exposure; CPR, cardiopulmonary resuscitation; PEA, pulseless electrical activity; VF, ventricular fibrillation; VT, ventricular tachycardia.

2 APPENDIX

ANAPHYLAXIS

Signs Anaphylaxis is a clinical diagnosis to be suspected if, after exposure to a potential allergen, the patient develops sudden onset and rapid progression of symptoms: hoarse voice, stridor, breathlessness, wheeze, fatigue, confusion, cyanosis, pallor, tachycardia, hypotension, dizziness, patchy erythema, urticaria, flushing and angioedema (swelling of eyelids, lips and throat). The diagnosis is supported if a patient has been exposed to an allergen known to affect them, but in up to 30% of cases there may be no obvious trigger. The risk of anaphylaxis after fluorescein angiography is ≈1:10,000 but evidence is unclear. Shellfish allergy is weakly predictive of indocyanine green allergy, but less certain with fluorescein.

Treatment

1. Call for resuscitation team, remove the cause if possible and lay patient flat (with or without legs raised) or semi-recumbent.
2. Give epinephrine (adrenaline) 0.5 mg intramuscularly (i.m.) (equivalent to 0.5 mL of 1:1,000 solution). If no clinical improvement, repeat after 5 minutes.
3. Establish airway, give high flow oxygen, apply monitoring (pulse oximetry, ECG and BP) and i.v. access.
4. Give rapid i.v. crystalloid fluid challenge (500–1,000 mL).
5. If respiratory and cardiovascular symptoms persist despite two appropriate doses of i.m. epinephrine (adrenaline), undertake a rapid Airway, Breathing, Circulation, Disability and Exposure (ABCDE) assessment, and give priority to treating the greatest threat to life. Critical care support is required.
6. Before discharge, arrange review by a senior clinician about the need for further treatment and duration of observation.

If at any time the person becomes unresponsive or unconscious, and breathing is absent or abnormal, start cardiopulmonary resuscitation (CPR) immediately.

Report adverse drug reactions that include an anaphylactic reaction to the Medicines and Healthcare products Regulatory Agency (MHRA yellow card scheme).

Source: Emergency treatment of anaphylaxis—Resuscitation Council (UK) May 2021 Guidelines.

APPENDIX 3

VISUAL STANDARDS FOR DRIVING

All UK drivers have a legal duty to notify the Driver and Vehicle Licensing Agency (DVLA) of any injury or illness that would have a likely impact on safe driving ability as per the guidance below. If they do not abide by this, they may receive a fine. Doctors and healthcare professionals should advise the individual of the impact of their medical condition for safe driving ability and their legal requirement to notify the DVLA. Doctors and healthcare professionals should notify the DVLA directly of an individual's medical condition or fitness to drive (**Table A3.1**), where the patient cannot or will not notify the DVLA.

Table A3.1: Guide to fitness to drive (United Kingdom)

Visual function	Group 1 entitlement (includes motor cars and motorcycles)	Group 2 entitlement (includes large lorries and buses)
Acuity	Must be able to read a car number plate made after September 2001 from 20 metres. Must have a visual acuity of at least 6/12 Snellen (with glasses or contact lenses, if necessary) using both eyes together or in the only eye if monocular. *Note:* Bioptic telescope devices are not acceptable for driving.	Must have a visual acuity of at least 6/7.5 Snellen in the best eye and at least 6/60 in the other eye. Glasses or contact lenses can be worn, but they cannot have a corrective power >+8 dioptres in any meridian of either lens.
Cataract	Must meet acuity and visual field minimum standards. If they do, no requirement to inform DVLA.	Must meet acuity and visual field minimum standards. If they do, no requirement to inform DVLA.

Table A3.1: Guide to fitness to drive (United Kingdom)—*Contd...*

Visual function	Group 1 entitlement (includes motor cars and motorcycles)	Group 2 entitlement (includes large lorries and buses)
Monocular vision	This is defined as no light perception in one eye. Drivers must not drive until they are clinically advised that they have adapted to the defect *and* they must meet the same visual acuity and visual field standards as binocular drivers. Only monocular people who fail to meet these requirements are required to notify DVLA.	This is defined as no light perception in one eye. Monocular patients are therefore not able to drive and must inform the DVLA. Please see DVLA online guidance for details on 'Grandfather Rights' to obtain licenses in exceptional scenarios.
Visual field defects	Driving must cease unless confirmed able to meet following standard, in general tested using a binocular Esterman test: Visual field of at least 120° on the horizontal meridian measured using a target equivalent to the white Goldman III4e settings. The extension should be at least 50° left and right. In addition, there should be no significant defect in the binocular field which encroaches within 20° of fixation above or below the horizontal meridian. The following are regarded as acceptable central loss: • Scattered single missed points • A single cluster of up to three adjoining points with no additional separate missed points within the central 20° area	Drivers must have an uninterrupted measurement of at least 160° on the horizontal plane with an extension of at least 70° left and at least 70° right. Visual field must extend at least 30° above and below the horizontal midline. It is acceptable to have a total of up to three missed points which may or may not be contiguous. There should be no defect present within a central 30° radius. There must be no other impairment of visual function, including no glare sensitivity, contrast sensitivity, or impairment of twilight vision.

Table A3.1: Guide to fitness to drive (United Kingdom)—*Contd...*		
Visual function	**Group 1 entitlement (includes motor cars and motorcycles)**	**Group 2 entitlement (includes large lorries and buses)**
	The following are regarded as acceptable peripheral defects: • A cluster of up to three adjoining missed points, unattached to any other defect on or across the horizontal meridian • A vertical defect of only a single point width, but any length, unattached to any other defect, on or across the horizontal meridian. Please see DVLA online guidance for exceptional scenarios where an individual with a field defect may be eligible to drive.	
Diplopia	Cease driving on diagnosis and inform DVLA. Can resume driving once confirmed to the DVLA that the diplopia is controlled by glasses or by a patch which the license holder undertakes to wear while driving. A stable uncorrected diplopia of 6 months' duration or more may be compatible with driving if there is a consultant/specialist's report indicating satisfactory functional adaptation.	Must not drive and must notify DVLA. Patches are not acceptable.
Night blindness	Must not drive and must notify DVLA. Acuity and field standards must be met, and cases will then be considered on an individual basis.	Must not drive and must notify DVLA. Group 2 acuity and field standards must be met and cases will then be considered on an individual basis.

Table A3.1: Guide to fitness to drive (United Kingdom)—*Contd...*

Visual function	Group 1 entitlement (includes motor cars and motorcycles)	Group 2 entitlement (includes large lorries and buses)
Colour blindness	Can drive and need not notify DVLA.	Can drive and need not notify DVLA.
Blepharospasm	Must not drive and must notify DVLA. Consultant opinion is sought by DVLA. If mild, driving may be allowed subject to satisfactory medical reports. Control of mild blepharospasm with botulinum toxin may be acceptable provided that treatment does not produce side effects such as uncontrollable diplopia. DVLA should be informed of any change or deterioration in condition.	Must not drive and must notify DVLA. Consultant opinion is sought by DVLA. If mild, driving may be allowed subject to satisfactory medical reports. Control of mild blepharospasm with botulinum toxin may be acceptable provided that treatment does not produce side effects such as uncontrollable diplopia. DVLA should be informed of any change or deterioration in condition.
Nystagmus	DVLA need not be notified, providing the vision standards for driving are achieved and providing any associated medical condition is declared.	DVLA need not be notified, providing the vision standards for driving are achieved and providing any associated medical condition is declared.

Abbreviation: DVLA – Driver and Vehicle Licensing Agency.

Source: DVLA, Swansea. 'Assessing fitness to drive – a guide for medical professionals'.

Readers are advised to check all details are correct before issuing advice, as they may be subject to change. Visit: https://www.gov.uk/government/publications/assessing-fitness-to-drive-a-guide-for-medical-professionals

APPENDIX 4

VISUAL CRITERIA FOR REGISTRATION AS SIGHT IMPAIRED

To register a UK patient severely sight impaired (blind) or sight impaired (partially sighted), the consultant should complete a Certificate of Visual Impairment (CVI). The following definitions depend on the VA and visual field defect.

Severely sight impaired (blind) Needs to fit one of the following categories with glasses/contact lenses as required:

- Binocular VA worse than 3/60 Snellen
- Binocular VA between 3/60 and 6/60 with visual field contraction
- Binocular VA better than 6/60 with a significant contracted field of vision especially if the contraction is in the lower part of the field or causing a bitemporal hemianopia, with significant functional impairment

Sight impaired (partially sighted) Needs to fit one of the following categories with glasses/contact lenses as required:

- Binocular VA 3/60 to 6/60 with full visual field
- Binocular VA 6/60 to 6/24 with moderate contraction of the visual field (e.g. media opacities or aphakia)
- Any VA if they have a gross visual field defect, e.g. homonymous hemianopia

Source: Department of Health, UK. 'Certificate of Visual Impairment: Explanatory notes for consultant ophthalmologists and hospital eye clinic staff in England'.

5 APPENDIX

SUTURES AND NEEDLES

Sutures

- Sutures can be divided into absorbable/non-absorbable, and monofilament/multifilament (braided) (**Table A5.1**).
- Absorbable sutures are absorbed by proteolysis of natural material or hydrolysis of synthetic materials; hydrolysis causes less tissue reaction. Non-absorbable sutures become encapsulated by fibrosis.
- Compared to multifilament sutures, monofilament sutures are more resistant to infection, have a lower coefficient of friction (easier to pass through tissue), lower tensile strength, lower flexibility, and are harder to tie.
- Sutures may be coated to reduce their coefficient of friction and dyed to increase their visibility.

Table A5.1: Summary of types of suture materials

Suture	Type	Tensile strength	Tissue reaction
Absorbable			
Polyglactin 910 (Vicryl)	Mono or multifilament	24–30 days	Mild
Polyglycolic acid (Dexon)	Multifilament	24–30 days	Mild
Plain gut*	Monofilament	5–7 days	Marked
Chromic gut*	Monofilament	10–21 days	Moderate
Nonabsorbable			
Polyamide (Nylon)	Monofilament	High; approximately 10% of strength lost per year	Mild
Silk	Multifilament	Moderate; lost by 1 year	Marked

Table A5.1: Summary of types of suture materials —*Contd...*			
Suture	**Type**	**Tensile strength**	**Tissue reaction**
Polypropylene (Prolene)	Mono or multifilament	High; maintains strength over 2 years	Minimal
Polyester (Mersilene)	Monofilament	High; maintains tensile strength indefinitely	Minimal

* These have been phased out of most high-income countries including UK, France, Germany, Spain, Austria and Japan.

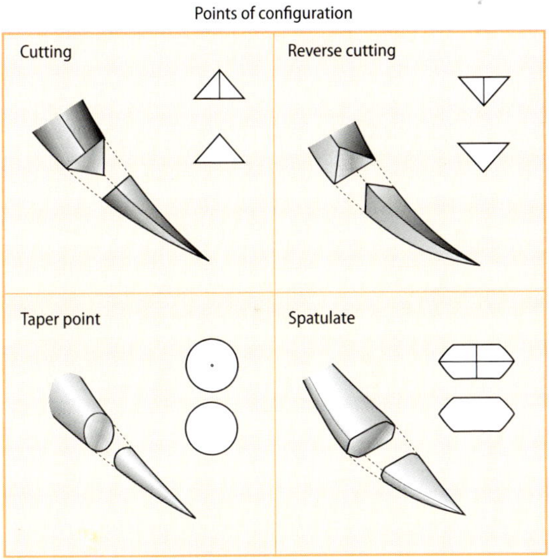

Fig. A5.1: Examples of types of needles.

Needles

- The needle is divided into three parts – the point, the body, and the swage.
- The point extends from the tip to the maximum cross-section of the body. There are five types – spatulate, round bodied/taper point, cutting point, reverse cutting point, and tapered spatulate (**Fig. A5.1**). The body incorporates the needle

length, and is the grasping area that transmits the penetrating force to the point. The body can be oval, round, triangular, side-flattened rectangular, or trapezoidal. The longitudinal shape of the body can be straight, half-curved, curved, or compound curved. The suture attaches to the swage, creating a continuous unit.

- A needle has five measurements:
  1. *Chord length*: linear distance from the point of a curved needle to the swage. This determines the width of the bite.
  2. *Needle length*: distance measured along the needle from the point to the swage; detailed on the packaging.
  3. *Radius*: distance from the body to the centre of the circle along which the needle curves; this determines bite depth.
  4. *Diameter*: thickness of the needle; a smaller-diameter needle requires less force and causes less trauma.
  5. *Bicurve:* two radii on a needle; the radius near the point is usually shorter than that near the swage.

Needles may be coated with silicone to permit easier passage through tissues. Needles are made of stainless steel; the tip should not be touched with the needle holders to avoid blunting.

Table A5.2 summarises the types of needle and suture materials recommended for use on named tissues.

Table A5.2: Selection of needle and suture material

Site	Suture types	Remove (days)	Needle type
Periocular skin	6/0 Nylon for most facial trauma.	Day 5	Reverse cutting point
	6/0 silk: more comfortable than Nylon but may produce more scarring. Used for some oculoplastic procedures.	Day 5	
	6/0 Vicryl: may be appropriate for young children if avoids general anaesthesia to remove sutures.	Absorbable	
Lid margin	6/0 silk	Day 5–7	Reverse cutting point

Table A5.2: Selection of needle and suture material —*Contd...*

Site	Suture types	Remove (days)	Needle type
Conjunctiva	8/0 Vicryl	Absorbable	Spatulate, round body
Sclera	7/0 Nylon behind the insertion of the muscles, 7/0 Nylon or 7/0 Vicryl between muscle insertions and the limbus. Avoid Vicryl for ruptured globe repair.	Permanent (Nylon) Absorbable (Vicryl)	Tapered spatulate
Cornea	10/0 Nylon	Usually weeks/month, depending on use	Tapered spatulate
Iris	10/0 Prolene	Permanent	Round bodied

6 APPENDIX

OPHTHALMIC SURGICAL INSTRUMENTS

Forceps Ophthalmic forceps have three parts: tip, shaft and handle. The term 'platform' refers to the last 5–7 mm of the shaft and includes the tip. There are three main types:

- Toothed: for holding tissues.
- Notched: also used for holding tissues but causes less trauma.
- Tying: for holding and tying sutures. Most are designed to close incrementally with increasing pressure.

Colibri forceps incorporate two types by adding a tying platform to the toothed forceps. The shaft can be straight, angled or curved.

Needle holders Hold like a pen, grasping at the junction of the upper one-third and lower two-thirds of the needle. Six main types are used during suturing. The type selected depends on the size of the needle used. Most needle holders have the option of being locking or non-locking. The platform that holds the needle can also be straight or curved. The handle can be flat or round.

Commonly used ophthalmic instruments are shown in **Fig. A6.1** and **Table A6.1**.

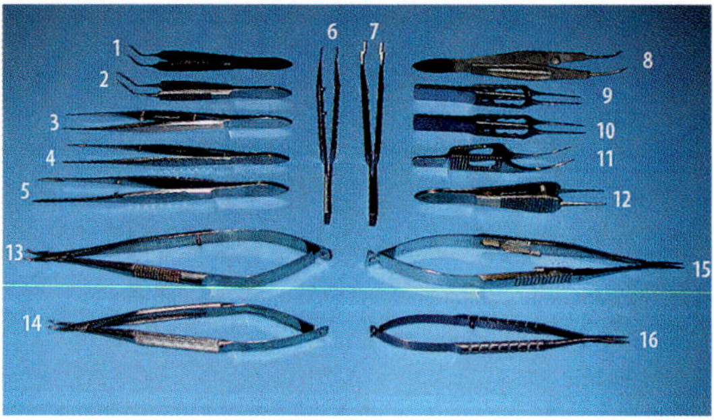

Fig. A6.1: Commonly used instruments.

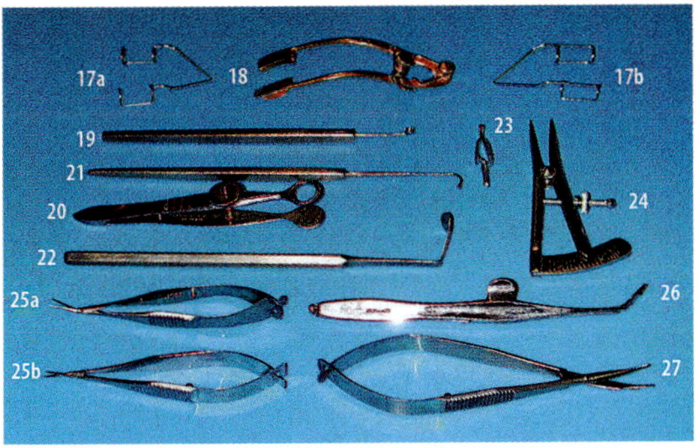

Fig. A6.1: Commonly used instruments. *continued...*

Table A6.1: Frequently used ophthalmic instruments		
Forceps	**Name**	**Notes**
1	Kelman McPherson	Long-angled shaft used for intraocular work, especially lens positioning.
2	Rhexis forceps	Long-angled shaft with further angle at tip. Used to grasp the lens capsule during capsulorrhexis. Commonly used version is Utrata forceps.
3	Jayles	Plain handle and small interdigitating teeth.
4	Toothed Castroviejo	The interdigitating teeth are forward angled.
5	Moorfields	Flat handled with grooves on the handle and at the tip to allow firm grasping of the conjunctiva.
6 and 7	Folding and insertion forceps	Designed to fold then insert intraocular lenses during cataract surgery.
8	Maxfines	Plain curved platform commonly used for removing corneal sutures.
9	Suture tying	Fine plain forceps used for suture tying.
10	Notched	Plain platform with curved notch at end. Various uses especially holding corneal or scleral wounds while suturing.

Table A6.1: Frequently used ophthalmic instruments—*Contd...*

Forceps	Name	Notes
11	Colibri	Ideal for holding the cornea or sclera while suturing.
12	St. Martins	Short wide flat handle, interdigitating teeth commonly used during strabismus surgery. Can damage conjunctiva.
13	Barraquer	Used for suturing skin and sclera. Round handled.
14	Troutman	Finer than Barraquer. Also round handled. Useful for suturing conjunctiva.
15	Castroviejo	It has a locking system that allows for a firm grasp; used for closing the sclera in vitreoretinal surgery and tying sutures tight over scleral explants. Flat handled.
16	Titanium micro needle holder	For use with fine sutures (e.g. 10/0 Nylon) during corneal surgery.
Instrument	**Name**	**Notes**
17	Kratz Barraquer lid speculum	Wire speculum that produces a fixed opening of the palpebral fissure. The Kratz Barraquer (17a) has open wires and Barraquer (17b) has closed wires; the former is a commonly used 'phaco speculum'. Pierce speculum is similar but allows adjustment of interpalpebral distance.
18	Langs lid speculum	Allows the width of the palpebral fissure to be adjusted; has guards to keep the eyelashes out of the operating field. Clark speculum is similar but has open wire loops to hold lids apart.
19 and 20	Curette and chalazion clamp	Clamp controls bleeding and provides a rigid surface for incision and then curettage of cyst contents.
21	Squint hook	Used for isolating extraocular muscles in squint and conventional retinal detachment surgery.

Table A6.1: Frequently used ophthalmic instruments—*Contd...*

Instrument	Name	Notes
22	Fison retractor	Commonly used to retract conjunctiva and Tenon's capsule.
23	Bulldog clamp	Used to clip sutures to avoid entanglement.
24	Calipers	The pointed tips of the caliper can be used to mark the sclera, measure corneal diameter, and extraocular muscle position. Should usually be checked against a ruler.
25	Vannas scissors	Fine scissors are suitable for intraocular use. They can be angled (25a) or straight (25b).
26	Dewecker scissors	Designed for cutting iris (iridectomy) but also suitable for prolapsed vitreous.
27	Westcott scissors	Curved tips allow easy dissection of Tenon's capsule down to sclera during strabismus and vitreoretinal surgery. Tips of blades can be rounded or pointed. Use the former for blind procedures such as subTenon's anaesthesia. Similar to Castroviejo scissors and often called 'spring scissors'.

7 APPENDIX

USE OF THE OPERATING MICROSCOPE

Operating microscopes have several important attributes including coaxial illumination, stereo-optics, fully adjustable eyepieces, and foot-controlled zoom and focussing.

The important steps in using the microscope are:

- Before surgery
  1. Set the eyepiece interpupillary distance and move the observer's viewing system to the correct side (left or right).
  2. If wearing spectacles during surgery, ensure the eyepiece focus is set to 0 and that the 'spacers' (adjustable pads that separate your eye from the eyepiece) are out.
  3. If not wearing spectacles, set the eyepiece focus to your refraction and put in the spacers so you can rest your eyebrow on them during surgery.
  4. Reset the microscope focus and XY to the centre of their travel (look for a reset or centre button).
  5. Ensure the patient is comfortably positioned under the microscope.
  6. Adjust the surgeon's chair as required.
  7. Scrub, prep and drape.
- At the start of surgery
  1. Adjust the position of the table, foot controls, microscope height, and importantly the eyepiece tilt so that your lower spine is straight or slightly extended, but never flexed.
  2. When comfortable, set any wheel locks on the surgeon's chair or mobile microscopes.
- During surgery
  1. Most microscopes are parfocal; that is, the focus and zoom are independent.
  2. However, increasing magnification reduces the depth of focus and may blur the image if the focal plane is far from the surgical plane.
  3. To prevent this, focus the microscope under low magnification then zoom in on a defined object such as a blood vessel, adjusting the focus to maintain a clear image.
  4. Zoom back out to the minimum magnification required to perform each task – this increases the depth of field (to

avoid focusing too often) and field of view (to see the effects of manipulations on neighbouring structures).
5. This also helps to overcome involuntary accommodation that is a common problem for inexperienced surgeons. If things start to blur transiently, zoom in, refocus, and zoom out. Alternatively, focus the microscope so that it moves from above down.
6. Some hand tremor is normal under the microscope; concentrate on breathing normally to help reduce excessive sympathetic activity. Avoid breath-holding during difficult manoeuvres.
7. Using arm rests and resting your hands on the patient's forehead may help to avoid excessive arm and upper body tension.
8. Avoid gripping the instruments too tightly as this reduces fine motor control and causes fatigue.

8 APPENDIX

DRUG USE IN PREGNANCY

Medications should only be used in pregnancy when the benefit to the mother outweighs the risk to the fetus, and should be prescribed using the lowest concentration at the minimum effective dose for the shortest duration of time. If possible, avoid medicines in the first trimester. As fetal medication exposure is dependent on systemic absorption, topical eye preparations are likely to be of low fetal risk. However, a small amount of systemic absorption may still occur through conjunctival vessels or nasal mucosa. The latter is more common with eye drops than ointment. Systemic absorption may be reduced by nasolacrimal occlusion or eyelid closure for a few minutes after instillation, by avoiding the instillation of different drops in succession (since this increases the percentage of drops entering the nose), and by blowing the nose after. However, the amount of systemic absorption remains highly variable, and is often unquantifiable. The number of applications and period of treatment are additional important factors which may influence the potential for fetal exposure, with most single application and short-term use products likely posing a minimal fetal risk.

Below is a table of medicines and diagnostic materials commonly used in ophthalmology. The recommendation categories presented are based on available pharmacokinetic and pregnancy safety data (June 2024). For some medicines, there are conflicting data, or the information is based on systemic (not topical exposure) studies. In some cases, the chance of systemic exposure may have been estimated based on the low doses used in general clinical practice.

Readers are advised not to rely solely on the table for forming patient-specific risk assessments. The potential fetotoxic effects of topical ocular medicines are often uncertain. Recommendations based on studies of systemic administration may not apply. Therefore, the guidance provided in the table must be interpreted alongside the potential risk of leaving a maternal condition inadequately treated. Readers are also advised to contact obstetricians with a specialist interest in co-existing medical conditions during pregnancy for further advice.

Note, absence of a medication from the table below does not imply safety.

Definitions for use in pregnancy categories are as follows (**Table A8.1**):

- Category 1 – Considered to be of low fetal risk, due to minimal systemic absorption and/or systemic concentrations.
- Category 2 – Possible low fetal risk, based on likelihood of minimal systemic absorption and/or systemic concentrations. However, adequate data to confirm this are lacking.
- Category 3 – Adverse effects may have been described in human studies, but consider use if clinical benefit outweighs risk.
- Category 4 – Human pregnancy exposure and outcome data too limited to provide an evidence-based risk assessment, however use may remain justifiable on a case-by-case basis.
- Category 5 – Avoid, unless there are no suitable alternatives. Known or highly suspected human teratogen.

For the most up-to-date information or for patient-specific risk assessments, contact the UK Teratology Information Service UKTIS (telephone: 0344 892 0909, available 9 AM to 5 PM, Monday to Friday, excluding bank holidays).

Open access UKTIS summary monographs are currently available for specific medications at www.uktis.org, with full versions available to National Health Service health professionals after creating a free account. Corresponding patient information may also be available via the Bumps website (www.medicinesinpregnancy.org).

Table A8.1: Recommendation Category

Medication Group	1	2	3	4	5
Lubricants (t)	Hypromellose Carbomers Carmellose Sodium chloride Acetylcysteine Trehalose	Polyvinyl alcohol[a] Povidone[a] Hydroxyethyl cellulose[a]	–	–	–
Antibacterials	Fusidic acid (t) Aminoglycosides (t)	Chloramphenicol (t)	Vancomycin[a] (s, t) Penicillins (s, t) Cephalosporins (s, t) Metronidazole (s) Erythromycin (s, t) Clindamycin[a] (s) Azithromycin[b] (s, t) Polymyxin B[a] (t) Tetracyclines[c] (s, ≤15 weeks' gestation) Quinolones (s, t) Aminoglycosides (s) Sulphonamides[d] (s) Trimethoprim[d] (s, t) Clarithromycin[b] (s)	Linezolid[a] (s, t)	Tetracyclines (s, >15 weeks' gestation)[c]

Table A8.1: Recommendation category—*Contd...*

Medication group	1	2	3	4	5
Antifungals	Clotrimazole (t) Miconazole (t)	Econazole (t)	Amphotericin[a] (i, t) Natamycin[a] (t) Fluconazole (s, stat dose)	Voriconazole[a] (s, t)	Fluconazole (s, 400–800 mg/day)[e]
Antivirals	Aciclovir (t)	–	Aciclovir (s) Famciclovir[a] (s) Valaciclovir[a] (s) Ganciclovir[a] (i, t)	Trifluorothymidine[a] (t)	–
Anti-amoebics (t)	–	Polyhexanide/PHMB[a]	–	Chlorhexidine[a] Hexamidine[a] Propamidine[a]	–
Intraocular pressure-lowering medications (t unless stated)	–	β-blockers Brimonidine[a] Apraclonidine[a] Brinzolamide[a] Dorzolamide[a] Latanoprost[a & f] Travoprost[a & f] Bimatoprost[a & f] Tafluprost[a & f] Glycerin[a] (s) Netarsudil[a & f]	Pilocarpine[a] Acetazolamide (s)	Mannitol[a] (iv)	–

Table A8.1: Recommendation category—*Contd...*

Medication group	1	2	3	4	5
Anti-inflammatory medications	–	–	NSAIDs[g & h] (s, t) Corticosteroids[i] (t, i, s) Low dose aspirin (s)	Ketorolac[a and h] (s, t)	–
Anti-allergy medications (t unless stated)	Sodium cromoglicate Azelastine Ketotifen	Olopatadine[a]	Chlorphenamine[j] (s) Cetirizine (s) Loratadine (s)	–	–
Local anaesthetics (t unless stated)	–	–	Lidocaine (inj, t)	Tetracaine (amethocaine)[a] Oxybuprocaine (benoxinate)[a] Proxymetacaine (proparacaine)[a]	Cocaine
Diagnostics and mydriatics (t unless stated)	Fluorescein	Tropicamide[a] Cyclopentolate[a] Rose Bengal[a] Phenylephrine[a] Lissamine green[a] Trypan blue[a] (i) Brilliant green[a](i) Indocyanine green[k] (iv)	Fluorescein[l] (iv) Atropine Hyoscine[a]	–	–

Table A8.1: Recommendation category—*Contd...*

Medication group	1	2	3	4	5
Monoclonal antibodies	–	–	Infliximab[m] (iv) Adalimumab[m] (s) Rituximab[m] (s)	Aflibercept[a & n] (i – standard and high dose) Bevacizumab[a] (i) Brolucizumab[a] (i) Faricimab[a] (i) Ranibizumab[a & n] (i)	–
Miscellaneous	Sodium citrate (t) Ascorbic acid[o](s, t) Ciclosporin (t) Sodium hyaluronate[p] (t)	Mitomycin C[a] (t) 5-fluorouracil[a & q] (t)	Paracetamol (s) Ciclosporin (s) Botulinum toxin[a] (inj) Verteporfin[a] (iv) Azathioprine (s) Tacrolimus (s) Dapsone[r] (s) Methotrexate (weekly dose ≤25 mg)[d & s] (s) Interferon alpha[a] (s, t)	Homatropine[a] (t)	Mycophenolate[t] (s) Cyclophosphamide (s) Methotrexate (weekly dose >25 mg)[d & s] (s)

Abbreviations: i - intravitreal; inj - injection; IV - intravenous; NSAIDs - non-steroidal anti-inflammatory drugs; s - systemic; t - topical.

Footnotes:

[a]Due to lack of data, use of equally effective but better studied alternatives may be more appropriate, where available.

[b]If a macrolide antibiotic is indicated in pregnancy, erythromycin may be preferred as there is more documented experience with its use.

[c]Avoid tetracyclines after the 15th week of gestation, if possible, due to the documented risk of discolouration of deciduous teeth and a possible risk of bone growth inhibition.

[d]High dose of folic acid supplementation (5 mg) is recommended.
[e]Since repeat exposure to high dose of fluconazole in the first trimester is suspected to be teratogenic, reserve for serious mycotic infections for which no suitable alternatives exist. As such, use may still be justifiable on a case-by-case basis.
[f]A disproportionality analysis of spontaneous adverse drug reaction reports identified an imprecise statistical signal linking miscarriage with prostaglandin eye drop use in pregnancy. This was based on five cases of pregnancy loss reported among 25 total reports of maternal latanoprost eye drop use in pregnancy. However, the level of evidence is weak, given the small patient numbers and because disproportionality analyses may be prone to identifying false positive associations.
[g]Seek information regarding the specific NSAID and formulation.
[h]Avoid if possible. Systemic or topical use of NSAIDs after 20 weeks' gestation could increase the risk of premature closure of the ductus arteriosus and oligohydramnios. If the maternal clinical condition requires short-term treatment (such as post-operative or for acute short-lived pain), limit to the lowest effective dose for the shortest duration possible.
[i]Seek information regarding the specific corticosteroid and formulation.
[j]Preferable to select a nonsedating antihistamine.
[k]Considered to be of possible low fetal risk because of documented evidence of minimal placental transfer.
[l]Although adverse fetal outcomes have been described in an uncontrolled study (including fetal anomalies), this does not provide convincing evidence of a causal relationship between adverse fetal outcome and the medication.
[m]Avoid live vaccines for 6 months in infants of patients exposed to immunosuppressant antibodies in pregnancy, due to a risk of neonatal immunosuppression.
[n]The risk of fetal exposure following ocular administration has not been systematically quantified, but is thought to be low.
[o]Use of recommended daily amounts in pregnancy is likely to be of low fetal risk.
[p]Animal reproductive toxicity data and a controlled human exposure safety study provide reassuring evidence of safety in pregnancy.
[q]Although concerns exist that intravenous administration of 5-fluorouracil in pregnancy may be teratogenic, it is probable that topical administration of a 1% eye drop solution will result in a minimal systemic concentration. However, pharmacokinetic data for the 1% eye drop preparation are not evident to confirm.
[r]Haemolytic anaemia has been described, which may confer a risk of kernicterus in the neonate.
[s]Women of childbearing potential must use at least one reliable form of contraception before, during and for 6 months after stopping treatment. Male patients should use reliable contraception during methotrexate treatment and for at least 6 months after stopping treatment.
[t]Women of childbearing potential must use at least one reliable form of contraception before, during and for 6 weeks after stopping treatment. Male patients should use reliable contraception during mycophenolate treatment and for at least 90 days after stopping treatment.

We are most grateful to J. Bloom and F. Hashmi, Medicines Information Department at Moorfields Eye Hospital, and J. Richardson and N. George, UK Teratology Information Service.

APPENDIX 9

READING TEST TYPES

Held at 15 inches = 38 cm

N4.5

As we walked along the edge of the river, the mild breeze rustling the trees which boughs were bent over the water by the weight of their leaves, I could not help but recall those happy memories of childhood.

N5

With the actual experience of it all being quite overwhelming. I could not help but wonder who had been here before me, what feet had trodden the same marble tiles that I stood on now.

N6

What a difference a day makes. One day, you find yourself hard up, wandering where you are going to get your next meal; the next day, just like a fairy-tale ending, a rich uncle claims you to be his long-lost nephew.

N8

But, it was the music lessons I looked forward to the most. That 1 hour spent in the music room was my escape from all the troubles around me. It just took a few bars on the piano for my spirits to lift.

N9

There is nowhere that can compare to Paris in the springtime. It is known as the most romantic city in the world and no wonder! The blossoms on the trees, the cafes by the riverside.

N10

Yet the face in the photograph was strangely familiar – the same arched brows, the same deep-set grey eyes, even the same twist to the mouth in that familiar.

N12

The little girl was playing on the swings with her mother tenderly watching over her. Her elder brother was amusing himself on the see-saw, all the while trying to gain.

N14

As the columns became broader, the

room became narrower, so that by the time we reached the end of the walk.

N18

The sand was a pearly white, much whiter than I had imagined it to be.

N24

Great flocks of birds were heading south for.

N36

Over the rooftops.

N48

Elephant trunks.

APPENDIX 10

AMSLER CHART

Chart to be held at a comfortable reading distance.

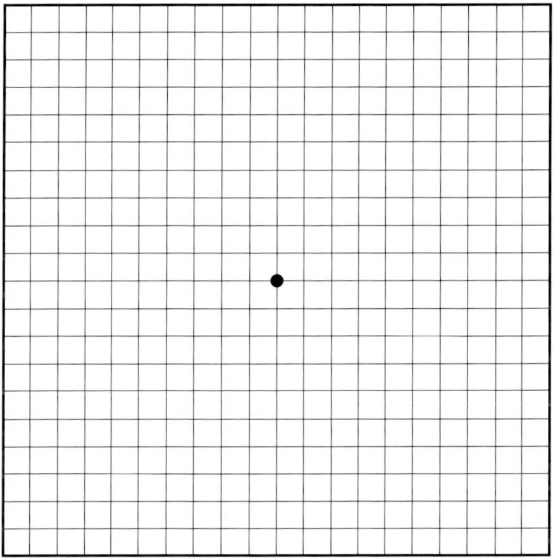

Fig. A10.1: Amsler chart.

VISUAL ACUITY CONVERSION

The three most commonly used VA eye charts and notations are Snellen VA, logarithm of the Minimum Angle of Resolution (logMAR) scores, and Early Treatment Diabetic Retinopathy Study (ETDRS) letter score. **Table A11.1** below provides approximate conversions between each VA method.

Table A11.1: Approximate Conversion Table for Visual Acuity

Snellen	Decimal	LogMAR*	ETDRS Letters
6/120	0.05	1.3	20
6/96	0.06	1.2	25
6/60	0.1	1.0	35
6/48	0.125	0.9	40
6/38	0.16	0.8	45
6/24	0.25	0.6	55
6/19	0.32	0.5	60
6/12	0.5	0.3	70
6/9.5	0.63	0.2	75
6/6	1.0	0.0	85
6/4.8	1.25	–0.1	90
6/3	2.0	–0.3	100

*logMAR = $\log_{10}$(1/enumerated Snellen fraction)

INDEX

Note: Page numbers in **bold**, ***bold italic*** or *italic* refer to tables, boxes or figures, respectively.

A

C

D

E

F

G

I

J

K

L

M

N

O

P

S

T

W